Eighth Edition

# INTERPLAY

## The Process of Interpersonal Communication

Eighth Edition

# INTERPLAY
## The Process of Interpersonal Communication

**Ronald B. Adler**   Santa Barbara City College

**Lawrence B. Rosenfeld**   University of North Carolina at Chapel Hill

**Russell F. Proctor II**   Northern Kentucky University

Original Contributions by Neil Towne

**Harcourt College Publishers**

Fort Worth   Philadelphia   San Diego   New York   Orlando   Austin   San Antonio
Toronto   Montreal   London   Sydney   Tokyo

| | |
|---|---|
| Publisher | Earl McPeek |
| Acquisitions Editor | Stephen Dalphin |
| Market Strategist | Laura Brennan |
| Developmental Editor | Laurie Runion |
| Project Editor | Joyce Fink |
| Art Director | Garry Harman |
| Production Manager | Linda McMillan |

Cover credit: © Terry Vine, Tony Stone Images

ISBN: 0-15-506956-X
Library of Congress Catalog Card Number: 00-102843

Some material in this work previously appeared in INTERPLAY: THE PROCESS OF INTERPERSONAL COMMUNICATION, Seventh Edition, copyright © 1998, 1995, 1992, 1989, 1986, 1983, 1980 by Harcourt, Inc.

Literary Credits appear on pages 447–48, which constitutes a continuation of the copyright page.

*Address for Domestic Orders*
Harcourt College Publishers, 6277 Sea Harbor Drive, Orlando, FL 32887-6777
800-782-4479

*Address for International Orders*
International Customer Service
Harcourt, Inc., 6277 Sea Harbor Drive, Orlando, FL 32887-6777
407-345-3800
(fax) 407-345-4060
(e-mail) hbintl@harcourt.com

*Address for Editorial Correspondence*
Harcourt College Publishers, 301 Commerce Street, Suite 3700, Fort Worth, TX 76102

*Web Site Address*
http://www.harcourtcollege.com

Harcourt College Publishers will provide complimentary supplements or supplement packages to those adopters qualified under our adoption policy. Please contact your sales representative to learn how you qualify. If as an adopter or potential user you receive supplements you do not need, please return them to your sales representative or send them to: Attn: Returns Department, Troy Warehouse, 465 South Lincoln Drive, Troy, MO 63379.

Printed in the United States of America

1 2 3 4 5 6 7 8 9   039   9 8 7 6 5 4 3 2

Harcourt College Publishers

# PREFACE

This edition of *Interplay* retains the approach that has been well received in the past: A readable, engaging, introduction to the subject of interpersonal communication built on a solid foundation of scholarship. This class-tested approach works well for the two primary audiences: faculty and students.

## Strong Academic Foundation

*Interplay* makes it clear that the academic study of interpersonal communication is based on solid scholarship that goes beyond—and often contradicts—"common sense." This edition cites almost 900 sources, the largest base of research of any introductory text in the field. In addition to the work cited within the text, numerous "Focus on Research" sidebars highlight work that readers will find especially interesting and noteworthy. New research profiles in this edition address topics including building relationships via e-mail, perceptions of racist speech, tattoos as identity management, misunderstandings about sexual overtures, and self-disclosure in personal ads. Material like this demonstrates that scholars do explore topics that are important in the "real world."

This edition continues *Interplay*'s commitment toward treating important topics in a balanced manner. For instance, both differences and similarities between male and female communication are explored, rather than favoring the increasingly questionable "men are from Mars, women from Venus" approach. The subject of intimacy is handled in a similarly evenhanded way, with self-disclosure and high intimacy presented as one approach to relationships, but not always the appropriate or necessary one. Alternatives to self-disclosure (e.g., equivocation, hinting, white lies) are identified, and their role in relationships is discussed. Similarly, Chapter 7 presents the pros and cons of various listening responses (e.g., paraphrasing, silent listening, questioning, supporting), and provides guidelines about which styles are most appropriate in a given situation.

## Student Appeal

Students who use *Interplay* will find that the academic study of interpersonal communication can be lively and engaging. We have worked hard to give the text a reader-friendly voice that explains concepts clearly without being simplistic, and a visual design aims to make the material inviting. An extensive and sophisticated array of cartoons and photos (most new to this edition) provide a mix of images that add a new dimension of meaning to the text. "Film Clip" sidebars throughout the book (over half of which are new to this edition) demonstrate how popular feature films illustrate communication principles. Finally, "Reflection" sidebars (again, most new to this edition) offer first-person accounts of how concepts in the text operate in everyday life.

## New to this Edition

This edition of *Interplay* contains expanded coverage on topics of current importance including the influence of new technology on interpersonal relationships, the influence of biological sex on communication, the nature of communication apprehension, and how cultural differences shape understanding and behavior. New and updated material in every chapter highlights scholarship on a multitude of topics including the value of communication skills in personal and occupational contexts, communication competence, nonverbal communication, relational dynamics, communication climate, and conflict.

Long-time users will notice some changes in organization and format. "Communication and the Self" (now Chapter 3) has been moved earlier in the book to reflect the central role of this topic. "Perceiving Others" is now Chapter 4. References that were formerly at the end of each chapter have now been consolidated in a single section to eliminate duplication and improve the flow of the book. Each chapter contains a list of recommended readings that point interested readers toward especially helpful sources on a variety of key topics.

## Instructional Resources

Within the text itself, end-of-chapter activities provide accessible ways for students to explore material. As in recent editions, activities are designated as "Skill Builders," "Invitations to Insight," and "Ethical Challenges."

In addition to the text, an array of ancillary tools is available to help instructors and students. A **new instructor's manual** by Derek Lane (University of Kentucky) includes activities and teaching strategies focusing on computer-mediated communication. A **computerized test bank** program is available for users in both Windows and Macintosh formats. **Two film resource guides** (*Communication in Film, Volumes I* and *II*) by Russell F. Proctor II are available free to adopters. These books offer teaching strategies for using dozens of feature films in conjunction with *Interplay*. A **web site** contains links to PowerPoint slides for lectures and additional resources.

## Acknowledgments

A product as ambitious as *Interplay* doesn't spring to life without the help of many people. We are grateful for the input of colleagues around the country who have helped us make this edition most useful for professors and

students: A product as ambitious as *Interplay* doesn't spring to life without the help of many people. We are grateful for the input of colleagues around the country who have helped us make this edition most useful for professors and students: Joyce Buttermore, Gulf Coast Community College; Marcia Dixson, Indiana University-Purdue University at Fort Wayne; Kimberly Batty-Herbert, Clovis Community College; Dave Engen, Eastern Michigan University; Steven Hartong, Eastern Michigan University; Derek Lane, University of Kentucky; Rebecca Mikesell, University of Scranton; Lori Montalbano-Phelps, Indiana University—Northwest; Heather Rosenfeld, Washburn University; Chuck Schilling, Fullerton College; Carol Shulman, Miami University; Charmaine Wilson, University of South Carolina—Aiken; and Richard Wiseman, California State University—Fullerton.

We remain grateful to colleagues whose suggestions for previous editions continue to benefit readers: Ruth Anderson, Nick Backus, Leonard Barchak, Donald Berg, Brian Betz, Vincent Bloom, Bruce Dorries, Robert Dretz, Veronica Duncan, Georgia Duran, Eric Eisenberg, George Enell, Leslye Evans, Mary Forestieri, Susan Fox, Ava Good, Barbara Gordon, Debra Grodin, Martha Haun, Kenneth Howard, Karen Inouye, Pam Johnson, Richard Joyce, Virginia Katz, Thurman Knight, Terri Main, John McGrath, Sandra Metts, Marilou Morris, Joe Munshaw, David Natharius, Nan Peck, Carol Peirce-Jones, Lynn Phelps, William Rawlins, Dirk Scheerhorn, Michael Schliessmann, Anntarie Lanita Simms, Dickie Spurgeon, Carolyn Stephens, Edwina Stoll, Todd Thomas, Eleanor Tucker, Anita Vaccaro, and Sonia Zamanou.

Our thanks go to the team of publishing professionals who have helped transform this edition of *Interplay* from concept to the product you are reading: Stephen Dalphin, Laurie Runion, Joyce Fink, Garry Harman, Linda McMillan, Janet Bollow, Laura Brennan, Caroline Robbins, and Jill Johnson.

Finally, we express our gratitude for the support of our families. We appreciate their indulgence during all the hours when we worked on *Interplay*. Now, perhaps we can spend less time writing *about* communication and more time with them!

R.B.A.
L.B.R.
R.F.P.

February, 2000

# BRIEF CONTENTS

# DETAILED CONTENTS

**PART II:  CREATING AND
RESPONDING TO MESSAGES**

# PART III   DIMENSIONS OF INTERPERSONAL RELATIONSHIPS

# CHAPTER

## 1

# Interpersonal Process

# After Studying the Material in This Chapter . . .

## You Should Understand:

1. The needs that effective communication can satisfy.

2. The qualities that make a transactional model of communication more accurate than linear or interactive models.

3. Quantitative and qualitative definitions of interpersonal communication.

4. Five key principles and three misconceptions about communication.

5. The characteristics of competent communication.

## You Should Be Able to:

1. Identify examples of the physical, identity, social, and practical needs you attempt to satisfy by communicating.

2. Demonstrate how the transactional communication model applies to your interpersonal communication.

3. Describe the degrees to which your communication is qualitatively impersonal and interpersonal, and describe the consequences of this combination.

4. Identify situations in which you communicate competently, and those in which your competence is less than satisfactory.

## Key Terms

| | | | |
|---|---|---|---|
| Behavior | Encoding | Noise | Self-monitoring |
| Channel | Environment | Physiological noise | Sender |
| Cognitive complexity | External noise | Psychological noise | Transactional communication model |
| Communication | Feedback | Qualitative interpersonal communication | |
| Communication competence | Interactive communication model | Quantitative interpersonal communication | |
| Content message | Linear communication model | Receiver | |
| Decoding | Message | Relational message | |
| Dyad | | | |

Everyone communicates. Students and professors, parents and children, employers and employees, friends, strangers, and enemies—all communicate. We have been communicating with others from the first weeks of life and will keep on doing so until we die.

Why study an activity you've done your entire life? There are three reasons. First, studying interpersonal communication will give you a new look at a familiar topic. For instance, in a few pages you will find that some people can go years—even lifetimes—without communicating in a truly interpersonal manner. In this sense, exploring human communication is rather like studying anatomy or botany—everyday objects and processes take on new meaning.

A second reason for studying the subject has to do with the staggering amount of time we spend communicating. For example, a study of over one thousand employees at *Fortune* 1000 companies revealed that workers send and receive an average of 178 messages every working day (Ginsburg, 1997). Another survey (Nellermoe et al., 1999) revealed that business professionals spent 80 percent of their business day communicating with colleagues and clients.

There is a third, more compelling reason for studying interpersonal communication. To put it bluntly, all of us could learn to communicate more effectively. Our friendships, jobs, and studies suffer because we fail to deal with others as effectively as is necessary. A group of senior executives cited lack of interpersonal skills as one of the top three skill deficits in today's workforce (Marchant, 1999). In a nationwide survey, "lack of effective communication" was identified as the cause of relational breakups more often than any other reason (National Communication Association, 1999). Most people realize that lack of effective communication with others can lead to serious problems in a person's life. When asked what causes marriages or other relationships to end, there are more Americans who believe that communication problems are "very

frequently" the cause than there are who attribute relational problems to money, relatives or in-laws, sexual problems, previous relationships (9 percent), or children (7 percent).

If you pause now and make a mental list of communication problems you have encountered, you'll see that, no matter how successful your relationships are at home, with friends, at school, and at work, there is plenty of room for improvement in your everyday life. The information that follows will help you improve the way you communicate with some of the people who matter most to you.

## Why We Communicate

Research demonstrating the importance of communication has been around longer than you might think. Frederick II, emperor of the Holy Roman Empire from 1220 to 1250, was called *stupor mundi*—"wonder of the world"—by his admiring subjects. Along with his administrative and military talents, Frederick was a leading scientist of his time. A medieval historian described one of his dramatic, if inhumane, experiments:

> He bade foster mothers and nurses to suckle the children, to bathe and wash them, but in no way to prattle with them, for he wanted to learn whether they would speak the Hebrew language, which was the oldest, or Greek, or Latin, or Arabic, or perhaps the language of their parents, of whom they had been born. But he labored in vain because all the children died. For they could not live without the petting and joyful faces and loving words of their foster mothers. (Ross & McLaughlin, 1949, p. 366)

Fortunately, contemporary researchers have found less dramatic ways to illustrate the importance of communication. In one study of isolation, five subjects were paid to remain alone in a locked room. One lasted for eight days. Three held out for two days, one commenting "Never again." The fifth subject lasted only two hours (Schachter, 1959, pp. 9–10).

The need for contact and companionship is just as strong outside the laboratory, as individuals who have led solitary lives by choice or necessity have discovered. W. Carl Jackson, an adventurer who sailed across the Atlantic Ocean alone in fifty-one days, summarized in a 1978 interview published in the *Wisconsin State Journal* the feelings common to most loners:

> I found the loneliness of the second month almost excruciating. I always thought of myself as self-sufficient, but I found life without people had no meaning. I had a definite need for somebody to talk to, someone real, alive, and breathing.

You might object to stories like this, claiming that solitude would be a welcome relief from the irritations of everyday life. It's true that all of us need solitude, often more than we get. On the other hand, each of us has a point beyond which we do not *want* to be alone. Beyond this point, solitude changes from a pleasurable to a painful condition. In other words, we all need people. We all need to communicate.

## Physical Needs

Communication is so important that its presence or absence affects physical health. In extreme cases communication can even become a matter of life or death. As a Navy pilot, Captain Eugene

McDaniel was shot down over North Vietnam and held as a prisoner of war for six years, often in solitary confinement. In his book *Scars and Stripes* (1975), he says POWs were likely to die much sooner if they couldn't communicate with one another. For this reason, McDaniel describes how he and other prisoners set up clandestine codes in which they sent messages by coughing, laughing, scratching, tapping on walls, and flapping laundry in code to spell out words. The inmates endured torture rather than give up these attempts to communicate. As McDaniel puts it,

> One thing I knew, I had to have communications with my own people here in this camp. . . . Communication with each other was what the North Vietnamese captors took the greatest pains to prevent. They knew, as well as I and the others did, that a man could stand more pain if he is linked with others of his own kind in that suffering. The lone, isolated being becomes weak, vulnerable. I knew I had to make contact, no matter what the cost.

Satisfying communication isn't just a necessity for prisoners of war. Evidence gathered by medical researchers (e.g., Cohen et al., 1997; Ruberman, 1992) and social scientists (e.g., Duck, 1991) shows that satisfying relationships can literally be a matter of life and death for people who lead normal lives. For example:

- People who lack strong relationships have two to three times the risk of early death, regardless of whether they smoke, drink alcoholic beverages, or exercise regularly.
- Terminal cancer strikes socially isolated people more often than those who have close personal relationships.
- Divorced, separated, and widowed people are five to ten times more likely to need mental hospitalization than their married counterparts.
- Pregnant women under stress and without supportive relationships have three times more complications than pregnant women who suffer from the same stress but have strong social support.
- Social isolation is a major risk factor contributing to coronary disease, comparable to

physiological factors such as diet, cigarette smoking, obesity, and lack of physical activity.
- Socially isolated people are four times more susceptible to the common cold than those who have active social networks.

Research like this demonstrates the importance of satisfying personal relationships, and it explains the conclusion of social scientists that communication is essential (Baumeister & Leary, 1995). Not everyone needs the same amount of contact, and the quality of communication is almost certainly as important as the quantity. Nonetheless, the point remains: Personal communication is essential for our well-being. To paraphrase a popular song, "people who need people" aren't "the luckiest people in the world": They're the *only* people!

## Identity Needs

Communication does more than enable us to survive. It is the way—indeed, the *only* way—we learn who we are. As you'll read in Chapter 3, our sense of identity comes from the way we interact with other people. Are we smart or stupid, attractive or ugly, skillful or inept? The answers to these questions don't come from looking in the mirror. We decide who we are based on how others react to us.

Deprived of communication with others, we would have no sense of identity. In his book *Bridges, Not Walls,* John Stewart (1999) dramatically illustrates this fact by citing the case of the famous "Wild Boy of Aveyron," who spent his early childhood without any apparent human contact. The boy was discovered in January 1800 while digging for vegetables in a French village garden. He showed no behaviors one would expect in a social human. The boy could not speak but uttered only weird cries. More significant than this absence of social skills was his lack of any identity as a human being. As author Roger Shattuck (1980, p. 37) put it, "The boy had no human sense of being in the world. He had no sense of himself as a person related to other persons." Only after the influence of a loving

"mother" did the boy begin to behave—and, we can imagine, think of himself—as a human. Contemporary stories support the essential role communication plays in shaping identity. In 1970, authorities discovered a twelve-year-old girl (whom they called "Genie") who had spent virtually all her life in an otherwise empty, darkened bedroom with almost no human contact. The child could not speak and had no sense of herself as a person until she was removed from her family and "nourished" by a team of caregivers (Rymer, 1993).

Like Genie and the boy of Aveyron, each of us enters the world with little or no sense of identity. We gain an idea of who we are from the way others define us. As Chapter 3 explains, the messages we receive in early childhood are the strongest, but the influence of others continues throughout life.

## Social Needs

Besides helping define who we are, some social scientists have argued, communication is the principal way relationships are created (Duck & Pittman, 1995). For example, after analyzing children's friendships, Julie Yingling (1994) asserted that children "talk friendships into existence." As Chapter 9 explains, sometimes we deal with social needs directly by discussing our relationships with others. But more often, communication satisfies a variety of social needs without our ever addressing them overtly. Rebecca Rubin and her associates (1988) identified six categories of social needs we satisfy by communicating: *pleasure* ("because it's fun," "to have a good time"), *affection* ("to help others," "to let others know I care"), *inclusion* ("because I need someone to talk to or be with," "because it makes me less lonely"), *escape* ("to put off doing something I should be doing"), *relaxation* ("because it allows me to unwind"), and *control* ("because I want someone to do something for me," "to get something I don't have").

As you look over this list of social motives, imagine how impossible life would be without communicating. Because relationships with others are so vital, some theorists have gone so far as to argue that communication is the primary goal of

## EVERYBODY NEEDS SOMEBODY: *AS GOOD AS IT GETS*

Melvin Udall (Jack Nicholson) is a crotchety, obsessive-compulsive hermit who locks himself in his apartment where, ironically, he writes romance novels. When people try to talk with him, Melvin drives them away with mean and offensive comments. He seems intent on disproving the notion that "no man is an island."

But one person—and one dog—break through Melvin's tough exterior. The person is Carol Connelly (Helen Hunt), a waitress who gives him attention and doesn't put up with his guff. As a result, Melvin ritualistically visits her restaurant every morning. The dog is named Verdell. Melvin is forced to babysit Verdell when his owner, Simon (Greg Kinnear), is hospitalized. The dog works his way into Melvin's heart and brings out his softest side.

When both Carol and Verdell temporarily exit Melvin's life, he must come to grips with the fact that he misses interacting with them. His social needs pull him into meaningful relationships with Carol and Simon, and he slowly becomes a more competent communicator through their love and support. The romance novelist finally finds romance in his own life, and he learns that it's not so bad to need—and be needed by—other people.

human existence. Anthropologist Walter Goldschmidt (1990) calls the drive for meeting social needs "the human career."

## Practical Needs

We shouldn't overlook the everyday, important functions communication serves. Communication is the tool that lets us tell the hairstylist to take just a little off the sides, direct the doctor to where it hurts, and inform the plumber that the broken pipe needs attention *now!*

Beyond these obvious needs, a wealth of research demonstrates that communication is an essential part of effectiveness in a variety of everyday settings. As the Focus on Research profile on page 9 explains, the abilities to speak and listen effectively have been identified as the most important factors in helping graduating college students gain employment and advance in their careers: more important than technical competence, work experience, and academic background. One survey of over four hundred employers identified "communication skills" as the top characteristic employers seek in job candidates (Job Outlook, 2000). It was rated as more important than technical competence, work experience, and academic background. In another survey, over 90 percent of the personnel officials at five hundred U.S. businesses stated that increased communication skills are needed for success in the twenty-first century (Peterson, 1998). *Harvard Business Review* subscribers rated "the ability to communicate" as the most important factor in making an executive promotable—more important than ambition, education, and the capacity for hard work (Bowman, 1964).

Communication is just as important outside of work, as a wealth of research demonstrates. In one study, married couples who were identified as effective communicators reported happier relationships than less skillful husbands and wives (Kirchler, 1988). In school, the grade-point averages of college students were related positively to their communication competence (Rubin & Graham, 1988), and school adjustment, drop-out rate, and overall school achievement and academic competency were found to be highly related to students' having strong, supportive relationships (Rosenfeld et al., 1998). In "getting acquainted" situations, communication competence played a major role in whether a

## FOCUS ON RESEARCH

### COMMUNICATION AND CAREER SUCCESS

Few goals are more important to career-minded students than getting hired and advancing in a rewarding career. To learn about the connection between communication and on-the-job success, researchers Jerry Winsor, Dan Curtis, and Ronald Stephens surveyed almost four hundred human resource managers from a variety of corporate, public, financial, service, insurance, retail, and wholesale organizations in the United States.

When asked to identify the skills they thought most helped graduating college students obtain employment, the personnel managers' list was headed by oral communication skills, followed in order by written communication skills and listening ability. Other factors such as work experience, specific degree held, recommendations, and grade-point average took a back seat to the communication-related top three.

According to human resource professionals, communication skills are just as important once candidates are hired. They identified interpersonal/human relations skills as most important for career success, followed closely by oral communication skills. Written communication skills came in third in importance, while enthusiasm and persistence/determination rounded out the top five.

When asked what courses they thought were most relevant for students seeking entry-level management positions, the managers ranked written communication number one, followed in order by interpersonal communication, management, and public speaking.

Finally, the researchers asked personnel managers to describe what they thought were the skills of the ideal manager. The top six qualities were all related to communication: the ability to listen effectively, work well with others one-on-one, operate effectively in small groups, gather accurate information from others before making a decision, write effective business reports, and give effective feedback. It goes without saying that most people would love to work for a boss with communication skills like these.

Winsor, J. L., Curtis, D. B., & Stephens, R. D. (1997). National preferences in business and communication education: An update. *Journal of the Association for Communication Administration, 3,* 170–179.

person was judged physically attractive, socially desirable, and good at the task of getting acquainted (Duran & Kelly, 1988).

Psychologist Abraham Maslow (1968) suggests that human needs fall into five categories, each of which must be satisfied before we concern ourselves with the next one. As you read on, think about the ways in which communication is often necessary to satisfy each need. The most basic needs are *physical:* sufficient air, water, food, and rest, and the ability to repro-

duce as a species. The second category of Maslow's needs involves *safety:* protection from threats to our well-being. Beyond physical and safety concerns are the *social* needs we have already mentioned. Beyond them, Maslow suggests that each of us has the need for *self-esteem:* the desire to believe that we are worthwhile, valuable people. The final category of needs involves *self-actualization:* the desire to develop our potential to the maximum, to become the best person we can be.

# The Communication Process

So far we have used the word communication as if its meaning were perfectly clear. In fact, most scholarly definitions of communication contain several common elements: A **sender encodes** ideas and feelings into some sort of message and then conveys them to a **receiver** by means of a **channel**—face-to-face speaking, writing, signing, telephoning, and so on. It's important to suggest that the telephone is a different channel than in-person conversation. The receiver then **decodes** the message.

This simple description doesn't even hint at the complexity of what happens as two or more people try to exchange messages. Consider, for example, the way in which various channels affect the relationship between communicators. As the Reflection on this page illustrates, the channel used to communicate can make an important difference. The new technology of computer-mediated communication (CMC) offers another example of how channels affect the way in which people interact. At first, theorists predicted that CMC would be less personal than face-to-face communication. With no nonverbal cues to go on, it seemed that CMC couldn't match the rich kind of interaction that happens in person, or even over the phone. Recent studies, however (e.g., Walther & Burgoon, 1992; O'Sullivan, 2000), have shown that CMC can be just as deep and complex as personal contact. This kind of research supports the suggestion of Steve Jobs, cofounder of Apple Computer, that personal computers be renamed "*inter*personal computers" (Kirkpatrick, 1992). Sociolinguist Deborah Tannen (1994) describes how the computer-mediated channel of electronic mail (e-mail) transformed the quality of two rela-tionships:

> E-mail deepened my friendship with Ralph. Though his office was next to mine, we rarely had extended conversations because he is shy. Face to face he mumbled, so I could barely tell he was speaking. But when we both got on e-mail, I started receiving long, self-revealing messages; we poured our hearts

out to each other. A friend discovered that e-mail opened up that kind of communication with her father. He would never talk much on the phone (as her mother would), but they have become close since they both got on line.

## A Linear View

Over a half-century ago, researchers viewed com-munication as something one person "does" to another (Shannon & Weaver, 1949). In this **linear communication model,** communication is like giving an injection (See Figure 1.1).

According to the linear model, interference with the message—termed **noise** in scientific jargon—interferes with accurate decoding. Three types of noise can disrupt communication: external, physiological, and psychological. **Exter-nal noise** includes those factors outside the receiv-er that make it difficult to hear, as well as many other kinds of distractions. For instance, too much cigarette smoke in a crowded room might make it hard for you to pay attention to another person,

---

## REFLECTION

### CHOOSING THE CHANNEL

I am a normal person in just about every way, except that I have a speech impediment. I have good days and bad days with my speech. On the bad days, I get the idea that strangers think I'm slow and incompetent, even though people who know me don't think I'm either.

E-mail has become a very satisfying way to communi-cate, especially with people I don't know very well. With e-mail, people can form opinions about me with-out thinking just about how I sound. I've found that my impediment isn't a problem once people know me, but at first I think it is a real barrier; and e-mail removes that barrier completely.

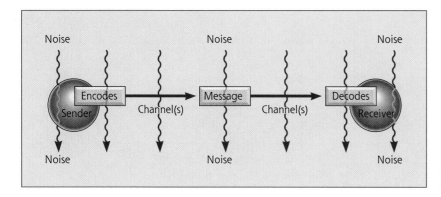

**Figure 1.1** Linear
Communication Model

and sitting in the rear of an auditorium might make a speaker's remarks unclear. External noise can disrupt communication almost anywhere in our model—in the sender, channel, message, or receiver. **Physiological noise** involves biological factors in the receiver that interfere with accurate reception: hearing loss, illness, and so on. **Psychological noise** refers to forces within the sender and receiver that make them less likely to communicate effectively. For instance, a woman who hears the word *gal* may become so irritated that she has trouble listening objectively to the rest of a speaker's message. Likewise, an insecure employee may interpret a minor suggestion the boss makes as ridicule or criticism.

The linear communication model does provide some useful information. For instance, it highlights how different channels can affect the way a receiver responds to a message. It also emphasizes the role of noise in interfering with effective transmission and reception of a message.

## An Interactive View

Despite its simplicity and usefulness, the linear view of communication isn't completely accurate. For one thing, it makes the questionable assumption that all communication involves encoding. We certainly do choose symbols to convey most verbal messages. But what about the many non-verbal cues that occur whether or not people speak: facial expressions, gestures, postures, vocal tones, and so on? Cues like these clearly do offer

information about others, although they are often unconscious or automatic (Kellermann, 1992). For this reason, it seems more accurate to replace the term *encoding* in our model with the broader label **behavior,** since it describes both deliberate and unintentional actions that can be observed and interpreted.

A more obvious problem of the linear model is its suggestion that communication flows in one direction, from sender to receiver. Although some types of messages (printed and broadcast material, for example) do flow in a one-way, linear manner, most types of communication—especially the interpersonal variety—are two-way exchanges. To put it differently, the linear view ignores the fact that receivers *react* to messages by sending other messages of their own.

For instance, consider the significance of a friend's yawn as you describe your romantic problems. Or imagine the blush you may see as you tell one of your raunchier jokes to a new acquaintance. Nonverbal behaviors like these show that most face-to-face communication is a two-way affair. The discernible response of a receiver to a sender's message is called **feedback.** Not all feedback is nonverbal, of course. Sometimes it is oral, as when you ask an instructor questions about an upcoming test or volunteer your opinion of a friend's new haircut. In other cases it is written, as when you answer the questions on a midterm exam or respond to a letter from a friend. Figure 1.2 makes the importance of feedback clear. It shows that most communication

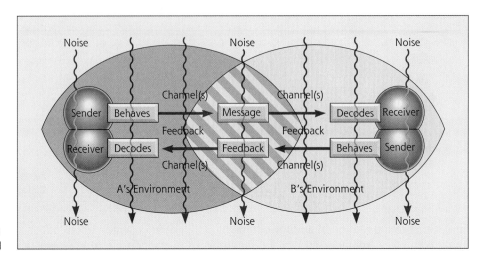

**Figure 1.2** Interactive Communication Model

is, indeed, a two-way affair in which we both send and receive messages.

The interactive communication model in Figure 1.2 also identifies a clue to the cause of many misunderstandings. Although we naively assume that conversational give-and-take will help people understand one another, your personal experience no doubt shows that misunderstandings often occur. Your constructive suggestion is taken as criticism; your friendly joke is taken as an insult; your hints are missed entirely. Such misunderstandings often arise because communicators occupy different **environments**—fields of experience that help them understand others' behavior. In communication terminology, *environment* refers not only to a physical location, but also to the personal experiences and cultural background that participants bring to a conversation. Environments aren't always obvious. For example, a recent study revealed that college students who have been enrolled in debate classes tend to become more argumentative and verbally aggressive than those who have not been exposed to this sort of environment (Colbert, 1993).

Consider just some of the factors that might contribute to different environments:

- A might belong to one ethnic group and B to another;
- A might be rich and B poor;

- A might be rushed and B have nowhere to go;
- A might have lived a long, eventful life, and B is young and inexperienced;
- A might be passionately concerned with the subject and B indifferent to it.

Notice how the model in Figure 1.2 shows that the environments of A and B overlap. On the one hand, this intersecting area represents the background that the communicators have in common. If this overlap didn't exist, communication would be impossible. On the other hand, there are some aspects of each communicator's environment that aren't shared, and these can generate noise that interferes with smooth interaction. For example, imagine the highly personal reactions that might come up when one person from a privileged background in society discusses racial politics with someone from an underrepresented group that has historically been the object of discrimination.

Even with the addition of feedback and environment, the model in Figure 1.2 isn't completely satisfactory. Notice that it portrays communication as a static activity, suggesting that there are discrete "acts" of communication beginning and ending at identifiable times, and that a sender's message causes some effect in a receiver. Furthermore, the model suggests that at any given moment a person is either sending or receiving.

## A Transactional View

Neither the linear nor the interactive model paints an accurate picture of most types of communication. The activity of communicating is best represented by a **transactional communication model.** There are several ways in which a transactional perspective differs from the more simplistic ones we've already discussed.

First, a transactional model reflects the fact that we usually send and receive messages simultaneously. Consider, for example, what might occur when you and your housemate negotiate how to handle household chores. As soon as you begin to hear the words sent by your partner, "I want to talk about cleaning the kitchen," you grimace and clench your jaw (sending a nonverbal message of your own while receiving the verbal one). This reaction leads your partner to defensively interject, "Now wait a minute. . . ." The simultaneous nature of most interaction explains why the terms *sender* and *receiver* have been replaced in Figure 1.3 by the broader term *communicator.*

Besides illustrating the simultaneous nature of face-to-face interaction, this example shows that it's difficult to isolate a single discrete "act" of communication from the events that precede and follow it. Your partner's comment about cleaning the kitchen (and the way it was presented) probably grew from exchanges you had in the past. Likewise, the way you'll act toward each other in the future depends on the outcome of this conversation. As communication researcher Steve Duck (1994c) puts it, relationships are best conceived as "unfinished business," not "done deals."

Perhaps the most important consequence of communication's transactional nature is the degree of mutual influence that occurs when we interact. To put it simply, communication isn't something we do *to* others; rather, it is an activity we do *with* them. In this sense, communication is rather like dancing—at least the kind of dancing we do with partners. Like dancing, communication depends on the involvement of a partner. And like good dancing, successful communication isn't something that depends just on the skill of one person. A great dancer who doesn't consider and adapt to the skill level of his or her partner can make both of them look bad. In communication and dancing, even two talented partners don't guarantee success. When two skilled dancers perform without coordinating their movements, the results feel bad to the dancers and

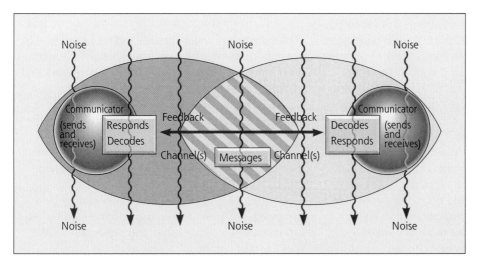

**Figure 1.3** Transactional Communication Model

look foolish to an audience. Finally, relational communication—like dancing—is a unique creation that arises out of the way in which the partners interact. The way you dance probably varies from one partner to another because of its cooperative, transactional nature. Likewise, the way you communicate almost certainly varies with different partners.

Psychologist Kenneth Gergen (1991) captures the transactional nature of communication well when he points out how our success depends on interaction with others. As he says, "one cannot be 'attractive' without others who are attracted, a 'leader' without others willing to follow, or a 'loving person' without others to affirm with appreciation" (p. 158).

The transactional nature of communication shows up dramatically in relationships between parents and their children. We normally think of "good parenting" as a skill that some people possess and others lack. We judge the ability of a mother and father in terms of how well their children turn out. In truth, the question of good parenting isn't quite so clear. Research summarized by Marianne Dainton and Laura Stafford (1993) shows that the quality of interaction between parents and children is a two-way affair, that children influence parents just as much as the other way around. For example, children who engage in what social scientists call "problematic behavior" evoke more high-control responses from their parents than do cooperative children, and youngsters with mild temperaments are less likely to provoke coercive reactions by their parents than more aggressive children. Parents with low self-esteem tend to send more messages that weaken the self-esteem of their children, who in turn are likely to act in ways that make the parents feel even worse about themselves. Thus, a mutually reinforcing cycle arises in which parents and children shape one another's feelings and behavior. In cases like this, it's at least difficult and probably impossible to identify who is the "sender" and who is the "receiver" of messages. It's more accurate to acknowledge that parents and children—just like

## REFLECTION

### IT TAKES TWO TO COMMUNICATE

Last week I got into a huge fight with my boss. After the initial argument was over, I spent the remaining part of the day trying to use the communication skills I've learned in my classes to find a resolution. The problem was, nothing I said to my boss made any difference. I felt like I was taking all the right steps, but they were completely ineffective.

After work, I couldn't stop thinking about the day's events. That's when I remembered some other lessons from class. I remembered that communication doesn't take place in a vacuum, which means that the history of my fight with the boss might make *anything* I might have said ineffective, at least for now. I remembered that not everyone communicates in the same way. This means that the techniques we have studied may not work with my boss, even though they work most of the time with most people. Finally, I realized that more communication isn't always better, and that sometimes you just need to know when to walk away. I guess I still have a lot to learn!

husbands and wives, bosses and employees, teachers and students, or any other people who communicate with one another—act in ways that mutually influence one another. The transactional nature of relationships is worth re-emphasizing: We don't communicate *to* others, we communicate *with* them.

By now we can see that, rather than a linear or interactive phenomenon, **communication** can be characterized as an ongoing, transactional process in which individuals exchange messages whose meanings are influenced by the history of the relationship and the experiences of the participants.

# Interpersonal Communication Defined

Now that you have a better understanding of the overall process of human communication, it's time to look at what makes some types uniquely interpersonal.

## Quantitative and Qualitative Definitions

Scholars have characterized interpersonal communication in a number of ways (Redmond, 1995). Most definitions focus on the number of people involved. A **quantitative** definition of interpersonal communication includes any interaction between two people, usually face to face. Social scientists call two persons interacting a **dyad,** and they often use the adjective **dyadic** to describe this type of communication. So, in a quantitative sense, the terms *dyadic communication* and *interpersonal communication* can be used interchangeably. Using a quantitative definition, a sales clerk and customer or a police officer ticketing a speeding driver would be examples of interpersonal acts, whereas a teacher and class or a performer and audience would not.

Dyadic communication *is* different from the kind of interaction that occurs in larger groups (Wilmot, 1995). For example, two-person exchanges are the earliest form of interaction we experience, and throughout life they are the most common type of communication. Unlike threesomes and other groups, dyads are complete and cannot be subdivided. As Wilmot puts it, "the loss of one is the loss of all." This indivisibility means that, unlike groups, the partners in a dyad can't form coalitions to get their needs met: They must work matters out with each other.

Despite the unique qualities of dyads, you might object to the quantitative definition of interpersonal communication. For example, consider a routine transaction between a sales clerk and customer, or the rushed exchange when you ask a stranger on the street for directions. Communication of this sort hardly seems interpersonal—or personal in any sense of the word. In fact, after transactions like this we commonly remark, "I might as well have been talking to a machine."

The impersonal nature of some two-person exchanges has led some scholars (e.g., Miller & Steinberg, 1975; Stewart & Logan, 1993) to argue that quality, not quantity, is what distinguishes interpersonal communication. Using a **qualitative** definition, interpersonal communication occurs when people treat one another as unique individuals, regardless of the context in which the interaction occurs or the number of people involved. When quality of interaction is the criterion, the opposite of interpersonal communication is *impersonal* interaction, not group, public, or mass communication.

Several features distinguish qualitatively interpersonal communication from less personal exchanges. The first is *uniqueness.* Whereas impersonal exchanges are governed by the kind of social rules we learn from parents, teachers, and Miss Manners, the way we communicate in a truly personal relationship is unlike our behavior with anyone else. In one relationship you might exchange good-natured insults, while in another you are careful never to offend your partner. Likewise, you might handle conflicts with one friend or family member by expressing disagreements as soon as they arise, whereas the unwritten rule in another relationship is to withhold resentments until they build up and then clear the air periodically. Communication scholar Julia Wood (1997) coined the term "relational culture" to describe people in close relationships who create their own unique ways of interacting.

A second characteristic of qualitatively interpersonal communication is *irreplaceability.* Because interpersonal relationships are unique, they can't be replaced. This explains why we usually feel so sad when a close friendship or love affair cools down. We know that no matter how many other relationships fill our lives, none of them will ever be quite like the one that just ended.

*Interdependence* is a third characteristic of qualitatively interpersonal relationships. Here, the fate of the partners is connected. You might be

# FOCUS ON RESEARCH

## COMPUTER-MEDIATED COMMUNICATION: IMPERSONAL, INTERPERSONAL, OR HYPERPERSONAL?

Here's a one-question, multiple-choice test. When compared with face-to-face interaction, communication via computer is:

(a) less personal
(b) more personal

According to communication researcher Joseph Walther, both (a) and (b) can be true. In a review of research spanning two decades, Walther maintains that computer-mediated communication (CMC) can vary from being quite impersonal, to what he terms "hyperpersonal," depending on the goals of the users.

Until the 1990s, most researchers believed that messages sent via computer were too impersonal and "lean" for solving complex problems and maintaining rich relationships. In some ways, they were right. CMC limits many of the "rich" nonverbal cues present when communicators can see one another and hear each other's voices. This can actually assist decision making in groups. After all, it's easier to express opinions when there are no frowns or dirty looks to worry about. Studies show that conducting meetings via computer can increase productivity, diminish status differences, and reduce conformity pressures. Walther notes, however, that this is true primarily among groups of strangers. When there is the potential for future interaction or ongoing relationships, people linked by computer tend to engage in many of the same interpersonal communication patterns as face-to-face communicators.

Sometimes CMC goes beyond normal patterns of interpersonal communication and becomes what Walther calls "hyperpersonal." Just as CMC may encourage people to express opinions they might otherwise withhold, it can also encourage them to disclose things they wouldn't normally share. This is particularly true in anonymous "chat room" conversations, where interactants can conceal their worst attributes and promote their best qualities. This ability to carefully manage impressions often leads to high levels of attraction, affection, and emotional expression; that is, hyperpersonal communication. Walther notes that "reports of exceedingly intimate interactions [in CMC] now abound."

The bottom line, according to Walther, is that CMC is not inherently impersonal or hyperpersonal. Instead, CMC can and does achieve the same interpersonal goals as face-to-face communication. It may, however, achieve those goals in different ways and at different rates. The key, says Walther, is that CMC "affords opportunities . . . to communicate as desired."

Walther, J. B. (1996). Computer-mediated communication: Impersonal, interpersonal, and hyperpersonal interaction. *Communication Research, 23*, 3–43.

able to brush off the anger, affection, excitement, or depression of someone you're not involved with interpersonally, but in an interpersonal relationship the other's life affects you. Sometimes interdependence is a pleasure, and at other times it is a burden. In either case, interdependence is a fact of life in qualitatively interpersonal relationships.

A fourth yardstick of interpersonal communication is *disclosure* of personal information. In impersonal relationships we don't reveal much about ourselves, but in many interpersonal ones

communicators feel more comfortable sharing their thoughts and feelings. This doesn't mean that all interpersonal relationships are warm and caring, or that all self-disclosure is positive. It's possible to reveal negative, personal information: "I'm really mad at you. . . ."

In impersonal communication we seek payoffs that have little to do with the people involved. You listen to professors in class or talk to potential buyers of your used car in order to reach goals that have little to do with developing personal relationships. By contrast, you spend time in qualitatively interpersonal relationships with friends, lovers, and others because of *intrinsic rewards* that come from your communication. It doesn't matter *what* you talk about: Developing the relationship is what's important.

Because interpersonal communication is characterized by the qualities of uniqueness, irreplace-

ability, interdependence, disclosure, and intrinsic rewards, it forms a small fraction of our interaction. The majority of our communication is relatively impersonal. We chat pleasantly with shopkeepers or fellow passengers on the bus or plane; we discuss the weather or current events with most classmates and neighbors; we deal with coworkers and teachers in a polite way, but considering the number of people with whom we communicate, interpersonal relationships are by far the minority.

The rarity of qualitatively interpersonal communication isn't necessarily unfortunate. Most of us don't have the time or energy to create personal relationships with everyone we encounter. In fact, the scarcity of interpersonal communication contributes to their value. Like precious and one-of-a-kind artwork, qualitatively interpersonal relationships are special because of their scarcity.

## Personal and Impersonal Communication: A Matter of Balance

Now that you understand the differences between qualitatively interpersonal and impersonal communication, we need to ask some important questions. Is personal communication better than the impersonal variety? Is more personal communication the goal?

Most relationships aren't either personal *or* impersonal. Rather, they fall somewhere between these two extremes. Consider your own communication and you'll find that there is often a personal element in even the most impersonal situations. You might appreciate the unique sense of humor of a grocery checker or spend a few moments sharing private thoughts with the person cutting your hair. And even the most tyrannical, demanding, by-the-book boss might show an occasional flash of humanity.

Just as there's a personal element in many impersonal settings, there is also an impersonal side to our relationships with the people we care about most. There are occasions when we don't

## REFLECTION

### THE DANGERS OF ROUTINES

My husband and I have been married for almost two years and we were together for almost three years before our wedding, so the novelty of being a couple is definitely behind us. We still love each other very much, but I have noticed that our familiarity and daily routines have led us to relate in less and less personal ways. Most of the time now, our conversations are predictable: "How was your day?" "What do you want to do Saturday night?" We have our daily routines about when to be alone and when to be together. One week is pretty much like the other. Even our sex is fairly predictable. We don't talk a lot about our feelings.

Reading this part of the chapter made me realize that qualitatively interpersonal communication is like being in good shape physically: If you don't use it, you lose it!

want to be personal: when we're distracted, tired, busy, or just not interested. In fact, interpersonal communication is rather like rich food—it's fine in moderation, but too much can make you uncomfortable. The blend of personal and interpersonal communication can shift in various stages of a relationship. The communication between young lovers who talk only about their feelings may change as their relationship develops. Several years later their communication has become more routine and ritualized, and the percentage of time they spend on personal, relational issues drops and the conversation about less intimate topics increases. Chapter 9 discusses how communication changes as relationships pass through various stages, and Chapter 10 describes various theories of self-disclosure. As you read this information, you will see even more clearly that, while interpersonal communication can make life worth living, it isn't possible or desirable all the time.

# Communication Principles

Before exploring the elements of interpersonal communication in the following chapters, we need to take a look at what communication is and what it isn't, at what it can and can't do. We begin by identifying several axioms of interpersonal communication.

## Communication Can Be Intentional or Unintentional

Some communication is clearly deliberate: You probably plan your words carefully before asking the boss for a raise or offering constructive criticism. Some scholars (e.g., Motley, 1990) argue that only intentional messages like these qualify as communication. However, others (e.g., Bavelas, 1990; Baxter & Montgomery, 1996) suggest that even unintentional behavior is communicative. Suppose, for instance, that a friend overhears you muttering complaints to yourself. Even though you didn't intend for her to hear your remarks, they certainly did carry a message. In addition to these slips of the tongue, we unintentionally send many nonverbal messages. You might not be aware of your sour expression, impatient shifting, or sigh of boredom, but others view them nonetheless. Scholars have debated without reaching consensus about whether unintentional behavior should be considered communication (see, e.g., Clevenger, 1991), and it's unlikely that they will ever settle this issue (Griffin, 1997).

In *Interplay* we will look at the communicative value of both intentional and unintentional behavior. This book takes the position that whatever you do—whether you speak or remain silent, confront or avoid, show emotion or keep a poker face—you provide information to others about your thoughts and feelings. In this sense, we are like transmitters that can't be shut off.

Of course, people who decode your message may not interpret it accurately. They might take your kidding seriously or underestimate your feelings. The message you intend to convey may not even resemble the one others infer from your actions. This explains why the best way to boost understanding is to negotiate a shared meaning with your communication partners. The perception-checking skills you learn in Chapter 4 and the listening skills introduced in Chapter 7 are tools that will allow you to make sure that the meaning of messages you send and receive are understandable by both you and others.

## All Messages Have a Content and a Relational Dimension

Virtually every verbal statement has a **content** dimension, the information it explicitly conveys: "Please pass the salt," "Not now, I'm tired," "You forgot to buy a quart of milk." In addition to this sort of obvious content, all messages also have a **relational** component (Dillard et al., 1999; Watzlawick et al., 1967) that expresses how you feel about the other person: whether you like or dislike the other person, feel in control or subordinate, feel comfortable or anxious, and so on. For instance, consider how many different **relational**

messages you could communicate by simply saying "Thanks a lot" in different ways.

Sometimes the content dimension of a message is all that matters. For example, you may not care how the directory assistance operator feels about you as long as you get the phone number you're seeking. In a qualitative sense, however, the relational dimension of a message is often more important than the content under discussion. This explains why disputes over apparently trivial subjects become so important. In such cases we're not really arguing over whose turn it is to take out the trash or whether to play tennis or swim. Instead, we're disputing the nature of the relationship. Who's in control? How important are we to each other? Chapter 9 explores several key relational issues in detail.

## Communication Is Irreversible

We sometimes wish that we could back up in time, erasing words or acts and replacing them with better alternatives. Unfortunately, such reversal is impossible. Sometimes, further explanation can clear up another's confusion or an apology can mollify another's hurt feelings, but other times

"We will all disregard that last remark."

Reprinted from the *Wall Street Journal,* Permission — Cartoon Features Syndicate

## REFLECTION

### HURTFUL WORDS CAN'T BE RETRACTED

I was adopted at the age of five. My adoptive parents were verbally abusive. On a few occasions, they said things to me in anger that I will never forget and which changed our relationship forever. "Nobody wanted you—you should be thankful that we took you in" was one of their major hurtful messages. Even though they would apologize later, no amount of explanations ease the pain those words have caused me.

no amount of explanation can erase the impression you have created. It is no more possible to "unreceive" a message than to "unsqueeze" a tube of toothpaste. Words said and deeds done are irretrievable.

## Communication Is Unrepeatable

Because communication is an ongoing process, an event cannot be repeated. The friendly smile that worked so well meeting a stranger last week may not succeed with the person you encounter tomorrow: It may feel stale and artificial to you the second time around, or it may be wrong for the new person or occasion. Even with the same person, it's impossible to recreate an event. Why? Because both you and the other person have changed. You've both lived longer. The behavior isn't original. Your feelings about each other may have changed. You need not constantly invent new ways to act around familiar people, but you should realize that the "same" words and behavior are different each time they are spoken or performed.

## Communication Misconceptions

Now that we've spent some time describing what communication is, we need to identify some

things it is not. Avoiding these common misconceptions (adapted from McCroskey & Richmond, 1996) can save you a great deal of trouble in your personal life.

## Not All Communication Seeks Understanding

Most people operate on the implicit but flawed assumption that the goal of all communication is to maximize understanding between communicators. While some understanding is necessary for us to coordinate our interaction, there are some types of communication in which understanding as we usually conceive it isn't the primary goal (Aune, in press). Consider, for example,

- *The social rituals we enact every day.* "How's it going?" you ask. "Great," the other person replies. The primary goal in exchanges like these is mutual acknowledgment: There's obviously no serious attempt to exchange information.
- *Many attempts to influence others.* A quick analysis of most television commercials shows that they are aimed at persuading viewers to buy products, not to understand the content of the ad. In the same way, many of our attempts at persuading others to act as we want don't involve a

desire to get the other person to understand what we want—just to comply with our wishes.

■ *Deliberate ambiguity and deception.* When you decline an unwanted invitation by saying "I can't make it," you probably want to create the impression that the decision is really beyond your control. (If your goal was to be perfectly clear, you might say, "I don't want to get together. In fact, I'd rather do almost anything than accept your invitation.") As Chapter 10 explains in detail, we often equivocate precisely because we want to obscure our true thoughts and feelings.

## More Communication Is Not Always Better

While failure to communicate effectively can certainly cause problems (Richmond, 1995), *too much* talking can also be a mistake. Sometimes excessive communication is simply unproductive, as when two people "talk a problem to death," going over the same ground again and again without making progress. There are other times when talking too much actually aggravates a problem. We've all had the experience of "talking ourselves into a hole"—making a bad situation worse by pursuing it too far. As some writers have put it, "More and more negative communication merely leads to more and more negative results" (McCroskey & Wheeless, 1976, p. 5). In one study, college roommates revealed that thinking and talking about conflicts can actually increase relational problems (Cloven & Roloff, 1991).

There are even times when *no* interaction is the best course. When two people are angry and hurt, they may say things they don't mean and will later regret. In such cases it's probably best to spend time cooling off, thinking about what to say and how to say it. Chapter 8 will help you decide when and how to share feelings.

## Communication Will Not Solve All Problems

Sometimes even the best-planned, best-timed communication won't solve a problem. For exam-

*"Let's stop this before we both say a lot of things we mean."*

ple, imagine that you ask an instructor to explain why you received a poor grade on a project you believe deserved top marks. The professor clearly outlines the reasons why you received the low grade and sticks to that position after listening thoughtfully to your protests. Has communication solved the problem? Hardly.

Sometimes clear communication is even the *cause* of problems. Suppose, for example, that a friend asks you for an honest opinion of the two-hundred-dollar outfit he has just bought. Your clear and sincere answer, "I think it makes you look fat," might do more harm than good. Deciding when and how to self-disclose isn't always easy. See Chapter 10 for suggestions.

## Effective Communication Is Not a Natural Ability

Most people assume that communication is an aptitude that people develop without the need for training—rather like breathing. Although nearly everyone does manage to function passably without much formal communication training, most people operate at a level of effectiveness far below their potential. In fact, communication skills are rather like athletic ability. Even the most inept of us can learn to be more effective with training and practice.

## Communication Competence

"What does it take to communicate better?" is probably the most important question to ask as you read this book. Answering it has been one of the leading challenges for communication scholars. While all the answers aren't in yet, research has identified a great deal of important and useful information about communication competence.

### Communication Competence Defined

Defining **communication competence** isn't as easy as it might seem. Although scholars are still struggling to agree on a precise definition, most would agree that effective communication involves achieving one's goals in a manner that, ideally, maintains or enhances the relationship in which it occurs (Wiemann et al., 1997). This definition may seem both vague and verbose, but a closer look shows that it suggests several important characteristics of communication competence.

**There Is No Single "Ideal" or "Effective" Way to Communicate**   Your own experience shows that a variety of communication styles can be effective. Some very successful communicators are serious while others use humor; some are gregarious while others are quieter, and some are more straightforward while others hint diplomatically. Just as there are many kinds of beautiful music or art, there are many kinds of competent communication. Furthermore, a type of communication that is competent in one setting might be a colossal blunder in another. The joking insults you routinely trade with one friend might offend a sensitive family member, and last Saturday night's romantic approach would probably be out of place at work on Monday morning. This means that there can be no surefire list of rules or tips that will guarantee your success as a communicator.

Because communication is transactional, something we do *with* others rather than *to* them, behavior that is competent in one relationship isn't necessarily effective in others. For example, a study by Laura Guerrero and her associates (1995) uncovered a variety of ways people deal with jealousy in their relationships. The approaches

## DILBERT                                                                  by Scott Adams

DILBERT reprinted by permission of United Feature Syndicate, Inc.

included keeping closer tabs on the partner, acting indifferent, decreasing affection, talking the matter over, and acting angry. The researchers found that no type of behavior was effective or ineffective in every relationship. They concluded that approaches that work with some people would be harmful to others. Findings like these demonstrate that competence is relational, not absolute.

A fascinating study on relational satisfaction illustrates that what constitutes satisfying communication varies from one relationship to another. Researchers Brent Burleson and Wendy Samter (1994) hypothesized that people with sophisticated communication skills (such as managing conflict well, giving ego support to others, and providing comfort to relational partners) would be better at maintaining friendships than less skilled communicators. To their surprise, the results did not support this guess. In fact, friendships were most satisfying when partners possessed matching skill levels. Apparently, relational satisfaction arises in part when our style matches those of the others with whom we interact.

Flexibility is especially important when members of different cultures meet. Some communication skills seem to be universal (Ruben, 1989). Every culture has rules that require speakers to behave appropriately, for example. But the definition of what kind of communication is appropriate in a given situation varies considerably from one culture to another (Chen & Sarosta, 1996). On an obvious level, customs like belching after a meal or appearing nude in public that might be appropriate in some parts of the world would be considered outrageous in others. But there are more subtle differences in competent communication. For example, qualities like self-disclosure and speaking clearly that are valued in the United States are likely to be considered overly aggressive and insensitive in many Asian cultures, where subtlety and indirectness are considered important (Kim et al., 1998). Even within a single society, members of various cocultures may have different notions of appropriate behavior. One study revealed that ideas of how good friends should communicate varied

from one ethnic group to another (Collier, 1996). As a group, Latinos valued relational support most highly, while African Americans prized respect and acceptance. Asian Americans emphasized a caring, positive exchange of ideas, and Euro-Americans prized friends who recognized their needs as individuals. Findings like these mean that there can be no surefire list of rules or tips that will guarantee your success as a communicator. They also suggest that competent communicators are able to adapt their style to suit the individual and cultural preferences of others (Chen, 1997).

**Competence Is Situational**   Because competent behavior varies so much from one situation and person to another, it's a mistake to think that communication competence is a trait that a person either possesses or lacks (Spitzberg, 1991). It's more accurate to talk about *degrees* or *areas* of competence. You and the people you know are probably quite competent in some areas and less so in others. For example, you might deal quite skillfully with peers, while feeling clumsy interacting with people much older or younger, wealthier or poorer, more or less attractive than yourself. In fact, your competence may vary from situation to situation. This means it's an overgeneralization to say, in a moment of distress, "I'm a terrible communicator!" It's more accurate to say, "I didn't handle this situation very well, but I'm better in others."

**Competence Can Be Learned**   To some degree, biology is destiny when it comes to communication style (Beatty & McCroskey, 1998; Horvath, 1995). Studies of identical and fraternal twins suggest traits including sociability, anger, and relaxation seem to be partially a function of our genetic makeup.

Fortunately, biology isn't the only factor that shapes how we communicate. Communication competence is, to a great degree, a set of skills that anyone can learn. Sometimes competence is studied systematically—for instance, in communication classes. People with high communication apprehension often benefit from communication skills training (Ayres & Hopf, 1993; Phillips, 1986). Even a modest amount of training can

FILM CLIP

## NOTHING BUT THE TRUTH? *LIAR LIAR*

Would the world be a better place if everyone told the truth, the whole truth, and nothing but the truth? The movie *Liar Liar* suggests the answer is no. Fletcher Reede (Jim Carrey) is a lawyer whose communication style is filled with half-truths, exaggerations, and flat-out lies. His son Max (Justin Cooper) becomes fed up with his father's fudging and makes a wish over his birthday cake—that his dad won't lie for an entire day.

Max's wish comes true and the laughs begin. A judge casually asks Reede, "How are you today, counselor?" and gets the answer, "I'm a little upset about a bad sexual episode last night." A policeman asks, "Do you know why I'm pulling you over?" and Reede replies, "That depends on how long you were following me." He passes by an officemate whose name he's forgotten and announces, "You're not important enough to remember!" We laugh because we know a competent communicator would never make such blunt and insensitive comments, even if they were true.

It's worth noting that Reede's lying isn't much better than his blunt truth telling. He dishes out insincere flattery (telling a secretary with an awful hairdo that "it completely accents your facial features") and breaks promises he never intended to keep.

What we learn from watching Fletcher Reede as a truth teller and a liar is that competent communication isn't as simple as following a set of rules like "always tell the truth." Instead, it is often a complicated and skillful mixture of many behaviors that vary according to the situation, taking into account ethical standards, the needs of each communicator involved, and the situation.

produce dramatic results. For example, after only thirty minutes of instruction, one group of observers became significantly more effective in detecting deception in interviews (deTurck & Miller, 1990). Even without systematic training, it's possible to develop communication skills through the processes of observation and trial and error. We learn from our own successes and failures, as well as from observing other models—both positive and negative. One study revealed that the passage of time does lead to improved communication skill: College students' communication competence increases over the course of their undergraduate studies (Rubin et al., 1990).

## Characteristics of Competent Communication

Despite the fact that competent communication varies from one situation to another, scholars have identified several common denominators that characterize effective communication in most contexts.

**A Large Repertoire of Skills**   As we've already seen, good communicators don't use the same approach in every situation. They know that sometimes it's best to be blunt and sometimes tactful, that there is a time to speak up and a time to be quiet. They understand that it's sometimes best to be serious and sometimes best to be playful.

## FOCUS ON RESEARCH

### FACE-TO-FACE OR CHANGE THE CHANNEL?

Assume for a moment that you feel a need to make a confession to your romantic partner. The confession might be about something you've done wrong, or something that would make your partner think poorly of you. How would you send your message—through a mediated channel (such as a phone call or an e-mail) or in a face-to-face conversation?

Patrick O'Sullivan conducted research to learn about preferences for face-to-face versus mediated channels for sending messages. He surveyed 133 undergraduates in premarital romantic relationships to learn how they would offer information to their partners in four categories: Confess (negative message about self), Boost (positive message about self), Accuse (negative message about partner), or Praise (positive message about partner).

In all four categories, the students said they would favor face-to-face over mediated interactions. Nevertheless, there were differences in the degrees to which they preferred face-to-face conversations. As might be expected, the respondents said they would have little trouble sending positive messages face-to-face, but medi-ated channels appealed to them more for sending negative messages. In particular, the students rated the "Confess" category as the one for which they would most likely use a mediated channel.

O'Sullivan concluded that "individuals recognize that mediated channels can help minimize the costs for them-selves or their partner associated with embarrassing or unattractive information." This research suggests that the channels people choose for sending their messages can be an important factor in their communica-tion competence.

O'Sullivan, P. B. 2000. What you don't know won't hurt ME: Impression management functions of communication channels in relationships. *Communication Monographs, 70.*

The chances of behaving competently increase with the number of options you have about how to communicate. For example, if you want to start a conversation with a stranger, your chances of success increase as you have more options available (Kelly & Watson, 1986). All it might take to get the conversational ball rolling is a self-introduction. In other cases, seeking assistance might work well: "I've just moved here. What kind of neighborhood is the Eastside?" A third strategy is to ask a question about some situational feature: "I've never heard this band before. Do you know anything about them?" You could also offer a sincere compliment and follow it up with a question: "Great shoes! Where did you get them?" Just as a golfer has a wide range of clubs to use for various situations, a competent communicator has a large array of behaviors from which to choose.

**Adaptability**    Having a large repertoire of possible behaviors is one ingredient of competent commu-nication, but you have to be able to choose the *right* one for a particular situation (see, e.g., Brash-ers & Jackson, 1999; Hample & Dallinger, 2000; Stamp, 1999). To repeat, an approach that works well in one situation might be disastrous some-where else. Effective communication means choos-ing the right response for the situation.

**Ability to Perform Skillfully**   Once you have chosen the appropriate way to communicate, you have to perform that behavior effectively. In communication, as in other activities, practice is the key to skillful performance. Much of the information in *Interplay* will introduce you to new tools for communicating, and the Skill Builder activities at the end of each chapter will help you practice them.

**Involvement**   Not surprisingly, effective communication occurs when the people care about one another and the topic at hand (Cegala et al., 1982). Rod Hart suggests that this involvement has several dimensions (adapted here from Knapp & Vangelisti, 2000). It includes commitment to the other person and the relationship, concern about the message being discussed, and a desire to make the relationship clearly useful. Notice that these characteristics involve two themes. The first is *commitment.* Good communicators care about the other person, about the subject, and about being understood. The second theme is *profitability.* The most effective communication produces good results for everyone involved.

**Empathy/Perspective Taking**   People have the best chance of developing an effective message when they understand the other person's point of view (see Ifert & Roloff, 1997). And since others aren't always good at expressing their thoughts and feelings clearly, the ability to imagine how an issue might look from another's perspective suggests why listening is such an important communication skill. Not only does it help you understand others, but it also provides information to develop strategies about how to best influence them. Empathy is such an important element of communicative competence that researcher Mark Redmond (1989, p. 594) flatly states that "by definition, a person cannot produce a message that is empathic that is not also communicatively competent."

**Cognitive Complexity**   **Cognitive complexity** is the ability to construct a variety of different frame-

works for viewing an issue. Cognitive complexity is an ingredient of communication competence because it allows us to make sense of people using a variety of frameworks. For instance, imagine that a longtime friend seems to be angry with you. One possible explanation is that your friend is offended by something you've done. Another possibility is that something has happened in another part of your friend's life that is upsetting. Or perhaps nothing at all is wrong, and you're just being overly sensitive. Researchers have found that a large number of constructs for interpreting the behavior of others leads to greater "conversational sensitivity," increasing the chances of acting in ways that will produce satisfying results (Burleson & Caplan, 1998).

**Self-Monitoring**   Psychologists use the term **self-monitoring** to describe the process of paying close attention to one's behavior and using these observations to shape the way one behaves. Self-monitors are able to detach a part of their consciousness to observe their behavior from a detached viewpoint, making observations such as

> "I'm making a fool out of myself."
> "I'd better speak up now."
> "This approach is working well. I'll keep it up."

It's no surprise that self-monitoring increases one's effectiveness as a communicator (see Kolb, 1998; Sypher & Sypher, 1983). The ability to ask yourself the question, "How am I doing?" and to change your behavior if the answer isn't positive is a tremendous asset for communicators. People with poor self-monitoring skill blunder through life, sometimes succeeding and sometimes failing, without the detachment to understand why.

How does your behavior as an interpersonal communicator measure up against the standards of competence described in this chapter? Like most people, you will probably find some areas of your life that are very satisfying and others that you would like to change. As you read on in this book, realize that the information in each chapter offers advice that can help your communication become more productive and rewarding.

Although the qualities described here do play an important role in communicative competence, they can be ineffective when carried to excess (Spitzberg, 1994). For example, too much self-monitoring can make a person so self-conscious that the concern for appearance ("How do I sound?" "How am I doing?") overshadows the need to be faithful to one's true beliefs. Likewise, an excess of empathy and cognitive complexity can lead you to see all sides of an issue so well that you're incapable of acting. In other words, there is a *curvilinear relationship* among most of the elements described in these pages: Both a deficiency and an excess can lead to incompetent communication.

## Summary

Communication is important for a variety of reasons. Besides satisfying practical needs, meaningful communication contributes to physical health, plays a major role in defining our identity, and forms the basis for our social relationships.

Early theorists viewed communication as a linear process in which senders aimed messages at passive receivers. This linear model was refined into an interactive one, which pictured communication as an exchange of messages between senders and receivers. More recently, communication has been characterized as an ongoing, transactional process in which individuals exchange messages whose meanings are influenced by the history of the relationship and the experiences of the participants.

Interpersonal communication can be defined quantitatively (by the number of people involved) or qualitatively (by the nature of interaction between them). In a qualitative sense, interpersonal relationships are unique, irreplaceable, interdependent, and intrinsically rewarding. Qualitatively interpersonal communication is relatively infrequent, even in many close relationships.

A variety of principles help explain the communication process. Messages can be intentional or unintentional. They almost always have both a content and a relational dimension. Once expressed, messages cannot be withdrawn. Finally, communication is unrepeatable.

To understand the communication process, it is important to recognize and avoid several common misconceptions. Despite the value of self-expression, more communication is not always better. In fact, there are occasions when more communication can increase problems. Even at its best, communication is not a panacea that will solve every problem. Effective communication is not a natural ability. While some people have greater aptitude at communicating, everyone can learn to interact with others more effectively.

Communication competence is the ability to get desired results from others in a manner that maintains the relationship on terms that are acceptable to everyone. There is no single ideal way to communicate: Flexibility and adaptability are characteristics of competent communicators, as are skill at performing behaviors, involvement with others, the ability to view issues from the other's point of view, cognitive complexity, and self-monitoring. The good news is, communication competency can be learned.

## Recommended Readings

**Is it impossible not to communicate?**

Michael T. Motley. "On Whether One Can(not) Communicate: An Examination via Traditional Communication Postulates." *Western Journal of Speech Communication* 54 (1990): 1–20.

Theodore Clevenger. "Can One Not Communicate? A Conflict of Models." *Communication Studies* 42 (1991): 340–353.

**The limits of communication:**

David Stiebel. *When Talking Makes Things Worse: Resolving Problems When Communication Fails.* Kansas City, MO: Andrews and McMeel, 1997

### Qualitative interpersonal communication:

Ted Spencer. "Transforming Relationships through Ordinary Talk." In *Dynamics of Relationships,* edited by Steve Duck. Thousand Oaks, CA: Sage, 1994.

John Stewart. "Interpersonal Communication: Contact between Persons." In *Bridges, Not Walls: A Book about Interpersonal Communication.* New York: McGraw-Hill, 1998.

### Computer-mediated interpersonal communication:

Joseph B. Walther. "Computer-Mediated Communication: Impersonal, Interpersonal, and Hyperpersonal Interaction." *Communication Research* 23 (1996): 3–43.

## Activities

**1. Invitation to Insight**
   How much time do you spend communicating? Conduct an informal study to answer this question by keeping a two-day log of your activities. Based on your findings, answer the following questions:
   a. What percentage of your waking time is spent speaking and listening to others?
   b. Using the explanation on pages 15-17, describe what percentage of your entire communication is qualitatively interpersonal.
   c. How satisfied are you with your findings? How would you like to change your every-day communication?

**2. Critical Thinking Probe**
   As you read in this chapter, face-to-face communication is transactional in nature: something we do *with* others and not *to* them. Explain how transactional communication differs from the more linear kinds that occur in mass media such as films, television, books, and newspapers. Is linear communication possible in face-to-face interaction?

**3. Invitation to Insight**
   How competent are you as a communicator? You can begin to answer this question by interviewing someone who knows you well: a family member, friend, or fellow worker, for example.
   a. Describe the characteristics of competent communicators outlined on pages 24-26 of this chapter. Be sure your interviewee understands each of them.
   b. Ask your interviewee to rate you on each of the observable qualities. (It won't be possible for others to evaluate internal characteristics, such as cognitive complexity and self-monitoring.) Be sure this evaluation reflects your communication in a variety of situations: It's likely you aren't uniformly competent—or incompetent—in all of them.
   c. If your rating is not high in one or more areas, discuss with your partner how you could raise it.
   d. Consider whether another person might rate you differently. Why might this happen?

**4. Skill Builder**
   Knowing how you want to communicate isn't the same as being able to perform competently. The technique of behavior rehearsal provides a way to improve a particular communication skill before you use it in real life. Behavior rehearsal consists of four steps:
   a. Define your goal. Begin by identifying the way you want to behave.
   b. Break the goal into the behaviors it involves. Most goals are made up of several verbal and nonverbal parts. You may be able to identify these parts by thinking about them yourself, by observing others, by reading about them, or by asking others for advice.
   c. Practice each behavior before using it in real life. You can practice a new behavior by rehearsing it alone and then with others before you put it into action. Another approach is to picture yourself behaving in

new ways. This mental image can boost effectiveness.

d. Try out the behavior in real life. You can increase the odds of success if you follow two pieces of advice when trying out new communication behaviors: Work on only one subskill at a time, and start with easy situations. Don't expect yourself suddenly to behave flawlessly in the most challenging situations. Begin by practicing your new skills in situations in which you have a chance of success.

# CHAPTER
## 2

# Culture and Communication

# After Studying the Material in This Chapter . . .

## You Should Understand:

1. The prevalence and importance of intercultural communication in today's world.

2. The role of perception in intercultural communication.

3. Five key values that help shape a culture's communication norms.

4. The factors that shape a culture's verbal codes, nonverbal codes, and decoding of messages.

5. The attitudes, knowledge, and skills required for intercultural communication competence.

## You Should Be Able to:

1. Identify the range and significance of intercultural contacts you are likely to experience.

2. Describe a set of cultural values different from yours that could result in different cultural communication patterns.

3. Identify your tolerance for ambiguity and your open-mindedness to different cultural communication patterns.

4. Develop a strategy for dealing with people of cultural backgrounds different from your own.

## Key Terms

Achievement culture

Coculture

Collectivistic culture

Culture

Ethnic group

Ethnocentrism

High-context culture

Individualistic culture

In-group

Intercultural communication

Interethnic communication

International communication

Interracial communication

Linguistic determinism

Linguistic relativism

Low-context culture

Nurturing culture

Out-group

Power distance

Prejudice

Race

Sapir-Whorf hypothesis

Stereotyping

Uncertainty avoidance

# Why Study Intercultural Communication?

Over three decades ago, Marshall McLuhan (1966) coined the metaphor of the world as a "global village" where members of every nation are connected by communication technology. Just like members of a traditional village, McLuhan suggested, the affairs and fates of the occupants of planet Earth are connected—for better or worse. This analysis has proven to be increasingly true in the years since McLuhan introduced it. Communication scholars Larry Samovar, Richard Porter, and Lisa Stefani (1998) outline a list of factors that make the citizens throughout the world at large, and the United States and Canada in particular, increasingly connected.

Demographic changes are transforming the United States into a microcosm of the global village. Immigration has made North American society increasingly multicultural and multiethnic. As Figure 2.1 shows, Latino residents total more than fifteen million, and demographic experts see this number growing (Judy & D'Amico, 1997). The

**Figure 2.1** *U.S. Population by Race, 1995 and 2050 (projected)*
Adapted from Shinagawa, L. H. (1997). *Atlas of American Diversity.* Newbury Park, CA: Sage/Altamira, 150.

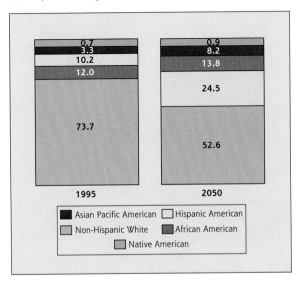

number of Asian Americans is over four million, many times the number only twenty years earlier. African Americans also account for a larger number and percentage of the U.S. population than ever before—over twenty million citizens. At the same time these groups are growing, the percentage of whites in the population is declining. In many cities—including Chicago, Miami, Los Angeles, San Diego, Dallas, Detroit, Washington, and Albuquerque—Euro-American students are now the minority in schools. Changes like these lead to a far more diverse workplace. In 1970, 54 percent of U.S. workers were white males. By 1980, the number had declined to 49 percent, and it fell to 43 percent by 1986. In the first years of the new millennium, white females, minorities, and immigrants will constitute almost 85 percent of those entering the workforce.

Relatively cheap transportation has reduced the barrier of distance, making international travel easier for more people than ever before. Author Erla Zwingle (1999, p. 12) describes some impressions that illustrate the degree to which worldwide travel and communication have blended cultures:

> That I should be sitting in a coffee shop in London drinking Italian espresso served by an Algerian waiter to the strains of the Beach Boys singing "I wish they all could be California girls. . . ." Or hanging around a pub in New Delhi that serves Lebanese cuisine to the music of a Filipino band in rooms decorated with barrels of Irish stout, a stuffed hippo head, and a vintage poster announcing the Grand Ole Opry concert to be given at the high school in Douglas, Georgia. Some Japanese are fanatics for flamenco. Denmark imports five times as much Italian pasta as it did ten years ago. The classic American blond Barbie doll now comes in some 30 national varieties—and this year emerged as Austrian and Moroccan.

By the early 1990s, over forty million Americans had traveled to other countries—almost twice the number who did so only a decade earlier Samovar et al., 1998). Likewise, the flow of travelers visiting the United States from abroad has steadily grown, to over thirty million visitors

cost no greater than exchanging computer messages with someone in the same town. Worldwide television programming from networks such as CNN brings images from around the world into the living room of anyone who tunes in. Unlike broadcasting in earlier times, technology now makes it possible to see events as they happen.

Economic integration also creates ties that bind nations and people. While national economies still exist, they are increasingly connected with and affected by developments around the world. Over a third of the profits of U.S. companies come from overseas operations. Some forty thousand U.S. firms do business internationally, and twenty-five thousand of them have overseas branches and affiliates. Even before the economies of the United States, Canada, and Mexico were integrated through the North American Free Trade Agreement in 1993, international trade resulted in four of every five new jobs created at home. Approximately 80 percent of U.S. manufacturers compete with firms from other nations. Just as U.S. companies seek out foreign markets, firms from around the world also do business in North America. More than five thousand foreign companies operate in the United States. Overseas investors own 64 percent of commercial property in downtown Los Angeles and over one million acres of U.S. farmland. Statistics like these demonstrate the flow of people, goods, and services around the world.

Native-born citizens also contribute to a diverse population. For example, African Americans now account for over 12 percent of the U.S. population, and legal changes have given members of this group significantly greater visibility and access to power and economic advantage formerly denied them. Members of many groups—homosexuals, people with disabilities, and women to name a few— achieved greater visibility and power by the end of the twentieth century. Approximately one million interracial marriages each year create families where diversity is a reality, not just an abstract term.

It is clear that people from varying backgrounds encounter and affect one another far more than ever before. Given these changes, it makes sense to examine how communication

annually by 1990. Visitors to the Grand Canyon, Disneyland, the Statue of Liberty, or Niagara Falls are likely to overhear their fellow tourists conversing in a symphony of languages, including Japanese, German, French, and Spanish.

Thanks to the growth in communication technology, even stay-at-homes have access to virtually the entire world. International telephone service makes it possible to reach out and touch someone in virtually every country around the globe, usually by simply punching a few numbers into a handy telephone touch pad. The Internet and World Wide Web allow users around the world to share information with one another instantaneously, at a operates when members of different cultures interact. Our examination will show that there is, indeed, a cultural dimension to human communication, that when people from different backgrounds interact, they face a set of challenges different from those that arise when members of the same culture try to communicate effectively. In this chapter we will outline some of those differences and offer suggestions on how to communicate most effectively when encountering people from different backgrounds.

# Fundamental Concepts

Before going any further, we need to clarify two important concepts: *culture* and *intercultural communication*. We also need to look at what distinguishes intercultural communication from interpersonal communication as we examine it in the rest of this book.

## Culture

Defining **culture** isn't an easy task. Almost fifty years ago, a survey of scholarly literature revealed five hundred definitions, phrasings, and uses of the concept (Kroeber & Kluckholn, 1952). For our purposes, Sarah Trenholm and Arthur Jensen (2000, p. 363) offer a clear and comprehensive definition of *culture*: "that set of values, beliefs, norms, customs, rules, and codes that socially define groups of people, giving them a sense of commonality."

This definition shows that culture is, to a great extent, a matter of *perception* and *definition*. When you identify yourself as a member of a culture, you must not only share certain characteristics, but you must also recognize yourself and others like you as possessing these features and see others who don't possess them as members of different categories. For example, eye color doesn't seem like a significant factor in distinguishing "us" from "them," while skin color plays a more important role, at least in some cases. It's not hard to imagine a society where the opposite were true. Social scientists

use the label **in-groups** to describe groups with which we identify and **out-groups** to label those that we view as different (Tajfel & Turner, 1992).

## Intercultural Communication

Having defined culture, we can go on to define **intercultural communication** as the process that occurs when members of two or more cultures exchange messages in a manner that is influenced by their different cultural perceptions and symbol systems (Samovar & Porter, 1995). Note that intercultural communication (at least as we'll use the term here) doesn't always occur when people from different cultures interact. The cultural backgrounds, perceptions, and symbol systems of the participants must have a significant impact on the exchange before we can say that culture has made a difference. Consider a few examples where culture does and doesn't play a role:

- A group of preschool children is playing together in a park. These three-year-olds don't recognize the fact that their parents may come from different countries, that their skins are different colors, or even that they don't speak the same language. Most of the time as the children play happily together, these differences are trivial. At this point we wouldn't say that intercultural communication is taking place. Only when different norms become apparent—about diet, sharing, or parental discipline, for example—do the children begin to think of one another as different.
- Members of a school basketball team—some Asian, some black, some Latino, and some white—are intent on winning the league championship. During a game, racial distinctions aren't important. There's plenty of communication, but it isn't fundamentally intercultural. Away from their games, the players are friendly when they encounter one another, but they rarely socialize. If they did, they might notice some fundamental differences in the way members of each group communicate.
- A husband and wife were raised in homes with different religious traditions. Most of the time

their religious heritage makes little difference, and the partners view themselves as a unified couple. Every so often, however—perhaps during the holidays or when meeting members of each other's family—the different backgrounds are highlighted. At those times we can imagine the partners feeling quite different from each other—thinking of themselves as members of separate cultures.

These examples show that, in order to view ourselves as a member of a culture, there has to be some distinction between "us" and "them," between in- and out-group. We may not always be able to say precisely what the differences are. We may have only a gut feeling that something is going on, and there are occasions when cultural influences are powerful but so subtle that they go unrecognized.

There are several notable types of intercultural communication, and the differences among them are more significant than they might first appear.

The term **race** refers to physical characteristics: skin color, facial features, hair texture, and so on. Hence, interracial communication occurs when communicators from different races interact. There's no question that race plays a major role in shaping one's identity and affecting one's communication. You can probably identify several personal encounters in which racial differences were significant. Nonetheless, it's important to note that not *every* interracial encounter is a case of intercultural communication—at least not as we've defined it here. Samovar and Porter (1995) cite the example of two neighbors: an Anglo-American and a third-generation Korean American whose family has been firmly acculturated in the mainstream North American lifestyle. Although the communicators are racially different, they share fundamentally the same cultural basis during their conversation. Likewise, many (though not all) interracial transactions occur in business, education, sports, and other contexts without skin color or other features playing a significant role.

Although the adjectives *racial* and *ethnic* are usually used interchangeably, the terms aren't synonymous. Communication scholars define an **ethnic group** as a collection of people who share customs, characteristics, language, common history, or geographic origin. in this sense, the United States is made up of many different ethnic groups: Irish Americans, Mexican Americans, Italian Americans, and so on. Interethnic communication occurs when members of ethnically different groups interact.

A comparison of race and ethnicity shows that the two concepts aren't always identical. Canada and the territory formerly called Yugoslavia provide examples of racially similar but ethnically different groups. French- and English-speaking Canadians may resemble one another physically, but anyone familiar with Canadian politics and culture will testify to the profound differences in heritage and attitudes between the two groups. Most former Yugoslavians are racially quite homogeneous, but this similarity did not prevent the ethnically different Serbs, Croats, and Moslems from slaughtering one another after the country devolved into a collection of ethnic enclaves.

An ethnic group may consist of several races. Jews are a good example. For instance, there are Ethiopian Jews from Africa, Semitic Jews from the Middle East, and Northern European Jews from Russia, Poland, and Ukraine. Likewise, most citizens in racially diverse countries such as Brazil or Cuba are ethnically similar. In contrast, a race may be composed of several ethnic groups. Although Japanese, Thais, Chinese, and Koreans resemble each other physically, their cultural differences are enormous.

When citizens from different countries or other political entities meet, **international communication** occurs. By now, you can see that international communication may or may not be interethnic, interracial, or intercultural. A look at any history book or daily newspaper provides a catalog of examples—some encouraging and many others depressing—that illustrate the frequency and significance of communication between citizens of different countries. Despite its

"Daddy, do we belong to an ethnic group?"

importance, international communication has not been a major field of study for communication scholars, most of whom are more interested in personal contacts than political differences.

Many social scientists use the term **coculture** to describe the perception of membership in a group that is part of an encompassing culture. For example, in American culture it is easy to recognize categories such as age (teen culture, senior citizens), ethnicity (Latino, Euro-American), gender, sexual orientation, physical disabilities, and religion. Some scholars (e.g., Tannen, 1990, 1994; Wood, 1997) and writers in the popular press (e.g., Gray, 1992) have even characterized men and women as belonging to different cocultures because their communication styles are so different. The Focus on Research profile on page 40 illustrates one such difference. Differences in accepted communication patterns and styles can present challenges when people from different cocultural backgrounds interact.

## Interpersonal and Intercultural Communication

At this point, you might be asking yourself whether there is any communication that isn't intercultural, or at least cocultural. After all, if every encounter is defined as being cross-cultural, the term has little

use. Indeed, there are many cases when communication isn't influenced by intercultural considerations. Even in an increasingly diverse world, there are still plenty of relationships in which people share a basically common background. The Irish marchers in a St. Patrick's Day parade, the suburban-bred group of men who play poker every other Friday night, and the members of a college sorority or fraternity are likely to share fundamentally similar personal histories and, therefore, have similar norms, customs, and values. Even when people with different cultural backgrounds communicate, shared values and experiences are often far more significant than the cultural backgrounds they bring to the relationship (Singer, 1998). David may be a Jewish male whose ancestors came from Eastern Europe while Lisa is a third-generation Japanese person whose parents are practicing Christians, but they have created a life together that usually is more significant than their differences and that leaves them able to comfortably deal with those differences when they do arise.

Rather than classifying some exchanges as intercultural and others as free from cultural influences, it's more accurate to talk about *degrees* of cultural significance (Lustig & Koester, 1999). Encounters can fit along a spectrum of "interculturalness." At the "most intercultural" end are situations where differences between the backgrounds and beliefs of communicators are high. A traveler visiting a new country for the first time with little knowledge of local society would be an obvious example. At the "least intercultural" end of the spectrum fall exchanges where cultural differences make little difference. A student from Los Angeles who attends a small liberal arts college in the Midwest might find life somewhat different, but the adjustment would be far less difficult than that for the international traveler. In between these extremes falls a whole range of encounters in which culture plays varying roles.

What is the relationship between intercultural communication and interpersonal relationships? William Gudykunst and Young Kim (1997) summarize an approach that helps answer this question.

Their thinking suggests that interpersonal and intercultural factors combine to form a two-by-two matrix in which the importance of interpersonal communication forms one dimension and intercultural significance forms the second one (Figure 2.2). This model shows that some interpersonal transactions (for example, a conversation between two siblings who have been raised in the same household) have virtually no intercultural elements. Other encounters (such as a traveler from Senegal trying to get directions from a Ukrainian taxi driver in New York City) are almost exclusively intercultural, without the personal dimensions that we have discussed throughout this book. Still other exchanges—the most interesting ones for our purposes—contain elements of both intercultural and interpersonal communication. This range of encounters is broad in the global village: Business people from different backgrounds try to wrap up a deal; U.S.-born and immigrant children learn to get along in school; health-care educators seek effective ways to serve patients from around the world; neighbors from different racial or ethnic back-grounds look for ways to make their streets safer and cleaner; suburban-bred teachers seek common ground with inner-city students—the list seems almost endless. In situations like these, communicators are trying to establish some degree of personal contact. When they do find ways of connecting that account for, and even transcend, cultural differences, communicators have created what Fred Casmir (1991) calls a "third culture": a unique relationship shared by two or more people.

## Cultural Values and Norms

Some cultural influences on communication are obvious. You don't have to be a scholar or researcher to appreciate how different languages or customs can make communication between groups both interesting and challenging. However, in addition to these obvious differences, some far less visible values and norms shape how members of cultures think and act (Gudykunst & Matsumoto, 1996). Unless communicators are

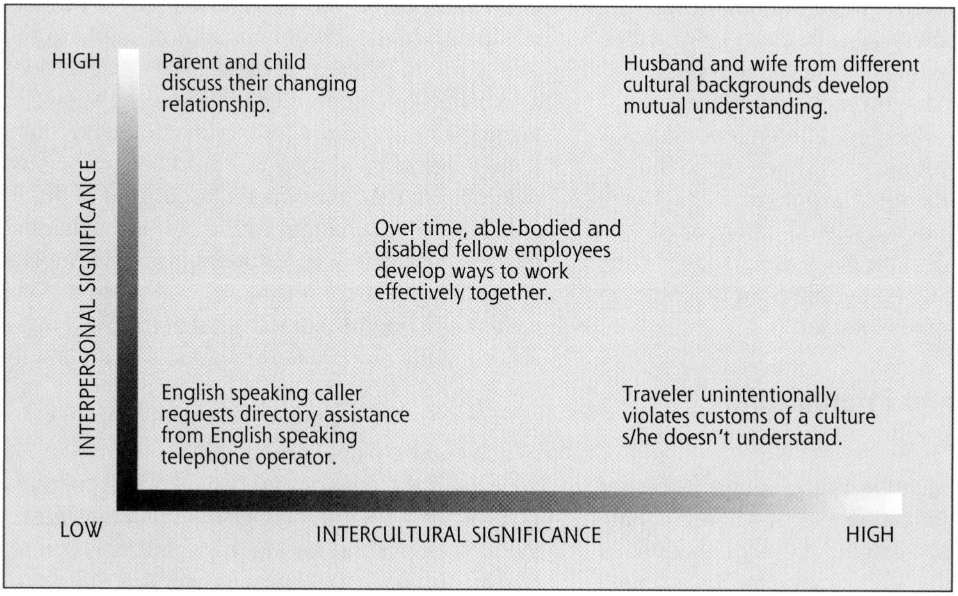

**Figure 2.2** Some Possible Interactions among Interpersonal and Intercultural Dimensions of Person-to-Person Communication

aware of these differences, they may see people from other cultures as different—or even offensive—without realizing that their apparently odd behavior comes from following a different set of beliefs and unwritten rules about the "proper" way to communicate.

## High- versus Low-Context

Anthropologist Edward Hall (1959) identified two distinct ways that members of various cultures deliver messages. A **low-context** culture uses language primarily to express thoughts, feelings, and ideas as clearly and logically as possible. To low-context communicators, the meaning of a statement lies in the words spoken. By contrast, a **high-context** culture relies heavily on subtle, often nonverbal cues to maintain social harmony (Ambady et al., 1996). Rather than upset others by speaking clearly, communicators in these societies learn to discover meaning from the context in which a message is delivered: the nonverbal behaviors of the speaker, the history of the relationship, and the general social rules that govern interaction between people. Table 2.1 summarizes some key differences between the way low- and high-context cultures use language.

Mainstream culture in the United States and Canada falls toward the low-context end of the scale. Longtime residents generally value straight talk and grow impatient with "beating around the bush." By contrast, most Asian and Middle Eastern cultures fit the high-context pattern. In many Asian societies, for example, maintaining harmony is important, so communicators avoid speaking clearly if that threatens another person's face. For this reason, communicators raised in Japanese or Korean cultures are less likely than Americans to offer a clear "no" to an undesirable request. Instead, they would probably use roundabout expressions like "I agree with you in principle, but . . ." or "I sympathize with you. . . ." As T. R. Reid (1999, p. 84) explains, "Japanese people avoid saying 'no,' not because they are dishonest, but because saying a flat 'no' might cause disappointment and ill-feeling. . . . So the Japanese fall back on their arsenal of euphemisms: 'That would be difficult.' 'We'll give your request careful thought.' 'Excuse me, but. . . .'"

To members of high-context cultures, communicators with a low-context style can appear overly talkative, lacking in subtlety, and redundant. On the other hand, to people from low-context backgrounds, high-context communicators often seem unexpressive, or even dishonest. It is easy to see how the clash between directness and indirectness can aggravate problems between

**Table 2.1**

| **High- and Low-Context Communication Styles** | |
| --- | --- |
| **Low Context** | **High Context** |
| Majority of information carried in explicit verbal messages, with less focus on the situational context. | Important information carried in contextual cues time, place relationship, situation. Less reliance on explicit verbal messages. |
| Self-expression valued. Communicators state opinions and desires directly and strive to persuade others to accept their own viewpoint. | Relational harmony valued and maintained by indirect expression of options. Communicators abstain from saying "no" directly. |
| Clear, eloquent speech considered praiseworthy. Verbal fluency admired. | Communicators talk "around" the point, allowing the other to fill in the missing pieces. Ambiguity and use of silence admired. |

## FOCUS ON RESEARCH

### WHEN WORDS WOUND: CULTURAL PERCEPTIONS OF RACIST SPEECH

Racist speech is cruel and painful in any form—but some words seem to wound more than others. Laura Leets wanted to know if cultural background plays a role in how people perceive racist messages, and on the impact those messages have on their targets.

Leets conducted a series of studies in which Euro-Americans and people of color—Asian American, African American, and Latino—were presented with examples of racist messages, all of which were aimed at people of color. Some of these messages were direct and blatantly offensive, while others were indirect and less overtly racist. In her first study, Leets found that Euro-

American participants judged the directly racist messages as more hurtful, while Asian American respondents rated the indirectly racist comments as more damaging.

Intrigued to see if this pattern applied to other groups, Leets later asked African American and Latino students to rate the hurtfulness of messages aimed at someone from their own ethnic background. Unlike Asian Americans, both Latinos and African Americans (as well as Euro-Americans) found the directly racist messages more offensive than the indirect ones.

Leets suggests that the traditional Asian tendency to favor high-context

messages explains why Asian Americans were more offended by indirectly racist speech. Adept at recognizing hints and nonverbal cues, low-context communicators are sensitive to messages that were overlooked by African Americans, Latinos, and Euro-Americans—all of whom were from cultural groups that rely more heavily on unambiguous, explicit, low-context messages.

Racism in any form has the potential to wound its targets. The research here illustrates that the kinds of messages that are most harmful vary from culture to culture.

Leets, L. (1999, May). *When words wound: Another look at racist speech.* Paper presented at the annual conference of the International Communication Association, San Francisco; Leets, L. & Giles, H. (1997). Words as weapons—When do they wound? *Human Communication Research 24,* 260–301.

straight-talking, low-context Israelis, who value speaking clearly, and their Arab neighbors, whose high-context culture stresses smooth interaction. The clash of cultural styles could lead to misunderstandings and conflicts between Israelis and their Palestinian neighbors. Israelis might view their Arab counterparts as evasive, while the Palestinians might perceive the Israelis as insensitive and blunt.

## Individualism versus Collectivism

Some cultures value the individual, while others place greater emphasis on the group. Members of an **individualistic culture** view their primary

responsibility as helping themselves, whereas communicators in **collectivistic cultures** feel loyalties and obligations to an in-group: one's extended family, community, or even the organization one works for (Triandis, 1995). Individualistic cultures also are characterized by self-reliance and competition, whereas members of a collectivistic culture are more attentive to and concerned with the opinions of significant others. The consequences of a culture's individualistic-collectivistic orientation is so powerful that some scholars (e.g., Andersen, 1999) have labeled it as the most fundamental dimension of cultural differences.

The United States is one of the world's more individualistic countries, along with Canada, Australia, and Great Britain. Latin American and Asian cultures are generally more collectivistic (Hofstede, 1984). Table 2.2 summarizes some differences between individualistic and collectivistic cultures.

Members of individualistic cultures tend to view themselves in terms of what they do, while people in collectivistic cultures are more likely to define themselves in terms of membership in an in-group. For instance, members of several cultures were asked to answer the question "Who am I?" twenty times (DeAngelis, 1992). North Americans were likely to answer by giving individual factors ("I am athletic"; "I am short"). By contrast, members of more collective societies—Chinese, Filipinos, Japanese, and some South Americans, for example—responded in terms of their relationships with others ("I am a father"; "I am an employee of _____ Corporation").

The difference between the team orientation of collectivistic cultures and the go-it-alone focus of individualistic ones has implications for the amount of honesty and directness a culture encourages or even tolerates. Communication researcher Stella Ting-Toomey (1988) suggests that in individualistic Western cultures, where there is a strong "I" orientation, the norm of speaking directly is honored; however, in collectivistic cultures, where the main desire is to build connections between the self and others, indirect approaches that maintain harmony are considered more desirable. "I gotta be me" could be the motto of a Westerner, but "If I hurt you, I hurt myself" is closer to the Asian way of thinking.

Individualistic and collectivistic cultures have very different approaches to handling disagreements. Individualistic societies are relatively tolerant of conflicts and use a direct, solution-oriented approach. By contrast, members of collectivistic cultures are less direct (Ting-Toomey, 1988). Collectivistic societies produce team players, while individualistic ones are far more likely to produce and reward superstars.

The difference between individualistic and collectivistic cultures also shows up in the level of comfort or anxiety their respective members feel when communicating. In societies where the need to conform is great, there is a higher degree of communication apprehension. For example, as a group, residents of China, Korea, and Japan exhibit a significantly higher degree of anxiety about speaking out in public than do members of individualistic cultures such as the United States and Australia (Klopf, 1984). It's important to realize that different levels of communication apprehension don't mean that shyness is a "problem" in some cultures. In fact, just the opposite is true: In these societies reticence is valued. When the goal is to avoid being the nail that sticks out, it's logical to feel nervous when you make yourself appear different by calling attention

**Table 2.2**

### The Self in Individualistic and Collectivist Cultures

| Individualistic Cultures | Collectivistic Cultures |
|---|---|
| Self is separate, unique individual; should be independent, self-sufficient. | People belong to extended families or in-groups; "we" or group orientation. |
| Individual should take care of himself/herself and immediate family. | Person should take care of extended family before self. |
| Many flexible group memberships; friends based on shared interests and activities. | Emphasis on belonging to a very few permanent in-groups, which have a strong influence over the person. |
| Reward for individual achievement and initiative; individual decision encouraged; individual credit and blame assigned. | Reward for contribution to group goals and well-being; cooperation with in-group members; group decisions valued; credit and blame shared. |
| High value on autonomy, change, youth, individual security, equality. | High value on duty, order, tradition, age, group security, status, and hierarchy. |

Adapted by Sandra Sudweeks from: Triandis, H. C. (1990) Cross-cultural studies of individualism and collectivism. In J. Berman (Ed.), *Nebraska symposium on motivation* (pp. 41–133). Lincoln: University of Nebraska Press; and Hall, E. T. (1959). *Beyond culture.* New York: Doubleday, 1959).

your way. A self-concept that includes "assertive" might make a Westerner feel proud, but in much of Asia it would more likely be cause for shame.

## Power Distance

For members of democratic societies, the principle embodied in the U.S. Declaration of Independence that "all men [and women] are created equal" is so fundamental that we accept it without question. However, not all cultures share this belief. Some operate on the assumption that certain groups of people (an aristocracy or an economic class, for example) and some institutions (such as a church or the government) have the right to control the lives of individuals. Geert Hofstede (1984) coined the term **power distance** to describe the degree to which members of a society accept an unequal distribution of power.

Cultures with low power difference believe in minimizing the difference between various social classes. Rich and poor, educated and uneducated groups may still exist, but there is a pervasive belief that one person is as good as another regardless of his or her station in life. Low power difference cultures also support the notion that

challenging authority is acceptable—even desirable. Members aren't necessarily punished for raising questions about the status quo. According to Hofstede's research, U.S. and Canadian societies have relatively low power distance, though not the lowest in the world. Austria, Denmark, Israel, and New Zealand proved to be the most egalitarian countries. At the other end of the spectrum are countries with a high degree of power distance: Philippines, Mexico, Venezuela, India, and Singapore.

The degree of power distance in a culture is reflected in key relationships (Lustig & Koester, 1999). Children who are raised in cultures with high power difference are expected to obey their parents and other authority figures to a degree that would astonish most children raised in the United States or Canada. Power automatically comes with age in many countries. For example, the Korean language has separate terms for *older brother, oldest brother, younger sister, youngest sister,* and so on. Parents in cultures with low power distance don't expect the same degree of unquestioning obedience. They are not surprised when children ask "why?" when presented with a request or demand.

Differences between high and low power distance cultures also show up in school (Yook & Albert, 1998). In societies that accept high power differences, students are expected to obey teachers without question. In these cultures, rote by-the-book learning is common. Students are discouraged from asking questions, because these might seem like attacks on the teacher's authority or knowledge. School is a different place in countries where low power distance is the norm. Students are more likely to be rewarded for showing initiative and for questioning their instructors.

On-the-job communication is different in low and high power distance societies. In countries with higher degrees of power distance, employees have much less input into the way they perform their work. In fact, workers from these cultures are likely to feel uncomfortable when given freedom to make their own decisions or when a more egalitarian boss asks for their opinion: They prefer to view their bosses as benevolent decision makers. The reverse is true when management from a culture with an egalitarian tradition tries to do business in a country whose workers are used to high power distance. They can be surprised to find that employees do not expect much say in decisions and do not feel unappreciated when they aren't consulted. They may regard dutiful, submissive, respectful employees as lacking initiative and creativity—traits that helped them gain promotions back home. Given these differences, it's easy to understand why multinational companies need to consider fundamental differences in communication values and behavior when they set up shop in a new country.

## Uncertainty Avoidance

The future is filled with uncertainty about every person and every relationship. Nobody knows for certain how others might act tomorrow, or even in the next few minutes, and the desire to resolve uncertainty seems to be a trait shared by people around the world (Berger, 1992). While uncertainty may be universal, cultures have different ways of coping with an unpredictable future. Hofstede (1984) uses the term **uncertainty avoidance** to reflect the degree to which members of a culture feel threatened by ambiguous situations and how much they try to avoid them. He developed an uncertainty avoidance index (UAI) to measure differing degrees of uncertainty avoidance around the world. Residents of some countries (including Singapore, Great Britain, Denmark, Sweden, Hong Kong, and the United States) proved to be relatively unthreatened by change, while others (such as natives of Belgium, Greece, Japan, and Portugal) found new or ambiguous situations discomfiting.

A culture's degree of uncertainty avoidance is reflected in the way its members communicate. In countries that avoid uncertainty, deviant people and ideas are considered dangerous, and intolerance is high (Samovar & Porter, 1995). People in these cultures are especially concerned with security, so they have a strong need for clearly defined rules and regulations. It's easy to imagine how most relationships in cultures with a high UAI—family, work, friendships, and romance—are likely to fit a predictable pattern. By contrast, people in a culture that is less threatened by the new and unexpected are more likely to tolerate—or even welcome—people who don't fit the norm. Following established rules and patterns isn't necessarily expected, and different behavior might even be welcomed.

When one person whose cultural conditioning has discouraged a tolerance for uncertainty meets another who welcomes the unexpected, the potential for discomfort increases (Lustig & Koester, 1999). For example, when a mainstream North American who is relatively comfortable with change and novelty spends time with someone from a high UAI culture such as Japan, both communicators may find the other behaving in disconcerting ways. The North American is likely to view the Japanese as rigid and overly controlled, while the Japanese would probably regard the North American as undisciplined, overly tolerant, and generally lacking self-control. On the other hand, if the communicators understand how their cultural conditioning affects their style, then they are more likely to understand, and maybe even learn from, the other's different style.

## CULTURAL COLLABORATION: *GUNG HO*

*Gung Ho* is the fictional story of a Japanese car company that attempts a collaborative business venture in the United States. Hunt Stevenson (Michael Keaton) is an auto worker who convinces Assan Motors to set up shop in Hadleyville, a small town whose car factory was shut down two years earlier. Assan assigns Kazihiro (Gedde Watanabe) to manage the American plant according to Japanese principles. He is met with resistance at nearly every turn, as the clash of cultures strains working and personal relationships.

While the movie may be guilty of exaggerating stereotypes about both cultures, it illustrates the conflicts that can occur when differing cultural systems intersect in the workplace. The American and Japanese workers hold opposing beliefs about various values: individuality vs. teamwork, personal satisfaction vs. corporate success, specialization vs. generalization, honesty vs. face-saving, and quality of life vs. work ethic. The conflict from these tensions builds throughout the movie, leading ultimately to the shutdown of the plant.

The saving grace comes from the friendship that develops between Stephenson and Kazihiro. As leaders of the two cultural factions, they discover that they have a great deal in common. Each comes to empathize with, appreciate, and in some cases adopt the other's values and leadership style. Focusing on their commonalities rather than their differences, they successfully reopen the plant by working collaboratively. The happy ending suggests that cultures can work together if they treat their differences as assets rather than liabilities.

## Achievement versus Nurturing

The term **achievement culture** describes societies that place a high value on material success and a focus on the task at hand, while **nurturing** is a descriptive term for cultures that regard the support of relationships as an especially important goal. Hofstede (1984, p. 176) referred to the first group as "masculine" and the second as "feminine," based on the stereotypical focus of each sex. In some ways, the terms "hard" and "soft" are more descriptive. "Hard" cultures that emphasize achievement include Japan, Switzerland, and Germany. "Softer," more nurturing cultures include the Scandinavian countries (Norway, Sweden, and Denmark), Spain, and France.

The portrait of an effective communicator varies from one type of culture to another. Most notably, achievement-oriented societies prescribe different roles for women and men. In these cultures, male virtues include assertiveness, indepen-

dence, and individuality. Women who exhibit these traits may be viewed unfavorably for "acting like a man." By contrast, in nurturing societies there is little difference between the expected behavior for men and women: The ideal profile for both sexes is one of cooperation, being a team player, and holding the belief that personal relationships are at least as important as material achievement.

As you think about the cultural values described here, realize that they don't just arise between people from different countries. In today's increasingly multicultural society, people from different cultural backgrounds are likely to encounter one another "at home," in the country they share. Consider the United States and Canada in the 1990s: Native Americans; Latinos from the Caribbean, Mexico, and South America; and Asians from China, Japan, Korea, Vietnam, and other countries mingle with first-generation and longtime residents whose ancestors came from Europe. This is a cultural mixture that often seems less like a melting pot than a salad bowl, in which the many "ingredients" retain much of their own identity. With this sort of diversity, it's no surprise that people bring some very different approaches to communicating as they encounter one another. Understanding these differences can help smooth the potentially bumpy interaction that can occur when people with different cultural backgrounds try to communicate.

## Codes and Culture

At this point, you probably have a healthy appreciation for the challenges that arise when two or more people try to communicate with one another. These challenges become even greater when the communicators use different verbal and nonverbal communication systems.

### Verbal Codes

Considering that many languages grew independently from one another, the world's tongues have a remarkable number of similarities (Brown, 1991). For example, all languages include a concept of the individual person, making it possible to distinguish the self from others. (If ants and other insects could speak, their language probably wouldn't include this sort of self-other distinction.) All languages enable their speakers to think and talk about abstractions (such as love and friendship) and things not physically present (such as your Aunt Bertha or the New Year's Eve party). All contain terms that reflect status (husband, sweetheart, leader, sister, and so on). All have rhetorical standards and figurative speech that enable them to be used for ceremonial purposes and special occasions. All are governed by some sort of phonetic, syntactic, semantic, and pragmatic rules as described in Chapter 5 of this book.

Despite these similarities, the many languages of the world differ in some important respects that affect the way their speakers communicate with one

another and with speakers of other tongues. The following sections outline some of those factors.

**Language and Identity**   The language that members of a culture and its various cocultures speak shapes the identity of the speakers. If you live in a culture where everyone speaks the same tongue, then language will have little noticeable impact on how you view yourself and others. But when some members of a society speak the dominant language and others speak a minority tongue, or when that second language is not prestigious, the sense of being a member of an out-group is strong. At this point the speaker of a nondominant tongue can react in one of two ways: either feel pressured to assimilate by speaking the "better" language, or refuse to accommodate to the majority language and maintain loyalty to the ethnic tongue (Giles et al., 1992). In either case, the impact of language on the self-concept is powerful. On one hand the feeling is likely to be "I'm not as good as speakers of the native language," and on the other the belief is "There's something unique and worth preserving in my language." A case study of Latino managers illustrates the dilemma of speaking a nondominant language (Banks, 1987). The managers, employees in an Euro-American organization, felt their Mexican identity threatened when they found that the road to advancement would be smoother if they deemphasized their Spanish and adopted a more colloquial English style of speaking.

Even the names a culture uses to identify its members reflect its values and shape the way its members relate to one another. When asked to identify themselves, individualistic Americans, Canadians, Australians, and Europeans would probably respond by giving their first name, surname, street, town, and country. Many Asians do it the other way around (Servaes, 1989). If you ask Hindus for their identity, they will give you their caste and village and then their name. The Sanskrit formula for identifying oneself begins with lineage and goes on to state family and house, and ends with one's personal name (Bharti, 1985). The same collectivist orientation is reflected in Chinese written language, where the pronoun *I* looks very similar to the word for *selfish* (Samovar & Porter, 1998). The Japanese language has no equivalent to the English pronoun *I*. Instead, different words are used to refer to one's self depending on the social situation, age, gender, and other social characteristics (Gudykunst, 1993).

Even within a language system, the labels that members of a coculture use to define themselves can both reflect and help define their sense of identity. In one study, Linda Larkey and her associates (1993) surveyed a cross-section of African Americans to identify the significance of the labels they used to identify themselves. The most commonly used terms revealed different orientations toward the user's sense of self as member of a distinct coculture. Communicators who identified themselves as "Black" generally were oriented toward the goals of unity and acceptability, while those who preferred "African American" tended to focus more on their blended heritage. The researchers detected a trend toward use of the term "African American," which they interpreted as a move toward self-determination in meeting the challenge of maintaining a positive identity.

**Verbal Communication Styles**  Using language is more than just a matter of choosing a particular group of words to convey an idea. Each language has its own unique style that distinguishes it from others. Matters like the amount of formality or informality, precision or vagueness, and brevity or detail are major ingredients in speaking competently. When a communicator tries to use the verbal style from one culture in a different one, problems are likely to arise.

Consider a simple example of differing cultural rules: Many Euro-American schoolteachers use quasi-questions that hint at the information they are seeking. The pragmatic rules that govern simple exchanges can also vary. For example, an elementary school instructor might encourage the class to speak up by making an incorrect statement that demands refutation: "So twelve divided by four is six, right?" Most Anglo students would recognize this as a way of testing their understanding. But this style of questioning is unfamiliar to many students raised in traditional African-American cultures, who aren't likely to respond until they are directly questioned by the instructor (Rubin, 1986). Given this sort of difference, it's easy to imagine how some teachers might view children who were not raised in the mainstream culture as unresponsive or slow, when they are simply playing by a different set of rules.

Gudykunst and Ting-Toomey (1988) describe three important types of cultural differences in verbal style. One is *directness*. We have already discussed how low-context cultures use language primarily to express thoughts, feelings, and ideas as clearly and logically as possible, while high-context cultures may speak less directly, using language to maintain social harmony. Rather than upset others by speaking clearly, communicators in low-context societies learn to discover meaning from the context in which a message is delivered rather than relying on just the spoken words.

Another way in which language styles can vary across cultures is in terms of whether they are *elaborate* or *succinct*. For instance, speakers of Arabic commonly use language that is much more rich and expressive than normally found in English. Strong assertions and exaggerations that

## FOCUS ON RESEARCH

### INSULT AND AGGRESSION IN A "CULTURE OF HONOR"

You're walking down the hallway at college and a stranger bumps into you. Rather than apologizing, the person who bumped you calls you an "asshole." How would you respond? If you're a white male student, your reaction might depend on whether you were raised in the southern or northern United States, according to Dov Cohen, Brian Bowdle, Richard Nisbett, and Norbert Schwarz. Previous research suggests that southern white males are brought up in a "culture of honor" in which "even small disputes become contests for reputation and social status." Cohen and his colleagues ran a series of experiments to see if they could provide further support for this notion.

The researchers recruited white male students to participate in studies that were supposedly about personality and judgment. After taking a battery of tests, the participants were sent down the hall for further testing—and that's when they were bumped and insulted by a research confederate. A variety of posttests measured the participants' immediate and delayed reactions to the bump insult.

The results confirmed the "culture of honor" hypotheses. Participants raised in the North were relatively unaffected by the bump insult; in fact, many of them found it humorous. Southern-raised participants, on the other hand, were more likely to be upset and primed for aggression after the hallway incident. Southerners were also more likely to think their masculinity had been threatened. The "chicken game," in which another research confederate walked straight at the participants, yielded similarly

predictable results: Previously bumped northerners "chickened out" and stepped aside far earlier than previously bumped southerners, who didn't bail out until they were within three feet of another hallway collision.

How important is a little bump-and-insult between strangers? It can be a potential trigger for larger conflicts, say Cohen and his associates: "Arguments that start over petty matters can quickly escalate into deadly conflicts once a challenge or insult has been issued." Indeed, research shows that more argument-related homicides occur in the South than in the North, and that white male homicide rates are higher in the South as well. This study helps explain these statistics by identifying some of the cultural rules that operate south of the Mason-Dixon line.

Cohen, D., Bowlie, B.F., Nisbett, R.E. & Schwarz, N. (1996). Insult, aggression, and the southern culture of honor: An experimental ethnography. *Journal of Personality and Social Psychology, 70,* 945–960.

would sound ridiculous in English are a common feature of Arabic. This contrast in linguistic style can lead to misunderstandings between people from different backgrounds:

First, an Arab feels compelled to overexert in almost all types of communication because others expect him [or her] to. If an Arab says exactly what he [or she] means without the expected assertion, other Arabs may still think that he [or she] means the opposite. For example, a simple "no" from a guest to the host's requests to eat more or drink more will not suffice. To convey the meaning that he [or she] is actually full, the guest must keep repeating "no" several times, coupling it with an oath such as "By God" or "I swear to God." Second, an Arab often fails to realize that others, particularly foreigners, may mean exactly what they say even though their language is simple. To the Arabs, a simple "no" may mean the indirectly expressed consent and encouragement of a coquettish woman. On the other hand, a simple consent may mean the rejection of a hypocritical politician. (Almaney & Alwan, 1982, p. 84)

Succinctness is most extreme in cultures where silence is valued. In many Native American cultures, for example, the favored way to handle ambiguous social situations is to remain quiet (Basso, 1970). When you contrast this silent style to the talkativeness that is common when people first meet in mainstream American cultures, it's easy to imagine how the first encounter between an Apache or Navajo and an Anglo might be uncomfortable for both people.

A third way that languages differ from one culture to another involves *formality* and *informality*. One guidebook for British readers who want to understand how Americans communicate describes the openness and informality that characterizes U.S. culture:

> Visitors may be overwhelmed by the sheer exuberant friendliness of Americans, especially in the central and southern parts of the country. Sit next to an American on an airplane and he will immediately address you by your first name, ask "So—how do you like it in the States?," explain his recent divorce in intimate detail, invite you home for dinner, offer to lend you money, and wrap you in a warm hug on parting. This does not necessarily mean he will remember your name the next day. Americans are friendly because they just can't help it; they like to be neighbourly and want to be liked. (Faul, 1994, pp. 3–4)

The informal approach that characterizes communication in countries like the United States is quite different from the great concern for propriety in many parts of Asia and Africa. Formality isn't so much a matter of using correct grammar as of defining social relationships. In Korea, for example, the language reflects the Confucian system of relational hierarchies (Yum, 1987). It has special vocabularies for different sexes, for different levels of social status, for different degrees of intimacy, and for different types of social occasions. For example, there are different degrees of

formality for speaking with old friends, non-acquaintances whose background one knows, and complete strangers. One sign of being a learned person in Korea is the ability to use language that recognizes these relational distinctions. When you contrast these sorts of distinctions with the casual friendliness many North Americans use even when talking with complete strangers, it's easy to see how a Korean might view American communicators as boorish and how an American might see Koreans as stiff and unfriendly.

**Language and Worldview**    Different linguistic styles are important, but some scholars argue that there may be even more fundamental differences that separate speakers of various languages. For almost 150 years, theorists have put forth the notion of **linguistic determinism:** that the worldview of a culture is shaped and reflected by the language its members speak. The best-known example of linguistic determinism is the notion that Eskimos have a large number (estimated at anywhere from seventeen to one hundred) of words for what most others would simply call "snow." Different terms are used to describe conditions such as a driving blizzard, crusty ice, and light powder. This example suggests how linguistic determinism operates. The need to survive in an Arctic environment led Eskimos to make distinctions that would be unimportant to residents of warmer environments, and once the language makes these distinctions, speakers are more likely to see the world in ways that match this broader vocabulary.

There is some doubt that Eskimos really do have so many words for snow (Martin & Pullum, 1991). Nonetheless, other examples offer support for the principle of linguistic determinism (Giles & Franklyn-Stokes, 1989). For instance, bilingual speakers seem to think differently when they change languages. In one study, French Americans were asked to interpret a series of pictures. When they spoke in French, their descriptions were far more romantic and emotional than when they used English to describe the same kind of images. Likewise, when students in Hong Kong were asked to

**"The Eskimos have eighty-seven words for
snow and not one for malpractice."**

complete a values test, they expressed more traditional Chinese values when they answered in Can-
tonese than when they spoke in English. In Israel,
both Arab and Jewish students saw bigger distinctions between their group and "outsiders" when
using their native language than when they spoke in
English, a neutral tongue. Examples like these show
the power of language to shape cultural identity—
sometimes for better and sometimes for worse.

Linguistic influences start early in life. English-
speaking parents often label the mischievous pranks
of their children as "bad," implying that there is
something immoral about acting wild. They are
inclined to say "Be good!" In contrast, French
adults are more likely to say *"Sois sage!"*—"Be
wise." The linguistic implication is that misbehaving
is an act of foolishness. Swedes would correct the
same action with the words *"Var snall!"*—"Be
friendly; be kind." In contrast, German adults use
the command *"Sei artig"*—literally, "Be of your own
kind." In other words, get back in step; conform to
your role as a child (Sinclair, 1954).

The best-known declaration of linguistic determinism is the **Sapir-Whorf hypothesis,** formulated
by Benjamin Whorf, an amateur linguist, and
anthropologist Edward Sapir (Hoijer, 1994; Whorf,

1956). Following Sapir's theoretical work, Whorf
found that the language spoken by Hopi Native
Americans represented a view of reality that is dramatically different from most tongues. For example,
the Hopi language makes no distinction between
nouns and verbs. Therefore, the people who speak
it describe the entire world as being constantly in
process. Whereas English speakers use nouns to
characterize people or objects as being fixed or
constant, the Hopi language represents them more
as verbs, constantly changing. In this sense English
represents the world rather like a collection of
snapshots, whereas Hopi reflects a worldview that
is more like a motion picture.

Recent scholarship has cast doubt on the extreme
linguistic deterministic viewpoint that it is *impossible*
for speakers of different languages to view the world
identically (see Pinker, 1994). The more moderate
notion of **linguistic relativism**—that language exerts a
strong influence on perceptions—does seem valid.
As one scholar put it, "the differences between languages are not so much in what *can* be said, but in
what it is *relatively easy* to say" (Hoijer in Steinfatt,
1989, p. 63). Some languages contain terms that
have no English equivalents (Rheingold, 1988). For
example, consider a few words in other languages
that have no simple translation in English:

- *Nemawashi* (Japanese): the process of inform-
  ally feeling out all the people involved with an
  issue before making a decision
- *Lagniappe* (French/Creole): an extra gift given in
  a transaction that wasn't expected by the terms
  of a contract
- *Lao* (Mandarin): respectful term used for older
  people, showing their importance in the family
  and in society
- *Dharma* (Sanskrit): each person's unique, ideal
  path in life and the knowledge of how to find it
- *Koyaanisquatsi* (Hopi): nature out of balance; a
  way of life so crazy it calls for a new way of living

Once words like these exist and become a
part of everyday life, the ideas that they represent
are easier to recognize. But even without such
terms, each of the concepts above is still possible

to imagine. Thus, speakers of a language that includes the notion of *lao* would probably treat its older members respectfully, and those who are familiar with *lagniappe* might be more generous. However, these words don't have to be in a language for a communicator to follow these principles. While language may shape thoughts and behavior, it doesn't dominate them absolutely.

## Nonverbal Codes

Just as with spoken and written languages, there are many elements of nonverbal communication that are shared by all humans, regardless of culture (Brown, 1991). For instance, people of all cultures convey messages through facial expressions and gestures. Furthermore, some of these physical displays have the same meaning everywhere. Crying is a universal sign of unhappiness or pain, and smiles signal friendly intentions. (Of course, smiles and tears may be insincere and manipulative, but their overt meanings are similar and constant in every culture.) The universality of many basic nonverbal behaviors was demonstrated in one study when inhabitants of the New Guinea rain forest, who had not been exposed to any media from the industrialized world, correctly identified the emotions on photos of U.S. citizens' faces (Ekman et al., 1969; Izard, 1971).

Despite nonverbal similarities, the range of differences in nonverbal behavior is tremendous. For example, the meaning of some gestures varies from one culture to another. Consider the use of emblems such as the "OK" sign made by joining thumb and forefinger to form a circle. This gesture is a cheery affirmation to most Americans, but it has very different meanings in other parts of the world (Knapp & Hall, 1997, p. 253). In France and Belgium it means "you're worth zero," in Japan it means "money," and in Greece and Turkey it is an insulting or vulgar sexual invitation. Given this sort of cross-cultural ambiguity, it's easy to visualize how an innocent tourist from the United States could wind up in serious trouble overseas without understanding why.

Less obvious cross-cultural differences can damage relationships without the communicators ever recognizing exactly what has gone wrong. Edward Hall (1959) points out that whereas North Americans traditionally conduct business at a distance of roughly four feet, people from the Middle East stand much closer. It is easy to visualize the awkward advance and retreat pattern that might occur when two diplomats or business-people from these cultures meet. The Middle Easterner would probably keep moving forward to close the gap that feels so wide, while the North

DILBERT reprinted by permission of United Feature Syndicate, Inc.

American would continually back away. Both would probably feel uncomfortable without knowing why.

Like distance, patterns of eye contact vary around the world. A direct gaze is considered appropriate for speakers in Latin America, the Arab world, and southern Europe. On the other hand, Asians, Indians, Pakistanis, and northern Europeans gaze at a listener peripherally or not at all. In either case, deviations from the norm are likely to make a culturally uneducated listener uncomfortable. Even within a culture, various cocultures can have different nonverbal rules. For example, some Native American cultures, such as the Hopi and Navajo, view direct eye contact as offensive, unlike the traditional attitude that looking others in the eye is a sign of honesty and self-confidence (Samovar & Porter, 1998).

## Decoding Messages

Given all the differences in verbal and nonverbal communication systems, it's easy to see how decoding is an especially big challenge for communicators from different cultural backgrounds. The following pages will show that the potential for misunderstanding is even greater than it might already seem.

**Translation**   Anyone who has tried to translate ideas from one language to another knows that the potential for misunderstanding is always present. Sometimes the results of a bungled translation can be amusing. For example, the American manufacturers of Pet milk unknowingly introduced their product in French-speaking markets without realizing that the word *pet* in French means "to break wind" (Ricks, 1983, p. 41). Likewise, the English-speaking representative of a U.S. soft drink manufacturer naively drew laughs from Mexican customers when she offered free samples of *Fresca* soda pop. In Mexican slang the word *fresca* means "lesbian."

Even choosing the right words during translation won't guarantee that nonnative speakers will use an unfamiliar language correctly. For example,

Japanese insurance companies warn their policy-holders who are visiting the United States to avoid their cultural tendency to say "excuse me" or "I'm sorry" if they are involved in a traffic accident (Sugimoto, 1991). In Japan, apologizing is a traditional way to express goodwill and maintain social harmony, even if the person offering the apology is not at fault. But in the United States an apology can be taken as an admission of guilt and result in Japanese tourists being held accountable after accidents for which they may not be responsible.

Difficult as they may be, translation and terminology constitute only one of many communication challenges facing members of different cultures and cocultures. Now we need to look at some more subtle challenges that can make decoding messages from members of other cultures a challenging task.

### REFLECTION

#### IDIOMS AND TRANSLATION

I hadn't realized how tricky it can be to learn a new language until I started tutoring some international students who have just arrived on campus from overseas. Most of them have an excellent textbook understanding of English, since they've been studying the language since elementary school. But knowing formal rules and vocabulary hasn't prepared them for the way everyday talk works.

Some of the idioms we take for granted as native English speakers don't make any sense. Yesterday I counted over twenty of them in just one class lecture: "Taking the bull by the horns," "beating around the bush," "shot down," "blowing your top," "up in the air," and so on. Until you can understand idioms like these, you miss a lot. And until you learn to use them, you sound like a textbook instead of a natural speaker.

**Attributional Variations**  As Chapter 4 will explain, attribution is the process of making sense of another person's behavior. Attribution is an unavoidable part of communicating: We *have* to form some sort of interpretation of what others' words and actions mean. But most behavior is so ambiguous that it can be interpreted in several ways, and people rarely make the effort to check or otherwise verify the accuracy of their interpretation. Furthermore, the usual tendency is to stick to the first attribution one makes. It's easy to see how this quick, sloppy attribution process can lead to making faulty interpretations—especially when communicators are from different cultural backgrounds.

In Table 2.3, a supervisor from the United States invites a subordinate from Greece to get involved in making a decision (Triandis, 1975, pp. 42–43). Since U.S. culture ranks relatively low on power distance, the supervisor encourages input from the employee. In Greece, however, the distance between bosses and their subordinates is much greater. Therefore, the Greek employee wants and expects to be told what to do. After all, it's the boss's job to give orders. Table 2.3 shows how the differing cultural beliefs shape both figures' attributions of the other's messages.

In fact, the report needed thirty days of regular work. So the Greek employee worked day and night, but at the end of the fifteenth day, he still needed one more day's work.

Culturally based attributions don't just occur between members of different nationalities. Even different use of dialects or accents by native-born

## REFLECTION

### ACCENT SHAPES ATTITUDES

Last semester I had a student from the hills of Appalachia in one of my classes. I could barely understand her accent, and she used "mountain" phrases that were unfamiliar to me. My first reaction: she *can't* be intelligent, given how she speaks! She turned out to be the smartest person in the class, asking the most insightful questions and demonstrating the firmest grasp of course material. We became friendly enough so that at the end of the semester I was able to openly thank her for helping me kill off a useless stereotype!

**Table 2.3**

| Culture Affects Attributions | |
|---|---|
| **Behavior** | **Attribution** |
| American: How long will it take you to finish the report? | American: I asked him to participate.<br>Greek: His behavior makes no sense. He is the boss. Why doesn't he tell me? |
| Greek: I do not know. How long should it take? | American: He refuses to take responsibility.<br>Greek: I asked him for an order. |
| American: You are in the best position to analyze time requirements. | American: I press him to take responsibility for his own actions.<br>Greek: What nonsense! I better give him an answer. |
| Greek: Ten days. | American: He lacks the ability to estimate time; this estimate is totally inadequate. |
| American: Take fifteen. It is agreed you will do it in fifteen days? | American: I offer a contract.<br>Greek: These are my orders. Fifteen days. |

members of the same country can affect a listener's evaluation of a speaker. Most cultures have a "standard dialect," which is spoken by high-status opinion leaders. For the most part, people who use the standard dialect are judged as being competent, intelligent, industrious, and confident (Ng, 1993). By contrast, nonstandard speakers are likely to be rated less favorably. The likely attribution is "this person doesn't even speak correctly. There must be something wrong with him/her." This sort of attributional stereotyping doesn't just involve language. Race, ethnicity, sex, and physical disabilities also can serve as triggers that evoke a whole set of attributions that may not be accurate. The notion that everyone who speaks with a country accent is an ignorant bumpkin, that all blacks are natural athletes, or that every woman is sensitive while every man is not are patently ridiculous when stated outright, yet many people operate in everyday life as if they were true.

**Patterns of Thought**   The way members of a culture are taught to think and reason shapes the way they interpret others' messages (Gudykunst & Kim, 1997). One important force that affects thinking is a culture's system of logic. Members of individualistic cultures such as the United States prize rationality and linear, logical thinking. They value the ability to be impartial—to analyze a situation from a detached perspective. They rely on facts, figures, and experts to make decisions. Members of individualistic societies tend to see the world in terms of dichotomies: good-bad, right-wrong, happy-sad, and so on. In contrast, members of collectivistic societies are more likely to be intuitive. They prefer to get a feel for the big picture and are less impressed by precision, classification, or detachment. Collectivistic cultures are also less prone to see the world in either-or terms. They accept the fact that people, things, or ideas can be both right and wrong, good and bad at the same time.

Don't misunderstand: These differing ways of thinking don't mean that members of individualistic cultures are never intuitive or that collectivists are never rational. The differences in ways of thinking are a matter of degree. Nonetheless, it's easy to imagine how an individualist raised in mainstream U.S. culture and someone from a more collectivistic European background or an extremely collectivistic Asian one could find their relationship perplexing. For instance, consider what might happen when a conflict arises between two romantic partners, friends, or coworkers. "Let's look at this rationally," the individualist might say. "Let's figure out exactly what happened. Once we decide whose fault the problem is, we can fix it." By contrast, the partner with a more collectivistic way of thinking might say, "Let's not get caught up in a lot of details or an argument about who

| Culture Affects Attributions | |
| --- | --- |
| **Behavior** | **Attribution** |
| In fact, the report needed 30 days of regular work. So the Greek employee worked day and night, but at the end of the fifteenth day, he still needed one more day's work. American: Where is the report? | American: I am making sure he fulfills his contract. Greek: He is asking for the report. (Both understand that it is not ready.) |
| Greek: It will be ready tomorrow. American: But we agreed that it would be ready today. | American: I must teach him to fulfill an agreement. Greek: The stupid, incompetent boss! Not only did he give me wrong orders, but he does not appreciate that I did a 30-day job in 16 days. |
| The Greek hands in his resignation. | The American is surprised. Greek: I can't work for such a man. |

is right or wrong. If we can get a feel for the problem, we can make things more harmonious." Although both partners might be speaking the same language, their modes of thinking about their relationship would be dramatically different.

# Developing Intercultural Communication Competence

Perhaps you've known people who find it easy to build relationships with strangers from other cultures. They seem comfortable with anyone, regardless of background. You probably have known other people who have a very hard time dealing with anyone who is different. What distinguishes competent and incompetent intercultural communicators? The rest of this chapter focuses on answering this question.

To a great degree, interacting successfully with strangers calls for the same ingredients of general communicative competence outlined in Chapter 1. It's important to have a wide range of behaviors and to be skillful at choosing and performing the most appropriate ones in a given situation. A genuine concern for others plays an important role. Cognitive complexity and the ability to empathize also help. Finally, self-monitoring is important, since the need to make mid-course corrections in your approach is often necessary when dealing with strangers.

But beyond these basic qualities, communication researchers have worked long and hard to identify qualities that are unique, or at least especially important, ingredients of intercultural communicative competence (Chen & Starosta, 1996; Koester et al., 1993; Martin, 1993). Most scholars acknowledge that intercultural competence has three elements. The first involves *motivation* and *attitude,* since intercultural communication requires a sincere desire to communicate effectively with strangers. The second requirement is *knowledge* of how other cultures communicate. The final requirement is *skill:* the ability to create and respond to messages effectively.

## Motivation and Attitude

Approaching strangers can take extra motivation and some special attitudes. The desire to communicate successfully is an important start. For example, people high in willingness to communicate with people from other cultures report a greater

number of friends from different backgrounds than those who are less willing to reach out (Kassing, 1997). But desire alone isn't sufficient. Some other ways of thinking are essential when dealing with people from other backgrounds. Following the terminology of Samovar, Porter, and Stefani (1999, p. 252), we call these attitudes "culture-general" because they are necessary when communicating competently with people from any background that is different from one's own.

**Tolerance for Ambiguity**   One of the most important concerns facing communicators is their desire to reduce uncertainty about one another (Berger, 1992). Even when we encounter others from the same background, we try to learn enough information to make attributions about who they are and what they want. Once the uncertainty has been reduced, it becomes easier to decide how to respond to them.

When we encounter communicators who speak a different language, the level of uncertainty is especially high. Consider the basic challenge of communicating in an unfamiliar language. Unless you can speak and understand the other language like a native, it's often difficult to know for certain what others are saying or to express your own ideas accurately. Pico Iyer (1990, pp.129–130)

"Excuse me. We're Americans. Would you please give us your table."

captures the ambiguity that arises from a lack of fluency when he describes his growing friendship with Sachiko, a Japanese woman he met in Kyoto:

> I was also beginning to realize how treacherous it was to venture into a foreign language if one could not measure the shadows of the words one used. When I had told her, in Asuka, *"Jennifer Beals ga suki-desu. Anata mo"* ("I like Jennifer Beals—and I like you"), I had been pleased to find a way of conveying affection, and yet, I thought, a perfect distance. But later I looked up suki and found that I had delivered an almost naked protestation of love. . . .
>
> Meanwhile, of course, nearly all her shadings were lost to me, and I felt sorry for her having to box her feelings into the few adjectives she knew, throwing heavy terms over subtle, fleeting nuances. . . . Once, when I had to leave her house ten minutes early, she said, "I very sad," and another time, when I simply called her up, she said, "I very happy"—and I began to think her unusually sensitive, or else prone to bold and violent extremes, when really she was reflecting nothing but the paucity of her English vocabulary. . . . Talking in a language not one's own was like walking on one leg; when two people did it together, it was like a three-legged waltz.

This kind of confusion discourages some communicators from seeking out contacts with people who speak different languages. But competent intercultural communicators accept—even welcome—this kind of ambiguity. Iyer (1990, pp. 220–221) describes the way the mutual confusion he shared with Sachiko actually helped their relationship develop:

> Yet in the end, the fact that we were both speaking in this pared-down diction made us both, I felt, somewhat gentler, more courteous, and more vulnerable than we would have been otherwise, returning us to a state of innocence.

Without a tolerance for ambiguity, the mass of often confusing and sometimes downright incomprehensible messages that bombard intercultural sojourners would be impossible to manage. Some people seem to come equipped with this sort of tolerance, while others have to cultivate it. One way or the other, that ability to live

## FILM CLIP

### LEARNING AND UNLEARNING PREJUDICE: *AMERICAN HISTORY X*

Derek Vinyard (Edward Norton) is an angry young man. When his fireman father is killed in an inner-city shooting, he sees the crime as a racial issue. Derek turns to a man named Cameron (Stacy Keach) for answers on how to vent his rage. Cameron tutors Derek in the ways of prejudice and encourages him to form a group of skinheads in his neighborhood. Derek's fury ultimately lands him in prison after he violently murders two black men who break into his car.

The hatred doesn't end once Derek's in prison. His younger brother Danny (Edward Furlong) picks up the crusade and comes under Cameron's wing. This greatly dismays Dr. Sweeney (Avery Brooks), a high school teacher who has taught both Danny and Derek and knows how bright they are. The boys are captivated by Sweeney's intelligence and wisdom, but they hold him at arm's length because he's African American.

Thus, Derek and Danny are caught between mentors: Cameron, who teaches hate, and Sweeney, who teaches respect. Sweeney continues to mentor Derek in prison, where (ironically) Derek is an outcast among whites and befriended by blacks. His positive exposure to people of other races leads him to revise his prejudices. By the time he leaves prison, Derek's attitude, motivation, and demeanor have changed. He's a better listener, less temperamental, and more open-minded. Derek's primary goal becomes to help his brother get out of the skinheads so Danny doesn't repeat his mistakes.

*American History X* is a challenging film. It illustrates how prejudice and intolerance are not inborn but learned—and that they can be unlearned with the proper attitude, motivation, and instruction.

with uncertainty is an essential ingredient of intercultural communication competence (Ruben & Kealey, 1979).

**Open-Mindedness**   Being comfortable with ambiguity is important, but without an open-minded attitude a communicator will have trouble interacting competently with people from different backgrounds. To understand open-mindedness, it's helpful to consider three traits that are incompatible with it. **Ethnocentrism** is an attitude that one's own culture is superior to others. An ethnocentric person might be aware of cultural differences and even be able to live comfortably with the notion that not everyone shares his or her standards. At the same time, this ethnocentric individual would think— either privately or openly—that anyone who did not belong to his or her in-group was somehow strange, wrong, or even inferior. Travel writer Rick Steves (1996, p. 9) describes how an ethnocentric point of view can interfere with respect for other cultural practices:

> Americans, like all groups, have their peculiar traits. It's fun to look at our culture from a grander perspective and see how others may question our sanity. For instance, we consider ourselves very clean and commonly criticize other cultures as dirty. In the bathtub we soak, clean, and rinse, all in the same water. (We would never wash our dishes that way.) A Japanese visitor, who uses clean water for each step, might find our way of bathing strange or even disgusting. Many cultures spit in public and blow their nose right onto the street. They couldn't imagine doing that into a small cloth, called a hanky, and storing that in their pocket to be used again and again.
>
> Too often we think of the world in terms of a pyramid of "civilized" (us) on the top and "primitive" groups on the bottom. If we measured things differently (maybe according to stress, loneliness, heart attacks, hours spent in traffic jams, or family togetherness) things stack up differently.

Ethnocentrism leads to an attitude of **prejudice**—an unfairly biased and intolerant attitude toward others who belong to an out-group.

(Note that the root term in *prejudice* is "pre-judge.") The key element of prejudice is its unfair nature. Everyone has personal biases, both positive and negative, but many of them are not unfair. Consider a few simple cultural examples: You might prefer Thai food to Chinese or like the blues more than rap music. You might think Asians are more attractive than Caucasians or vice versa. There's nothing inherently unfair about these personal preferences. On the other hand, when personal preferences are based on irrational beliefs, they cross the line and become prejudices. To say that blacks are lazy or Jews cheap without any valid evidence to support these claims is downright prejudiced.

An important element of prejudice is **stereotyping**—exaggerated generalizations about a group. Stereotypical prejudices include the obvious exaggerations that all women are emotional, all men are sex-crazed and insensitive goons, all older people are out of touch with reality, and all immigrants are welfare parasites. Stereotyping can even be a risk when it comes to knowledge of cultural characteristics like individualism or collectivism. Not all members of a group are equally individualistic or collectivistic. For example, a close look at Americans of European and Latin descent showed differences within each group (Oetzel, 1998). Some Latinos were more independent than some Euro-Americans, and vice versa. It's important to remember that obvious factors like ethnicity are just one factor in a person's communication style. A host of other variables are also important: family-of-origin, peer influences, education, and so on.

It's encouraging to know that open-minded communicators can overcome preexisting stereotypes and learn to appreciate people from different backgrounds as individuals. In one study, college students who were introduced to strangers from different cultural backgrounds developed attitudes about their new conversational partners based more on their personal behavior than on preexisting expectations about how people from those backgrounds might behave (Manusov et al., 1997).

## Knowledge and Skill

Without open-mindedness and a tolerance for ambiguity, satisfying intercultural communication isn't likely to occur. But attitude alone isn't enough to guarantee success in intercultural encounters. Communicators need to possess enough knowledge of other cultures to know what approaches are appropriate. For example, research by Mary

## REFLECTION

### RULES OF EXPRESSIVENESS

One of my favorite professors at another college was an African American. About halfway through the semester I heard he was also the pastor in a local church, so I asked him if I could watch him preach. When I visited the church one Sunday, I couldn't believe the familiar-looking man at the altar was the same person I saw in class every Monday, Wednesday, and Friday. It was like comparing Clark Kent and Superman! My professor's style in the classroom wasn't much different from most white faculty members. He was basically calm and well organized. He spoke clearly and not especially loudly. In front of his congregation (which was 100 percent African American), he was much more animated. His voice was like a musical instrument, sometimes quiet and sometimes shouting. He used his whole body as he spoke, moving around a great deal and using his arms to emphasize his message. The congregation didn't just sit quietly like the people at the church I attend back home. They would shout back to the minister and exclaim when he made a point. They sang along with the choir loudly and enthusiastically, not like the meek mumbles I grew up with.

The difference between my professor's style in a mostly white college and an all-black church really showed me how interculturally competent he is.

Jane Collier (1996) revealed how ethnic background influences what people consider the most important qualities in a friendship. Collier found that Latinos were most likely to value relational support and bonding with friends. By contrast, Asian Americans placed a greater value on helping one another achieve personal goals. For African Americans in the study, the most important quality in a friend was respect for and acceptance of the individual. Euro-Americans reported that they valued friends who met their task-related needs, offered advice, shared information, and had common interests.

This research suggests how knowledge of others' cultural background might help you become a more competent intercultural communicator. If, for example, you understand that a potential friend's background is likely to make displays of respect especially important, you could adjust your communication accordingly.

Unlike the culture-general attitudes we have discussed so far, knowledge of how to communicate with people from different backgrounds is usually "culture specific," to use Samovar, Porter, and Stefani's terminology (1998). The rules and customs that work with one group might be quite different from those that succeed with another. The ability to "shift gears" and adapt one's style to the norms of another culture or coculture is an essential ingredient of communication competence (Kim et al., 1996).

How can a communicator acquire the culture-specific information that leads to competence? One important element is what Stella Ting-Toomey (1999) and others label as *mindfulness*—awareness of one's own behavior and that of others. Communicators who lack this quality blunder through intercultural encounters *mindlessly*, oblivious of how their own behavior may confuse or offend others, and how behavior that they consider weird may be simply different.

Charles Berger (1979) suggests three strategies for moving toward a more mindful, competent style of intercultural communication. *Passive observation* involves noticing what behaviors are used by members of a different culture and using these insights to communicate in ways that are most effective. *Active strategies* include reading, watching films, asking experts and members of the other culture how to behave, as well as taking academic courses (Carrell, 1997). The third strategy, *self-disclosure*, involves volunteering personal information to people from the other culture with whom one wants to communicate. One type of self-disclosure is to confess one's cultural ignorance: "This is very new to me. What's the right thing to do in this situation?" This approach is the riskiest of the three described here, since some cultures may not value candor and self-disclosure as much as others.

Along with knowledge, a competent intercultural communicator has to have enough skill to use this information when interacting with others. There are several skills and ways of thinking that can help boost the chances of a successful intercultural encounter.

**Display of Respect**   Respect is an important dimension of relational communication in every culture and coculture, but methods for demonstrating that respect are culture specific. A competent communicator has to learn *who* deserves displays of respect in a particular culture and *how* to display that attitude.

Even in a country with low power distance such as the United States, respect is important. The North American idea that all people are "created equal" means that everyone is entitled to the same degree of attention and consideration. Other, less egalitarian cultures have communication rules that are more elaborate. In many Asian cultures, for example, older people are especially respected. In other countries one's level of education helps determine displays of respect. In Italy, for instance, all university graduates have a title (e.g., *avvocato* for *lawyers* and *ingegnere* for people in technical fields) and usually prefer to be addressed by it in formal settings (Axtell, 1990). A communicator who isn't aware of these customs and doesn't follow them is likely to offend others without ever knowing why.

## FOCUS ON RESEARCH

### THE CHALLENGES OF COCULTURE COMMUNICATION

Cautious. Guarded. Fearful. Uncomfortable. Stifled. This is how some members of "nondominant" groups say they feel when interacting with members of the dominant culture in the United States. Mark Orbe collected these and other responses from nondominant group members in the process of learning the strategies they use to survive and succeed in what he described as "oppressive environments."

Nondominant groups are those that have not traditionally had access to or influence upon the dominant culture. "In this country," says Orbe, "these groups include, but are not limited to, people of color, women, gays/lesbians/bisexuals, people with disabilities, lower/working class, and the young and elderly."

Orbe conducted in-depth and focus-group interviews with twenty-seven participants whom he personally knew or who were recommended to him by those he first interviewed. The participants represented a wide array of nondominant groups. The communication strategies identified by the respondents were as diverse as their backgrounds. Some said they manage their discomfort around members of the dominant culture by avoiding interaction with them ("I don't get involved too much"). Others said they restrict their self-expression in various ways ("Basically you tend not to act like yourself"). Still others said they don't alter their communication ("I really don't think that I communicate with them any differently"), or they use confrontational tactics ("I really don't let anyone walk all over me—even if that means stepping on some toes"). Orbe believes one "revelatory phrase" captured the standpoint of the respondents in this study. It came from a woman who was describing her reaction to the "good old boys" at a town council board meeting. She said she felt left out "because it was their world."

The idea that some citizens of the same country regard themselves as living in different and unequal worlds illustrates, clearly and painfully, the difficulties and challenges of cocultural communication in the United States.

Orbe, M.P. (1996). Laying the foundation for co-cultural communication theory: An inductive approach to studying "non-dominant" communication strategies and the factors that influence them. *Communication Studies, 47,* 157–176.

**Interaction Management**   Interaction management is part of every communication transaction. It involves controlling the flow of conversation, determining who will speak and for how long, and passing conversational control from one person to another. When two members of the same culture converse, their interaction management is usually unconscious and relatively smooth. For example, in mainstream U.S. culture, a speaker can signal that he or she is finishing a statement by gazing at the other person while decreasing the loudness of speech, slowing its tempo, drawling on the last syllable, or pausing (Knapp & Hall, 1997).

However, familiar clues don't necessarily have the same meaning in other cultures. The following account shows how a microsecond's difference in the length of a conversational pause can cause problems between English-speaking Canadians and Athabaskans, a Native American culture:

> When an English speaker pauses, he waits for the regular length of time (around one second or less), that is, his regular length of time, and if the Athabaskan

does not say anything, the English speaker feels he is free to go on and say anything else he likes. At the same time the Athabaskan has been waiting his regular length of time before coming in. He does not want to interrupt the English speaker. This length of time we think is around one and one-half seconds. It is just enough longer that by the time the Athabaskan is ready to speak the English speaker is already speaking again. So the Athabaskan waits again for the next pause. Again, the English speaker begins just enough before the Athabaskan was going to speak. The net result is that the Athabaskan can never get a word in edgewise (an apt metaphor in this case), while the English speaker goes on and on. (Scollon & Wong-Scollon, 1990, p. 273)

**Task and Relational Role Behaviors**   Task role behaviors are ways of interacting that help people or groups accomplish the job at hand. Since many intercultural encounters involve accomplishing some sort of task, the ability to take care of business in a manner that fits the communication style of another culture can make the difference between a smooth, positive relationship and causing discomfort or even offense. Task-related skills can involve a number of considerations: What kinds of demands can authority figures impose on their subordinates without overstepping their roles? How honest should fellow workers be with one another? What is the proper behavior for service providers and their clientele? What is the proper mix of business and personal communication? Some societies—many in Latin America and the Middle East, for example—don't make the distinction between business and personal relationships that is more common in Europe, North America, and Asia. When doing business with a Mexican or Saudi Arabian, a "let's get down to work" attitude before discussing each other's family and perhaps even sharing a meal would seem rude.

Relational harmony is important in every context, whether among the closest of friends or family members or between strangers who are just beginning an association. The communication style that helps build and maintain close relationships in North America can have quite the opposite effect in other cultures (Stewart & Bennett, 1991). Some differences in relational role behavior are rather obvious—at least once they are explained. For instance, in many countries around the Mediterranean, in the Middle East, and in Latin America, it is customary to greet others with an embrace and even a kiss. In some cultures, members of the same sex who are friends walk hand in hand. Understanding these rules can offer clues about how to behave with strangers and how to react when they act in ways that have very different meanings back home.

Relational role behaviors can vary between cocultures in the same society. For instance, several studies suggest that white Americans disclose more personal information than do African Americans, who in turn reveal more than do Mexican Americans. Other research suggests that the differences have more to do with social class than race—that African Americans and whites from lower socioeconomic classes disclose equally, for example (Gudykunst & Kim, 1997).

Differences like these can be even greater when members of one culture encounter people from another. As a group, North Americans value being direct, clear, and personal. This low-context, informal approach can leave communicators from high-context, hierarchical cultures feeling uncomfortable. North Americans are much more likely than members of most other cultures to clarify a relationship by asking "Where do we stand?" or "What are you thinking?" These questions might seem rude and overly personal in other societies. Rules for expressing feelings—both verbally and nonverbally—also vary from one culture to another. North Americans fall in about the middle of the expressiveness scale: To Arabs and Latin Americans they often seem cold, while Japanese people are likely to see them as lacking restraint. Understanding and using appropriate role behavior can help communicators from different backgrounds build and maintain comfortable, satisfying relationships.

# Summary

The growing diversity of American culture and the increased exposure to people from around the world make an understanding of intercultural communication essential. In order to understand this phenomenon, it is important to understand the meaning and differences of various concepts: culture, coculture, ethnicity, race, and international communication.

Intercultural communication occurs when members of two or more cultures or other groups exchange messages in a manner that is influenced by their different cultural perceptions and symbol systems. In other words, intercultural communication requires the perception of differences, not just their existence.

A number of fundamental values shape communication. When members of different cultures interact, these values can affect interaction in ways that may be felt but not understood. These values include an emphasis on high- or low-context communication, individualism or collectivism, high or low power distance, relatively more or less avoidance of uncertainty, and either achievement or nurturing.

The codes that are used by members of a culture are often the most recognizable factors that shape communication between people from different backgrounds. Verbal codes include language spoken and the worldview created by it, as well as verbal communication style. Nonverbal codes also differ significantly, as do the attributions that cultural conditioning generate.

Intercultural communicative competence involves three dimensions. The first is attitude: Regardless of the cultures involved, motivation to communicate is an important ingredient in successful interaction. Open-mindedness and tolerance of ambiguity are two elements of a competence-inducing attitude. Knowledge and skill are the other two key ingredients of intercultural communicative competence. These dimensions go hand in hand, since neither alone is sufficient. Whereas motivation is culture-general, knowledge and skill are usually culture-specific, requiring different information and abilities, depending on the cultures involved. Dimensions of knowledge and skill include displays of respect, interaction management, task role behavior, and relational role behavior.

# Recommended Readings

**Cultural influences on business practices:**

Terri Morrison, Wayne A. Conway, and George A. Borden. *Kiss, Bow, or Shake Hands: How to Do Business in Sixty Countries.* Holbrook, MA: Adams Media, 1994.

Geert Hofstede. *Cultures and Organizations.* New York: McGraw-Hill, 1997.

**Dimensions of intercultural communication:**

Judith N. Martin, Thomas K. Kakayama, and Lisa A. Flores. *Readings in Cultural Contexts.* Mountain View, CA: Mayfield, 1998.

Larry A. Samovar and Richard E. Porter. *Intercultural Communication: A Reader.* 9th ed. Belmont, CA: Wadsworth, 1999.

**Individualism and collectivism:**

Harry C. Triandis. *Individualism and Collectivism.* Boulder, CO: Westview, 1995.

**Intercultural communication competence:**

Myron W. Lusting and Jolene Koester. *Intercultural Competence: Interpersonal Communication across Cultures.* 3rd ed. New York: Longman, 1999.

**Perception and culture:**

Marshall R. Singer. *Perception and Identity in Intercultural Communication.* Yarmouth, ME: Intercultural Press, 1998.

# Activities

1. **Invitation to Insight**

   What in-groups do you belong to? You can best answer this question by thinking about whom you regard as belonging to out-groups. Based on your observations, consider the criteria you use to define in- and out-groups. Do you rely on race? Ethnicity? Age? Lifestyle? How do your judgments about in- and out-group membership affect your communication with others?

2. **Critical Thinking Probe**

   Identify one of your important interpersonal relationships. Consider how that relationship might be different if you and your partner adopted values and norms that were opposite from the ones you already hold. For example, if your communication is low context, how would things be different if you shifted to a high-context style? If you are tolerant of uncertainty, what might happen if you avoided any surprises? Based on your answers, consider the advantages and disadvantages of the cultural values and norms you hold. Think about the pros and cons of cultures that have differing values and norms.

3. **Ethical Challenge**

   Some cultural differences seem charming. However, others might seem alien—even inhumane. Explore the question of whether there are (or should be) any universal norms of behavior by identifying what rights and practices, if any, should be prohibited or honored universally.

4. **Skill Builder**

   Use the criteria on pages 54-60 to evaluate your intercultural communication competence. Identify one culture with which you currently interact or could interact with in the future. Collect information on communication rules and norms in that culture through library research and personal interviews. Based on your findings, describe the steps you can take to communicate more effectively with the culture's members.

# CHAPTER
# 3

# Communication and the Self

# After Studying the Material in This Chapter . . .

## You Should Understand:

1. The influences that shape development of the self-concept.

2. The subjective, resistant nature of the self-concept.

3. The role of self-fulfilling prophecies in shaping the self-concept and influencing communication.

4. How it is possible to change one's self-concept.

5. The nature and extent of identity management.

## You Should Be Able to Identify:

1. The key elements of your self-concept.

2. The most important forces that have shaped your self-concept.

3. The influence you have on shaping the self-concept of others.

4. The elements of yourself that you may inaccurately perceive as favorable or unfavorable.

5. Any self-fulfilling prophecies that you impose on yourself or on others, and that others impose on you.

6. Steps you can take to change undesirable elements of your self-concept.

7. The differences between your perceived self and various presenting selves.

8. The identity management strategies you use, and the ethical implications of those strategies.

## Key Terms

| | | | |
|---|---|---|---|
| Cognitive conservatism | Perceived self | Reflected appraisal | Self-fulfilling prophecy |
| Face | Presenting self | Self-concept | Significant other |
| Facework | Reference groups | Self-esteem | Social comparison |
| Identity management | | | |

Who are you? Before reading on, take a few minutes to answer this question by trying a simple exercise. First, make a list of the ten words or phrases that describe the most important features of who you are. Some of the items on your list may involve social roles: student, son or daughter, employee, and so on. Or you could define yourself through physical characteristics: fat, skinny, tall, short, beautiful, ugly. You may focus on your intellectual characteristics: smart, stupid, curious, inquisitive. Perhaps you can best define yourself in terms of moods, feelings, or attitudes: optimistic, critical, energetic. Or you could consider your social characteristics: outgoing, shy, defensive. You may see yourself in terms of belief systems: pacifist, Christian, vegetarian, libertarian. Finally, you could focus on particular skills (or lack of them): swimmer, artist, carpenter. In any case, choose ten words or phrases that best describe you, and write them down.

Next, choose the one item from your list that is the most fundamental to who you are and copy it on another sheet of paper. Then pick the second most fundamental item and record it as number two on your new list. Continue ranking the ten items until you have reorganized them all.

Now comes the most interesting part of the experience: Find a place where you won't be disturbed, and close your eyes. Take a few moments to relax, and then create a mental image of yourself. Try to paint a picture that not only captures your physical characteristics, but also reflects the attitudes, aptitudes, feelings, and/or beliefs included on your list. Take plenty of time to create this image.

Now recall (or peek at) your second list, noticing the item you ranked as number ten—the one least essential to your identity. Keeping your mental image in focus, imagine that this item suddenly disappeared from your personality or physical makeup. Try to visualize how you would be different without that tenth item. How would it affect the way you act? The way you feel? The way others behave toward you? Was it easy to give up that item? Do you like yourself more or less without

it? Take a few minutes with your eyes closed to answer these questions.

Without regaining the item you've just given up, continue your fantasy by removing item number nine. What difference does its absence make for you?

Slowly, at your own pace, continue the process by jettisoning one item at a time until you have given them all up. Notice what happens at each step of the process. After you've gone through your entire list, reclaim the items one by one until you are back to where you started.

How do you feel after trying this exercise? Most people find the experience a powerful one. They say that it clarifies how each of the items selected is fundamental to their identity. Many people say that they gain a clear picture of the parts of themselves they value and the parts with which they are unhappy.

Dump the contents of your purse or wallet on the table in front of you. Spread the items out so you can look at each one separately. Now, pretend you found the purse or wallet—that it is not yours—and you're trying to figure out what kind of person owns it.

- Look at the driver's license and any other photos of you. Do they accurately reflect your appearance? What do you like or dislike about the way this person looks? Would you want to have this person for a friend?
- Are there any family pictures? If so, what do they tell you about this person? If there are none, what might this suggest?
- Are there any membership cards from social or work groups? Can you guess the person's leisure activities and job? Is there a college identification card?
- Are there receipts? If there are, to what stores, for what goods or services, and for how much?
- How much money does the wallet contain? How many credit cards? What can you conclude about this person's financial state?
- What other items provide clues about who this person is?

Take your time and consider each item. See how much you can find out about this person. Then ask yourself: Am I the person these items suggest I am? If not, what information needs to be included to accurately reflect who you are?

# Communication and the Self-Concept

The items you examined are less significant than your reactions to them. The way you regard yourself in the first exercise offers clues about **self-concept:** the relatively stable set of perceptions you hold of yourself. One way to understand the self-concept is to imagine a special mirror that not only reflects physical features, but also allows you to view other aspects of yourself—emotional states, talents, likes, dislikes, values, roles, and so on. The reflection in that mirror would be your self-concept.

Any description of your self-concept that you constructed in this exercise is only a partial one. To make it complete, you'd have to keep adding items until your list ran into hundreds of words. Take a moment now to explore some of the many parts of your self-concept simply by responding to the question "Who am I?" over and over again. The resulting list will demonstrate the fact that the self-concept contains many dimensions. Physical appearance (attractive, unusual), skills (athletic, clumsy), social talents (gregarious, shy), roles (parent, student), intellectual traits (smart, intuitive), and emotional states (happy, confused)—all these and more make up your self-concept.

Of course, not every dimension of your self-concept list is equally important. For example, the most significant part of one person's self-concept might consist of social roles, whereas for another it might be physical appearance, health, friendships, accomplishments, or skills.

**Self-esteem** is the part of the self-concept that involves evaluations of self-worth. A hypothetical communicator's self-concept might include being quiet, argumentative, or serious. His or her self-

esteem would be determined by how he or she felt about these qualities. High or low self-esteem has a powerful affect on communication behavior, as Figure 3.1 shows. People who feel good about themselves have positive expectations about how they will communicate. These feelings increase the chance that communication will be successful, and successes contribute to positive self-evaluations, which reinforce self-esteem. Of course, the same principle can work in a negative way with communicators who have low self-esteem.

## How the Self-Concept Develops

Researchers generally agree that the self-concept does not exist at birth (Rosenblith, 1992). An infant lying in a crib has no notion of self, no notion—even if verbal language were miraculously made available—of how to answer the question "Who am I?" At about six or seven months, the child begins to recognize "self" as distinct from surroundings. If you've ever watched children at this age, you've probably marveled at how they can stare with great fascination at a foot, hand, and other body parts that float into view, almost as if they were strange objects belonging to someone else. Then the connection is made, almost as if the child were realizing "The hand is me," "The foot is me." These first revelations form the child's earliest concept of self. At this early stage, the self-concept is almost exclusively physical, involving the child's basic realization of existing and of possessing certain body parts over which some control is exerted.

As the child develops, this rudimentary sense of identity expands into a much more complete and sophisticated picture that resembles the self-concept of adults. This evolution is almost totally a product of social interaction (Wachs, 1992).

Two complementary theories describe how interaction shapes the way individuals view themselves: reflected appraisal and social comparison (Burkitt, 1992).

**Reflected Appraisal**   Before reading on, try the following exercise: Either by yourself or aloud

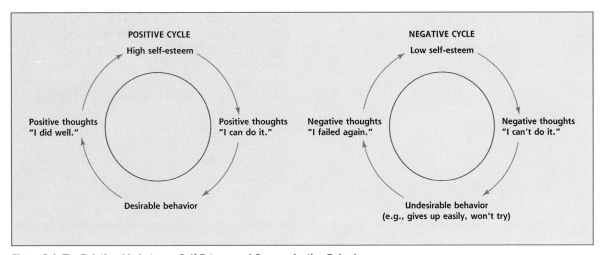

*Figure 3.1* **The Relationship between Self-Esteem and Communication Behavior**

Adapted from Johnson, H.M. (1998). *How do I love me?* (3rd ed.) Salem, WI: Sheffield Publishing Co., 3, 5.

with a partner, recall someone you know or once knew who helped enhance your self-concept by acting in a way that made you feel accepted, worthwhile, important, appreciated, or loved. This person needn't have played a crucial role in your life, as long as the role was positive. Often, one's self-concept is shaped by many tiny nudges as well as a few giant shoves. For instance, you might recall a childhood neighbor who took a special interest in you or a grandparent who never criticized or questioned your youthful foolishness.

After thinking about this supportive person, recall someone who acted in either a big or small way to diminish your self-esteem. For instance, teachers recall students who yawn in the middle of their classes. (The students may be tired, but it's difficult for teachers not to think that they are doing a poor, boring job.)

After thinking about these two types of people, you should begin to see that everyone's self-concept is shaped by **reflected appraisal:** perceptions of the judgments of those around her or him. To the extent that you have received supportive messages, you have learned to appreciate and value yourself. To the degree that you have received critical signals, you are likely to feel less valuable, lovable, and capable (Felson, 1985). Your self-concept can be seen, at least in part, as a product of the messages you've received throughout your life.

Social scientists use the term **significant other** to describe a person whose evaluations are especially influential. Messages from parents, of course, are an early and important influence on the self-concept. Supportive parents are more likely to raise children with healthy self-concepts. By contrast, parents with poor, negative, or deviant self-concepts tend to have unhappy children who view themselves in primarily negative ways (Fitts, 1971) and who go on to have unsatisfying relationships (Vangelisti & Crumley, 1998). Interestingly, if one parent has a good self-concept and the other a poor self-concept, the child is most likely to choose the parent with the more positive self-concept as a model. If neither parent has a strong self-concept, the child may seek an adult outside the family with whom to identify.

Along with family, the messages from many other significant others shape our self-concept. A teacher from long ago, a special friend or relative, or even a barely known acquaintance whom you respected can all leave an imprint on how you view yourself. To see the importance of significant

## THE POWER OF A PARENT: BOYZ IN THE HOOD

How important is a parent in shaping a child's self-concept? The movie *Boyz in the Hood* offers dramatic answers to this question. Tre Styles (Cuba Gooding, Jr.) is an angry young man being raised on the mean streets of South Central Los Angeles by his father, Fury (Lawrence Fishburne). Tre becomes pals with his neighbors Ricky (Morris Chestnut) and Doughboy (Ice Cube), who are half-brothers. The three young men take different paths in life, due in large part to the parenting they receive.

Tre is the only one of the three with a father to guide him. Tre sometimes resents his father's discipline, but Fury explains, "I'm trying to teach you how to be responsible, unlike your little friends across the street." Fury also fills Tre's mind and heart with messages about how to be a leader and how much he is loved. Tre becomes a strong young man who is able to resist the pressures of the streets that surround him.

Ricky receives words of approval and affection from his mother, which help boost his self-esteem. He also looks to Fury and Tre for guidance and direction that he never received from his absentee father. Doughboy, on the other hand, is told by his mother from an early age that he will never amount to anything. Their mother's words become self-fulfilling prophecies for each son. Ricky becomes a star football player while Doughboy struggles, angry and aimlessly, through life. At the movie's conclusion, the moral to the story is clear: A parent's appraisal can make all the difference in the world.

others, ask yourself how you arrived at your opinion of yourself as a student, as a person attractive to others, as a competent worker, and you will see that these self-evaluations were probably influenced by the way others regarded you. As we grow older, the power of messages from significant others remains (Voss et al., 1999). For example, teenage girls whose close friends are overly concerned with weight loss are more likely to view their appearance negatively and become prone to extreme weight-loss behaviors such as radical diets and bulimia (Paxton et al., 1999).

You might argue that not every part of your self-concept is shaped by others, that there are certain objective facts recognizable by self-observation alone. After all, nobody needs to tell you whether you are taller than others, speak with an accent, have curly hair, and so on. These facts are obvious. Indeed, some features of the self *are* immediately apparent. But the *significance* we attach to them—that is, the rank we assign them in the hierarchy of our list and the interpretation we give them—depends greatly on the opinions of others. After all, many of your features are readily observable, yet you don't find them important at all because nobody has regarded them as significant.

**Social Comparison**   So far, we have looked at the way others' messages shape the self-concept. In addition to using these messages, each of us forms our self-image by the process of **social comparison**: evaluating ourselves in terms of how we compare with others.

Two types of social comparison need highlighting. In the first, we decide whether we are *superior* or *inferior* by comparing ourselves to others. Are we attractive or ugly? A success or failure? Intelligent or stupid? It depends against whom we measure ourselves.

You might feel just ordinary or inferior in terms of talent, friendships, or attractiveness if you compare yourself with an inappropriate reference group. In one study, young women's perceptions of their bodies changed for the worse after watching just thirty minutes of televised images of the "ideal" female form (Myers & Biocca, 1992). You'll probably never be as beautiful as a Hollywood star, as agile as a professional athlete, or as wealthy as a millionaire. When you consider the matter logically, these facts don't mean you're worthless.

## FAMILY COMPARISONS

I'm the second-born son in my family. My older brother has always been a straight-*A* student. In high school, he was a National Merit Scholarship Finalist and one of the top ten students in his graduating class. The teachers always loved him, but I often have felt jealous of his accomplishments. When I used to get mad at him, I'd call him "Mister Perfect." I've earned a mixture of *A*s and *B*s throughout my school career, which both my family and teachers assured me was just fine. Still, I have been convinced that nobody ever thinks of me as being especially smart, thanks to the comparisons they make with my brother.

College has been the first time that I haven't attended a school where he preceded me. I'm slowly coming to realize that I am a pretty good student. Having the chance to judge myself against other, more normal students is making a big difference in how I regard myself academically.

Nonetheless, many people judge themselves against unreasonable standards and suffer accordingly (Grodin & Lindolf, 1995). You'll read more about how to avoid placing perfectionistic demands on yourself in Chapter 8.

In addition to feelings of superiority and inferiority, social comparison provides a way to decide if we are the *same as* or *different from* others. Research by psychologists William McGuire and Alice Padawer-Singer (1976) revealed that children were more likely to focus on characteristics such as birthplace, ethnic background, height, weight, or other physical features when those traits were different from the majority of their classmates. This principle of distinctiveness illustrates the power of social comparison to shape identity. A child who is interested in ballet and who lives in a setting where such a preference is regarded as weird will start to accept this label if there is no support from others. Likewise, adults who want to improve the quality of their relationships but are surrounded by friends and family who don't recognize or acknowledge the importance of these matters will think of themselves as oddballs. Thus, it's easy to recognize that the **reference groups** against which we compare ourselves play an important role in shaping our view of ourselves.

At first glance, social comparison theory seems rather deterministic. Besides being influenced by how others see us, we also are shaped by how we measure up to others. At second glance, however, the concept of social comparison offers a way of reshaping an unsatisfying self-concept.

To some degree, we're in control of who we choose for comparison. It's possible to seek out people with whom we compare favorably. This technique may bring to mind a search for a community of idiots in which you would appear as a genius, but there are healthier ways of changing your standards for comparison. For instance, you might decide that it's foolish to constantly compare your athletic prowess with professionals or campus stars, your looks with movie idols, and your intelligence with members of Phi Beta Kappa. Once you place yourself alongside a truly representative sample, your self-concept may improve.

## Characteristics of the Self-Concept

Now that you have a better idea of how your self-concept has developed, we can take a closer look at some of its characteristics.

**The Self-Concept Is Subjective**   The way we view ourselves is often at odds with others' perceptions—and often with the observable facts. In one study (Myers, 1980), a random sample of men were asked to rank themselves on their ability to get along with others. Defying mathematical laws, all subjects—every last one—put themselves in the top half of the population. Sixty percent rated themselves in the top 10 percent of the population, and an amazing 25 percent believed they were in the top 1 percent. In the same study, 70 percent of the men ranked the quality of their leadership in the top quarter of the population, whereas only 2 percent thought they were below average. Sixty percent said they were in the top quarter for athletic abilities, whereas only 6 percent viewed themselves as below average.

There are several reasons why some people have a self-concept that others would regard as unrealistically favorable. First, a self-estimation might be based on obsolete information. Perhaps your jokes used to be well received, or your grades were high, or your work was superior, but now the facts have changed. A self-concept might also be excessively favorable due to distorted feed-

back from others. A boss may claim to be an excellent manager because assistants pour on false praise in order to keep their jobs. A child's inflated ego may be based on the praise of doting parents.

There are also times when we view ourselves more harshly than the facts warrant. We have all experienced a temporary case of the "uglies," convinced we look much worse than others say that we really appear. Research confirms what common sense suggests—people are more critical of themselves when they are experiencing these negative moods than when they are feeling more positive (Brown & Mankowski, 1993). While everyone suffers occasional bouts of self-doubt that affect communication, some people suffer from long-term or even permanent states of excessive self-doubt and criticism (Gara et al., 1993). It's easy to understand how this chronic condition can influence the way these people approach and respond to others.

What are the reasons for such excessively negative self-evaluations? As with unrealistically high self-esteem, one source for an overabundance of self-put-downs is obsolete information. A string of past failures in school or with social relations can linger to haunt a communicator long after they have occurred. Similarly, we've known slender students who still think of themselves as fat and clear-complexioned people who still behave as if they were acne-ridden.

Distorted feedback also can lead to an excessively negative self-concept. Growing up in an overly critical family is one of the most common causes of a negative self-image. In other cases, the remarks of cruel friends, uncaring teachers, excessively demanding employers, or even memorable strangers can have a lasting effect. As you read earlier, the impact of significant others and reference groups in forming a self-concept can be great.

Along with obsolete information and distorted feedback, another cause for a strongly negative self-concept is the myth of perfection that is common in our society. From the time most of us learn to understand language, we are exposed to models who appear to be perfect at whatever they do. This myth is clearest when we examine the stories commonly told to children. In these stories the hero and heroine are wise, brave, talented, and victorious, whereas villains are totally evil and doomed to failure. This kind of model is easy for a child to understand, but it hardly paints a realistic picture of the world. Unfortunately, many parents perpetuate the myth of perfection by refusing to admit that they are ever mistaken or unfair. Children, of course, accept this perfectionist facade for a long time, not being in a position to dispute the wisdom of such powerful beings. From the behavior of the adults around them comes the clear message: "A well-adjusted, successful person has no faults."

Thus, children learn that in order to gain acceptance, they must pretend to "have it all together," even though they know they haven't. Given this naive belief that everyone else is perfect and the knowledge that you aren't, self-esteem will naturally suffer. We'll have a great deal to say about perfection and other irrational ideas, both in this chapter and in Chapter 8. In the meantime, don't get the mistaken impression that it's wrong to aim at perfection as an *ideal*. We're only suggesting that achieving this state is usually not possible and to expect that you should do so will certainly lead to unnecessarily low self-esteem.

A final reason people often sell themselves short is also connected to social expectations.

Curiously, the perfectionistic society to which we belong rewards those people who downplay the strengths we demand they possess (or pretend to possess). We term these people "modest" and find their behavior agreeable. On the other hand, we consider some of those who honestly appreciate their own strengths to be "braggarts" or "egotists," confusing them with the people who boast about accomplishments they do not possess (Miller et al., 1992). This convention leads most of us to talk freely about our shortcomings while downplaying our accomplishments. It's all right to proclaim that you're miserable if you have failed to do well on a project, but it's boastful to express your pride at a job well done. It's fine to remark that you feel unattractive, but it's egocentric to say that you think you look good.

After a while we begin to believe the types of statements we repeatedly make. The self-put-downs are viewed as modesty and become part of our self-concept, whereas the strengths and accomplishments go unmentioned and are forgotten. In the end, we see ourselves as much worse than we are.

Self-esteem may be based on inaccurate thinking, but it still has a powerful effect on the way we relate to others. Table 3.1 summarizes

**Table 3.1**

| Characteristics of Communicators with Positive and Negative Self-Esteem | |
| --- | --- |
| **Persons with Positive Self-Esteem** | **Persons with Negative Self-Esteem** |
| 1. Are likely to think well of others. | 1. Are likely to disapprove of others. |
| 2. Expect to be accepted by others. | 2. Expect to be rejected by others. |
| 3. Evaluate their own performance more favorably. | 3. Evaluate their own performance less favorably. |
| 4. Perform well when being watched: are not afraid of others' reactions. | 4. Perform poorly when being watched: are sensitive to possible negative reactions. |
| 5. Work harder for people who demand high standards of performance. | 5. Work harder for undemanding, less critical people. |
| 6. Are inclined to feel comfortable with others they view as superior in some way. | 6. Feel threatened by people they view as superior in some way. |
| 7. Are able to defend themselves against negative comments of others. | 7. Have difficulty defending themselves against others' negative comments: are more easily influenced. |

Reported by D. E. Hamachek. (1982). *Encounters with others: Interpersonal relationships and you.* New York: Holt, Rinehart and Winston.

some important differences between communicators with positive and negative self-esteem. Differences like these make sense when you realize that people who dislike themselves are likely to believe that others won't like them either. Realistically or not, they imagine that others are constantly viewing them critically, and they accept these imagined or real criticisms as more proof that they are indeed unlikable people. To use the well-known terminology of psychiatrist Eric Berne, they adopt an "I'm not OK—you're OK" orientation to life. This low self-esteem is sometimes manifested in hostility toward others, since the communicator takes the approach that the only way to look good is to put others down.

**A Healthy Self-Concept Is Flexible**   People change. From moment to moment, we aren't the same. We wake up in the morning in a jovial mood and turn grumpy before lunch. We find ourselves fascinated by a conversational topic one moment, then suddenly lose interest. You might be a relaxed conversationalist with people you know but at a loss for words with strangers. You might be patient when explaining things on the job but have no tolerance for such explanations at home.

The self-concepts of most communicators react to these changes. For example, between the ages of fourteen and twenty-three, the self-esteem of about two-thirds of the males in one study increased, while about one-third of the males felt less good about themselves (Block & Robins, 1993). The same study revealed that about 57 percent of women in the same age group grew to feel *less* good about themselves, while the self-esteem of the remaining 43 percent increased. After they approach the age of thirty, most people's self-concepts don't change so radically, at least not without a conscious effort, such as psychotherapy (Adler, 1992).

As we change in these and many other ways, our self-concept must also change in order to stay realistic. An accurate self-portrait today would not be exactly the same as the one we had a year ago, a few months ago, or even yesterday. This does not mean that you change radically from day to day. The fundamental characteristics of your personality will stay the same for years, perhaps for a lifetime. However, it is likely that in other important ways you are changing—physically, intellectually, emotionally, and spiritually.

**The Self-Concept Resists Change**   Although we change and a realistic self-concept should reflect this change, the tendency to resist revision of our self-perception is strong. Once a communicator fastens onto a self-concept—whether it be positive or negative—the tendency is to seek out people who confirm it. Numerous studies (e.g., Bower, 1992; Nicotera, 1993; Swann et al., 1992) show that both college students and married couples with high self-esteem seek out partners who view them favorably, while those with negative self-concepts are more inclined to interact with people who view them unfavorably. This tendency to seek information that conforms to an existing self-concept has been labeled **cognitive conservatism** (Greenwald, 1980; Greenwald & Pratkanis, 1984; Kihlstrom & Klein, 1994). We are understandably reluctant to revise a favorable self-concept. If you were a thoughtful, romantic partner early in a relationship, it would be hard to admit that you might have become less considerate and attentive lately. Likewise, if you used to be a serious student, acknowledging that you have slacked off isn't easy.

Curiously, the tendency to cling to an outmoded self-perception holds even when the new image would be more favorable. We can recall literally scores of attractive, intelligent students who still view themselves as the gawky underachievers they were in the past. The tragedy of this sort of cognitive conservatism is obvious. People with unnecessarily negative self-esteem can become their own worst enemies, denying

themselves the validation they deserve and need to enjoy satisfying relationships.

Once the self-concept is firmly rooted, only a powerful force can change it. At least four requirements must be met for an appraisal to be regarded as important (Gergen, 1971). First of all, the person who offers a particular appraisal must be *someone we see as competent to offer it.* Parents satisfy this requirement extremely well because as young children we perceive that our parents know so much about us—sometimes more than we know about ourselves. Second, *the appraisal must be perceived as highly personal.* The more the other person seems to know about us and adapts what is being said to fit us, the more likely we are to accept judgments from this person. In addition, the appraisal must be *reasonable in light of what we believe about ourselves.* If an appraisal is similar to one we give ourselves, we will believe it; if it is somewhat dissimilar, we will probably still accept it; but if it is completely dissimilar, we will probably reject it.

Finally, appraisals that are *consistent* and *numerous* are more persuasive than those that contradict usual appraisals or those that occur only once. As long as only a *few* students yawn in class, a teacher can safely disregard them as a reflection on his or her teaching ability. In like manner, you could safely disregard the appraisal of the angry date who tells you in no uncertain terms what kind of person behaves as you did. Of course, when you get a second or third similar appraisal in a short time, the evaluation becomes harder to ignore.

## The Self-Fulfilling Prophecy and Communication

The self-concept is such a powerful influence on the personality that it not only determines how you see yourself in the present but also can actually affect your future behavior and that of others. Such occurrences come about through a phenomenon called the self-fulfilling prophecy.

A **self-fulfilling prophecy** occurs when a person's expectations of an event and her or his subsequent behavior based on those expectations make the outcome more likely to occur than would otherwise have been true. Self-fulfilling prophecies occur all the time, although you may never have given them that label. For example, think of some instances you may have known:

> You expected to become nervous and botch a job interview and later did so.
> You anticipated having a good (or terrible) time at a social affair and found your expectations being met.
> A boss explained a new task to you, saying that you probably would find it difficult, and indeed you did.

In each of these cases, there is a good chance that the event occurred because it was predicted to occur. You needn't have botched the interview, the party might have been boring only because you helped make it so, and you might have done better on the job if your boss hadn't spoken up. In other words, what helped make each event occur was the expectation of it.

**Types of Self-Fulfilling Prophecies**   There are two types of self-fulfilling prophecies. *Self-imposed prophecies* occur when your own expectations influence your behavior. You've probably had the experience of waking up in a cross mood and saying to yourself, "This will be a bad day." Once you made such a decision, you may have acted in ways that made it come true. If you avoid the company of others because you expect they had nothing to offer, your suspicions would have been confirmed—nothing exciting or new is likely to happen. On the other hand, if you approach the same day with the idea that it could be a good one, this expectation may well be met. Smile at people, and they're more likely to smile back. Enter a class determined to learn something, and you probably will—even if it's how not to instruct students! In these cases and other similar ones, your attitude has a great deal to do with how you see yourself and how others see you.

## REFLECTION

### GETTING WHAT I EXPECT

I had the following interaction with a friend, and it's my best example of a self-fulfilling prophecy: how someone's beliefs about himself can affect how he behaves and, in turn, create the expected outcome. I asked my friend, "From whom can you get love? Anyone?" "No, not anyone. The person needs to be a woman." I asked, "Any woman?" "No, she needs to be between eighteen and forty years of age." I asked, "Any woman between eighteen and forty?" "No, she needs to have long red hair." I asked, "Any woman between eighteen and forty with long red hair?" "No, she needs to have blue eyes." I asked, "Any woman between eighteen and forty, with long red hair and blue eyes?" "No, she also needs to be between five-foot-three and five-foot-seven." I asked, "Any woman between eighteen and forty, with long red hair and blue eyes, between five-foot-three and five-foot-seven?" "No, she also needs a college degree." I asked, "Any woman between eighteen and forty, with long red hair and blue eyes, between five-foot-three and five-foot-seven, with a college degree?" "No, she needs to have a degree in the helping professions, such as teaching, nursing, or social work." I asked, "Any woman between eighteen and forty, with long red hair and blue eyes, between five-foot-three and five-foot-seven, with a college degree in the helping professions?" "No, there's one more requirement. She has to love me—first." I asked, "And what's the problem?" "I'm unlovable."

Research has demonstrated the power of self-imposed prophecies. In one study, communicators who believed they were incompetent proved less likely than others to pursue rewarding relationships and more likely to sabotage their existing relationships than did people who were less critical of themselves (Kolligan, 1990). On the other

## FOCUS ON RESEARCH

### SMILE: IT CAN CHANGE YOUR MOOD

Most people believe that mood determines behavior. If you're in a good mood, you smile and laugh; if you're in a bad mood, nothing will make you grin. While there is certainly truth to this notion, researchers Chris Kleinke, Thomas Peterson, and Thomas Rutledge found the opposite can also be true. Putting a smile on your face, even if you're not in a good mood, can lead to a more positive disposition.

The researchers asked participants in their study to fill out questionnaires that identified their pre-experiment moods. They were then randomly assigned to one of three groups. In the first group, participants were asked to mimic pictures of people with positive facial expressions. The second group mimicked pictures of people with negative facial expressions; the third group maintained neutral facial expressions while looking at the pictures. At the end of the experiment, the participants were asked to fill out the mood-assessing questionnaire once again.

As predicted, participants who mimicked pictures of smiling people reported more positive moods after engaging in the experiment. Those who mimicked scowls developed more negative moods; those who held neutral facial expressions had little or no change in disposition. This study offers a measure of support for the concept of a self-imposed, self-fulfilling prophecy. Acting happy, even if you're not feeling happy, might help you become happy—because behavior can sometimes determine mood.

Kleinke, C. L., Peterson, T. R., & Rutledge, T. R. (1998). Effects of self-generated facial expressions on mood. *Journal of Personality and Social Psychology, 74*, 272–279.

hand, students who perceive themselves as capable achieved more academically (Zimmerman et al., 1992). In another study, subjects who were sensitive to social rejection tended to expect rejection, perceive it where it might not have existed, and overreact to their exaggerated perceptions in ways that jeopardized the quality of their relationships (Downey & Feldman, 1996). Research also suggests that communicators who feel anxious about giving speeches seem to create self-fulfilling prophecies about doing poorly, which causes them to perform less effectively (MacIntyre & Thiviegre, 1995).

A second category of self-fulfilling prophecies occurs when one person's expectations govern another's actions (Blank, 1993). The classic exam-ple was demonstrated by Robert Rosenthal and Lenore Jacobson in a study they described in their book *Pygmalion in the Classroom* (1968). The experimenters told teachers that 20 percent of the children in a certain elementary school showed unusual potential for intellectual growth. The names of these 20 percent were drawn by means of a table of random numbers—much as if they were drawn out of a hat. Eight months later these unusual or "magic" children showed significantly greater gains in IQ than did the remaining children, who had not been singled out for the teachers' attention. The change in the teachers' behavior toward these allegedly "special" children led to changes in the intellectual performance of these randomly selected children. Among other things, the teachers gave the "smart" students more time to answer questions, and provided more feedback to them. These children did better not because they were any more intelligent than their classmates, but because their teachers—significant others—communicated the expectation that they could. In other words, it wasn't just what the teachers *believed* that made a difference; it was how these beliefs were conveyed by the teachers' *behavior.*

To put this phenomenon in context with the self-concept, we can say that when a teacher communicates to a child the message "I think you're bright," the child accepts that evaluation and changes his or her self-concept to include it. Unfortunately, we can assume that the same principle holds for students whose teachers send the message "I think you're stupid."

This type of self-fulfilling prophecy has been shown to be a powerful force for shaping the self-concept and thus the behavior of people in a wide range of settings. In medicine, patients who unknowingly receive placebos—substances such as injections of sterile water or doses of sugar pills that have no curative value—often respond just as favorably to treatment as those who have actually received a drug. The patients believe they have taken a substance that will help them feel better, and this belief actually brings about a "cure." In psychotherapy, Rosenthal and Jacobson describe several studies suggesting that patients who believe they will benefit from treatment do so regardless of the type of treatment they receive. Similarly, when a doctor believes a patient will improve, the patient may do so precisely because of this expectation, whereas another person for whom the physician has little hope often fails to recover. The patient's self-concept as sick or well—as shaped by the doctor—apparently plays an important role in determining the actual state of health.

Notice that it isn't just the observer's *belief* that creates a self-fulfilling prophecy for the person who is the target of the expectations. The observer must *communicate that belief* in order for the prediction

to have any effect. If parents have faith in their children but the kids aren't aware of that confidence, they won't be affected by their parents' expectations. If a boss has concerns about an employee's ability to do a job but keeps those worries to herself, the subordinate won't be influenced. In this sense, the self-fulfilling prophecies imposed by one person on another are as much a communication phenomenon as a psychological one.

**Influence of Self-Fulfilling Prophecies** The influence of self-fulfilling prophecies on communication can be strong, acting either to improve or to harm relationships. If you assume that another person is unlikable, then you'll probably act in ways that communicate your feelings. In such a case, the other person's behavior will probably match your expectations: We usually don't go out of our way to be nice to people who aren't nice to us. If, on the other hand, you treat the other person as likable, the results are likely to be more positive.

In business, the power of the self-fulfilling prophecy was proved as early as 1890. A new tabulating machine had just been installed at the U.S. Census Bureau in Washington, D.C. To use the machine, the bureau's staff had to learn a new set of skills that the machine's inventor believed to be quite difficult. He told the clerks that after some practice they could expect to punch about 550 cards per day; to process any more would jeopardize their psychological well-being. Sure enough, after two weeks the clerks were processing the anticipated number of cards and reporting feelings of stress if they attempted to move any faster.

Later, an additional group of clerks was hired to operate the same machines. These workers knew nothing of the devices, and no one had told them about the upper limit of production. After only three days, the new employees were each punching over 2,000 cards per day with no ill effects. Again, the self-fulfilling prophecy seemed to be in operation. The original workers believed themselves capable of punching only 550 cards

*"I don't sing because I am happy. I am happy because I sing."*

and so behaved accordingly, whereas the new clerks had no limiting expectations as part of their self-concepts and so behaved more productively (Rosenthal & Jacobson, 1968).

The self-fulfilling prophecy operates in families as well. If parents tell a child long enough that she can't do anything right, her self-concept will soon incorporate this idea, and she may fail at many or most of the tasks she attempts. On the other hand, if a child is told he is a capable, lovable, or kind person, there is a much greater chance of his behaving accordingly.

The self-fulfilling prophecy is an important force in interpersonal communication, but we don't want to suggest that it explains all behavior. There are certainly times when the expectation of

an event's outcome won't bring it about. Your hope of drawing an ace in a card game won't in any way affect the chance of that card turning up in an already shuffled deck, and your belief that good weather is coming won't stop the rain from falling. In the same way, believing you'll do well in a job interview when you're clearly not qualified for the position is unrealistic. Similarly, there will probably be people you don't like and occasions you won't enjoy, no matter what your attitude is. To connect the self-fulfilling prophecy with the "power of positive thinking" is an oversimplification.

In other cases, your expectations will be borne out because you're a good predictor and not because of the self-fulfilling prophecy. For example, children are not equally well-equipped to do well in school, and in such cases it would be wrong to say that a child's performance was shaped by a parent or teacher, even though the behavior did match what was expected. In the same way, some workers excel and others fail, some patients recover and others don't, in agreement with or contrary to our predictions, but not because of them.

Keeping these qualifications in mind, you will find it important to recognize the tremendous influence that self-fulfilling prophecies have on our lives. To a great extent, we are what we believe we are. In this sense, we and those around us constantly create our self-concepts and, therefore, ourselves through communication.

## Changing Your Self-Concept

You've probably begun to realize that it is possible to change an unsatisfying self-concept. In the next sections we'll discuss some methods for accomplishing such a change.

**Have Realistic Expectations**　It's important to realize that some of your dissatisfaction might come from expecting too much of yourself. If you demand that you handle every act of communication perfectly, you're bound to be disappointed. Nobody is able to handle every conflict productively, to be totally relaxed and skillful in conversations, always to ask perceptive questions, or to be 100 percent helpful when others have problems. Expecting yourself to reach such unrealistic goals is to doom yourself to unhappiness at the start.

It's important to judge yourself in terms of your own growth and not against the behavior of others. Rather than feeling miserable because you're not as talented as an expert, realize that you probably are a better, wiser, or more skillful person than you used to be and that this growth is a legitimate source of satisfaction. Perfection is fine as an ideal, but you're being unfair to yourself if you actually expect to reach it.

**Have a Realistic Perception of Yourself**   One source of low self-esteem is inaccurate self-perception. As you've already read, such unrealistic pictures sometimes come from being overly harsh on yourself, believing that you're worse than the facts indicate. Of course, it would be foolish to deny that you could be a better person than you are, but it's also important to recognize your strengths. A periodic session of "bragging"—acknowledging the parts of yourself with which you're pleased and the ways you've grown—is often a good way to put your strengths and shortcomings into perspective.

Unrealistically low self-esteem also can come from the inaccurate feedback of others. Perhaps you are in an environment where you receive an excessive number of negative messages, many of which are undeserved, and a minimum of encouragement. For example, we've known many women who have returned to college after years spent in homemaking, where they received virtually no recognition for their intellectual strengths. It's amazing that these women have the courage to come to college at all, for their self-esteem is so low; but they do come, and most are thrilled to find that they are much brighter and more intellectually competent than they suspected. In the same way, workers with overly critical supervisors, children with cruel "friends," and students with unsupportive teachers are all prone to suffering from low self-esteem due to excessively negative feedback.

If you fall into this category, it's important to put into perspective the unrealistic evaluations you receive and then to seek out supportive people who will acknowledge your assets as well as point out your shortcomings. Doing so is often a quick and sure boost to your self-esteem.

**Have the Will to Change**   Often we say we want to change, but aren't willing to do the necessary work. In such cases the responsibility for not growing rests squarely on your shoulders. At other times we maintain an unrealistic self-concept by claiming that we "can't" be the person we'd like to be, when in fact we're simply not willing to do what's required. You *can* change in many ways, but only if you are willing to put out the effort.

**Have the Skill to Change**   Trying is often not enough. There are times when you would change if you knew how to do so.

First, you can seek advice—from books such as this one, the suggested readings at the end of each chapter, and other printed sources. You also can get advice from instructors, counselors, and other experts, as well as from friends. Of course, not all the advice you receive will be useful, but if you read widely and talk to enough people, you have a good chance of learning the things you want to know.

A second method of learning how to change is to observe models—people who handle themselves in the ways you would like to master. It's often been said that people learn more from models than in any other way, and by taking advantage of this principle you will find that the world is full of teachers who can show you how to communicate more successfully. Become a careful observer. Watch what people you admire do and say, not so you can copy them but so you can adapt their behavior to fit your own personal style.

At this point you might be overwhelmed by the difficulty of changing the way you think about yourself and the way you act. Remember, we never said that this process would be easy (although it sometimes is). But even when change is difficult, it's possible if you are serious. You don't need to be perfect, but you *can* improve your self-concept and raise your self-esteem, and, as a result, your communication—*if you choose to.*

## Presenting the Self: Communication as Identity Management

So far, we have described how communication shapes the way communicators view themselves. In the remainder of this chapter we turn the tables and focus on the topic of **identity management**—the communication strategies people use to influence how others view them. In the following pages you will see that many of our messages are aimed at creating desired impressions.

## Public and Private Selves

To understand why identity management exists, we have to discuss the notion of self in more detail. So far, we have referred to the "self" as if each of us had only one identity. In truth, each of us possesses several selves, some private and others public. These selves are often quite different.

The **perceived self** is the person you believe yourself to be in moments of honest self-examination. The perceived self may not be accurate in every respect. For example, you might think you are much more (or less) intelligent than an objective test would measure. Accurate or not, the perceived self is powerful because we believe it reflects who we are. We can call the perceived self "private" because you are unlikely to reveal all of it to another person. You can verify the private nature of the perceived self by thinking of elements of your self-perception that you would not disclose. For example, you might be reluctant

"Hah! <u>This</u> is the Old King Cole nobody ever sees."

to share some feelings about your appearance ("I think I'm rather unattractive"), your goals ("The most important thing to me is becoming rich"), or your motives ("I care more about myself than about others").

In contrast to the perceived self, the **presenting self** is a public image—the way we want to appear to others. In most cases the presenting self we seek to create is a socially approved image: diligent student, loving partner, conscientious worker, loyal friend, and so on. Sociologist Erving Goffman (1959, 1971) used the word **face** to describe this socially approved identity, and he coined the term **facework** to describe the verbal and nonverbal ways in which we act to maintain our own presenting image and the images of others. He argued that each of us can be viewed as a kind of playwright who creates roles that we want others to believe, as well as the performer who acts out those roles. Goffman suggested that each of us maintains face by putting on a *front* when we are around others whom we want to impress.

In contrast, behavior in the *back region*—when we are alone—may be quite different. You can recognize the difference between front and backstage behavior by recalling a time when you observed a driver, alone in his or her car, behaving in ways that would never be acceptable in public. All of us engage in backstage ways of acting that we would never exhibit in front of others. Just recall how you behave in front of the bathroom mirror when the door is locked, and you will appreciate the difference between public and private behavior. If you knew someone was watching, would you behave differently?

## Characteristics of Identity Management

Now that you have a sense of what identity management is, we can look at some characteristics of this process.

**We Strive to Construct Multiple Identities**   It is an oversimplification to suggest we use identity management strategies to create just one identity. In the course of even a single day, most people play a variety of roles: "respectful student," "joking friend," "friendly neighbor," and "helpful worker," to suggest just a few. We even play a variety of roles around the same person. As you grew up, you almost certainly changed characters as you interacted with your parents. In one context you acted as responsible adult ("You can trust me with the car!") and at another time you were the helpless child ("I can't find my socks!"). At some times—perhaps on birthdays or holidays—you were a dedicated family member, and at other times you may have played the role of rebel. Likewise, in romantic relationships we switch among many ways of behaving, depending on the context: friend, lover, business partner, scolding critic, apologetic child, and so on.

The ability to construct multiple identities is one element of communication competence. For example, the style of speaking or even the language itself can reflect a choice about how to construct one's identity. Recall the African-American professor/Baptist minister described in the Reflection on page 57. On campus his manner of speaking was typically professorial; but a visit to hear him preach one Sunday revealed a speaker whose style was much more animated and theatrical, reflecting his identity in that context. Likewise, one scholar pointed out that bilingual Latinos in the United States often choose whether to use English or Spanish depending on the kind of identity they are seeking in a given conversation (Scotton, 1983).

**Identity Management Is Collaborative**   As we perform like actors trying to create a front, our "audience" is made up of other actors who are trying to create their own characters. Identity-related communication is a kind of process theater in which we improvise scenes where our character reacts with others.

You can appreciate the collaborative nature of identity management by thinking about how you might handle a gripe with a friend or family member who has failed to pass along a phone message that arrived while you were away from home. Suppose that you decide to raise the issue tactfully in an effort to avoid seeming like a nag (desired role for yourself: "nice person"), and also to save the other person from the embarrassment of being confronted (hoping to avoid suggesting that the other person's role is "screw-up"). If your tactful bid is accepted, the dialog might sound like this:

> **You:** By the way, Jenny told me she called yesterday. If you wrote a note, I guess I missed seeing it.
>
> **Other:** Oh, . . . sorry. I meant to write a note, but as soon as I hung up the doorbell rang, and then I had to run off to class.
>
> **You** (in friendly tone of voice): That's okay. I sure would appreciate from now on if you'd leave me a note.
>
> **Other:** No problem.

In this upbeat conversation, both you and the other person accepted one another's bids for identity as basically thoughtful people. As a result, the conversation ran smoothly. Imagine, though,

how differently the outcome would be if the other person didn't accept your role as "thoughtful person":

> **You:** By the way, Jenny told me she called yesterday. If you wrote a note, I guess I missed seeing it.
>
> **Other** (defensively): Okay, so I forgot. It's not that big a deal. You're not perfect yourself, you know!

Your first bid as "nice, face-saving person" was rejected. At this point you have the choice of persisting in trying to play the original role: "Hey, I'm not mad at you, and I know I'm not perfect!" Or, you might switch to the new role of "unjustly accused person," responding with aggravation: "I never said I was perfect. But we're not talking about me here. . . ."

As this example illustrates, collaboration doesn't mean the same thing as agreement (Stewart & Logan, 1998). The small issue of the phone message might mushroom into a fight in which you and the other person both adopt the role of combatants. The point here is that virtually all conversations provide an arena in which communicators construct their identities in response to the behavior of others. As you read in Chapter 1, communication isn't made up of discrete events that can be separated from one another. Instead, what happens at one moment is influenced by what each communicator brings to the interaction, and what happened in their relationship up to that point.

**Impression Management Can Be Deliberate or Unconscious**   There's no doubt that sometimes we are highly aware of managing impressions. Most job interviews and first dates are clear examples of deliberate identity management. But in other cases we unconsciously act in ways that are really small public performances. For example, experimental subjects expressed facial disgust in reaction to eating sandwiches laced with a supersaturated solution of salt water only when there was another person present; when they were alone, they made no faces upon eating the same snack (Brightman et al., 1975). Another

## REFLECTION

### MULTIPLE "ME'S"

An assignment in my English class showed me how much I change my identity in different relationships. We had to write letters to two different people describing how we were doing in life. I wrote the first one to my grandmother, and the other to my best friend. I was amazed at the difference between the two. I was much more positive and superficial with my grandma. I talked about events: school, work, and what I was doing with other members of our family. When writing to my friend, I talked about my nonfamily relationships and shared a lot of information that would probably have shocked and confused my grandmother.

This assignment helped me realize that I show different sides of myself to different people. It's not that I lie to anybody. It's just that I have different identities in different relationships.

study showed that communicators engage in facial mimicry (such as smiling or looking sympathetic in response to another's message) only in face-to-face settings, when their expressions can be seen by the other person. When they are speaking over the phone and their reactions cannot be seen, they do not make the same expressions (Chovil, 1991). Studies like these suggest that most of our behavior is aimed at sending messages to others—in other words, identity management.

You can see by now that much identity management is unconscious. The experimental subjects described in the last paragraph didn't consciously think, "Somebody is watching me eat this salty sandwich so I'll make a face" or "Since I'm in a face-to-face conversation, I'll show I'm sympathetic by mimicking the facial expressions of my conversational partner." Decisions like these are often instantaneous and outside our conscious awareness.

Despite the claims of some theorists, it seems an exaggeration to suggest that *all* behavior is aimed at making impressions. Young children certainly aren't strategic communicators. A baby spontaneously laughs when pleased and cries when sad or uncomfortable, without any notion of creating an impression in others. Likewise, there are almost certainly times when we, as adults, act spontaneously. But when a significant other questions the presenting self we try to present, the likelihood of acting to prop it up increases. This process isn't always conscious: At a nonconscious level of awareness we monitor others' reactions, and swing into action when our face is threatened—especially by significant others (Leary & Kowalski, 1990).

**People Differ in Their Degree of Identity Management**   Some people are much more aware of their identity management behavior than others (Snyder, 1979). These high self-monitors have the ability to pay attention to their own behavior and others' reactions, adjusting their communication to create the desired impression. By contrast, low self-monitors express what they are thinking and feeling without paying much attention to the impression their behavior creates.

There are certainly advantages to being a high self-monitor (Hamachek, 1992). People who pay attention to themselves are generally good actors who can create the impression they want, acting interested when bored or friendly when they really feel quite the opposite. This allows them to handle social situations smoothly, often putting others at ease. They are also good "people-readers" who can adjust their behavior to get the desired reaction from others. Along with these advantages, there are some potential drawbacks to being an extremely high self-monitor. Their analytical nature may prevent them from experiencing events completely, since a portion of their attention will always be viewing the situation from a detached position. High self-monitors' ability to act makes it difficult to tell how they are really feeling. In fact, because high self-monitors change roles often, they may have a hard time knowing *themselves* how they really feel.

People who score low on the self-monitoring scale live life quite differently from their more self-conscious counterparts. They have a more simple, focused idea of who they are and who they want to be. Low self-monitors are likely to have a narrower repertoire of behaviors, so they can be expected to act in more or less the same way regardless of the situation. This means that low self-monitors are easier to read than high self-monitors. "What you see is what you get" might be their motto. While this lack of flexibility may make their social interaction less smooth in many situations, low self-monitors can be counted on to be straightforward communicators.

By now it should be clear that neither extremely high nor low self-monitoring is the ideal. There are some situations when paying attention to yourself and adapting your behavior can be useful, and other times when reacting without considering the effect on others is a better approach. This need for a range of behaviors demonstrates once again the notion of communicative competence outlined in Chapter 1—flexibility is the key to successful relationships.

## Why Manage Impressions?

Why bother trying to shape others' opinions? Sometimes we create and maintain a front to follow social rules. As children we learn to act politely, even when bored. Likewise, part of growing up consists of developing a set of manners for various occasions, such as meeting strangers, attending school, and going to church. Young children who haven't learned all the do's and don'ts of polite society often embarrass their parents by behaving inappropriately ("Mommy, why is that man so fat?"), but by the time they enter school, behavior that might have been excusable or even amusing just isn't acceptable. Good manners are often aimed at making others more comfortable.

For example, able-bodied people often mask their discomfort upon encountering someone who is disabled by acting nonchalant or stressing similarities between themselves and the disabled person (Coleman & DePaulo, 1991).

Social rules govern our behavior in a variety of settings. For example, it would be impossible to keep a job without meeting certain expectations. Salespeople are supposed to treat customers with courtesy. Employees need to appear reasonably respectful when talking to the boss. Some forms of clothing would be considered outrageous at work. By agreeing to take on a job, you are signing an unwritten contract that dictates you will present a certain face at work, whether or not that face reflects the way you might be feeling at a particular moment.

Even when social roles don't dictate the proper way to behave, we often manage impressions for a second reason: to accomplish personal goals. You might, for example, dress up for a visit to traffic court in the hope that your front (responsible citizen) will convince the judge to treat you sympathetically. You might be sociable to your neighbors so they will agree to your request that they keep their dog off your lawn.

Identity management sometimes aims at achieving one or more of the relational goals we discussed in Chapter 1: affiliation, control, respect, and immediacy. For instance, you might act more friendly and lively than you feel upon meeting a new person so that you will appear likable. You could sigh and roll your eyes when arguing politics with a classmate to gain an advantage in an argument. You might smile and preen to show the attractive stranger at a party that you would like to get better acquainted. In situations like these, you aren't being deceptive as much as "putting your best foot forward."

All these examples show that it is difficult—perhaps even impossible—*not* to create impressions. After all, you have to send some sort of message. If you don't act friendly when meeting a stranger, you have to act aloof, indifferent, hostile, or in some other manner. If you don't act

## FOCUS ON RESEARCH

### THE BODY AS BILLBOARD: THE CASE OF HIV/AIDS TATTOOS

The use of tattoos to stigmatize wearers has a long history. In thirteenth-century Japan, criminals were tattooed to mark their status as lawbreakers. Nineteenth-century British army deserters were marked with a *D*, and soldiers judged to be of bad character were labeled with a *BC*. So why would some people *choose* to tattoo themselves in an apparent act of self-stigmatization?

Daniel Brouwer examined the reasons some HIV-positive people advertise their health status with tattoos reading "POZ," or ones that bear a plus sign and the letters *HIV*. Through an analysis of written texts and an interview with one "POZ" tattoo wearer, Brouwer uncovered benefits of these indelible labels that, in the eyes of their wearers, are valuable enough to offset the costs of publicly announcing one's life-threatening, infectious condition.

At the most obvious level, these tattoos convey important information about the health status of the wearer to medical workers. Beyond being a practical announcement, though, Brouwer found that the tattoos are a vehicle for identity management, intended for both the wearer and others. One tattoo wearer listed the messages his visible label conveys: the refusal to internalize shame; a commitment to safer sex practices; a challenge to stereotypes about weak "AIDS victims"; and an educational tool that generates discussion by making the condition visible.

Paradoxically, tattoos that seem to stigmatize wearers can offer a certain freedom and control over their lives. As Brouwer discovered, announcing one's status visibly allows the wearer to admit being infected both to self and to others. This, in turn, provides the chance to live life without the anxiety, emotional exhaustion, guilt, and shame of having to maintain such an enormous secret.

Brouwer, D. (1998). The precarious visibility politics of self-stigmatization: The case of HIV/AIDS tattoos. *Text and Performance Quarterly, 18,* 114–136.

businesslike, you have to behave in an alternative way: casual, goofy, or whatever. Often the question isn't whether or not to present a face to others; it's only which face to present.

## How Do We Manage Impressions?

How do we create a public face? In an age in which technology provides many options for communicating, the answer depends in part on the communication channel chosen.

**Face-to-Face Identity Management**  In face-to-face interaction, communicators can manage their front in three ways: manner, appearance, and setting. *Manner* consists of a communicator's words and nonverbal actions. Your manner plays a major role in shaping how others view you. Chapters 5 and 6 will describe in detail how your words and nonverbal behaviors create impressions. Since you *have* to speak and act, the question isn't whether or not your manner sends a message; rather, it's whether or not these messages will be intentional.

Along with manner, a second dimension of identity management is *appearance*—the personal items people use to shape an image. Sometimes appearance is part of creating a professional image. A physician's white lab coat and a police officer's uniform set the wearer apart as someone special. A tailored suit or a rumpled outfit creates a very different impression in the business world. Off the job, clothing is just as important. We choose clothing that sends a message about ourselves, sometimes trendy and sometimes traditional. Some people dress in ways that accent their sexuality, while others hide it. Clothing can say, "I'm an athlete," "I'm wealthy," or "I'm an environmentalist." Along with dress, other aspects of appearance play a strong role in impression management. Are you suntanned or pale? What is your hairstyle?

A final way to manage impressions is through the choice of *setting*—physical items we use to influence how others view us. In modern Western society, the automobile is a major part of identity management. This explains why many people lust after cars that are far more expensive and powerful than they really need. A sporty convertible or fancy imported sedan doesn't just get drivers from one place to another; it also makes statements

about the kind of people they are. The physical setting we choose and the way we arrange it is another important way to manage impressions. What colors do you choose for the place you live? What artwork is on your walls? What music do you play? If possible, we choose a setting that we enjoy, but in many cases we create an environment that will present the desired front to others. If you doubt this fact, just recall the last time you straightened up the house before important guests arrived. Backstage you might be comfortable with a messy place, but your public front—at least to some people—is quite different.

**Identity Management in Mediated Communication** Most of the preceding examples involve face-to-face interaction, but identity management is just as pervasive and important in other types of communication. Consider the care you probably

*"On the Internet, nobody knows you're a dog."*

## MANAGING IMPRESSIONS IN CYBERSPACE: *YOU'VE GOT MAIL*

Joe Fox (Tom Hanks) and Kathleen Kelly (Meg Ryan) are thirty-something New Yorkers who detest each other—or at least they think they do. Face-to-face, Kathleen despises Joe because his discount bookstore chain threatens to bankrupt Kathleen's family-owned bookshop. She also hates Joe's arrogant, self-absorbed style of communicating.

But in cyberspace, Joe seems like a different person. Unknown to both Joe and Kathleen, they have been communicating anonymously for months after meeting in an on-line chat room, using the names "NY152" and "Shopgirl." The e-mail messages Joe sends Kathleen are tender and self-disclosing. She falls for NY152 without knowing that the enchanting messages are written by the same man she can't stand in person.

Joe learns of Kathleen's cyber identity before she learns of his, and he realizes the need to change his face-to-face presentational style. He begins revealing his softer side in their in-person encounters. In true Hollywood fashion, Kathleen and Joe ultimately find love in person. For students of communication, this romance illustrates the idea that each of us has many identities, and the way we present ourselves can shape the fate of our relationships.

about considerations like these because they instinctively know that the *way* a message is presented can say as much as the words it contains.

At first glance, the new technology of computer-mediated communication (CMC) seems to limit the potential for identity management. E-mail messages, for example, appear to lack the "richness" of other channels. They don't convey the tone of your voice, postures, gestures, or facial expressions. Recently, though, communication scholars have begun to recognize that what is missing in computer-mediated communication can actually be an *advantage* for communicators who want to manage the impressions they make. E-mailers can choose the desired level of clarity or ambiguity, seriousness or humor, logic or emotion. Unlike face-to-face communication, electronic correspondence allows a sender to say difficult things without forcing the receiver to respond immediately, and it permits the receiver to ignore a message rather than give an unpleasant response. Options like these show that CMC can serve as a tool for identity management at least as well as face-to-face communication.

Like e-mail, personal pages on the World Wide Web provide opportunities for their creators to manage their identities. Every Web surfer has encountered pages "under construction." Some observers have pointed out that the construction involves much more than what appears on the computer screen: Personal home page designers are also constructing their public identities (Chandler, 1998). The words, images, and sounds that Web designers choose make a statement about who they are—or at least how they want to be regarded by others.

Designers create identity both by what they *include* and what they *exclude* from their home page. Consider how featuring or withholding the following kinds of information affects how Web surfers might regard the creator of a home page: age, personal photo, educational or career accomplishments, sexual orientation, job title, personal interests, personal philosophy and religious beliefs, and organizations to which the page creator

take when drafting a résumé for a potential employer, a thank you letter in response to a gift, or a love note to a sweetheart. Besides giving careful thought to the wording of your message, you probably make strategic decisions about its appearance. Will you use plain white paper or something more distinctive? Will you type your words or handwrite them? People think carefully belongs. You can easily think of a host of other kinds of material that could be included or excluded, and the effect that each would have on how others regard the page creator.

Communicators who want to manage impressions don't always prefer computer-mediated channels. People are generally comfortable with face-to-face interaction when they feel confident that others support the image they want to present. On the other hand, people are more likely to prefer mediated channels when their own self-presentation is threatened (O'Sullivan, 2000).

## Identity Management and Honesty

At first, identity management might sound like an academic label for manipulation or phoniness. There certainly are situations where impression management is dishonest. A manipulative date who pretends to be affectionate in order to gain sexual favors is clearly unethical and deceitful. So are job applicants who lie about their academic records to get hired or salespeople who pretend to be dedicated to customer service when their real goal is to make a quick buck. Joseph Walther (1996) reports "the strange case of the electronic lover" in which a male computer bulletin board user misrepresented himself as a female therapist named Joan to women who were seeking counseling.

But not all cases of identity management are so clearly wrong. In a job interview, is it legitimate to act more confident and reasonable than you really feel? Likewise, are you justified in acting more attentive than you feel in a boring conversation out of courtesy to the other person? Situations like these suggest that managing impressions doesn't necessarily make you into a liar. In fact, it is almost impossible to imagine how we could communicate effectively without making decisions about which front to present in one situation or another. It would be ludicrous to act the same way with strangers as you do with close friends, and nobody would show the same face to a two-year-old as he or she would to an adult.

Each of us has a repertoire of faces—a cast of characters—and part of being a competent

communicator is choosing the best role for a situation. Imagine yourself in each of the following situations, and choose the most effective way you could act, considering the options:

- You offer to teach a friend a new skill, such as playing the guitar, operating a computer program, or sharpening up a tennis backhand. Your friend is making slow progress with the skill, and you find yourself growing impatient.
- At a party you meet someone who you find very attractive, and you are pretty sure that the feeling is mutual. On one hand you feel an obligation to spend most of your time with the person you came with, but the opportunity here is very appealing.
- At work you face a belligerent customer. You don't believe that anyone has the right to treat you this way.
- A friend or family member makes a joke about your appearance that hurts your feelings. You aren't sure whether or not to make an issue of the remark or to pretend that it doesn't bother you.

In each of these situations—and in countless others every day—you have a choice about how to act. It is an oversimplification to say that there is only one honest way to behave in each circumstance and that every other response would be insincere and dishonest. Instead, identity management involves deciding which face—which part of yourself—to reveal. For example, when teaching a new skill you may choose to display the "patient" side of yourself instead of the "impatient" side. In the same way, at work you have the option of being either hostile or nondefensive in difficult situations. With strangers, friends, or family you can choose whether or not to disclose your feelings. Which face to show to others is an important decision, but in any case you are sharing a real part of yourself.

## Summary

The self-concept is a relatively stable set of perceptions individuals hold about themselves. It begins to develop soon after birth, being shaped by both verbal and nonverbal messages from significant others and from reflected appraisals based on comparisons with reference groups. The self-concept is subjective and can vary substantially from the way a person is perceived by others. Although the self may evolve over time, the self-concept resists change.

A self-fulfilling prophecy occurs when a person's expectations of an event influence the outcome. One type of prophecy consists of predictions by others, while another category is self-imposed. Self-fulfilling prophecies can be both positive and negative.

It is possible to change one's self-concept in ways that lead to more effective communication. It is necessary to have realistic expectations about how much change is possible and to begin with a realistic assessment of oneself. Willingness to exert the effort to change is important and in some cases change requires new information or skill.

Identity management consists of an individual's strategic communication designed to influence others' perceptions of herself or himself. Identity management aims at presenting one or more faces to others, which may be different from private, spontaneous behavior that occurs outside of others' presence. Some communicators are high self-monitors who are highly conscious of their own behavior, while others are less aware of how their words and actions affect others.

Identity management occurs for two reasons. In many cases it is based on following social rules and conventions. At other times it aims at achieving a variety of content and relational goals. In either case, communicators engage in creating impressions by managing their manner and appearance, along with the settings in which they interact with others. Although identity management might seem manipulative, it can be an authentic form of communication. Since each person has a variety of faces that she or he can reveal, choosing which one to present is a central concern of competent communicators.

# Recommended Readings

**Self-concept construction in communication:**

Jodi O'Brien and Peter Kollock, eds. *The Production of Reality: Essays and Readings on Social Interaction.* 2nd ed. Thousand Oaks, CA: Sage, 1997.

**Early influences on the self-concept:**

J. F. Rosenblith. *In the Beginning: Development from Conception to Age Two.* Newbury Park, CA: Sage, 1992.

**Constructing the self in contemporary society:**

Kenneth J. Gergen. *The Saturated Self: Dilemmas of Identity in Contemporary Life.* New York: Basic Books, 1991.

**Identity management and communication:**

William R. Cupach and Sandra Metts. *Facework.* Thousand Oaks, CA: Sage, 1994.

# Activities

1. **Invitation to Insight/Ethical Challenge**
   Choose someone with whom you have an important interpersonal relationship, and explore how you influence each other's self-concepts.
   a. Interview your partner to discover how your words and deeds influence his or her self-concept. Identify specific incidents to illustrate these influences, and discuss which specific parts of the self-concept you have affected.
   b. Now share with your partner how his or her behaviors have affected your self-concept. Again, be specific about identifying the incidents and the parts of your self-concept that were affected.
   c. Once you recognize the power you have to shape another's self-concept, ask yourselves what responsibility each of you has to treat the other person in a supportive manner when you are faced with delivering a potentially critical message.

d. Based on the information exchanged so far, discuss whether you are satisfied with the way you have affected each other's self-concepts. Identify any ways you could communicate more effectively.

2. **Invitation to Insight**
What reference groups do you use to define your self-concept? What is the effect of using these groups as a basis for judging yourself? How might you view yourself differently if you used other reference groups as a basis for comparison?

3. **Critical Thinking Probe**
What social forces affect the development of self-concept in childhood and beyond? To what degree do these forces contribute to healthy or unhealthy self-concepts? Identify three specific messages to illustrate your answer to these questions. Then discuss how individuals can reduce the effect of unhealthy forces in their everyday lives.

4. **Invitation to Insight**
Describe two incidents in which self-fulfilling prophecies you have imposed on yourself have affected your communication. Explain how each of these predictions shaped your behavior, and describe how you might have behaved differently if you had made a different prediction. Next, describe two incidents in which you imposed self-fulfilling prophecies on others. What effect did your prediction have on these people's actions?

5. **Skill Builder**
Identify one communication-related part of your self-concept you would like to change.

Use the guidelines on pages 79–81 to describe how you could make that change.
a. Decide whether your expectations for change are realistic. Don't expect to become a new person: Becoming a *better* one should be enough.
b. Recognize your strengths as well as your shortcomings. You may not be as bad as you think you are!
c. Decide whether you are willing to make the necessary effort to change. Good intentions are an important start, but hard work also is necessary.
d. Develop a specific plan to change the way you behave. You may want to consult books and experts as well as observing models to gain a clear idea of your new goals and how to achieve them.

6. **Ethical Challenge**
You can gain a clearer sense of the ethical implications of impression management by following these directions:
a. Make a list of the different presenting selves you try to communicate at school, to family members, to friends, and to various types of strangers.
b. Which of these selves are honest, and which are deceptive?
c. Are any deceptive impressions you try to create justified? What would be the consequences of being completely candid in the situations you have described?
d. Based on your answers to these questions, develop a set of guidelines to distinguish ethical and unethical impression management.

# CHAPTER

# 4

# Perceiving Others

# After Studying the Material in This Chapter . . .

## You Should Understand:

1. How the processes of selection, organization, and interpretation affect a communicator's perception of others.

2. How physiological and cultural factors, social roles, and self-concepts lead communicators to perceive one another and other phenomena differently.

3. Common factors that can distort interpersonal perception.

## You Should Be Able to:

1. Describe the factors that shape your perceptions of important people and events, and explain how these and other factors could lead another person to perceive the same people and events differently.

2. Describe an interpersonal issue from the other person's point of view, showing how and why the other person experiences the issue differently.

3. Use perception checking to clarify your understanding of another person's point of view.

## Key Terms

| | | | |
|---|---|---|---|
| Androgynous | Interpretation | Punctuation | Stereotyping |
| Attribution | Narrative | Selection | Sympathy |
| Empathy | Organization | Self-serving bias | |
| Halo effect | Perception checking | Standpoint theory | |

"Look at it my way. . . ."
"Put yourself in my shoes. . . ."
"YOU DON'T UNDERSTAND ME!"
"YOU'RE DRIVING ME CRAZY!"

Statements like these reflect one of the most common communication challenges. We talk to (or at) one another until we're hoarse and exhausted, yet we still don't really understand one another. Research confirms this fact: Typical dyads can interpret and explain only 25 to 50 percent of each other's behavior accurately (Spitzberg, 1993), and spouses consistently overestimate the degree to which they agree with their partners (Sillars et al., 1992). Some communication scholars (e.g., Eisenberg, 1984) have suggested complete understanding could lead to more disagreement and dissatisfaction, not smoother relationships. Nonetheless, failing to share each other's view of the world can leave us feeling isolated and alone, despairing that our words don't seem able to convey the depth and complexity of what we think and feel.

In this chapter we focus on the process of perception. We begin by exploring how our views of others may be inherently inaccurate, and how our distorted perceptions of them can affect our communication.

## The Perception Process

We need to begin our discussion of perception by examining the gap between "what is" and what we know. At one time or another you've probably seen photos of sights invisible to the unaided eye: perhaps an infrared photo of a familiar geographic area or the vastly enlarged image of a minute object taken by an electron microscope. You've also noticed how certain animals are able to hear sounds and smell odors that are not apparent to humans. Experiences like these remind us that there is much more going on in the world than we are able to experience with our limited senses, and that our idea of reality is in fact only a partial one.

Even within the realm of our senses, we're aware of only a small part of what is going on around us. For instance, most people who live in large cities find that the noises of traffic, people, and construction soon fade out of their awareness. Others can take a walk through the forest without distinguishing one bird's call from another or noticing the differences between various types of vegetation. On a personal level, we've all had the experience of failing to notice something unusual about a friend—perhaps a new hairstyle or a sad expression—until it's called to our attention.

Sometimes our failure to recognize some events while noticing others comes from not paying attention to important information. But in other cases it's simply impossible to be aware of everything, no matter how attentive we might be: There is just too much going on.

How do we make sense of the world? How do our ways of perceiving affect our understanding of others, and our communication with them? We will begin to answer these questions by taking a look at the three steps by which we attach meaning to our experiences: selection, organization, and interpretation.

## Selection

Since we're exposed to more input than we can possibly manage, the first step in perception is the **selection** of which data we will attend to. There are several factors that cause us to notice some messages and ignore others.

Stimuli that are *intense* often attract our attention. Something that is louder, larger, or brighter stands out. This explains why—other things being equal—we're more likely to remember extremely tall or short people and why someone who laughs or talks loudly at a party attracts more attention (not always favorable) than do more quiet guests.

*Repetitious stimuli, repetitious stimuli, repetitious stimuli, repetitious stimuli, repetitious stimuli,*

*repetitious stimuli* also attract attention.* Just as a quiet but steadily dripping faucet can come to dominate our awareness, people to whom we're frequently exposed become noticeable.

Attention is also frequently related to CONTRAST or CHANGE in stimulation. Put differently, unchanging people or things become less noticeable. This principle offers an explanation (excuse?) for why we take consistently wonderful people for granted when we interact with them frequently. It's only when they stop being so wonderful or go away that we appreciate them.

*Motives* also determine how we perceive people. For example, someone on the lookout for a romantic adventure will be especially aware of attractive potential partners, whereas the same person in an emergency might be oblivious to anyone but police or medical personnel.

Selection isn't an objective process: Paying attention to some things and ignoring others

---

* The graphic demonstrations of factors influencing perception in this and the following paragraph are borrowed from Dennis Coon's *Introduction to Psychology.* 7th ed. (1995). St. Paul, MN: West, 137.

invariably distorts our observations. Some of these distortions are due to *omission.* Consider, for example, the times a friend has asked you to describe "what happened" at a party or some other event. It would be impossible to describe everything that occurred: the clothes everyone wore, the number and type of drinks each person had, the sequence of musical numbers played, every word spoken by every guest, and so on.

As these examples show, many of the details we omit are trivial. In other cases, however, we leave out important information. This kind of omission results in *oversimplification.* A long, thoughtful explanation winds up being described simply as "he said 'no.'" "What's she like?" you might ask and get the answer "She's from England" or "She's a biochemist" or "She's a lesbian." Any one of these descriptions might be true as far as it goes, but each ignores the fact that the person being described also may be a single parent, a genius, a neurotic, or a top-notch skier, along with a host of other significant characteristics. The tendency to oversimplify when selecting information to notice reminds us of the person who, when asked to describe the novel *War and Peace,* replied, "It's about Russia."

## Organization

After selecting information from the environment, we must arrange it in some meaningful way in order to make sense of the world. We call this stage **organization.** The raw sense data we perceive can be organized in more than one way. For instance, consider the picture of the boxes in Figure 4.1. How many ways can you view the figure? Most people have a hard time finding more than one perspective, although Figure 4.2 shows that there are four ways to view the image.

Like these boxes, we create ways of organizing all the information we select from the environment. We do this by using *perceptual schema,* cognitive frameworks that allow us to organize the raw data we have selected.

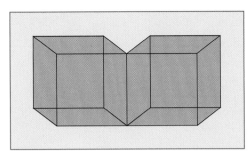

**Figure 4.1**

Four types of schemata can help us classify others (Andersen, 1993). *Physical constructs* classify people according to their appearance: beautiful or ugly, fat or thin, young or old, and so on. *Role constructs* use social position, such as student, attorney, and wife. *Interaction constructs* focus on social behavior: friendly, helpful, aloof, and sarcastic, for example. The final organizing scheme uses *psychological constructs:* generous, nervous, insecure, and so on.

These schemata are useful in two ways: First, they allow us to form impressions of others. Imagine that you've just met a new person in class or at a party. Without these constructs, you would have no way to answer the question "What's this person like?" Once you have classified others using various perceptual constructs, they become a useful way to predict future behavior. If you've classified a professor, for example, as "friendly," you'll handle questions or problems one way; if your analysis is "mean," your behavior will probably be quite different.

The kinds of constructs we use strongly affect the way we relate to others. Young children usually don't classify people according to their skin color. They are just as likely to identify an Anglo, Black, or Asian by age, size, or personality. As they become more socialized, however, they learn that one common organizing principle in today's society is ethnicity, and their perceptions of others change. What constructs do you use to classify the people you encounter in your life? Consider how your relationships might change if you used different schema.

Once we have selected an organizing scheme to classify people, we use that scheme to make generalizations about members of the groups who fit our categories. For example, if you are especially aware of gender, you might be alert to the differences between the way men and women behave or the way they are treated. If religion plays an important part in your life, you might think of members of your faith differently than you do others. If ethnicity is an important issue for you, you probably tune into the differences

**Figure 4.2**

## FOCUS ON RESEARCH

### PERCEIVING PREJUDICE: THE ROLE OF EXPECTATIONS

When have you been a victim of prejudice? This question isn't as easy to answer as it might first seem, as demonstrated by a series of experiments on perceptions of racial prejudice and gender bias by Mary Inman and Robert Baron. In one phase of the study, white and black students were presented with stories in which a prejudicial act might or might not have taken place. For example, a man promised a hotel room over the phone is later denied the room when he shows up in person. Four race combinations were used for each story:

white perpetrator/black victim, white perpetrator/white victim, black perpetrator/white victim, and black perpetrator/black victim. In almost all instances, participants were more likely to label white-on-black behavior (white perpetrator and black victim) as prejudice than any other combination. In addition, females were more likely than males, and blacks were more likely than whites, to label an action as prejudiced.

From these results, the researchers conclude that a prototypic or "model"

stereotype exists regarding racism (whites oppress blacks, men oppress women, and not the reverse), and that "participants who belong to traditionally oppressed groups (blacks, women) may be more sensitive to potential prejudice." In other words, we don't view the people and events in our lives neutrally and objectively. Rather, the expectations we carry in our minds and the groups to which we belong affect how we think about the world and how we feel about others' behavior.

Inman, M. L., & Baron, R. S. (1996). Influence of prototypes on perceptions of prejudice. *Journal of Personality and Social Psychology, 70,* 727–739.

between members of various ethnic groups. There's nothing wrong with generalizations as long as they are accurate. In fact, it would be impossible to get through life without them. But when generalizations lose touch with reality, they lead to **stereotyping**—exaggerated beliefs associated with a categorizing system. Stereotypes may be based on a kernel of truth, but they go beyond the facts at hand and make claims that usually have no valid basis.

Two characteristics distinguish stereotypes from reasonable generalizations. The first involves *categorizing others on the basis of easily recognized but not necessarily significant characteristics*. For example, perhaps the first thing you notice about a person is his or her skin color. The second feature that characterizes stereotypes is *ascribing a set of characteristics to most or all members of a*

*group*. For example, you might assume that all older people are doddering or that all men are insensitive to women's concerns.

Stereotypes can plague interracial communication (Allen, 1995; Buttny, 1997). Surveys of college student attitudes show that many blacks characterize whites as "demanding" and "manipulative," while many whites describe blacks as "loud" and "ostentatious." Many African-American women report having been raised with stereotypical characterizations of whites (e.g., "most whites cannot be trusted"). One black college professor reported a personal story revealing a surprising set of stereotypical assumptions from a white colleague. "As the only African American at a university-sponsored party for faculty a few years ago, I was appalled when a white professor (whom I had just met) asked me to sing a Negro spiritual" (Hecht et al.,

# Farcus

by David Waisglass
Gordon Coulthart

© 1993 Farcus Cartoons

WAISGLASS/COULTHART

"There are two types of people in this world . . .
those who generalize, and those who don't"

1993). Although it's possible that behavior like this can be motivated by a desire to be friendly, it is easy to see how it can be offensive.

Once we hold stereotypes like these, we seek out isolated behaviors that support our inaccurate beliefs. For example, men and women in conflict with each other often remember only behaviors of the opposite sex that fit their gender stereotypes (Allen, 1998). They then point to these behaviors—which might not be representative of how the other person typically behaves—as "evidence" to suit their stereotypical and inaccurate claims: "Look! There you go criticizing me again. Typical for a woman!"

One way to avoid the kinds of communication problems that come from excessive stereotyping is to "decategorize" others, giving yourself a chance to treat people as individuals instead of assuming that they possess the same characteristics as every other member of the group to which you assign them.

Perceptual differences don't just involve the general categories we use to classify others. We also can organize specific communication transactions in different ways, and these differing organizational schemes can have a powerful effect on our relationships. Communication theorists have used the term **punctuation** to describe the determination of causes and effects in a series of interactions (Watzlawick et al., 1967). You can begin to understand how punctuation operates by visualizing a running quarrel between a husband and wife. The husband accuses the wife of being a nag, while she complains that he is withdrawing from her. Notice that the order in which each partner punctuates this cycle affects how the dispute looks. The husband begins by blaming the wife: "I withdraw because you nag." The wife organizes the situation differently, starting with the husband: "I nag because you withdraw." Once the cycle gets rolling, it is impossible to say which accusation is accurate, as Figure 4.3 (p. 100) indicates. The answer depends on how the sequence is punctuated.

Anyone who has seen two children argue about "who started it" can understand that haggling over causes and effects isn't likely to solve a conflict. In fact, the kind of finger pointing that goes along with assigning blame will probably make matters worse. Rather than argue about whose punctuation of an event is correct, it's far more productive to recognize that a dispute can look different to each party and then move on to the more important question of "What can we do to make things better?"

## Interpretation

Once we have selected and organized our perceptions, we **interpret** them in a way that makes some sort of sense. Interpretation plays a role in virtually every interpersonal act. Is the person who smiles at you across a crowded room interested in

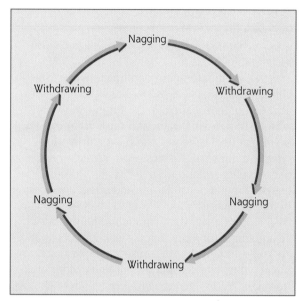

**Figure 4.3** The way a communication sequence is punctuated affects its perceived meaning. Which comes first, the nagging or the withdrawing?

romance or simply being polite? Is a friend's kidding a sign of affection or irritation? Should you take an invitation to "drop by any time" literally or not?

There are several factors that cause us to interpret a person's behavior in one way or another. The first is our *degree of involvement* with the person. Research suggests that we sometimes view people with whom we have or seek a relationship more favorably than those whom we observe from a detached perspective (Manusov, 1993). One study revealed how this principle operates in everyday life. A group of male subjects was asked to critique presentations by women who allegedly owned restaurants. Half of these presentations were designed to be competent and half of them incompetent. The men who were told they would be having a casual date with the female speakers judged their presentations—whether competent or not—more highly than those who didn't expect any involvement with the speakers (Adler, 1992).

Of course, in an unhappy relationship, we sometimes view our partner more critically than would an independent observer. This fact suggests that *relational satisfaction* is a second factor that influences our interpretation. The behavior that seems positive when you are happy with a partner might seem completely different when the relationship isn't satisfying. For example, couples in unsatisfying relationships are more likely than satisfied partners to blame one another when things go wrong (Bradbury & Fincham, 1990; Manusov, 1993). They are also more likely to believe that their partners are selfish and have negative intentions. To see how this principle operates, recall the husband-wife quarrel we discussed earlier. Suppose the wife suggests that they get away for a weekend vacation. If the marriage has been troubled, the husband might interpret his wife's idea as more nagging ("You never pay attention to me"), and the fight will continue. If the relationship is solid, he is more likely to view the suggestion as a bid for a romantic getaway. It wasn't the event that shaped the interpretation, it was the couple's relational dissatisfaction.

A third factor that influences interpretations is *past experience*. What meanings have similar events held? If, for instance, you've been gouged by landlords in the past, you might be skeptical about an apartment manager's assurances that careful housekeeping will ensure the refund of your cleaning deposit.

*Assumptions about human behavior* also influence interpretations. "People do as little work as possible." "In spite of their mistakes, people generally do the best they can." Such beliefs shape the way you interpret another's actions.

*Expectations* are another factor that shape our interpretations. If you imagine your boss is unhappy with you, you'll probably feel threatened by a request to "see me in my office Monday morning." On the other hand, if you imagine that your work will be rewarded, your weekend will be filled with pleasant anticipation.

*Knowledge of others* affects the way we interpret their actions. If you know a friend has just behavior becomes especially noticeable) and the organization of events (when there's a fight, the assumption is that Jason started it). As with all communication, perception is an ongoing process in which it is hard to pin down beginnings and endings.

## Influences on Perception

How we select, organize, and interpret data about others is influenced by a variety of factors. Some of our perceptual judgments are affected by physiology, others by cultural and social factors, and still others by psychological factors.

### Physiological Influences

Visit a large camera store and you'll be confronted by an impressive array of equipment: everything from cheap pocket models to sophisticated systems including lenses, filters, tripods, and timers.

---

### REFLECTION

#### PROBLEMATIC PUNCTUATION

When I was living with my parents, my father always was asking where I was going or where I had been. I interpreted his questions as too nosy, and I usually responded with hostility or silence. This made him even more concerned about what I was doing.

Now I recognize that each of us was punctuating this situation differently. He saw me as being the problem: "I ask you what you're doing because you never tell me." I saw him as the cause of the problem: "I never tell you what I'm doing because you're always pestering me." Each of us believed we were right and the other was wrong. Who started the cycle? Either way, we both lost. Now I realize how understanding our different ways of punctuating the situation kept us from understanding one another.

---

been jilted by a lover or fired from a job, you'll interpret his aloof behavior differently than if you were unaware of what happened. If you know an instructor is rude to all students, then you won't be likely to take her remarks personally.

Such evidence shows that our judgments often say more about our own attitudes than about the other people involved. Research shows that couples in unsatisfying relationships are more likely than satisfied partners to blame one another when things go wrong (Fincham et al., 1987, 1988). They are also more likely to believe that their partners are selfish and have negative intentions.

Although we have talked about selection, organization, and interpretation separately, the three phases of perception can occur in differing sequences. For example, a parent's or babysitter's past interpretations (such as "Jason is a troublemaker") can influence future selections (his

YOU KIDS TODAY HAVE IT EASY. WHEN I WAS A KID EVERYTHING WAS HUGE. MY DAD WAS NEARLY FOUR TIMES BIGGER THAN ME. YOU COULDN'T EVEN SEE THE TOPS OF COUNTERS......THEN GRADUALLY EVERYTHING BECAME SMALLER UNTIL IT WAS THE MANAGEABLE SIZE IT IS TODAY....

Some cameras can photograph miniature items at close range, and others can capture distant objects clearly. With the right film, it's even possible to take pictures of objects invisible to the unaided eye. There's only one world "out there," but different equipment allows us to see different parts of it. In the same way, each person's perceptual equipment gives a different image of the world. Sometimes these pictures are so dissimilar that it seems as if we're not talking about the same events at all.

**The Senses**    The differences in how each of us sees, hears, tastes, touches, and smells stimuli can affect interpersonal relationships. Consider the following everyday situations:

> "Turn down that radio! It's going to make me go deaf."
> "It's not too loud. If I turn it down, it will be impossible to hear it."

> "It's freezing in here."
> "Are you kidding? We'll suffocate if you turn up the heat!"

> "Why don't you pass that truck? The highway is clear for half a mile."
> "I can't see that far, and I'm not going to get us killed."

These disputes aren't just over matters of opinion. The sensory data we receive is different. Differences in vision and hearing are the easiest to recognize, but other gaps also exist. There is evidence that identical foods taste different to various individuals (Bartoshuk, 1980). Odors that please some people repel others (Montcrieff, 1966). Likewise, temperature variations that leave some of us uncomfortable are inconsequential to others. Remembering these differences won't eliminate them; rather, they remind us that other people's preferences aren't crazy, just different.

**Age**    Older people view the world differently than younger ones because of a greater scope and number of experiences. Developmental differences also shape perceptions. Developmental psychologists (Piaget, 1952; Lourenco & Machado, 1996) describe a series of stages that children pass through on their way to adulthood. Younger children are incapable of performing mental feats that are natural to the rest of us. Until they approach the age of seven, for example, they aren't able to take another person's point of view. This fact helps explain why youngsters often seem egocentric, selfish, and uncooperative. A parent's exasperated "Can't you see I'm too tired to play?" just won't make sense to a four-year-old full of energy, who imagines that everyone else must feel the same.

**Health**    Recall the last time you came down with a cold, flu, or some other ailment. Do you remember how differently you felt? You probably had much less energy. It's likely that you felt less sociable and that your thinking was slower than usual. Such changes have a strong impact on how you relate to others. It's good to realize that someone else may be behaving differently because of illness. In the same way, it's important to let others know when you feel ill so they can give you the understanding you need.

**Fatigue**    Just as illness can affect your relationships, so can excessive fatigue. When you've been working long hours or studying late for an exam, the world can seem quite different than when you are well rested. Again, it's important to recognize that you or someone else may behave differently when fatigued. Trying to deal with important issues at such times can get you into trouble.

**Hunger**    Our digestive system often rules our behavior. One experiment demonstrated this fact (McClelland & Atkinson, 1948). Subjects were denied food for up to fourteen hours. During this time they were asked to describe what they saw projected on a screen at very low light levels. In truth, no image at all was projected. Despite this fact, the subjects did report seeing objects. As their hunger grew, the number of food-related observations increased.

Our own experience confirms that we often grow grumpy when hungry, and sleepy after stuffing ourselves. These facts suggest that conducting important business at the wrong time in our eating schedules can create interpersonal problems.

**Biological Cycles**   Are you a "morning person" or a "night person"? Most of us can answer this question pretty easily, and there's a good physiological reason why. Each of us has a daily cycle in which all sorts of changes constantly occur, including variations in body temperature, sexual drive, alertness, tolerance to stress, and mood (Palmer, 1976; Touitou, 1998). Most of these changes are due to hormonal cycles. For instance, adrenal hormones, which affect feelings of stress, are secreted at higher rates during some hours. In the same manner, the male and female sex hormones enter our systems at variable rates. We often aren't conscious of these changes, but they surely affect the way we relate toward each other. For example, Jeffrey Larson and his associates (1991) discovered that couples with mismatched waking and sleeping patterns (e.g., an evening person and a morning person) reported significantly more conflict, and less sexual intimacy, and less time spent conversing on important topics than couples with matched sleeping patterns. Once we're aware that our own daily cycles and those of others influence our feelings and behavior, it becomes possible to run our lives so that we deal with important issues at the most effective times.

For some women, the menstrual cycle plays a role in shaping feelings and thus affects communication. But women aren't the only ones whose communication is affected by periodic changes in mood. Many men also go through recognizable mood cycles, but theirs aren't marked by obvious physical changes. These men, sometimes unaware, seem to go through biologically regulated periods of good spirits followed by equally predictable times of depression (Ramey, 1972). The average length of this cycle is about five weeks, although in some cases it's as short as sixteen days or as long as two months. However

long it may be, this cycle of ups and downs is quite regular.

Although neither men nor women can change these emotional cycles, simply learning to expect them can be a big help in improving communication. When you understand that a bad mood is predictable from physiological causes, you can plan for it. You'll know that every few weeks your patience will be shorter, and you'll be less likely to blame your bad moods on innocent bystanders. The people around you also can learn to expect your periodic lows. If they can attribute them to biology, maybe they will be more understanding and empathic.

## Psychological Influences

Along with physiology, our psychological state also influences the way we perceive others.

**Mood**   Our emotional state strongly influences how we view people and events, and therefore how we communicate. An experiment using hypnotism dramatically demonstrated this fact (Lebua & Lucas, 1945). Each subject was shown the same series of six pictures, each time having been put in a different mood. The descriptions of the pictures differed radically depending on the emotional state of the subject. For example, these are descriptions by one subject in various emotional states while describing a picture of children digging in a swampy area:

*Happy mood:* "It looks like fun, reminds me of summer. That's what life is for, working out in the open, really living—digging in the dirt, planting, watching things grow."

*Anxious mood:* "They're going to get hurt or cut. There should be someone older there who knows what to do in case of an accident. I wonder how deep the water is."

*Critical mood:* "Pretty horrible land. There ought to be something more useful for kids of that age to do instead of digging in that stuff. It's filthy and dirty and good for nothing."

Such evidence shows that our judgments often say more about our own attitudes than about the other people involved.

Although there's a strong relationship between mood and happiness, it's not clear which comes first: the perceptual outlook or the amount of relational satisfaction. There is some evidence that perception leads to satisfaction rather than the opposite order (Fletcher et al., 1987). In other words, the attitude/expectation we bring to a situation shapes our level of happiness or unhappiness. Of course, once started, this process can create a spiral. If you're happy about your relationship, you will be more likely to interpret your partner's behavior in a charitable way. This, in turn, can lead to greater happiness. Of course, the same process can work in the opposite direction. One remedy to serious distortions—and unnecessary conflicts—is to monitor your own moods. If you're aware of being especially critical or sensitive, you can avoid overreacting to others.

**Self-Concept**   A final factor that influences perception is the self-concept. For example, the recipient's self-concept has proved to be the single greatest factor in determining whether people who are being teased interpret the teaser's motives as being friendly or hostile, and whether they respond with comfort or defensiveness (Alberts et al., 1996). The same goes for happiness and sadness or any other opposing emotions. The way we feel about ourselves strongly influences how we interpret others' behavior.

Besides distorting the facts about others, our self-concepts also lead us to distorted views of ourselves. As Chapter 3 explains, the self-concept is not objective. "It wasn't my fault," you might be tempted to say, knowing deep inside that you were responsible. "I look horrible," you might think as you look into the mirror, despite the fact that everyone around you sincerely insists you look terrific.

Such distortions usually revolve around the desire to maintain a self-concept that has been threatened. Chapter 3 describes the tendency to maintain a presenting self-image, which is often an idealized form of the person we privately believe ourselves to be. If you want to view yourself as a good student or musician, for example, then an instructor who gives you a poor grade or a critic who doesn't appreciate your music *must* be wrong, and you'll find evidence to show it. If you want to think of yourself as a good worker or parent, then you'll find explanations for the problems in your job or family that shift the responsibility away from you. Of course, the same principle works for people with excessively negative self-images: They'll go out of their way to explain any information that's favorable to them in terms that show they really are incompetent or undesirable.

## Cultural Influences

Culture plays a major role in shaping our perceptions of the world and its inhabitants. This fact was demonstrated in studies exploring the domination of vision in one eye over the other (Bagby, 1957). Researchers used a binocularlike device that projects different images to each eye. The subjects were twelve United States and twelve Mexican natives. Each was presented with ten pairs of photographs, each pair containing one picture from U.S. culture (for instance, a baseball game) and one from Mexican culture (such as a bullfight). After viewing each pair of images, the subjects reported what they saw. The results clearly illustrated the power of culture to influence perceptions: Subjects had a strong tendency to see the image from their own background.

Cultural selection, organization, and interpretation exert a powerful influence on the way we view others' communication. Even beliefs about the very value of talk differ from one culture to another (Giles et al., 1992). Western cultures tend to view talk as desirable and use it for social purposes as well as to perform tasks. Silence has a negative value in these cultures. It is likely to be interpreted as lack of interest, unwillingness to communicate, hostility, anxiety, shyness, or a sign

## REFLECTION

### CULTURAL DIFFERENCES IN HUMOR

I was born and raised in Russia. One thing I find very different here is the way people use humor. When I first arrived in Texas, I noticed that my host family joked and teased me a lot. I was often offended and hurt. The problem was that neither my host family nor I understood the differences in meaning people attach to the same way of behaving. In Russia, people don't tease to express affection. In the United States, though, joking is often a way to show friendship. Once I realized this cultural difference, I was much better at socializing.

of interpersonal incompatibility. Westerners are uncomfortable with silence, which they find embarrassing and awkward.

On the other hand, Asian cultures tend to perceive talk quite differently. For thousands of years, Asian cultures have discouraged the expression of thoughts and feelings. Silence is valued, as Taoist sayings indicate: "In much talk there is great weariness" or "One who speaks does not know; one who knows does not speak." Unlike Westerners, who are uncomfortable with silence, Japanese and Chinese people believe that remaining quiet is the proper state when there is nothing to be said. To Asians, a talkative person is often considered a show-off or a fake.

It's easy to see how these different views of speech and silence can lead to communication problems when people from different cultures meet. Both the "talkative" Westerner and the "silent" Asian are behaving in ways they believe are proper, yet each views the other with disapproval and mistrust. Only when they recognize the different standards of behavior can they adapt to one another, or at least understand and respect their differences.

Author Anne Fadiman (1997, p. 33) explains why Hmong immigrants from the mountains of Laos preferred their traditional shamanistic healers, called *txiv neeb,* to American doctors.

> A *txiv neeb* might spend as much as eight hours in a sick person's home; doctors forced their patients, no matter how weak they were, to come to the hospital, and then might spend only twenty minutes at their bedsides. *Txiv neebs* were polite and never needed to ask questions; doctors asked about their sexual and excretory habits. *Txiv neebs* could render an immediate diagnosis; doctors often demanded samples of blood (or even urine or feces,

which they liked to keep in little bottles), took X rays, and waited for days for the results to come back from the laboratory—and then, after all that, sometimes they were unable to identify the cause of the problem. *Txiv neebs* never undressed their patients; doctors asked patients to take off all their clothes, and sometimes dared to put their fingers inside women's vaginas. *Txiv neebs* knew that to treat the body without treating the soul was an act of patent folly; doctors never even mentioned the soul.

Perceptual differences don't just occur between residents of different countries. Within a single national culture, regional and ethnic differences can create very different realities. In a fascinating series of studies, Peter Andersen, Myron Lustig, and Janis Andersen (1987a, 1987b) discovered that climate and geographic latitude were remarkably accurate predictors of communication predispositions. People living in southern latitudes of the United States were found to be more socially isolated, less tolerant of ambiguity, higher in self-esteem, more likely to touch others, and more likely to verbalize their thoughts and feelings. This sort of finding helps explain why communicators who travel from one part of a country to another find that their old patterns of communicating don't work as well in their new location. A southerner whose relatively talkative, high-touch style seemed completely normal at home might be viewed as pushy and aggressive in a new, northern home.

Of course, geography isn't the only factor that shapes perception. The gap between cultures often extends beyond dissimilar norms to a wide range of different experiences and feelings. Chapter 2 describes the multitude of factors that lead people from different cultural backgrounds to experience the world in ways that often bear little resemblance to one another.

## Social Influences

Within a culture, our personal point of view plays a strong role in shaping perceptions. Social scientists have developed **standpoint theory** to describe how a person's position in a society shapes his or

## FILM CLIP

### FROM ANOTHER STANDPOINT:
### *WHITE MAN'S BURDEN*

A group of well-to-do people are dining together, debating social problems. Thaddeus Thomas (Harry Belafonte) concludes their discussion with a question: "Are these a people who are beyond being helped?" Viewers of *White Man's Burden* realize at this point that the movie is reversing stereotypical roles of blacks and whites in our society. The dinner guests are rich black people who see poor white people as the problem to be solved.

The movie explores what the United States might be like if blacks were the privileged majority and whites were the disadvantaged minority. Louis Pinnock (John Travolta) is a white man who works at a factory owned by Thomas. Pinnock gets fired over a misunderstanding and begs Thomas—unsuccessfully—for his job back. Pinnock and other whites are in one-down positions throughout the movie. Black people mistrust and mistreat them; they are the butts of racist comments and jokes.

*White Man's Burden* offers a provocative illustration of standpoint theory. The film asks viewers to look at U.S. society through a different set of perceptual lenses and a new set of assumptions. For some, it provides a glimpse into privileges and disadvantages they might not have seen because of the limitations of their perceptual standpoints.

her view of society in general, and of specific individuals (Harding, 1991; Orbe, 1998). Standpoint theory is most often applied to the difference between the perspectives of privileged social groups and people who have had less power. Unless one has been disadvantaged, it can be difficult to imagine how the world might look differ-

"How is it gendered?"

ent to someone who has been treated badly because of race, ethnicity, gender, sexual orientation, or socioeconomic class. After some reflection, though, it is easy to undersand how being marginalized can make the world seem like a very different place. The Film Clip describing *White Man's Burden* offers an instructive look at the importance of standpoints.

**Gender Roles**   Physiological differences aren't the only factor that shapes the differing perceptions of men and women. Personal experiences and social expectations also are powerful. For example, Jordan Singer and associates (1988) found that women and men judge the same behaviors quite differently. Some types of behavior that men found innocuous were judged by women as being harassing. Not surprisingly, much of the difference came from experience: Women who reported having been harassed were

more likely to find harassment in subsequent interactions. Experience wasn't the only factor, though: Younger women were more likely to perceive harassment than older ones who, presumably, had a different set of expectations about what kinds of communication are and aren't appropriate. Also, attitudes play a role: People who disapprove of socializing and dating between coworkers are more likely to perceive harassment than those who accept this sort of relationship (Solomon & Williams, 1997).

Early theorizing by Sandra Bem (1974) suggested that stereotypical masculine and feminine behaviors are not opposite poles of a single continuum, but rather two separate sets of behavior. With this view, an individual can act in a masculine manner, a feminine manner, or exhibit both types of characteristics. The masculine-feminine dichotomy, then, is replaced with four psychological sex types, including masculine, feminine, **androgynous** (combining masculine and feminine traits), and undifferentiated (neither masculine nor feminine). Combining the four psychological sex types with the traditional physiological sex types produces the eight categories listed in Table 4.1 (p. 108).

Each of these eight psychological sex types perceives interpersonal relationships differently. For example, masculine males probably see their interpersonal relationships as opportunities for competitive interaction, as opportunities to win something. Feminine females probably see their interpersonal relationships as opportunities to be nurturing, to express their feelings and emotions. Androgynous males and females, on the other hand, probably differ little in their perceptions of their interpersonal relationships.

Androgynous individuals probably see their relationships as opportunities to behave in a variety of ways, depending on the nature of the relationships themselves, the context in which a particular relationship takes place, and the myriad other variables affecting what might constitute appropriate behavior. These variables are usually ignored by the sex-typed masculine males and

**Table 4.1**

| Bem's Sex Types | | |
| --- | --- | --- |
| | **Male** | **Female** |
| Masculine | Masculine males | Masculine females |
| Feminine | Feminine males | Feminine females |
| Androgynous | Androgynous males | Androgynous females |
| Undifferentiated | Undifferentiated males | Undifferentiated females |

feminine females, who have a smaller repertoire of behaviors.

**Occupational Roles**   The kind of work we do also governs our view of the world. Imagine five people taking a walk through a park. One, a botanist, is fascinated by the variety of trees and plants. The zoologist is on the lookout for interesting animals. The third, a meteorologist, keeps an eye on the sky, noticing changes in the weather. The fourth, a psychologist, is totally unaware of the goings-on of nature, concentrating instead on the interaction among the people in the park. The fifth, a pickpocket, quickly takes advantage of the others' absorption to collect their wallets. There are two lessons in this little story: The first, of course, is to watch your wallet carefully. The second is that our occupational roles frequently govern our perceptions.

Even within the same occupational setting, the different roles of participants can affect their experience. Consider a typical college classroom: The experiences of the instructor and students are often quite dissimilar. Having dedicated a large part of their lives to their work, most professors see their subject matter—whether French literature, physics, or communication—as vitally important. Students who are taking the course to satisfy a general education requirement may view the subject as one of many obstacles standing between them and a degree, or as a chance to meet new people.

Another difference centers on the amount of knowledge people possess. To an instructor who has taught the course many times, the material probably seems extremely simple; but to students encountering it for the first time, it may seem strange and confusing. Toward the end of a semester or quarter, the instructor might be pressing onward hurriedly to cover all the course material, while the students are fatigued from their studies and ready to move more slowly. We don't need to spell out the interpersonal strains and stresses that come from such differing perceptions.

The most dramatic illustration of how occupational roles shape perception is from the early 1970s. Stanford psychologist Philip Zimbardo (1971) recruited a group of well-educated middle-class young men. He randomly chose eleven to serve as "guards" in a mock prison set up in the basement of Stanford's psychology building. He issued the guards uniforms, handcuffs, whistles, and billy clubs. The remaining ten subjects became "prisoners" and were placed in rooms with metal bars, bucket toilets, and cots.

Zimbardo let the guards establish their own rules for the experiment. The rules were tough: no talking during meals and rest periods and after lights out. They took head counts at 2:30 A.M. Troublemakers received short rations.

Faced with these conditions, the prisoners began to resist. Some barricaded their doors with beds. Others went on hunger strikes. Several ripped off their identifying number tags. The guards reacted to the rebellion by clamping down hard on protesters. Some turned sadistic, physically and verbally abusing the prisoners. They threw

## FOCUS ON RESEARCH

### SAME STORY, DIFFERENT REACTIONS: MALE AND FEMALE PERCEPTIONS

Name a movie you loved that one of your friends hated. This is probably easy to do, since even close friends have different tastes and preferences. Some differences in reactions, however, run much deeper, as Brenda Cooper found with student responses to the movie *Thelma and Louise*. She concluded that males and females tend to perceive and interpret the film differently from one another.

*Thelma and Louise* is a 1991 movie about two women who go on a weekend trip to get away from the men in their lives. Their adventure becomes a nightmare when Thelma is sexually assaulted and Louise kills the would-be rapist. As the women flee to

Mexico, according to Cooper, "they strike back against the men they encounter along the way and, in the process, discover in themselves strength they didn't know existed."

Cooper collected and analyzed seventy-three essays about *Thelma and Louise* from students at two universities. Beyond the fact that most of the women liked the movie and most of the men didn't, their essays showed that they selected, organized, and interpreted information in the film quite differently.

For instance, the female students saw the movie as a statement about sexism and women's marginalized status

in society. The male students didn't see these themes at all; instead, they saw the movie as an unfair exercise in male bashing. Other elements of the movie—the rape scene, the portrayal of men, the women's friendship, and the film's conclusion—were perceived differently depending on the sex of the viewer.

*Thelma and Louise* is a controversial film because most viewers react to the story based on their own point of view. Of course, what's true for this film also applies to everyday life: We perceive events and one another through the lenses of our social roles and personal experiences.

Cooper, B. (1999). The relevancy of gender identity in spectators' interpretations of *Thelma and Louise*. *Critical Studies in Mass Communication, 16*, 20–41.

prisoners into solitary confinement. Others forced prisoners to call each other names and clean out toilets with their bare hands.

Within a short time the experiment had become reality for both prisoners and guards. Several inmates experienced stomach cramps and lapsed into uncontrollable weeping. Others suffered from headaches, and one broke out in a head-to-toe rash after his request for early "parole" was denied by the guards.

The experiment was scheduled to go on for two weeks, but after six days Zimbardo realized that what had started as a simulation had become

too intense. "I knew by then that they were thinking like prisoners and not like people," he said. "If we were able to demonstrate that pathological behavior could be produced in so short a time, think of what damage is being done in 'real' prisons."

This dramatic exercise, in which twenty-one well-educated middle-class citizens turned almost overnight into sadistic bullies and demoralized victims, tells us that how we think is a function of our roles in society. It seems that *what* we are is determined largely by society's designation of *who* we are.

**Shared Narratives** Our interaction with other individuals and groups creates a shared perception of the world. Communication scholars have come to call this kind of shared perspective a **narrative** (Shaw, 1997). This term reflects the notion that humans make sense of the world by spinning a kind of story to explain events and behavior. Shared narratives help communicators make sense of themselves and others.

Narratives evolve without any conscious strategy by the participants, but once they take hold, they offer a framework for explaining behavior and shaping future communication. For example, one analysis of how fathers are described by their daughters revealed four distinct visions: "Knight in Shining Armor," "Buddy," "Authoritarian," and "Shadow" (Endres, 1997). Once a daughter has established one of these views of her father, it is easy to see how that perception could explain the father's behavior and shape the daughter's future communication with him.

Narratives also operate on the job. One study of sense making in organizations illustrates how the process operates (Sias, 1996). Researchers located employees who had participated in office discussions about "differential treatment"—cases where a fellow worker had received "differential treatment" from management about matters such as time off, pay, or work assignments. The researchers then analyzed the conversations employees held with fellow workers about the differential treatment. The analysis revealed that these conversations were the place in which workers created and reinforced the meaning of the employee's behavior and management's response. For example, consider the way workers made sense of Jane Doe's habit of taking late lunches. As Jane's coworkers discuss her behaviors, they might decide that her late lunches aren't fair—or they might agree that late lunches aren't a big deal. Either way, discussion of office events *defines* those events. Once defined, coworkers tend to seek reinforcement for their perceptions by keeping a mental scorecard rating their fellow employees and management. ("Did you notice that Bob came

"You are fair, compassionate, and intelligent, but you are <u>perceived</u> as biased, callous, and dumb."

© The New Yorker Collection 1997 Robert Mankoff from cartoonbank.com. All Rights Reserved.

in late again today?" "Did you notice that the boss chose Jane to go on that trip to New York?") Although most of us like to think we make judgments about others on our own, this research suggests that sense making is an *interactive* process. In other words, reality in the workplace and elsewhere isn't "out there"; rather, we create it with others through communication.

Research on long-term happy marriages demonstrates that shared narratives don't have to be accurate to be powerful (Martz et al., 1998; Murray et al., 1996). Couples who report being happily married after fifty or more years seem to collude in a relational narrative that doesn't always jibe with the facts. They agree that they rarely have conflict, although objective analysis reveals that they have had their share of disagreements and challenges. Without overtly agreeing to do so, they choose to blame outside forces or unusual circumstances for problems, instead of attributing responsibility to one another. They offer the most charitable interpretations of one another's behavior, believing that their spouse acts with good intentions when things don't go well. They seem willing to forgive, or even forget transgressions. Examining this research, Judy Pearson (2000, p. 186) asks

> Should we conclude that happy couples have a poor grip on reality? Perhaps they do, but is the reality of one's marriage better known by outside onlookers than by the players themselves? The conclusion is evident. One key to a long happy marriage is to tell yourself and others that you have one and then to behave as though you do!

## Common Tendencies in Perception

By now it's obvious that many factors distort the way we interpret the world. Social scientists use the term **attribution** to describe the process of attaching meaning to behavior. We attribute meaning to both our own actions and to the actions of others, but we often use different yardsticks. Research has uncovered several perceptual errors that lead to inaccurate attributions (Hamachek, 1992).

### We Judge Ourselves More Charitably Than We Do Others

In an attempt to convince ourselves and others that the positive face we show to the world is true, we tend to judge ourselves in the most generous terms possible. Social scientists have labeled this tendency the **self-serving bias.** On the one hand, when others suffer, we often blame the problem on their personal qualities. When we're the victims, on the other hand, we find explanations outside ourselves (Sedikides et al., 1998). Consider a few examples:

- When *they* botch a job, we think they weren't listening well or trying hard enough; when *we* make the mistake, the problem was unclear directions or not enough time.
- When *he* lashes out angrily, we say he's being moody or too sensitive; when *we* blow off steam, it's because of the pressure we've been under.
- When *she* gets caught speeding, we say she should have been more careful; when *we* get

### REFLECTION

#### RESPONSIBILITY AT WORK

As a camp counselor last summer, I definitely was guilty of the self-serving bias. I remember one time when another staff member failed to have the materials ready for an arts and crafts project. I was indignant! I thought of her as a flake, and let her know that she had let me down.

The next week, I was the one who didn't get the materials ready on time. I had to hunt around for the stuff, and then I stopped to talk to one of the other counselors and eat a snack. (Well, I was famished!) When the kids arrived before I had the materials set up, I explained all the good reasons why I wasn't ready. Now I realize that I was using the self-serving bias to justify my behavior.

the ticket, we deny we were driving too fast or say "Everybody does it."

Not surprisingly, the self-serving bias is especially common in troubled relationships. In one study (Schutz, 1999), couples in conflict were more likely to blame their partner for the problem than to accept responsibility for their role in the problem. The researchers point out that these results came from couples dealing with ordinary relational challenges. They observe that the self-serving bias is likely to be even stronger in troubled relationships. Interestingly, there are a few occasions where the self-serving bias is less powerful. For example, men tend to be more charitable when making judgments about women they don't know well (Kluwer et al., 1998).

We don't always fall into the kind of perceptual tendencies described in this section. Sometimes, for instance, people *are* responsible for their misfortunes, or our problems *are not* our fault. Likewise, the most obvious interpretation of a

situation may be the correct one. Nonetheless, a large amount of research has shown again and again that our perceptions of others are often distorted in the ways we have described. The moral, then, is clear: Don't assume your negative appraisal of a person is accurate or unbiased.

## We Are Influenced by the Obvious

Being influenced by what is most obvious is understandable. As you read earlier, we select stimuli from our environment that are noticeable—that is, intense, repetitious, unusual, or otherwise attention grabbing. The problem is that the most obvious factor is not necessarily the only cause—or the most significant one—of an event. For example:

- When two children (or adults, for that matter) fight, it may be a mistake to blame the one who lashes out first. Perhaps the other one was at least equally responsible, teasing or refusing to cooperate.
- You might complain about an acquaintance whose malicious gossiping or arguing has become a bother, forgetting that by putting up with that kind of behavior you have been at least partially responsible.

- You might blame an unhappy work situation on the boss, overlooking other factors beyond her control—such as a change in the economy, the policy of higher management, or demands of customers or other workers.

These examples show that it is important to take time to gather all the facts.

## We Cling to First Impressions

Labeling people according to our first impressions is a part of the perception process that is difficult to avoid. Such labels are a way of making quick interpretations: "She seems cheerful." "He seems sincere." "They sound awfully conceited."

If impressions are accurate, they can be useful ways of deciding how to respond best to people in the future. However, problems arise when the labels we attach are inaccurate, for once we form an opinion of someone, we tend to hang onto it and make any conflicting information fit our image.

Social scientists have coined the term **halo effect** to describe the power of a first impression to influence subsequent perceptions. The power of the halo effect has been demonstrated by research on how employers rate job applicants (Dougherty et al., 1994). Interviewers typically form strong impressions of candidates in the first few minutes after meeting them. Once these impressions are formed, they often ask questions that confirm their image of the applicant. For example, when an interviewer forms a positive impression, she might ask leading questions aimed at supporting her positive views ("What lessons did you learn from that setback?"), interpret answers in a positive light ("Ah, taking time away from school to travel was a good idea!"), encourage the applicant ("Good point!"), and sell the company's virtues ("I think you would like working here"). Likewise, applicants who create a negative first impression are operating under a cloud that may be impossible to dispel.

Given the almost unavoidable tendency to form first impressions, the best approach is to keep an open mind and be willing to change your opinion if events prove you mistaken.

## We Assume Others Are Like Us

People commonly imagine that others possess the same attitudes and motives that they do. The frequently mistaken assumption that others' views are similar to our own applies in a wide range of situations. For example:

- You've heard a slightly raunchy joke that you found funny. You assume that it won't offend a friend. It does.
- You've been bothered by an instructor's tendency to get off the subject during lectures. If you were a professor, you'd want to know if you were creating problems for your students; so you decide that your instructor will probably be grateful for some constructive criticism. Unfortunately, you're wrong.
- You lost your temper with a friend a week ago and said some things you regret. In fact, if someone said those things to you, you would consider the relationship finished. Imagining that your friend feels the same way, you avoid making contact. In fact, your friend feels that he was partly responsible and has avoided you because he thinks you're the one who wants to end things.

These examples show that others don't always think or feel the way we do and that assuming similarities can lead to problems. Sometimes you can find out the other person's real position by asking directly, sometimes by checking with others, and sometimes by making an educated guess after you've thought the matter out. All these alternatives are better than simply assuming everyone would react the way you do.

## We Favor Negative Impressions

What do you think about Harvey? He's handsome, hardworking, intelligent, and honest. He's also conceited.

Did the last quality make a difference in your evaluation? If it did, you're not alone. Research shows that when people are aware of both the positive and negative characteristics of another, they tend to be more influenced by the undesirable traits (Kellermann, 1989). In one study, researchers found that job interviewers were likely to reject candidates who revealed negative information even when the total amount of information was highly positive (Regan & Totten, 1975).

This attitude sometimes makes sense. If the negative quality clearly outweighs any positive ones, you'd be foolish to ignore it. For example, a surgeon with shaky hands and a teacher who hates children would be unsuitable for their jobs, whatever their other virtues. But much of the time it's a bad idea to pay excessive attention to negative qualities and overlook good ones. Some people make this mistake when screening potential friends or dates. They find some who are too outgoing or too reserved, others who aren't intelligent enough, and still others who have a strange sense of humor. Of course, it's important to find people you truly enjoy, but expecting perfection can leave you lonely.

# Perceiving Others More Accurately

After reading this far, you can appreciate how flawed our perceptions of one another can be. It's easy to understand how these distorted perceptions can interfere with our communication. What we need, then, are tools to improve the accuracy of our attributions. The following section will introduce two such tools.

## Perception Checking

With the likelihood for perceptual errors so great, it's easy to see how a communicator can leap to the wrong conclusion and make inaccurate assumptions. Consider the defense-arousing potential of incorrect accusations like these:

"Why are you mad at me?" (Who said you were?)

"What's the matter with you?" (Who said anything was the matter?)

"Come on now. Tell the truth." (Who said you were lying?)

Even if interpretations like these are correct, dogmatic, mind-reading statements are likely to generate defensiveness. The skill of perception checking provides a better way to share your interpretations. A complete perception check has three parts:

1. A description of the behavior you noticed;
2. Two possible interpretations of the behavior;
3. A request for clarification about how to interpret the behavior.

Perception checks for the preceding three examples would look like this:

"When you stomped out of the room and slammed the door [behavior], I wasn't sure whether you were mad at me [first interpretation] or just in a hurry [second interpretation]. How did you feel? [request for clarification]"

"You haven't laughed much in the last couple of days [behavior]. It makes me wonder whether something's bothering you [first interpretation] or whether you're just being quiet [second interpretation]. What's up? [request for clarification]"

"You said you really liked the job I did [behavior], but there was something about your voice that made me think you may not like it [first interpretation]. "Maybe it's just my imagination, though [second interpretation]. "How do you really feel? [request for clarification]"

**Perception checking** is a tool to help us understand others accurately instead of assuming that our first interpretation is correct. Because its goal is mutual understanding, perception checking is a cooperative approach to communication. Besides leading to more accurate perceptions, it signals an attitude of respect and concern for the other person, saying, in effect, "I know I'm not qualified to judge you without some help."

Sometimes an effective perception check won't need all of the parts listed above to be effective:

"You haven't dropped by lately. Is anything the matter?" [single interpretation combined with request for clarification].

"I can't tell whether you're kidding me about being cheap or if you're serious [behavior combined with interpretations]. Are you mad at me?"

"Are you sure you don't mind driving? I can use a ride if it's no trouble, but I don't want to take you out of your way" [no need to describe behavior].

The straightforward approach of perception checking has the best chance of working in what Chapter 2 identifies as *low-context cultures,* ones in which members use language as clearly and logically as possible. The dominant cultures of North America and Western Europe fit into this category, and members of these groups are most likely to appreciate the kind of straight talking that perception checking embodies. On the other hand, members of *high-context cultures* (more common in Latin America and Asia) value social harmony over clarity. High-context communicators are more likely to regard candid approaches like perception checking as potentially embarrassing, preferring instead less direct ways of understanding one another. Thus, a "let's get this straight" perception check that might work well with a Euro-American manager who was raised to value clarity but it could be a serious mistake with a Mexican-American or Asian-American boss who has spent most of his or her life in a high-context culture.

## Building Empathy

Perception checking can help you decode messages more accurately, but it doesn't provide enough information for us to claim that we fully understand another person. For example, a professor who uses perception checking might learn that a student's reluctance to ask questions is due to confusion and not lack of interest. This information would be helpful, but imagine how

### REFLECTION

#### T-SHIRT PROVOKES STEREOTYPING

I don't have a physical disability, but I recently got a glimmer of what life with a disability might be like. I participated in a disability awareness day on our campus and spent the afternoon in a wheelchair. It was interesting to see how many things I take for granted about getting from place to place.

However, I think I learned more in the days that followed from a simple T-shirt. I got the shirt as part of the disability day activities, and I've worn it around town a lot. The only thing it has on the front is the international disability symbol (a person in a wheelchair). People stare at me strangely when I have the shirt on. Someone in my family even asked me to stop wearing it because he said it was embarrassing. I'm afraid that says a lot about some of the ugly stereotypes we still have about physical disabilities.

much more effective the professor would be if she could get a sense of how it feels to be confused, and consider how the material that is so familiar to her appears to the student who is examining it for the first time. Likewise, parents whose perception checks reveal that their teenager's outlandish behavior grows from a desire to be accepted by others don't necessarily understand (or perhaps recall) what it feels like to crave that acceptance.

**Empathy Defined**   What we need, then, to understand others more completely is **empathy**— the ability to recreate another person's perspective, to experience the world from his or her point of view. It is impossible to achieve total empathy, but with enough effort and skill, we can come closer to this target (Long et al., 1999).

"How would you feel if the mouse did that to you?"

As we'll use the term here, empathy has three dimensions (Stiff et al., 1988). On one level, empathy involves *perspective taking*—the ability to take on the viewpoint of another person. This understanding requires a suspension of judgment so that for the moment you set aside your own opinions and take on those of the other person. Besides cognitive understanding, empathy also has an *affective* dimension—what social scientists term *emotional contagion*. In everyday language, emotional contagion means that we experience the same feelings that others have. We know their fear, joy, sadness, and so on. A third ingredient of empathy is a genuine *concern* for the welfare of the other person. Not only do we think and feel as others do, but we have a sincere interest in their well-being.

The linguistic roots of the word *empathy* shed light on the word's meaning. *Empathy* is derived from two Greek words that mean "feeling (in)side," which suggests that empathy means *experiencing* the other's perception—in effect, temporarily becoming that person. This kind of understanding is very different from **sympathy**. The Greek roots for *sympathy* mean "feeling with." As

this definition implies, when you feel sympathetic you stand beside the other person. You feel compassion, but you do not share the other person's emotions. Despite your concern, sympathy involves less identification than does empathy. When you sympathize, the confusion, joy, or pain belongs to another. When you empathize, the experience becomes your own, at least for the moment.

The ability to empathize seems to exist in a rudimentary form in even the youngest children (Goleman, 1995). Virtually from birth, infants become visibly upset when they hear another baby crying, and children who are a few months old cry when they observe another child in tears. Young children have trouble distinguishing others' distress from their own. If, for example, one child hurts its finger, another baby might put its own finger in its mouth as if she was feeling pain. Researchers report cases in which children who see their parents in tears wipe their own eyes, even though they are not crying.

Although infants and toddlers may have a basic capacity to empathize, studies with twins suggest that the degree to which we are born with the ability to sense how others are feeling seems to vary according to genetic factors. Although some people may have an inborn edge, environmental experiences are the key to developing the ability to understand others. Specifically, the way in which parents communicate with their children seems to affect their ability to understand others' emotional states. When parents point out to children the distress that others feel from their misbehavior ("Look how sad Jessica is because you took her toy. Wouldn't you be sad if someone took away your toys?"), those children gain a greater appreciation that their acts have emotional consequences than when parents simply label behavior as inappropriate ("That was a mean thing to do!").

**The Value of Empathy**   As you read in Chapter 1, the ability to empathize is so important that it is generally considered to be an essential ingredient of communicative competence. Empathy can profit both the person who is doing the empathizing and the person who is being understood (Redmond, 1986).

The recipient of empathy receives several payoffs. The first is increased *self-esteem*. Others usually respond to your point of view with judgments such as "That's right, . . . " or "No, it's not that way at all. . . ." An empathic response is different: It suggests the listener is willing to accept you as you are, without any evaluations. It's flattering to find that someone is interested enough in your position to hear you out without passing judgment. The act of being understood also can be very *comforting,* whether or not the other person's reflections offer any additional help. When others empathize, a common thought is "I'm not alone." Finally, the target of empathy learns to *trust* the empathizer in a way that probably would not be otherwise possible.

Desirable as it is, too much empathy can lead to burnout. Studies focusing on human service workers at a psychiatric hospital showed that a high degree of responsiveness to the needs of others led to several symptoms of burnout: depersonal-

## FILM CLIP

### TRYING ON OTHERS' SHOES: *THE DOCTOR*

Jack McKee (William Hurt) is an ace surgeon and a first-class egotist. He treats his patients with a breezy self-assurance, brushing aside their concerns with jokes and indifference. It's not that McKee is mean-spirited: He just views his patients as objects upon which he can practice his skill, and not as human beings with feelings.

McKee receives a major attitude adjustment when his nagging cough is diagnosed as throat cancer and his surgeon treats him with the same mechanical indifference that he had bestowed on his patients. As McKee suffers the indignities of a hospital patient and confronts his mortality, his attitude toward the human side of medical care predictably changes.

The film—which should become a part of the medical school curriculum—shows the general public how walking a mile in another person's shoes can lead to greater tolerance and understanding.

ization of the person being helped, emotional exhaustion, reduced feelings of personal accomplishment, and, ultimately, less emotional commitment to the needy person (Miller et al. 1988). This evidence doesn't mean that empathizing is a guaranteed path to burnout. Rather, it suggests that in addition to being concerned for others, it's necessary to take care of your own needs as well.

## Empathy and Ethics

The "golden rule" of treating others as we want to be treated points to the clear relationship between the ability to empathize and the ethical principles that enable society to function in a matter that we consider civilized. Researcher Martin Hoffman

(1991) cites research showing the link between empathy and ethical altruism. Bystanders who feel empathy for victims are more likely to intervene and offer help than those who are indifferent. On a larger scale, studies in the United States and Germany have revealed a relationship between feelings of empathy and the willingness of people to favor the moral principle that resources should be allocated according to people's needs.

A look at criminal behavior also demonstrates the link between empathy and ethics. Typically, people who commit the most offensive crimes against others, such as rape and child abuse, are not inhibited by any sense of how their offenses affect the victims (Goleman, 1995). Promising new treatments attempt to change behavior by instilling the ability to imagine how others are feeling. In one program, offenders read emotional descriptions of crimes similar to the ones they have committed and watch videotapes of victims describing what it was like to be assaulted. They also write accounts of what their offense must have felt like to the victim, read these stories to others in therapy groups, and even experience simulated reenactments of the crime in which they play the role of the victim. Through strategies like these, social scientists try to help offenders develop the ethical compass that makes it more difficult to be indifferent to causing pain in others.

**Requirements for Empathy**   Empathy may be valuable, but it isn't always easy to achieve. In fact, research shows that it's hardest to empathize with people who are different from us radically: in age, sex, socioeconomic status, intelligence, and so forth (Cronkhite, 1976). In order to make such perceptual leaps, you need to develop several skills and attitudes.

*Open-mindedness*   Perhaps the most important characteristic of an empathic person is the ability and disposition to be open-minded—to set aside for the moment beliefs, attitudes, and values and to consider those of the other person. Open-mindedness is especially difficult when the other person's position is radically different from your own. The temptation is to think (and sometimes say) "That's crazy!" "How can you believe that?" or "I'd do it this way. . . ."

Being open-minded is often difficult because people confuse *understanding* another's position with *accepting* it. These are quite different matters. To understand why a friend disagrees with you, for example, doesn't mean you have to give up your position and accept hers.

*Imagination*   Being open-minded often isn't enough to allow empathy. You also need enough imagination to be able to picture another person's background and thoughts. A happily married or single person needs imagination to empathize with the problems of a friend considering divorce. A young person needs it to empathize with a parent facing retirement. A teacher needs it to understand the problems facing students, just as students can't be empathic without trying to imagine how their instructor feels.

Making the effort to put oneself in another's position can produce impressive results. In one study (Regan & Totten, 1975), college students were asked to list their impressions of people either shown in a videotaped discussion or described in a short story. Half of the students were instructed to empathize with the people as much as possible, and the other half were not given any instructions about empathizing. The results were impressive: Students who did not practice empathy were prone to explain a person's behavior in terms of personality characteristics. For example, they might have explained a cruel statement by saying the speaker was mean, or they might have attributed a divorce to the partners' lack of understanding. The empathic students, on the other hand, were more aware of possible elements in the situation that might have contributed to the reaction. For instance, they might have explained a person's unkind behavior in terms of job pressures or personal difficulties instead of simply labeling that person as mean. In other words, practicing empathy seems to make people more understanding.

*Commitment*   Because empathizing is often difficult, a third necessary quality is a sincere desire to understand another person. Listening to unfamiliar, often confusing information takes time and isn't always fun. If you aim to be empathic, be willing to face the challenge.

By now, you can see the tremendous challenges that face us when we want to understand one another. Physiological distortion, psychological interference, social and cultural conditioning all insulate us from our fellow human beings. But the news isn't all bad: With a combination of determination and skill, we can do a better job of bridging the gulf of understanding that separates us and, as a result, enjoy more-satisfying interpersonal  relationships.

## Summary

Many communication challenges arise because of differing perceptions. The process of interpersonal perception is a complex one, and a variety of factors cause each person's view of reality to vary.

Perception involves three phases: selection, organization, and interpretation. Because communication is a process, these phases may occur simultaneously or in any order. A number of influences can affect how we select, organize, and interpret others' behavior. Physiological factors include age, health, fatigue, hunger, and biological cycles. Psychological factors such as mood and self-concept also have a strong influence on how we regard others. In addition, cultural influences shape how we recognize and make sense of others' words and actions. Finally, social influences, such as sex roles and occupational roles, play an important part in the way we view those with whom we interact.

Our perceptions are often affected by common perceptual tendencies. We often are influenced by obvious stimuli, even if they are not the most important factors. We cling to first impressions, even if they are mistaken. We assume others are similar to us. We favor negative impressions over positive ones. Finally, we are more likely to blame others than ourselves for misfortunes.

One way to verify the accuracy of interpretations is through perception checking. Instead of jumping to conclusions, communicators who check their perceptions describe the behavior they noticed, offer two equally plausible interpretations, and ask for clarification from their partner.

Empathy is the ability to experience the world from another person's perspective. There are three dimensions to empathy: perspective taking, emotional involvement, and concern for the other person. Empathy has benefits for both the empathizer and the recipient. Some evidence suggests that there may be hereditary influences on the ability to empathize but that this ability can be developed with practice. Requirements for empathy include open-mindedness, imagination, and commitment.

## Recommended Readings

**Empathy:**

William E. Ickes, ed. *Empathic Accuracy*. New York: Guilford, 1997.

**The perception process:**

Dean E. Hewes, ed. *The Cognitive Bases of Interpersonal Perception*. Mahwah, NJ: Lawrence Erlbaum Associates, 1995.

**Personal narrative:**

Em Griffin. "Narrative Paradigm." In *A First Look at Communication Theory*. 4th ed. New York: McGraw-Hill, 2000, 295–304.

**Understanding and overcoming stereotyping:**

C. Neil Macrae, Charles Stangor, and Miles Hewstone, eds. *Stereotypes and Stereotyping*. New York: Guilford, 1996.

# Activities

### 1. Critical Thinking Probe

Complete the following sentences:

a. Women _____
b. Men _____
c. Latinos _____
d. Anglos _____
e. African Americans _____
f. Older people _____

Now ask yourself the degree to which each of your responses was a stereotype and/or a generalization. Is it possible to make generalizations about the groups listed above? How could your answers to these questions change the way you perceive and respond to people in these groups?

### 2. Invitation to Insight

You can get a better appreciation of the importance of punctuation by using the format pictured in Figure 4.3 to diagram the following situations:

a. A father and daughter are growing more and more distant. The daughter withdraws because she interprets her father's coolness as rejection. The father views his daughter's aloofness as a rebuff and withdraws further.
b. The relationship between two friends is becoming strained. One jokes to lighten up the tension, and the other becomes more tense.
c. A couple is on the verge of breaking up. One partner frequently asks the other to show more affection. The other withdraws physical contact.

Explain how each of these situations could be punctuated differently by each participant. Next, use the same procedure to identify how an event from your experience could be punctuated in at least two different ways. Describe the consequences of failing to recognize the plausibility of each of these punctuation schemes.

### 3. Invitation to Insight

Choose one of the following situations, and describe how it could be perceived differently by each person. Be sure to include the steps of selection, organization, and interpretation. List any relevant physiological influences, cultural factors, and social influences, as well as suggesting how the communicators' self-concepts might have affected their perceptions.

a. A customer complains to a salesperson about poor service in a busy store.
b. A parent and teenager argue about the proper time for returning home after a Saturday night date.
c. A quiet student feels pressured when called upon by an instructor to speak up in class.
d. A woman and a man argue about whether to increase balance in the workplace by making special efforts to hire employees from underrepresented groups.

### 4. Invitation to Insight

Pages 111–114 of this chapter outline several common perceptual tendencies. Describe instances in which you committed each of them, and explain the consequences of each one. Which of these perceptual tendencies are you most prone to make, and what are the potential results of making it? How can you avoid these tendencies in the future?

### 5. Skill Builder

Improve your perception-checking ability by developing complete perception-checking statements for each of the following situations. Be sure your statements include a description of the behavior, two equally plausible interpretations, and a request for verification.

a. You made what you thought was an excellent suggestion to your boss. He or she said "I'll get back to you about that right away." It's been three weeks, and you haven't received a response yet.
b. You haven't received the usual weekly phone call from your family in over a month. Last

time you spoke, you had an argument about where to spend the holidays.

6. **Skill Builder**

You can develop your empathy skills by putting yourself in the shoes of someone with whom you have an interpersonal relationship. With that person's help, describe *in the first person* how the other person views an issue that is important to him or her. In other words, try as much as possible to become that person and see things from his or her perspective. Your partner will be the best judge of your ability to make this perceptual jump, so use his or her feedback to modify your account. After completing the exercise, describe how your attempt changed the way you might relate to the other person.

# CHAPTER
## 5

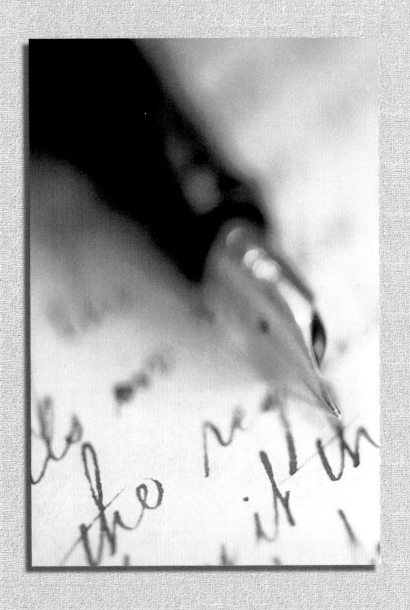

# Language

# After Studying the Material in This Chapter . . .

## You Should Understand:

1. The symbolic nature of language.

2. That meanings are in people, not words.

3. The types of rules that govern the use of language.

4. The influence of language on identity, credibility and status, affiliation, attraction, interest, power, and attitudes about sexism and racism.

5. The factors that influence precision and vagueness in language.

6. The language patterns that reflect a speaker's level of responsibility for his or her statements.

7. Three forms of disruptive language.

8. The relationship between language use and gender roles.

## You Should Be Able to:

1. Identify cases in which you have attributed meanings to words instead of people.

2. Analyze a real or potential misunderstanding in terms of semantic or pragmatic rules.

3. Describe how principles presented in the section of this chapter titled "The Impact of Language" operate in your life.

4. Construct a message at the optimal level of specificity or vagueness for a given situation.

5. Construct statements that acknowledge your responsibility for the content of messages.

6. Rephrase disruptive statements in less inflammatory terms.

7. Identify the masculine and feminine characteristics of your speech.

## Key Terms

| | | | |
|---|---|---|---|
| Abstraction ladder | Euphemism | "It" statement | Semantic rules |
| "But" statement | Factual statement | Opinion statement | Static evaluation |
| Convergence | Hedges | Phonological rules | Syntactic rules |
| Disclaimer | Hesitations | Powerless speech mannerisms | Tag question |
| Divergence | "I" language | | "We" language |
| Emotive language | Inferential statement | Pragmatic rules | "You" language |
| Equivocal language | Intensifier | Relative language | |

"I don't know what you mean by 'glory,'" Alice said.

Humpty Dumpty smiled contemptuously. "Of course you don't—till I tell you. I meant 'there's a nice knock-down argument for you!'"

"But 'glory' doesn't mean 'a nice knock-down argument,'" Alice objected.

"When I use a word," Humpty Dumpty said, in a rather scornful tone, "it means just what I choose it to mean—neither more nor less."

"The question is," said Alice, "whether you can make words mean so many different things."

"The question is," said Humpty Dumpty, "which is to be master—that's all."

—Lewis Carroll, *Through the Looking Glass*

Like Alice, at one time or another everyone has felt trapped in a linguistic wonderland. Words shift meanings until we don't know what others, or even we ourselves, are saying. Although language is an imperfect vessel with which to convey ideas, it also is a marvelous tool. On an everyday level, it allows us to carry on the normal activities that make civilized life possible. Language is a foundation for our personal relationships, and it is a tool for understanding and expressing our spiritual nature. To appreciate the tremendous importance of language, imagine how impossible life would be without it. Most physical disabilities are troublesome, but not completely debilitating: We could survive without eyesight or hearing, and life would still be possible without a limb. But without the ability to use language, we would hardly be human—at least not in the usual sense of the word.

In this chapter we will explore the relationship between words and ideas. We will describe some important characteristics of language and show how these characteristics affect our day-to-day communication. We will outline several types of troublesome language and show how to replace them with more effective kinds of speech. Finally, we will look at the power language has to shape and reflect our attitudes toward others.

# The Nature of Language

We begin our survey by looking at some features that characterize all languages. These features explain both why language is such a useful tool and why it can be so troublesome.

## Language Is Symbolic

Words are arbitrary symbols that have no meaning in themselves. For example, the word *five* is a kind of code that represents the number of fingers on your hand only because we agree that it does. As Bateson and Jackson (1964, p. 271) point out, "There is nothing particularly five-like in the number 'five.'" To a speaker of French, the symbol *cinq* would convey the same meaning; to a computer, the same value would be represented by the electronically coded symbol "00110101."

Even sign language, as "spoken" by most deaf people, is symbolic in nature and not the pantomime it might seem. Because this form of communication is symbolic and not literal, there are hundreds of different sign languages used around the world that have evolved independently whenever significant numbers of deaf people have come in contact (Sacks, 1989). These distinct languages include American Sign Language, British Sign Language, French Sign Language, Danish Sign Language, Chinese Sign Language, and Australian Aboriginal and Mayan sign languages.

Despite the fact that symbols are arbitrary, people often act as if they had some meaning in themselves. S. I. Hayakawa (1964) points out the vague sense we often have that foreign languages are rather odd and that the speakers really ought to call things by their "right" names. To illustrate the mistaken belief that words are inherently connected to the things they label, Hayakawa describes the little boy who was reported to have said "Pigs are called pigs because they are such dirty animals" (p. 27).

## Language Is Rule-Governed

The only reason symbol-laden languages work at all is that people agree on how to use them. The linguistic agreements that make communication possible can be codified in rules. Languages contain several types of rules. **Phonological rules** govern how sounds are combined to form words. For instance, the words *champagne, double,* and *occasion* have the same meaning in French and English, but are pronounced differently.

Whereas phonological rules determine how spoken language sounds, **syntactic rules** govern the way symbols can be arranged. For example, in English, syntactic rules require every word to contain at least one vowel and prohibit sentences such as "Have you the cookies brought?" which would be a perfectly acceptable arrangement in German.

Although most of us aren't able to describe the syntactic rules that govern our language, it's easy to recognize their existence by noticing how odd a statement that violates them appears. Sometimes, however, apparently ungrammatical speech is simply following a different set of syntactic rules. For example, Black English, which is spoken by some members of the African-American community, treats forms of the verb *to be* differently than does standard English (Rathus, 1993, p. 295). The expression "I be angry," which would be ungrammatical in standard English, is perfectly correct in

Black English, where it would be equivalent to "I've been angry for a while."

**Semantic rules** also govern our use of language. Whereas syntax deals with structure, semantics governs meaning. Semantic rules reflect the ways in which speakers of a language respond to a particular symbol. Semantic rules are what make it possible for us to agree that "bikes" are for riding and "books" are for reading, and they help us know whom we will encounter when we use rooms marked "men" and "women." Without semantic rules, communication would be impossible: Each of us would use symbols in unique ways, unintelligible to others.

Semantic rules help us understand the meaning of individual words, but they often don't explain how language operates in everyday life. Consider the statement "Let's get together tomorrow." The semantic meaning of the words in this sentence is clear enough, yet the statement could be taken in several ways. It could be a request ("I hope we can get together"), a polite command ("I want to see you"), or an empty cliché ("I don't really mean it"). We learn to distinguish the accurate meanings of such speech acts through **pragmatic rules** that tell us what uses and interpretations of a message are appropriate in a given context. When these rules are understood by all players in the language game, smooth communication is possible. For example, one rule specifies that the relationship between communicators plays a large role in determining the meaning of a statement. Our example, "I want to see you," is likely to mean one thing when uttered by your boss and another entirely when it comes from your lover. Likewise, the setting in which the statement is made plays a role. Saying "I want to see you" will probably have a different meaning at the office than the same words uttered at a cocktail party. Of course, the nonverbal behaviors that accompany a statement also help us decode its meaning.

The *coordinated management of meaning (CMM)* theory describes some types of pragmatic rules that operate in everyday conversations. It suggests that we use rules at several levels to create our own messages and interpret others' statements (Cronen et al., 1988). Table 5.1 uses a CMM framework to illustrate how two people might wind up confused because they are using different rules at several levels. In situations like this, it's important to make sure that the other person's use of language matches yours before jumping to conclusions about the meaning of his or her statements. The skill of perception checking described in Chapter 4 can be a useful tool at times like this.

## Language Is Subjective

If the rules of language were more precise and if everyone followed them, we would suffer from fewer misunderstandings. You respond to a "while you were out" note and spend a full day trying to reach Barbara, only to find you called the wrong Barbara. You have an hour-long argument about "feminism" with a friend, only to discover that you were using the term in different ways and that you really were in basic agreement. You tease a friend

**Table 5.1**

| Pragmatic Rules Govern the Use and Meaning of a Statement   Notice how the same message ("You look very pretty today") takes on different meaning depending on which of a variety of rules are used to formulate and interpret it. | | |
|---|---|---|
| | **Boss** | **Employee** |
| **Content** Actual words and behaviors | "You look very pretty today." | |
| **Speech Act** The intent of a statement | Compliment an employee | Unknown |
| **Relational Contract** The perceived relationship between communicators | Boss who treats employees like family members | Subordinate employee, dependent on boss's approval for advancement |
| **Episode** Situation in which the interaction occurs | Casual conversation | Possible come-on by boss? |
| **Life script** Self-concept of each communicator | Friendly guy | Woman determined to succeed on own merits |
| **Cultural archetype** Cultural norms that shape member's perceptions and actions | Middle-class American | Middle-class American |

Adapted from Pearce, W.B., & Cronen, V. (1980). *Communication, action, and meaning.* New York: Praeger. Used by permission.

in what you mean to be a playful manner, but he takes you seriously and is offended.

These problems occur because people attach different meanings to the same word or words. Ogden and Richards (1923) illustrated this point graphically in their well-known "triangle of meaning" (see Figure 5.1). This model shows that there is only an indirect relationship—indicated by a broken line—between a word and the thing or idea it represents. An example of this indirect and often confusing relationship between words and ideas explains the decision of Crayola corporation to rename its "Indian red" crayon (Brown, 1999). Many observers regarded the name as an offensive reference to the skin color of Native Americans, although the company pointed out that the name actually came from a reddish-brown pigment commonly found in the country of India.

A far greater uproar arose when the newly appointed Washington, D.C. ombudsman, David Howard, used the word *niggardly* to describe his approach to budgeting (Henneberger, 1999). Howard, who is white, was accused by some African-American critics of uttering an unforgivable racial slur. His defenders pointed out that the word, which means "miserly," is derived from Scandinavian languages, and that it has no link to the racial slur it resembles. Even though the criticisms eventually died away, they illustrate that, correct or not, the meanings people associate with words have far more significance than do their dictionary definitions.

The Ogden and Richards model is oversimplified in that not all words refer to physical "things" or referents. For instance, some referents are abstract ideas (such as *love*), while others (like *angry* or *exciting*) aren't even nouns. Despite these shortcomings, the triangle of meaning is useful since it clearly demonstrates that meanings are in people, not words. Hence, an important task facing communicators is to establish a common understanding of the words they use to exchange messages. In this sense, communication—at least the effective kind—requires us to negotiate the meaning of our language (Duck, 1994c).

## The Impact of Language

### Naming and Identity

"What's in a name?" Juliet asked rhetorically. If Romeo had been a social scientist, he would have answered, "A great deal." Research has demonstrated that names are more than just a simple means of identification: They shape the way others think of us, the way we view ourselves, and the way we act (Marcus, 1976).

At the most fundamental level, some research suggests that even the phonetic sound of a person's name affects the way we regard him or her, at least when we don't have other information available. One recent study revealed that reasonably accurate predictions about who will win an election (at least in the United States) can be made on the basis of some phonetic features of the candidate's surnames (Smith, 1998). Names that were simple, easily pronounced, and rhythmic were judged more favorably than ones that lacked these qualities. For

**Figure 5.1**  **Ogden and Richards' Triangle of Meaning**

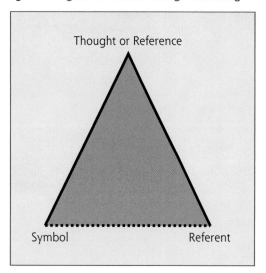

Thought or Reference

Symbol                    Referent

example, in one series of local elections, the winning candidates had names that resonated with voters: Sanders beat Pekelis, Rielly defeated Dellwo, Grady outpolled Schumacher, Combs trounced Bernsdorf, and Golden prevailed over Nuffer. Names don't guarantee victory, but in 78 election races, 48 outcomes supported the value of having an appealing name.

Different names have different connotations. In one study, psychologists asked college students to rate over a thousand names according to their likability, how active or passive they seemed, and their masculinity or femininity. In spite of the large number of subjects, the responses were quite similar. Michael, John, and Wendy were likable and active and were rated as possessing the masculine or feminine traits of their sex. Percival, Isadore, and Alfreda were less likable, and their sexual identity was less clear. Other research also suggests that names have strong connotative meanings. Common names are generally viewed as being more active, stronger, and better than unusual ones (Marcus, 1976).

The preconceptions we hold about people because of their names influence our behavior toward them. Researchers asked a number of teachers to read several essays supposedly written by fifth-grade students. The researchers found that certain names—generally the most popular ones, such as Lisa, Michael, and Karen—received higher grades regardless of which essay they were attached to, whereas less-popular names—Elmer,

Bertha, and Hubert—were consistently graded as inferior. There was one exception to the link between popular names and high grades: Unpopular Adelle received the highest evaluation of all. The researchers speculated that the teachers saw her as more "scholarly."

It's not surprising to find that the attitudes others hold toward a person because of his or her name have an effect on that person's self-concept. Over forty years ago, researchers found that students at Harvard who had unusual names were more likely to be neurotic and to flunk out of school. The negative effect of unusual names seems to be more damaging to men than women, perhaps owing to our social convention that makes such labels acceptable for women. At any rate, research such as this makes it clear that the question "What shall we name the baby?" is important for more than just aesthetic reasons.

The labels we choose for ourselves and encourage others to use say a great deal about who we think we are and how we want others to

view us. For many people, changes in age lead to changes in names. The diminutive that seemed to fit as a child doesn't fit as well in adolescence or adulthood. Thus, Vinnie may become Vince, and Danny may insist on being called Dan or Daniel. It still may be fine for close friends to use diminutives, but not others. The shift to more formal, adult names may not be as pronounced for some women: It's not uncommon to meet an adult Betsy or Susie. But when being taken seriously is the goal in a world where women are all too often treated with less respect than they deserve, having a serious name can be an asset. A male president of the United States may have been elected without changing his name from Bill to William, but it's hard to imagine a female public figure who would risk being called Cindy or Babs. Contemporary female officeholders prove the point: Names like Lizzie Dole or Sandy O'Connor just don't sound right.

Many women in Western society, aware of the power of names to influence identity, are aware

"My mother is black, my father is African-American, and my grandfather is Negro. I can hardly wait to find out about me."

## FOCUS ON RESEARCH

### WHAT'S IN A NAME?: MARRIED WOMEN'S NAME CHOICES AND SENSE OF SELF

In the late twentieth century, many women have resisted the traditional practice of taking their husband's last name upon marriage. Instead, some have kept their birth name (remaining, for example, Jane Doe instead of becoming Jane Snow). Others have hyphenated their own name and their husband's (Jane Doe-Snow). A few husbands and wives have even combined elements of their former names to create a new hybrid word (Snowdoe).

Many advocates of these nontraditional approaches have argued that a woman who gives up her birth name is sacrificing her sense of identity.

Some have suggested that doing so can be demoralizing and result in a loss of self-esteem. Communication professors Laura Stafford and Susan Kline decided to examine these claims by measuring differences between women who took their husband's names ("name-changers") upon marriage and those who keep their birth names ("name-keepers").

The researchers recruited 110 well-educated married women with an average age of thirty-one years, both name-changers and name-keepers. They used a variety of measuring instruments to evaluate each

woman's feelings about herself and her relationship.

Contrary to what linguistic reformers might have expected, the results showed that there were no significant differences between name-changers and name-keepers in terms of self-esteem, relationship dependency, autonomy, or feelings about the balance of control in their marriages. The researchers conclude: "The findings here suggest that scholars who study women's experiences need to be careful not to assume that women's married name choices are associated with perceptions of loss of personal self."

Stafford, L., & Kline, S. L. (1996). Married women's name choices and sense of self. *Communication Reports 9*, 85–92.

that choosing how to identify themselves after marriage can be a significant decision. They may follow the tradition of taking their husband's last name, hyphenate their own name and their husband's, or keep their birth name. One study by Karen Foss and Belle Edson (1989) revealed that a woman's choice is likely to reveal a great deal about herself and her relationship with her husband. Surveys revealed that women who took their husband's names placed the most importance on relationships, with social expectations of how they should behave rated second and issues of self coming last. On the other hand, women who kept their birth names put their personal concerns

ahead of relationships and social expectations. Women with hyphenated names fell somewhere between the other groups, valuing self and relationships equally. Despite these findings, the study profiled in the Focus on Research appearing on this page suggests that the results of name keeping or name changing aren't as profound as they might seem.

## Credibility and Status

The words we use and the way we pronounce them have a powerful influence on whether others accept or reject our ideas. In the classic musical

*My Fair Lady,* Professor Henry Higgins transforms Eliza Doolittle from a lowly flower girl into a high-society woman by replacing her cockney accent with an upper-crust speaking style. The power of speech to influence status is real. In 1971, British researcher Howard Giles conducted experiments that demonstrated (if any proof was necessary) that in Britain, judgments of attractiveness and status are strongly influenced by style of speech. Other research by social psychologists in North America shows that the same principle applies in the New World (see Giles & Poseland, 1975). For example, speakers of Black English have shorter job interviews and receive fewer job offers than applicants who speak standard English (Terrell & Terrell, 1983).

Vocabulary is just as important as accent in shaping perceptions. Scholarly speaking is a good example of this phenomenon. One illustration is the Dr. Fox hypothesis (Cory, 1980): "An apparently legitimate speaker who utters an unintelligible message will be judged competent by an audience in the speaker's area of apparent expertise." The Dr. Fox hypothesis got its name from one Dr. Myron L. Fox, who delivered a talk followed by a half-hour discussion on "Mathematical Game Theory as Applied to Physical Education." The audience included psychiatrists, psychologists, social workers, and educators. Questionnaires collected after the session revealed that these educated listeners found the lecture clear and stimulating.

Despite his warm reception by this learned audience, Fox was a complete fraud. He was a professional actor whom researchers had coached to deliver a lecture of double-talk—a patchwork of information from a *Scientific American* article mixed with jokes, non sequiturs, contradictory statements, and meaningless references to unrelated topics. When wrapped in a linguistic package of high-level professional jargon, however, the meaningless gobbledygook was judged as important information. In other words, Fox's credibility came more from his style of speaking than from the ideas he expressed.

## Affiliation, Attraction, and Interest

Accent and vocabulary aren't the only ways in which language reflects the status of relationships. Speech also can be a way of building and demonstrating solidarity with others. An impressive body of research has demonstrated that communicators who want to show affiliation with one another adapt their speech in a variety of ways, including their choice of vocabulary, rate of talking, number and placement of pauses, and level of politeness (Aune & Kikuchi, 1993; Giles et al., 1991). On an individual level, close friends and lovers often develop a set of special terms that serve as a way of signifying their relationship (Bell & Healey, 1992; Bell et al., 1987). Using the same vocabulary serves to set these people apart from others, reminding themselves and the rest of the world of their relationship. The same process works among members of larger groups, ranging from street gangs to military personnel. Communication researchers call the process of adapting one's speech style to match that of others with whom the communicator wants to identify **convergence.**

When two or more people feel equally positive about one another, their linguistic convergence will be mutual. But when communicators want or need approval, they often adapt their speech to accommodate the other person's style, trying to say the "right thing" or speak in a way that will help them fit in. We see this process when immigrants who want to gain the reward of material success in a new culture strive to master the host language. Likewise, employees who seek advancement tend to speak more like their superiors, supervisors adopt the speech style of managers, and managers converge toward their bosses.

The principle of speech accommodation works in reverse, too. Communicators who want to set themselves apart from others adopt the strategy of **divergence,** speaking in a way that emphasizes their differences. For example, members of an ethnic group, even though fluent in the

## REFLECTION

### WORD CHOICE AND ATTITUDE

I've taken two communication classes this year and they were completely different. I just figured out a big reason why. In one class my professor used language that made it sound as if communication had nothing to do with us. He would always refer to "people" or "communicators" as if they were from another planet, or at least another species. One day he announced that his lecture topic would be "How men and women speak when *they* are together." If men and women are *they*, who are *we?*

My other professor talked about how *we* communicate. "Does watching violence on television make *us* more aggressive?" she would ask. "Do movies teach *us* how to be husbands or wives or parents?" The two different ways of using language seemed trivial at first, but now I can see that they said a lot about how each professor approached the course.

dominant language, might use their own dialect as a way of showing solidarity with one another—a sort of "us against them" strategy. Divergence also occurs in other settings. For example, a physician or attorney who wants to establish credibility with his or her client might speak formally and use professional jargon to create a sense of distance. The implicit message here is "I'm different (and more knowledgeable) than you."

## Power

Communication researchers have identified a number of language patterns that add to or detract from a speaker's power to influence others. Notice the difference between these two statements:

Excuse me, sir. I hate to say this, but I. . . uh . . . I guess I won't be able to turn in the assignment on time. I had a personal emergency and . . . well . . . it was just impossible to finish it by today. I'll have it in your mailbox on Monday, OK?

I won't be able to turn in the assignment on time. I had a personal emergency and it was impossible to finish it by today. I'll have it in your mailbox on Monday.

Whether or not the professor finds the excuse acceptable, it's clear that the second one sounds more confident, whereas the tone of the first is apologetic and uncertain. Table 5.2 (p. 134) identifies several **powerless speech mannerisms** illustrated in the statements you just read. A number of studies have shown that speakers whose talk is free of these mannerisms are rated as more competent, dynamic, and attractive than speakers who sound powerless (Ng & Bradac, 1993). One study revealed that even a single type of powerless speech mannerism can make a person appear less authoritative or socially attractive (Hosman, 1989).

Powerful speech that gets the desired results in mainstream North American and European culture doesn't succeed everywhere with everyone (Samovar & Porter, 1998). In Japan, saving face for others is an important goal, so communicators there tend to speak in ambiguous terms and use hedge words and qualifiers. In most Japanese sentences the verb comes at the end of the sentence so the "action" part of the statement can be postponed. Traditional Mexican culture, with its strong emphasis on cooperation, also uses hedging to smooth over interpersonal relationships. By not taking a firm stand with their speech mannerisms, Mexicans believe they will not make others feel ill at ease. The Korean culture represents yet another group of people who prefer "indirect" (for example, *perhaps, could be*) over "direct" speech.

Even in North American culture, simply counting the number of powerful or powerless statements won't always reveal who has the most control in a relationship. Social rules often mask the real distribution of power. A boss who wants to be pleasant might say to a secretary, "Would you mind retyping this letter?" In truth, both boss and secretary know this is an order and not a request, but the questioning form makes the medicine less bitter. Sociolinguist Deborah Tannen (1994, p. 101) describes how politeness can be a face-saving way of delivering an order:

> I hear myself giving instructions to my assistants without actually issuing orders: "Maybe it would be a good idea to . . .;" "It would be great if you could. . ." all the while knowing that I expect them to do what I've asked right away. . . . This rarely creates problems, though, because the people who work for me know that there is only one reason I mention tasks—because I want them done. I *like* giving instructions in this way; it appeals to my sense of what it means to be a good person . . . taking others' feelings into account.

As this quotation suggests, high-status speakers—especially higher-status women, according to Tannen—often realize that politeness is an effective way to get their needs met while protecting the face of the less powerful person. The importance of achieving both content and relational goals helps explain why a mixture of powerful and polite speech is usually most effective (Geddes,

1992). Of course, if the other person misinterprets politeness for weakness, it may be necessary to shift to a more powerful speaking style.

## Racism and Sexism

Sexist language can affect the self-concepts of women and men, often in subtle ways. Suzanne Romaine (1999, p. 95) offers several examples of how linguistic terms can stereotype men and women. To say that a woman *mothered* her children focuses on her nurturing behavior, but to say that a man *fathered* a child talks only about his biological role. We are familiar with terms like *working mother*, but there is no term *working father* because we assume that men are the breadwinners.

Beyond just stereotyping, sexist language can stigmatize women. For example, the term *unmarried mother* is common, but we do not talk about *unmarried fathers* because there is no stigma attached to this status for men. Whereas there are over two hundred English words for promiscuous women, there are only twenty for men (Stanley, 1977). Differences in definitions of the terms *woman* and *man* in the *Oxford English Dictionary* indicate discriminatory treatment. The definition of

**Table 5.2**

| Examples of Less Powerful Language | |
|---|---|
| **Type of Usage** | **Example** |
| Hedges | "I'm kinda disappointed. . . ." <br> "I think we should. . . ." <br> "I guess I'd like to. . . ." |
| Hesitations | "Uh, can I have a minute of your time?" <br> "Well, we could try this idea. . . ." <br> "I wish you would—er—try to be on time." |
| Intensifiers | "So that's how I feel. . . ." <br> "I'm not very hungry." |
| Polite forms | "Excuse me, sir. . . ." |
| Tag questions | "It's about time we got started, isn't it?" <br> "Don't you think we should give it another try?" |
| Disclaimers | "I probably shouldn't say this, but. . . ." |

woman is an adult female being, a female servant, a ladylove or mistress, and a wife. *Man* is defined as a human being, the human creature regarded abstractly, an adult male endowed with manly qualities, and a person of importance or position (O'Donnell, 1973).

While sexist language usually defines the world as made up of superior men and inferior women, racist language reflects a worldview that classifies members of one racial group as superior and others as inferior. Not all language that might have racist overtones is deliberate. For example, the connotations of many words favor whites over people of color (Person-Lynn, 1994). Words and images associated with "white" are usually positive, whether it's the cowboy hero in white clothing or connotations of white as "pure," "clean," "honorable," "innocent," "bright," and "shiny." The words and images associated with "black" are often negative, a concept that reaches from the black hat of the villain cowboy and the black cat that causes bad luck to words and phrases like *black market, blackball,* and *blacklist.*

Using racist labels can have ugly consequences. Although experimental subjects who

heard a derogatory label used against a member of a minority group expressed annoyance at this sort of slur, the negative emotional terms did have an impact (Giles & Franklyn-Stokes, 1989; Kirkland et al., 1987). Not only did the unwitting subjects rate the minority individual's competence lower when that person performed poorly, but they also found fault with others who associated socially with the minority person—even members of the subject's own ethnic group.

Many linguistic changes beginning in the late 1960s aimed at teaching speakers and writers a new vocabulary in order to overcome linguistic biases that had plagued speech. For example, "Black is beautiful" was an effort to reduce perceived status differences between blacks and whites. Changes in writing style also were designed to counter the sexual prejudices inherent in language, particularly eliminating the constant use of *he* and introducing various methods either to eliminate reference to a particular sex or to make reference to both sexes (Miller & Swift, 1972). Words that use *man* generically to refer to humanity at large often pose problems, but only to the unimaginative. Consider the following substitutions: *mankind* may be replaced with *humanity, human beings, human race,* and *people; man-made* may be replaced with *artificial,*

"No, I'm not a salesgirl. Are you a salesboy?"

*manufactured,* and *synthetic; manpower* may be replaced with *labor, workers,* and *workforce;* and *manhood* may be replaced with *adulthood.* In the same way, *Congressmen* are *members of Congress; firemen* are *firefighters; chairmen* are *presiding officers, leaders,* and *chairs; foremen* are *supervisors; policemen* and *policewomen* are both *police officers;* and *stewardesses* and *stewards* are both *flight attendants.*

# Uses (and Abuses) of Language

By now, it's apparent that language can shape the way we perceive and understand the world. Next we will look at some specific types of usage and explore both the value and the potential problems that can arise.

## Precision and Vagueness

Most people assume that the goal of language is to make our ideas clear to one another. When clarity *is* the goal, we need language skills to make our ideas understandable to others. Sometimes, however, we want to be less than perfectly clear. The following pages will point out some cases where ambiguity and vagueness serve useful purposes as well as cases where perfect understanding is the goal.

**Equivocation**  **Equivocal language** consists of words that have more than one commonly accepted definition. Some equivocal misunderstandings are amusing, as the following newspaper headlines illustrate:

> Police Begin Campaign to Run Down Jaywalkers
>
> Teacher Strikes Idle Kids
>
> 20-Year Friendship Ends at the Altar

Other equivocal misunderstandings are trivial. We recall eating dinner at a Mexican restaurant and ordering a "tostada with beans." Instead of

## REFLECTION

### EQUIVOCAL EXPRESSION

Last week I told my friend I was planning on going to the mountains over vacation. She immediately said that she would love to go too. I laughed sarcastically and said I wasn't making any more plans with her because she always changes her mind. It wasn't the first time I have heard her say that she would love to do something with me and then not follow up.

My friend became very quiet and then said, "I'm not making any plans to go to the mountains. I'm only telling you that I would love to go there." After thinking about what she said, I realize that I have been misunderstanding her. I now realize that my friend's saying she would "love to" do something doesn't mean she wants to make plans with me. She is expressing a desire, but not making a commitment.

being served a beef tostada with beans on the side, we were surprised to see the waiter bring us a plate containing a tostada *filled* with beans. As with most equivocal misunderstandings, hindsight showed that the phrase *tostada with beans* has two equally correct meanings.

Other equivocal misunderstandings can be more serious. A nurse gave one of her patients a scare when she told him that he "wouldn't be needing" his robe, books, and shaving materials anymore. The patient became quiet and moody. When the nurse inquired about the odd behavior, she discovered that the poor man had interpreted her statement to mean he was going to die soon. In fact, the nurse meant he would be going home shortly.

Some equivocal misunderstandings can go on for a lifetime. Consider the word *love.* J. A. Lee

(1973; Hendrick et al., 1998) points out that people commonly use that term in six very different ways: *eros* (romantic love), *ludus* (game-playing love), *storge* (friendship love), *mania* (possessive, dependent love), *pragma* (logical love), and *agape* (all-giving, selfless love). Imagine the conflicts that would occur between a couple who sincerely pledged their love to one another, each with a different kind of love in mind. We can imagine them asking one another, "If you really love me, why are you acting like this?" and never realizing that each of them views the relationship differently.

It's difficult to catch every equivocal statement and clarify it. For this reason, the responsibility for interpreting statements accurately rests in large part with the receiver. Feedback of one sort or another—for example, paraphrasing and questioning—can help clear up misunderstandings: "You say you love me, but that you want to see other people. In my book, 'love' is exclusive. What about you?"

Despite its obvious problems, equivocal language has its uses. As Chapter 10 describes in detail, there are times when using language that is open to several interpretations can help you avoid the kind of honesty and clarity that can embarrass both the speaker and listener. For example, if a friend proudly shows you a newly completed painting and asks your opinion about it, you might respond equivocally by saying, "Gee, it's really unusual. I've never seen anything like it," instead of giving a less ambiguous but more hurtful response such as, "This may be the ugliest thing I've ever seen!"

**Abstraction**   High-level abstractions are convenient ways of generalizing about similarities between several objects, people, ideas, or events. Figure 5.2 is an abstraction ladder that shows how to describe the same phenomenon at various levels of abstraction.

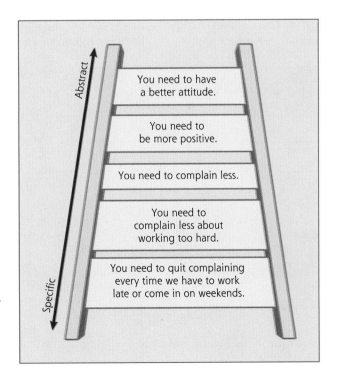

**Figure 5.2** Abstraction Ladder
A boss gives feedback to an employee about career advancement at various levels of specificity

We use higher-level abstractions all the time. For instance, rather than saying "Thanks for washing the dishes," "Thanks for vacuuming the rug," and "Thanks for making the bed," it's easier to say "Thanks for cleaning up." In such everyday situations, abstractions are a useful kind of verbal shorthand.

Like equivocation, high-level abstractions also can help communicators find face-saving ways to avoid confrontations and embarrassment by being deliberately unclear (Eisenberg, 1984; Eisenberg & Witten, 1987). If a friend apologizes for being late and making you wait, you can choose to brush off the incident instead of making it an issue by saying, "Don't worry. It wasn't the end of the world"— a true statement, but less specific than saying "To tell you the truth, I was mad at the time, but I've cooled off now." If your boss asks your opinion of a new idea that you think is weaker than your own approach but you don't want to disagree, you could respond with a higher level abstraction by saying "It *might* work. . . ."

Although vagueness does have its uses, highly abstract language can cause four types of problems. The first is stereotyping. Imagine someone who has had one bad experience and, as a result, blames an entire group: "Marriage counselors are worthless," "New Yorkers are all rude," or "Men are no good." Overly abstract expressions like these can cause people to *think* in generalities, ignoring uniqueness. As you learned in Chapter 3, expecting people to act in a certain way can become a self-fulfilling prophecy. If you expect the worst of people, you have a good chance of getting it.

Besides narrowing your own options, excessively abstract language also can confuse others. Telling the hairstylist "not too short" or "more casual" might produce the look you want, or it might lead to an unpleasant surprise.

Overly abstract language can lead to problems of a more serious nature. For instance, accusations of sexual assault can arise because one person claims to have said "no" when the other person insists no such refusal was ever conveyed. In response to this sort of disagreement, specific rules of sexual conduct have become more common in work and educational settings. Perhaps the best known code of this type is the one developed at Ohio's Antioch College (1996). The policy uses low-level abstractions to minimize the chances of anyone claiming confusion about a partner's willingness. For example, the code states:

- If sexual contact and/or conduct is not mutually and simultaneously initiated, then the person who initiates sexual contact/conduct is responsible for getting verbal consent of the other individual(s) involved.
- Verbal consent [for sexual activity] should be obtained with each new level of physi-

**"Be honest with me, Roger. By 'mid-course correction' you mean divorce, don't you."**

cal and/or sexual behavior. . . . Asking "Do you want to have sex with me?" is not enough. The request for consent must be specific to each act.

- If someone has initially consented but then stops consenting during a sexual interaction, she/he should communicate withdrawal of consent verbally (example: saying "no" or "stop") and/or through physical resistance (example: pushing away). The other individual(s) must stop immediately.

Some critics have ridiculed rules like these as being unrealistically legalistic and chillingly inappropriate for romantic relationships. Whatever their weaknesses, the Antioch code illustrates how low-level abstractions can reduce the chances of a serious misunderstanding. Specific language may not be desirable or necessary in many situations, but in an era when misinterpretations can lead to accusations of physical assault, it does seem to have a useful place.

You can make your language—and your thinking—less abstract and more clear by learning to make *behavioral descriptions* of your problems, goals, appreciations, complaints, and requests. We use the word *behavioral* because such descriptions move down the abstraction ladder to describe the specific, observable objects and actions we're thinking about. Table 5.3 (p. 140) shows how behavioral descriptions are much more clear and effective than vague, abstract statements.

**Euphemism**    Euphemisms (from a Greek word meaning "to use words of good omen") are innocuous terms substituted for blunt ones. For example, young adolescent girls often use euphemistic terms ("my friend," "it") to discuss their own menstruation without feeling embarrassed (Kissling, 1996). Euphemisms can also soften the impact of information that might be unpleasant. It's easy to imagine how a relational breakup might be easier to handle with the explanation "I'm not ready for commitment" than with "I'm bored with you." When choosing how to broach difficult subjects, the challenge is to be as

## FILM CLIP

### SHOOTING FROM THE HIP: *BULWORTH*

When it comes to equivocation and euphemisms, most politicians are masters of the art. To get elected, candidates carefully monitor their language to avoid offending party members, lobbyists, and financial backers. The result is that political speeches often sound bland and generic. Many a voter has wished that politicians would quit being cautious and just "tell it like it is."

Enter Jay Bulworth (Warren Beatty). A suave senator from California, Bulworth gets into financial trouble and decides to put out a contract on his own life so his daughter can collect the insurance money. Knowing his days are numbered, he no longer cares about what he says or how he says it. Bulworth tells a church full of African Americans that rich, white politicians have been using them for years. He accuses movie industry leaders of making exorbitant sums of money for producing "mostly crap." On national television, he berates the insurance lobby that has bankrolled his elections.

The story is reminiscent of the film *Network,* in which a news anchor contemplating suicide starts shooting from the hip in his nightly broadcasts. *Bulworth* and *Network* are entertaining because it's fun to watch politicians and newscasters using language that is frank and blunt. Audiences also know it's unlikely they'll ever hear such language from these people in the real world.

kind as possible without sacrificing either your integrity or the clarity of your message. (The guidelines for self-disclosure outlined in Chapter 10 will help you.)

**Relative Language**    Relative language gains meaning by comparison. For example, do you attend a large or a small school? This depends on

**Table 5.3**

| | Abstract Description | Behavioral Description | | | Remarks |
|---|---|---|---|---|---|
| | | Who Is involved | In What circumstances | Specific Behaviors | |
| **Problem** | I'm no good at meeting strangers. | People I'd like to date | At parties and in school | I think, "They'd never want to date me." Also, I don't originate conversations. | Behavioral description more clearly identifies thoughts and behaviors to change. |
| **Goal** | I'd like to be more assertive. | Telephone and door-to-door solicitors | When I don't want the product or can't afford it | Instead of apologizing, I want to keep saying "I'm not interested" until they go away. | Behavioral description clearly outlines how to act; abstract description doesn't. |
| **Appreciation** | "You've been a great boss." | (no clarification necessary) | When I've needed to change my schedule because of school exams or assignments | "You've rearranged my hours cheerfully." | Give both abstract and behavioral descriptions for best results. |
| **Complaint** | "I don't like some of the instructors around here." | Professors A and B | In class, when students ask questions the professors think are stupid | They either answer in a sarcastic voice (you might demonstrate) or accuse us of not studying hard enough. | If talking to A or B, use only behavioral description. With others, use both abstract and behavioral descriptions. |
| **Request** | "Quit bothering me!" | You and your friends, X and Y | When I'm studying for exams | "Instead of asking me again and again to party with you, I wish you'd accept my comment that I need to study tonight." | Behavioral description will reduce defensiveness and make it clear that you don't always want to be left alone. |

what you compare it to. Alongside a campus such as Ohio State University, with over fifty thousand students, your school may look small, but compared with a smaller institution, it may seem quite large. Relative words such as *fast* and *slow*, *smart* and *stupid*, *short* and *long* are clearly defined only through comparison.

Using relative terms without explaining them can lead to communication problems. Have you ever responded to someone's question about the weather by saying it was warm, only to find out the person thought it was cold? Have you followed a friend's advice and gone to a "cheap" restaurant, only to find that it was twice as expensive as you expected? Have classes you heard were "easy" turned out to be hard? The problem in each case resulted from failing to link the relative word to a more measurable term.

One way to avoid the pitfalls of relative language is to use numbers to define relative terms. For instance, when a friend says that she just saw a good movie, you could ask her, "On a scale of 1 to 10, how would you rate it?" You might be surprised when she says, "About a 6"—after all, you might have thought "good" meant "great," while your friend simply meant the movie was "okay." Using numbers can also help explain what you mean when describing how smart your brother is, how much pain you're in, or how quickly you need a report finished.

**Static Evaluation**   "Mark is a nervous guy." "Karen is short-tempered." "You can always count on Wes." Descriptions or evaluations that contain the word *is* contain a **static evaluation**—the usually mistaken assumption that people or things are totally consistent and unchanging. Instead of labeling Mark as permanently and completely nervous, it would probably be more accurate to outline the situations in which he behaves nervously: "Mark acts nervously until you get to know him." The same goes for Karen, Wes, and the rest of us: We are more changeable than the way static, everyday language describes us.

Edward Sagarian (1976) writes about an unconscious language habit that imposes a static view of others. Why is it, he asks, that we say "He *has* a cold" but say "He *is* a convict" or a genius, a slow learner, or any other set of behaviors that are also not necessarily permanent? Sagarian argues that such linguistic labeling leads us to typecast others and in some cases forces them to perpetuate behaviors that could be changed.

Alfred Korzybski (1933) suggested the linguistic device of dating to reduce static evaluation. He suggested adding a subscript whenever appropriate to show the transitory nature of a referent. For example, a teacher might write the following as an evaluation of a student: "Susan$_{May\ 12}$ had difficulty cooperating with her classmates." Although the actual device of subscripting is awkward in writing and impractical in conversation, the idea it represents can still be used. Instead of saying "I'm shy," a more accurate statement might be "I haven't approached any new people since I moved here." The first statement implies that your shyness is an unchangeable trait, rather like your height, while the second one suggests that you are capable of changing.

## The Language of Responsibility

Besides providing a way to make the content of a message clear or obscure, language reflects the speaker's willingness to take responsibility for his or her beliefs and feelings. This acceptance or rejection of responsibility says a great deal about the speaker, and it can shape the tone of a relationship. To see how, read on.

**"It" Statements**   Notice the difference between the sentences of each set:

> "It bothers me when you're late."
> "I'm worried when you're late."

> "It's nice to see you."
> "I'm glad to see you."

> "It's a boring class."
> "I'm bored in the class."

As their name implies, **"it" statements** replace the personal pronoun *I* with the less immediate construction *it's*. By contrast, **"I" language** clearly identifies the speaker as the source of a message. Communicators who use "it" statements avoid responsibility for ownership of a message, instead attributing it to some unidentified body. This habit isn't just imprecise; more important, it's an unconscious way to avoid taking a position. You can begin to appreciate the increased directness of "I" language by trying to use it instead of the less direct and more evasive "it" statements in your own conversations.

**"But" Statements**   Statements that take the form "X-but-Y" can be quite confusing. A closer look at the **"but" statement** explains why. *But* has the effect of canceling the thought that precedes it:

> "You're really a great person, but I think we ought to stop seeing each other."
> "You've done good work for us, but we're going to have to let you go."

> "This paper has some good ideas, but I'm giving it a grade of *D* because it's late."

These "buts" often are a strategy for taking responsibility for one's ideas. "Buts" *can* be a face-saving strategy worth using at times. When the goal is to be absolutely clear, however, the most responsible approach will deliver the central idea without the distractions that can come with "but" statements.

**"I," "You," and "We" Language**   We've already seen that "I" language is a way of accepting responsibility for a message. **"You" language** is quite different. It expresses a judgment of the other person. Notice how each of the following statements implies that the subject of the complaint is doing something wrong:

> "You left this place a mess!"
> "You didn't keep your promise!"
> "You're really crude sometimes!"

Despite its name, "you" language doesn't have to contain the pronoun *you*, which is often implied rather than stated outright:

> "That was a stupid joke!" ["Your jokes are stupid!"]
> "Don't be so critical!" ["You're too negative!"]
> "Mind your own business!" ["You're too nosy!"]

Whether the judgment is stated outright or implied, it's easy to see why "you" language can arouse defensiveness. A "you" statement implies that the speaker is qualified to judge the target—not an idea that most listeners are willing to accept, even when the evaluation is correct.

Fortunately, "I" language provides a more accurate and less provocative way to express a complaint (Kubany, et al., 1992; Winer & Majors, 1981). "I" language shows that the speaker takes responsibility for the accusation by describing his or her reaction to the other's behavior without making any judgments about its worth. A complete "I" statement has three parts: It describes (1) the other person's behavior, (2) your feelings, and

(3) the consequences the other's behavior has for you:

> "I get embarrassed [feeling] when you talk about my bad grades in front of our friends [behavior]. I'm afraid they'll think I'm stupid [consequence]."
> "When you didn't pick me up on time this morning [behavior], I was late for class and wound up getting chewed out by the professor [consequences]. That's why I got so mad [feeling]."
> "I haven't been very affectionate [consequence] because you've hardly spent any time with me in the past few weeks [behavior]. I'm confused [feeling] about how you feel about me."

When the chances of being misunderstood or getting a defensive reaction are high, it's a good idea to include all three elements in your "I" message. In some cases, however, only one or two of them will get the job done:

> "I went to a lot of trouble fixing this dinner, and now it's cold. Of course I'm mad!" (The behavior is obvious.)
> "I'm worried because you haven't called me up." ("Worried" is both a feeling and a consequence.)

Despite its obvious advantages, even the best constructed and delivered "I" messages won't always succeed. As Thomas Gordon (1970, p. 145) points out, "nobody welcomes hearing that his behavior is causing someone a problem, no matter how the message is phrased." Furthermore, "I" language in large doses can start to sound egotistical (Proctor, 1989). Research shows that self-absorbed people, also known as "conversational narcissists," can be identified by their constant use of first-person singular pronouns (Raskin & Shaw, 1988; Vangelisti et al., 1990). For this reason, "I" language works best in moderation.

One way to avoid overuse of "I" language is to consider the pronoun *we*. **"We" language** implies that the issue is the concern and responsibility of both the speaker and receiver of a message. Consider a few examples:

> "We have a problem. We can't seem to talk about money without fighting."

> "We aren't doing a very good job of keeping the apartment clean, are we?"
> "We need to talk to your parents about whether we'll visit them for the holidays."

It's easy to see how "we" language can help build a constructive climate. Besides being immediate, it suggests a kind of "we're in this together" orientation (Gorham, 1988). Couples who use "we" language are more satisfied than those who rely more heavily on "I" and "you" pronouns (Honeycutt, 1999; Sillars et al., 1997). On the other hand, using the pronoun *we* can be presumptuous since you are speaking for the other person as well as for yourself. It's easy to imagine someone responding to the statement "We have a problem . . . " by saying "Maybe *you* have a problem, but don't tell me *I* do!"

As Table 5.4 (p. 144) summarizes, all three pronouns—*I, you,* and *we*—have their advantages and drawbacks. Given this fact, what advice can we give about the most effective pronouns to use in interpersonal communication? A study by Russell Proctor and James Wilcox (1993) offers an answer. The researchers found that "I"/"We" combinations (for example, "I think that we . . . " or "I would like to see us . . .") were strongly endorsed by college students, particularly for confrontational conversations in romantic relationships. Anita Vangelisti and her associates (1990) made a similar observation: Unlike conversational narcissists, nonnarcissists combine their "I" references with references to other persons, objects, and events. Since too much of any pronoun comes across as inappropriate, combining pronouns is generally a good idea. If your "I" language reflects your position without being overly self-absorbed, your "you" language shows concern for others without judging them, and your "we" language includes others without speaking for them, you will probably come as close as possible to the ideal mix of pronouns.

## Disruptive Language

Not all linguistic problems come from misunderstandings. Sometimes people understand one

**Table 5.4**

| Pronoun Uses and Their Effects | | | |
|---|---|---|---|
| **Pronoun** | **Pros** | **Cons** | **Recommendation** |
| "I" Language | ■ Takes responsibility for personal thoughts, feelings, and wants.<br>■ Less defense-provoking than evaluate "you" language. | ■ Can be perceived as egotistical, narcissistic, and self-absorbed. | ■ Use descriptive "I" messages in conflicts when the other person does not perceive a problem.<br>■ Combine "I" with "we" language in conversations. |
| "We" Language | ■ Signals inclusion, immediacy, cohesiveness, and commitment. | ■ Can speak improperly for others. | ■ Combine with "I" language, particularly in personal conversations.<br>■ Use in group settings to enhance sense of unity.<br>■ Avoid when expressing personal thoughts, feelings, and wants. |
| "You" Language | ■ Signals other-orientation, particularly when the topic is positive. | ■ Can sound evaluative and judgmental, particularly during confrontations. | ■ Use "I" language during confrontations.<br>■ Use "You" language when praising or including others. |

another perfectly and still wind up in conflict. Of course, not all disagreements can, or should be, avoided. But eliminating three bad linguistic habits from your communication repertoire can minimize the kind of clashes that don't need to happen, allowing you to save your energy for the unavoidable and important struggles.

**Fact-Opinion Confusion** **Factual statements** are claims that can be verified as true or false. By contrast, **opinion statements** are based on the speaker's beliefs. Unlike matters of fact, they can never be proven or disproven. Consider a few examples of the difference between factual and opinion statements:

| Fact | Opinion |
|---|---|
| It rains more in Seattle than in Portland. | The climate in Portland is better than in Seattle. |
| Kareem Abdul-Jabbar is the all-time leading scorer in the National Basketball Association. | Kareem is the greatest basketball player in the history of the game! |
| The United States is the only industrialized country without universal health care. | The quality of life in the United States is lower than in any other industrial country when it comes to health care. |

When factual and opinion statements are set side by side like this, the difference between them is clear. In everyday conversation, however, we often present our opinions as if they were facts, and in doing so we invite an unnecessary argument. For example:

- ■ "That was a dumb thing to say!"
- ■ "Spending that much on _____ is a waste of money!"
- ■ "You can't get a fair shake in this country unless you're a white male."

Notice how much less antagonistic each statement would be if it were prefaced by a qualifier such as "In my opinion . . ." or "It seems to me. . . ."

**Fact-Inference Confusion**   Labeling your opinions can go a long way toward relational harmony, but developing this habit won't solve all linguistic problems. Difficulties also arise when we confuse factual statements with **inferential statements**— conclusions arrived at from an interpretation of evidence.

Arguments often result when we label our inferences as facts:

A: Why are you mad at me?

B: I'm not mad at you. Why have you been so insecure lately?

A: I'm not insecure. It's just that you've been so critical.

B: What do you mean, "critical"? I haven't been critical. . . .

Instead of trying to read the other person's mind, a far better course is to identify the observable behaviors (facts) that have caught your attention and to describe the interpretations (inferences) that you have drawn from them. After describing this train of thought, ask the other person to comment on the accuracy of your interpretation:

"When you didn't return my phone call [fact], I got the idea that you're mad at me [inference]. Are you?" (question)

"You've been asking me a lot lately whether I still love you [fact], and that makes me think you're feeling insecure [inference]. Is that right?" (question)

**Emotive Language**   **Emotive language** seems to describe something but really announces the speaker's attitude toward it. If you approve of a friend's roundabout approach to a difficult subject, you might call her "tactful"; if you don't like it, you might accuse her of "beating around the bush." Whether the approach is good or bad is more a matter of opinion than of fact, although this difference is obscured by emotive language.

You can appreciate how emotive words are really editorial statements when you consider these examples:

| If You Approve, Say | If You Disapprove, Say |
| --- | --- |
| thrifty | cheap |
| traditional | old-fashioned |
| extrovert | loudmouth |
| cautious | coward |
| progressive | radical |
| information | propaganda |
| eccentric | crazy |

"Sorry, Chief, but of course I didn't mean 'bimbo' in the perjorative sense."

Not surprisingly, research shows that the relational climate suffers when communicators use emotive language. A study by Jess Alberts (1988) indicated that when dealing with problems, dissatisfied couples were more likely to use personal, emotive comments but that satisfied partners described the other's behaviors in neutral terms.

## Male and Female Language Use

So far we have discussed language use as if it were identical for both sexes. According to some theorists and researchers (e.g., Tannen, 1990), this is an oversimplification. They have argued that there are significant differences between the way men and women speak. Other scholars have suggested that any differences are not significant (Canary & Emmers-Sommer, 1997). What are the similarities and differences between male and female language use?

## Content

While there is certainly variation within each sex, on the average men and women discuss a different range of topics. The first research on conversational topics was conducted over seventy years ago. Despite the changes in male and female roles since then, the results of more recent studies are remarkably similar (Bischoping, 1993; Clark, 1998; Fehr, 1996). These studies analyzed the communication of women and men ranging in age from seventeen to eighty, exploring the topics each discussed with friends of the same sex. Certain subjects were common to both sexes: Work, movies, and television proved to be frequent topics for both groups. Both men and women reserved discussions of sex and sexuality for members of the same sex. Along with the similarities, there were significant differences in the conversations of men and women, especially when talking to friends. Female friends spent much more time discussing relationship problems; family, health, and reproductive matters; weight; food; clothing; and men. Women also reported discussing other women frequently. Men, on the other hand, were more likely to discuss sports, hobbies, and activities. Both men and women were equally likely to discuss personal appearance, sex, and dating in same-sex conversations.

## Reasons for Communicating

Both men and women, at least in the dominant cultures of the United States and Canada, use language to build and maintain social relationships. Regardless of the sex of the communicators, the goal of almost all ordinary conversations include making the conversation enjoyable by being friendly, showing interest in what the other person says, talking about topics that interest the other person (Clark, 1998). *How* men and women accomplish these goals is often different, though. Although most communicators try to make their interaction enjoyable, men are more likely than women to emphasize making conversation fun.

## FILM CLIP

### MEN AND WOMEN IN CONVERSATION: *WHEN HARRY MET SALLY*

Harry Burns (Billy Crystal) and Sally Albright (Meg Ryan) are strangers who first get together for purely functional reasons: a cross-country car ride in which they share gas costs and driving. She sizes him up as crude and insensitive; he views her as naive and obsessive. By the time they finish their journey, they are glad to part ways.

But the car ride is just the start of their relationship—and the beginning of a look at male and female communication styles. In their conversations, Harry and Sally often exhibit communication patterns similar to those found in gender-related research. For instance, Harry tends to treat discussions as debates. He regularly tells jokes and enjoys having the first and last word. He rarely asks questions but is quick to answer them. Harry self-discloses with his buddy Jess (Bruno Kirby), but only while watching a football game or taking swings in a batting cage.

Sally, on the other hand, self-discloses with her female friends at restaurants, by phone, while shopping—just about any-place. She regularly asks questions of Harry but seems troubled by his competitive answers and approach to sex (Sally: "So you're saying that a man can be friends with a woman he finds unattractive?" Harry: "No, you pretty much want to nail them too"). In the language of Deborah Tannen, Sally's communication is about "rapport" while Harry's is about "report."

The story ends with a strong sense of hope for cross-sex communication. This is due in part to Harry's learning to "speak a different language." The rancor of his early interactions with Sally softens when he expresses empathy (much to her surprise) in a chance bookstore meeting. Near movie's end, he offers warm and detailed descriptions of why he enjoys being with and around her. Clearly they are friends as well as lovers, which seems to make their communication stronger. It also helps them fulfill a goal of most movies: the ending suggests they have a good chance to live "happily ever after."

Their discussions involve a greater amount of joking and good-natured teasing. By contrast, women's conversations focus more frequently on feelings, relationships, and personal problems (Samter et al., 1994). When a group of women was surveyed to find out what kinds of satisfaction they gained from talking with their friends, the most common theme mentioned was a feeling of empathy—"To know you're not alone," as some put it (Sherman & Haas, 1984). Whereas men commonly described same-sex conversations as something they *liked*, females characterized their woman-to-woman talks as a kind of contact they *needed*. The greater frequency of female conversations reflects their importance. Nearly 50 percent of the women surveyed by Sherman and Haas said they called friends at least once a week just to talk, whereas less than half as many men did so. In fact, 40 percent of the men surveyed reported that they never called another man just to chat.

Because they use conversation to pursue social needs, female speech often contains statements showing support for the other person, demonstrations of equality, and efforts to keep the conversation going (Clark, 1998). With these goals, it's not surprising that traditionally female speech often contains statements of sympathy and empathy: "I've felt just like that myself," "The same thing happened to me!" Women are also inclined to ask lots of questions that invite the other person

## DIFFERENT ROLES, DIFFERENT LANGUAGE

As the first woman in a formerly all-male architectural firm, I feel like something of a guinea pig. Most of the partners and associates have made me feel welcome, but a small group treats me with what seems like a condescending attitude. The structural, mechanical, and electrical engineers we use as consultants are even worse. I don't think they've ever worked with a woman who wasn't a secretary. I've found that with these guys I have changed the way I speak. I try to use more powerful language with fewer hesitations and hedges. I make more statements and ask fewer questions. In other words, I sound more like a stereotypical man.

I don't know yet whether this approach will make any difference. The point is, I sound like a different person when I'm at work than in any other setting. It's not really an act: It's more an effort to sound professional. I guess if someone dresses differently when they go to work, there's nothing wrong with sounding different too.

to share information: "How did you feel about that?" "What did you do next?" The importance of nurturing a relationship also explains why stereotypically female speech is tentative. Saying "This is just my opinion . . ." is less likely to put off a conversational partner than a more definite "Here's what I think. . . ."

Men's speech is often driven by quite different goals than women's. Men are more likely to use language to accomplish the job at hand than to nourish relationships. This explains why men are less likely than women to disclose their vulnerabilities, which would be a sign of weakness. When someone else is sharing a problem, most language experts suggest that instead of empathizing, men are prone to offer advice: "That's nothing to worry about . . ." "Here's what you need to do. . . ." Besides taking care of business, men are more likely than women to use conversations to exert control, preserve their independence, and enhance their status. This explains why men are more prone to dominate conversations and one-up their partners. Men often interrupt their conversational partners to assert their own experiences or point of view. (Women interrupt too, but they usually do so to offer support, which is quite a different goal.)

Differences like these begin early in childhood. Sociolinguist Deborah Tannen (1990) summarizes a variety of studies showing that boys use talk to assert control over one another, while girls' conversations are aimed at maintaining harmony. Transcripts of conversations between preschoolers aged two to five show that girls are far more cooperative than boys (Sachs, 1987). They preceded their proposals for action by saying "let's," as in "Let's go find some" or "Let's turn back." By contrast, boys gave orders like "Lie down" or "Gimme your arm."

## Conversational Style

Research suggests that women behave somewhat differently in conversations than do men (for summaries, see Wood, 1997; Turner et al., 1995). For example, Mulac (1998) reports that men are more likely than women to use judgmental adjectives ("Reading can be a drag"), directives ("Think of some more"), and "I" references ("I have a lot to do"). Women are more likely to use intensive adverbs ("He's *really* interested), emotional references ("If he really cared about you . . ."), uncertainty verbs ("It seems to me . . ."), and contradictions ("It's cold, but that's okay"). Mulac summarizes style differences by claiming that men's speech is more typically direct, succinct (to-the-point), personal, and task-oriented. By con-

## FOCUS ON RESEARCH

### THE IMPACT OF POWER AND SEX ON THE USE OF THREATS

Some studies have revealed that women are more likely to use affiliative, "powerless" language than men. Joseph Scudder and Patricia Hayes Andrews wanted to determine whether gender differences in the use of threats—one type of powerful speech—arise because women care more than men about building positive relationships or because a lack of power has left many women with few alternatives to being "nice."

The researchers placed male-male and female-female dyads in a car buying-selling simulation in which the

participants could make actual money, depending on the favorability of the price they could negotiate with their partner. Power—the extent to which the seller/buyer was dependent on the other person—was manipulated to create five conditions: (1) sellers with very high power were paired with buyers with very low power, (2) sellers with high power were paired with buyers with low power, (3) sellers and buyers with moderate power were paired, (4) sellers and buyers with low power were paired, and (5) sellers and buyers with very low power were paired.

In four of the five conditions, men and women did not differ in their use of threats: The negotiator's bargaining position influenced his or her negotiating style far more than her or his sex. The authors conclude that "Results of this study provide substantial support for the notion that women, like men, will use more powerful language [threats] when placed in positions of enhanced power." Power, not gender, appears to be the important variable affecting the use of at least one form of powerful language.

Scudder, J. N. & Andrews, P. H. (1995). A comparison of two alternative models of powerful speech: The impact of power and gender upon the use of threats. *Communication Research Reports, 12,* 25–33.

trast, female speech is characterized by being more indirect, elaborate, and focused on relationships. Some theorists have argued that such differences cause women's speech to be less powerful than men's, although research does not back up this claim (Grob et al., 1997).

Other studies have revealed that men and women behave differently in different conversational settings. For example, in mixed-sex dyads men talk longer than women, while in same-sex situations women speak for a longer time. In larger groups men talk more, while in smaller settings

women do more of the speaking. In same-sex conversations there are other differences: Women use more questions, justifiers, intensive adverbs, personal pronouns, and adverbials. Men use more directives, interruptions, and filler words to begin sentences (Mulac et al., 1988).

An accommodating style isn't always a disadvantage. Although one study revealed that women who spoke tentatively were actually more influential with men than those who used more powerful speech, this tentative style was less effective in persuading women (Carli, 1990). (Language use had no effect on men's persuasiveness.) This research suggests that women who are willing and able to be flexible in their approach can persuade both other women and men—at least as long as they are not dealing with an audience consisting of both sexes.

## Nonsex Variables

Despite the differences in the way men and women speak, the link between sex and language use isn't as clear-cut as it might seem. Some observers (e.g., Gray, 1992) have claimed that differences are so great that men might as well have come from Mars and women from Venus. A more sober look at research suggests that the differences are not nearly so dramatic. For example, one analysis of over 1,200 research studies found that only 1 percent of variance in communication behavior resulted from sex differences (Canary & Hause, 1993). There is no significant difference between male and female speech in areas such as use of profanity, use of qualifiers, such as "I guess" or "this is just my opinion," tag questions, and vocal fluency (Grob et al., 1997; Zahn, 1989). Some on-the-job research shows that male and female supervisors in similar positions behave the same way and are equally effective. In light of the considerable similarities between the sexes and the relatively minor differences, communication scholars Julia Wood and Kathryn Dindia (1998) suggest that the "men are from Mars, women from Venus" claim should be replaced by the metaphor that "men are from North Dakota, women are from South Dakota."

A growing body of research explains some of the apparent contradictions in similarities and differences between female and male speech by pointing out that factors other than communicator sex influence language use. For example, social philosophy plays a role. Feminist wives talk more than their husbands do, while nonfeminist wives talk less. Orientation toward problem solving also plays a role in conversational style: Whether a speaker has a cooperative or competitive orienta-

tion has greater influence on interaction than sex (Fisher, 1983). Sexual orientation may be more powerful than biological sex in determining speech mannerisms. In gay and lesbian relationships, the conversational styles of partners reflect power differences in the relationship (e.g., who is earning more money) more than the biological sex of the communicators (Steen & Schwartz, 1995).

The speaker's occupation also influences speaking style. For example, male day-care teacher's speech to their students resembles the language of female teachers more closely than it resembles the language of fathers at home (Gleason, 1983). Overall, doctors interrupt their patients more often than the reverse, although male patients interrupt female physicians more often than they do male physicians (Zimmerman & West, 1975). At work, task differences exert more powerful effects on whether speakers use sex-inclusive language (such as "he or she" instead of just "he") than biological sex (Rubin et al., 1994). A close study of trial transcripts showed that the speaker's experience on the witness stand and occupation had more to do with language use than did biological sex. The researcher concluded, "So-called women's language is neither characteristic of all women nor limited only to women" (O'Barr, 1982).

Another powerful force that influences the way individual men and women speak is their *gender role.* Recall the various sex types described in Chapter 4 (pages 107–108): masculine, feminine, and androgynous. Remember that these sex types don't necessarily line up neatly with biological sex. There are "masculine" females as well as "feminine" females, "feminine" males as well as "masculine" males, and androgynous communicators who combine traditionally masculine and feminine characteristics. Research shows that these sex roles can influence a communicator's style more than his or her biological sex. Donald Ellis and Linda McCallister (1980) found that masculine sex-type subjects used significantly more dominance language than did either feminine or androgynous group members. Feminine members expressed slightly more submissive behaviors and more equivalence behaviors than the androgynous group members, and their submissiveness and equivalence were much greater than the masculine subjects'.

By now it should be clear that there are differences between the way men and women speak, but that these differences are determined by a wide variety of factors that may have little or nothing to do with biological sex. As men and women grow to have equal opportunities and more similar social experiences, we can expect that there will be fewer differences in the ways they speak.

## Summary

Language is both a marvelous communication tool and the source of many interpersonal problems. Every language is a collection of symbols governed by a variety of rules. Because of its symbolic nature, language is not a precise vehicle: Meanings rest in people, not in words themselves.

Besides conveying meanings about the content of a specific message, language both reflects and shapes the perceptions of its users. Terms used to name people influence the way they are regarded. The terms used to label speakers and the language they use shape others' evaluations of the speakers' credibility and status. Language also reflects the level of affiliation, attraction, and interest of a speaker toward a subject. In addition, language patterns reflect and shape a speaker's perceived power. Finally, language reflects and influences racist and sexist attitudes.

When used carelessly, language can lead to a variety of interpersonal problems. The level of precision or vagueness of messages can affect a receiver's understanding of them. Both precise messages and vague, evasive messages have their uses in interpersonal relationships, and a competent communicator has the ability to choose the optimal level of precision for the situation at hand. Language also acknowledges or avoids the speaker's acceptance of responsibility for his or her positions, and competent communicators know how to use "I," "you," and "we" statements to accept the optimal level of responsibility and relational harmony. Some language habits—confusing facts with opinions or inferences and using emotive terms—can lead to unnecessary disharmony in interpersonal relationships.

The relationship between communicator sex and language is a confusing one. There are many differences in the ways men and women speak: The content of their conversations varies, as do their reasons for communicating and their conversational style. However, not all differences in language use can be accounted for by the speaker's sex. Occupation, social philosophy, and orientation toward problem solving also influence the use of language, and psychological gender can be more of an influence than biological sex.

## Recommended Readings

**Overview of language:**

Donald G. Ellis. *From Language to Communication.* Hillsdale, NJ: Lawrence Erlbaum Associates, 1992.

**Language and the human mind:**

Steven Pinker. *The Language Instinct.* New York: Harper, 1995.

**Male and female language use:**

Daniel J. Canary and Tara M. Emmers-Sommer. *Sex and Gender Differences in Personal Relationships.* New York: Guilford, 1997. See also Daniel J. Canary and Kathryin Dindia, eds. *Sex Differences and Similarities in Communication: Critical Essays and Empirical Investigations of Sex and*

*Gender in Interaction.* Mahwah, NJ: Lawrence Erlbaum Associates, 1998.

**Sexism and language:**

Suzanne Romaine. *Communicating Gender.* Mahwah, NJ: Lawrence Erlbaum Associates, 1999.

# Activities

1. **Invitation to Insight**
   For each of the following scenes, describe one syntactic, one semantic, and one pragmatic rule:
   a. Asking an acquaintance out for a first date.
   b. Declining an invitation to a party.
   c. Responding to a stranger who has just said "excuse me" after bumping into you in a crowd.

2. **Invitation to Insight**
   Recall an incident in which you were misunderstood. Explain how this event illustrated the principle "Meanings are in people, not words."

3. **Ethical Challenge**
   The information about the impact of language on pages 128–136 shows how the words a communicator chooses can shape others' perceptions. Create two scenarios for each type of linguistic influence listed below. The first should describe how the type of influence could be used constructively, and the second should describe an unethical application of this knowledge.
   a. Naming and identity
   b. Credibility and status
   c. Attraction and interest
   d. Power
   e. Racism and sexism

4. **Skill Builder**
   Translate the following into behavioral language:
   a. An abstract goal for improving your interpersonal communication (for example, "Be more assertive," or "Stop being so sarcastic").

   b. A complaint you have about another person (for instance, that he or she is "selfish" or "insensitive").

   In both cases, describe the person or people involved, the circumstances in which the communication will take place, and the precise behaviors involved. What difference will using the behavioral descriptions be likely to make in your relationships?

5. **Invitation to Insight**
   Are there ever situations in your life when it is appropriate to be *less* clear and *more* vague? Use the information on pages 136–142 to answer this question and to decide whether vagueness is the most competent approach to the situation.

6. **Skill Builder**
   You can develop your skill at delivering "I" and "we" messages by following these steps:
   a. Visualize situations in your life when you might have sent each of the following messages:
   "You're not telling me the truth!"
   "You only think of yourself!"
   "Don't be so touchy!"
   "Quit fooling around!"
   "You don't understand a word I'm saying!"
   b. Write alternatives to each statement, using "I" language.
   c. Think of three "you" statements you could make to people in your life. Transform each of these statements into "I" and "we" language, and rehearse them with a classmate.

7. **Invitation to Insight**
   What role do the types of disruptive language described on pages 143–146 play in your life? Recall incidents when you have confused facts and opinions, confused facts and inferences, and used emotive language. Discuss the consequences of each type of language use, and describe how the results might have been different if you had used language more carefully.

8. **Invitation to Insight**

   Some authors believe that differences between male and female communication are so great that they can be characterized, "men are from Mars, women are from Venus." Other researchers believe the differences aren't nearly so dramatic and would describe them as "men are from North Dakota, women are from South Dakota." Which approach seems more accurate to you? Offer experiences from your life to support your point of view.

# CHAPTER
## 6

# Nonverbal Communication

# After Studying the Material in This Chapter . . .

## You Should Understand:

1. The five distinguishing characteristics of nonverbal communication.

2. The functions that nonverbal communication can serve.

3. The nonverbal behaviors that suggest a communicator is attempting an act of deception.

4. The various types of nonverbal communication.

## You Should Be Able to:

1. Describe your nonverbal behavior in any situation.

2. Identify nonverbal behavior that repeats, substitutes for, complements, accents, regulates, or contradicts a verbal message.

3. Analyze the attitudinal messages in examples of your own nonverbal behavior.

4. Share appropriately your interpretation of another's nonverbal behavior.

## Key Terms

| | | | |
|---|---|---|---|
| Affect displays | Illustrators | Nonverbal communication | Proxemics |
| Chronemics | Intimate distance | Paralanguage | Public distance |
| Disfluencies | Kinesics | Personal distance | Social distance |
| Emblems | Manipulators | Personal space | Territory |

P*eople don't always say what they mean. . . but their body gestures and movements tell the truth!*

Will he ask you out? Is she encouraging you? Know what is really happening by understanding the secret language of body signals. You can:

Improve your sex life . . .
Pick up your social life . . .
Better your business life . . .

*Read* Body Language *so that you can penetrate the personal secrets, both of intimates and total strangers . . .*

Does her body say that she's a loose woman?
Does her body say that she's a phony?
Does her body say that she's a manipulator?
Does her body say that she's lonely?

Unless you've been trapped in a lead mine or doing fieldwork in the Amazon Basin, claims like these are probably familiar to you. Almost every drugstore, supermarket, and airport bookrack has its share of "body language" paperbacks. They promise that, for only a few dollars and with a fifth-grade reading ability, you can learn secrets that will change you from a fumbling social failure into a self-assured mind reader who can uncover a person's deepest secrets at a glance.

Observations like these are almost always exaggerations or fabrications. Don't misunderstand: There *is* a scientific body of knowledge about **nonverbal communication**, and it *has* provided many fascinating and valuable clues to human behavior. That's what this chapter is about. It's unlikely the next few pages will turn you instantly into a rich, sexy, charming communication superstar, but don't go away. Even without glamorous promises, a quick look at some facts about nonverbal communication shows that it's an important and valuable field to study.

## Nonverbal Communication Defined

If *non* means "not" and *verbal* means "with words," then it seems logical that *nonverbal communication* would involve "communication without words." This definition is an oversimplification, however, because it fails to distinguish between *vocal* communication (by mouth) and *verbal* communication (with words). Some nonverbal messages have a vocal element. For example, the words "I love you" have different meanings depending on the way they are spoken. A better definition of nonverbal communication is "messages expressed by nonlinguistic means."

These nonlinguistic messages are important because what we *do* often conveys more meaning than what we *say*. Albert Mehrabian (1972), a psychologist working in the field of nonverbal behavior, claimed that 93 percent of the emotional impact of a message comes from a nonverbal source, whereas only a paltry 7 percent is verbal. Anthropologist Ray Birdwhistell (1970) described a 65–35 percent split between actions and words. Although social scientists have disputed these figures (e.g., Hegstrom, 1979; Lapakko, 1997), the point remains: Nonverbal communication contributes a great deal to shaping perceptions.

You might ask how nonverbal communication can be so powerful. At first glance, it seems as if meanings come from words. To answer this question, recall a time when you have observed speakers of an unfamiliar language communicating. Although you can't understand the words being spoken, there are plenty of clues that give you an idea of what is going on in the exchange. By tuning into their facial expressions, postures, gestures, vocal tones, and other clues you probably can make assumptions about the way the communicators feel about one another at the moment and get some ideas about the nature of their relationship. Researchers have found that subjects who hear content-free speech—ordinary speech that has been electronically manipulated so that the words are unintelligible—can consistently recognize the emotion being expressed, as well as identify its strength (Knapp & Hall, 1997).

# Characteristics of Nonverbal Communication

The many types of nonverbal communication share some characteristics. As Table 6.1 shows, these characteristics are quite different from verbal, linguistic means of communication. We will now take a look at some of the fundamental characteristics of nonverbal communication.

## All Behavior Has Communicative Value

Some theorists have suggested that *all* nonverbal behavior communicates information. They argue that it is impossible *not* to communicate. You can understand the impossibility of non-communication by recalling a recent time you spent with another person. Suppose you were told not to communicate any messages at all while with that partner. What would you have done? Closed your eyes? Withdrawn into a ball? Left the room? You can probably see that even these behaviors communicate messages that mean

you're avoiding contact. One study (DePaulo, 1992) took just this approach. When communicators were told not to express nonverbal clues, others viewed them as dull, withdrawn, uneasy, aloof, and deceptive.

The impossibility of not communicating is extremely significant because it means that each of us is a kind of transmitter that cannot be shut off. No matter what we do, we send out messages that say something about ourselves and our relationships with others. If, for instance, others were observing you now, what nonverbal clues would they get about how you're feeling? Are you sitting forward or reclining back? Is your posture tense or relaxed? Are your eyes wide open, or do they keep closing? What does your facial expression communicate now? Can you make your face expressionless? Don't people with expressionless faces communicate something to you? Even uncontrollable behaviors can convey a message. You may not intend to show that you're embarrassed, but your blushing can still be a giveaway. Of course, not all behaviors (intentional or not) will be interpreted correctly: Your trembling hands might be taken as a sign of nervousness when you're really just shivering from the cold. But whether or not your behavior is intentional, and whether or not it is interpreted accurately, all nonverbal behavior has the potential to create messages.

**Table 6.1**

| Some Differences Between Verbal and Nonverbal Communication | |
|---|---|
| **Verbal Communication** | **Nonverbal Communication** |
| ■ Mostly voluntary and conscious | ■ Often unconscious |
| ■ Usually content-oriented | ■ Usually relational |
| ■ Can be clear or vague | ■ Inherently ambiguous |
| ■ Primarily shaped by culture | ■ Primarily shaped by biology |
| ■ Discontinuous/intermittent | ■ Continuous |
| ■ Single-channel (words only) | ■ Multi-channeled |

Adapted from p. 16 of: Andersen, P. (1999). *Nonverbal communication: forms and functions.* Mountain View, CA, Mayfield.

Although nonverbal behavior reveals information, we aren't always conscious of what we are communicating nonverbally. In one study, less than a quarter of experimental subjects who had been instructed to show increased or decreased liking of a partner could describe the nonverbal behaviors they used (Palmer & Simmons, 1995). Furthermore, just because communicators are nonverbally expressive doesn't mean that others will tune in to the abundance of unspoken messages that are available. One study comparing the richness of e-mail to in-person communication confirmed the greater amount of information available in face-to-face conversations, but it also showed that some communicators (primarily men) failed to recognize these messages (Dennis et al., 1999).

Whether or not we are aware of nonverbal behavior, it has great communicative power—often more than the words we speak (Burgoon et al., 1996). In a variety of settings (including job interviews, therapy sessions, and first meetings), adults rely more on nonverbal messages than on words when interpreting the messages of others. Nonverbal cues are especially likely to carry weight when they contradict a speaker's words. In one series of experiments, friendly, neutral, and unfriendly verbal messages were paired with conflicting nonverbal behaviors (Argyle et al., 1971). Raters who judged the verbal and nonverbal messages separately found them equal in strength. But when the two messages were combined, the nonverbal statements carried as much as 12.5 times more weight than the verbal ones. This study shows that, when verbal and nonverbal messages contradict each other, we tend to believe the nonverbal.

## Nonverbal Communication Is Primarily Relational

Some nonverbal messages serve utilitarian functions. For example, a police officer directs the flow of traffic, or a team of street surveyors uses hand motions to coordinate their work. But nonverbal communication also serves in a far more common (and more interesting) series of *social* functions.

One important social function of nonverbal communication involves identity management. Chapter 3 discusses how we strive to create an image of ourselves as we want others to view us. Nonverbal communication plays an important role

"I tell you, Mr. Arthur, this survey has no way of registering a nonverbal response!"

Reproduced by Special Permission of *Playboy* Magazine. Copyright ©1977 by *Playboy.*

in this process—in many cases, a role that is more important than that of verbal messages. For example, consider what happens when you attend a party where you are likely to meet strangers you would like to get to know better. Instead of projecting your image verbally ("Hi! I'm attractive, friendly, and easygoing"), you behave in ways that will present this identity. You might smile a lot and perhaps try to strike a relaxed pose. It's also likely that you dress carefully—even if the image involves looking as if you hadn't given a lot of attention to your appearance.

Along with identity management, nonverbal communication allows us to define the kind of relationships we want to have with others (Burgoon & Le Poire, 1999). You can appreciate this fact by thinking about the wide range of ways you could behave when greeting another person. You could

wave, shake hands, nod, smile, clap the other person on the back, give a hug, or avoid all contact. Each one of these behaviors sends a message about the nature of your relationship with the other person.

Nonverbal behavior can be more powerful than words in defining the kind of relationship you are seeking. You can appreciate this fact by recalling the times and ways you learned that someone is upset with you. Most of the time the first clues don't come from direct statements, but from nonverbal clues. Perhaps the message is conveyed via a lack of eye contact, different facial expressions than usual, an increase in distance, or decreased touch. In any case, the change in behavior clearly proves the power of nonverbal communication to define the status of a relationship.

Nonverbal messages perform another valuable social function: They convey emotions that we may be unwilling or unable to express, or ones we may not even be aware of. In fact, nonverbal communication is much better suited to expressing attitudes and feelings than it is ideas. You can prove this for yourself by imagining how you could express each item on the following list nonverbally:

1. "I'm tired."
2. "I'm in favor of capital punishment."
3. "I'm attracted to another person in the group."
4. "I think prayer in the schools should be allowed."
5. "I'm angry at someone in this room."

This experience shows that, short of charades, ideas don't lend themselves to nonverbal expressions nearly as well as attitudes do. This explains why it's possible to understand the attitudes or feelings of others, even if you aren't able to understand the subject of their communication.

As technology develops, an increasing number of Internet messages will include the sender's voice. Until then, e-mail messages offer fewer nonverbal cues about the speaker's feelings than do face-to-face encounters, or even telephone conversations. New e-mail users soon learn that their messages can be and often are misunder-

## FILM CLIP

### TWO PERSONALITIES IN THE SAME BODY: *ALICE* AND *THE MAN IN THE IRON MASK*

In both *Alice* and *The Man in the Iron Mask*, we see gifted actors switching between different personalities. In so doing, they illustrate the powerful role of nonverbal behavior in personal relationships.

*The Man in the Iron Mask*, loosely based on the Dumas novel, is set in prerevolutionary France. King Louis XIV (Leonardo DiCaprio) is a heartless despot who presides over his decadent court, indifferent to the fate of his starving subjects. In an attempt to protect his sovereignty, Louis has banished his twin brother, Philippe (also DiCaprio), to a prison where he wears the notorious iron mask. DiCaprio's contrasting portrayals of Louis and Phillipe remind us how gesture, posture, facial expression, vocal tone, and other nonverbal behaviors reflect personality.

Alice (Mia Farrow) is a sweet, meek socialite who lives a life of dull luxury in Manhattan with her emotionally distant husband (William Hurt). One day she meets a dark, handsome stranger (Joe Mantegna) and begins thinking about having an affair. Her Chinese herbalist, Dr. Yang (Keye Luke), gives her a potion that releases her from all inhibitions. As we watch Alice's transformation from repressed persona to uninhibited tigress, we again appreciate the fundamental way nonverbal behavior offers clues about a person's identity.

common ones. (Because of formatting limitations that come with e-mail, emoticons appear sidewise instead of in an up-and-down orientation.) Note that, like most nonverbal messages, emoticons can have multiple meanings.

:-) Basic smile. Most commonly used to indicate humorous intent ("No offense intended.")

:-D Big smile.

;- ) Wink and grin. Sometimes used to indicate sarcasm or say, "Don't hit me for what I just said."

:-( Frown.

:-I Indifference.

:-@ Screaming, swearing, very angry.

:-| Disgusted, grim.

:~-( Crying.

:-/ or :-\ Skeptical.

:- O Surprised, yelling, realization of an error ("Oops!").

Symbols like these may be helpful, but they clearly aren't an adequate substitute for the rich mixture of nonverbal messages that flow in face-to-face exchanges, or even in telephone conversations. As Internet technology improves, more and more computer users will be able to communicate via voice, and even see one another as they communicate. This technology will help the Internet become a more useful tool for communicating relational messages.

## Nonverbal Communication Is Ambiguous

Chapter 5 pointed out how some language can be ambigious. (For example, the equivocal statement "that nose piercing really makes you stand out" could be a compliment or a criticism, and the vague statement "I'm almost done" could mean you have to wait a few minutes or an hour. Most nonverbal behavior has the potential to be even more ambiguous than verbal statements like these. To understand why, consider how you would interpret silence from your companion during an evening together. Consider all the possible meanings of this nonverbal behavior: warmth, anger, preoccupation, boredom, nervousness, thoughtfulness—the possibilities are many. The ambiguity of

stood. Probably the biggest problems arise from joking remarks taken as serious statements. To solve these problems, e-mail correspondents have developed a series of symbols—called *emoticons* or *smileys*—that can be created using keyboard characters to simulate nonverbal dimensions of a message. The list below contains some of the most

## FOCUS ON RESEARCH

### COMMUNICATING SEXUAL CONSENT: NONVERBAL CUES AREN'T ENOUGH

Does a kiss mean "I like you a lot" or "I want to have sex"? Does pulling away from a romantic partner mean "Stop now" or "Keep trying"? Questions such as these aren't easy to answer because they involve ambiguous nonverbal cues. Grace Lim and Michael Roloff conducted research to find out if verbal messages are clearer than nonverbal messages for communicating sexual consent.

Lim and Roloff surveyed one hundred college students about sexual consent in twelve dating scenarios. The scenarios included partners rebounding from broken relationships, under-

graduates dating graduate teaching assistants, and the use of alcohol. The researchers wanted to discover under what conditions verbal consent (e.g., "Do you want to have sex with me?") was considered clearer than nonverbal consent (e.g., kissing as an indicator of a desire to have sex). In every scenario, verbal consent was seen as less ambiguous than nonverbal consent. This doesn't mean that romantic partners don't rely on nonverbal signals; many of the respondents indicated that they interpret nonverbal cues (such as kissing) as signs of sexual willingness. However,

nonverbal messages were far less likely to be misunderstood when accompanied by verbal statements.

The conclusions of this research seem obvious: Verbal messages are clearer than nonverbal messages in matters of sexual consent. That they are obvious, however, doesn't mean they are practiced. Using clearer and less ambiguous verbal messages could reduce a variety of unfortunate outcomes, ranging from a spoiled evening to lawsuits to date rape.

Lim, G. Y., & Roloff, M. E. (1999). Attributing sexual consent. *Journal of Applied Communication Research, 27*, 1–23.

nonverbal behavior was illustrated when one supermarket chain tried to emphasize its customer-friendly approach by instructing employees to smile and make eye contact with customers (Curtis, 1998). Several clerks filed grievances when some customers mistook the service-with-a-smile approach as sexual come-ons.

Not all nonverbal behavior is equally ambiguous. In laboratory settings, subjects are better at identifying positive facial expressions, such as happiness, love, surprise, and interest, than negative ones, like fear, sadness, anger, and disgust (Druckmann et al., 1982). In real life, however, spontaneous nonverbal expressions are so ambiguous that observers are frequently unable to

identify accurately what they mean (Motley, 1993; Motley & Camden, 1988).

Because nonverbal behavior is so ambiguous, caution is wise when you are responding to nonverbal cues. Rather than jumping to conclusions about the meaning of a sigh, smile, slammed door, or yawn, it's far better to use the kind of perception-checking approach described in Chapter 4. "When you yawned, I got the idea I might be boring you. But maybe you're just tired. What's going on?" The ability to consider more than one possible interpretation for nonverbal behavior illustrates the kind of cognitive complexity that Chapter 1 identified as an element of communication competence. In fact, research has demonstrated that cognitively complex people are better at decoding nonverbal behavior than those who jump to conclusions about its meaning (Woods, 1996). Popular advice on the subject notwithstanding, it's usually *not* possible to read a person like a book.

# Functions of Nonverbal Communication

This chapter deals with nonverbal communication, but don't get the idea that our words and actions are unrelated. Quite the opposite is true: Verbal and nonverbal communication are interconnected, although not always in the same way. Let's take a look at the various relationships between our words and other types of expression.

## Repeating

First, nonverbal behavior may repeat a verbal message. If someone asked you for directions to the nearest drugstore, you could say "Go north about two blocks" and then repeat your instructions nonverbally by pointing north. This kind of repetition is especially useful when we're describing an idea with a visual dimension, such as size, shape, or direction. Repeating is so much a part of face-to-face interaction that many people regard it as a required part of communication (Kendon, 1994).

## Substituting

We can substitute nonverbal messages for verbal ones that we communicate. For instance, the more you know someone, the easier it is to use nonverbal expressions as a kind of shorthand to substitute for words. When you see a familiar friend wearing a certain facial expression, it isn't necessary to ask, "What kind of day did you have?" In the same way, experience has probably shown you that certain kinds of looks, gestures, and other clues say, far better than words, "I'm angry at you" or "I feel great."

Some nonverbal behaviors—called **emblems**—are culturally understood substitutes for verbal expressions. Nodding the head up and down is an accepted way of saying yes in most cultures. Likewise, a side-to-side head shake is a nonverbal way of saying no, and a shrug of the shoulders is commonly understood as meaning "I don't know" or "I'm not sure." Remember, however, that some emblems—such as the thumbs-up gesture—vary from one culture to another (it means "Good job!" in the United States, the number 1 in Germany, and the number 5 in Japan), and other nonverbal signs can be ambiguous even within a single culture. For example, a wink might mean something entirely different to the person on the receiving end than it does to the person winking.

## Complementing and Accenting

Whereas nonverbal emblems convey meaning independent of words, **illustrators** serve the functions of complementing and accenting verbal statements. Illustrators are behaviors that have no meaning of their own. Snapping your fingers, running your fingers through your hair, or pounding one fist into the other can accompany a positive statement in one instance and a negative one in others: The meaning of such gestures is specific to their context.

Emblems are used consciously; you roll your eyes and circle your finger around one ear to signal "He's crazy" in the United States (in

Argentina, it means you have a phone call). Illustrators are usually unconscious (Ekman et al., 1984). We rarely plan the smiles and frowns, sighs and laughs, and all the other nonverbal behaviors that so richly complement and accent our words. Social scientists use the term **affect displays** to describe these unintentional messages.

## Regulating

Nonverbal behaviors sometimes help control verbal interaction by regulating it. The best example of such regulation is the wide array of turn-taking signals in everyday conversation (see, for instance, Drummond & Hopper, 1993; Rosenfeld, 1987). Research has shown that three nonverbal signals indicate a speaker has finished talking and is ready to yield to a listener: (1) changes in vocal intonation—a rising or falling in pitch at the end of a clause; (2) a drawl on the last syllable or the stressed syllable in a clause; and (3) a drop in vocal pitch or loudness when speaking a common expression such as "you know." You can see how these regulators work by observing almost any conversation.

Eye contact is another way of regulating verbal communication. Lack of visual contact is one way to signal turn taking or even to exclude an unwanted person from a conversation. Speakers make surprisingly little eye contact during a conversation, but they commonly focus on another person when coming to the end of their turn. Children (and some socially insensitive adults) have not learned all the subtle signals of such turn taking. Through a rough series of trial and error (*very* rough in some homes), children finally learn how to "read" other people well enough to avoid interrupting behaviors.

## Contradicting

Nonverbal behavior can often *contradict* the spoken word. If you said "Go north about two blocks" and pointed south, your nonverbal message would be contradicting what you said.

Although sending such incongruous messages might sound foolish at first, there are times when we deliberately do just this. One deliberate use of *mixed messages* (as they're often called) is to send a message politely but clearly that might be difficult to handle if it were expressed in words. For instance, think of a time when you became bored with a conversation while your companion kept rambling on. At such a time the most straightforward statement would be, "I'm tired of talking to you and want to go meet someone else." Although it might feel good to be so direct, this kind of honesty is impolite for anyone over five years of age. Instead of being blunt in situations like this, a face-saving alternative is to express your disinterest nonverbally. While nodding politely and murmuring, "uh-huh" and "no kidding?" at the appropriate times, you can signal a desire to leave by looking around the room, turning slightly away from the speaker, or even making a point of yawning. In most cases such clues are enough to end the conversation without the awkwardness of expressing outright what's going on.

## FILM CLIP

### LEARNING A VISUAL VOCABULARY:
### *AT FIRST SIGHT*

Virgil Adamson (Val Kilmer) has been blind since he was three years old. He works as a massage therapist in a small resort town where Amy Benic (Mira Sorvino) stops for a visit. Despite his lack of sight, Virgil's other senses are strong and keen. He introduces Amy to touch she has never felt and sounds she has never heard—and soon they fall in love.

Amy learns of a surgical procedure that can restore Virgil's sight; he reluctantly agrees to undergo an operation. When the bandages are removed, he opens his eyes to a world that is confusing and terrifying (he cries, "There's something wrong—this can't be seeing!"). A therapist (Nathan Lane) explains that Virgil lacks a "visual vocabulary," which keeps him from making connections between the foreign things he sees, the familiar things he hears and touches, and the words that represent them.

The movie, based on a true story, illustrates how sighted people can take for granted their understanding of nonverbal messages. Virgil often asks Amy, "What does that face mean?" He is unfamiliar with the relational cues being sent in a coy smile, a pained grimace, or an embarrassed blush. Amy even has to teach Virgil when not to look, such as when he stares at a homeless person on the street. Ultimately, they both learn that assigning meaning to sensory information and nonverbal behavior is not a natural ability—it is a skill that must be learned and honed.

## Deceiving

Deception is perhaps the most interesting type of nonverbal communication, and one that social scientists have studied extensively. As Chapter 10 explains in detail, the vast majority of messages we exchange are not completely truthful. As you will read there, not all deception is self-serving or malicious: Much of it is aimed at saving the face of the communicators involved. For example, you might tell a "white lie" to avoid hurting the feelings of a friend who asks your opinion: "That new tattoo looks, uh, really nice." In a situation like this, it's easy to see how nonverbal factors can make the face-saving deception either succeed or fail.

Some people are better at hiding deceit than others. For example, most people—especially women—become more successful liars as they grow older (Buller & Burgoon, 1994). High self-

monitors are usually better at hiding their deception than communicators who are less self-aware (Burgoon et al., 1994), and raters judge highly expressive liars as more honest than those who are more subdued (Burgoon et al., 1995). Not surprisingly, people whose jobs require them to act differently than they feel, such as actors, lawyers, diplomats, and salespeople, are more successful at deception than the general population (Riggio & Friedman, 1983).

It's easiest to catch liars who haven't had a chance to rehearse, when they feel strongly about the information being hidden, or when they feel anxious or guilty about their lies (Andersen, 1999). Imagine, for example, that you want to decline an unwanted invitation with a face-saving lie. Your chances of getting away with the deception are best if you had advance notice of the invitation. If you are caught unprepared, your excuse for not attending is likely to be less persuasive. Trust (or lack of it) also plays a role in which deceptive messages are successful: People who are suspicious that a speaker may be lying pay closer attention to the speaker's nonverbal behavior (e.g., talking faster than normal, shifted posture) than people who are not suspicious (Millar & Millar, 1998). Table 6.2 outlines some conditions under which liars are likely to betray themselves nonverbally. See if they match your personal experience.

Decades of research have revealed that there are no surefire nonverbal clues that indicate deception. Nonetheless, there are some clues that may reveal less-than-totally-honest communication (Andersen, 1999). For example, deceivers typically make more speech errors than truth-tellers: stammers, stutters, hesitations, false starts, and so on. Vocal pitch often rises when people tell lies, and liars hesitate more (Rockwell et al., 1997). Deceivers tend to blink their eyes more often, fidget with their hands, shift their posture, and blink their eyes more rapidly. Despite clues like these, it's a mistake to assume that every tongue-tied, fidgeting, eye-blinking person is a liar.

How good are people at detecting lies? The range of effectiveness in uncovering deceptive messages is broad, ranging from 45 to 70 percent (Kalbfleisch, 1992). Age plays an important role: Children use a speaker's words to make sense of a message, while adults rely more on nonverbal clues to form impressions. Most studies show that women are consistently more accurate than men at detecting lying and what the underlying truth really is (McCornack & Parks, 1990). Despite their overall accuracy at detecting lies, however, women are more inclined to fall for the deception of intimate partners.

It isn't always easy to detect deception. Some research shows that people who probe the messages of deceptive communicators are no better at detecting lies than those who don't investigate the truth of a statement (DePaulo, 1994). One explanation for this surprising finding is that deceivers who are questioned become more vigilant about revealing the truth; their greater caution results in a better cover-up. Generally, the more time we spend around communicators who are less than totally honest, the better the chance that we will catch their deception (Burgoon et al., 1998). For example, you are likely to suspect that

**Table 6.2**

| Circumstances in Which a Deceiver Leaks Nonverbal Clues to Deception | |
|---|---|
| **Leakage Most Likely** | **Leakage Least Likely** |
| Wants to hide emotions being experienced at the moment | Wants to hide information unrelated to emotions |
| Feels strongly about the information being hidden | Has no strong feelings about the information being hidden |
| Feels apprehensive about the deception | Feels confident about the deception |
| Feels guilty about being deceptive | Experiences little guilt about the deception |
| Gets little enjoyment from being deceptive | Enjoys the deception |
| Needs to construct the message carefully while delivering it | Knows the deceptive message well and has rehearsed it |

Based on material from: Ekman, P. (1981). Mistakes when deceiving. In T. A. Sebeok & R. Rosenthal (Eds.), *The Clever Hans phenomenon: Communication with horses, whales, apes, and people* (pp. 269–278). New York: New York Academy of Sciences, 1981.

something unusual is happening when a normally quiet person starts chattering, or when a talkative one suddenly turns quiet.

There is one exception to the rule that familiarity helps us become better lie detectors: Intimate partners aren't very good at recognizing one another's lies (Kalbfleisch, 1992). Perhaps an element of wishful thinking interferes with our accurate decoding of these messages. After all, we would hate to think that a lover would lie to us. When intimates *do* become suspicious, however, their ability to recognize deception increases (McCornack & Levine, 1990).

# Types of Nonverbal Communication

So far, we've talked about the characteristics of nonverbal communication and the ways unspoken messages relate to our use of words. Now it's time to look at the many types of nonverbal communication.

## Face and Eyes

The face and eyes are probably the most noticeable parts of the body. However, the nonverbal messages from the face and eyes are not the easiest to read (Carroll & Russell, 1996). The face is a tremendously complicated channel of expression to interpret, for several reasons.

First, it's hard to describe the number and kind of expressions commonly produced by the face and eyes. For example, researchers have found that there are at least eight distinguishable positions of the eyebrows and forehead, eight more of the eyes and lids, and ten for the lower face (Ekman & Friesen, 1974a, 1975). When you multiply this complexity by the number of emotions we experience, you can see why it would be almost impossible to compile a dictionary of facial expressions and their corresponding emotions.

The eyes themselves can send several kinds of messages. Gazes and glances are usually sig-

nals of the looker's interest. However, the *type* of interest can vary. Sometimes, as mentioned earlier, looking is a conversational turn-taking signal that says "I'm finished talking. Now it's your turn." Gazing also is a good indicator of liking (Druckmann et al., 1982). Sometimes, eye contact *reflects* liking that already exists, and at other times it actually creates or *increases* liking—hence the expression "making eyes." In other situations, eye contact indicates interest, but not attraction or approval. A teacher who glares at a rowdy student or a police officer who "keeps an eye on" a suspect is both signaling interest with his or her eyes.

In addition to influencing verbal responses, research by Stephen Davis and Jamie Kieffer (1998) details at least one effect of eye contact on an important nonverbal behavior: tipping. They found that customers in both small towns and urban areas leave larger tips when their servers (whether male or female) maintain eye contact with them. The authors speculate that good eye contact makes the atmosphere of the restaurant friendlier, and makes the customers feel as if they are dining at home.

"I knew the suspect was lying because of certain telltale discrepancies between his voice and non verbal gestures. Also his pants were on fire."

## Body Movement

Another way we communicate nonverbally is through the physical movement of our bodies: our posture, gestures, physical orientation to others, and so on. Social scientists use the term **kinesics** to describe the study of how people communicate through bodily movements.

To appreciate the communicative value of kinesic messages, stop reading for a moment and notice how you're sitting. What does your position say nonverbally about how you feel? Are there any other people near you now? What messages do you get from their present posture? By paying attention to the postures of those around you, as well as to your own, you'll find another channel of nonverbal communication that reveals how people feel about themselves and others.

The English language indicates the deep links between posture and communication. English is full of expressions that tie emotional states with body postures:

> "I won't take this lying down!"
> "He can't stand on his own two feet."
> "She has to carry a heavy burden."
> "Take a load off your back."
> "You're all wrapped up in yourself."
> "Don't be so uptight!"

Such phrases show an awareness of posture, even if it's often unconscious. The main reason we miss most posture messages is that they aren't too obvious. It's seldom that people who feel weighed down by a problem hunch over dramatically. When we're bored, we usually don't lean back and slump enough to embarrass the person with whom we're bored. In interpreting posture, then, the key is to look for small changes that might be shadows of the way people feel.

Gestures are a fundamental element of communication—so fundamental, in fact, that people who have been blind from birth use them (Iverson, 1999; Iverson & Goldin-Meadow, 1997). Gestures are sometimes intentional—for example, a cheery wave or thumbs up. In other cases, however, our gestures are unconscious. Occasionally an unconscious gesture will consist of an unambiguous emblem, such as a shrug that clearly means "I don't

"I've had eye contact with women before, Marcia—
but never like this."

know." More often, however, there are several possible interpretations to gestures (Krauss et al., 1991). A group of ambiguous gestures consists of what we usually call *fidgeting*— movements in which one part of the body grooms, massages, rubs, holds, fidgets, pinches, picks, or otherwise manipulates another part. Social scientists call these behaviors **manipulators**. Social rules may discourage us from performing more manipulators in public, but people still do so without noticing.

Research reveals what common sense suggests—that an increased use of manipulators is often a sign of discomfort (Ekman & Friesen, 1974b). But not *all* fidgeting signals uneasiness. People also are likely to use manipulators when relaxed. When they let their guard down (either alone or with friends), they will be more likely to fiddle with an earlobe, twirl a strand of hair, or clean their fingernails. Whether or not the fidgeting person is hiding something, observers are likely to interpret manipulators as a signal of dishonesty. Since not all people who fidget are liars, it's important not to jump to conclusions about the meaning of a person's use of manipulators.

The amount of gesturing can be a measure of power and status (Andersen, 1999). Pointing, for example, is judged by observers as one indicator of power, since it implies at least some ability to order other people around. People who gesture more are rated by observers as being in positions of control and power, whereas those who gesture less are judged by observers as being subordinate.

Gestures can produce a wide range of reactions in receivers (Druckmann et al., 1982). In many situations, the right kinds of gestures can increase persuasiveness. Increasing hand and arm movements, leaning forward, fidgeting less, and keeping limbs open all make a speaker more effective at influencing others (Leathers, 1992). Even more interesting is the fact that persuasiveness increases when one person mirrors another's movements. When persuader and audience are reasonably similar, reciprocating the other person's gestures has a positive effect, whereas acting in a contrary manner is likely to have the opposite result.

People who gesture appropriately often create impressions that differ from those of less-expressive

spontaneously delivering and to consider how they reflect the attitudes you already feel. Impression management has its uses, but it is a tricky process.

## Touch

Contemporary research confirms the value of touch for infants (Whitman et al., 1999). Studies at the University of Miami's School of Medicine, for example, have shown that premature babies grow faster and gain more weight when massaged (Adler, 1993). The same institute's researchers demonstrated that massage can help premature children gain weight, make colicky children sleep better, and boost the immune function of cancer and HIV patients. Massage helps newborn babies thrive, and it also helps depressed mothers of newborns feel better and smooth the delivery process (Mwakalyelye & DeAngelis, 1995). Research shows that touch between therapists and clients has the potential to encourage a variety of beneficial changes: more self-disclosure, client self-acceptance, and better client-therapist relationships (Driscoll et al., 1988). In addition, patients with dementia who were administered

people: They are rated as being more warm, casual, agreeable, and energetic. They also are viewed as more enthusiastic, considerate, approachable, and likable. On the other hand, less-expressive people are viewed as more logical, cold, and analytic. Not only are they less persuasive, they are also viewed as less likable in general.

As with almost any nonverbal behavior, the context in which gestures occur makes all the difference in the results they produce. Animated movements that are well received in a cooperative social setting may seem like signals of aggression or attempts at domination in a more competitive setting. Fidgeting that might suggest deviousness in a bargaining session could be appropriate when you offer a nervous apology in a personal situation. In any case, trying to manufacture insincere, artificial gestures (or any other nonverbal behaviors) will probably backfire. A more useful goal is to recognize the behaviors you find yourself hand massage on each hand, along with intermittent gentle touch on the arm and shoulder and calm soothing speech, decreased their anxiety and dysfunctional behavior (Kim & Buschmann, 1999).

Touch also plays a large part in how we respond to others. For instance, in a laboratory task, subjects evaluated partners more positively when they were touched (appropriately, of course) by them (Burgoon et al., 1992). Besides increasing liking, touch also boosts compliance. In a study by Chris Kleinke (1977), subjects were approached by a female confederate who requested that they return a dime left in the phone booth from which they had just emerged. When the request was accompanied by a light touch on the subject's arm, the probability that the subject would return the dime increased significantly. In a similar experiment (Willis & Hamm, 1980), subjects were asked by a male or female confederate to sign a petition or complete a rating scale. Again, subjects were more likely to cooperate when they were touched lightly on the arm. In the rating-scale variation of the study, the results were especially dramatic: 70 percent of those who were touched complied, whereas only 40 percent of the untouched subjects were willing to cooperate (indicating a predisposition not to comply).

An additional power of touch is its on-the-job utility. One study showed that fleeting touches on the hand and shoulder resulted in larger tips for restaurant waiters (Crusco & Wetzel, 1984). Perhaps this research is what led the Waiters Association in 1996 to advise its members to touch diners briefly when presenting the bill or returning change ("Tipping Tips," 1996). And the latest wrinkle to this research on touch in restaurants indicates that both women and men in taverns, whether in same-sex or different-sex dyads, increase their alcohol consumption when touched by the waitress (Kaufman & Mahoney, 1999).

In contemporary society, unwanted touching is cause for concern, and even legal action. In the United States, touching is generally more appropriate for women than for men (Derlega et

## REFLECTION

### CULTURE SHAPES FAMILY COMMUNICATION

My mother's side of the family is from Sicily, and they fit the Italian cultural mode perfectly. They are very emotional and expressive. My dad's side of the family is British. They are reserved, polite, and nonaggressive. You can imagine what happens when both sides of the family get together, which (thank goodness) isn't very often. My mom's relatives yell and gesture almost constantly. My dad's parents sit quietly, looking frightened and uncomfortable. Everybody knows that the different communication styles come from their backgrounds, but that doesn't make it any less weird.

al., 1989; Jones, 1986). Males touch their male friends less than they touch their female friends, and also less than females touch their female friends. Although women are generally more comfortable about touching than men, sex isn't the only factor that shapes contact. In general, the degree of touch comfort goes along with openness to expressing intimate feelings, an active interpersonal style, and satisfactory relationships (Fromme et al., 1989).

The amount of touching usually decreases with age (Knapp & Hall, 1997). Sixth graders touch each other less than do first graders. Parents touch their older children less often than their younger ones. As young children, most North Americans receive at least a modest amount of physical contact from their parents. The next time most can expect to receive this level of physical caring won't come until they have chosen a partner. Even then, the nurturing seemingly brought by physical contact will most often come only from that partner—a heavy demand for one person to carry.

## Voice

Social scientists use the term **paralanguage** to describe the way a message is spoken. Vocal rate, pitch, tone, volume, and so on can give the same word or words many meanings. For example, note how many meanings come from a single sentence just by shifting the emphasis from one word to another:

*This* is a fantastic communication book.
(Not just any book, but *this* one in particular.)

This is a *fantastic* communication book.
(This book is superior, exciting.)

This is a fantastic *communication* book.
(The book is good as far as communication goes; it may not be so great as literature or as drama.)

This is a fantastic communication *book.*
(It's not a play or record; it's a book.)

There are many other ways our voice communicates—through its tone, speed, pitch, volume, number and length of pauses, and **disfluencies** (such as stammering and use of "uh," "um," and "er"). All these factors can do a great deal to reinforce or contradict the message that words convey.

The impact of paralinguistic cues is strong. In fact, listeners pay more attention to paralanguage than to the content of the words when asked to determine a speaker's attitudes (Burns & Beier, 1973). Furthermore, when vocal factors contradict a verbal message (as when a speaker shouts "I am *not* angry!"), listeners judge the speaker's intention from the paralanguage, not the words themselves (Mehrabian & Weiner, 1967). Vocal changes that contradict spoken words are not easy to conceal. If the speaker is trying to hide fear or anger, the voice will probably sound higher and louder, and the rate of talk may be faster than normal. Sadness produces the opposite vocal pattern: quieter, lower-pitched speech delivered at a slower rate (Ekman, 1985).

Paralanguage can affect behavior in many ways, some of which are rather surprising. Studies by

David Buller and Kelly Aune (1988, 1992) revealed that communicators are most likely to comply with requests delivered by speakers whose rate was similar to their own. However, speaking rate isn't constant. For example, it changes when a speaker's first message doesn't seem to get the desired results. Charles Berger and Patrick diBattista (1993) discovered that when communicators gave directions that weren't followed, the wording of their second attempts didn't change significantly. Instead, they simply slowed down and spoke louder.

Sarcasm is one approach in which we use both emphasis and tone of voice to change a statement's meaning to the opposite of its verbal message. Experience this reversal yourself with the following three statements. First say them literally, and then say them sarcastically.

**Figure 6.1** A Comparison of the Ideal Speaker's Voice Types in Mexico and the United States

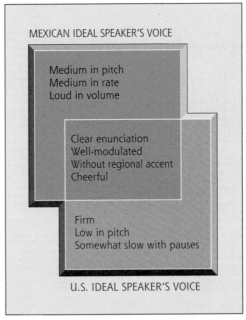

Reproduced from page 62 of: Valentine, C. A. and Saint Damian, B. (1988). Communicative power: Gender and culture as determinants of the ideal voice. In C. A. Valentine and N. Hoar (Eds.), *Women and communicative power: theory, research, and practice.* Annandale, VA: Speech Communication Association.

1. "You look terrific!"
2. "I really had a wonderful time on my blind date."
3. "There's nothing I like better than calves' brains on toast."

As with other nonverbal messages, people often ignore or misinterpret the vocal nuances of sarcasm. Members of certain groups—children, people with weak intellectual skills, and poor listeners—are more likely to misunderstand sarcastic messages than are others (Andersen, 1992).

Communication through paralanguage isn't always intentional. Our voices often give us away when we're trying to create an impression different from our actual feelings. For example, you've probably had the experience of trying to sound calm and serene when you were really seething with inner nervousness. Maybe your deception went along perfectly for a while—just the right smile, no telltale fidgeting of the hands, posture appearing relaxed—and then, without being able to do a thing about it, right in the middle of your relaxed comments, your voice squeaked! The charade was over.

In addition to reinforcing or contradicting messages, some vocal factors influence the way a speaker is perceived by others. People who speak more slowly are judged as having greater conversational control than fast talkers (Tusing & Dillard, 2000). Communicators with more attractive voices are rated more highly than those whose speech sounds less attractive (Francis & Wales 1994; Zuckerman & Driver, 1989). Just what makes a voice attractive can vary. As Figure 6.1 shows, culture can make a difference. Surveys indicate that there are both similarities and differences between what Mexicans and U.S. citizens view as the "ideal" voice. Howard Giles and his associates (1992) found that age combines with accent to form preferences by listeners. Older-sounding communicators whose language was accent-free were rated as most competent, while older-sounding speech by people who did not speak in a culturally standard way was judged least competent.

## Proxemics and Territoriality

**Proxemics** is the study of how people use the space around them. Each of us carries around a sort of invisible bubble of **personal space** wherever we go. We think of the area inside this bubble as our own—almost as much a part of us as our own bodies. Our personal bubbles vary in size according to the culture in which we were raised, the person we're with, and the situation. It's precisely the varying size of our personal space—the distance we put between ourselves and others—that gives a nonverbal clue to our feelings.

D. Russell Crane (1987) and other researchers tested over one hundred married couples, asking partners to walk toward one another and stop when they reached a "comfortable conversational distance." Then they gave each partner a battery of tests to measure their marital intimacy, desire for change, and potential for divorce. The researchers discovered that there was a strong relationship between distance and marital happiness. The average space between distressed couples was about 25 percent greater than that between satisfied partners. On average, the happy couples stood 11.4 inches apart, while the distance between unhappy spouses averaged 14.8 inches.

## REFLECTION

### ASYMMETRICAL SPATIAL BUBBLES

Over vacation I stayed in a high-rise San Francisco hotel where I spent a lot of time in crowded elevators. Being jammed in with total strangers made me realize that being inches away from someone, or even making body contact, isn't always an invasion of intimate space. As long as the crowded elevator forced us to stand very close and everybody was facing in one direction, the proximity didn't feel intimate at all. Of course, if any of the elevator riders had turned around and stood face to face with a stranger, the whole situation would have been very different!

In another study, Mark Snyder (1980) reported that the distance subjects unconsciously placed between themselves and others was a good indication of their prejudices. All the subjects were polled on their attitudes about homosexuality. Half the interviewers, who were confederates of the experimenter, wore "Gay and Proud" buttons and mentioned their membership in the Association of Gay Psychologists. The other interviewers wore no buttons and simply identified themselves as graduate students. Despite their expressions of tolerance, subjects seated themselves almost a foot farther away from the apparently gay interviewers of the same sex.

Preferred spaces are largely a matter of cultural norms. For example, people living in hyper-dense Hong Kong manage to live in crowded residential quarters that most North Americans would find intolerable (Chan, 1999).

Anthropologist Edward T. Hall (1969) has defined four distances that North American communicators use in everyday interaction. He says that we choose a particular one depending upon how we feel toward others at a given time and that by "reading" which distance people select, we can get some insight into their feelings.

**Intimate Distance**   The first of Hall's zones begins with skin contact and ranges out to about eighteen inches. We usually use **intimate distance** with people who are emotionally close to us, and then mostly in private situations—making love, caressing, comforting, protecting. By allowing people to move into our intimate distance, we let them enter our personal space. When we let them in voluntarily, it's usually a sign of trust: We've willingly lowered our defenses. On the other hand, when someone invades this most personal area without our consent, we usually feel threatened.

**Personal Distance**   The second spatial zone, **personal distance**, ranges from eighteen inches at its closest point to four feet at its farthest. Its closer phase is the distance at which most couples stand in public. If someone thought to be sexually attractive stands this near one partner at a party, the other partner is likely to become alert. This "moving in" often is taken to mean that something more than casual conversation is taking place. The far range of personal distance runs from about two and a half to four feet. It's the zone just beyond the other person's reach. As Hall puts it, at this distance we can keep someone "at arm's length." His choice of words suggests the type of communication that goes on at this range: The contacts are still reasonably close, but they're much less personal than the ones that occur a foot or so closer.

Test this zone for yourself. Start a conversation with someone at a distance of about three feet, and slowly move a foot or so closer. Do you notice a difference? Does this distance affect your conversation?

**Social Distance**   The third zone is **social distance**. It ranges from four to about twelve feet out. Within it are the kinds of communication that usually occur in business situations. Its closer phase, from four to seven feet, is the distance at which conver-

sations usually occur between salespeople and customers or between people who work together. Most people feel uncomfortable when a salesclerk comes as close as three feet, whereas four or five feet nonverbally signals "I'm here to help you, but I don't mean to be too personal or pushy."

We use the far range of social distance—seven to twelve feet—for more focal and impersonal situations. At this range we sit across the desk from our boss (or other authority figures). Sitting at this distance signals a far different and less relaxed type of conversation than if we were to pull a chair around to the boss's side of the desk and sit just three feet away.

Choosing the optimal distance can have a powerful effect on how we regard and respond to others. For example, students are more satisfied with teachers who reduce (at appropriate levels, of course) the distance between themselves and their classes. They also are more satisfied with the course itself and are more likely to follow the teacher's instructions (Hackman & Walker, 1990). Likewise, medical patients are more satisfied with physicians who are not standoffish (Conlee et al., 1993; Grant et al., 2000).

**Public Distance**  **Public distance** is Hall's term for the farthest zone, running outward from twelve feet. The closer range of public distance is the one that most teachers use in the classroom. In the farther reaches of public space—twenty-five feet and beyond—two-way communication is almost impossible. In some cases it's necessary for speakers to use public distance to reach a large audience, but we can assume that anyone who chooses to use it when more closeness is possible is not interested in a dialogue.

When our spatial bubble is invaded, we respond with what are called *barrier behaviors,* strategies designed to create a barrier (or fix a broken one) between ourselves and other people. Invade someone's personal space, and notice the reaction. At first the person is most likely simply to back away, probably without realizing what is happening. Next your partner might attempt to put an object between you, such as a desk, a chair, or some books clutched to the chest, all in an effort to get some separation. Then the other person will probably decrease eye contact (the "elevator syndrome," in which we can crowd in and even touch one another so long as we avoid eye contact). Furthermore, your reluctant partner might sneeze, cough, scratch, and exhibit any variety of behaviors to discourage your antisocial behavior. In the end, if none of these behaviors achieves the desired goal of getting some space between the two of you, the other person might leave or "counterattack," gently at first ("Move back, will you?"), then more forcefully (probably with a shove).

While personal space is the invisible bubble we carry around, the area that serves as an extension of our physical being, **territory** remains stationary. Any geographical area such as a room, house, neighborhood, or country to which we assume some kind of "rights" is our territory. What's interesting about territoriality is that there is no real basis for the assumption of proprietary rights, of "owning" some area, but the feeling of ownership exists nonetheless. My room in my house is *my room* whether I'm there or not (unlike my personal space, which is carried around with me), and it's my room because I say it's my room. Although I could probably make a case for my room *really being* my room (as opposed to belonging to another family member or to the mortgage holder), what about the desk I sit at in class? I feel the same about the desk. It's *my desk,* even though it's certain that the desk is owned by the school and is in no way really mine.

Generally, we grant people with higher status more personal territory and greater privacy. We knock before entering our supervisor's office, whereas the supervisor can usually walk into our work area without hesitating. In traditional schools, professors have offices, dining rooms, and even toilets that are private, whereas the students, who are presumably less important, have no such sanctuaries. In the military, greater space and privacy usually come with rank: Privates sleep forty to a barracks, sergeants have their own private rooms, and generals have government-provided houses.

## Time

Social scientists use the term **chronemics** to describe the study of how humans use and structure time. The way we handle time can express both intentional and unintentional messages. Social psychologist Robert Levine (1988; Levine & Norenzayan, 1999) describes several ways that time can communicate. For instance, in cultures like those of the United States, Canada, and northern Europe, which value time highly, waiting can be an indicator of status. "Important" people (whose time is supposedly more valuable than others) may be seen by appointment only, while it is acceptable to intrude without notice on lesser beings. To see how this rule operates, consider how natural it is for a boss to drop into a subordinate's office unannounced, while the employee would never intrude into the boss's office without an appointment. A related rule is that low-status people must never make more-important people wait. It would be a serious mistake to show up late for a job interview, although the interviewer might keep you cooling your heels in the lobby. Important people are often whisked to the head of a restaurant or airport line, while presumably less-exalted ones are forced to wait their turn.

The use of time depends greatly on culture. In some cultures, punctuality is critically important, while in others it is barely considered (Levine & Norenzayan, 1999). Punctual mainlanders often

## FOCUS ON RESEARCH

### IT'S ABOUT TIME: THE SIGNIFICANCE OF DATE STAMPING IN E-MAIL MESSAGES

What is the primary difference between face-to-face communication and e-mail? Many people would say that computer communication eliminates the nonverbal cues that are present in face-to-face interaction. Joseph Walther and Lisa Tidwell don't buy this distinction. They note that e-mail messages can convey a variety of nonverbal signals through emoticons, capitalized letters ("I need it NOW"), or linguistic disclosures ("I'm blushing"). They also studied a nonverbal cue that some may have overlooked: The time-date stamp in the header of e-mail messages. Walther and Tidwell believe these chronemic markers affect perceptions in computer-mediated communication, just as the use of time affects face-to-face interaction.

Walther and Tidwell surveyed 160 regular e-mail users from a variety of organizations. The respondents were sent four different versions of a fictional e-mail exchange between

Ted Parks (identified as a vice president in a large manufacturing firm) and Sheila Smith (identified as an assistant manager in the accounts payable department of the same company). The primary differences in the four versions were (1) The content of the messages (either social or task-oriented) and (2) The time-date header of Ted's message and Sheila's reply. The header on Ted's message was either 9:58 A.M. (i.e., during business hours) or 9:58 P.M. (i.e., after hours). Sheila's reply was stamped at either 10:04 A.M. the same day (a near-immediate reply) or 10:04 A.M. the following day (a twenty-four-hour delay). An attached questionnaire allowed the researchers to determine the respondents' perceptions of dominance and intimacy in the e-mail exchanges.

As expected, the social messages were regarded as more intimate than the task messages. Their degree of perceived intimacy, however, was affected by when the message was

sent and how quickly a reply was issued. For instance, task messages sent at night were regarded as non-intimate; if they got an immediate reply, they were also regarded as highly dominant. Slow replies generally made the sender seem less influential but the relationship more intimate (suggesting that people in intimate relationships can "get away" with delayed responses, while strangers and nonintimates cannot). Social exchanges after-hours suggested greater relational equality; greater dominance by the sender was associated with "talking shop" in the evening.

The authors were quick to point out that the study did not account for differences related to sex and power (Ted and Sheila never switched roles). While these variables need to be addressed in future research, the current study clearly shows that computer-mediated communication does contain nonverbal cues.

Walther, J. B., & Tidwell, L. C. (1995). Nonverbal cues in computer-mediated communication, and the effect of chronemics on relational communication. *Journal of Organizational Computing, 5,* 355–378.

report welcoming the laid-back Hawaiian approach to time. One psychologist discovered the difference between North and South American attitudes when teaching at a university in Brazil (Levine, 1988). He found that some students arrived halfway through a two-hour class and that most of them stayed put and kept asking questions when the class was scheduled to end. A half hour after the official end of the period, the professor finally closed off discussion, since there was no indication that the students intended to leave. This flexibility of time is quite different from what is common in most North American colleges and universities!

Even within a culture, rules of time vary. Sometimes the differences are geographic. In New York City, the party invitation may say 9:00 P.M., but nobody would think of showing up before 10:30 P.M. In Salt Lake City, guests are expected to show up on time, or perhaps even a bit early. Even within the same geographic area, different groups establish their own rules about the use of time. Consider your own experience. In school, some instructors begin and end class punctually, while others are more casual. With some people, you feel comfortable talking for hours in person or on the phone, while with others time seems precious and not to be "wasted."

## Physical Attractiveness

The importance of beauty has been emphasized in the arts for centuries. More recently, social scientists have begun to measure the degree to which physical attractiveness affects interaction between people. Recent findings, summarized by Knapp and Hall (1997), indicate that women who are perceived as attractive have more dates, receive higher grades in college, persuade males with greater ease, and receive lighter court sentences. Both men and women whom others view as attractive are rated as being more sensitive, kind, strong, sociable, and interesting than their less-fortunate brothers and sisters. Who is most likely to succeed in business? Place your bet on the attractive job applicant. Attractiveness is at least partly in the mind of the beholder. Some evidence suggests that, as we get to know more about people and like them, we start to regard them as better looking (Bazil, 1999).

The influence of attractiveness begins early in life. For example, preschoolers were shown photographs of children their own age and asked to choose potential friends and enemies. The researchers found that children as young as three agreed as to who was attractive ("cute") and unat-

tractive ("homely"). Furthermore, they valued their attractive counterparts—both of the same and the opposite sex—more highly. Also, preschool children rated by their peers as pretty were most liked, and those identified as least pretty were least liked. Children who were interviewed rated good-looking children as having positive social characteristics ("He's friendly to other children") and unattractive children negatively ("He hits other children without reason").

Teachers also are affected by students' attractiveness. Vicki Ritts and her colleagues (1992) found that physically attractive students are usually judged more favorably—more intelligent, friendly, popular. Even the parents of attractive students benefit from their childrens' good looks: They are judged by strangers as caring more about education than are parents of less attractive youngsters.

Fortunately, attractiveness is something we can control without having to call the plastic surgeon.

We view others as beautiful or ugly, not just on the basis of the "original equipment" they come with, but also on *how they use that equipment.* Posture, gestures, facial expressions, and other behaviors can increase the attractiveness of an otherwise unremarkable person. Exercise can improve the way each of us looks. Finally, the way we dress can make a significant difference in the way others perceive us, as you'll now see.

## Clothing

Besides protecting us from the elements, clothing is a means of nonverbal communication. One writer has suggested that clothing conveys at least ten types of messages to others (Thourlby, 1978):

1. economic level
2. educational level
3. trustworthiness
4. social position
5. level of sophistication
6. economic background
7. social background
8. educational background
9. level of success
10. moral character

Research shows that we do make assumptions about people based on their style of clothing. For example, the way people are dressed affects judg-

### REFLECTION

#### CLOTHING AND CUSTOMER SERVICE

I always have thought that people judged one another by their clothing, but I never thought about how this rule applied to me until I tried an experiment. One day I went to a local department store dressed in a pair of jeans, a T-shirt, and tennis shoes. Not one salesperson asked me if I needed help. The next day I went back to the same store wearing the clothes I wear at work in a law office. This time, I got attention from every single associate in the store. I was the same person, but I might as well have been two different people to the staff.

ments of their credibility. In one experiment, college students judged victims of sexual harassment differently depending on their attire. Victims dressed in black were rated as less honest and more aggressive than those dressed in light colors (Vrij & Akehurst, 1999). In another study, a man and a woman were stationed in a hallway so that anyone who wished to go by had to avoid them or pass between them. In one condition the conversationalists wore

## FOCUS ON RESEARCH

### DRESSING FOR SUCCESS: STUDENT RESPONSES TO TEACHERS' ATTIRE

Most people would agree that how an instructor dresses shouldn't have much to do with his or her effectiveness as a teacher. Despite this fact, two studies suggest that the clothing worn by graduate teaching assistants (GTAs) makes a difference in how students perceive and respond to them.

Tracy Morris and her colleagues wanted to know if GTAs, who are sometimes only a few years older than the undergrads they teach, would be perceived differently depending on the apparel they wore. The researchers had GTAs dress in three different styles: professional (business suits), casual professional (sweaters/slacks/skirts), or casual (jeans/T-shirts). They found that student perceptions of the GTA's expertise decreased as attire became more casual. On the other hand, the GTAs who dressed casually were seen as more interesting, extroverted, and sociable than those who dressed more formally.

In a later study, K. David Roach asked 355 undergraduates to complete surveys about their GTAs' clothing. The students also answered questions about their perceptions of their GTAs, what they learned from their courses, and their own classroom behavior. Results showed positive correlations between the formality of GTAs' clothing and the ratings students gave them. Students also reported that they behaved better and learned more in classes where GTAs dressed professionally.

The results suggest some clothing strategies for graduate teaching assistants. If appearing competent and maintaining order are the primary goals, more formal attire might be a good idea. If being perceived as outgoing and sociable is important, casual clothing might help the cause. It's also possible that mixing and matching attire according to the educational goals of the session might be the best approach of all.

Morris, T. L., Gorham, J., Cohen, S. H., & Huffman, D. (1996). Fashion in the classroom: Effects of attire on student perceptions of instructors of college classes. *Communication Education, 45,* 135–48; Roach, K. D. (1997). Effects of graduate teaching assistant attire on student learning, misbehaviors, and ratings of instruction. *Communication Quarterly, 45,* 125–141.

"formal daytime dress"; in the other, they wore "casual attire." Passersby behaved differently toward the couple, depending on the style of clothing: They responded positively to the well-dressed couple and negatively when the same people were casually dressed (Fortenberry et al., 1978). Similar results in other situations show the influence of clothing. We are more likely to obey people dressed in high-status attire. Pedestrians were more likely to return lost coins to well-dressed people than to those dressed in low-status clothing (Bickman, 1974). We are also more likely to follow the lead of high-status dressers, even when it comes to violating social rules. Eighty-three percent of the pedestrians in one study followed a well-dressed jaywalker who violated a "wait" crossing signal, whereas only forty-eight percent followed a confederate dressed in lower-status clothing (Lefkowitz et al., 1955).

Communicators who wear special clothing often gain persuasiveness (Lawrence & Watson, 1991). For example, experimenters dressed in uniforms resembling police officers were more successful than those dressed in civilian clothing in requesting pedestrians to pick up litter and in persuading them to lend a dime to an overparked motorist (Bickman, 1974). The Focus on Research on page 180 provides other examples of how attire can affect attitudes.

Despite the frequency of our clothing-based assumptions, they aren't always accurate. The stranger wearing wrinkled, ill-fitting clothes might be a worker on vacation, a normally stylish person on the way to clean a fireplace, or even an eccentric millionaire. As we get to know others better, the importance of clothing shrinks (Hoult, 1954), which suggests that clothing is especially important in the early stages of a relationship, when making a positive first impression is necessary in order to encourage others to get to know us better. This advice is equally important in personal situations and in employment interviews. In both cases, your style of dress (and personal grooming) can make all the difference between the chance to progress and outright rejection.

One setting in which dress is significant is in employment interviews (Kwon & Johnson, 1999). Janelle Johnson conducted a 1981 study in which thirty-eight personnel representatives involved in recruiting and interviewing in the Southwest were asked several questions about their attitudes toward applicants' appearance. One question was, "What is the most predominant factor influencing your initial impression of interviewees?" Choices were physical attractiveness, résumé, appearance (dress), and manners. The majority of respondents (45 percent) indicated appearance as the most influential factor (followed by résumé with 33 percent and the other two items with 11 percent each).

Another question Johnson's study asked was how the first impression created by the applicant affected the rest of the interview. Choices were not at all, not significantly, somewhat significantly, significantly, or the most important factor affecting the rest of the interview. The majority of respondents indicated that their first impression

## REFLECTION

### SIDE-BY-SIDE VS. HEAD-TO-HEAD

After three years in college I've met with plenty of professors during their office hours to discuss papers and exams. I have noticed that some of them sit behind their desks, so that we discuss my work across a barrier. Other professors will set up their offices or move their chairs so that we sit next to one another while looking at the work.

The two layouts seem to make a difference. Having that barrier between us leaves me feeling like conferences are more adversarial than collaborative, and I definitely feel like there's a greater power difference in this setup. I don't know whether the furniture layout causes my feelings or whether professors who want to exert more power choose to set up their offices in a way that reflects their attitudes. Either way, I've come to think that the significance of office design goes beyond aesthetics.

affected the rest of the interview either somewhat (42 percent) or significantly (37 percent).

## Environment

We conclude our look at nonverbal communication by examining how physical settings, architecture, and interior design affect communication. Begin by recalling the different homes you've visited lately. Were some of these homes more comfortable to be in than others? Certainly a lot of your feelings were shaped by the people you were with, but there are some houses in which it seems impossible to relax, no matter how friendly the hosts. We've spent what seemed like endless evenings in what Knapp and

Hall (1997) call "unliving rooms," where the spotless ashtrays, furniture coverings, and plastic lamp covers seemed to send nonverbal messages telling us not to touch anything, not to put our feet up, and not to be comfortable. People who live in such houses probably wonder why nobody ever seems to relax and enjoy themselves at their parties. One thing is quite certain: They don't understand that the environment they have created can communicate discomfort to their guests.

The impressions that home designs communicate can be remarkably accurate. Edward Sadalla (1987) showed ninety-nine students slides of the insides or outsides of twelve upper-middle-class homes and then asked them to infer the personality of the owners from their impressions. The students were especially accurate after glancing at interior photos. The decorating schemes communicated accurate information about the home owners' intellectualism, politeness, maturity, optimism, tenseness, willingness to take adventures, family orientations, and reservedness. The home exteriors also gave viewers accurate perceptions of the owners' artistic interests, graciousness, privacy, and quietness.

Besides communicating information about the designer, an environment can also shape the kind of interaction that takes place in it. In one experiment, subjects working in a "beautiful" room were more positive and energetic than those working in "average" or "ugly" spaces (Maslow & Mintz, 1956). Inner-city adults and children who have access to landscaped public spaces interact in ways that are much more pro-social than do those who have to interact in more barren environments (Taylor et al., 1998). Students saw professors who occupied well-decorated offices as being more credible than those occupying less attractive work areas (Teven & Comadena, 1996). Physicians have shaped environments to improve the quality of interaction with their patients. According to environmental psychologist Robert Sommer (1969), simply removing a doctor's desk made patients feel almost five times more at ease during office

visits. Sommer also found that redesigning a convalescent ward of a hospital greatly increased the interaction between patients. In the old design, seats were placed shoulder to shoulder around the edges of the ward. By grouping the chairs around small tables so that patients faced each other at a comfortable distance, the amount of conversations doubled.

Even the design of an entire building can shape communication among its users. Architects have learned that the way housing projects are designed controls to a great extent the contact neighbors have with each other. People who live in apartments near stairways and mailboxes have many more neighbor contacts than do those living in less heavily traveled parts of the building, and tenants generally have more contacts with immediate neighbors than with people even a few doors away. Architects now use this information to design buildings that either encourage communication or increase privacy, and house hunters can use the same knowledge to choose a home that gives them the neighborhood relationships they want.

So far, we've talked about how designing an environment can shape communication, but there's another side to consider: Watching how people use an already existing environment can be a way of telling what kind of relationships they pursue. For example, Sommer watched students in a college library and found that there's a definite pattern for people who want to study alone. While the library was uncrowded, students almost always chose corner seats at one of the empty rectangular tables. After each table was occupied by one reader, new readers would choose a seat on the opposite side and at the far end, thus keeping the maximum distance between themselves and the other readers. One of Sommer's associates tried violating these "rules" by sitting next to and across from other female readers when more-distant seats were available. She found that the approached women reacted defensively, signaling their discomfort through shifts in posture, gesturing, or moving away.

# Summary

Nonverbal communication consists of messages expressed by nonlinguistic means such as distance, touch, body posture and orientation, expressions of the face and eyes, movement, time, vocal characteristics, clothing, and physical environment.

Nonverbal communication is pervasive; in fact, nonverbal messages are always available as a source of information about others. Most nonverbal behavior suggests messages about attitudes and feelings, in contrast to verbal statements, which are better suited to expressing ideas. While many nonverbal behaviors are universal, their use and significance vary from one culture to another. Nonverbal communication serves many functions. It can repeat, substitute for, complement, accent, regulate, and contradict verbal messages. Nonverbal communication can also be used as a tool to enhance the success of deceptive verbal messages.

Nonverbal messages differ from verbal statements in several ways. They involve multiple channels, are continuous instead of discrete, are usually more ambiguous, and are more likely to be unconscious. When presented with conflicting verbal and nonverbal messages, communicators are more likely to rely on the nonverbal ones.

Nonverbal messages can be communicated in a variety of ways: Through the face and eyes, body movement, touch, voice, distance, time, physical appearance, clothing, and environment.

# Recommended Readings

**Survey of nonverbal communication:**

Peter Andersen. *Nonverbal Communication: Forms and Functions.* Mountain View, CA: Mayfield, 1999.

**Nonverbal communication in relationships:**

Maureen Keeley and Allan J. Hart. "Nonverbal Behavior in Dyadic Interactions." In *Dynamics of Relationships,* edited by Steve Duck. Thousand Oaks, CA: Sage, 1994.

**Nonverbal deception:**

David B. Buller. "Deception." In *Strategic Interpersonal Communication,* edited by John A. Daly and John M. Wiemann. Hillsdale, NJ: Lawrence Erlbaum Associates, 1994.

**Proxemics:**

Edward T. Hall. *The Hidden Dimension.* Garden City, NY: Anchor Books, Doubleday, 1969.

**Time as a form of nonverbal communication:**

Robert A. Levine. *A Geography of Time, or How Every Culture Keeps Time Just a Little Differently.* New York: Basic Books, 1997.

**Touch:**

Ashley Montagu. *Touching: The Human Significance of the Skin.* 3rd ed. New York: Harper & Row, 1986.

# Activities

1. **Invitation to Insight**
   Demonstrate for yourself that it is impossible to avoid communicating nonverbally by trying *not* to communicate with a friend or family member. (You be the judge of whether to tell the other person about this experiment beforehand.) See how long it takes for your partner to inquire about what is going on and to report on what he or she thinks you might be thinking and feeling.

2. **Critical Thinking Probe**
   Interview someone from a culture different from your own, and learn at least three ways in which nonverbal codes differ from the environment where you were raised. Together, develop a list of ways you could violate unstated but important rules about nonverbal behavior in

your partner's culture in three of the following areas:

a. Eye contact
b. Posture
c. Gesture
d. Facial expression
e. Distance
f. Voice
g. Touch
h. Time
 i. Clothing
 j. Environmental design
k. Territory

Describe how failure to recognize different cultural codes could lead to misunderstandings, frustrations, and dissatisfaction. Discuss how awareness of cultural rules can be developed in an increasingly multicultural world.

3. **Invitation to Insight**

   Using the videotape of a television program or film, identify examples of the following nonverbal functions:

   a. Repeating
   b. Substituting
   c. Complementing
   d. Accenting
   e. Regulating
    f. Contradicting
   g. Deceiving

   If time allows, show these videotaped examples to your classmates.

4. **Skill Builder**

   Sharpen your ability to distinguish between observing and interpreting nonverbal behaviors by following these directions:

   a. Sit or stand opposite a partner at a comfortable distance. For a one-minute period, report your observations of the other person's behavior by repeatedly completing the statement "Now I see (*nonverbal behavior*)." For example, you might report

"Now I see you blinking your eyes . . . now I see you looking down at the floor . . . now I see you fidgeting with your hands. . . ." Notice that no matter what your partner does, you have an unending number of nonverbal behaviors to observe.

   b. For a second one-minute period, complete the sentence "Now I see (*nonverbal behavior*), and I think _____," filling in the blank with your interpretation of the other person's nonverbal behavior. For instance, you might say "Now I see you look away, and I think you're nervous about looking me in the eye . . . now I see you smiling and I think you're imagining that you agree with my interpretation. . . ." Notice that by clearly labeling your interpretation, you give the other person a chance to correct any mistaken hunches.

   c. Repeat the first two steps, changing roles with your partner.

5. **Invitation to Insight**

   Learn more about the nonverbal messages you send by interviewing someone who knows you well: a friend, family member, or coworker. Ask your interview subject to describe how he or she knows when you are feeling each of the following emotions, even though you may not announce your feelings verbally:

   a. Anger or irritation
   b. Boredom or indifference
   c. Happiness
   d. Sadness
   e. Worry or anxiety

   Which of these nonverbal behaviors do you display intentionally, and which are not conscious? Which functions do your nonverbal behaviors perform in the situations your partner described: repeating, substituting, complementing, accenting, regulating, contradicting, and/or deceiving feelings?

6. **Invitation to Insight**

Explore your territoriality by listing the spaces you feel you "own," such as the space in which you park your car, parts of the place you live, and seats in a particular classroom. Describe how you feel when your territory is invaded and identify things you do to "mark" it.

# Listening

## After Studying the Material in This Chapter . . .

### You Should Understand:

1. The importance of listening.

2. The error of common myths which suggest that listening is easy.

3. The habits of people who listen ineffectively.

4. The reasons for listening to others.

5. The components of the listening process.

6. The differences among the listening responses introduced in this chapter.

7. The advantages and disadvantages of various listening styles.

### You Should Be Able to:

1. Identify specific instances when you listen to understand and retain information, to build and maintain relationships, to help others, and to evaluate.

2. Identify the circumstances in which you listen ineffectively, and the poor listening habits you use in these circumstances.

3. Identify the response styles you commonly use when listening to others.

4. Demonstrate a combination of listening styles you could use to respond effectively to another person.

### Key Terms

| | | | |
|---|---|---|---|
| Advising | Empathizing | Paraphrasing | Sincere questions |
| Ambushing | Evaluating | Pseudolistening | Stage hogging |
| Analyzing | Filling in gaps | Questioning | Supporting |
| Attending | Hearing | Remembering | Understanding |
| Closed questions | Insulated listening | Responding | |
| Counterfeit questions | Listening | Selective listening | |
| Defensive listening | Open questions | Silent listening | |

The grizzled army sergeant faced a roomful of new Signal Corps cadets, about to begin their training as radio operators.

"The equipment is a snap to operate," he explained. "All you have to do to send a message is to push this button on the microphone, and your voice goes out to anyone who's tuned in. Go ahead . . . give it a try."

Each recruit picked up a microphone and began speaking. The sound of thirty amplified voices all transmitting at the same time created a loud, painful squeal.

"OK, soldiers," the sergeant announced. "You just learned the first principle of radio communication. Any fool can send a message. The only way communication works is if you're willing and able to *receive* one too."

The sergeant's lesson was a good one for every communicator. Speaking is important, but without listening, a message might as well never be sent. In this chapter you will learn just how important listening is in interpersonal communication. You will learn about the many factors that make good listening difficult and find reasons for tackling those challenges. You will learn what really happens when listening takes place. Finally, you will read about a variety of listening responses that you can use to increase your own understanding, improve your relationships, and help others.

## The Importance of Listening

How important is listening? If we use frequency as a measure, it ranks at the top of the list. As far back as 1926, Paul Rankin (1952) found that adults spent about 70 percent of their waking time communicating. Writing occupied 9 percent of that time, reading 16 percent, speaking 30 percent, and listening 45 percent. One writer put Rankin's findings in perspective this way: We listen a book a day, speak a book a week, read a book a month, and write a book a year (Loban, 1996). One survey, illustrated in Figure 7.1 (Barker et al.,

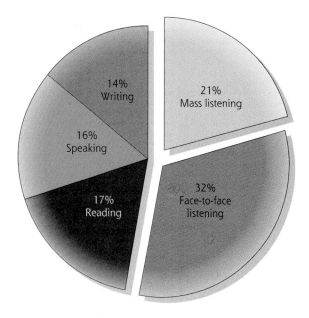

*Figure 7.1* **Types of Communication Activities**

1981), suggests that listening may be even more important today than it was at the time of Rankin's study. This is confirmed by Brown (1982), Keefe (1971), and Steil (1991), all of whom report that executives spend approximately 60 percent of their communication time listening.

Besides being the most frequent form of communication, listening is arguably a more valued skill than speaking. Andrew Wolvin and Carolyn Coakley (1991, 1996) summarize numerous studies that find listening to be the most important communication skill for entry-level workers, subordinates, supervisors, and managers on several dimensions: job and career success, productivity, upward mobility, communication training, and organizational effectiveness. When one thousand human resource executives were asked to identify skills of the ideal manager, the ability to listen effectively ranked at the top of the list (Winsor et al., 1997). In problem-solving groups, effective listeners are judged as having the most leadership skills (Johnson & Bechler, 1998). When a diverse group of senior executives was asked what skills were most important on the job, listening was

## FOCUS ON RESEARCH

### PERCEPTIONS OF MANAGERS' LISTENING ABILITY

Most experts and laypeople would agree that good managers need to be good talkers, but a study by communication researcher Judi Brownell suggests that they also need to be good listeners.

Using the previous research, Brownell developed a twenty-six-item survey that assessed several dimensions of listening ability: hearing, understanding, interpreting, evaluating, remembering, and responding. She administered this test to 827 employees in six hospitality organizations. The survey identified thirty-six managers who were perceived to be "good listeners" and another thirty-six who were viewed as "poor listeners."

Managers who were rated as particularly effective listeners were generally younger (between the ages of twenty-four and thirty-four) than bosses who didn't listen so well. Perceived good listeners had been in their current managerial position a shorter length of time (less than six years), had participated in some kind of listening training, and were more satisfied with their current position. Also, the percentage of women perceived as particularly effective listeners was higher than the percentage of men.

One important lesson from this research concerns the role of training in developing effective listening skills. Training isn't a surefire guarantee of being perceived as an effective listener—twenty-one of the thirty-six "good listeners" had received training. On the other hand, *not* having any training significantly increases the chances of being perceived as an ineffective listener: thirty-two of the thirty-six "poor listeners" had not had any training. These results suggest that listening is a communication skill that can be developed and improved.

Brownell, J. (1990). Perceptions of effective listeners: A management study. *Journal of Business Communication, 27,* 401–416.

identified more often than any other skill, including technical competence, computer knowledge, creativity, and administrative talent (Marchant, 1999).

The business world is not the only setting in which listening is vital. When a group of adults was asked to rank various communication skills according to their importance, listening topped the family/social list as well as the career list (Wolvin, 1984). In committed relationships, listening to personal information in everyday conversations is considered an important ingredient of satisfaction (Prager & Buhrmester, 1998).

Unfortunately, there is no connection between how well most communicators *think* they listen and how competent they really are in their ability to understand others (Carrell & Willmington, 1996). Virtually everyone acknowledges the importance of listening, but people rarely view themselves as needing to improve their own skills in receiving and understanding. A study by Judi Brownell (1990) illustrates this point vividly. A group of managers in her study were asked to rate their listening skills. Astonishingly, not one of the managers described himself or herself as a "poor" or "very poor" listener, while 94 percent rated themselves as "good" or "very good." As the Focus on Research on this page explains, the favorable self-ratings contrasted sharply with the perceptions of the managers' subordinates, many of whom said their bosses' listening skills were weak. As you'll soon read, some poor listening is inevitable.

The good news is that listening can be improved through instruction and training (McGee & Cegala, 1998; Spinks & Wells, 1991).

**Reasons for Listening**    A first step in becoming a better listener is to realize that there are actually four different reasons to listen: The most obvious is to *understand and retain information*. People who can understand and retain more information have a greater chance of becoming successful, however that term is defined (Floyd, 1985). Understanding the instructions and advice of superiors and colleagues, learning about the needs and reactions of subordinates, and discovering the concerns of clients and other members of the public are important in virtually every job.

A second type of listening involves *evaluating the quality of messages*. In their interesting book *Teaching as a Subversive Activity,* Neil Postman and Charles Weingartner (1969) discuss this function of listening in their chapter called "Crap Detecting." They define a crap detector as someone who not only functions in a society, but also *observes* it, noting its obsessions, fears, strengths, and weaknesses. Critical listeners are able to hear a speaker's words and understand the ideas without necessarily accepting them or agreeing with them. The ability to listen analytically and critically differs radically from empathic and supportive listening, but it is equally important.

The third reason for listening is especially relevant for interpersonal communication: *building and maintaining relationships*. Research shows that effective listening "builds better relationships, and poor listening weakens relationships, or prevents relationships from developing at all" (Kaufmann, 1993, p. 4). In one survey, marital counselors identified "failing to take the other's perspective when listening" as one of the most frequent communication problems in the couples with which they work (Vangelisti, 1994; see also Long et al., 1999).

The fourth type of listening involves *helping others*, another important interpersonal skill. Lis-

tening is an essential tool professionals use to help their clients. Doctors, lawyers, teachers, managers, supervisors, clergy, and therapists must listen carefully so they can offer sound and appropriate assistance. Professionals aren't the only people we call on for help; we also seek the counsel of friends and family. When others listen to us with empathy and concern, we can gain different and useful perspectives for solving problems.

## The Challenge of Listening

Despite its importance, listening is misunderstood by most people. Many believe if they've heard another person's message, they've engaged in listening—it's as simple as that. What these people fail to realize is that good listening is not simple; it's a challenge. The challenge can be met, but only by those who don't buy into popular misconceptions about listening. Let's look at several of these misconceptions.

### Hearing Is Not Listening

**Hearing** is the process wherein sound waves strike the eardrum and cause vibrations that are transmitted to the brain. **Listening** occurs when the brain reconstructs these electrochemical impulses

I just say?" The ability to repeat a statement doesn't guarantee understanding, of course: It means only that the listener has heard the message and can replay it from short-term storage.

People who confuse listening with hearing often fool themselves into thinking that they're really understanding others, when in fact they're simply receiving sounds. As you'll see by reading this chapter, true listening involves much more than the passive act of hearing.

into a representation of the original sound and then gives them meaning. Barring illness, injury, or cotton plugs, hearing cannot be stopped. Your ears will pick up sound waves and transmit them to your brain whether you want them to or not.

However, listening is not so automatic. Many times we hear but do not listen. Sometimes we deliberately do not listen. Instead of paying attention to words or other sounds, we avoid them. Often we block irritating sounds, such as a neighbor's lawn mower or the roar of nearby traffic. We also stop listening when we find a subject unimportant or uninteresting. Boring stories, TV commercials, and nagging complaints are common examples of messages we avoid.

There are also cases when we honestly believe we're listening although we're merely hearing. For example, recall times when you think you've "heard it all before." It's likely that in these situations you might claim you were listening when in fact you had closed your mental doors to new information.

You may also remember times when you were able to repeat on demand what a person just told you, like children do when their parents pause during a lecture and ask, "Are you listening? What did

## Listening Is Not Easy

Another common myth is that listening is like breathing—a natural activity that people do without conscious effort. The fact is, there are numerous obstacles that must be hurdled to become an effective listener, and doing so sometimes involves time, concentration, and work. Researchers have identified several barriers to listening (Golen, 1990; Hulbert, 1989). A look at some of these barriers will show why good listening is so tough.

**Hearing Problems**    If a person suffers from a physical impairment that prevents either hearing sounds at an adequate volume or receiving certain auditory frequencies, then listening will obviously suffer. Once a hearing problem has been diagnosed, it's often possible to treat it. The real tragedy occurs when a hearing loss goes undiagnosed. Both the person with the defect and those with whom she or he interacts can become frustrated and annoyed at the ineffective communication that takes place. If you suspect that you or someone you know might have a hearing loss, it's wise to have a physician or audiologist perform an examination.

**Information Overload**   The sheer amount of speech most of us encounter every day makes it impossible to listen carefully to everything we hear. We often spend five or more hours a day listening to people talk. If you add these hours to the amount of time we devote to radio and TV, you can see that it's virtually impossible for us to keep our attention totally focused for so long. Therefore, we periodically let our attention wander.

**Personal Concerns**   A third reason we don't always listen carefully is that we're often wrapped up in personal concerns of more immediate importance to us than the messages others are sending. It's hard to pay attention to someone else when we're anticipating an upcoming test or thinking about the wonderful time we had last night with our friends. When we still feel that we have to "listen" politely to others, listening becomes a charade.

**Rapid Thought**   Listening carefully is also difficult because our minds are so active. Although we're capable of understanding speech at rates up to 600 words per minute (Drullman & Smoorenburg, 1997), the average person speaks much more slowly—between 100 and 140 words per

minute. Therefore, we have a lot of "spare time" to spend with our minds while someone is talking. The temptation is to use this time in ways that don't relate to the speaker's ideas, such as thinking about personal interests, daydreaming, planning a rebuttal, and so on. The trick is to use this spare time to understand the speaker's ideas better, rather than let your attention wander.

**Noise**   Finally, our physical and mental worlds often present distractions that make it hard for us to pay attention to others. The sounds of other conversations, traffic, and music, as well as the kinds of psychological noise discussed in Chapter 1, all interfere with our ability to hear well. For example, research has supported the commonsense suspicion that background noise from a television set reduces the ability of a communicator to understand messages (Armstrong et al., 1991). Also, fatigue or other forms of discomfort can distract us from paying attention to a speaker's remarks. For instance, consider how the efficiency of your listening decreases when you are seated in a crowded, hot, stuffy room full of moving people and other noises. In such circumstances even the best intentions aren't enough to ensure cogent understanding.

Before going any further, we want to make it clear that intensive listening isn't always desirable, even when circumstances permit. Given the number of messages to which we're exposed, it's impractical to expect yourself to listen well 100 percent of the time. Many of the messages sent to us aren't even worthwhile: long-winded stories, radio chatter, or remarks we've heard many times before. Hence, nonlistening behaviors are often reasonable. Our main concern is that you have the ability to be an accurate receiver when it really does matter.

## All Listeners Do Not Receive the Same Message

When two or more people are listening to a speaker, we tend to assume that they are each hearing and understanding the same message. In

"You haven't been listening. I keep telling you that I don't want a product fit for a king."

fact, such uniform comprehension isn't the case. Recall our discussion of perception in Chapter 4, where we pointed out the many factors that cause each of us to perceive an event in a different manner. Physiological factors, social roles, cultural background, personal interests, and needs all shape and distort the raw data we hear into very different messages.

Because every person interprets data uniquely, we have to accept the fact that we can never completely understand another person. As John Stewart (1983) and Benjamin Broome (1991) note, even the most active, empathic listener cannot actually "lay aside" the self and truly "walk in another's shoes." We bring our personal perspective and experiences with us into every interaction, and they affect the way we make sense of others' words and actions. It's no wonder that dyads typically achieve only 25 to 50 percent accuracy in interpreting or representing each other's behavior (Spitzberg, 1993). Our listening is always colored and limited by our unique view of the world.

## Poor Listening Habits

Most people possess one or more bad habits that keep them from understanding others' messages. As you read about the following poor listening behaviors, see which ones describe you.

**Pseudolistening** is an imitation of the real thing. "Good" pseudolisteners give the appearance of being attentive: They look you in the eye, nod and smile at the right times, and even answer you occasionally. Pseudolisteners use a polite facade to mask thoughts that have nothing to do with what the speaker is saying.

**Stage hogs** are interested only in expressing their ideas and don't care about what anyone else has to say. These people allow you to speak from time to time, but only so they can catch their breath and use your remarks as a basis for their own babbling. Research on "conversational narcissism" (Vangelisti et al., 1990) shows that self-centered stage hogs ask questions, but not other-oriented, information-seeking ones. Rather, these conversa-

### REFLECTION

#### SELECTIVE LISTENING

An incident last week showed me how much of a selective listener I am. At work, the overnight express crew came into work for their usual pickup. They chatted away like always, and I responded automatically. I was busy going through my closing procedures, and wasn't listening very carefully. All of a sudden I heard the supervisor say "You know, we're always hiring, and even our part-time employees get full health benefits." It was like an alarm went off inside my head. I immediately dropped what I was doing and started asking her questions.

This experience helped me realize how much of a selective listener I am. Much of the time I barely pay attention to what other people are saying, but when the subject is important to me, I tune right in.

tional narcissists ask **counterfeit questions** to demonstrate their superiority and hold the floor.

**Selective listeners** respond only to the parts of a speaker's remarks that interest them, rejecting everything else. Unless and until you bring up one of these pet subjects, you might as well be talking to a tree.

People who **fill in gaps** like to think that what they remember makes a whole story. These people manufacture information so that when they retell what they listened to, they can give the impression they "got it all." The message that's left is actually a distorted (not merely incomplete) version of the real message.

The habit of **insulated listening** is almost the opposite of selective listening. Instead of looking for something, these listeners avoid it. Whenever a topic arises they'd rather not deal with, insulated listeners simply fail to hear or acknowledge it.

**REDEEMING A POOR LISTENER:**
*JERRY MAGUIRE*

Jerry Maguire (Tom Cruise) is a high-powered pro sports agent with a bulging Rolodex and a stable of multi-millionaire athletes. He is so successful that he doesn't have time to truly listen to any of his clients. In an early scene, Maguire juggles the callers on his multiline office phone, slinging clichés as he switches between athletes. He pretends to care about them, but he really only cares about making a buck and beating out other agents.

Maguire's listening skills aren't much better in his personal life. Dorothy Boyd (Renee Zellweger) gives up everything to follow Jerry and his dreams, but she too gets lost on the back burner of his egocentric life. In true Hollywood fashion, Maguire only learns the importance of listening when he is close to losing the most important people in his life.

As the film ends, Jerry is redeemed by the love of Dorothy, her son, and the few friends he has left. Fans of the story can only hope he now understands that genuine listening can go a long way toward preserving the things that matter most in life.

People who engage in **defensive listening** take innocent comments as personal attacks. It's fair to assume that many defensive listeners are suffering from shaky self-images, and avoid facing this by projecting their own insecurities onto others.

An **ambusher** will listen carefully to you, but only because he or she is collecting information that will be used to attack what you have to say. Needless to say, using this kind of strategy will justifiably initiate defensiveness on the other's side.

# Components of Listening

By now, you can begin to see that there is more to listening than sitting quietly while another person speaks. In truth, *listening*—at least listening effectively—consists of five separate elements: hearing, attending, understanding, remembering, and responding.

## Hearing

As we have already discussed, hearing is the physiological aspect of listening. It is the non-selective process of sound waves impinging on the ear. Hearing is the most fundamental part of listening. It can be diminished by physiological disorders, background noise, and auditory fatigue, a temporary loss of hearing caused by continuous exposure to the same tone or loudness. People who spend an evening at a rock concert may experience auditory fatigue and, if they are exposed often enough, permanent hearing loss.

## Attending

While hearing is a physiological process, **attending** is a psychological one, and is part of the process of selection that we described in Chapter 4. We would go crazy if we attended to every sound we hear, so we filter out some messages and focus on others. Needs, wants, desires, and interests determine what is attended to. Not surprisingly, research shows that we attend most carefully to messages when there's a payoff for doing so (Smeltzer & Watson, 1984). If you're planning to see a movie, you'll listen to a friend's description more carefully than you otherwise would. And when you want to get better acquainted with others, you'll pay careful attention to almost anything they say, in hopes of improving the relationship.

Surprisingly, attending doesn't just help the listener: It also benefits the message sender. Participants in one study viewed brief movie segments and then described them to listeners who varied in their degree of attentiveness to the speaker. Later

"Excuse me, Doc, my attention wandered. What
type of deficit disorder did you say I had?"

on, the researchers tested the speakers' long-term recall of details from the movie segment. Those who had recounted the movie to attentive listeners remembered more details of the movie (Pasupathi et al., 1998).

## Understanding

Paying attention—even close attention—to a message doesn't guarantee that you'll understand what's being said. **Understanding** is composed of several elements. First, of course, you must be aware of the syntactic and grammatical rules of the language. But beyond this basic ability, understanding a message depends on several other factors. One is your knowledge about the source of the message. Such background will help you decide, for example, whether a friend's insulting remark is a joke or a serious attack. The context of a message also helps

you understand what's being said. A yawning response to your comments would probably have a different meaning at midnight than at noon.

Finally, understanding often depends on the listener's mental abilities. Generally speaking, the ability to make sense of messages is closely related to the listener's intelligence (Bostrom & Waldhart, 1980). As early as 1948, Ralph Nichols related successful understanding to factors that included verbal ability, intelligence, and motivation. Timothy Plax and Lawrence Rosenfeld (1979) found that the personality traits of listeners also affect their ability to understand messages. People good at interpreting disorganized messages were especially secure, sensitive to others, and willing to understand the speaker. Listeners successful at understanding disorganized speech proved to be more insightful and versatile in their thinking.

EAR

EYES

UNDIVIDED
ATTENTION

HEART

Calligraphy by Angie Au.

**Figure 7.2**
The Chinese characters that make up the verb "to listen" tell us something significant about this skill.

## Remembering

The ability to recall information once we've understood it, or **remembering**, is a function of several factors: the number of times the information is heard or repeated, how much information there is to store in the brain, and whether the information may be "rehearsed" or not.

Early research on listening revealed that people remember only about half of what they hear *immediately* after hearing it (Barker, 1971). They forget half even if they work hard at listening. This situation would probably not be too bad if this half were retained, but it isn't. Within two months, half of the half is forgotten, bringing what we remember down to about 25 percent of the original message. However, this loss doesn't take two months: People start forgetting immediately (within eight hours, the 50 percent remembered drops to about 35 percent). Given the amount of information we process every day—from teachers, friends, radio, TV, and other sources—the *residual message* (what we remember) is a small fraction of what we hear.

This high rate of forgetfulness isn't as depressing as it might seem. While most people recall very few details of their conversations, they do retain an overall impression about the speaker, especially in important relationships (Fisher & Adams, 1994). The more intensity, intimacy, trust, and commitment in the relationship, the more we pay attention to what others are saying. Thus, high recall is one characteristic of healthy interpersonal relationships.

## Responding

All the steps we have discussed so far—hearing, attending, understanding, and remembering—are internal activities. A final part of the listening process involves **responding** to a message—giving observable feedback to the speaker (Bostrom, 1996; Cooper et al., 1997). One study of 195 critical incidents in banking and medical settings showed that a major difference between effective and ineffective listening was the kind of feedback offered (Lewis & Reinsch, 1988). Good listeners showed that they were attentive by nonverbal behaviors such as keeping eye contact and reacting with appropriate facial expressions. Their verbal behavior—for example, answering questions and exchanging ideas—also demonstrated their attention. It's easy to imagine how other responses would signal less effective listening. A slumped posture, bored expression, and yawning send a clear message that you are not tuned in to the speaker.

Adding responsiveness to our listening model demonstrates the fact we discussed in Chapter 1, that communication is transactional in nature. Listening isn't just a passive activity. As listeners, we are active participants in a communication transaction. At the same time that we receive messages, we also send them.

## Types of Listening Responses

Of the five components of listening described above, it's responding that lets us know if others are truly tuned in to what we're saying. Think for a moment of someone you consider a good listener.

Why did you choose that person? It's probably because of the way she or he behaves while you are speaking: making eye contact and nodding when you're talking, staying attentive while you're telling an important story, reacting with an exclamation when you say something startling, expressing empathy and support when you're hurting, and offering another perspective or advice when you ask for it. As Figure 7.3 illustrates, listening responses like these range from reflective feedback that invites the speaker to talk without concern of evaluation, to more directive responses that evaluate the speaker's messages. We'll spend the remainder of the chapter looking at each of these response styles in detail.

## Silent Listening

There are times when the best response is no response. This is certainly true when you don't want to encourage a speaker to keep talking. For instance, recall times when a boss or instructor droned on and on when you needed to leave for an appointment, or instances when a friend retold the story of a love affair gone bad for what seemed like the tenth time. In situations like these, a verbal response would only encourage the speaker to continue—precisely the opposite reaction you would be seeking. At times like these, the best response may be **silent listening**—staying attentive and nonverbally responsive without offering any verbal feedback.

Silent listening isn't just an avoidance strategy. It also can be the right approach when you are open to the other person's ideas but your interjections wouldn't be appropriate. If you are part of a large audience hearing a lecture, asking questions and offering comments would probably be disruptive. On a more personal scale, when a friend tells you a joke, butting in to ask for clarification ("There was a priest, a rabbi, and a *what?*") would probably spoil your friend's rhythm.

There are even times when silent listening can help others solve their problems. Sonia Johnson (1987) describes a powerful activity she calls "hearing into being." The process is simple: In brainstorming sessions, each participant has a half hour of uninterrupted floor time. "When we are free to talk without threat of interruption, evaluation, and the pressure of time," notes Johnson, "we move quickly past known territory out into the frontiers of our thought" (p. 132). Johnson, who uses the technique in feminist seminars, reports that some women burst into tears when they first experience "hearing into being" because they are not used to being listened to so seriously and completely. Ask yourself: When was the last time you talked, uninterrupted, to an attentive partner for more than a few minutes? How would you like the chance to develop your ideas without pausing for another's comments? Silent listening is a response style that many of us could profit from using—and receiving—more often.

*Figure 7.3* **Types of Listening Responses**

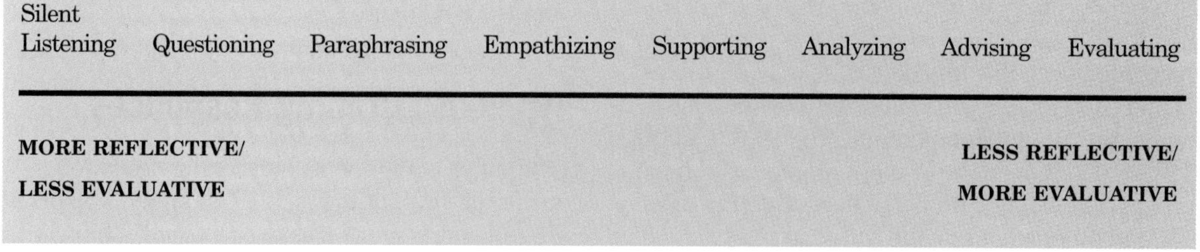

| Silent Listening | Questioning | Paraphrasing | Empathizing | Supporting | Analyzing | Advising | Evaluating |
|---|---|---|---|---|---|---|---|

**MORE REFLECTIVE/ LESS EVALUATIVE**                **LESS REFLECTIVE/ MORE EVALUATIVE**

## FOCUS ON RESEARCH

### LISTENING TO A FRIEND IN NEED: THE VALUE OF NOT INTRUDING

Imagine that one of your friends just had something bad happen—perhaps a relational breakup or a low exam grade. The only reason you know about the bad news is because someone else told you. Would you bring up the subject to your friend and express regret? Would you offer support or advice? According to research by Ruth Anne Clark and Jesse Delia, those well-meaning approaches might not be what your friend really wants or needs.

Clark and Delia asked 113 college students to imagine themselves in six different unpleasant situations (e.g., bad test score, brother in a car accident, dad unemployed). The students were then asked how they would like to be approached by a friend who learned of the distressing situation from someone else. The results were somewhat surprising. Although some respondents said they would want and expect their friend to bring up the subject, the majority reported they would rather their friend not mention the troubling situation. The researchers found that "participants displayed a strong preference to determine for themselves whether to discuss their problem with a friend."

The conclusions suggest there is value in being a silent listener around a troubled friend, or at most asking noncommittal questions such as, "How's it going?" If and when your friend feels like talking is the best—and perhaps the only—time to use the other listening responses discussed in this section of the text.

Clark, R. A., & Delia, J. G. (1997). Individuals' preferences for friends' approaches to providing support in distressing situations. *Communication Reports, 10,* 115–121.

## Questioning

Regarded as "the most popular piece of language" (Goodman & Esterly, 1990), **questioning** occurs when the listener asks the speaker for additional information. There are several reasons to ask sincere, nondirective questions:

- *To clarify meanings.* By now you know that people who share words do not always share meanings. Good listeners don't assume they know what their partners mean; they ask for clarification with questions such as these: "What did you mean when you said he had been 'unfair' to you?" "You said she's 'religious'—how do you define that term?" "You said you were going 'fast'—could you be more specific?" Of course, be sure to use an appropriate tone of voice

when asking such questions, or else they might sound like an inquisition.

- *To learn about others' thoughts, feelings, and wants.* A caring listener may want to inquire about more than just the "facts." Opinions, emotions, and even hopes are buried inside many messages; with sensitivity, a sincere question can draw these out. "What do you think about the new plan?" "How did you feel when you heard the news?" and "Were you hoping for something different?" are examples of such probes. When inquiring about personal information, it is usually best to ask **open questions** that allow a variety of extended responses rather than **closed questions** that only allow a limited range of answers. For instance, "How did you feel?" is an open question that allows a variety of responses, while "Did

you feel angry?" is a closed question that requires only a yes or no answer (and may direct respondents toward feelings they weren't experiencing).

■ *To encourage elaboration.* People are sometimes hesitant to talk about themselves, or perhaps they aren't sure if others are interested. Remarks such as "Tell me more about that," "Try me again—I'm not sure I understand," and "Keep going—I'm following you" convey concern and involvement. Notice that none of these examples ends with a question mark. Unlike the television show *Jeopardy,* questioning responses need not be phrased in the form of a question. We can encourage elaboration simply by acknowledging that we are listening.

■ *To encourage discovery.* People in the helping professions—clergy, counselors, therapists, and so on—often ask questions to prod their clients into discovering solutions for their problems. "Playing counselor" can be a dangerous game, but there are times when you can use questions to encourage others to explore their thoughts and feelings. "So, what do you see as your options?" may prompt an employee to come up with creative problem-solving alternatives. "What would be your ideal solution?" might help a friend get in touch with various wants and needs. Most importantly, encouraging dis-

covery rather than dispensing advice indicates you have faith in the other person's ability to think for herself or himself. This may be the most important message that you can communicate as an effective listener.

■ *To gather more facts and details.* Just because your conversational partner tells you something doesn't mean you understand the whole story. As long as your questions aren't intrusive (and you'll need to monitor others' nonverbal behavior to determine this), people often appreciate listeners who want to learn more. Questions such as "What did you do then?" and "What did she say after that?" can help a listener understand the larger story.

Not all questions are genuine requests for information. Whereas **sincere questions** are aimed at understanding others, **counterfeit questions** are really disguised attempts to send a message, not receive one. As such, they really fit better at the "more evaluative" end of the listening response continuum pictured in Figure 7.3 on page 198. It's also likely that they'll lead to a defensive communication climate, as discussed in Chapter 11.

Counterfeit questions come in several varieties:

■ *Questions that trap the speaker.* When your friend says, "You didn't like that movie, did

LISTING **201**

you?" you're being backed into a corner. It's clear that your friend disapproves, so the question leaves you with two choices: You can disagree and defend your position, or you can devalue your reaction by lying or equivocating— "I guess it wasn't perfect." Consider how much easier it would be to respond to the sincere question, "What did you think of the movie?"

Adding a tag question such as "did you?" or "isn't that right?" to the end of a question can be a tip-off that the asker is looking for agreement, not information. While some listeners use these tag endings to confirm and facilitate understanding (Coates, 1986), our concern here is when tags are used to coerce agreement: "You said you'd call at five o'clock, but you forgot, didn't you?" Similarly, questions that begin with "Don't you" (such as "Don't you think he would make a good boss?") direct others toward a desired response. As a simple solution, changing "Don't you?" to "Do you?" makes the question less leading.

■ *Questions that make statements.* "Are you finally off the phone?" is more of a statement than a question—a fact unlikely to be lost on the targeted person. Emphasizing certain words also can turn a question into a statement: "You lent money to *Tony?*" We also use questions to offer advice. The person who responds with, "Are you going to stand up to him and give him what he deserves?" clearly has stated an opinion about what should be done.

■ *Questions that carry hidden agendas.* "Are you busy Friday night?" is a dangerous question to answer. If you say "No," thinking the person has something fun in mind, you won't like hearing "Good, because I need some help moving my piano." Obviously, such questions are not designed to enhance understanding; they are setups for the proposal that follows. Other examples include "Will you do me a favor?" and "If I tell you what happened, will you promise not to get mad?" Because they are strategic rather than spontaneous, these questions are likely to provoke defensiveness (Gibb, 1961). Wise communicators answer questions that mask hidden agendas cautiously with responses such as "It depends" or "Let me hear what you have in mind before I answer."

■ *Questions that seek "correct" answers.* Most of us have been victims of question askers who only want to hear a particular response. "Which

# Calvin and Hobbes     by Bill Watterson

shoes do you think I should wear?" can be a sincere question—unless the asker has a predetermined preference. When this happens, the asker isn't interested in listening to contrary opinions, and "incorrect" responses get shot down. Some of these questions may venture into delicate territory. "Honey, do you think I'm overweight?" is usually a request for a "correct" answer—and the listener must have a fair amount of rhetorical sensitivity to determine an appropriate response.

■ *Questions based on unchecked assumptions.* "Why aren't you listening to me?" assumes the other person isn't paying attention. "What's the matter?" assumes that something *is* wrong. As Chapter 4 explained, perception checking is a much better way of confirming assumptions. As you recall, a perception check offers a description and interpretations, followed by a sincere request for clarification: "When you kept looking over at the TV, I thought you weren't listening to me, but maybe I was wrong. *Were* you paying attention?"

No question is inherently sincere or counterfeit. As Chapter 5 explained, the meaning and intent of any statement is shaped by its context. Moreover, a slight change in tone of voice or facial expression can turn a sincere question into a counterfeit one, and vice versa. Nonetheless, the types of questions in the list above are usually closer to statements than requests for information.

Counterfeit questions aren't all bad: They can be powerful tools for making a point. Lawyers use them to get confessions in the courtroom, and journalists ask them to uncover concealed information. Our point is that they usually get in the way of effective listening and relationship building—after all, most people don't like feeling trapped or "grilled" in a conversation.

## Paraphrasing

**Paraphrasing** is feedback that restates, in your own words, the message you thought the speaker sent. You may wonder, "Why would I want to

restate what's already been said?" Consider this simple exchange:

> "Drive down to the traffic signal and turn left."
> "So you want me to go to that traffic light that's by the high school and turn left?"
> "No, that's way too far. I meant that you should drive to the four-way stop by the park and turn there."

By paraphrasing, the listener learned that to the speaker, "signal" meant "stop sign," not "traffic light." Note that the listener rephrased rather than repeated the message. In effective paraphrasing you restate what you think the speaker has said in your own words as a way of cross-checking the meaning you've assigned to the message. It's important that you paraphrase, not "parrotphrase." If you simply repeat the speaker's comments verbatim, you'll sound foolish or hard-of-hearing—and just as important, you still might misunderstand what's been said.

**Types of Paraphrasing Statements**  Restating another person's message in a way that sounds natural can sometimes be a difficult skill to master. Here are three approaches to get you started:

1. **Change the speaker's wording.**

*Speaker:* "Bilingual education is just another failed idea of bleeding heart liberals."
*Paraphrase:* "Let me see if I've got this right. You're mad because you think bilingual ed sounds good, but it doesn't work?"

2. **Offer an example of what you think the speaker is talking about.**
   When the speaker makes an abstract statement, you may suggest a specific example or two to see if your understanding is accurate.

*Speaker:* "Lee is such a jerk. I can't believe the way he acted last night."
*Paraphrase:* "You think those jokes were pretty offensive, huh?"

3. **Reflect the underlying theme of the speaker's remarks.**

When you want to summarize the *theme* that seems to have run through another person's conversation, a complete or partial perception check is appropriate:

*Paraphrase:* "You keep reminding me to be careful. Sounds like you're worried that something might happen to me. Am I right?"

There are several reasons why paraphrasing assists listening. First, as the preceding examples illustrate, paraphrasing allows you to find out if the message received is the message sent. Second, paraphrasing often draws out further information from the speaker, much like questioning (in fact, a good paraphrase often ends with a question such as "Is that what you meant?"). Third, paraphrasing is an ideal way to take the heat out of intense discussions. When conversations begin to boil, it is often because the people involved believe they aren't being heard. Rather than escalating the conflict, try paraphrasing the other person: "OK, let me be sure I understand you. It sounds like you're concerned about . . . ." Paraphrasing usually short-circuits a defensive spiral because it assures the other person of your involvement and concern. When you take the time to restate and clarify a speaker's message, your commitment to listening is hard to deny.

There are two levels at which you can paraphrase messages. The first involves feedback of factual information; the second involves reflecting personal information.

**Paraphrasing Factual Information**    Summarizing facts, data, and details is important during personal or professional conversations. "We've agreed that we'll take another few days to think about our choices and make a decision on Tuesday—right?" might be an effective way to conclude a business lunch. A questioning tone should be used; a listener wants to be sure that meaning has been shared. Even personal topics are sometimes best handled on a factual level: "So your main problem is that our friends take up all the parking spaces in front of your place. Is that it?" While this "neutral"

---

response may be difficult when you are under attack, it helps to clarify facts before you offer your reaction. It is also a good idea to paraphrase instructions, directions, and decisions before acting on what you *think* has been said.

**Paraphrasing Personal Information**    While restating factual information is relatively easy, it takes a sensitive ear to listen for others' thoughts, feelings, and wants. The "underlying message" is often the more important message, and effective listeners try to reflect what they hear at this level. Listening for thoughts, feelings, and wants addresses the cognitive (rational), affective (emotional), and behavioral (desired action) domains of human experience. Read the following statement as if a married, female friend is talking to you, and listen for all three components:

> Bob has hardly been home all week—he's been so busy with work. He rushes in just long enough to eat dinner, then buries himself at his desk until bedtime. Then he tells me today that he's going fishing Saturday with his buddies. I guess men are just like that—job first, play second, family third.

What is the speaker thinking, feeling, and wanting? Paraphrasing can help you find out: "Sounds like you're unhappy (feeling) because you think Bob's ignoring you (thought) and you want him to spend more time at home (want)." Recognize that you may not be accurate; the speaker might reply, "No, I really don't want him to spend more time at home—I just want him to pay attention to me when he's here." Recognize also that you could identify an entirely different think-feel-want set: "So you're frustrated (feeling) because you'd like Bob to change (want), but you think it's hopeless because men have different priorities (thought)." The fact that these examples offer such different interpretations of the same message demonstrates the value of paraphrasing.

Your paraphrases don't have to be as long as the examples in the preceding paragraph. In many cases, you'll want to reflect only one or two of the think-feel-want components. The key is giving feedback that is appropriate for the situation and offering it in a way that assists the listening process. Because paraphrasing is an unfamiliar way of responding, it may feel awkward at first. If you start by paraphrasing occasionally and then gradually increase the frequency of such re-sponses, you can begin to see the benefits of this method.

It's also a good idea to mix paraphrasing with other listening responses. The dialogue on pages 206–207 shows how paraphrasing, questioning, and empathizing—three response styles from the "more reflective" end of the listening continuum—can be combined in an everyday conversation.

## Empathizing

**Empathizing** is a response style listeners use when they want to show that they *identify* with a speaker. As discussed in Chapter 4, empathy involves per-spective taking, emotional contagion, and genuine concern. When listeners put the attitude of empathy into verbal and nonverbal responses, they engage in empathizing. Sometimes these responses can be quite brief: "Uh-huh," "I see," "Wow!" "Ouch!" "Whew!" "My goodness." In other cases, empathizing is expressed in statements like these:

> "I can see that really hurts."
> "I know how important that was to you."
> "It's no fun to feel unappreciated."
> "I can tell you're really excited about that."
> "Wow, that must be rough."
> "I think I've felt that way, too."
> "Looks like that really made your day."
> "This means a lot to you, doesn't it?"

Empathizing falls near the middle of the listening response continuum pictured in Figure 7.3. It is different from the less-evaluative responses at the left end of the spectrum, which attempt to neutrally gather information. It is also different from the more evaluative styles at the right end of the spectrum, which offer more direction than reflection. To understand how empathizing compares to other types of responses, consider these examples:

> "So your boss isn't happy with your performance and you're thinking about finding a new job." (Paraphrasing)
> "Ouch—I'll bet it hurt when your boss said you weren't doing a good job." (Empathizing)
> "Hey, you'll land on your feet—your boss doesn't appreciate what a winner you are." (Supporting)

Notice that empathizing identifies with the speaker's emotions and perceptions more than paraphrasing does, yet offers less evaluation and agreement than supporting responses. In fact, it's possible to empathize with others while disagreeing with them. For instance, the response "I can see you feel strongly about that issue" legitimizes a speaker's feelings without assenting to that person's point of view (it could be said to either a friend or a foe at a business meeting). Empathizing is therefore an important skill not only for interacting with people with whom you agree, but also for responding to those who see the world differently from you.

Perhaps a better way to explain empathizing is to describe what it *doesn't* sound like. Many listeners believe they are empathizing when, in fact, they are offering responses that are evaluative and directive. Listeners are probably *not* empathizing when they display the following behaviors:

■ *Denying others the right to their feelings.* Consider this common response to another person's problem: "Don't worry about it." While the remark may be intended as a reassuring comment, the underlying message is that the speaker wants the person to feel differently. The irony is that the direction probably won't work— after all, it's unlikely that people can or will stop worrying just because you tell them to do so. Other examples of denying feelings are "It's nothing to get so upset about" and "That's a silly way to feel." Research suggests that men are more likely than women to offer these kinds of responses (Goldsmith & Fulfs, 1999). Research also shows that empathizing is more effective than denying the feelings and perspectives of others (Samter et al., 1987).

■ *Minimizing the significance of the situation.* Think about the times someone said to you, "Hey, it's only _____." You can probably fill in the blank a variety of ways: "a game," "words," "a test," "a party." How did you react? You probably thought the person who said it just didn't understand. To someone who has been the victim of verbal abuse, the hurtful message wasn't "just words"; to a child who didn't get an invitation, it wasn't "just a party" (see Burleson, 1984); to a student who has flunked an important exam, it wasn't "just a test" (see Burleson & Samter, 1985). When you minimize the significance of someone else's experience, you aren't empathizing. Instead, you are interpreting the event from your perspective and then passing judgment—rarely a helpful response.

■ *Self-defending.* When your response to others' concerns is to defend yourself ("Don't blame me; I've done my part"), it's clear you are more concerned with yourself than with the other person. Chapter 11 offers detailed advice for responding nondefensively to criticism. Until then, realize that justifying yourself isn't compatible with understanding and identifying with others.

■ *Raining on the speaker's parade.* Most of the preceding examples deal with difficult situations or messages about pain. However, empathizing involves identifying with others' joys as well as their sorrows. Many of us can recall coming home with exciting news, only to be told "A 5-percent raise? That isn't so great." "An *A*-minus? Why didn't you get an A?" "Big deal—I got one of those years ago." Taking the wind out of someone's sails is the opposite of empathizing.

Authors Florence Wolff and Nadine Marsnik (1992) believe that empathizing requires "fine skill and exquisite tuning to another's moods and feelings" (p. 100). Research suggests that cognitive complexity and flexibility are needed to offer these nonjudgmental, other-oriented responses (Applegate, 1990). Fortunately, research also indicates that the ability to offer such responses can be learned (Clinton & Hancock, 1991). The exercises at the end of this chapter can offer you valuable practice in developing your skill as an empathic communicator.

## Supporting

So far, we have looked at listening responses that put a premium on being reflective and non-evaluative. However, there are times when other people want to hear more than a reflection of how they feel: They would like to know how you feel about them. **Supporting** responses reveal the listener's solidarity with the speaker's situation. There are several types of support:

| | |
|---|---|
| Agreement | "You're right—the landlord is being unfair." |
| | "Yeah, that class was tough for me too." |
| Offers to help | "I'm here if you need me." |
| | "Let me try to explain it to him." |

# REFLECTION

## REFLECTIVE LISTENING IN EVERYDAY LIFE

The following conversation between two friends shows how reflective responses from the "more reflective" end of the listening continuum—paraphrasing, questioning, and empathizing—can help both the speaker and the listener. Notice how Jill comes to a conclusion about her problem without advice from Mark: He simply serves as an empathic reflector of her thoughts, feelings, and wants. Notice also how Mark might have misunderstood Jill if he hadn't asked questions, offered clarifying paraphrases, and empathized with her situation. This combination of listening styles enhances Mark and Jill's communication and strengthens their relationship.

**Jill:** I've had the strangest feeling about my boss lately.

**Mark:** What's that? [A simple question invites Jill to go on.]

**Jill:** I'm starting to think maybe he has this thing about women—or maybe it's just about me.

**Mark:** You mean he's coming on to you? [Mark paraphrases what he thinks Jill has said.]

**Jill:** Oh no, not at all! But it seems like he doesn't take women—or at least me—seriously. [Jill corrects Mark's misunderstanding and explains herself.]

**Mark:** What do you mean? [Mark asks another simple question to get more information.]

**Jill:** Well, whenever we're in a meeting or just talking around the office and he asks for ideas, he always seems to pick men. He gives orders to women—men too—but he never asks the women to say what *they* think.

**Mark:** Gee, that must hurt—it's no fun to feel ignored. So you think maybe he doesn't take women seriously, is that it? [Mark empathizes with Jill, then offers a paraphrase.]

**Jill:** Yeah. Well, he sure doesn't seem interested in their ideas. But that doesn't mean he's a total woman hater or a male chauvinist pig. I know he counts on some women in the office. Our accountant, Teresa, has been there forever, and he's always saying he couldn't live without her. And when Brenda got the new computer system up and running last month, I know he appreciated that. He gave her a day off and told everybody how she saved our lives.

**Mark:** Now you sound confused. [He reflects her apparent feeling.]

**Jill:** I *am* confused. I don't think it's just my imagination. I mean I'm a good producer, but he has never—not once—asked me for my ideas about how to improve sales or

*(continued)*

| | | |
|---|---|---|
| Praise | "I don't care what the boss said: I think you did a great job!" | "I know you'll do a great job." |
| | "You're a terrific person! If she doesn't recognize it, that's her problem." | "Although it's probably hard to look at it this way, maybe you've learned something really important that can help you in the future." |
| Reassurance | "The worst part seems to be over. It will probably get easier from here." | |
| | | Diversion | "Let's catch a movie and get your mind off this." |

anything. And I can't remember a time when he's asked any other women. But maybe I'm overreacting.

**Mark:** You're not positive whether you're right, but I can tell that this has you concerned. [Mark paraphrases Jill's central theme and reflects her feeling.]

**Jill:** Yes. But I don't know what to do about it.

**Mark:** Maybe you should . . . [starts to offer advice, but catches himself and decides to ask a sincere, nonleading question instead]. So what are your choices?

**Jill:** Well, I could just ask him if he's aware that he never asks women their opinions. But that might sound too aggressive and angry.

**Mark:** And you're *not* angry? [He tries to clarify how Jill is feeling.]

**Jill:** Not really. I don't know whether I should be angry because he's not taking ideas seriously, or whether he just doesn't take *my* ideas seriously, or whether it's nothing at all.

**Mark:** So you're mostly confused. [He reflects Jill's apparent feeling again.]

**Jill:** Yes! I don't know where I stand with my boss, and not being sure is starting to get to me. I wish I knew what he thinks of me. Maybe I could just tell him I'm confused about what is going on here and ask him to clear it up. But what if it's nothing? Then I'll look insecure.

**Mark:** [He thinks Jill should confront her boss, but isn't positive that this is the best approach, so he paraphrases what Jill seems to be saying.] And that would make you look bad.

**Jill:** I'm afraid maybe it would. I wonder if I could talk it over with anybody else in the office and get their ideas . . .

**Mark:** See what they think . . .

**Jill:** Yeah. Maybe I could ask Brenda. She's easy to talk to, and I do respect her judgment. Maybe she could give me some ideas about how to handle this.

**Mark:** Sounds like you're comfortable with talking to Brenda first.

**Jill:** (warming to the idea) Yes! Then if it's nothing, I can calm down. But if I do need to talk to the boss, I'll know I'm doing the right thing.

**Mark:** Great. Let me know how it goes.

This conversation shows how a reflective listening style can open up an important, unexplored area of concern. The emotional responses we have to problems are often more important than the problems themselves. In the dialogue, Jill's feelings of insecurity are far more important than the specifics of one project or another. By encouraging Jill to express those feelings and by offering reflective responses, Mark helps her tackle the biggest problem that was bothering her.

"That reminds me of the time we . . . ."

There's no question about the value of receiving support when faced with personal problems. "Comforting ability" and social support have been shown to be among the most important communication skills a friend—or a teacher or a parent—can have (Burleson, 1984, 1994; Rosenfeld et al., 1998, 1999). The value of personal support is clear when big problems arise, but research shows that smaller, everyday distresses and upsets can actually take a bigger toll on mental health and physical well-being (Ekenrode, 1984). Perhaps that's why senior citizens who are taught to use the Internet discover quickly that it provides a network of social support (Cody et al., 1999). Like all of us, these

## FILM CLIP

### LOVING THROUGH LISTENING: *DEAD MAN WALKING*

Sister Helen Prejean (Susan Sarandon) is a nun who serves in an inner-city neighborhood. She receives a letter from death-row inmate Matthew Poncelet (Sean Penn) and decides to visit him in prison. He fills the profile for everything she is not: uneducated, angry, bigoted, rude, and insecure. Nonetheless, Sister Helen agrees to help Poncelet appeal his murder conviction and death sentence—and her world turns upside down.

Sister Helen's highest goal is to get Matthew to take responsibility for his actions and to come to peace with God, the murder victims' parents, and himself. She does this not by pushing or persuading, but by giving him her time and her ear. In their early meetings, Prejean comes with no agenda; she tells Poncelet, "I'm here to listen. Whatever you want to talk about is fine with me." She asks open-ended questions and allows Poncelet to arrive at his own conclusions. He admits to being surprised that she "didn't come down here preaching fire and brimstone," so he slowly opens his life to her.

As time goes on, Sister Helen comes to realize that Poncelet is, indeed, guilty of the awful crimes for which he has been convicted. Her pain is obvious as she confronts the grieving families of his victims, none of whom can understand or accept why she is willing to help a murderer. What they don't appreciate is that she never wavers in her abhorrence for his deeds, but she remains steadfast in separating her hate for the crime from her concern and love for Poncelet. As such, she provides viewers with proof that unconditional positive regard can be achieved, and can heal.

"silver surfers" need the listening ears of others, either in person or in cyberspace.

Men and women differ in the way they act when the opportunity to support others arises. Women are more prone than men to give supportive responses when presented with another person's problem (Hale et al., 1997; Trobst et al., 1994) and are more skillful at composing such messages (Burleson, 1982). By contrast, men tend to respond to others' problems by offering advice, or by diverting the topic (Barbee et al., 1990; Derlega et al., 1994). In a study of sororities and fraternities, Woodward and his colleagues (1996) found that sorority women frequently respond with emotional support when asked to help; also, they rated their sisters as being better at listening nonjudgmentally, and on comforting and showing concern for them. Fraternity men, on the other hand, fit the stereotypical pattern of offering help by challenging their brothers to evaluate their attitudes and values.

For both men and women, a supporting response can sometimes be helpful. In other instances, this kind of comment isn't helpful at all; in fact, it can even make things worse. Telling a person who is obviously upset that everything is all right, or joking about a serious matter, can trivialize the problem. People might see your comments as a put-down, leaving them feeling worse than before. As with the other styles we'll discuss, supporting can be helpful, but only in certain circumstances (Goldsmith & Fitch, 1997):

- Make sure your expression of support is sincere. Phony agreement or encouragement is probably worse than no support at all, since it adds the insult of your dishonesty to whatever pain the other person is already feeling.
- Be sure the other person can accept your support. Sometimes people are so upset that they aren't ready or able to hear anything positive.
- Focus on "here and now" rather than "then and there." While it's sometimes true that "You'll feel better tomorrow," it sometimes isn't (you can

ZITS Partnership © 1999. Reprinted with special permission of King Features Syndicate.

probably remember times when you felt *worse* the next day). More importantly, focusing on the future avoids supporting in the present. Even if the prediction that "Ten years from now, you won't remember her name" proves correct, it gives little comfort to someone experiencing heartbreak today. "Everything is going to turn out fine" and "There are other fish in the sea—you'll land one soon" are variations on the same theme—they are promises that may not come true. Their intentions may be good, but they usually don't offer the support that's needed.

## Analyzing

In **analyzing** a situation, the listener offers an interpretation of a speaker's message ("I think what's really bothering you is . . ."; "She's doing it because . . ."; or "Maybe the problem started when he . . ."). Interpretations are often effective in helping people who have problems to consider alternative meanings of a situation—meanings they would have never thought of without your assistance. Sometimes an analysis helps clarify a confusing problem, providing an objective understanding of the situation. Research suggests that analytic listeners are able to hear the concerns of emotionally upset others without experiencing similar emotions, which can be an advantage in problem solving (Weaver & Kirtlye, 1995).

In other cases, an analysis can create more problems than it solves. There are two reasons

why: First, your interpretation may not be correct, in which case the problem holder may become even more confused by accepting it. Second, even if your analysis is accurate, sharing it with the problem holder might not be useful. There's a chance that it will arouse defensiveness (analysis implies being superior and in a position to evaluate). Besides, the problem holder may not be able to understand your view of the problem without working it out personally.

How can you know when it's helpful to offer an analysis? There are several guidelines to follow:

- Offer your interpretation in a tentative way rather than as absolute fact. There's a big difference between saying "Maybe the reason is . . ." and insisting "This is the truth."
- Your analysis ought to have a reasonable chance of being correct. An inaccurate interpretation—especially one that sounds plausible—can leave a person more confused than before.
- Make sure that the other person will be receptive to your analysis. Even if you're completely accurate, your thoughts won't help if the problem holder isn't ready to consider them.
- Be sure that your motive for offering an analysis is truly to help the other person. It can be tempting to offer an analysis to show how brilliant you are or even to make the other person feel bad for not having thought of the right

## FOCUS ON RESEARCH

### COMMUNICATION IN A HIV/AIDS SUPPORT GROUP

Being a supportive listener can be difficult when a friend has lost a job or flunked a test, but those problems seem trivial when compared to the prospect of a life-threatening illness. People wrestling with potentially terminal diseases usually need a listening ear. One outlet is a support group, where people share their similar concerns with one another.

Carol Stringer Cawyer and Athena Smith-Dupré decided to study one particular support group, composed of people "facing the stigmas and difficulties that occur when living with HIV/AIDS." Some in the group had HIV or AIDS; others worked with or were related to people who did.

To provide a vivid depiction of support-group communication, Cawyer collected her data through participant observation. She joined

the weekly group for a three-month period; in fact, she was told in her first session that she "must be willing to disclose some of her own feelings" in the sessions. She took notes during the meetings and wrote follow-up observations after leaving each session.

Group members used a variety of listening styles when responding to one another. Sometimes members would offer empathic statements that communicated, "We know how you feel" and "We have felt that way too." Some gave advice in the form of educational information; others tried to put things in perspective by describing situations that were worse than anything a speaker had described. Questions were asked, help was offered, and even disagreements occurred. Regardless of

which type of listening response was used, the members were clearly invested in listening and being listened to. The authors noted high levels of nonverbal attentiveness: "Head nods, smiles, and pats communicate that they are listening and supportive." Often the members cried together.

As Chapter 1 pointed out, communication will not solve all problems. Support groups such as this cannot take away all the personal and social difficulties associated with HIV/AIDS. Talking and listening to others can make a difference, however, as Cawyer and Smith-Dupré observed: "In a situation that emphasizes how little control individuals have over life and death, communication is a valuable way to give and receive social support."

Cawyer, C. S., & Smith-Dupré, A. (1995). Communicating social support: Identifying supportive episodes in an HIV/AIDS support group. *Communication Quarterly, 43*, 243–258.

answer in the first place. Needless to say, an analysis offered under such conditions isn't helpful.

## Advising

When approached with another's problem, the most common reaction is **advising** (Notarius & Herrick, 1988). Advice can be offered in at least three conditions. First, when it's requested in a

straightforward manner: "What do you think I should do?" In other cases, an ambiguous statement might sound like a request for suggestions (Goldsmith, 1994). Ambiguous statements of this sort include requests for opinions ("What do you think of Jeff?"), soliciting information ("Would that be an example of sexual harassment?"), and announcement of a problem ("I'm really confused . . ."). Finally, advice is sometimes offered even when it hasn't been solicited. ("You look awful. You ought to get more sleep!") Advice isn't always as helpful as it might seem. In interviews with bereaved people who had recently lost a loved one, almost half of the mourners received sympathy gestures consisting of advice, yet the suggestions were rated as helpful only three percent of the time (Davidowitz & Myrick, 1984). Advice is most welcome under two conditions: when it has been requested, and when the advisor seems concerned with respecting the face needs of the recipient (Goldsmith, 2000; Goldsmith & Fitch, 1997).

There are several reasons why advice isn't always helpful. First, it may not offer the best suggestion about how to act. In fact, it might even be harmful. There's often a temptation to tell others how you would behave in their place, but it's important to realize that what's right for one person may not be right for another. A related consequence of advising is that it often allows others to avoid responsibility for their decisions. A partner who follows a suggestion of yours that doesn't work out can always pin the blame on you. Finally, people often don't want advice: They may not be ready to accept it, and instead may simply need to talk out their thoughts and feelings. Research suggests that unsolicited advice threatens the presenting self of the recipient (Goldsmith, 2000). In effect, the advisor who gives advice without being asked to do so seems to be suggesting that there's something wrong with the recipient . . . not a welcome message.

Before offering advice, then, be sure four conditions are present:

- Be sure the other person really wants to hear your suggestions. The best indicator is a clear request for advice. If you're not sure whether the other person is seeking your opinion, it may be best to ask.
- Consider whether the person seeking your advice is truly ready to accept it. This way, you can avoid the frustration of making good sug-

gestions, only to find that the person with the problem had another solution in mind all the time.
- Be confident that your advice is correct. Resist the temptation to act like an authority on matters you know little about or to make suggestions when you aren't positive that they are the best choice. Realize that while a particular course of action worked for you, it probably won't be correct for everybody.
- Be certain that the receiver won't blame you if the advice doesn't work out. You may be offering the suggestions, but the choice and responsibility for accepting them is up to the recipient of your advice.

## Evaluating

An **evaluating** response appraises the sender's thoughts or behaviors in some way. The evaluation may be favorable ("That's a good idea" or "You're on the right track now") or unfavorable ("An attitude like that won't get you anywhere"). In either case, it implies that the person evaluating is in some way qualified to pass judgment on the speaker's thoughts or actions.

Sometimes negative evaluations are purely critical. How many times have you heard responses such as "Well, you asked for it!" or "I *told* you so!" or "You're just feeling sorry for yourself"? Although such comments can sometimes serve as a verbal slap that "knocks sense" into the problem holder, they usually make matters worse by arousing defensiveness in that person. After all, suggesting that someone is foolish or mistaken is an attack on the presenting image that most people would have a hard time ignoring or accepting.

Other times, negative evaluations are less critical. These involve what we usually call constructive criticism, which is intended to help the problem holder improve in the future. Friends give this sort of response about the choice of everything from clothing, to jobs, to friends. Another common setting for constructive criticism is school, where instructors evaluate students' work in order to help them master concepts and skills. Even constructive criticism can arouse defensiveness because it may threaten the self-concept of the person at whom it is directed.

Evaluations have the best chance of being received when two conditions exist:

- The person with the problem should have requested an evaluation from you. Occasionally, an unsolicited judgment may bring someone to his or her senses, but more often this sort of uninvited evaluation will trigger a defensive response.
- Your evaluation should be genuinely constructive and not designed as a put-down. If you are tempted to use evaluations as a weapon, don't fool yourself into thinking that you are being helpful. Often, statements such as, "I'm telling you this for your own good" simply aren't true.

## Which Style to Use?

By now, it should be clear that there are many ways to respond as a listener. You also can see that each style has advantages and disadvantages. This leads to the important question: Which style is best? There isn't a simple answer to this question. Research shows that all response styles can help others accept their situation, feel better, and have a sense of control over their problems (Albrecht & Adelman, 1987; Burleson, 1994).

As a rule of thumb, it's probably wise to begin with responses from the left and middle of the listening response continuum: silent listening, questioning, paraphrasing, empathizing, and supporting. Once you've gathered the facts and demonstrated your interest and concern, it's likely that the speaker will be more receptive to (and perhaps even ask for) your analyzing, advising, and evaluating responses.

You can boost the odds of choosing the best style in each situation by considering three factors. First, think about the *situation,* and match your response to the nature of the problem. People sometimes need your advice. In other cases your encouragement and support will be most helpful, and in still other instances your analysis or judg-

ment may be truly useful. And, as you have seen, there are times when your questioning and paraphrasing can help others find their own answer.

Besides considering the situation, you also should think about the *other person* when deciding which approach to use. As the Focus on Research article on page 199 demonstrates, it's important to be sure that the other person is open to receiving *any* kind of help. Furthermore, you need to be confident that you will be regarded as someone whose support is valuable. The same response that would be accepted with gratitude when it comes from one communicator can be regarded as unhelpful when it's offered by someone else (Clark et al., 1998; Sullivan, 1996).

It's also important to match the type of response you offer with the style of the person to whom it is directed. Some people are able to consider advice thoughtfully, while others use suggestions to avoid making their own decisions. Many communicators are extremely defensive and aren't capable of receiving analysis or judgments without lashing out. Still others aren't equipped to think through problems clearly enough to profit from questioning and paraphrasing. Sophisticated listeners choose a style that fits the person.

Finally, think about *yourself* when deciding how to respond. Most of us reflexively use one or two styles. You may be best at listening quietly, posing a question, or paraphrasing from time to time. Or perhaps you are especially insightful and can offer a truly useful analysis of the problem. Of course, it's also possible to rely on a response style that is *unhelpful.* You may be overly judgmental or too eager to advise, even when your suggestions aren't invited or productive. As you think about how to respond to another's problems, consider your weaknesses as well as your strengths.

## Summary

Listening is both more frequent and less emphasized than speaking. Despite its relative invisibility, listening is at least as important as speaking.

Understanding of listening suffers from several misconceptions, which communicators need to correct. Listening—at least listening effectively—is quite different from merely hearing a message. Skillful listening is not easy; rather, it is a challenge that requires much effort and talent. Several barriers can hamper effective listening: hearing problems, information overload, rapid thought, and both internal and external noise. Even careful listening does not mean that all listeners will receive the same message. A wide variety of factors discussed in this chapter can result in widely varying interpretations of even simple statements.

There are a variety of reasons why we listen to others. At the most basic level, we listen to understand and retain information. Perhaps more importantly, we listen to build and maintain our interpersonal relationships. We may listen to help others, and also to evaluate their messages. Listening consists of several components: hearing, attending to a message, understanding the statement, recalling the message after the passage of time, and responding to the speaker.

Listening responses can be placed on a continuum. More reflective/less evaluative responses include silent listening, questioning, paraphrasing, and empathizing. These put a premium on gathering information and showing interest and concern. Less reflective/more evaluative responses include supporting, analyzing, advising, and evaluating. These put a premium on offering input and direction. It is possible to use the "more reflective" listening responses to help people arrive at their own decisions without offering advice or evaluation. The most effective listeners use several styles, depending on the situation, the other person, and their own personal skills and motivation.

## Recommended Readings

**Overview of listening:**

Andrew D. Wolvin and Carolyn G. Coakley. *Listening*. 5th ed. Boston: McGraw-Hill, 1996.

**Listening and social support:**

Terence L. Albrecht, Brant R. Burleson, and Deana Goldsmith. "Supportive Communication." In *Handbook of Interpersonal Communication*, 2nd ed., edited by Mark L. Knapp and Gerald R. Miller. Newbury Park, CA: Sage, 1994.

**Listening in various contexts:**

Michael Purdy and Deborah Borisoff. *Listening in Everyday Life: A Personal and Professional Approach*. Lanham, MD: University Press of America, 1996.

## Activities

1. **Invitation to Insight**
   You can overcome believing in some common myths about listening by recalling specific instances when:
   a. you heard another person's message but did not attend to it.
   b. you attended to a message but forgot it almost immediately.
   c. you attended and remembered a message but did not understand it accurately.
   d. you understood a message but did not respond sufficiently to convey your understanding to the sender.

2. **Invitation to Insight**
   Keep a three-day journal of your listening behavior, noting the time you spend listening in various contexts. In addition, analyze your reasons for listening. Which goal(s) were you trying to achieve?
   a. To understand and retain information
   b. To build and maintain relationships
   c. To help
   d. To evaluate

3. **Critical Thinking Probe**
   Communication problems can arise from factors that aren't easily observed. Based on your experience, decide which of the following

steps in the listening process cause the greatest difficulties:

a. Hearing
b. Attending
c. Understanding
d. Remembering
e. Responding

Discuss your findings with your friends, and develop a list of remedies that can help minimize listening problems in the areas you identified.

4. **Skill Builder**

Explore the benefits of passive listening by using a "Talking Stick." Richard Hyde (1993) developed this exercise from the Native American tradition of "council." Gather a group of people in a circle, and designate a particular item as the talking stick. Participants will then pass the stick around the circle. Participants may speak

a. only when holding the stick;
b. for as long as they hold the stick; and
c. without interruption from anyone else in the circle.

When a member is through speaking, the stick passes to the left and the speaker surrendering the stick must wait until it has made its way around the circle before speaking again.

After each member of the group has had the chance to speak, discuss how this experience differs from more common approaches to listening. Decide how the desirable parts of this method could be introduced in everyday conversations.

5. **Invitation to Insight**

Check your understanding of counterfeit questions and nonempathic responses by looking again at Jill and Mark's conversation on pages 206–207. Create examples of poor responses that Mark could have given Jill by showing how and where he could have:

a. asked a question that was really a statement;
b. asked a question with a hidden agenda;
c. asked a question that begged for a "correct" answer;
d. asked a question based on an unchecked assumption;
e. denied Jill the right to her feelings;
f. minimized the significance of the situation; and
g. focused on "then and there" rather than "here and now."

In each case, speculate how Jill might have reacted to Mark's response.

6. **Ethical Challenge**

What responsibility do communicators have to listen as carefully and thoughtfully as possible to other speakers? Are there ever cases where the poor listening habits listed on pages 194–195 (for example, pseudolistening, stage hogging, and defensive listening) are justified? How would you feel if you knew that others weren't listening to you?

7. **Skill Builder**

Practice your ability to paraphrase in order to understand others by following these steps.

a. Choose a partner, and designate one of yourselves as A and the other as B. Find a subject on which you and your partner seem to disagree—a personal dispute, a philosophical or moral issue, or perhaps a matter of personal taste.
b. A begins by making a statement on the subject. B's job is to paraphrase the idea. In this step B should feed back only what he or she heard A say, without adding any judgment or interpretation. B's job here is simply to *understand* A—not to agree or disagree with A.
c. A responds by telling B whether or not the response was accurate, and by making any necessary additions or corrections to clarify the message.
d. B then paraphrases the revised statement. This process should continue until A is sure that B understands him or her.

e. Now B and A reverse roles and repeat the procedure in steps a–d. Continue the conversation until both partners are satisfied that they have explained themselves fully and have been understood by the other person.

After the discussion has ended, consider how this process differed from typical conversations on controversial topics. Was there greater understanding here? Do the partners feel better about one another? Finally, ask yourself how your life might change if you used more paraphrasing in everyday conversations.

8. **Skill Builder**

Explore the various types of listening responses by completing the following steps.

a. Join with two partners to form a trio. Designate members as A, B, and C.

b. A begins by sharing a current, real problem with B. The problem needn't be a major life crisis, but it should be a real one. B should respond in whatever way seems most helpful. C's job is to categorize each response by B as silent listening, questioning, paraphrasing, empathizing, supporting, analyzing, advising, or evaluating.

c. After a four- to five-minute discussion, C should summarize B's response styles. A then describes which of the styles were most helpful and which were not helpful.

d. Repeat the same process two more times, switching roles so that each person has been in all of the positions.

e. Based on their findings, the threesome should develop conclusions about what combination of response styles can be most helpful.

# CHAPTER
## 8

# Emotions

# After Studying the Material in This Chapter . . .

## You Should Understand:

1. The four components of emotion.

2. The factors that influence the expression of emotion in contemporary society.

3. The influence of sex and culture on emotional expressiveness and sensitivity.

4. The relationships among activating events, thoughts, emotions, and communication behavior.

5. Seven fallacies that lead to unnecessarily debilitative emotions which can interfere with effective communication.

6. The steps in the rational-emotive approach for coping with debilitative emotions.

## You Should Be Able to:

1. Observe the physical and cognitive manifestations of some of the emotions you experience.

2. Label your own emotions accurately.

3. Identify the degree to which you express your emotions and the consequences of this level of expression.

4. Follow the guidelines in this chapter in deciding when and how to express your emotions in an important relationship.

5. Realize which of your emotions are facilitative and which are debilitative.

6. Identify the fallacious beliefs that have caused you to experience debilitative emotions in a specific situation.

7. In a specific situation, apply the rational-emotive approach to managing your debilitative emotions.

## Key Terms

| | | | |
|---|---|---|---|
| Debilitative emotions | Fallacy of catastrophic expectations | Fallacy of overgeneralization | Mixed emotions |
| Facilitative emotions | | | Primary emotions |
| Fallacy of approval | Fallacy of causation | Fallacy of perfection | Self-talk |
| | Fallacy of helplessness | Fallacy of should | |

At one time or another, you have probably imagined how different life would be if you became disabled in some way. Although the thought of losing your eyesight, hearing, or mobility might be frightening, it can remind you to appreciate the faculties you do have. Now, have you ever considered how life would be if you somehow lost your ability to experience emotions?

Although life without feelings wouldn't be as dramatic as other disabilities, its effects would be profound. An emotionless world would be free of boredom, frustration, fear, and loneliness. But the cost of such a pain-free existence would be the loss of emotions like joy, pride, and love. Few of us would be willing to make that sort of trade-off.

The role of emotions in human affairs is apparent to social scientists and laypeople alike. When Yale University psychologist Robert Sternberg (1985) asked people to describe an "intelligent person," one of the skills listed was the ability to understand and get along with others. This ability to get along was described by psychologist Daniel Goleman (1995) as one aspect of "emotional intelligence." Goleman makes the claim that intellectual ability is not the only way to measure one's talents, and that success in the world depends in great part on the ability to understand and manage one's own emotions and to be sensitive to others' emotions.

Because emotions are such an important part of human communication, we will take a close look at them in the following pages. We will explore what feelings are, discuss the ways they are handled in contemporary society, and see how recognizing and expressing them can improve relationships. We will look at some guidelines that should give you a clearer idea of when and how to express your emotions constructively. Finally, we will explore a method for coping with troublesome, debilitating feelings that inhibit rather than help your communication.

# What Are Emotions?

Suppose an extraterrestrial visitor asked you to explain emotions. How would you answer? You might start by saying that emotions are things that we feel. But this doesn't say much, for in turn you would probably describe feelings as synonymous with emotions. Social scientists generally agree that there are several components to the phenomena we label as feelings.

## Physiological Changes

When a person has strong emotions, many bodily changes occur. For example, the physical components of fear include an increased heartbeat, a rise in blood pressure, an increase in adrenaline secretions, an elevated blood sugar level, a slowing of digestion, and a dilation of pupils. Some of these changes are recognizable to the person having them. These physiological messages can offer a significant clue to your emotions once you become aware of them. A churning stomach or tense jaw can be a signal that something is wrong.

## Nonverbal Reactions

Not all physical changes that accompany emotions are internal. Feelings are often apparent by observable changes. Some of these changes involve a person's appearance: blushing, sweating, and so on. Other changes involve behavior: a distinctive facial expression, posture, gestures, different vocal tone and rate, and so on.

Although it's reasonably easy to tell when someone is feeling a strong emotion, it's more difficult to be certain exactly what that emotion might be. A slumped posture and sigh may be a sign of sadness, or it may signal fatigue. Likewise, trembling hands might indicate excitement, or they may be an outward sign of fear. As you learned in Chapter 6, nonverbal behavior is usually ambiguous, and it's dangerous to assume that it can be "read" with much accuracy.

Although we usually think of nonverbal behavior as the reaction to an emotional state, there may

## CHANGING EMOTIONS BY CHANGING BEHAVIOR

When I was a kid, my dad used a technique on me whenever he saw I was getting tense. He would say to me, "Loosen your jaw." In almost every case, I found that my jaw was indeed clenched and stiff. By moving my jaw and letting it fall loose, I would feel more relaxed and less uptight. I still hear his voice every time I get stressed, and I still loosen my jaw to feel less nervous about the situation.

"What the hell was _that_? Something just swept over me—like contentment or something."

be times when the reverse is true—when nonverbal behavior actually _causes_ emotions. As you read in Chapter 3 (see page 77), people actually create emotional states by altering their facial expressions. When volunteers were coached to smile, they actually reported feeling better, and when they altered their expressions to look unhappy, they felt worse than before (Kleinke et al., 1998). Previous research by Paul Ekman and his colleagues (1983) produced the same results, with subjects feeling afraid, angry, disgusted, amused, sad, surprised, and contemptuous when they created facial expressions that mimicked those feelings. As behavioral scientists like to say, it can be easier to act yourself into new ways of feeling than to feel yourself into new ways of acting.

## Cognitive Interpretations

Although there may be cases in which there is a direct connection between physical behavior and emotional states, in most situations the mind plays an important role in determining how we feel. On page 219 you read that some physiological components of fear are a racing heart, perspiration, tense muscles, and elevated blood pressure. Interestingly enough, these symptoms are similar to the physical changes that accompany excitement, joy, and other emotions. In other words, if we were to measure the physical condition of someone having a strong emotion, we would have a hard time knowing whether that person was trembling with fear or quivering with excitement. The recognition that the bodily components of most emotions are similar led some psychologists to conclude that the experience of fright, joy, or anger comes primarily from the _label_ we give to the same physical symptoms at a given time (Valins, 1966). Psychologist Philip Zimbardo (1977, p. 53) offers a good example of this principle:

> I notice I'm perspiring while lecturing. From that I infer I am nervous. If it occurs often, I might even label myself a "nervous person." Once I have the label, the next question I must answer is "Why am I nervous?" Then I start to search for an appropriate explanation. I might notice some students leaving the room, or being inattentive. I am nervous because I'm not giving a good lecture. That makes me nervous. How do I know it's not good? Because

I'm boring my audience. I am nervous because I am a boring lecturer and I want to be a good lecturer. I feel inadequate. Maybe I should open a delicatessen instead. Just then a student says, "It's hot in here, I'm perspiring and it makes it tough to concentrate on your lecture." Instantly, I'm no longer "nervous" or "boring."

In his book *Shyness* (1977), Zimbardo discusses the consequences of making inaccurate or exaggerated attributions such as these. In a survey of more than five thousand people, over 80 percent described themselves as having been shy at some time in their lives, whereas more than 40 percent considered themselves presently shy. Most significantly, those who labeled themselves "not shy" behaved in virtually the *same way* as their shy counterparts. They would blush, perspire, and feel their hearts pounding in certain social situations. The biggest difference between the two groups seemed to be the label with which they described themselves. This is a significant difference. Someone who notices the symptoms we've described and thinks, "I'm such a shy person!" will most likely feel more uncomfortable and communicate less effectively than another person with the same symptoms who thinks, "Well, I'm a bit shaky (or excited) here, but that's to be expected."

We'll take a closer look at ways to reduce unpleasant emotions through cognitive processes later in this chapter.

### Verbal Expression

As you read in Chapter 6, nonverbal behavior is a powerful way of communicating emotion. In fact, nonverbal actions are better at conveying attitudes than they are at expressing ideas. But sometimes words are necessary to express feelings. Is your friend's uncharacteristically short temper a sign of anger at you, or does it mean something less personal? Is a lover's unenthusiastic response a sign of boredom with you or the result of a long workday? Is a new acquaintance mistaking your friendliness as a come-on? There are times—especially in our low-context culture—when you can't rely on per-

ceptiveness to make sure a message is communicated and understood accurately.

The ability to communicate clearly about feelings has been characterized as part of "emotional intelligence." Daniel Goleman (1995) identifies a wide range of problems that arise for people who aren't able to talk about emotions constructively, including social isolation, unsatisfying relationships, feelings of anxiety and depression, and misdirected aggression. Research by John Gottman and his associates (1997) has shown that the way parents talk to their children about emotions has a powerful effect on the children's development. The researchers identified two distinct parenting styles, "emotion coaching" and "emotion dismissing." They show how the coaching approach gives children skills for communicating about feelings in later life that lead to much more satisfying relationships. Later in this chapter you will find some guidelines for effectively communicating about emotions.

## Types of Emotions

So far our discussion has implied that although emotions may differ in tone, they are similar in most other ways. In truth, emotions vary in many respects.

### Primary and Mixed Emotions

Emotions are rather like colors: Some are simple, whereas others are blends. Robert Plutchik's (1984) "emotion wheel" (Figure 8.1 p. 222) illustrates the difference. For example, jealousy can be viewed as a combination of several different emotions: distress, anger, disgust, contempt, fear, and even shame. Likewise, loneliness can include feelings of anger toward self and others, estrangement, and depression. Plutchik has identified eight **primary emotions,** which are inside the perimeter of the wheel. He suggests that these primary feelings can combine to form other, **mixed emotions,** some of which are listed outside the circle.

Whether or not you agree with the specific emotions Plutchik identifies as primary and

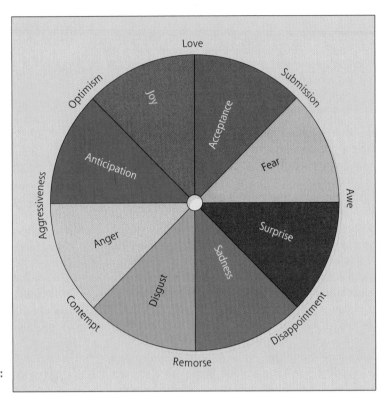

**Figure 8.1** The Emotion Wheel: Primary and Mixed Emotions

## Intense and Mild Emotions

Another way emotions are like colors is in their intensity. Figure 8.2 illustrates this point clearly. Each vertical slice represents the range of a primary emotion from its mildest to its most intense state. The model in Figure 8.2 shows the importance of choosing language that describes the intensity of your feelings clearly. To say you're "annoyed" when a friend breaks an important promise, for example, would probably be an understatement. In other cases, people chronically overstate the strength of their feelings. To them, everything is "wonderful" or "terrible." The problem with this sort of exaggeration is that when a truly intense emotion comes along, they have no words left to describe

secondary, the wheel suggests that many feelings need to be described in more than a single term.

it adequately. If chocolate chip cookies from the local bakery are "fantastic," how does it feel to fall in love?

## Influences on Emotional Expression

Each of us is born with the disposition to reveal our emotions, at least nonverbally. But over time, a wide range of differences develops in emotional expression. In the next few pages, we will look at some influences that shape how people communicate their feelings.

### Culture

Over 100 years of research has confirmed the fact that certain basic emotions are experienced by people around the world (Gudykunst & Young,

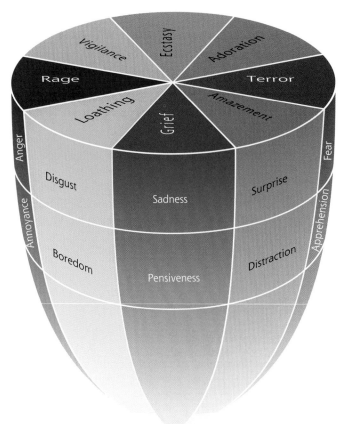

***Figure 8.2*** **Intensity of Emotions**

1992). No matter where a person is born and regardless of his or her background, the ability to feel happiness, sadness, surprise, anger, disgust, and fear seems to be universal. People from all cultures also express these emotions in the same way, at least in their facial expressions. A smile or scowl, for example, is understood everywhere.

Of course, this doesn't mean that the same events generate the same emotion in all cultures. The notion of eating snails might bring a smile of delight to some residents of France, though it would cause many North Americans to grimace in disgust. More to the point of this book, research has shown that fear of strangers and risky situations is more likely to frighten people living in the United States and Europe than those in Japan, while Japanese are more apprehensive about relational communication than are Americans and Europeans (Ting-Toomey, 1991).

There are also differences in the degree to which people in various cultures display their feelings (Aune & Aune, 1996). For example, social scientists have found support for the notion that people from warmer climates are more emotionally expressive than those who live in cooler places (Pennebaker et al., 1996). Over 2,900 respondents representing 26 nationalities reported that people from the southern part of their countries were more emotionally expressive than northerners.

Cultural background influences the way we interpret others' emotions as well as the way we express our own. In one experiment (Matsumoto,

1993), an ethnically varied group of students—Euro-American, African-American, and Asian-American—identified the type, intensity, and appropriateness of emotional expression in fifty-six photos representing eight social situations (e.g., alone, with a friend, in public, with someone of higher status). Results indicated that ethnicity led to considerable differences in the way subjects gauged others' emotional states. For example, blacks perceived the emotions in the photos as more intense than the Euro-American, Asian, and Latino respondents; Asians perceived them the least intense. Also, blacks reported a greater frequency of anger expressions than the other groups. Ethnicity also shaped ideas about appropriate rules for expressing one's own emotions. For example, Euro-Americans perceived the display of emotions as more appropriate than did the other groups; Asians perceived their display as least appropriate. These findings remind us that, in a multicultural society, one element of communicative competence is the ability to understand our own cultural filters when judging others' behaviors.

One of the most significant factors that influences emotional expression is the position of a culture on the individualism–collectivism spectrum. Members of collective cultures (such as Japan and India) prize harmony among members of their "in-group," and discourage expression of any negative emotions that might upset relationships among people who belong to it. By contrast, members of highly individualistic cultures like the United States and Canada feel comfortable revealing their feelings to people with whom they are close (Gallois, 1993; Matsumoto, 1991). Individualists and collectivists also handle emotional expression with members of out-groups differently: Whereas collectivists are quite frank about expressing negative emotions toward outsiders, individualists are more likely to hide such emotions as dislike (Triandis, 1994). It's easy to see how differences in display rules can lead to communication problems. For example, individualistic North Americans might view collective Asians as less than candid, whereas a person raised in

### REFLECTION

#### E-MAIL AS A SAFE CHANNEL FOR EMOTIONAL EXPRESSION

I've never been very close with my sister, but last year both of us got on-line and started sending e-mail messages to each other. At first we "talked" about once a week; now it's almost daily. What's interesting is that my sister doesn't show her emotions very much in person, but in her e-mails she "bares her soul" to me.

Last week we got together in person for the first time in months. I thought we would pick right up at the same level of emotional exchange that had become the norm in our on-line discussions. Wrong! In face-to-face conversation, it still seemed hard for her to express her feelings. It was kind of hard for me, too.

Funny thing is, she sent me an e-mail after she got home telling me how much she enjoyed our get-together. It was warm and touching. It was also something she would never say to me in person.

Asia could easily regard North Americans as overly demonstrative.

### Sex

Even within our culture, the ways in which men and women express their emotions vary in some significant areas (Kunkel & Burleson, 1999). Research on emotional expression suggests that there is at least some truth in the cultural stereotype of the inexpressive male and the more demonstrative female. As a group, women are more likely than men to verbally and nonverbally express a wide range of feelings. On the Internet, the same differences between male and female emotional expressiveness apply. For example, women were more likely to use emoticons to clarify their feelings than were men (Witmer & Katzman, 1999).

Whether on the Internet or in face-to-face conversations, men tend to be less emotionally expressive, particularly when it comes to revealing feelings of vulnerability, including fear, sadness, loneliness, and embarrassment. On the other hand, men are less bashful about revealing their strengths and positive emotions, and both sexes feel and express anger equally (Goldsmith & Fulfs, 1999).

Differences between the sexes also exist in the sensitivity to others' emotions. Women are consistently better than men at detecting nonverbal emotional cues. In fact, sex is the best predictor of the ability to detect and interpret emotional expressions—better than academic background, amount of foreign travel, cultural similarity, or ethnicity (Swenson & Casmir, 1998).

One's sex isn't the only variable that affects emotional sensitivity. A second factor is whether the other person is of the same or different sex. For example, men are more likely to express feelings (especially positive ones) with women than with other men (Floyd, 1997a). People generally are better at recognizing emotions of members of the same sex.

Of course, these sex differences are statistical averages, and many men and women don't fit these profiles. Furthermore, sex isn't the *only* variable that affects emotional sensitivity. A third factor that influences sensitivity to others' emotions is the person or people with whom we are communicating. For example, dating and married couples are significantly better at recognizing each other's emotional cues than are strangers.

A final factor is the difference in power between the two communicators. People who are less powerful learn—probably from necessity—to read the more powerful person's signals. One experiment revealed that "women's intuition" should be relabeled "subordinate's intuition." In opposite-sex twosomes, the person with less control—regardless of sex—was better at interpreting the leader's nonverbal signals than vice versa (Snodgrass, 1985).

## Social Conventions

In mainstream U.S. society the unwritten rules of communication discourage the direct expression of most emotions (Shimanoff, 1984). Count the number of genuine emotional expressions you hear over a two- or three-day period and you'll discover that such expressions are rare. People are generally comfortable making statements of fact and often delight in expressing their opinions, but they rarely disclose how they feel.

Not surprisingly, the emotions that people *do* share directly are usually positive. Communicators are reluctant to send messages that embarrass or threaten the face of others (Shimanoff, 1988). Historians offer a detailed description of the ways contemporary society discourages expressions of anger. When compared to past centuries, Americans today strive to suppress this "unpleasant"

## FILM CLIP

### A LIFETIME OF UNEXPRESSED EMOTIONS: *THE REMAINS OF THE DAY*

Stevens (Anthony Hopkins) is a reserved and proper head butler in a 1930s English mansion. In the tradition of formal British service, Stevens shows little or no emotion as he performs his duties. His sense of professional obligation is so strong that when his father is dying in an upstairs room, Stevens doesn't abandon his downstairs post at an important dinner party.

Miss Kenton (Emma Thompson), the mansion's housekeeper, is smitten with Stevens. He is probably smitten with her, too, but he doesn't let it show. In a highly charged scene, Kenton catches Stevens leafing through a book in his den. She asks him what he's reading and he refuses to show her. She seductively pursues him around the room, then grabs the book—only to discover it's a romance novel. Rather than acknowledging the passion he feels for both the book and Miss Kenton, he stiffly explains that he reads only to improve his vocabulary. The moment is fraught with emotion, yet it ends with Stevens solemnly asking Kenton "not to disturb the few moments I have to myself."

The scene is a metaphor for Stevens' life. It's not that he has no emotions; it's that he represses them so others can't see them. Although this makes him an excellent butler, it handicaps his personal relationships. By movie's end, it's clear that his life without expressed emotions is hardly a life at all.

("I love you") or face-saving ones ("I'm sorry I yelled at you"). They also willingly disclosed both positive and negative feelings about absent third parties ("I like Fred," "I'm uncomfortable around Gloria"). On the other hand, the husbands and wives rarely verbalized face-threatening feelings ("I'm disappointed in you") or hostility ("I'm mad at you") (Shimanoff, 1985).

Surprisingly, social rules even discourage too much expression of positive feelings (Duck, 1992). A hug and kiss for Mother is all right, but many young men feel more comfortable shaking hands with Dad. Affection toward friends becomes less and less frequent as we grow older, so that even a simple statement such as, "I like you" is seldom heard between adults. Feelings of love are even more risky, at least when we aren't sure the other person feels the same way about us. Saying "I love you" is easiest in established romantic relationships between men and women, and it is not uncommon in friendships between two women; however, it is judged as far less appropriate in friendships between men—probably because of the possibility of the expression being mistaken as a homosexual come-on (Floyd, 1997b).

### Social Roles

Expression of emotions is also limited by the requirements of many social roles. Salespeople are taught always to smile at customers, no matter how obnoxious. Teachers are portrayed as paragons of rationality, supposedly representing their field of expertise and instructing their students with total impartiality. Students are often rewarded for asking "acceptable" questions and otherwise being submissive creatures (Trenholm & Rose, 1980).

The result of all these restrictions is that many of us lose the ability to feel deeply. Just as a muscle withers away when it is unused, our capacity to recognize and act on certain emotions decreases without practice. It's hard to cry after spending most of one's life fulfilling the role society expects of a man even when the tears are inside. After years of denying anger, the ability to recognize

emotion in almost every context, including childraising, the workplace, and personal relationships (Stearns & Stearns, 1986). Research supports this analysis. One study of married couples revealed that the partners shared complimentary feelings

## FOCUS ON RESEARCH

### MANAGING EMOTIONS ON THE JOB: THE WORLD OF 911 CALL TAKERS

On the phone is a hysterical person whose house is being burglarized. You're a 911 operator and it's your job to stay calm and assist the caller. How do you handle this emotionally charged situation while keeping your own emotions in check? That's what Sarah Tracy and Karen Tracy wanted to learn in their research on "emotion labor" at an emergency call center in a large western U.S. city. They observed and took notes at a call center; they attended training sessions; they went on ride-alongs in ambulances; they conducted in-depth interviews; they even went to a pub where call takers, fire dispatchers, and police officers unwind. They found that "a routine part of the call-taker job is to channel callers' feelings of anger and hysteria while dealing with a jumble of their own feelings including: sadness, irritation and anxiety, disgust, amusement, and powerlessness."

Call takers are instructed to be calm and professional on the phone. Offline, they're supposed to detach themselves from the trauma of the situations they assisted. Call takers in the study repeatedly said "you can't take it personal" or get "too wrapped up" in callers' personal situations. (In fact, they seldom learn the outcome of a caller's dilemma.) To help process their emotions, call takers use strategies such as making faces or gestures during a call while their voices stay even-keeled, using self-talk (coaching themselves to stay cool and to empathize with the caller), and joking with fellow employees about callers.

It may sound strange for emergency call takers to be tossing pencils in the air or chuckling with coworkers about traumatic situations, but these coping mechanisms allow them to manage their jumbled and sometimes frayed emotions. After all, as the researchers discovered, "acting in a neutral manner . . . is demanding work."

Tracy, S. J., & Tracy, K. (1998). Emotion labor at 911: A case study and theoretical critique. *Journal of Applied Communication Research 26*, 390–411.

that feeling takes real effort. For someone who has never acknowledged love for one's friends, accepting that emotion can be difficult indeed.

## Fear of Self-Disclosure

In a society that discourages the expression of feelings, emotional self-disclosure can seem risky. For a parent, boss, or teacher whose life has been built on the image of confidence and certainty, it may be frightening to say, "I'm sorry. I was wrong."

Moreover, someone who musters up the courage to share feelings such as these still risks unpleasant consequences. Others might misunderstand: An expression of affection might be construed as a romantic invitation, and a confession of uncertainty might appear to be a sign of weakness. Another risk is that emotional honesty might make others feel uncomfortable. This may be one reason why some people find it easier to express their emotions via computer (see the Focus on Research on page 228.) Finally, there's always a chance that emotional honesty could be used against you, either out of cruelty or thoughtlessness. Chapter 10 discusses alternatives to complete disclosure and suggests circumstances when it can be both wise and ethical to keep your feelings to yourself.

## FOCUS ON RESEARCH

### INITIATING ROMANTIC RELATIONSHIPS VIA COMPUTER

For many people, the most difficult part of a romantic relationship is getting it started. As relational researchers have found, the initiating stage can be awkward and tense for even the most gregarious person. Consider, then, how difficult this stage can be for those who are shy. What are the options for people who find it hard to talk with others? Bradford Scharlott and William Christ researched one alternative: computer-dating systems. Their findings suggest that technology might provide assistance for those who normally have trouble getting the relational ball rolling.

Scharlott and Christ studied the uses and users of Matchmaker, an on-line dating system. Matchmaker is a sophisticated version of a computer bulletin board. Newcomers answer a series of questions about themselves, then ask the system computer to "Make Me a Match." The system produces a list of names of others whose answers closely match those of the user. The user then has the option to contact these people "personally" through e-mail—and in many cases, a relationship begins. Scharlott and Christ placed a seventy-four-question survey on the Matchmaker system in San Antonio, Texas. Several of the items focused on shyness with statements such as, "It is hard for me to act natural when I am meeting new people" and "I feel tense when I am with people I don't know very well." Of the 150 registered subscribers, 102 responded to the survey.

Shyness appears to be an important variable in explaining how and why some people use Matchmaker.

Seventy-four percent of the high-shyness users indicated that their main purpose for joining Matchmaker was to find a romantic or sexual relationship, while only 46 percent of the low-shyness users joined for that reason. Shyer users were more likely to agree that Matchmaker allowed them to explore new aspects of their personalities; they also expressed a greater appreciation for the system's anonymous, nonthreatening environment for making matches. Scharlott and Christ conclude that "many shy users employ Matchmaker to overcome inhibitions that may prevent them from initiating relationships in face-to-face settings." Computer-dating systems might not be the answer for everyone, but they may offer some hope for people who find relationship initiation particularly intimidating.

Scharlott, B. W., & Christ, W. G. (1995). Overcoming relationship-initiation barriers: The impact of a computer-dating system on sex role, shyness, and appearance inhibitions. *Computers in Human Behavior, 11*, 191–204.

## Emotional Contagion

Along with cultural rules, social roles, and self-induced fears, our emotions are also affected by the feelings of those around us through **emotional contagion,** the process by which emotions are transferred from one person to another. As Daniel Goleman (1995, p. 115) observed, "We catch feelings from one another as though they were some kind of social virus."

Most of us recognize the degree to which emotions are "infectious." You can almost certainly recall instances in which being around a calm person leaves you feeling more at peace, or when your previously sunny mood was spoiled by contact with a grouch. Researchers have demonstrated that this process can occur quickly, and with little or no verbal communication. In one study (Sullins, 1991), two volunteers completed a survey that identified their moods. They spent two

unsupervised minutes together, ostensibly waiting for the researcher to return to the room. At the end of that time, they completed another emotional survey. Time after time, the brief exposure resulted in the less-expressive partner's moods coming to resemble the feelings of the more-expressive one. If an expressive communicator can shape another person's feelings with so little input in such a short time, it's easy to understand how emotions can be even more "infectious" with prolonged contact.

distress—are more likely to get a host of ailments, including cancer, asthma, and heart disease (DeAngelis, 1992; Mayne, 1999). On the other hand, people who are *overly* expressive also suffer physiologically. When people lash out verbally, their blood pressure jumps an average of 20 points, and in some people it increases by as much as 100 points (Mayne, 1999; Siegman & Snow, 1997). The key to health, then, is to learn how to express emotions *constructively*. In a few pages, you will find guidelines for this important communication skill.

Beyond the physiological benefits, another advantage of expressing emotions effectively is the chance of improving relationships (Kennedy-Moore & Watson, 1999). As Chapter 10 explains, self-disclosure is one path (though not the only one) to intimacy. Even on the job, many managers and organizational researchers are contradicting generations of tradition by suggesting that constructively expressing emotions can lead to career success as well as helping workers feel better (Nelton, 1996).

Despite its benefits, expressing emotions effectively isn't a simple matter. It's obvious that showing every feeling of boredom, fear, anger, or frustration would get you in trouble. Even the indiscriminate sharing of positive feelings—love,

## Guidelines for Expressing Emotions

A wide range of research supports the value of expressing emotions appropriately. At the most basic physiological level, people who know how to share their feelings are healthier than those who don't. On one hand, under-expression of feelings can lead to serious ailments. Inexpressive people—those who value rationality and self-control, try to control their feelings and impulses, and deny

affection, and so on—isn't always wise. On the other hand, withholding emotions can be personally frustrating and can keep relationships from growing and prospering.

The following suggestions can help you decide when and how to express your emotions. Combined with the guidelines for self-disclosure in Chapter 10, they can improve the effectiveness of your emotional expression.

## Recognize Your Feelings

Answering the question "How do you feel?" isn't as easy for some people as others. Communication researchers Melanie and Steven Booth-Butterfield (1998) found that some people (whom they term "affectively oriented") are much more aware of their own emotional states and use information about those feelings when making important decisions. By contrast, people with a low affective orientation are usually unaware of their emotions, and tend to reject feelings as useful, important information. The researchers summarize scholarship showing a relationship between awareness of feelings and a wide range of valuable traits, including positive relationships between parents and children, the ability to comfort others, sensitivity to nonverbal cues, and even skillful use of humor. In other words, being aware of one's feelings is an important ingredient in communication skill.

As you read earlier in this chapter, there are a number of ways in which feelings become recognizable. Physiological changes can be a clear sign of your emotional state. Monitoring nonverbal behaviors is another excellent way to keep in touch with your feelings. You can also recognize your emotions by monitoring your thoughts, as well as the verbal messages you send to others. It's not far from the verbal statement "I hate this!" to the realization that you're angry (or bored, nervous, or embarrassed).

## Choose the Best Language

Most people suffer from impoverished emotional vocabularies. Ask them how they're feeling and

the response will almost always include the same terms: *good* or *bad, terrible* or *great,* and so on. Take a moment now and see how many feelings you can write down. After you've done your best, look at Table 8.1 and see which ones you've missed from this admittedly incomplete list.

Many communicators think they are expressing feelings when, in fact, their statements are emotionally counterfeit. For example, it sounds emotionally revealing to say, "I feel like going to a show" or "I feel we've been seeing too much of each other." But in fact, neither of these statements has any emotional content. In the first sentence the word *feel* really stands for an intention: "I *want* to go to a show." In the second sentence the "feeling" is really a thought: "I *think* we've been seeing too much of each other." You can recognize the absence of emotion in each case by adding a genuine word of feeling to it. For instance, "I'm *bored* and I want to go to a show" or "I think we've been seeing too much of each other and I feel *confined.*"

Relying on a small vocabulary of feelings is as limiting as using only a few terms to describe colors. To say that the ocean in all its moods, the sky as it varies from day to day, and the color of your true love's eyes are all "blue" only tells a fraction of the story. Likewise, it's overly broad to use a term like *good* or *great* to describe how you feel in situations as different as earning a high grade, finishing a marathon, and hearing the words "I love you" from a special person.

There are several ways to express a feeling verbally:

- Through *single words:* "I'm angry" (or "excited," "depressed," "curious," and so on).
- By describing *what's happening to you:* "My stomach is tied in knots," "I'm on top of the world."
- By describing *what you'd like to do:* "I want to run away," "I'd like to give you a hug," "I feel like giving up."

Sometimes communicators express feelings in a coded manner. This happens most often

**Table 8.1**

**Descriptions of Emotional States**

| | | | | | |
|---|---|---|---|---|---|
| afraid | concerned | exhausted | hurried | nervous | sexy |
| aggravated | confident | fearful | hurt | numb | shaky |
| amazed | confused | fed up | hysterical | optimistic | shocked |
| ambivalent | content | fidgety | impatient | paranoid | shy |
| angry | crazy | flattered | impressed | passionate | sorry |
| annoyed | defeated | foolish | inhibited | peaceful | strong |
| anxious | defensive | forlorn | insecure | pessimistic | subdued |
| apathetic | delighted | free | interested | playful | surprised |
| ashamed | depressed | friendly | intimidated | pleased | suspicious |
| bashful | detached | frustrated | irritable | possessive | tender |
| bewildered | devastated | furious | jealous | pressured | tense |
| bitchy | disappointed | glad | joyful | protective | terrified |
| bitter | disgusted | glum | lazy | puzzled | tired |
| bored | disturbed | grateful | lonely | refreshed | trapped |
| brave | ecstatic | happy | loving | regretful | ugly |
| calm | edgy | harassed | lukewarm | relieved | uneasy |
| cantankerous | elated | helpless | mad | resentful | vulnerable |
| carefree | embarrassed | high | mean | restless | warm |
| cheerful | empty | hopeful | miserable | ridiculous | weak |
| cocky | enthusiastic | horrible | mixed up | romantic | wonderful |
| cold | envious | hostile | mortified | sad | worried |
| comfortable | excited | humiliated | neglected | sentimental | wacky |

when the sender is uncomfortable about revealing the feeling in question. Some codes are verbal ones, as when the sender hints more or less subtly at the message. For example, an indirect way to say, "I'm lonesome" might be "I guess there isn't much happening this weekend, so if you're not busy, why don't you drop by?" Such a message is so indirect that your real feeling may not be recognized. For this reason, people who send coded messages stand less of a chance of having their emotions understood—and their needs met.

## Share Multiple Feelings

Many times the feeling you express isn't the only one you're experiencing. For example, you might often express your anger but overlook the confusion, disappointment, frustration, sadness, or embarrassment that preceded it. To understand the importance of expressing multiple emotions, consider the following examples. For each one, ask yourself two questions: How would I feel? What feelings might I express?

- An out-of-town friend has promised to arrive at your house at six o'clock. When he hasn't arrived by nine, you are convinced that a terrible accident has occurred. Just as you pick up the phone to call the police and local hospitals, your friend breezes in the door with an offhand remark about getting a late start.
- You and your companion have a fight just before leaving for a party. Deep inside, you know you were mostly to blame, even though you aren't willing to admit it. When you arrive at the party, your companion leaves you to flirt with several other attractive guests.

## REFLECTION

### CHOOSING THE EMOTION TO EXPRESS FIRST

Not long ago our seventeen-year-old daughter spent the entire night out— without telling us about her plans to stay at a friend's. By 2:00 A.M. we were in a panic. We frantically called the police and the local hospitals, but she couldn't be found anywhere. My wife and I spent the entire sleepless night praying that she was all right and imagining all the awful things that might have happened to her.

When our daughter's car came up the driveway at 7:30 A.M., I was never so relieved in my life! But as soon as she walked in the door and I realized she was okay, I really let her have it. "What were you thinking? How irresponsible can you be?" You can imagine how I sounded, and how defensively she reacted.

After a couple of minutes I could see our "conversation" headed in the wrong direction, and that it was at least partly my fault. I had only shared my anger, and not the feelings of relief, concern, and love that were even more important. "Let's start over," I suggested. Then I explained to her how worried we were all night long, and how relieved we were to know that she was safe. What a difference! Our daughter still knew how angry we were, but she also understood that the anger came from love and concern. This experience taught me how important it is to share mixed feelings. Hearing the positive ones makes negative feelings a lot easier to accept.

In situations like these you would probably feel several emotions. Consider the case of the overdue friend. Your first reaction to his arrival would probably be relief— "Thank goodness, he's safe!" But you would also be likely to feel anger— "Why didn't he phone to tell me he'd be late?" The second example would probably leave you with an even greater number of emotions: guilt at contributing to the fight, hurt and perhaps embarrassment at your friend's flirtations, and anger at this sort of vengefulness.

Despite the commonness of experiencing several emotions at the same time, we often communicate only one feeling—usually, the most negative one. In both of the preceding examples you might show only your anger, leaving the other person with little idea of the full range of your feelings. Consider the different reaction you would get by showing *all* your emotions in these situations as well as others.

### Recognize the Difference between Feeling and Acting

Just because you feel a certain way doesn't mean you must always act on it. In fact, there is compelling evidence that people who act out angry feelings—even by hitting an inanimate punching bag—actually feel worse than those who experience anger without lashing out (Bushman et al., 1999).

Recognizing the difference between feeling and acting can liberate you from the fear that getting in touch with certain emotions will commit you to some disastrous course of action. If, for instance, you think, "I'm so nervous about the interview that I want to cancel it and pretend that I'm sick," it becomes possible to explore why you feel so anxious and then work to remedy the problem. Pretending that nothing is the matter, on the other hand, will do nothing to diminish your anxiety, which can then block your chances for success.

### Accept Responsibility for Your Feelings

As you'll soon read, people don't make us like or dislike them, and believing that they do denies the responsibility each of us has for our own emotions. It's important to make sure that your emotional expressions don't blame others for the way you feel. The "I" language described in Chapter 5 makes it clear that you are owning up to your feelings. For example, instead of saying "You're making me angry," it's more accurate to say, "I'm feeling angry." Instead of "You hurt my feelings," a more responsible statement is, "I feel hurt when you do that."

## Choose the Best Time and Place to Express Your Feelings

Often the first flush of a strong feeling is not the best time to speak out. If you're awakened by the racket caused by a noisy neighbor, storming over to complain might result in your saying things you'll regret later. In such a case, it's probably wiser to wait until you have thought out carefully how you might express your feelings in a way that would be most likely to be heard.

Even after you've waited for the first flush of feeling to subside, it's still important to choose the time that's best suited to the message. Being rushed or tired or disturbed by some other matter is probably a good reason for postponing the expression of your feeling. Often, dealing with your emotions can take a great amount of time and effort, and fatigue or distraction will make it difficult to follow through on the matter you've started. In the same manner you ought to be sure that the recipient of your message is ready to hear you out before you begin.

There are also cases where you may choose to *never* express your feelings. If you think telling an instructor that her lectures leave you bored into a stupor, you might decide to answer her question "How's class going?" with an innocuous "Okay." And even though you may be irritated by the arrogance of a police officer stopping you for speeding, the smartest approach might be to keep your feelings to yourself.

## Express Your Feelings Clearly

When people do decide to express their feelings, they often do so in an unclear way, either out of confusion or discomfort. When communicators know and understand one another as well as the

characters in the film *Smoke* (described on page 234), clarity may not be important. But most of the time, ambiguous statements and nonverbal cues are easy to misinterpret.

One key to making your emotions clear is to realize that you most often can summarize them in a few words—hurt, glad, confused, excited, resentful, and so on. Once you have summarized your emotions, you can go on to explain why you feel as you do. The list in Table 8.1 on page 231 offers some examples of words to use in clear emotional statements.

A second way to prevent confusion is to avoid overqualifying or downplaying your emotions— "I'm a *little* unhappy" or "I'm *pretty* excited" or "I'm *sort of* confused." Of course, not all emotions are strong ones. We do feel degrees of sadness and joy, for example, but some communicators

## FILM CLIP

### THE POTENTIAL OF UNVERBALIZED FEELINGS: *SMOKE*

The film *Remains of the Day* (see page 226) described the tragedy of unexpressed feelings. At one time or another, most people have probably had thoughts such as, "I wish I told him I loved him" or "If only I said I was hurt instead of pouting." While clear emotional expression can be valuable, the film *Smoke* shows that the communication of affection, especially between men, can be like the title of this film: sometimes barely visible, elusive, yet powerful.

The story is filled with an interesting, if not motley, collection of characters. Paul Benjamin (William Hurt) is a forlorn writer still recovering from the death of his wife. Rashid Cole (Harold Perrineau, Jr.) is a bright young man in search of himself and his father (Forest Whitaker). Auggie Wren (Harvey Keitel) is a cigar store owner who befriends Benjamin, hires Cole, and helps his old girlfriend Ruby (Stockard Channing) through a difficult relationship with her (and perhaps his) daughter.

In this story, children are furious with their parents. Friends care deeply for each other. Enemies make amends. Affection is felt on a variety of levels. In some scripts, these emotions would be expressed verbally— "I hate you"; "You mean so much to me"; "I'm sorry"; "I love you"—but not in this movie. Rashid and Auggie "make up" by cursing each other with smiles on their faces. Rashid buries the hatchet with his dad by fighting him, then eating with him in silence. Auggie "tells" Benjamin he cares by showing him photographs, shooting the bull, and sharing stories. Auggie doesn't like it when Ruby cries in appreciation for the money he gives her; he just wants her to know he's concerned. The characters banter, swear, goad each other, and smoke together—and love one another. They don't need to say it; they communicate it quite clearly.

have a tendency to discount almost every feeling. Do you?

Finally, you express yourself most clearly when you make it clear that your feeling is centered on a specific set of circumstances, rather than the whole relationship. Instead of saying "I resent you," say "I get resentful when you don't keep your promises." Rather than "I'm bored with you," say "I get bored when you talk about money."

## Managing Difficult Emotions

Perceiving others more accurately isn't the only challenge communicators face. At times we view *ourselves* in a distorted way. These distorted self-perceptions can generate a wide range of feelings— insecurity, anger, and guilt, to name a few—that interfere with effective communication. To begin understanding how this process works, read on.

### Facilitative and Debilitative Emotions

We need to make a distinction between **facilitative emotions,** which contribute to effective functioning, and **debilitative emotions,** which hinder or prevent effective performance. A classic example

## FEELING NERVOUS ISN'T NECESSARILY DEBILITATIVE

I have always been a singer. My mom describes me as a ham, and sure enough, I usually jump center stage whenever the opportunity arises. I've sung in school shows, at weddings, and in bands. I even dressed up in funny costumes and delivered singing telegrams for a while.

Because I perform so much, people assume that I'm confident. The truth is, I get very nervous whenever I sing in front of an audience. I get butterflies in my stomach and sweaty palms. Sometimes I even feel nauseous. I've grown used to these feelings, so I don't let them keep me from performing. In fact, I might worry if I *didn't* feel nervous!

of a debilitative emotion is *communication apprehension*—feelings of anxiety that plague some people at the prospect of communicating in an unfamiliar or difficult context such as giving a speech, meeting strangers, or interviewing for a job. (See the Focus on Research profile on page 237 for an account of how debilitative emotions can plague job-seekers.)

Not surprisingly, debilitative emotions like communication apprehension can lead to a variety of problems in personal, business, educational and even medical settings (Bourhis & Allen, 1992). When people become anxious, they generally speak less, which means their needs aren't met; and when they do manage to speak up, they are less effective than their more confident counterparts (Patterson & Ritts, 1997).

The difference between facilitative and debilitative emotions often isn't one of quality so much as *degree*. For instance, a certain amount of anger

or irritation can be constructive, since it often stimulates a person to improve the unsatisfying conditions. Rage, on the other hand, usually makes matters worse. The same is true for fear. A little bit of nervousness before a job interview may boost you just enough to improve your performance (mellow athletes or actors usually don't do well), but a job candidate who is visibly nervous isn't likely to impress potential employers (Ayres & Crosby, 1995). Even a little suspicion can make people more effective communicators. One study revealed that couples who doubted that their relational partners were telling the truth were better at detecting deception than were trusting mates (McCornack & Levine, 1990). Of course, an extreme case of paranoia would have the opposite and debilitative effect, reducing the ability to interpret the partner's behavior accurately. One big difference, then, between facilitative and debilitative emotions is their *intensity*.

A second characteristic of debilitative feelings is their extended *duration*. Feeling depressed for a while after the breakup of a relationship or the loss of a job is natural. Spending the rest of one's life grieving over the loss accomplishes nothing. In the same way, staying angry at someone for a wrong inflicted long ago can be just as punishing to the grudge holder as to the wrongdoer.

## Thoughts Cause Feelings

The goal, then, is to find a method for getting rid of debilitative feelings while remaining sensitive to the more facilitative emotions. Fortunately, such a method—termed a *rational-emotional* approach—does exist (Dryden et al., 1999; Ellis, 1999; Ellis & Greiger, 1977). This method is based on the idea that the key to changing feelings is to change unproductive thinking. Let's see how it works.

For most people, emotions seem to have a life of their own. People wish they could feel calm when approaching strangers, yet their voices quiver. They try to appear confident when asking for a raise, but their eyes twitch nervously. Many

ZITS Partnership © 1999. Reprinted with special permission King Features Syndicate.

people would say that the strangers or the boss *makes* them feel nervous, just as they would say that a bee sting causes them to feel pain:

| Activating Event | | Consequence |
|---|---|---|
| bee sting | ⟶ | physical pain |
| meeting strangers | ⟶ | nervous feelings |

When looking at emotions in this way, people may believe they have little control over how they feel. However, the causal relationship between physical pain and emotional discomfort (or pleasure) isn't as great as it seems. Cognitive psychologists and therapists argue that it is not *events,* such as meeting strangers or being jilted by a lover, that cause people to feel poorly, but rather the *beliefs they hold* about these events.

Ellis tells a story that clarifies this point. Imagine yourself walking by a friend's house and seeing your friend come to a window and call you a string of vile names. (You supply the friend and the names.) Under the circumstances, it's likely that you would feel hurt and upset. Now imagine that instead of walking by the house, you were passing a mental institution when the same friend, who was obviously a patient there, shouted the same offensive names at you. In this case, your reaction would probably be quite different; most likely, you'd feel sadness and pity.

In this story the activating event—being called names—was the same in both cases, yet the emotional consequences were very different. The reason for different feelings has to do with the pattern of thinking in each case. In the first instance you would most likely think that your friend was angry with you and that you must have done something terrible to deserve such a response. In the second case you would probably assume that your friend had experienced some psychological difficulty, so you would probably feel sympathetic. This example illustrates that people's *interpretations* of events determine their feelings:

| Activating Event | Thought or Belief | Consequences |
|---|---|---|
| being called names | ⟶ "I've done something wrong." | ⟶ hurt, upset |
| being called names | ⟶ "My friend must be sick." | ⟶ pity, sympathy |

The same principle applies in more common situations. For example, the words "I love you" can be interpreted in a variety of ways. They could be taken at face value as a genuine expression of deep affection. They might also be decoded in a variety of other ways; for example, as an attempt at manipulation, a sincere but mistaken declaration uttered in a moment of passion, or an attempt to make the recipient feel better. One study revealed that women are more likely than men to regard expressions of love as genuine statements, instead

## FOCUS ON RESEARCH

### SELF-TALK AFFECTS PERFORMANCE IN JOB INTERVIEWS

Employment interviews can be nerve-racking for even the most confident communicators, and they are even more difficult for people with high levels of communication anxiety—what researchers call "communication apprehension" (CA). Joe Ayres and his graduate student colleagues at Washington State University conducted research to better understand what causes some people to become especially apprehensive during the process of meeting prospective employers.

The research team conducted focus group interviews with high-CA and low-CA students to learn what goes through their minds before, during, and after an employment interview. The differences between the groups were startling. High-CA students avoided thinking about an interview in advance; therefore, they did little in the way of research or preparation. When they did think about an upcoming interview, high-CA students dwelled on negative self-talk: "I won't do well"; "I don't know why I'm doing this."

During interviews, high-CA candidates continued to flood their minds with similar downbeat thoughts. After the interview was finished, their self-talk was equally negative. It's no surprise that thoughts like these created negative self-fulfilling prophecies that led to poor interview performances in classroom role-plays. It's not that low-CA students are free of anxiety about interviews; they simply channel it into productive activities such as research, preparation, rehearsal, and visualization of positive outcomes. We can imagine them thinking, "I'll do a lot better if I prepare."

This research reinforces the importance of rational, constructive self-talk. On the job, as in personal relationships, the way we think affects the way we communicate.

Ayres, J., Keereetaweep, T., Chen, P., & Edwards, P. A. (1998). Communication apprehension and employment interviews. *Communication Education, 47,* 1–17.

of attributing them to some other cause (Booth-Butterfield & Trotta, 1994). It's easy to imagine how different interpretations of a statement like "I love you" can lead to different emotional reactions:

| Event | Thought | Feeling |
|-------|---------|---------|
| Hearing "I love you" → | "This is a genuine statement" → | Delight (perhaps) |
| Hearing "I love you" → | "S/he's just saying this to manipulate me" → | Anger |

The key, then, to understanding and changing feelings lies in the pattern of thought, which manifests itself through **self-talk** (Vocate, 1994). To understand how self-talk works, pay attention to the part of you that, like a little voice, whispers in your ear. Take a moment now and listen to what the voice is saying.

Did you hear the voice? It was quite possibly saying "What little voice? I don't hear any voices!" This little voice talks to you almost constantly:

"Better pick up a loaf of bread on the way home."
"I wonder when he's going to stop talking."
"It sure is cold today!"
"Are there two or four cups in a quart?"

At work or at play, while reading the paper or brushing our teeth, we all tend to think. This thinking voice rarely stops. It may fall silent for a while when you're running, riding a bike, or meditating, but most of the time it rattles on.

# Irrational Thinking and Debilitative Emotions

This process of self-talk is essential to understanding the debilitative feelings that interfere with effective communication. Many debilitative feelings come from accepting a number of irrational thoughts—we'll call them *fallacies* here—that lead to illogical conclusions and, in turn, to debilitating feelings. We usually aren't aware of these thoughts, which makes them especially powerful (Bargh, 1988).

**The Fallacy of Perfection**   People who accept the **fallacy of perfection** believe that a worthwhile communicator should be able to handle any situation with complete confidence and skill. Although such a standard of perfection can serve as a goal and a source of inspiration (rather like making a hole in one for a golfer), it's totally unrealistic to expect that you can reach or maintain this level of behavior. The truth is, people simply aren't perfect. Perhaps the myth of the perfect communicator comes from believing too strongly in novels, TV, or films. In these media, perfect characters are often depicted—the perfect mate or child, the totally controlled and gregarious host, the incredibly competent professional. Although these fabrications are certainly appealing, real people will inevitably come up short compared to them.

People who believe that it's desirable and possible to be a perfect communicator come to think that people won't appreciate them if they are imperfect. Admitting mistakes, saying "I don't know," or sharing feelings of uncertainty or discomfort thus seem to be social defects. Given the desire to be valued and appreciated, these people are tempted at least to try to *appear* perfect. They assemble a variety of social masks, hoping that if they can fool others into thinking that they are perfect, perhaps they'll find acceptance. The costs of such deception are high. If others ever detect that this veneer of confidence is false, the person hiding behind it is considered a phony. Even if the facade goes undetected, the performance consumes a great deal of psychological energy and diminishes the rewards of approval.

The irony for perfectionists is that their efforts are unnecessary. Research by Eliot Aronson (1995) and others suggests that the people we regard most favorably are those who are competent but not perfect. Why? First, many people understand that the acts of would-be perfectionists are manifestations of a desperate struggle. It's obviously easier to like someone who is not trying to deceive you than someone who is. Second, most people become uncomfortable around a person regarded as perfect. Knowing they don't measure up to certain standards, most people are tempted to admire this superhuman only from a distance.

Not only can subscribing to the myth of perfection keep others from liking you, but it also acts as a force to diminish self-esteem. How can you like yourself when you don't measure up to your own standards? You become more liberated each

time you comfortably accept the idea that you are not perfect. For example, like everyone else, you sometimes have a hard time expressing yourself. Like everyone else, you make mistakes from time to time, and there is no reason to hide it. You are honestly doing the best you can to realize your potential, to become the best person you can be.

**The Fallacy of Approval**   Another mistaken belief is based on the idea that it is vital—not just desirable—to obtain everyone's approval. Communicators who subscribe to the **fallacy of approval** go to incredible lengths to seek acceptance from others, even to the extent of sacrificing their own principles and happiness. Adherence to this irrational myth can lead to some ludicrous situations, such as feeling nervous because people you really don't like seem to disapprove of you, or feeling apologetic when you are not at fault.

The myth of acceptance is irrational. It implies that some people are more respectable and more likable because they go out of their way to please others. Often, this implication simply isn't true. How respectable are people who have compromised important values simply to gain acceptance? Are people highly thought of who repeatedly deny their own needs as a means of buying approval? Genuine affection and respect are hardly due such characters. In addition, striving for universal acceptance is irrational because it is simply not possible. Sooner or later, a conflict of expectations is bound to occur. One person approves of a certain kind of behavior, whereas another approves of only the opposite course of action.

Don't misunderstand: Abandoning the fallacy of approval doesn't mean living a life of selfishness. It's still important to consider the needs of others. It's also pleasant—one might even say necessary—to strive for the respect of certain people. The point is that the price is too high if you must abandon your own needs and principles in order to gain this acceptance.

**The Fallacy of Should**   One huge source of unhappiness is the inability to distinguish between

what *is* and what *should be,* or the **fallacy of should**. For instance, imagine a person who is full of complaints about the world:

> "There should be no rain on weekends."
> "People ought to live forever."
> "Money should grow on trees."
> "We should all be able to fly."

Beliefs such as these are obviously foolish. However pleasant such wishing may be, insisting that the unchangeable should be altered won't affect reality one bit. Yet many people torture themselves by engaging in this sort of irrational thinking: They confuse "is" with "ought." They say and think:

> "That guy should drive better."
> "She shouldn't be so inconsiderate."
> "They ought to be more friendly."
> "He should work harder."

In each of these cases, the person *prefers* that people behave differently. Wishing that things were better is perfectly legitimate, and trying to change them is, of course, a good idea; but it is unreasonable for people to *insist* that the world operate just as they want it to. Parents wish that their children were always considerate and neat. Teachers wish that their students were totally fascinated with their subjects and willing to study diligently. Consumers wish that inflation weren't such a problem. As the old saying goes, those wishes and a quarter (now more like a dollar) will get you a cup of coffee.

Becoming obsessed with shoulds yields three bad consequences. First, this preoccupation leads to unnecessary unhappiness. People who are constantly dreaming about the ideal are seldom satisfied with what they have. For instance, partners in a marriage who focus on the ways in which their mate could be more considerate, sexy, or intelligent have a hard time appreciating the strengths that drew them together in the first place.

Second, the obsession keeps you from changing unsatisfying conditions. One employee, for example, constantly complains about the problems on the job: The quality of teaching should be improved, pay ought to be higher, the facilities should be upgraded, and so on. This person could be using the same energy to improve such conditions. Of course, not all problems have solutions; but when they do, complaining is rarely very productive. As one college manager puts it, "Rather than complain about the cards you are dealt, play the hand well."

Finally, this obsession tends to build a defensive climate in others. Imagine living around someone who insisted that people be more punctual, work harder, or refrain from using certain language. This kind of carping is obviously irritating. It's much easier to be around people who comment without preaching.

**The Fallacy of Overgeneralization**   The **fallacy of overgeneralization** occurs when a person bases a belief on a *limited amount of evidence*. Consider the following statements:

> "I'm so stupid! I can't understand how to do my income tax."
> "Some friend I am! I forgot my best friend's birthday."

In these cases people have focused on a single shortcoming as if it represented everything. Sometimes people forget that despite their difficulties, they have solved tough problems, and that although they can be forgetful, they're often caring and thoughtful.

A second, related category of overgeneralization occurs when we *exaggerate shortcomings:*

> "You *never* listen to me."
> "You're *always* late."
> "I can't think of *anything*."

Upon closer examination, such absolute statements are almost always false and usually lead to discouragement or anger. It's better to replace overgeneralizations with more accurate messages:

> "You often don't listen to me."
> "You've been late three times this week."
> "I haven't had any ideas I like today."

## REFLECTION

### THINKING ABOUT AN ANNOYING FRIEND

My friend Maria talks about her personal life at length, but when I talk about myself for more than a couple of minutes, she has few comments and quickly turns the conversation back to her favorite topic: herself.

Until lately Maria's egocentric focus was beginning to hurt my feelings. When Maria talks about herself, I think that what I have to say isn't interesting or that she doesn't care about me as a friend. I feel neglected, as if our relationship is one-sided.

Lately I've started to think about other reasons Maria talks so much. For example, she's told me that I am a great listener and that I help her by lending an ear. Also, I've realized that Maria seldom gets to talk about herself (she spends all day talking to customers on the phone and is engaged to a very talkative guy).

So now I have started to take Maria's self-centered approach less personally. I still wish she would listen to me more, but I don't think that her egocentrism is making me resentful. It's my choice whether to accept her as she is, speak up about what I want, or see less of her.

**The Fallacy of Causation**   People who live their lives in accordance with the **fallacy of causation** believe they should do nothing that can hurt or in any way inconvenience others because it will cause undesirable feelings. For example, you might visit friends or family out of a sense of obligation rather than a genuine desire to see them because, you believe, not to visit them will hurt their feelings. Did you ever avoid objecting to behavior that you found troublesome because you didn't want to cause anger? You may, on occasion, have pretended to be attentive—even though you were running late for an appointment and in a rush—because you didn't want a person to feel embarrassed for "holding you up." Then there were the times when you substituted praise for more honest negative responses in order to avoid causing hurt.

A reluctance to speak out in such situations often results from assuming that one person can cause another's emotions—that others, for example, are responsible for your feeling disappointed, confused, or irritated, or that you are responsible for others feeling hurt, angry, or upset. Actually, this assumption is incorrect. We may *act* in provocative ways, but each person is responsible for the way he or she *reacts*.

To understand why each person is responsible for his or her own feelings, consider how strange it sounds to suggest that people *make* you fall in love with them. Such a statement simply doesn't make sense. It would be more correct to say that people first act in one way or another; then you may or may not fall in love as a result of these actions.

In the same way, it's not accurate to say that people *make* you angry, upset, or even happy. Behavior that upsets or pleases one person might not bring any reaction from another. If you doubt this fact, think about people you know who are affected differently by the same behaviors that you find so bothersome. (You may scream "Idiot!" when you're driving and someone switches lanes in front of you without signaling, while the person with you in the car may not even notice, or may notice but not care.) The contrast between their reactions and yours shows that responses are determined more by our own temperament and thinking than by others' behavior.

**The Fallacy of Helplessness**  The **fallacy of help-lessness** suggests that satisfaction in life is determined by forces beyond our control. People with this outlook continuously see themselves as victims:

> "There's no way a woman can get ahead in this society. It's a man's world, and the best thing I can do is to accept it."

> "I was born with a shy personality. I'd like to be more outgoing, but there's nothing I can do about that."

> "I can't tell my boss that she is putting too many demands on me. If I did, I might lose my job."

The error in such statements becomes apparent once a person realizes that few paths are completely closed. In fact, most "can't" statements may be more correctly restated in one of two ways.

The first is to say that you *won't* act in a certain way, that you *choose* not to do so. For instance, you may choose not to stand up for your rights or to follow unwanted requests, but it is usually inaccurate to claim that some outside force keeps you from doing so. The other way to rephrase a "can't" is to say that you *don't know how* to do something. Examples of such a situation include not knowing how to complain in a way that reduces defensiveness, or not being aware of how to conduct a conversation. Many difficulties a person claims can't be solved do have solutions: The task is to discover those solutions and to work diligently at applying them.

When viewed in this light, many "can'ts" are really rationalizations to justify an unwillingness to change. Research supports the dangers of helpless thinking (Marangoni & Ickes, 1989). Lonely people tend to attribute their poor interpersonal relationships to uncontrollable causes. "It's beyond my control," they think. For example, lonely people are more negative than nonlonely ones about ever finding a mate. Also, they expect their relational partners to reject them. Notice the self-fulfilling prophecy in this attitude: Believing that your relational prospects are dim can lead you to act in ways that make you an unattractive prospect. Once you persuade yourself that there's no hope, it's easy to give up trying. On the other hand, acknowledging that there is a way to change—even though it may be difficult—puts the responsibility for the predicament on your shoulders. Knowing that you can move closer to your goals makes it difficult to complain about the present. You can become a better communicator.

**The Fallacy of Catastrophic Expectations**   Some fearful people operate on the assumption that if something bad can happen, it probably will. This is the **fallacy of catastrophic expectations**—a position similar to Murphy's Law. These statements are typical of such an attitude:

> "If I invite them to the party, they probably won't want to come."
> "If I speak up in order to try to resolve a conflict, things will probably get worse."
> "If I apply for the job I want, I probably won't be hired."
> "If I tell them how I really feel, they'll probably just laugh at me."

Once you start imagining terrible consequences, a self-fulfilling prophecy can begin to build. One study revealed that people who believed that their romantic partners would not change for the better were likely to behave in ways that contributed to the breakup of the relationship (Metts & Cupach, 1990).

It's undoubtedly naive to blithely assume that all your interactions with others will succeed, but it's equally wrong to assume they will fail. One consequence of this attitude is that you'll be less likely to be expressive at important times. To carry the concept to its logical extreme, imagine people who fear *everything:* How could they live their lives? They wouldn't step outside in the morning to see what kind of day it was for fear they'd be struck by lightning or a falling airplane. They wouldn't drive a car for fear of a collision. They wouldn't engage in any exercise for fear the strain might cause a heart attack. Do these examples seem ridiculous? Consider whether you've ever withdrawn from communicating because you were afraid of consequences that were actually likely. A certain amount of prudence is wise, but carrying caution too far can lead to a life of lost opportunities.

One way to escape from the myth of catastrophic failure is to reassess the consequences that would follow if you failed in your efforts to communicate. Failing in a given situation usually isn't as bad as it seems. What if people do laugh? Suppose you don't get the job? What if others do get angry at certain remarks? Are these matters really that serious? Trying something may, of course, lead to failure, but not trying something guarantees you don't get the job, or the better relationship, or whatever it is you want.

## Minimizing Debilitative Emotions

How can you overcome irrational thinking? Social scientists have developed a simple yet effective approach (Burns, 1999; Dryden et al., 1999; Needleman, 1999). When practiced conscientiously, it can help you cut down on the self-defeating thinking that leads to many debilitative emotions.

**Monitor Your Emotional Reactions**   The first step is to recognize when you're having debilitative emotions. (Of course, it's also nice to be aware of

"So the prince and the princess lowered their expectations and lived reasonably contentedly forever after."

pleasant feelings when they occur!) As we suggested earlier, one way to notice feelings is through physical stimuli: butterflies in the stomach, racing heart, hot flashes, and so on. Although such reactions might be symptoms of food poisoning, more often they reflect a strong emotion. You also can recognize certain ways of behaving that suggest your feelings: Stomping instead of walking normally, being unusually quiet, and speaking in a sarcastic tone of voice are some examples.

It may seem strange to suggest that it's necessary to look for emotions—they ought to be immediately apparent. However, the fact is that we often suffer from debilitative feelings for some time without noticing them. For example, at the end of a trying day you've probably caught yourself frowning and realized that you've been wearing that mask for some time without knowing it.

**Note the Activating Event**   Once you're aware of how you're feeling, the next step is to figure out what activating event triggered your response. Sometimes it is obvious. If your sweetheart keeps calling you by the name of a former lover, you're likely to become upset. In other cases, however, the activating event isn't so apparent.

Sometimes there isn't a single activating event but rather a series of small incidents that finally build toward a critical mass and trigger a debilitative feeling. This sort of thing happens when someone teases you over and over about the same thing, or when you suffer a series of small disappointments.

The best way to begin tracking down activating events is to notice the circumstances in which you have debilitative feelings. Perhaps they occur when you're around *specific people*. For example, you may feel tense or angry every time you encounter a person with whom you have struggled in the past (Gayle & Priess, 1999). Until those issues are dealt with, feelings about past events can trigger debilitative emotions, even in apparently innocuous situations.

In other cases, you might discover that being around certain *types of individuals* triggers debilitative emotions. For instance, you might become

nervous around people who seem more intelligent or self-confident than you are. In other cases, certain *settings* can stimulate unpleasant emotions: parties, work, school. Sometimes the *topic* of conversation is the factor that sets you off, whether politics, religion, sex, or some other subject.

**Record Your Self-Talk**   This is the point at which you analyze the thoughts that are the link between the activating event and your feelings. If you're serious about getting rid of debilitative emotions, it's important actually to write down your self-talk when first learning to use this method. Putting your thoughts on paper will help you see whether or not they make any sense.

Monitoring your self-talk might be difficult at first. This is a new skill, and any new activity seems awkward. If you persevere, however, you'll find you will be able to identify the thoughts that lead to your debilitative feelings. Once you get in the habit of recognizing this internal monologue, you'll be able to identify your thoughts quickly and easily.

**Dispute Your Irrational Beliefs**   Disputing your irrational beliefs is the key to success in the rational-emotive approach. Use the discussion of irrational fallacies on pages 238–242 to find out which of your internal statements are based on mistaken thinking.

You can do this most effectively by following three steps. First, decide whether each belief you've recorded is rational or irrational. Next, explain why the belief does or doesn't make sense. Finally, if the belief is irrational, write down an alternative way of thinking that is more sensible and that can leave you feeling better when faced with the same activating event in the future.

After reading about this method for dealing with unpleasant emotions, some readers have objections:

*"This rational-emotive approach sounds like nothing more than trying to talk yourself out of feeling bad."* This accusation is totally correct. After all, since we talk ourselves into feeling bad,

what's wrong with talking ourselves out of bad feelings, especially when they are based on irrational thoughts? Rationalizing may be an excuse and a self-deception, but there's nothing wrong with being rational.

*"The kind of disputing we just read sounds phony and unnatural. I don't talk to myself in sentences and paragraphs."* There's no need to dispute your irrational beliefs in any special literary style. You can be just as colloquial as you want. The important thing is to clearly understand what thoughts led you into your debilitative feeling so you can clearly dispute them. When the technique is new to you, it's a good idea to write or talk out your thoughts in order to make them clear. After you've had some practice, you'll be able to do these steps in a quicker, less formal way.

*"This approach is too cold and impersonal. It seems to aim at turning people into cold-blooded, calculating, emotionless machines."* This is simply not true. A rational thinker can still dream, hope, and love: There's nothing necessarily irrational about feelings like these. Rational people usually indulge in a bit of irrational thinking once in a while. But they usually know what they're doing. Like healthy eaters who occasionally treat themselves to a snack of junk food, rational thinkers occasionally indulge themselves in irrational thoughts, knowing that they'll return to their healthy lifestyle soon with no real damage done.

*"This technique promises too much. There's no chance I could rid myself of all unpleasant feelings, however nice that might be."* We can answer this by assuring you that rational-emotive thinking probably won't totally solve your emotional problems. What it can do is to reduce their number, intensity, and duration. This method is not the answer to all your problems, but it can make a significant difference—which is not a bad accomplishment.

## Summary

Emotions have several dimensions. They are signaled by internal physiological changes, manifested by verbal and nonverbal reactions, and defined in most cases by cognitive interpretations. Some emotions are primary, while others are combinations of two or more emotions. Some are intense, while others are relatively mild.

There are several reasons why people do not verbalize many of the emotions they feel. Some cultures encourage and others discourage the expression of emotions. Social rules discourage the expression of some feelings, particularly negative ones. Many social roles do not allow expression of certain feelings. Some people express emotions so rarely that they lose the ability to recognize when they are feeling them. Finally, fear of the consequences of disclosing some emotions leads people to withhold expression of them.

Since total expression of feelings is not appropriate for adults, several guidelines help define when and how to share emotions effectively. Self-awareness, clear language, and expression of mixed feelings are important. Willingness to accept responsibility for feelings instead of blaming them on others leads to better reactions. Choosing the proper time and place to share feelings is also important.

While some emotions are facilitative, other debilitative feelings inhibit effective functioning. Many of these debilitative emotions are caused by various types of irrational thinking. It is often possible to communicate more confidently and effectively by identifying troublesome emotions, identifying the activating event and self-talk that triggered them, and replacing any irrational thoughts with a more logical analysis of the situation.

## Recommended Readings

**Research on communication and emotion:**

Peter A. Andersen and Laura K. Guerrero, eds. *Handbook of Communication and Emotion: Research, Theory, Applications, and Contexts.* San Diego: Academic Press, 1998.

**Cultural influences on emotions:**

Peter N. Stearns and Jan Lewis, eds. *An Emotional History of the United States.* New York: New York University Press, 1998.

**Emotions and health:**

Aron W. Siegman and Timothy W. Smith, eds., *Anger, Hostility, and the Heart.* Hillsdale, NJ; Lawrence Erlbaum Associates, 1994.

**Overcoming debilitative self-talk:**

William Glasser. *Choice Theory.* New York: HarperCollins, 1999.

**Emotional expression in families:**

John M. Gottman, Lynn F. Katz, and Carole Hooven. *Meta-emotion: How Families Communicate Emotionally.* Mahwah, NJ: Lawrence Erlbaum Associates, 1997.

# Activities

1. **Invitation to Insight**
   Discover your emotional range by reviewing the list of feelings in Table 8.1 on page 231. Use the information there to complete the following steps:
   a. Focus on an important personal relationship.
   b. Identify the ten emotions that play the most important role in the relationship you are analyzing.
   c. Identify how you express each emotion in your "top ten." Focus both on the *frequency* with which you express the feeling and the *ways* you express it.
   d. Decide how satisfied you are with the insights you gained by answering questions b and c above.

2. **Skill Builder**
   Choose an important emotion you experience in one of your relationships. This relationship needn't be highly personal. You might, for example, focus on an employer, a professor, or a neighbor. Use the guidelines on pages 229–234 to determine whether and how you might express this emotion.

3. **Ethical Challenge**
   According to the rational-emotive approach, we cause our own feelings by interpreting an event in one way or another. If this is true, it is a fallacy to claim we "make" others feel happy or sad. Do you accept this position? To what degree are you responsible for communicating in ways that "cause" others to feel happy or sad? Use a specific incident from your life to illustrate your answer.

4. **Invitation to Insight**
   Explore whether you subscribe to the fallacy of helplessness by completing the following lists. Describe two important (to you) communication-related difficulties you have for each of the following: communicating with family members, people at school or at work, strangers, and friends. Use the following format for each difficulty:
   I can't _____,
   because _____.
   Now read the list, but with a slight difference. For each "can't," substitute the word "won't." Note which statements are actually "won'ts."

   Read the list again, only this time substitute "I don't know how to" for your original "can't." Rewrite any statements that are truly "don't know hows," and decide what you could do to learn the skill that you presently lack.

   Based on your experience, decide whether you subscribe to the fallacy of helplessness, and what you could do to eliminate this sort of debilitative thinking from your life.

5. **Skill Builder**
   Choose an important situation in which you experience debilitative emotions that interfere with your ability to communicate effectively. Use the four steps on pages 242–243 to challenge the rationality of your beliefs. Report on how the rational-emotive approach affects your communication in this important situation.

# CHAPTER 9

# Dynamics of Interpersonal Relationships

# After Studying the Material in This Chapter . . .

## You Should Understand:

1. The reasons why people choose others as potential relational partners.

2. The stages of relational development and the characteristics of movement between these stages.

3. The dialectical tensions that can arise as communicators attempt to satisfy conflicting needs.

4. The ways content and relational messages are communicated in interpersonal relationships.

5. The strategies that can be used to gain compliance in a relationship.

## You Should Be Able to:

1. Identify the social needs that you and the other person are trying to satisfy at a given point in one of your interpersonal relationships.

2. Identify the bases of interpersonal attraction in one of your relationships.

3. Describe the current stage of an important personal relationship and predict whether and how that relationship might move to a more satisfying stage.

4. Identify the dialectical tensions that influence your communication goals, the strategies you use to manage these tensions, and alternative strategies you might consider using.

5. Choose the most promising compliance-gaining strategy you could use in a given situation.

## Key Terms

Avoiding

Bonding

Circumscribing

Comparison level (CL)

Comparison level of alternatives (CL$_{alt}$)

Compliance-gaining strategy

Connection-autonomy dialectic

Conventionality-uniqueness dialectic

Dialectical tensions

Differentiating

Direct request

Exchange theory

Experimenting

Expression-privacy dialectic

Face maintenance strategy

Inclusion-seclusion dialectic

Indirect appeal

Initiating

Integrating

Integration-separation dialectic

Intensifying

Interpersonal relationship

Metacommunication

Norm of reciprocity

Openness-closedness dialectic

Predictability-novelty dialectic

Relational appeal

Relational maintenance

Revelation-concealment dialectic

Stability-change dialectic

Stagnating

Terminating

There's no question that personal relationships matter. To understand just how important they are, imagine how your life would suffer without them: no friends, family, fellow workers, or romantic partners. Almost as bad would be poor relationships with these key people. It's no surprise that respondents to one survey identified *interpersonal relationships* as more important than anything else in making their lives meaningful (Campbell et al., 1976).

What does it mean to have a relationship with another person? Communication theorist Charles Berger (1993) offers some basic conditions. For a relationship to exist, the people must be aware of each other and take each other into account. This means that the ritualistic or automated exchanges like those between customers and the person who takes orders at a fast-food restaurant wouldn't count: You might as well be dealing with a machine. Another basic ingredient of a relationship is some degree of influence: At least one person must affect the other in some way. For example, teachers affect students (and vice versa), and family members certainly influence one another for better or worse. Berger suggests that a third ingredient of relationships is some agreement about the social form and expectations that govern the interaction. You can appreciate the importance of shared relational definitions by imagining yourself far from home, asking a stranger for directions. The way you and that person relate to each other would define the relationship. For example, is the encounter merely an exchange of information, or is it more personal? Until you and the other person work out this fundamental question, the relationship wouldn't be defined.

Most people intuitively understand the important role communication plays in the development and maintenance of interpersonal relationships. The quality of interaction helps shape the quantity of communication. For instance, Virginia Richmond (1995) found that satisfied couples talk more with one another than do less satisfied couples, especially about certain "important" topics, such as their life together at home, their sexual relationship, and their recreational time. The quality of communication is certainly as important as quantity. Besides helping to create relational satisfaction, communication reflects the kind of relationship that exists: what kinds of feelings partners hold about one another, and where the relationship is headed.

This chapter introduces some of the dynamics that characterize interpersonal relationships and the communication that occurs within them. After reading it, you will see that relationships aren't fixed or unchanging. Rather, they can, and often do, change over time. In other words, a relationship is less a *thing* than a *process.* You might establish a businesslike pattern with a fellow worker and later find that the relationship has changed into a friendship. Likewise, professors and students might begin interacting according to traditional roles and later find their communication develops into some other form. The same phenomenon is true in close relationships. For example, the quality of interaction in a family usually changes when children reach late adolescence. Patterns that worked well enough between grown-ups and youngsters don't fit so well when all the family members are adults (Preto, 1999). New definitions of power, affection, and respect may become necessary. In a sense, the relationship is reinvented. To see how, read on.

## Why We Form Relationships

Why do we form relationships with some people and not with others? Sometimes we have no choice: Children can't select their parents, and most workers aren't able to choose their colleagues. In many other cases, however, we seek out some people and actively avoid others. Social scientists have collected an impressive body of research on interpersonal attraction (see, for example, Byrne, 1997; Poole et al., 1987).

### Appearance

Most people claim that we should judge others on the basis of how they act, not how they look. How-

## FOCUS ON RESEARCH

### NOT UP CLOSE, YET PERSONAL: MAKING FRIENDS IN CYBERSPACE

Some social critics have argued that new communication technologies are making the world an increasingly impersonal place. Malcolm Parks and Kory Floyd disagree, and they have data to back their claim. In one of the first systematic surveys of on-line personal relationships, Parks and Floyd found that computer-mediated communication can be far more personal than many might have imagined.

Their study examined the relationships created through Internet discussion groups (commonly called "newsgroups"). Newsgroup participants post electronic messages that reach thousands of people connected by computers around the world. After reading posted messages, participants can establish individual contact (usually through e-mail) with people

they meet in cyberspace. Parks and Floyd surveyed 176 discussion group participants, representing twenty-four randomly selected newsgroups.

The primary finding of the study was that e-mail is an important channel for starting and maintaining personal relationships. Almost two-thirds of the respondents said they had formed a personal relationship with someone they had met for the first time through an Internet newsgroup. The electronic friends characterized their relationships in ways that sound remarkably similar to traditional friendships: interdependence (e.g., "We would go out of our way to help each other"); breadth ("Our communication ranges over a wide variety of topics"); depth ("I feel I could confide in this person about almost anything"); and commit-

ment ("I am very committed to maintaining this relationship"). More than half the respondents communicated with their cyberspace partners at least weekly by e-mail. Perhaps more interesting, two-thirds of them augmented their e-mailing with another channel of communication, contacting their partners by postal mail, telephone, and even face-to-face visits.

Parks and Floyd acknowledge that their survey is only a first step in studying the new frontiers of interpersonal communication in cyberspace. They recommend, however, a revised starting point for understanding computer-mediated communication. It is not about "relationships lost"; it is about "relationships liberated and found."

Parks, M. R., & Floyd, K. (1996). Making friends in cyberspace. *Journal of Communication, 46,* 80–97.

ever, the reality is quite the opposite (Hatfield & Sprecher, 1986). Appearance is especially important in the early stages of a relationship. In one study, a group of over seven hundred men and women were matched as blind dates, allegedly for a "computer dance." After the party was over, they were asked whether or not they would like to date their partners again. The result? The more physically attractive the person (as judged in advance by independent raters), the more likely he or she was seen as desirable. Other factors—social skills

and intelligence, for example—didn't seem to affect the decision (Walster et al., 1966).

The influence of physical attractiveness begins early in life. Infants as young as six months prefer images of attractive faces to less appealing ones (Rubenstein et al., 1999). From age five on, overweight boys are viewed by peers as less attractive; tall, thin ones are judged as introverted and nervous; and muscular and athletic youngsters are seen as outgoing, active, and popular (Aboud & Mendelson, 1998; Lemer & Gillert, 1969; Staffieri,

1967). The same princi[...]
Handsome men and be[...]
more sensitive, kind, int[...]
modest, sociable, outgo[...]
less attractive counterpa[...]
Adults are more likely to[...]
they view as attractive (M[...]
Senior citizens also rate g[...]
more desirable than those[...]
(Larose & Standing, 1998)[...]

Although we might as[...]
ple are radically different fr[...]
attractive, the truth is that w[...]
beautiful. Langlois and Rog[...] (1990) presented raters with two types of photos: Some were images of people from North European, Asian, and Latino backgrounds, while others were computer-generated images that combined the characteristics of several individuals. Surprisingly, the judges consistently preferred the composite photos of both men and women. When the features of eight or more individuals were combined into one image, viewers rated the picture as more attractive than the features of a single person or of a smaller combination of people. Thus, we seem to be drawn to people who represent the most attractive qualities of ourselves and those people we know. In other words, beautiful people aren't different from the rest of us. Rather, they're "radically similar."

Even if your appearance isn't beautiful by societal standards, consider these encouraging facts: First, ordinary-looking people with pleasing personalities are likely to be judged as being attractive (Berscheid & Walster, 1978). Second, physical factors become less important as a relationship progresses. As Hamachek (1982, p. 59) puts it, "Attractive features may open doors, but apparently, it takes more than physical beauty to keep them open."

## Similarity

It's comforting to know someone who likes the same things you like, has similar values, and may even be of the same race, economic class, or educational standing. The basis for this sort of relationship, commonly known as the *similarity thesis,* is the most frequently discussed of the several bases of relationship formation (Buss, 1985). For example, friends in middle and high school report being similar to each other in many ways, including having mutual friends, enjoying the same sports, liking the same social activities, and using (or not using) alcohol and cigarettes to the same degree (Aboud & Mendelson, 1998; Urberg et al., 1998). For adults, similarity is more important to relational happiness than even communication ability: Friends who have low levels of communication skills are just as satisfied with their relationships as are friends having high levels of skills (Burleson & Samter, 1996).

There are several reasons why similarity is a strong foundation for relationships. First, the other person serves as an external indication—a social validation—that we are not alone in our thinking, that we're not too "weird." Someone else *did* like the same controversial book you liked. Therefore, this other person offers good support for you, reinforcing your own sense of what is right.

Second, when someone is similar to you, you can make fairly accurate predictions—whether the person will want to eat at the Mexican restaurant or hear the concert you're so excited about. This ability to make confident predictions reduces uncertainty and anxiety (Duck & Barnes, 1992).

There's a third explanation for the similarity thesis. It may be that when we learn that other peo-

ple are similar to us, we assume they'll probably like us, so we in turn like them. The self-fulfilling prophecy creeps into the picture again.

Similarity turns from attraction to dislike when we encounter people who are like us in many ways but who behave in a strange or socially offensive manner (Cooper & Jones, 1969; Taylor & Mette, 1971). For instance, you have probably disliked people others have said were "just like you" but who talked too much, were complainers, or had some other unappealing characteristic. In fact, there is a tendency to have stronger dislike for similar but offensive people than for those who are offensive but different. One likely reason is that such people threaten our self-esteem, causing us to fear that we may be as unappealing as they are. In such circumstances, the reaction is often to put as much distance as possible between ourselves and this threat to our ideal self-image.

## Complementarity

The old saying "opposites attract" seems to contradict the principle of similarity we just described.

In truth, though, both are valid. Differences strengthen a relationship when they are *complementary*—when each partner's characteristics satisfy the other's needs. For instance, couples are more likely to be attracted to each other when one partner is dominant and the other passive (Winch, 1958). Relationships also work well when the partners agree that one will exercise control in certain areas ("You make the final decisions about money") and the other will take the lead in different ones ("I'll decide how we ought to decorate the place"). Strains occur when control issues are disputed.

Studies that have examined successful and unsuccessful couples over a twenty-year period show the interaction between similarities and differences. When partners are radically different, the dissimilar qualities that at first appear intriguing later become cause for relational breakups (Felmlee, 1998). Partners in successful marriages were similar enough to satisfy each other physically and mentally, but were different enough to meet each other's needs and keep the relationship interesting (Kelley, 1977). The successful couples found ways to keep a balance between their similarities and differences while adjusting to the changes that occurred over the years.

## Rewards

Some relationships are based on an economic model called **exchange theory** (Homans, 1961; Thibaut & Kelley, 1959). This approach suggests that we often seek out people who can give us rewards that are greater than or equal to the costs we encounter in dealing with them. Social exchange theorists define rewards as any outcomes we desire. They may be tangible (a nice place to live, a high paying job) or intangible (prestige, emotional support, companionship). Costs are undesirable outcomes: unpleasant work, emotional pain, and so on. A simple formula captures the social exchange explanation for why we form and maintain relationships:

$$\text{Rewards} - \text{Costs} = \text{Outcome}$$

According to social exchange theorists, we use this formula (often unconsciously) to calculate whether a relationship is a "good deal" or "not worth the effort," based on whether the outcome is positive or negative.

At its most blatant level, an exchange approach seems cold and calculating; but in some types of relationships it seems quite appropriate. A healthy business relationship is based on how well the parties help one another, and some friendships are based on an informal kind of barter: "I don't mind listening to the ups and down of your love life because you rescue me when the house needs repairs." Even close relationships have an element of exchange. Friends and lovers often tolerate each other's quirks because the comfort and enjoyment they get make the less-than-pleasant times worth accepting.

Costs and rewards don't exist in isolation: We define them by comparing a certain situation with alternatives. For example, consider a hypothetical woman we will call Gloria, who is struggling to decide whether to remain in a relationship with Raymond, her longtime boyfriend. Ray does love

"I'd like to buy everyone a drink. All I ask in return is that you listen patiently to my shallow and simplistic views on a broad range of social and political issues."

Gloria, but he's not perfect: He has a hair trigger temper, and he has become verbally abusive from time to time. Also, Gloria knows that Raymond was unfaithful to her at least once. In deciding whether or not to stay with Raymond, Gloria will use two standards. The first is her **comparison level** (**CL**)—her standard of what behavior is acceptable. If Gloria believes that relational partners have an obligation to be faithful and treat one another respectfully at all times, then Raymond's behavior will fall below her comparison level. On the other hand, if Gloria adopts a "nobody's perfect" standard, she is more likely to view Raymond's behavior as meeting or exceeding her comparison level.

Gloria also will rate Raymond according to her **comparison level of alternatives** (**CL$_{alt}$**). This standard refers to a comparison between the rewards she is receiving in her present situation and those she could expect to receive in others. If, for example, Gloria views her choices as staying with Raymond or being alone, her CL$_{alt}$ would be

## REFLECTION

### BALANCING RELATIONAL ACCOUNTS

Toni and I are comanagers of a restaurant. She's a terrible bookkeeper, so I wind up doing a lot of paperwork that's really her job. She can be very moody at times, and when she gets in a bad mood I have to be careful what I say. Also, Toni hates to confront people, so I have to handle all the personnel problems, like firing employees who don't work out.

Why do I put up with her? Because Toni does a lot for me. She's always there when I need to talk about a problem. If I want to take an extra day off to go skiing, she'll cover for me. I don't have any relatives nearby, and she goes out of her way to include me in her family on holidays. We're sort of an odd couple, but I think it works because each of us gets at least as much out of the relationship as we put in.

lower than her present situation; but if she is confident that she could find a kinder partner, her $CL_{alt}$ would be higher than the status quo.

Table 9.1 outlines all the possible combinations of the outcomes (the present situation), comparison levels, and comparison levels of alternatives. Social exchange theorists suggest that communicators unconsciously use this calculus to decide whether to form and stay in relationships. At first this information seems to offer little comfort to communicators who are in unsatisfying relationships such as those where $CL > CL_{alt} >$ outcome. But there are alternatives to being stuck in situations where the costs outweigh the rewards. First, you might make sure that you are judging your present relationship against a realistic comparison level. Expecting a situation to be perfect can be a recipe for unhappiness. (Recall

the discussion of the "fallacy of shoulds" in Chapter 8.) If you decide that your present situation truly falls below your comparison level, you might explore whether there are other alternatives you haven't considered. And finally, the skills introduced throughout *Interplay* may help you negotiate a better relationship with the other person.

## Competency

We like to be around talented people, probably because we hope their skills and abilities will rub off on us. On the other hand, we are uncomfortable around those who are *too* competent—probably because we look bad by comparison (Bales, 1958).

Elliot Aronson and his associates (1966) demonstrated how competence and imperfection combine to affect attraction by having subjects evaluate tape recordings of candidates for a quiz program. One was a " perfect" candidate who answered almost all the questions correctly and modestly admitted that he was an honor student, athlete, and college yearbook editor. The "average" candidate answered fewer questions correctly, had average grades, was a less successful athlete, and was a low-level member of the yearbook staff. Toward the end of half the tapes, the candidates committed a blunder, spilling coffee all over themselves. The remaining half of the tapes contained no such blunder. These, then, were the four experimental conditions: (1) a person with superior ability who blundered; (2) a person with superior ability who did not blunder; (3) an average person who blundered; and (4) an average person who did not blunder.

The students who rated the attractiveness of these four types of people revealed an interesting and important principle of interpersonal attraction. The most attractive person was the superior candidate who blundered. Next was the superior person who did not blunder. Third was the average person who did not blunder. The least attractive person was the average person who committed the blunder.

**Table 9.1**

**Calculating Relational Costs and Rewards**

| Relative Value of Outcome, CL, $CL_{alt}$ | State of the Relationship |
|---|---|
| Outcome > CL > $CL_{alt}$ | Satisfying<br>Stable<br>Dependent |
| Outcome > $CL_{alt}$ > CL | Satisfying<br>Stable<br>Nondependent |
| $CL_{alt}$ > CL > Outcome | Not satisfying<br>Break off relationship<br>Happy elsewhere |
| $CL_{alt}$ > Outcome > CL | Satisfying<br>Unstable<br>Happier elsewhere |
| CL > $CL_{alt}$ > Outcome | Not satisfying<br>Break off relationship<br>Continue unhappy |
| CL > Outcome > $CL_{alt}$ | Highly unsatisfying<br>Can't break away<br>Dependent and unhappy |

Adapted from: Roloff, M. E. (1981). *Interpersonal communication: The social exchange approach.* Beverly Hills, CA: Sage; and Griffin, E. M. (1997). *A first look at communication theory* (3rd ed.). New York: McGraw-Hill.

Aronson's conclusion was that we like people who are somewhat flawed because they remind us of ourselves. However, there are some qualifications to this principle. People with especially positive or negative self-esteem find "perfect" people more attractive than those who are competent but flawed (Helmreich et al., 1970). Furthermore, women tend to be more impressed by uniformly superior people, whereas men find desirable but "human " subjects especially attractive (Deaux, 1972). On the whole, though, the principle stands: The best way to gain the liking of others is to be good at what you do but also to admit your mistakes.

## Proximity

As common sense suggests, we are likely to develop relationships with people with whom we interact frequently. In many cases, proximity leads to liking. For instance, we're more likely to develop friendships with close neighbors than with distant ones, and the chances are good that we'll choose a mate with whom we cross paths often. Facts like these are understandable when we consider that proximity allows us to get more information about other people and benefit from a relationship with them. Also, people in close proximity may be more similar to us than those not close—for example, if we live in the same neighborhood, odds are we share the same socioeconomic status.

Familiarity, on the other hand, can breed contempt. Evidence to support this fact comes from police blotters as well as university laboratories. Thieves frequently prey on nearby victims, even though the risk of being recognized is greater. Most aggravated assaults occur within the family or among close neighbors. The same principle

## FILM CLIP

### A *TITANIC* RELATIONSHIP

The movie *Titanic* is one of the most popular motion pictures of all time. Part of the film's success is due to the well-known story of the ill-fated ocean liner, as well as the special effects that brought the story to life for millions of viewers. At the movie's heart, however, is a relationship between two star-crossed lovers: Jack (Leonardo DiCaprio) and Rose (Kate Winslet).

Why are Rose and Jack attracted to each other? Many concepts from this chapter are involved:

- Appearance: Without question, these are two stunningly attractive people (as fans of the movie will quickly acknowledge).
- Similarity: On a ship filled with older, staid passengers, Jack and Rose are two young people looking for adventure and romance.
- Complementarity: Rose is rich, educated, and proper; Jack is poor, unbridled, and street-smart. Both seem attracted to the novelty and risk of interacting with someone so different.
- Rewards: In a theme seen in other movies, such as *The Prince and the Pauper* and *Trading Places*, Jack and Rose gain insights and excitement from experiencing how "the other half" lives during their brief relationship.
- Proximity: Rose and Jack are trapped on the same ship and are in almost constant contact with each other once their relationship begins.

Other attraction factors, such as competency and disclosure, also are illustrated in the movie. Although their relationship only lasts a few days, it's easy to see why these two young lovers fall for each other so quickly and deeply.

holds in more routine contexts: You are likely to develop strong personal feelings, either positive or negative, toward others you encounter frequently.

## Disclosure

Telling others important information about yourself can help build liking (Derlega et al., 1993). Sometimes the basis of this attraction comes from learning about ways we are similar, either in experiences ("I broke off an engagement myself") or in attitudes ("I feel nervous with strangers, too"). Self-disclosure also increases liking because it indicates regard. Sharing private information is a form of respect and trust—a kind of liking that we've already seen increases attractiveness.

Not all disclosure leads to liking. Research shows that the key to satisfying self-disclosure is *reciprocity*: getting back an amount and kind of information equivalent to that which you reveal (Altman, 1973; Derlega et al., 1976; Dindia, 2000). A second important ingredient in successful self-disclosure is *timing*. It's probably unwise to talk about your sexual insecurities with a new acquaintance or express your pet peeves to a friend at your birthday party. The information you reveal ought to be appropriate for the setting and stage of the relationship (Archer & Berg, 1978; Wortman et al., 1976). Chapter 10 contains more information on the subject of self-disclosure.

# Communication and Relational Dynamics

A relationship is a process, not a static thing. Even the most stable relationships vary from day to day and over longer periods of time. Communication scholars have attempted to describe and explain how communication creates and reflects the changing dynamics of relational interaction. The following pages describe two very different characterizations of relational development and interaction.

## Developmental Models of Interpersonal Relationships

One of the best-known models of relational stages was developed by Mark Knapp (Knapp & Vangelisti, 2000; see also Avtgis et al., 1998), who broke the

waxing and waning of relationships into ten steps (see Figure 9.1). Other researchers have suggested that any model of relational communication ought to contain a third area of **relational maintenance**—communication aimed at keeping relationships operating smoothly and satisfactorily. Figure 9.1 shows how Knapp's ten stages fit into this three-part view of relational communication. This model seems most appropriate for describing communication between romantic partners, but in many respects it works well for other types of close relationships.

**Initiating**    The goals in the **initiating** stage are to show that you are interested in making contact and to demonstrate that you are a kind of person worth talking to. Communication during this stage is usually brief, and it generally follows conventional formulas: handshakes, remarks about innocuous subjects such as the weather, and friendly expressions. Such behavior may seem superficial and meaningless, but it is a way of signaling that you're interested in building some kind of relationship with the other person. It allows us

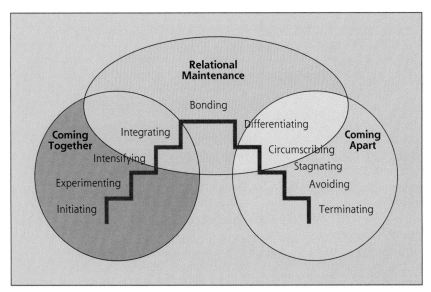

**Figure 9.1** Stages of Relational Development

From *Interpersonal Communication and Human Relationships* (4th Ed.) by Mark L. Knapp and Anita L. Vargelsti. Copyright © 2000 by Allyn and Bacon. Adapted by permission.

to say, without saying, "I'm a friendly person, and I'd like to get to know you."

Initiating a relationship requires a fair measure of skill. One study revealed several strategies that are both efficient and socially acceptable ways to learn about others (Douglas, 1987). The first is *networking*—getting information about the other person from a third party who helps the first moments of contact go well. Another strategy is *offering*—putting yourself in a favorable position to be approached by the desired partner. Offering strategies might include picking a seat in class near the person you'd like to meet, or hanging around the hors d'oeuvres at a party until the attractive person drops by for a snack. A third technique is *approaching*—signaling your desire for contact, either verbally or nonverbally. Typical approaches include smiles and self-introductions. (Incredibly, there are people who never even try such seemingly obvious strategies, instead waiting for interesting people to approach them.) A final initiating strategy is *sustaining*—behaving in ways to keep the conversation going. Asking questions is a typical sustaining technique.

Other styles proved less effective, either because they didn't work or because they were socially inappropriate. Expressing feelings ("Do you like me?") was too forward for most initial contacts. Remaining silent (either to be coy or from an inability to know what to say) didn't work. Seeking favors that were inconvenient to the other person was rarely successful. Finally, diminishing oneself ("I'm such a dope!") seldom met with success.

**Experimenting**    After making contact with a new person, we generally begin the search for common ground. This search usually begins with the basics: "Where are you from? What's your major?" From there we look for other similarities: "You're a runner too? How many miles do you run a week?"

It usually doesn't take long for communicators who are interested in one another to move from initiating to **experimenting**. The shift seems to occur even more rapidly in cyberspace than in person. Laurie Pratt and her associates (1999) found

THE FAR SIDE © 1991 FARWORKS, INC. All rights reserved. Used by permission.

that people who develop relationships via e-mail begin asking questions about attitudes, opinions, and preferences more quickly than those in face-to-face contact. It probably helps that e-mailers can't see each others' nonverbal reactions—they don't have to worry about blushing, stammering, or looking away if they realize that they asked for too much information too quickly.

The hallmark of experimenting is small talk. We tolerate the ordeal of small talk because it serves several functions. First, it is a useful way to find out what interests we share with the other person. It also provides a way to "audition" the other person—to help us decide whether a relationship is worth pursuing. In addition, small talk is a safe way to ease into a relationship. You haven't risked much as you decide whether to proceed further. Finally, small talk *does* provide some kind of link to others. It's often better than being alone.

The kind of information we look for during the experimentation stage depends on the nature of the relationship we are seeking (Miller, 1998; Stewart et al., in press). For example, both men and women who are seeking short-term relationships look for someone with an exciting personality and a good sense of humor. Qualities of being trustworthy and romantic become more important when people seek long-term relationships.

**Intensifying**   At the next stage, the kind of qualitatively interpersonal relationship defined in Chapter 1 begins to develop. Dating couples use a wide range of communication strategies to express their feelings of attraction (Tolhuizen, 1989). In this **intensifying** stage, about a quarter of the time they express their feelings directly, using metacommunication to discuss the state of the relationship. More often they use less direct methods of communication: spending an increasing amount of time together, asking for support from one another, doing favors for the partner, giving tokens of affection, hinting and flirting, expressing feelings nonverbally, getting to know the partner's friends and family, and trying to look more physically attractive.

Although commitment grows as a relationship intensifies, communication between partners shows that doubts can still remain. Romantic partners use a variety of strategies to test each other's commitment (Baxter & Wilmot, 1985; Bell & Buerkel-Rothfuss, 1990). These approaches include asking direct questions, "testing" the partner by presenting challenges that require proof of commitment, hinting in order to gain expressions of commitment, asking third parties for information, and attempting to make the partner jealous. While these behaviors are frequent in the early stages of a relationship, they decline as the partners spend more time together.

The intensifying stage is usually a time of relational excitement and even euphoria. For romantic partners, it's often filled with starstruck gazes, goosebumps, and daydreaming. As a result, it's a stage that's regularly depicted in movies and romance novels—after all, we love to watch lovers in love. The problem, of course, is that the stage doesn't last forever. Sometimes romantic partners who stop feeling goosebumps begin to question whether they're still in love. While it's possible that they're not, it also could be that they've simply moved on to a different stage in their relationship—such as integrating.

**Integrating**   As the relationship strengthens, the individuals enter an **integrating** stage. They begin to take on an identity as a social unit. Invitations begin to come addressed to a couple. Social circles merge. The partners share each other's commitments: "Sure, we'll spend Thanksgiving with your family." Common property may begin to be designated—our apartment, our car, our song (Baxter, 1987). Partners develop their own personal idioms (Bell & Healey, 1992) and forms of play (Baxter, 1992). They develop routines and rituals that reinforce their identity as a couple—jogging together, eating at a favorite restaurant, expressing affection

## FOCUS ON RESEARCH

### RELATIONAL RITUALS

Do you and your sweetheart have an anniversary date you celebrate regularly? Do you and your friends have a monthly night out together? Do you have a television show that you watch every week with the same person? If so, researchers Carol Bruess and Judy Pearson would say you've discovered the importance of relational rituals.

Bruess and Pearson surveyed seventy-nine married couples and conducted in-depth interviews with twenty of them. The researchers questioned the couples about the rituals they maintain with their spouses and their friends. Interestingly, many of the ritual categories that emerged

were common to both marriages and friendships. Even more interesting were the examples of rituals that the researchers provided from the interviews, such as:

- "Whoever goes in and brushes their teeth first always puts toothpaste on the other's toothbrush. . . . If we're upset with each other we might set the tube next to the brush, not put paste on it."

- "Every year on the day after Thanksgiving, my friends and I go shopping. It's an all day and night affair. It's not considered a success unless you buy enough to warrant using one of those twenty-five cent shopping bags."

- "We were married on the 26th of May. We have a monthly contest to see who says, 'Happy Anniversary' first on the 26th day of the month. Rules are: no waking spouse, said anytime after midnight, and must be person to person."

Bruess and Pearson found that "both in friendships and marriages, a unique culture is created by relationship members through symbolic enactments." You might smile as you read about the rituals above because they sound silly. You also might smile because they provide a glimpse of people in meaningful, satisfying relationships who have created a culture together.

Bruess, C. J. S., & Pearson, J. C. (1997). Interpersonal rituals in marriage and adult friendship. *Communication Monographs, 64,* 25–46.

---

with a goodnight kiss, and worshipping together (Afifi & Johnson, 1999; Bruess & Pearson, 1997). As these examples illustrate, the stage of integrating is a time when we give up some characteristics of our former selves and become different people.

As we become more integrated with others, our sense of obligation to them grows (Roloff et al., 1988). We feel obliged to provide a variety of resources such as class notes and money, whether or not the other person asks for them. When intimates do make requests of one another, they are relatively straightforward. Gone are the elaborate explanations, inducements, and apologies. In

short, partners in an integrated relationship expect more from one another than they do in less intimate associations.

**Bonding**   During the **bonding** stage, the partners make symbolic public gestures to show the world that their relationship exists. These gestures can take the form of a contract to be business partners or a license to be married. Bonding typically generates social support for the relationship. Custom and law both impose certain obligations on partners who have officially bonded.

Bonding usually marks an important turning point in relationships. Up to now the relationship may have developed at a steady pace: Experimenting gradually moved into intensifying and then into integrating. Now, however, there is a spurt of commitment. The public display and declaration of exclusivity make this a critical period in the relationship. Although most people would agree that turning points do occur, research shows that couples don't always agree about what specific events marked those points in their relationships. About 45 percent of the time, the partners do not identify the same events as turning points (Baxter & Bullis, 1986).

**Differentiating**   Now that the two people have formed this commonality, they need to reestablish individual identities. How are we different? How am I unique? Former identifications as "we" now emphasize "I." **Differentiating** often occurs when a relationship begins to experience the first, inevitable feelings of stress. Whereas happy employees might refer to "our company," the description might change to "this company" when a raise or some other request isn't forthcoming.

We see this kind of differentiation when parents argue over the misbehavior of a child: "Did you see what *your* son just did?"

Differentiation also can be positive, for people need to be individuals as well as parts of a relationship. The key to successful differentiation is maintaining commitment to a relationship while creating the space for being individuals as well (we'll describe this later in the chapter as the connection-autonomy dialectic). Partners use a variety of strategies to gain privacy from each other (Burgoon et al., 1989; Petronio, 2000). Sometimes they confront the other person directly, explaining that they don't want to continue a discussion. In other cases they are less direct, offering nonverbal cues, changing the topic, or leaving the room.

**Circumscribing**   So far, we have been looking at the growth of relationships. Although some reach a plateau of development, going on successfully for as long as a lifetime, others pass through several stages of decline and dissolution. In the **circumscribing** stage, communication between members decreases in quantity and quality (Duck, 1987). Subtle hints of dissatisfaction grow more evident. Working later at the office, seeking less and less romance, and more and more arguing begin to form a pattern that is hard to ignore (Kellermann et al., 1991). Ironically, both partners in a circumscribed relationship still cooperate in one way: suppressing the true status of the relationship. They hide its decline from others and even from themselves (Vaughn, 1987). Restrictions and restraints characterize this stage, and dynamic communication becomes static. Rather than discuss a disagreement (which requires some degree of energy on both parts), members opt for withdrawal: either mental (silence or daydreaming and fantasizing) or physical (where people spend less time together). Circumscribing doesn't involve total avoidance, which comes later. Rather, it entails a certain shrinking of interest and commitment.

**Stagnating**   If circumscribing continues, the relationship begins to **stagnate**. Members behave toward each other in old, familiar ways without much feeling. No growth occurs. The stagnating relationship is a hollow shell of its former self. We see stagnation in many workers who have lost enthusiasm for their job yet continue to go through the motions for years. The same sad event occurs for some couples who unenthusiastically have the same conversations, see the same people, and follow the same routines without any sense of joy or novelty.

**Avoiding**   When stagnation becomes too unpleasant, people in a relationship begin to create distance between each other by **avoiding**. Sometimes they do it under the guise of excuses ("I've been sick lately and can't see you") and sometimes directly ("Please don't call me; I don't want to see you now "). In either case, by this point the handwriting is on the wall about the relationship's future.

**Terminating**   **Termination** has its own distinguishable pattern and distinctiveness (Battaglia et al., 1998). Characteristics of this stage include summary dialogues of where the relationship has gone and the desire to dissociate. The relationship may end with a cordial dinner, a note left on the kitchen table, a phone call, or a legal document stating the dissolution. Depending on each person's feelings, this terminating stage can be quite short or it may be drawn out over time, with bitter jabs at each other. In either case, termination doesn't have to be totally negative. Understanding each other's investments in the relationship and needs for personal growth may dilute the hard feelings.

Baxter (1982) and Cody (1982) found that the strategy partners use to disengage depends on the degree of intimacy their relationship had reached. In the least intimate relationships, one partner simply withdraws (physically or emotionally) from the other. In slightly more intimate relationships, one partner is likely to request they see less of each other. When intimacy has been greater, the disengaging partner makes an effort to explain the reason for leaving in a way that takes the other's feelings into account. In the most intimate relationships, the initiator expresses grief over the disengagement. In fact, Cody (1982) found that the more intimate the relationship, the greater the feeling of obligation to justify terminating it.

How do the individuals deal with each other after a romantic relationship has ended? The best predictor of whether the individuals will become friends is whether they were friends before their romantic involvement (Metts et al., 1989). The way the couple split up also makes a difference. It's no surprise to find that friendships are most possible when communication during the breakup was positive: expressions that there were no regrets for time spent together and other attempts to minimize hard feelings. When communication during termination was negative (manipulative, complaining to third parties), friendships were less likely.

Survivors of terminated relationships offer a number of reasons why their relationships didn't last (Cupach & Metts, 1986). These reasons are summarized in Table 9.2. The tendency is to blame the breakup on the other person more than on oneself, although divorced women are more likely to blame themselves, with men more likely to pin the responsibility on their ex-wives or on outside forces.

## Dialectical Perspectives on Relational Dynamics

Stage-related views like the one described in the preceding pages characterize communication as differing in important ways at various points in the life of a relationship. According to the stage approach, what happens during initiating, experimenting, or intensifying is different from the kind of communication that occurs during differentiating, circumscribing, or avoiding.

Not all theorists agree that relational stages are the best way to explain interaction in rela-

**Table 9.2**

### Reasons Offered for Relationship Termination

I. **Characteristics of the individuals themselves**
"My former husband decided he was unhappy."
"I began to feel lonely."
"She said she felt trapped."
"He was too conservative."

II. **Lack of fulfillment of relational roles**
"He found no joy in being a father."
"There were no sexual relations."
"He tried to tell me what I had to do to be his wife."
"She went back to school."

III. **Unsatisfactory relational cohesiveness and intimacy**
"We no longer wanted the same things in life."
"We did nothing together as a couple."
"We had different needs."

IV. **Poor regulation of interaction**
"He wouldn't listen."
"All our discussions ended in arguments."
"He threatened me."

V. **Third-party involvements**
"I had an affair with an exciting older man."
"When I found out she'd been seeing other guys, I was very hurt."
"The unexpected pregnancy was more than we could handle."
"I lost my job."

Adapted from: Cupach, W. R., & Metts, S. (1986). Accounts of relational dissolution: A comparison of marital and non-marital relationships. *Communication Monographs, 53,* 311–354.

tionships. Some suggest that communicators grapple with the same kinds of challenges whether a relationship is brand new or has lasted decades. Their focus, then, is on the ongoing maintenance of relationships (e.g., Lee, 1998). They argue that communicators seek important but apparently incompatible goals. The struggle to achieve these goals creates **dialectical tensions**: conflicts that arise when two opposing or incompatible forces exist simultaneously. For example, the desire to satisfy your own needs and meet the expectations of a relational partner can create a

**Table 9.3**

| Dialectical Tensions | | | |
|---|---|---|---|
| | Dialectic of Integration-Separation | Dialectic of Stability-Change | Dialectic of Expression-Privacy |
| **Internal Manifestations** | Connection-Autonomy | Predictability-Novelty | Openness-Closedness |
| **External Manifestations** | Inclusion-Seclusion | Conventionality-Uniqueness | Revelation-Concealment |

From: Baxter, L. A. (1994). A dialogic approach to relationship maintenance. In D. J. Canary & L. Stafford (Eds.)., *Communication and relational maintenance* (p. 240). San Diego, CA: Academic Press.

tension when what you want doesn't match the other person's goals (Veroff et al., 1998).

In recent years, communication scholars such as Leslie Baxter and Barbara Montgomery (1996), William Rawlins (1992), and Brian Spitzberg (1993) have identified several dialectical forces that make successful communication challenging. They suggest that the struggle to manage these dialectical tensions creates the most powerful dynamics in relational communication. In the following pages we will discuss three powerful dialectical tensions, which are summarized in Table 9.3. As the table shows, we experience dialectical challenges both *internally, vis à vis* our partners, and *externally* as we and our relational partners face other people whose desires clash with our own.

**Integration versus Separation**   No one is an island. Recognizing this fact, we seek out involvement with others. But, at the same time, we are unwilling to sacrifice our entire identity to even the most satisfying relationship. The conflicting desires for connection and independence are embodied in the **integration-separation dialectic.** This set of apparently contradictory needs creates communication challenges that can show up both within a relationship and when relational partners face the world.

Internally, the struggle shows up in the **connection-autonomy dialectic.** We want to be close to others, but at the same time we seek independence. Sociolinguist Deborah Tannen (1986) captures the insoluble integration-separation dialectic nicely by evoking the image of two porcupines trying to get through a cold winter:

> They huddle together for warmth, but their sharp quills prick each other, so they pull away. But then they get cold. They have to keep adjusting their closeness and distance to keep from freezing and from getting pricked by their fellow porcupines—the source of both comfort and pain.
>
> We need to get close to each other to have a sense of community, to feel we're not alone in the world. But we need to keep our distance from each other to preserve our independence, so others don't impose on or engulf us. This duality reflects the human condition. We are individual and social creatures. We need other people to survive, but we want to survive as individuals.

Baxter (1994) describes the consequences for relational partners who can't successfully manage the conflicting needs for connection and autonomy. Some of the most common reasons for relational breakups involve failure of partners to satisfy one another's needs for connection: "We barely spent any time together"; "S/he wasn't committed to the

## REFLECTION

### ONE PLUS ONE MAKES THREE

I've been to a lot of weddings in the last few years, and several couples have included a ceremony that got me thinking about dialectical challenges in a marriage. There are usually three candles in a holder—two that are lit on the outsides and a center one that isn't. The bride and groom each take an outside candle and light the center one, symbolizing that they've created a new union together.

The part that comes next is most interesting to me. Some couples blow out their own individual candles, leaving only the center one burning. Others leave their own individual candles burning.

I like the symbolism of leaving all three candles burning. It reminds me of the autonomy-connection tension we talked about in class. If only the center one is burning, there's connection without autonomy. If only the outside ones are burning, it's autonomy without connection. Leaving all three lit says to me that being a couple is important, but so is being an individual.

relationship"; "We had different needs." But other relational complaints involve excessive demands for connection: "I was feeling trapped"; "I needed freedom."

In accounts of relational turning points, both men and women in heterosexual romantic pairs cited the connection-autonomy dialectic as one of the most significant factors affecting their relationship (Baxter & Erbert, 1999). This dialectical tension was crucial in negotiating turning points related to commitment, conflict, disengagement, and reconciliation. Research also shows that managing the dialectical tension between connection and auton-omy is as important during divorce as it is at the beginning of a marriage, as partners seek ways to salvage and reconcile the unbreakable bonds of their personal history (including finances, children, and friends) with their new independence (Pam & Pearson, 1998).

Parents and children must deal constantly with the conflicting tugs toward connection and auto-nomy, as Chapter 10 describes in some detail. These struggles don't end when children grow up and leave home. Parents experience the mixed feelings of relief at their new freedom and longings to stay connected to their adult children. Likewise, grown children typically feel excitement at being on their own, and yet miss the bonds that had been taken for granted since the beginning of their lives (Blacker, 1999; Fulmer, 1999; Lomranz, 1995).

The tension between integration and separation also operates externally, when people within a relationship struggle to meet the often contradictory needs of the **inclusion-seclusion dialectic.** They struggle to reconcile a desire for involvement with the "outside world" with the desire to live their own lives, free of what can feel like interference from others. For example, when the end of a busy week comes, does a couple accept the invitation to a party (and sacrifice the chance to spend quality time with one another), or do they decline the invitation (and risk losing contact with valued friends)? Does a close-knit nuclear family choose to take a much anticipated vacation together (disappointing their relatives), or do they attend a family reunion (losing precious time to enjoy one another without any distractions)?

**Stability versus Change** Stability is an important need in relationships, but too much of it can lead to feelings of staleness. The **stability-change dialectic** operates both between partners and when they face others outside the relationship.

Within a relationship, the **predictability-novelty dialectic** captures another set of tensions. While nobody wants a completely unpredictable

*"And do you, Rebecca, promise to make love only to Richard, month after month, year after year, and decade after decade, until one of you is dead?"*

relational partner ("You're not the person I married!"), humorist Dave Barry (1990, p. 47) exaggerates only slightly when he talks about the boredom that can come when husbands and wives know each other too well:

> After a decade or so of marriage, you know *every-thing* about your spouse, every habit and opinion and twitch and tic and minor skin growth. You could write a seventeen-pound book solely about the way your spouse *eats*. This kind of intimate knowledge can be very handy in certain situa-tions—such as when you're on a TV quiz show where the object is to identify your spouse from the sound of his or her chewing—but it tends to lower the passion level of a relationship.

At an external level, the **conventionality-uniqueness dialectic** captures the challenges that people in a relationship face when trying to meet others' expectations as well as their own. On one hand, stable patterns of behavior do emerge that enable others to make useful judgments like "happy family" or "dependable organization." But those blanket characterizations can stifle people in relationships, who may sometimes want to break away from the expectations others hold of them. For example, playing the role of "happy family" or "perfect couple" during a time of con-flict can be a burden.

**Expression versus Privacy**   Disclosure is one char-acteristic of interpersonal relationships. Yet, along with the drive for intimacy, we have an equally important need to maintain some space between ourselves and others. These sometimes conflicting drives create the **expression-privacy dialectic.**

The internal struggle between expression and privacy shows up in the **openness-closedness**

## FOCUS ON RESEARCH

### GOING PUBLIC OR STAYING PRIVATE: DIALECTICAL TENSIONS OF BATTERED WOMEN

For many couples, the expression-privacy dialectic centers on decisions to reveal or conceal good news about their relationship. "Should we tell our friends that we're dating?" or "Is it time for you to meet my family?" are questions they might ask about sharing positive relational information with others. For some couples, however, the concealed news isn't so pleasant. Lara Dieckmann looked into the world of battered women and found that most of them wrestle with the dialectic of staying private or going public about the abuse in their relationships.

Dieckmann conducted in-depth interviews at an agency for battered women in Chicago. She also talked with shelter volunteers and drew upon her experience as a legal advocate for battered women. Her goal was to interpret "abused women's experience in relation to their social and political context and with reference to their own words."

A word that Dieckmann used to describe the women's experience is balance—that is, their need to constantly balance the competing demands of privacy and publicity, secrecy and disclosure, safety and danger. Telling others about partner abuse can be the first step in disengaging from a violent relationship, but it can also threaten a woman's self-esteem, security, and very life. Con-sider, for example, the dilemma of a battered woman who wants to reach out to friends and family for help, but fears that her mate will find out and react violently. Or imagine the spouse whose shame at confessing to being victimized conflicts with the desire to share her problem.

From the outside, it can be hard to understand why victims of abuse keep quiet about their awful situations. But understanding the dialectical tension between openness and privacy can help us appreciate the dilemmas often faced by partners in abusive relationships.

Dieckmann, L. E. (2000). Private secrets and public disclosures: The case of battered women. In S. Petronio (Ed.), *Balancing the secrets of private disclosures* (pp. 275–286). Mahwah, NJ: Lawrence Erlbaum.

**dialectic.** What do you do in an intimate relationship when a person you care about asks an important question that you don't want to answer? "Do you think I'm attractive?" "Are you having a good time?" Your commitment to the relationship may compel you toward honesty, but your concern for the other person's feelings and a desire for privacy may lead you to be less than completely honest. This dialectic raises so many communication challenges that Chapter 10 explores it in depth.

The same conflicts between openness and privacy operate externally in the **revelation-concealment dialectic.** If you and a long-time fellow worker haven't been getting along, do you answer the boss's question "How's it going?" honestly, or keep your disagreement to yourselves?

Although all of the dialectical tensions play an important role in managing relationships, some occur more frequently than others. In one study (Pawlowski, 1998), young married couples reported that autonomy-connection was the most frequent tension (30.8 percent of all reported contradictions). Predictability-novelty was second (occurring 21.7 percent of the time), and inclu-

## FILM CLIP

### DIALECTICAL TENSIONS IN MALE/FEMALE RELATIONSHIPS: *THE BROTHERS MCMULLEN*

Gender research suggests that when it comes to dialectical tensions, males and females in romantic relationships often have competing goals. The data generally indicate that men want autonomy while women want connection; men are more closed while women are more open; men like novelty while women prefer predictability.

Exhibit A: The Brothers McMullen. At first blush, the three brothers—Barry (Edward Burns), Patrick (Mike McGlone), and Jack (Jack Mulcahy)—live up to male stereotypes. Barry is a carefree bachelor who doesn't want commitment. Patrick has mixed emotions about two women and doesn't know how to say what he feels (at least to them). Jack is married but is having an affair. Respectively, they typify autonomy, closedness, and novelty.

But it's not that simple. By movie's end, Barry recognizes and acts on his need for an intimate relationship. Patrick gets in touch with his feelings and declares them to the woman he loves. Jack returns to his marriage after his affair proves unfulfilling. The moral to the story? Dialectical tensions are a part of every human relationship. While there may be gender-based tendencies, every person in a relationship must come to grips with both the push and the pull of relational dialectics.

Erbert (1999) found that autonomy-connection and openness-closedness were the most important factors affecting relational turning points for heterosexual partners.

**Strategies for Managing Dialectical Tensions**
Managing the dialectical tensions outlined in these pages and summarized in Table 9.3 presents communication challenges. There are a number of ways these challenges can be managed (Griffin, 2000).

1. *Denial*   In the strategy of denial, communicators respond to one end of the dialectical spectrum and ignore the other. For example, a couple caught between the conflicting desires for stability and novelty might find their struggle for change too difficult to manage and choose to follow predictable, if unexciting patterns of relating to one another.
2. *Disorientation*   In this mode, communicators feel so overwhelmed and helpless that they are unable to confront their problems. In the face of dialectical tensions they might fight, freeze, or even leave the relationship. A couple who discovers soon after the honeymoon that living a "happily ever after" conflict-free life is impossible might become so terrified that they would come to view their marriage as a mistake.
3. *Alternation*   Communicators who use this strategy choose one end of the dialectical spectrum at some times, and the other end on different occasions. Friends, for example, might manage the autonomy-connection dialectic by alternating between times when they spend a large amount of time together and other periods when they live independent lives.
4. *Segmentation*   Partners who use this tactic compartmentalize different areas of their relationship. For example, a couple might manage the openness-closedness dialectic by sharing almost all their feelings about mutual friends with one another, but keeping certain parts of their past romantic histories private.

sion-seclusion was third (21.4 percent). Less common were tensions between openness-closedness (12.7 percent), conventionality-uniqueness (7.5 percent), and revealment-concealment (6 percent). Research by Baxter and

5. *Balance*  Communicators who try to balance dialectical tensions recognize that both forces are legitimate and try to manage them through compromise. As Chapter 12 points out, compromise is inherently a situation in which everybody loses at least a little of what he or she wants. A couple caught between the conflicting desires for predictability and novelty might seek balance by compromising with a lifestyle that is neither as predictable as one wants nor as surprise filled as the other seeks—not an ideal outcome.

6. *Integration*  With this approach, communicators simultaneously accept opposing forces without trying to diminish them. Barbara Montgomery (1993) describes a couple who accept both the needs for predictability and novelty by devising a "predictably novel" approach: Once a week they would do something together that they had never done before. Similarly, Dawn Braithwaite and her colleagues (1998) found that step-families often manage the tension between the "old family" and the "new family" by adapting and blending their family rituals.

7. *Recalibration*  Communicators can respond to dialectical challenges by reframing them so that the apparent contradiction disappears. Consider how a couple who felt hurt by one another's unwillingness to share parts of their past might redefine the secrets as creating an attractive aura of mystery instead of being a problem to be solved. The desire for privacy would still remain, but it would no longer compete with a need for openness about every aspect of the past.

8. *Reaffirmation*  This approach acknowledges that dialectical tensions will never disappear. Instead of trying to make them go away, reaffirming communicators accept—or even embrace—the challenges they present. The metaphorical view of relational life as a kind of roller-coaster reflects this orientation, and communicators who use reaffirmation view dialectical tensions as part of the ride.

## Characteristics of Relational Development

Whether you analyze a relationship in terms of stages or dialectical dynamics, two characteristics are true of every interpersonal relationship.

**Relationships Are Constantly Changing**  Relationships are rarely stable for long periods of time. In fairy tales a couple may live "happily ever after," but in real life this sort of equilibrium is less common. Consider a husband and wife who have been married for some time. Although they have formally bonded, their relationship will probably shift forward and backward along the spectrum of stages, and different dialectical tensions will become more or less important at different times.

Richard Conville (1991) captures this constant change by describing relational cycles in which the partners continually move through a series of stages before returning back to ones they previously encountered, although at a new level. He pictures this movement as a kind of helix, as shown in Figure 9.2 (p. 270). According to Conville, we move from security (integration in Knapp's terminology) to disintegration (differentiating) to alienation (circumscribing) to resynthesis (intensifying, integrating) to a new level of security. This cycle repeats itself again and again. This back-and-forth movement reflects the three dialectical contradictions identified by Baxter and others.

**Movement Is Always to a New Place**  Even though a relationship may move back to a stage it has experienced before, it will never be the same as before. For example, most healthy long-term relationships will go through several phases of experimenting, as the partners try out new ways of behaving with one another. Though each phase is characterized by the same general features, the specifics will feel different each time. Similarly, how partners manage the openness-closedness dialectic regarding one issue at one time will affect how this dialectic is experienced and managed at another time with the same or different

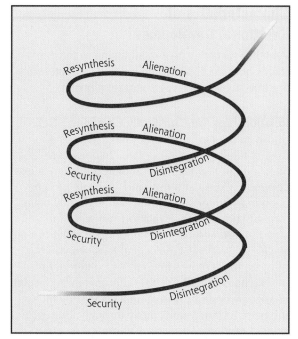

***Figure 9.2*** **A Helical Model of Relational Cycles**

relational issues. As you learned in Chapter 1, communication is irreversible. Partners can never go back to "the way things were." Sometimes this fact may lead to regrets, but sometimes it can make relationships exciting since it lessens the chance for boredom and can lead to novelty and growth (Montgomery, 1993).

# Communicating about Relationships

By now, it is clear that relationships are complex, dynamic, and important. How do communicators address relational issues with one another?

## Content and Relational Messages

As you learned in Chapter 1, every message has a *content* and a *relational* dimension. The most obvious component of most messages is their con-

tent—the subject being discussed. The content of statements like "It's your turn to do the dishes" or "I'm busy Saturday night" is obvious.

Content messages aren't the only information being exchanged when two people communicate. In addition, every message—both verbal and nonverbal—also has a second, *relational* dimension, which makes statements about how the communicators feel toward one another (Dillard et al., 1999; Watzlawick et al., 1967). These relational messages deal with one or more social needs: intimacy, affinity, respect, and control. Consider the two examples we just mentioned:

- Imagine two ways of saying "It's your turn to do the dishes," one that is demanding and another that is matter-of-fact. Notice how the different nonverbal messages make statements about how the sender views control in this part of the relationship. The demanding tone says, in effect, "I have a right to tell you what to do around the house," whereas the matter-of-fact one suggests, "I'm just reminding you of something you might have overlooked."
- You can easily imagine two ways to deliver the statement "I'm busy Saturday night," one with little affection and the other with much liking.

Like these messages, every statement we make goes beyond discussing the subject at hand and says something about the way the speaker feels about the recipient. You can prove this fact by listening for the relational messages implicit in your own statements to others and theirs to you.

Most of the time we are unaware of the relational messages that bombard us every day. Sometimes these messages don't capture our awareness because they match our belief about the amount of control, liking, or intimacy that is appropriate in a relationship. For example, you probably won't be offended if your boss tells you to drop everything and tackle a certain job, because you agree that supervisors have the right to direct employees. However, if your boss delivered the order in a condescending, sarcastic, or abusive tone of voice, you would probably be offended. Your complaint wouldn't be with the order itself, but with the way it was delivered. "I may work for this company," you might think, "but I'm not a slave or an idiot. I deserve to be treated like a human being."

## Expression of Relational Messages

Exactly how are relational messages communicated? As the boss-employee example suggests, they are usually expressed nonverbally. To test this fact for yourself, imagine how you could act while saying "Can you help me for a minute?" in a way that communicates each of the following relationships:

superiority
helplessness
friendliness
aloofness
sexual desire
irritation

Although nonverbal behaviors are a good source of relational messages, remember that they are ambiguous. The sharp tone you take as a personal insult might be due to fatigue, and the interruption you take as an attempt to ignore your ideas might be a sign of pressure that has nothing to do with you. Before you jump to conclusions about relational clues, it is a good idea to verify the accuracy of your interpretation with the other person: "When you cut me off, I got the idea you're angry at me. Is that right?"

Not all relational messages are nonverbal. Social scientists use the term **metacommunication** to describe messages that refer to other messages. In other words, metacommunication is communication about communication. Whenever we discuss a relationship with others, we are metacommunicating: "I wish we could stop arguing so much," or "I appreciate how honest you've been with me." Verbal metacommunication is an

### REFLECTION

#### SENDING THE WRONG RELATIONAL MESSAGE

I work 30 hours a week and have a full course load at school, so I am very busy. Sometimes when my little brother wants to hang out and talk, I give him the brush-off. While he's telling me about his day, I keep typing on the computer or reading a book. After a while I sigh and start replying automatically, "yeah, yeah." Last night he asked "Why don't you like me any more?" I realized that, in my obsession with staying on top of my work, I've been giving him the wrong impression. I explained to him why I've been so preoccupied. It's hard for him to accept that he can't always be the center of my world, but I think he understands that my brush-offs mean "I'm busy" and not "I don't like you."

essential ingredient in successful relationships. Sooner or later, there are times when it becomes necessary to talk about what is going on between you and the other person. The ability to focus on the kinds of issues described in this chapter can be the tool for keeping your relationship on track. Despite its importance, overt metacommunication isn't a common feature of most relationships (Wilmot, 1987). In fact, there seems to be an aversion to it, even among many intimates. When ninety people were asked to identify the taboo subjects in their personal relationships, the most frequent topics involved metacommunication (Baxter & Wilmot, 1985). For example, people were reluctant to discuss the state of their current relationships and the norms ("rules") that governed their lives together. Other studies suggest that when metacommunication does occur, it sometimes threatens the recipient and provokes conflict (Hocker & Wilmot, 1995).

# Compliance Gaining in Interpersonal Relationships

Whether the goal is gaining control, affection, or respect, we use communication to get what we seek. Researchers have identified over sixty ways we try to gain others' compliance (Kellerman & Cole, 1994). Sometimes the choice of approaches is conscious: If you are trying to impress a potential boss or romantic partner, you will probably think carefully about what to say or do. Once relationships develop, we still do our share of strategizing. A teenager who wants to borrow the family car, a spouse who wants to propose a vacation that his or her mate might not like, and a friend who needs to explain why he or she forgot to show up for a date are all likely to weigh their words before speaking. In other cases we don't consciously strategize, but even then it's likely that as competent communicators we consider a number of ways to get what we seek before choosing what we hope will be the best approach.

Skill at compliance gaining develops early in childhood (Dillard, 1990; Monastersky, 2000). By the age of one, most infants understand that they can influence the actions of others through their behavior. Some (though certainly not all) of their tears and tantrums, laughter and cuddles, gestures, and other movements are conscious attempts to get something from others. They form rough but often effective requests, or perhaps commands: "Feed me!" "Pick me up!" "I want it *now*!" By age three, children develop primitive strategies to get what they want. They are able to adapt their messages in terms of simplicity, politeness, and topic. For example, one child might find that politeness pays dividends, so "please" and "thank you " become means to an end. Another might find that saying "I love you" puts grown-ups in a better mood. These decisions aren't conscious, of course. Rather, they are scripts that develop from a process of trial and error.

By the time a child reaches kindergarten age-specific personalized strategies and scripts replace generalized ones. A child realizes that the approach that works with Dad may fail miserably with Mom and that what may be regarded as cute at home is a misdemeanor at school. As children grow up, they become even more skillful at creating messages that gain cooperation or agreement from others. They are able to consider a variety of approaches and choose the one that appears most likely to produce the desired results.

## Types of Compliance-Gaining Strategies

Social scientists use the term **compliance-gaining strategies** to define the tactics we use to persuade others to think or act in a desired way. Over the past quarter century, researchers have devised a variety of ways to describe compliance-gaining strategies (see, for example, Table 9.4; Gass & Seiter, 1999; Goss & O'Hair, 1988). The particular strategies we use to get what we seek from others can vary from one type of relationship to another. For example, dating couples who want to intensify their relationship use the strategies listed in Table 9.4. When the goal is to increase the level of physical intimacy, a

**Table 9.4**

| Compliance Strategies Used to Intensify Dating Relationships (Listed in Order of Frequency) |
| --- |

| Percent of Use | |
| --- | --- |
| 39.2% | *Increased contact:* Interact with partner more often and for longer periods of time. |
| 29.1% | *Relationship negotiation:* Initiate or engage in direct give-and-take discussion of relationship. |
| 26.1% | *Social support and assistance:* Ask for advice, assistance, or support. |
| 17.6% | *Increase rewards:* Compliment, do favors, perform tasks to increase rewards. |
| 16.6% | *Direct relational bid:* Direct request or bid, without discussion, for a more serious exclusive relationship. |
| 16.1% | *Token of affection:* Give gifts, cards, flowers, sentimental items to partner. |
| 15.1% | *Personalized communication:* Self-disclosure or use of language that reflects uniqueness of relationship (e.g., pet names). |
| 14.1% | *Verbal expressions of affection:* Directly express feeling of affection to partner. |
| 13.1% | *Suggestive actions:* Hint, flirt, play hard to get, and other deceptive or non-open methods to communicate feelings. |
| 12.1% | *Nonverbal expressions of affection:* Touching, sustained eye contact, etc. |
| 11.6% | *Social enmeshment:* Get to know friends and family of the partner or get the partner to know one's own friends and family. |
| 9.5% | *Accept definitional bid:* Agree to a direct request for a more serious/exclusive relationship. |
| 9.5% | *Personal appearance:* Attempt to look physically attractive for one's partner. |

From: Tolhuizen, J. H. (1989). Communication strategies for intensifying dating relationships: Identification, use and structure. *Journal of Social and Personal Relationships, 6,* 413–434.

wide range of approaches can be used, including logic, pleading, bargaining, flattery, and physical impositions (Christopher & Frandsen, 1990). Whatever the approach, skill in compliance-gaining communication can help people get what they seek in ways that don't compromise the other person's feelings of self-worth (Ifert & Roloff, 1997).

The following list of approaches combines most of the elements in previous taxonomies. As you read each category, think of times when you have used it, or when it has been used by others to gain your compliance.

**Direct Requests**   The most straightforward way to gain compliance is to ask for it, or make a **direct request.** We usually preface a request with a reason: "I have to work late tonight, . . ." and then make a polite request: "so could you pick up a few things downtown for me?" (Tracy, 1984). Along with its simplicity and honesty, this approach is a

surprisingly effective way to get what you want. College students have reported that the best way to get social support is to ask for it (Conn & Peterson, 1989). This approach even works well with strangers. One famous study illustrates its power (Langer, 1978). Experimenters waiting in line to use a copying machine asked to move ahead of others by asking, "May I use the Xerox machine because I'm in a rush?" Over 90 percent of the customers let the requester go ahead. People were almost as willing to comply when the reason was a lame one: "May I use the Xerox machine because I have to make some copies?" Even without a reason for letting the requester cut in, over 60 percent of the people complied.

**Indirect Appeals**   When it is awkward or ineffective to make a direct request, we often use **indirect appeals,** hoping that the other person will infer or assume our real intent (Goss & O'Hair,

1988). Indirect appeals usually take the form of hints: "You're driving downtown? What a coincidence—I was just going to catch a bus myself!" "You're tired of that sweater? I think it's great!"

While hints are strategic by definition, they are often a sensible and ethical way to seek compliance. Asking others directly may make them uncomfortable or put them on the spot. For example, it's usually inappropriate to invite yourself to a party, but hinting that you're free gives the host a chance to include you—or pretend not to have noticed the unspoken request. The risk of hints is that the other person might not recognize them. Nonetheless, they are a useful part of a repertoire for getting what you want from others.

Indirect approaches are especially useful when a direct approach would risk physical harm. Researchers who have studied abusive relationships have found that battered wives are more likely to use indirect approaches with their husbands than are spouses in nonviolent marriages (Rudd & Burant, 1995).

**Reciprocity**   Even if others aren't inclined to do what we want just because we ask them, they will often comply because of the powerful social **norm of reciprocity**—the convention that obligates us to return the favors others have extended to us—even when we dislike the other person (Cialdini, 1988; Garko, 1990). If I have given you a ride or helped you study, you are likely to do me a favor when I ask, even though you might prefer not to.

When used in a manipulative manner, the norm of reciprocity provides a good way to trick people into doing things they otherwise wouldn't do. For instance, a devious person might offer to lend you cash, knowing you don't need it, so that you'll feel obliged to extend a loan the next time he asks. But in many cases reciprocity is a kind of social lubricant that keeps relationships running. By supporting others, we wind up feeling altruistic and helping ourselves. In this sense, reciprocity can be a win-win approach, in which both people profit.

**Reward and Punishment**   Sometimes we comply because there's a clear payoff for doing so: "If you fix dinner tonight, I'll wash the dishes and pay for a movie later." The flip side of rewards, of course, is punishments: "If you try anything like that again, we're through!"

Not all threats and promises have immediate outcomes. Sometimes they lay out more general consequences. A dentist might counsel a patient to floss daily in order to avoid oral surgery or tooth loss later in life. Likewise, an English teacher might tell students that people who can't read or write are headed for dead-end jobs.

Rewards or punishments may be blatant: "I'll give you five dollars for washing my dirty clothes," or "If you don't pay the rent on time, I'm moving out." Sometimes the positive or negative consequences we project are more subtle: acting more friendly when another person cooperates or becoming less talkative when things don't go our way.

*"It's only a suggestion, but let's not forget who's making it."*

Reprinted by permission of Jerry Marcus.

Not surprisingly, communication in a relationship is more satisfying when positive compliance-gaining strategies prevail over negative ones (Grant et al., 1994). Still, some relationships are better suited than others to the use of power-based appeals of reward and punishments. For example, a boss might reasonably persuade an employee to work harder by suggesting that promotions go to workers who make an extra effort on the job. But even in relationships where power is distributed unevenly, rewards and punishments aren't used as often as we might think. One study compared the compliance-gaining methods of parents on prime-time family television shows with the approaches used by real-life parents. Television parents used commands 39 percent of the time—much more often than in real families (Haefner & Comstock, 1990).

**Face Maintenance**   Rewards aren't always obvious. Sometimes we appeal to others by stroking their egos, inducing them to comply because it makes them feel better about themselves. **Face-maintenance strategies** lead others to act in ways that reinforce their presenting self and at the same time provide what we want (Goss & O'Hair, 1988). For example, you might get a friend to help you work on a tough assignment by saying, "You're so smart and so good at explaining things. I know I could do better if you gave me a hand." Since the desire to maintain a presenting self is strong, others may provide what you are seeking for their sake, because it enhances their image. Your friend might not feel like helping you study, but lending a hand lets her think, "I really *am* pretty smart, and I'm helpful too. I'm a pretty good person!"

Face-maintenance strategies aren't always cynical attempts to manipulate others. They are often ways to shape others in a socially desirable manner. Research findings indicate, for example, that when a person feels guilty, soliciting compliance with a positive self-feeling message—"You'll feel really good about yourself if you help out"—is a more effective strategy than a direct request (Boster et al.,

1999). A parent might urge a child to perform a task by using this approach: "Now that you're six years old, I know you can clean up your room without me having to nag you." Likewise, a boss might give an employee an important assignment by saying, "I know I can count on you to do a good job." In cases like these, face maintenance can create a self-fulfilling prophecy. By creating idealized images of other people, we can induce them to become the person they (and we) want themselves to be.

**Relational Appeals**   Sometimes we comply with others out of respect or affection. **Relational appeals** fall into this category. They consist of strategies that rely on the target's relationship with the person making the request. Some referent appeals are straightforward requests for help: "I know you think those jokes are funny, but I'm embarrassed when you tell them. Would you stop telling them, for me?"

Other referent appeals may be just as sincere, but more calculating: "If you really care about me, you won't drink and drive." In every case, a relational appeal offers no other reason for complying beyond honoring the wishes of someone whose feelings are important to you. These appeals are most effective in intimate relationships, where the partners already feel a strong obligation to support one another (Roloff et al., 1988). This explains why the requests of intimate partners are less elaborate than those of mere acquaintances. They contain fewer apologies, explanations, and inducements. Simply making the request seems to include this implied reasoning: "You owe it to me to do what I ask."

## Which Strategy to Choose?

There is no single best compliance-gaining strategy. As you learned in Chapter 1, competent communicators have a wide repertoire of strategies and are skillful at choosing the best one for the circumstances. Sometimes, the best strategy varies by culture. For example, a study comparing compliance-gaining strategies in the United States and Colombia found that, whereas giving explanations or reasons is an often-used strategy in the United States, invoking shared obligations is more powerful in Colombia where relational connectedness and duties are paramount (Fitch, 1994).

Some skill at compliance gaining comes with age. Research shows that, as children become older, they become more skillful and flexible in their compliance-gaining approaches. Between the ages of two and five, preschoolers become more skilled at adjusting to one another and managing conflicts (Haslett, 1983). The flexibility in choosing the best approach continues to develop with age. A study of five-, nine-, and thirteen-year-old girls showed that the number and variety of appeals grew as the children grew older (Finley & Humphreys, 1974).

Once we have developed the skill to consider alternate ways to gain compliance, we weigh a number of factors in choosing the most promising approach. Some factors to weigh include the level of intimacy (spouse versus neighbor), dominance (employee versus boss), resistance (agreeable versus reluctant target), rights (reasonable versus unreasonable request), personal benefits of the persuader (high or low reward), and the consequence of rejection (Cody & McLaughlin, 1980; Cody et al., 1983).

In addition to these factors, there are several potential obstacles to compliance that need to be taken into account when selecting a strategy. Danette Ifert and Michael Roloff (1998) identified six of them. First, the person of whom you are making a request may not possess what you are asking for: "I don't have any." Second, your request may be seen as an imposition: "I'm too busy"; "I have other plans." Third, your request could be interpreted as inappropriate: "It's none of your business"—perhaps because it's viewed as your own responsibility: "Do it yourself." Fourth, there may be no incentive to comply: "Why should I do what you ask?" Fifth, the person may simply balk at complying, "I don't want to," without giving a reason. And sixth, you may get a request to postpone your own request: "I can't do it now, but maybe later"; "Can you wait a week?"

Although there is no single "best" strategy for gaining compliance, three principles can help you choose the best approach for a given situation (Cody et al., 1981).

### Which Strategy Has the Best Chance for Immediate Success?

Since your goal is to gain the other's cooperation, you need to choose the approach that promises to have the best chance of success. This means you must tailor your approach to the personal characteristics of the person involved. The approach that might work with a friend might fail with a professor, or even another friend. Unlike public speakers who often have to persuade a diverse audience, you can tailor your approach to the characteristics of the single person you want to reach. For example, Vincent Waldron and James Applegate (1998) found that using person-centered tactics during verbal disagreements—that is, adapting to the other person's feelings, motivations, and understandings—increased persuasiveness.

As you analyze the other person, consider all the appeals listed on pages 272–275 and then select the one that seems most promising. Is the other person likely to prefer a straightforward request, or would an indirect approach work better? Are you better off using logic to support your bid, or should you ask for compliance as a personal favor? Do your respective social roles make the promise of reward or punishment appropriate, or should you try a different tack?

### How Will the Strategy Affect the Long-Term Well-Being of the Relationship?

As you consider which approach to use, don't focus exclusively on short-term gains. Be sure to communicate in a way that keeps the long-term quality of the relationship comfortable. For example, you might be able to persuade a reluctant partner to give up studying to join you for an evening on the town by using a combination of relational and face-maintaining appeals ("I really was looking forward to spending the evening with you") and threats ("If you don't go tonight, don't expect me to party next time you ask"). Even if you succeed in this short-term goal, pestering the other person to do something that really isn't appealing is probably not worth the cost.

**Does the Strategy Conform to Your Values and Personal Style?**   Some approaches are clearly unethical. For example, Scott Christopher and Michael Frandsen (1990) point out the unfortunate fact that some dating partners rely on ridicule, guilt, alcohol, and persistence to gain sexual favors. Most people would agree that telling outright lies isn't justified, although you may feel justified using the kinds of equivocation and "white lies" described in Chapter 10. In any case, you should feel comfortable with whatever approaches you take. One test is whether you would be embarrassed to confess your strategy to the other person involved if he or she confronted you.

In addition to ethical considerations, the strategies you use should fit your personal style of communicating. You probably feel more comfortable with some of the strategies listed above than with others. Your preferred style might be to make straightforward requests, perhaps backing them up with evidence. Or you might be more inclined to demonstrate the desirability of cooperating by emphasizing the face-maintaining benefits and other rewards.

Don't rule out a particular strategy just because you aren't used to using it. You may feel a bit awkward trying a seldom-used approach, but it still may be the best for a particular situation. Compliance gaining, like any skill, takes time to develop. Whatever strategy you use, short- and long-term success probably depend on your sincerity. If you are going to compliment the other person, be sure your praise is sincere. If you ask the other person to comply because the request is personally important, be sure you mean what you say. If you seem to be deceiving or manipulating the other person, your chances for success will shrink, as will your ability to be persuasive in the future.

## Summary

Several conditions must be satisfied for a personal relationship to exist: The people must be aware of each other and take each other into account, there must be mutual influence, and there must be some agreement about the social form and expectations that govern the interaction. The last condition suggests that relationships change over time—that they are continually in process.

There are several explanations for why we form relationships with some people and not others. These explanations include appearance (physical attractiveness), similarity, complementarity, rewards, competency, proximity, and disclosure. The explanation for which there is the most evidence is similarity: In general, people are attracted to people who are like themselves.

Some theorists argue that interpersonal relationships may go through as many as ten stages of growth and deterioration. They suggest that communication may reflect more than one stage at a given time, although one stage will be dominant. Other models describe the dynamics of interpersonal communication in terms of dialectical tensions: mutually opposing, incompatible desires that can never be completely resolved. Both models characterize relationships as constantly changing, so that communication is more of a process than a static thing.

Messages have both content and relational dimensions. While the content aspect of a message may be obvious, the relational aspect is less clear. Relational messages sometimes are expressed overtly via metacommunication; however, more frequently they are conveyed nonverbally.

Communicators use a variety of compliance-gaining strategies to achieve their relational goals. These strategies include direct requests, indirect appeals, reciprocity, promising or delivering rewards and punishments, acting in ways that maintain the other's face, and making relational appeals. The choice of a particular compliance-gaining strategy depends on several short- and long-term considerations.

Whatever the lens through which you view relationships—models of attraction, stages of development, dialectical tensions, or compliance-gaining strategies—the point is that our relationships are continually in process, constantly changing. Accepting that change is inevitable, and understanding the characteristics and qualities of your relationship increases your chances of improving them.

## Recommended Readings

**The nature of interpersonal relationships:**

Richard Conville and L. Edna Rogers, eds., *The Meaning of "Relationship" in Interpersonal Communication.* New York: Praeger, 1998.

**Relational stages:**

Mark L. Knapp and Anita L. Vangelisti. Chapter 2: "Stages of Coming Together and Coming Apart" in *Interpersonal Communication and Human Relationships,* 4th ed. Boston: Allyn & Bacon, 2000.

**Relational dialectics:**

Barbara M. Montgomery and Leslie A. Baxter, eds., *Relating: Dialectical Approaches to Studying Personal Relationships.* Mahwah, NJ: Lawrence Erlbaum Associates, 1998.

**Compliance gaining:**

Robert B. Cialdini. *Influence: Science and Practice.* Glenview, IL: Scott-Foresman, 1988.

## Activities

1. **Invitation to Insight**
   Identify examples of complementary, symmetrical, and parallel distributions of control in relationships you have observed or in ones in which you have been involved. You may choose

different relationships to describe each type of control, or you may describe how a single relationship exhibited each distribution of power at a different time.

2. **Invitation to Insight**
   What attracts you to others? Choose five *voluntary* relationships you are currently involved in. (Attraction usually isn't an issue in involuntary relationships, such as with families and job partners.) Describe which factors listed on pages 249–257 of this chapter first attracted you to the other person and which factors encouraged you to maintain the relationship.

3. **Critical Thinking Probe**
   Some critics claim that Knapp's model of relational stages is better suited to describing romantic relationships than it is other types. Use a variety of romantic and nonromantic interpersonal relationships from your experience to evaluate the breadth of his model. If the model does not describe the developmental path of all types of interpersonal relationships, can you suggest alternative models?

4. **Invitation to Insight**
   How do you manage the dialectical tensions in your important relationships? Is there a pattern to what you and the other person do, or does it depend on the type of relationship you have? Identify at least two dialectical tensions in two different relationships—one relationship, perhaps, with a person with whom you work closely, and the other with a romantic partner. How is each tension managed? Which approach do you and your partner tend to use (denial, disorientation, alternation, segmentation, balance, integration, recalibration, or reaffirmation)? What seem to be the conditions that determine which method you and your partner use?

5. **Ethical Challenge**
   As you read on pages 262–268, we often face conflicting goals when we communicate in an attempt to meet our own needs and those of

others. Use the information on these pages to identify a situation in which your personal goals conflict with those of another person. What obligation do you have to communicate in a way that helps the other person reach his or her goals? Is it possible to honor this obligation and still try to satisfy your own needs?

6. **Skill Builder**

Identify three unexpressed relational messages in one or more of your interpersonal relationships.
   a. Describe how you could have used metacommunication to express each one. Consider skills you learned in other chapters, such as perception checking, "I" language, and paraphrasing.
   b. Discuss the possible benefits and drawbacks of this kind of metacommunication

in each of the situations you identified. Based on your discussion here, what principles do you believe should guide your decision about whether and when to focus explicitly on relational issues?

7. **Ethical Challenge**

Identify the six compliance-gaining strategies described on pages 272–275 that you use most often. Describe specific instances in which you used each one. Based on your description, discuss whether these strategies are ethical. In answering this question, consider how willing you would be to disclose your strategies to the people at whom they are directed. Also, consider how you would feel if others used these strategies with you.

# CHAPTER
## 10

# Intimacy and Distance in Relationships

# After Studying the Material in This Chapter . . .

## You Should Understand:

1. Four dimensions of intimacy.

2. The dialectical forces that encourage both intimacy and privacy in relationships.

3. How notions of intimacy are shaped by gender and cultural influences.

4. The characteristics of and reasons for self-disclosure.

5. The types, functions, and extent of equivocation, white lies, and hints.

6. The risks and benefits of self-disclosure.

## You Should Be Able to:

1. Identify the optimal blend of intimacy and distance in your personal relationships.

2. Identify the degree to which you engage in self-disclosure with individuals in your life and the circumstances in which you do so.

3. Use the Johari Window model to represent the level of self-disclosure in one of your relationships.

4. Express the reasons you self-disclose in a selected relationship.

5. Compose responses to a situation that reflect varying degrees of candor and equivocation.

6. Name the potential risks and benefits of disclosing in a selected situation.

7. Use the guidelines in this chapter to decide whether or not to disclose important information in one of your relationships.

## Key Terms

| | | | |
|---|---|---|---|
| Equivocal language | Johari Window | Self-disclosure | White lie |
| Intimacy | Lie | Social penetration model | |

# Intimacy and Distance: Striking a Balance

The musical group Three Dog Night said it well: One *can* be the loneliest number. For most of us, the desire to connect with others is a powerful force. As Chapter 1 explained, strong attachments with others not only make us happier, they also can make us healthier and help us live longer (see also Prager & Buhrmester, 1998).

In their book *Intimacy: Strategies for Successful Relationships*, C. Edward Crowther and Gayle Stone (1986) offer a reminder of just how important close relationships can be. As part of a study of people who were dying in hospices and hospitals in the United States and England, Crowther and Stone asked each person what mattered most in his or her life. Fully 90 percent of these terminally ill patients put intimate relationships at the top of the list. As a fifty-year-old mother of three children who was dying of cancer put it, "You need not wait until you are in my condition to know nothing in life is as important as loving relationships" (p. 13).

## Dimensions of Intimacy

What does it mean to be intimate? A scene from the Broadway musical *Fiddler on the Roof* raises this question:

**Him:**  Do you love me?
**Her:**  Do I love you? For twenty years I've cleaned the house, raised the kids, given your dinner parties, washed your clothes. After all these years, why ask?
**Him:**  But do you love me?
**Her:**  For twenty years I've lived with you, argued with you, worried with you, worried *about* you, slept with you! What do you think love is?
**Him:**  Then do you love me?

This dialogue raises some good questions. Does intimacy mean spending time together? Sharing feelings? Having sex? Going through thick and thin? Are intimacy and love identical? *Webster's New Collegiate Dictionary* defines

---

## REFLECTION

### BUILDING A RELATIONSHIP ON-LINE

This is a personal reflection from and about two authors of this textbook, Lawrence Rosenfeld and Russ Proctor. The two of us have never met in person, nor have we talked on the phone. Our only contact while working on several editions of this book has been through the exchange of e-mail messages.

This arrangement probably sounds impersonal, but in fact our relationship has grown from a professional partnership into a very satisfying friendship. In addition to working on the textbook you are reading, we have exchanged stories about our families, tales from our classrooms, and ideas about the communication field.

Both of us marvel at the fact that it's possible to have a solid friendship in the absence of ever speaking to one another.

---

*intimacy* as arising from "close union, contact, association, or acquaintance." This definition suggests that a key element of intimacy is closeness, one feature that "ordinary people" have reported as characterizing their intimate relationships (Register & Henley, 1992). This closeness can occur in a variety of relationships (Berscheid et al., 1989). When researchers asked several hundred college students to identify their "closest, deepest, most involved, and most intimate relationship," the answers were varied. Roughly half (47 percent) identified a romantic partner. About a third (36 percent) chose a friendship. Most of the rest (14 percent) cited a family member.

Another form of intimacy is *physical*. Even before birth, the developing fetus experiences a kind of physical closeness with its mother that will never happen again: "Floating in a warm fluid, curling inside a total embrace, swaying to the undulations of the moving body and hearing the beat of the pulsing heart" (Morris, 1973, p. 7). As they grow up, fortunate children are continually nourished by physical intimacy: being rocked, fed, hugged, and held. As we grow older, the opportunities for physical intimacy are less regular, but still possible and important. Some physical intimacy is sexual, but this category also can include affectionate hugs, kisses, and even struggles. Companions who have endured physical challenges together— for example, in athletics or during emergencies— form a bond that can last a lifetime.

In other cases, intimacy comes from *intellectual* sharing. Not every exchange of ideas counts as intimacy, of course. Talking about next week's midterm with your professor or classmates isn't likely to forge strong relational bonds. But when you engage another person in an exchange of important ideas, a kind of closeness develops that can be powerful and exciting.

If we define intimacy as being close to another person, then *shared activities* can provide another way to achieve this state (Wood & Inman, 1993). Shared activities can include everything from working side by side at a job to meeting regularly for exercise workouts. When people spend time together they can develop unique ways of relating that transform the relationship from an impersonal one to one with interpersonal qualities. Leslie Baxter (1992) found that both same-sex friendships and opposite-sex romantic relationships were characterized by several forms of play. Partners invented private codes, fooled around by acting like other people, teased one another, and played games—everything from having punning contests to arm wrestling.

The amount and type of intimacy can vary from one relationship to another (Speicher, 1999). Some intimate relationships exhibit all four qualities: emotional disclosure, physical intimacy, intellectual exchanges, and shared activities. Other intimate relationships exhibit only one or two. Of course, some relationships aren't intimate in any way. Acquaintances, roommates, and coworkers

may never become intimate. In some cases, even family members develop smooth but relatively impersonal relationships.

Not even the closest relationships always operate at the highest level of intimacy. At some times, you might share all of your thoughts or feelings with a friend, family member, or lover; at other times, you might withdraw. You might freely share your feelings about one topic and stay more aloof regarding another one. The same principle holds for physical intimacy, which waxes and wanes in most relationships.

Despite the fact that no relationship is *always* intimate, living without *any* sort of intimacy is hardly desirable. For example, one study revealed that subjects who fear intimacy in dating relationships anticipate less satisfaction in a long-term relationship and report feeling more distant from even long-time dating partners (Sherman & Thelen, 1996).

## The Dialectics of Intimacy and Distance

Intimacy is certainly important, but so is distance. It's impossible to have a close relationship with everyone: There simply isn't enough time and energy. Even if we could seek intimacy with everyone we encounter, few of us would want that much closeness. Consider the range of everyday contacts that don't require any sort of intimacy. Some are based on economic exchange (the people at work or the shopkeeper you visit several times a week), some are based on group membership (church or school), some on physical proximity (neighbors, carpooling), and some grow out of third-party connections (mutual friends, child care). Simply engaging in conversational give-and-take can be a kind of enjoyable recreation, not too different from the kind of impromptu "jamming" of musicians who gather together to create music without revealing any personal information (Eisenberg, 1990).

These examples suggest that intimacy isn't essential, even with people whom we encounter often. It's possible to have a very satisfying relationship with some friends, neighbors, coworkers, or even some family members without involving a high degree of closeness (Weiss, 1998). You can probably think of several satisfying relationships that include moderate or even low amounts of intimacy. This doesn't mean that intimacy is unimportant—just that it isn't the *only* measure of relational satisfaction.

Some scholars have pointed out that an obsession with intimacy can lead to *less* satisfying relationships (Bellah et al., 1985; Parks, 1982; Sennett, 1974). People who consider intimate communication as the only kind worth pursuing place little value on relationships that don't meet this standard. This can lead them to regard interaction with strangers and casual acquaintances as superficial, or at best as the groundwork for deeper relationships. When you consider the pleasure that can come from polite but distant communication, the limitations of this view become clear. Intimacy is definitely rewarding, but it isn't the only way of relating to others.

Even the kinds of social niceties that are often polite but insincere serve an important social function (Sennett, 1974). Behaving civilly to people whom you don't like provides the lubrication that keeps public life from degenerating into a series of nasty squabbles. You may not like your landlord and your teacher (and they may not like you!), but good manners can help you take care of necessary business. When no conflicts exist, social conventions provide a way to make contact with strangers and acquaintances without expending the energy required to build a personal relationship. Although casual remarks about the weather or current events may not create deeply personal relationships, they can provide a satisfying way of connecting with others.

Another look at two of the dialectical tensions introduced in Chapter 9 remind us that all relationships—even the closest ones—require some distance. We value privacy as well as disclosure, and autonomy is just as important as connection. On a short-term basis, the desire for intimacy waxes and wanes. Lovers often go through periods of much sharing alternating with times of

Reprinted by permission of Peter Steiner.

relative withdrawal. Likewise, they experience periods of passion and then times of little physical contact. Friends have times of high disclosure, when they share almost every feeling and idea, and then disengage for days, months, or even longer. Figure 10.1 (p. 286) illustrates some patterns of variation in openness uncovered in a study by C. Arthur VanLear (1991). College students reported the degree of openness in one of their important relationships—a friendship, a romantic relationship, or marriage—over a range of thirty conversations. The graphs show a definite pattern of fluctuation between disclosure and privacy in every stage of the relationships.

The dialectical tension between intimacy and distance makes intuitive sense. Intimacy is rather like chocolate. We may enjoy or even crave it, but too much of a good thing can extinguish the desire for more. Despite this fact, the tension between the opposing drives of openness and closedness can be a dilemma for many friends, coworkers, family members, and lovers. For example, many former couples report that the breakup of their relationships was caused in great part by their inability to manage the contradictions between the desires for intimacy and distance (Baxter, 1994; Kramer, 1997).

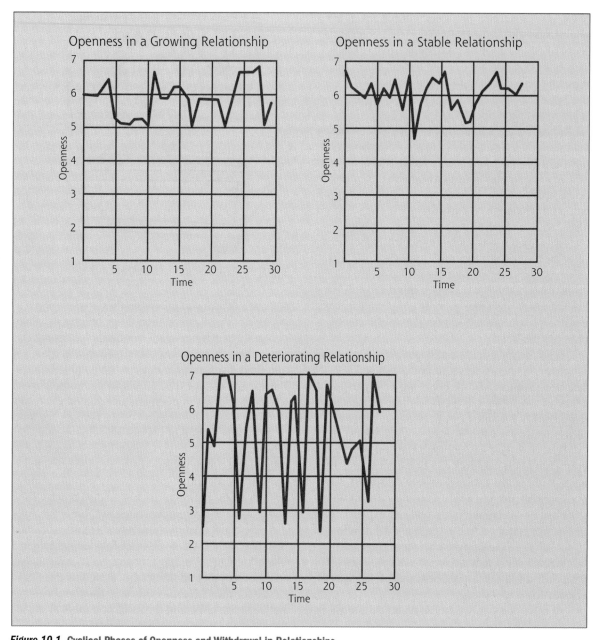

**Figure 10.1** Cyclical Phases of Openness and Withdrawal in Relationships

Adapted from: VanLear, C. A. (1991). Testing a cyclical model of communicative openness in relationship development: Two longitudinal studies. *Communication Monographs, 58,* 337–361. Used by permission of the National Communication Association.

The ideal level of intimacy can change over time. In his book *Intimate Behavior,* Desmond Morris suggests that each of us repeatedly goes through three stages: "Hold me tight," "Put me down," and "Leave me alone" (Morris, 1973). This cycle becomes apparent in the first years of life, when children move from the "hold me tight" phase that characterizes infancy into a new "put me down" stage of exploring the world by crawling, walking, touching, and tasting. This move for independence isn't all in one direction: The same three-year-old who insists "I can do it myself" in August may cling to parents on the first day of preschool in September.

As children grow into adolescents, the "leave me alone" orientation becomes apparent. Teenagers who used to happily spend time with their parents now may groan at the thought of a family vacation, or even the notion of sitting down at the dinner table each evening. More time is spent alone or with friends. Although this time can be painful for parents, most developmental experts recognize it as a necessary phase in moving from childhood to adulthood.

Families that are most successful at communicating during this difficult period tend to be those willing to explore new boundaries for control and autonomy. According to Patricia Noller (1995), adolescents are most likely to be healthy and well adjusted when their parents are open to renegotiating family rules and roles, when they can explore alternative identities without excessive criticism and abuse, and when they are encouraged to take responsibility for their lives. Specific styles and strategies for communicating during this challenging time are outlined in Chapters 11 and 12.

In adult relationships, the same cycle of intimacy and distance repeats itself. In marriages, for example, the "hold me tight" bonds of the first year are often followed by a desire for independence. This need for autonomy can manifest itself in a number of ways, such as the desire to make separate friends, to engage in activities that don't include the spouse, or to make a career move that might disrupt the relationship. As the discussion of relational stages in Chapter 9 explained, this movement from closeness to autonomy may lead to the breakup of relationships; however, it also can be part of a cycle that continuously redefines the relationship in new forms that recapture or even surpass the intimacy that existed in the past.

Given the equally important needs for intimacy and distance, the challenge is to communicate in a manner that provides the best possible mix of intimate and nonintimate relationships (Petronio, 1991). The material in the rest of this chapter can help you find the optimal level of intimacy in your relationships.

# Influences on Intimacy and Distance

What is the ideal amount of intimacy? The answer to this question varies according to who is giving the answer. You know from personal experience that different people seek different levels of intimacy. What factors lead to these differences? Two of the most powerful influences are gender and culture.

## Male and Female Intimacy Styles

Until recently, most social scientists believed that women were better than men at developing and maintaining intimate relationships. This view grew from the assumption that the disclosure of personal information is the most important ingredient of intimacy. Most research *does* show that women (taken as a group, of course) are somewhat more willing than men to share their most personal thoughts and feelings (Dindia & Allen, 1992), although the differences aren't as dramatic as most people believe (Dindia, 2000b).

In terms of the amount and depth of information exchanged, female-female relationships are at the top of the disclosure list. Male-female relationships come in second, while relationships between men typically involve less disclosure than do any other type. At every age, women disclose more than men, and the information they reveal is more personal and more likely to involve disclosure of feelings. While both sexes are equally likely to reveal negative information, men are less likely to share positive feelings.

Through the mid-1980s many social scientists interpreted the relatively lower rate of male self-disclosure as a sign that men were unwilling or unable to develop close relationships. Some (for example, Weiss & Lowenthal, 1975) argued that the female trait of disclosing personal information and feelings made them more "emotionally mature" and "interpersonally competent" than men. The title of one book captured this attitude of female superiority and male deficiency: *The Inexpressive Male: A Tragedy of American Society* (Balswick, 1988). Personal-growth programs and self-help books urged men to achieve closeness by learning to open up and share their feelings.

But more recent scholarship has begun to show that emotional expression isn't the *only* way to develop close relationships (Floyd, 1996; Inman, 1996; Johnson, 1996). Whereas women place a somewhat higher value on talking about personal matters as a measure of closeness, men are more likely to create and express closeness by doing things together. In one study, more than

75 percent of the men surveyed said that their most meaningful experiences with friends came from shared activities (Swain, 1989). They reported that through shared activities they "grew on one another," developed feelings of interdependence, showed appreciation for one another, and demonstrated mutual liking. Likewise, men regarded practical help as a measure of caring. The film *Diner,* profiled on page 291, and the study described in the Focus on Research on page 289 offer more details about ways in which many men achieve intimacy with one another. Materials like these show that, for many men, closeness grows from activities that don't always depend heavily

Sally Forth by Greg Howard © 1991. Reprinted with special permission King Features Syndicate.

# FOCUS ON RESEARCH

## MALE STYLES OF INTIMACY

In contemporary culture, the phrase "I love ya', man" has become more of a beer commercial joke than an expression of sincere affection among men. According to communication researchers Julia Wood and Christopher Inman, men in the real world are much more likely to create and express feelings of intimacy through actions than by words.

Wood and Inman first began exploring male intimacy styles when men in their classes at the University of North Carolina objected to the claim of some social scientists that women achieve closer relationships than men. Several argued that helping one another face challenges (on the football field, for example) and being there for one another at tough times

(such as when a girlfriend walked out) were good measures of closeness. "We know we're close. We just don't need to talk about those feelings" was their position. Female students, on the other hand, insisted that shared activities were no substitute for what they termed "really personal communication."

Intrigued by the very different notions of closeness, Inman and Wood reviewed four decades of research, much of which suggests that women are "intimacy experts." They suggest that this traditional opinion may result from "circular logic" which equates closeness with self-disclosure. Once this premise is accepted, they argue, women—who generally disclose more than men—appear to have

closer relationships than males who demonstrate their feelings by deeds more than words.

When this circular logic is abandoned, Wood and Inman suggest, there is ample evidence to support the notion that men are just as interested in and capable of developing close relationships as are women. The key, they argue, is to recognize that men often achieve and express intimacy through actions: shared activities and performing favors for one another. The authors conclude, "To persist in dismissing ways of interacting that men seem to prefer and to excel in impoverishes understanding of human connections."

Wood, J. T., & Inman, C. C. (1993). In a different mode: Masculine styles of communicating closeness. *Journal of Applied Communication Research, 21,* 279–295. Also see: Inman, C. (1996). Friendships among men: Closeness in the doing. In J. T. Wood (Ed.), *Gendered relationships* (pp. 95–110). Mountain View, CA: Mayfield.

on disclosure: A friend is a person who does things *for* you and *with* you. Of course, it's important not to assume that all men who value shared activities are reluctant to share feelings, or that doing things together isn't important to women. Recent scholarship offers convincing evidence that, in many respects, the meaning of intimacy is more similar than different for men and women (Goldsmith & Fulfs, 1999).

Whatever differences do exist between male and female styles of intimacy help explain some

of the stresses and misunderstandings that can arise between the sexes. For example, a woman who looks for emotional disclosure as a measure of affection may overlook an "unexpressive" man's efforts to show he cares by doing favors or spending time with her. Fixing a leaky faucet or taking a hike may look like ways to avoid getting close, but to the man who proposes them, they may be measures of affection and bids for intimacy. Likewise, differing ideas about the timing and meaning of sex can lead to misunderstandings.

Whereas many women think of sex as a way to *express* an intimacy that has already developed, men are more likely to see it as a way to *create* that intimacy (Reissman, 1990). In this sense, the man who encourages sex early in a relationship or after a fight may not just be a testosterone-crazed lecher: He may view the shared activity as a way to build closeness. By contrast, the woman who views personal talk as the pathway to intimacy may resist the idea of physical closeness before the emotional side of the relationship has been discussed.

## Cultural Influences on Intimacy

Historically, the notions of public and private behavior have changed dramatically (Adamopoulos, 1991; Gadlin, 1977). What would be considered intimate behavior today was quite public at times in the past. For example, in sixteenth-century Germany, the new husband and wife were expected to consummate their marriage upon a bed carried by witnesses who would validate the marriage (Adamopoulos & Bontempo, 1986)! Conversely, in England as well as in colonial America, the customary level of communication between spouses was once rather formal—not much different from the way acquaintances or neighbors spoke to one another.

Today, the notion of intimacy varies from one culture to another. In one study, researchers asked residents of Great Britain, Japan, Hong Kong, and Italy to describe their use of thirty-three rules that regulated interaction in social relationships (Argyle & Henderson, 1985). The rules governed a wide range of communication behaviors: everything from the use of humor, to handshaking, to the management of money. The results showed that the greatest differences between Asian and European cultures involved the rules for dealing with intimacy, including showing emotions, expressing affection in public, sexual activity, and respecting privacy.

Disclosure is especially high in mainstream North American society. In fact, natives of the United States are more disclosing than members of any other culture studied (Gudykunst, 1986). They are likely to disclose more about themselves to acquaintances and even to strangers. By contrast, Germans and Japanese tend to disclose little about themselves, except in personal relationships with a select few. Within American culture, intimacy varies from one group to another. For example, working class black men are much more disclosing than their white counterparts. By contrast, upwardly mobile black men communicate more like white males with the same social agenda, disclosing less with their male friends.

In some cultures, such as Taiwan and Japan (described as "collectivist" in Chapter 2), there is an especially great difference in the way people communicate with members of their "in-groups" (such as family and close friends) and with those they view as outsiders (Triandis, 1994). They generally do not reach out to strangers, often waiting until they are properly introduced before entering into a conversation. Once introduced, they address outsiders with a degree of formality. They go to extremes to hide unfavorable information about in-group members from outsiders, on the principle that one doesn't wash dirty laundry in public. By contrast, members of other cultures, such as the United States and Australia (characterized as "individualistic" in Chapter 2), make less of a distinction between personal and casual

## FILM CLIP

### INDIRECTLY EXPRESSING INTIMACY: *DINER*

*Diner* is set in the late 1950s, but update a few of the details and it could—and almost certainly does—take place today. A group of guys have been out of high school for a year or two. Billy (Timothy Daly) has gone away to college. Boogie (Mickey Rourke) is working his way through school while holding down a job. Shrevie (Daniel Stern) has married his high school sweetheart, Beth (Ellen Barkin). Eddie (Steve Gutenberg) is engaged but isn't quite sure why he is getting married. Fenwick (Kevin Bacon) is probably the smartest of the group, but he is drowning the unhappiness of his life in booze.

Viewed from one perspective, the film looks like an indictment of the lack of intimacy among men. The guys have been friends for years, but they never verbalize their obvious caring for one another. Their relationships with women seem distant at best: Shrevie confesses that marriage has taken the fun out of sex, and the strongest emotion he seems to feel toward his wife is anger when she forgets to replace his records on the shelf in alphabetical order. Boogie tries to pay back his gambling debts by seducing women while his friends watch in hiding. Eddie states that he will only marry his fiancée if she passes a football trivia test. On the surface, these characters are failing miserably at interpersonal communication.

However, a closer viewing of the film shows some strong examples of close relationships. Fenwick swallows his pride and asks his sanctimonious brother for money to save Boogie from a beating from the small-time hoods who have loaned him money. Boogie confesses his seductive strategy to Beth, when he could have gotten away with his plan and paid off his debt. Under director Barry Levinson's guidance, the buddies from the diner behave in ways that make their affection—even their love for one another—obvious. This story is a clear illustration of the traditionally male approaches to intimacy discussed in this chapter. The friends may not talk about their feelings toward one another, but by shared activities and the exchange of favors they show they care. They know, and we know too.

relationships. They are more familiar with strangers and disclose more personal information, making them excellent "cocktail party conversationalists." Social psychologist Kurt Lewin (1936) captured the difference nicely when he noted that Americans were easy to meet but difficult to get to know, while Germans were difficult to meet but then easy to know well.

Differences like these mean that the level of self-disclosure that is appropriate in one culture may seem completely inappropriate in another one. If you were raised in the United States, you might view people from other cultures as undisclosing and perhaps standoffish. But the amount of personal information that the non natives reveal might actually be quite personal and revealing, according to the standards of their culture. The converse is also true: To members of other cultures, North Americans probably appear like exhibitionists who spew personal information to anyone within earshot.

Chapter 2 offered detailed information about intercultural communication competence. At this point it's worth restating the point that, when communicating with people from different cultures, it's important to consider their norms for appropriate

## REFLECTION

### INTIMACY VARIES BY CULTURE

Growing up, my family hosted a number of foreign exchange students from around the world. It was interesting to see how some of them were comfortable with American ways of expressing intimacy—and some of them weren't. One of our German guests said he liked the way Americans share their feelings openly because he was used to keeping his emotions to himself and didn't like it. On the other hand, we hosted a Japanese student who (after quite a bit of prodding!) told us that she thought Americans are far too public with their displays of emotion and affection. Her bubbly Japanese friend, however, disagreed. We concluded that a person's rules about expressing intimacy are indeed influenced by culture, but they are also a product of one's personality and family of origin.

intimacy. On one hand, don't mistakenly judge them according to your own standards. Likewise, be sensitive about honoring their standards when talking about yourself. In this sense, choosing the proper level of intimacy isn't too different from choosing the appropriate way of dressing or eating when encountering members of a different culture: What seems familiar and correct at home may not be suitable with strangers.

## Self-Disclosure in Relationships

One way we judge the strength of relationships is by the amount of information we share with others. "We don't have any secrets," some people proudly claim. Opening up certainly is important. As Chapter 1 explained, one ingredient in qualitatively interpersonal relationships is disclosure. Chapter 9

showed that we find others more attractive when they share certain private information with us. Given the obvious importance of self-disclosure, we need to take a closer look at the subject. Just what is it? When is it desirable? How can it best be done?

### A Definition of Self-Disclosure

You might argue that aside from secrets, it's impossible *not* to make yourself known to others. After all, every time you open your mouth to speak, you're revealing your tastes, interests, desires, opinions, beliefs, or some other bit of information about yourself. Even when the subject isn't a personal one, your choice of what to talk about tells the listener something about who you are. Chapter 6 discussed the fact that each of us communicates nonverbally even when we're not speaking. For instance, a yawn may mean that you're tired or bored, a shrug of your shoulders may indicate uncertainty or indifference, and how close or how far you choose to stand from your listener may be taken as a measure of your friendliness or comfort.

If every verbal and nonverbal behavior in which you engage is self-revealing, how can self-disclosure be distinguished from any other act of communication? Psychologist Paul Cozby (1973) begins to answer this question. He suggests that in order for a communication act to be considered self-disclosing, it must meet the following criteria: (1) It must contain personal information about the sender, (2) the sender must communicate this information verbally, and (3) another person must be the target. Put differently, the subject of self-disclosing communication is the *self,* and information about the self is *purposefully communicated to another person.*

Although this definition is a start, it ignores the fact that some messages intentionally directed toward others are not especially revealing. For example, telling an acquaintance "I don't like clams" is quite different from announcing that "I don't like you." Let's take a look at several factors that further distinguish self-disclosure from other types of communication.

**Honesty**   It almost goes without saying that true self-disclosure has to be honest. It's not revealing to say "I've never felt this way about anyone before" to every Saturday night date, or to preface every lie with the statement "Let me be honest . . . ."

What about times when individuals do not know themselves well enough to present accurate information? Are these unintentionally false statements self-disclosing? For our purposes, the answer is yes. As long as you are honest and accurate to the best of your knowledge, the communication can qualify as an act of self-disclosure. On the other hand, painting an incomplete picture of yourself (telling only part of what's true) is not a self-disclosive act. We'll talk more about the relationship between honesty and disclosure later in this chapter.

**Depth**   A self-disclosing statement is generally regarded as being personal—containing relatively "deep" rather than "surface" information. Of course, what is personal and intimate for one person may not be for another. You might feel comfortable admitting your spotty academic record, short temper, or fear of spiders to anyone who asks, whereas others would be embarrassed to do so. Even basic demographic information, such as age, can be extremely revealing for some people.

**Availability of Information**   Self-disclosing messages must contain information that the other person is not likely to know at the time or be able to obtain from another source without a great deal of effort. For example, describing your conviction for a drunk-driving accident might feel like an act of serious disclosure, for the information concerns you, is offered intentionally, is honest and accurate, and is considered personal. However, if the other person could obtain that information elsewhere without much trouble—from a glance at the morning newspaper or from various gossips, for example—your communication would not be an act of self-disclosure.

**Context of Sharing**   Sometimes the self-disclosing nature of a statement comes from the setting in which it is uttered (Myers, 1998; Officer & Rosenfeld, 1985; Wambach & Brothen, 1997). For instance, relatively innocuous information about family life seems more personal when a teacher shares it with the class. This sort of sharing creates a more personal atmosphere because it changes the relationship from a purely "business" level to a more personal one.

We can summarize our definitional tour by saying that **self-disclosure** (1) has the self as subject, (2) is intentional, (3) is directed at another person, (4) is honest, (5) is revealing, (6) contains information generally unavailable from other sources, and (7) gains much of its intimate nature from the context and culture in which it is expressed.

Although many acts of communication may be self-revealing, this definition makes it clear that few of our statements may be classified as self-disclosure. Pearce and Sharp (1973) estimate that as little as 2 percent of our communication qualifies as self-disclosure. Other research confirms this. For example, most conversations—even among friends—focus on everyday mundane topics and disclose little or no personal information (Dindia et al., 1997; Duck & Miell, 1986). Even partners in intimate relationships don't talk about personal matters with a high degree of frequency (Duck, 1991).

## Degrees of Self-Disclosure

Although our definition of self-disclosure is helpful, it doesn't reveal the important fact that not all self-disclosure is equally revealing—that some disclosing messages tell more about us than others.

Social psychologists Irwin Altman and Dalmas Taylor (1973; Taylor & Altman, 1987) describe two ways in which communication can be more or less disclosing. Their **social penetration model** is pictured in Figure 10.2. The first dimension of self-disclosure in this model involves the *breadth* of information volunteered—the range of subjects being discussed. For example, the breadth of disclosure in your relationship with a fellow worker will expand as you begin revealing information about your life away from the job, as well as on-the-job details. The second dimension of disclosure is the *depth* of the information being volunteered—the shift from relatively non-revealing messages to more personal ones.

Depending on the breadth and depth of information shared, a relationship can be defined as casual or intimate. In a casual relationship, the breadth may be great, but not the depth. A more intimate relationship is likely to have high depth in at least one area. The most intimate relationships are those in which disclosure is great in both breadth and depth. Altman and Taylor see the development of a relationship as a progression from the periphery of their model to its center, a process that typically occurs over time. Each of your personal relationships probably has a different combination of breadth of subjects and depth of revealingness. Figure 10.3 pictures a student's self-disclosure in one relationship.

*Figure 10.2* Social Penetration Model

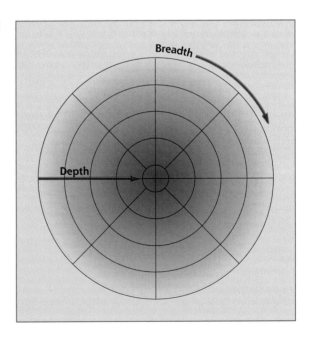

What makes the disclosure in some messages deeper than others? One way to measure depth is by how far it goes on two of the dimensions that define self-disclosure. Some revelations are certainly more *significant* than others. Consider the difference between saying "I love my family" and "I love you." Other statements qualify as deep disclosure because they are *private*. Sharing a secret that you've told only a few close friends is certainly an act of self-disclosure, but it's even more revealing to divulge information that you've never told anyone.

Another way to classify the depth of disclosure is to look at the types of information that can be revealed. *Clichés* are ritualized, stock responses to social situations—virtually the opposite of self-disclosure: "How are you doing?" "Fine." "We'll have to get together soon." Despite their apparent superficiality, clichés serve several useful functions. They can give speakers time to size each other up and decide whether it's desirable to carry the conversation any further. They also can serve as codes for messages we don't express directly, such as "I want to acknowledge your presence," when two acquaintances encounter one another. Other unstated messages often contained in clichés include " I'm interested in talking if you feel like it" or "Let's keep the conversation light and impersonal; I don't feel like disclosing much about myself right now." In all these cases, clichés can serve as a valuable kind of shorthand that makes it easy to keep the social wheels greased and can indicate the potential for further, possibly more profound conversation.

Another kind of message involves communicating *facts*. Not all factual statements qualify as self-disclosure: They must fit the criteria of being intentional, significant, and not otherwise known: "This isn't my first try at college. I dropped out a year ago with terrible grades." "I'm practically engaged" (on meeting a stranger while away from home). "That idea everyone thought was so clever

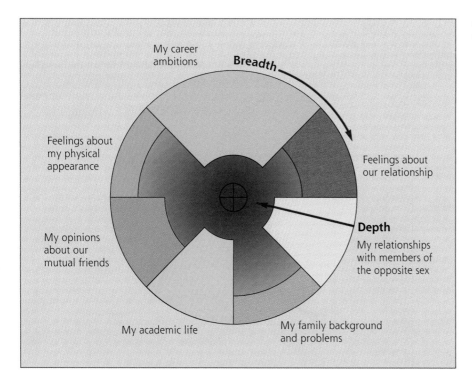

**Figure 10.3** Sample Model of Social Penetration

wasn't really mine. I read it in a book last year." Facts like these can be meaningful in themselves, but they also have a greater significance in a relationship. Disclosing important information suggests a level of trust and commitment that signals a desire to move the relationship to a new level.

*Opinions* can be a revealing kind of self-disclosure: "I don't think you're telling me what's on your mind." "I think Chris is a great person." Opinions like these often reveal more about a person than facts alone do. If you know where the speaker stands on a subject, you can get a clearer picture of how your relationship might develop. Likewise, every time you offer a personal opinion, you are giving others valuable information about yourself.

The fourth level of self-disclosure—and usually the most revealing one—involves the expression of *feelings*. At first glance, feelings might appear to be the same as opinions, but there's a big difference. As we saw, "I don't think you're telling me about what's on your mind" is an opinion. Notice how much more we learn about the speaker by looking at three different feelings that could accompany this statement: "I don't think you're telling me what's on your mind . . .

> *and I'm suspicious."*
> *and I'm angry."*
> *and I'm hurt."*

What is the optimal amount of self-disclosure? You might suspect that the correct answer is "the more the better," at least in personal relationships. However, research has shown that the matter isn't this simple. For example, there seems to be a curvilinear relationship between openness and satisfaction in marriage, so a moderate amount of openness produces better results than either extreme disclosure or withholding (Pearson, 1993). This relationship is described in Figure 10.4.

Other factors help determine the "best" level of openness. The amount of *perceived* disclosure is a better measure of happiness than the *actual* amount, and couples tend to overestimate the amount of personal information their partners reveal. One good measure of happiness is how well the level of disclosure matches the expectations of communicators: If we get what we believe is a reasonable amount of candor from others, we are happy. If they tell us too little—or even too much—we become less satisfied. Finally, the fit between the amount of information offered by communicators is important. Unmarried couples are happiest, for example, when their levels of openness are roughly equal. For married couples, however, the relationship isn't as clear. Although married couples who are very disclosive of their feelings report greater happiness and more effective conflict resolution than those who are less

**Figure 10.4**
**Relationship between Self-Disclosure and Relational Satisfaction**

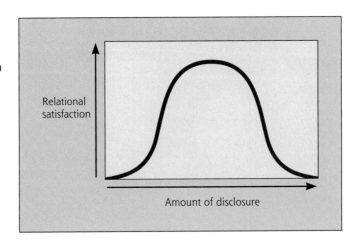

## REFLECTION

### MY MOST EMBARRASSING MOMENT—NOT

At a party I attended recently, we played an ice-breaker game: "Describe your most embarrassing moment." I sat there for awhile, trying to decide which story to tell (I have lots!). I was very conscious of the impression I might make. I wanted to paint myself in just the right light because I didn't know these people very well. I needed a story that would make me appear capable, good-humored, but not too full of myself. It needed to be about a one-time mistake, not a character flaw. I wasn't about to tell a story that would make me look incompetent, stupid, or strange, so I came up with a lame one about being embarrassed at a surprise party for me.

On the ride home, I realized I never even considered telling about the moments in my life that were truly the most embarrassing. A few of them I haven't told to even my closest friends. Just thinking about them makes me feel embarrassed all over again.

goals, your secrets, your needs—everything (see Figure 10.5).

Of course, you aren't aware of everything about yourself. Like most people, you're probably discovering new things about yourself all the time. To represent this, we can divide the frame containing everything about you into two parts: the part you know about and the part of which you are not aware (see Figure 10.6).

We also can divide the frame containing everything about you in another way. In this division, one part represents the things about you that others know, and the second part contains the things about you that you keep to yourself. Figure 10.7 (p. 298) represents this view.

disclosive (Vito, 1999), among some married couples, there is high marital satisfaction when one spouse enjoys disclosing and the other is a good listener (Rosenfeld & Bowen, 1991). These factors, as well as others, lead to the guidelines for when to self-disclose, found on pages 313–314 of this chapter.

## A Model of Self-Disclosure

One way to illustrate how self-disclosure operates in communication is to look at a model called the **Johari Window,** developed by Joseph Luft and Harry Ingham (Luft, 1969).

Imagine a frame that contains everything there is to know about you: your likes and dislikes, your

Figure 10.6

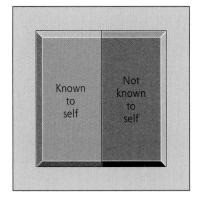

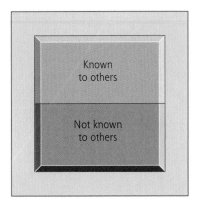

**Figure 10.7**

When we place these two divided frames one atop the other, we have a Johari Window. By looking at Figure 10.8, you can see that it divides everything about you into four parts.

Part 1 represents the information of which both you and the other person are aware. This part is your *open area*. Part 2 represents the *blind area:* information of which you are unaware but that the other person knows. You learn about information in the blind area primarily through feedback. Part 3 of the Johari Window represents your *hidden area:* information that you know but aren't willing to reveal to others. Items in this hidden area become public primarily through self-disclosure, which is

**Figure 10.8**

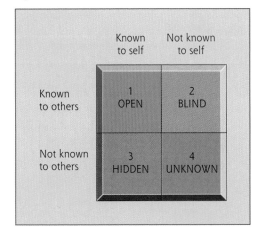

the focus of this chapter. Part 4 of the Johari Window represents information that is *unknown* to both you and to others. At first the unknown area seems impossible to verify. After all, if neither you nor others know what it contains, how can you be sure it exists at all? We can deduce its existence because we are constantly discovering new things about ourselves. For example, it is not unusual to discover that you have an unrecognized talent, strength, or weakness. Items move from the unknown area either directly into the open area when you share your insight, or through one of the other areas first.

The relative size of each area in our personal Johari Windows changes from time to time according to our moods, the subject we are discussing, and our relationship with the other person. Despite these changes, most people's overall style of disclosure could be represented by a single Johari Window. Figure 10.9 pictures windows representing four extreme interaction styles.

Style 1 depicts a person who is neither receptive to feedback nor willing to self-disclose. This person takes few risks and may appear aloof and uncommunicative. The largest quadrant is the unknown area: Such people have a lot to learn about themselves, as do others.

Style 2 depicts a person who is open to feedback from others but does not voluntarily self-disclose. This person may fear exposure, possibly because of a distrust of others. People who fit this pattern may appear highly supportive at first. After all, they want to hear *your* story, and they appear willing to deny themselves by remaining quiet. Then this first impression fades, and eventually you see them as distrustful and detached. A Johari Window describing such people has a large hidden area.

Style 3 in Figure 10.9 describes people who discourage feedback from others but disclose freely. Like the people pictured in Style 1, they may distrust others ' opinions. They certainly seem self-centered. Their largest quadrant is the blind area: They do not encourage feedback and thus fail to learn much about how others view them.

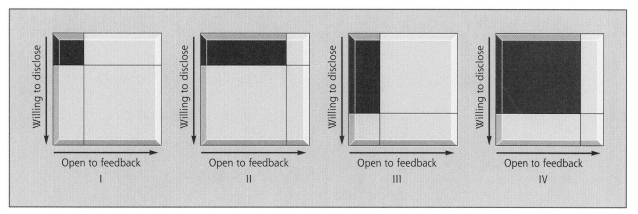

*Figure 10.9* **Four Styles of Disclosure**

Style 4 depicts people who are both willing to disclose information about themselves and be open to others' ideas. They are trusting enough to seek the opinions of others and share their own. In extreme, this communication style can be intimidating and overwhelming because it violates the usual expectations of how nonintimates ought to behave. In moderation, however, this open style provides the best chance for developing highly interpersonal relationships.

Interpersonal communication of any significance is virtually impossible if the individuals involved have small open areas. Going a step further, you can see that a relationship is necessarily limited by the individual who is less willing to disclose. Figure 10.10 illustrates this situation with Johari Windows. *A*'s window is set up in reverse so that *A*'s and *B*'s open areas are adjacent. Notice that the amount of communication (represented by the arrows connecting the two open areas) is dictated by the size of the smaller open area of *A*. The arrows originating from *B*'s open area and being turned aside by *A*'s hidden and blind areas represent unsuccessful attempts to communicate.

You probably have found yourself in situations that resemble Figure 10.10. Perhaps you have experienced the frustration of not being able to get to know someone who was too reserved. Perhaps you have blocked another person's attempts to

build a relationship with you in this way. Whether you picture yourself more like Person *A* or more like Person *B*, the fact is that self-disclosure on both sides is an important ingredient in the development of most interpersonal relationships.

## Reasons for Self-Disclosure

Although the amount of self-disclosure varies from one person and relationship to another, all of us share important information about ourselves at one time or another. What leads us to open up? Derlega and Grzelak (1979) present a variety of reasons that a person might have for disclosing in any particular situation. We can build upon their work and divide these reasons into several categories.

**Catharsis** Sometimes you might disclose information in an effort to "get it off your chest." In a moment of candor you might, for instance, share your regrets about having behaved badly in the past.

**Self-Clarification** Sometimes you can clarify your beliefs, opinions, thoughts, attitudes, and feelings by talking about them with another person. This sort of "talking the problem out" occurs in many psychotherapies, but it also goes on in other relationships, ranging all the way from good friends to interaction with bartenders or hairdressers.

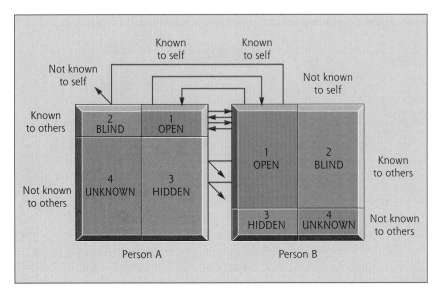

**Figure 10.10** How Limited Disclosure Blocks Communication

**Self-Validation** If you disclose information ("I think I did the right thing") with the hope of seeking the listener's agreement, you are seeking validation of your behavior—confirmation of a belief you hold about yourself. On a deeper level, this sort of self-validating disclosure seeks confirmation of important parts of your self-concept.

**Reciprocity** A well-documented conclusion from research is that one act of self-disclosure increases the odds that the other person will reveal personal information (Derlega et al., 1993; Dindia, 2000b). There is no guarantee that revealing personal information about yourself will trigger self-disclosures by others, but your own honesty can create a climate that makes the other person feel safer, and perhaps even obligated to match your level of candor. Sometimes revealing personal information will cause the other person to do so within the same conversation (Dindia, 2000b). It's easy to imagine how telling a partner how you feel about the relationship ("I've been feeling bored lately") would generate the same degree of candor ("You know, I've felt the same way!"). Reciprocity doesn't always occur on a turn-by-turn basis: Telling a friend today about your job-related problems might help her feel comfortable

opening up to you later about her family history, when the time is right for this sort of disclosure.

**Impression Formation** Sometimes we reveal personal information to make ourselves more attractive, and research shows that this strategy seems to work. One study revealed that both

"Bob, as a token of my appreciation for this wonderful lunch I would like to disclose to you my income-tax returns for the past four years."

## FOCUS ON RESEARCH

### SELF-DISCLOSURE IN PERSONAL ADS

Imagine approaching someone you want to date and saying, "I'm looking for someone with a good career and a strong sense of spirituality who wants a long-term romantic relationship." You'd probably scare the person off—unless you sent the message through a newspaper advertisement. Roxanne Parrott and her colleagues found that self-disclosures such as these are the norm rather than the exception in personal ads.

The researchers analyzed the content of 261 personal advertisements in a large southeastern U.S. newspaper. They discovered that every ad contained disclosures in three categories: appearance (e.g., height, weight, ethnicity); background (e.g., education, occupation, marital status); and attitude/values (e.g., hobbies, personality, sexual preferences). Although this kind of information is often exchanged on first dates, those who meet through personal ads know these facts *before* the date begins.

The researchers found that many principles of face-to-face interpersonal communication also operate in the construction of personal ads. For instance, the ads appeared to follow the reciprocity norm of self-disclosure—"I'll tell you some things about myself and expect that you'll reveal personal information in return." (It is worth noting that ad writers typically wrote less about themselves than about what they were seeking in a partner.) Also, ad writers seemed to subscribe to the principle that similarity leads to attraction: Most of what they revealed about themselves matched the qualities they were looking for in respondents.

This study demonstrates that mediated self-disclosures are both similar to and different from face-to-face disclosures. As the authors note, it also shows us that "personal ads are a rich source of human communication behavior."

Parrott, R., Lemieux, R., Harris, T., & Foreman, L. (1997). Interfacing interpersonal and mediated communication: Use of active and strategic self-disclosure in personal ads. *Southern Communication Journal, 62,* 319–332.

men's and women's attractiveness was associated with the amount of self-disclosure in conversations (Stiles et al., 1996). Consider a couple on their first date. It's not hard to imagine how one or both partners might share personal information to appear more sincere, interesting, sensitive, or curious about the other person. The same principle applies in other situations. A salesperson might say, "I'll be honest with you . . ." primarily to show that she is on your side, and a new acquaintance might talk about the details of his past in order to seem more friendly and likable.

### Relationship Maintenance and Enhancement

Research demonstrates that we like people who disclose personal information to us. In fact, the relationship between self-disclosure and liking works in several directions: We like people who disclose personal information to us, we reveal more about ourselves to people we like, and we tend to like others more after we have disclosed to them (Dindia, 2000b).

Beyond fostering liking, disclosure (appropriate, of course) can keep relationships healthy (Fitzpatrick & Sollie, 1999). There is a strong relationship between the amount and quality of self-disclosure and the level of marital satisfaction (Fincham & Bradbury, 1989; Rosenfeld & Bowen, 1991; Vito, 1999). Not surprisingly, partners who reveal personal information to one another avoid the sorts of misunderstandings that lead to unhappiness. The same principle applies in other relationships. For example, the bond between grandparents and grandchildren grows stronger when the honesty and depth of sharing between them are high (Downs, 1988). Even relative strangers who work together in groups are more productive, cohesive, and committed to their job when they are encouraged to share their feelings about the task at hand (Elias et al., 1989).

**Social Influence**   As you learned in Chapter 9, self-disclosure can be an effective compliance-gaining strategy. Revealing personal information may increase your control over the other person and sometimes over the situation in which you and the other person find yourselves. For example, an employee who tells the boss that another firm has made overtures probably will have an increased chance of getting raises and improvements in working conditions.

People sometimes reveal personal information to help others. This behavior is common in self-help groups such as Alcoholics Anonymous. On a larger scale, one study revealed that guests who chose to self-disclose on the television show *Donahue* indicated that their primary motive was "evangelical": They felt a calling to address injustices and remedy stereotypes (Priest & Dominick, 1994).

**Manipulation**   Although some of the preceding reasons might strike you as manipulative, they often aren't premeditated strategies. However, there are cases when an act of self-disclosure is calculated in advance to achieve a desired result. Of course, if a disclosure's hidden motive ever becomes clear to the receiver, the result will most likely be quite unlike the intended one.

To determine which of these reasons for self-disclosing are most important, Lawrence Rosenfeld and Leslie Kendrick (1984) asked college students to describe which ones would be their reasons for disclosing in a variety of situations. The situations varied in three respects:

The target of the self-disclosure (friend or stranger)

The setting (alone or in a group)

Intimacy (intimate or nonintimate)

For example, the *friend alone/intimate* situation was "It's evening, and you are alone with your boyfriend or girlfriend in his or her home." The *friend alone/nonintimate* situation was "You are in the library with a friend." The *group of strangers/nonintimate* situation was "You are introduced to a group of strangers."

The study showed that the most important reasons for disclosing depend on whether the other person is a stranger or a friend. When the target was a friend, the students being surveyed disclosed to maintain and enhance the relationship, to clarify their own feelings, and to both reciprocate their partner's revelations and encourage their partner to reciprocate their own disclosures. When the target was a stranger, subjects disclosed primarily to encourage the other person to disclose, as well as to reciprocate the other's revelations. This makes sense: Reciprocity of information provides a basis for deciding whether to continue the relationship and how personal it is likely to be. The second reason for disclosing to strangers was impression formation: to reveal information that made the discloser look good.

## Alternatives to Self-Disclosure

While self-disclosure plays an important role in interpersonal relationships, it isn't the only type of communication available. To understand why complete honesty isn't always an easy or ideal choice, consider some familiar dilemmas:

Your friend, who is headed out the door for an important job interview, says, "I know I'll never get this job! I'm really not qualified, and besides I look terrible." You agree with your friend's assessment.

A romantic partner asks why you haven't been affectionate lately. "Are you getting bored with me?" your partner asks. If you were to be completely honest, you would reply "Yes."

You've just been given a large, extremely ugly lamp as a gift by a relative who visits your home often. How would you respond to the question, "Where will you put it?"

Situations like these highlight some of the issues that surround deceptive communication. On one hand, our moral education and common sense lead us to abhor anything less than the truth. James Jaksa and Michael Pritchard (1994) point out that the very existence of a society seems based on a foundation of truthfulness. While isolated cultures do exist where deceit is a norm, they are dysfunctional and constantly on the verge of breakdown.

Although honesty is desirable in principle, it often has risky, potentially unpleasant consequences. It's tempting to side-step situations where self-disclosure would be difficult, but examples like the ones you just read show that avoidance isn't always possible. Research and personal experience show that communicators—even those with the best intentions—aren't always completely honest when they find themselves in situations when honesty would be uncomfortable (O'Hair & Cody, 1993). Three common alternatives to self-disclosure are lies, equivocation, and hinting. We will take a closer look at each one.

## Lying

A **lie** is a deliberate attempt to hide or misrepresent the truth. To most of us, lying seems to be a breach of ethics. While lying to gain unfair advantage over an unknowing victim seems clearly wrong, another kind of mistruth—the "white lie"—isn't so easy to dismiss as completely unethical. **White lies** are defined (at least by the people who tell them) as being unmalicious, or even helpful to the person to whom they are told.

Whether or not they are innocent, white lies are certainly common. In one study, 130 subjects were asked to keep track of the truthfulness of their everyday conversational statements (Turner et al., 1975). Only 38.5 percent of these statements—slightly more than a third—proved to be totally honest. In another study, both students and community members reported lying regularly, with the number of weekly lies ranging from zero to forty-six (DePaulo et al., 1996). Communication researchers have identified a variety of ways that people convey untruthful messages—for example, they are less complete, direct, clear, and personalized (Burgoon et al., 1996).

**Reasons for Lying**    What reasons do people give for being so deceitful? When subjects in DePaulo's study were asked to give a lie-by-lie account of their motives for concealing or distorting the truth, five major reasons emerged.

## FOCUS ON RESEARCH

### SELF-DISCLOSURE AS DECEPTION: THE RUSE OF A SOVIET SPY

Glenn Souther was a Soviet spy who doubled as a student at Virginia's Old Dominion University. He successfully deceived peers and instructors alike, including communication professor Virginia Cooper. Souther was a student of Cooper's, her research assistant, and even a frequent visitor in her home. When Cooper learned of Souther's ruse (after his graduation), she decided to study the methods he had used to form impressions that hid his identity.

Professor Cooper had an excellent source of data: She had saved four hours of audio tape from a group project in which Souther had participated. The audio tapes were transcribed, then content analyzed by Cooper and her assistants.

Their analysis suggests that Souther "was skilled in relationship deception due, in part, to his strategic disclosures that projected a plausible false image." In essence, Souther generated trust by revealing a large amount of personal information. In virtually every category, he made more disclosing statements than any other members of the group. This, believes Cooper, was part of Souther's strategy: He disclosed so much that he appeared "transparent." As a result, when his spy role became public years later, the people who thought they knew him so well were deeply shocked.

It's worth noting that Souther's approach was probably successful because he employed it in the low-context, individualistic culture of the United States, where directness and self-disclosure are generally prized. If he had used the same tactics in a different cultural setting—Japan or Germany, for instance—chances are good he wouldn't have been a well-disguised spy.

Cooper, V. W. (1994). The disguise of self-disclosure: The relationship ruse of a Soviet spy. *Journal of Applied Communication Research, 22,* 338–347.

*To Save Face*   Over half of the lies were justified as a way to prevent embarrassment. Such lying is often given the approving label "tact" and is used "when it would be unkind to be honest but dishonest to be kind" (Bavelas, 1983). Sometimes a lie saves face for the recipient, as when you pretend to remember someone at a party in order to save the person from the embarrassment of being forgotten. Married couples are especially likely to lie in order to protect the feelings of their spouse (Metts, 1989). In other cases, a self-serving lie protects the teller from humiliation. For instance, you might cover up your mistakes by blaming them on outside forces: "You didn't receive the check? It must have been delayed in the mail." Manipulative people, less highly socialized people, and people with less gratifying same-sex relationships tell more self-serving lies, whereas people with higher quality same-sex relationships tell relatively more lies aimed at preserving the face of others (Kashy & DePaulo, 1996).

*To Avoid Tension or Conflict*   Sometimes it seems worthwhile to tell a small lie to prevent a large conflict. For example, you might say you're not upset at a friend's teasing to prevent the hassle that would result if you showed your annoyance. It's often easier to explain your behavior in dishonest terms than to make matters worse. You might explain your apparent irritation by saying "I'm not mad at you; it's just been a tough day."

*To Guide Social Interaction*   Sometimes we lie to make everyday relationships run smoothly. For instance, you might pretend to be glad to see someone you actually dislike or fake interest in a dinner companion's boring stories to make a social event pass quickly. Children who aren't skilled at or interested in these social lies are often a source of embarrassment for their parents.

*To Expand or Reduce Relationships*   Some lies are designed to make a relationship grow: "You're going downtown? I'm headed that way. Can I give you a ride?" "I like science fiction too. What have you read lately?" One study (Rowatt et al., 1999) illustrated the pervasiveness of lying to expand relationships: A majority of college students (both men and women) willingly lied to improve their chances of getting a date with an attractive partner. Exaggerations and untruths covered a wide range of topics including their attitudes about love, personality traits, income, past relationships, career skills, and intelligence— all in the direction of making themselves more similar to the attractive prospects.

Romance isn't the only area where people lie to enhance relationships. You might try to impress a potential employer by calling yourself a management student when you've only taken a course or two in business. Sometimes we tell untruths to reduce interaction with others. Lies in this category often allow the teller to escape unpleasant situations: "I really have to go. I should be studying for a test tomorrow." In other cases, people lie to end a relationship entirely: "You're really great, but I'm just not ready to settle down yet."

*To Gain Power*   We sometimes tell lies to show that we're in control of a situation. Turning down a last-minute request for a date by claiming you're busy can be one way to put yourself in a one-up position, saying, in effect, "Don't expect me to sit around waiting for you to call." Lying to get confidential information—even for a good cause—also falls into the category of achieving power.

This five-part scheme isn't the only way to categorize lies. Exaggerations, for example, aren't covered in this scheme. Table 10.1 provides another list of reasons for distorting the truth.

**Table 10.1**

| Some Reasons for Lying | |
| --- | --- |
| **Reason** | **Example** |
| Acquire resources | "Oh, please let me add this class. If I don't get in, I'll never graduate on time!" |
| Protect resources | "I'd like to lend you the money, but I'm short myself." |
| Initiate and continue interaction | "Excuse me, I'm lost. Do you live around here?" |
| Avoid conflict | "It's not a big deal. We can do it your way. Really." |
| Avoid interaction | "That sounds like fun, but I'm busy Saturday night." |
| Leave taking | "Oh, look what time it is! I've got to run!" |
| Present a competent image | "Sure, I understand. No problem." |
| Increase social desirability | "Yeah, I've done a fair amount of skiing. |
| Exaggeration | "You think *this* is cold? Let me tell you about how cold it was on that trip. . . . |

Adapted from categories originally presented in Camden, C., Motley, M. T., & Wilson, A. (1984). White lies in interpersonal communication: A taxonomy and preliminary investigation of social motivations. *Western Journal of Speech Communication, 48*, 315.

Most people think white lies are told for the benefit of the recipient. In the study cited above, the majority of subjects claimed such lying was "the right thing to do." Other research paints a less flattering picture of who benefits most from lying. One study found that two out of every three lies are told for "selfish reasons" (Hample, 1980). Other research by Paula Lippard (1988) seems to indicate that this figure is too conservative. Of 322 lies recorded, 75.8 percent were for the benefit of the liar. Less than 22 percent were for the benefit of the person hearing the lie, while a mere 2.5 percent were intended to aid a third person.

Before we become totally cynical, however, the researchers urge a charitable interpretation. After all, most intentional communication behavior—truthful or not—is designed to help the speaker achieve a goal. Therefore, it's unfair to judge white lies more harshly than other types of messages. If we define selfishness as the extent to which some desired resource or interaction is denied to the person hearing the lie or to a third party, then only 111 lies (34.5 percent) can be considered truly selfish. This figure may be no worse than the degree of selfishness in honest messages.

Another measure of the acceptability of lying is the fact that most people are willing to accept many lies without challenging them. In fact, there are some circumstances when lies are judged as more appropriate than the undiluted truth (Hubbell, 1999; McCornack, 1992). For example, Peter Andersen (1999; 297–298) outlines the conditions when we are most likely to let statements that we know are untruthful go unchallenged:

1. *When we expect others to lie.* (You listen with amusement to a friend or relative's tall tales, even though you know they are exaggerations.)
2. *When the lie is mutually advantageous.* (A fellow employee's self-serving account of a job mix-up might get you off the hook, too.)
3. *When a lie helps us avoid embarrassment.* (You assure your host that a meal was delicious, even though it tasted awful.)

## REFLECTION

### WITHHOLDING THE TRUTH FROM MY PARENTS

I've been going out with a guy for several months. He's African American and I'm white, which is no problem for us. I haven't told my parents about his race, though, because they would be very uncomfortable.

Even though I'm not lying to my family, I feel uncomfortable not telling them an important part of the truth. Still, I have decided to only tell them once I'm sure this relationship will become more serious. There's just no point in getting them upset over nothing.

4. *When the lie helps us avoid confronting an unpleasant truth.* (One spouse might not threaten the tenuous stability of the marriage by challenging a partner's suspected infidelity.)
5. *When we have asked the other person to lie.* (A patient might tell the doctor "Don't let me know if it's malignant.")

**Effects of Lies on the Recipient**   What are the consequences of learning that you've been lied to? In an interpersonal relationship, the discovery can be traumatic. As we grow closer to others, our expectations about their honesty grow stronger (Buller, 1988; Stiff et al., 1989). After all, discovering that you've been deceived requires you to redefine not only the lie you just uncovered but also many of the messages you previously took for granted. Was last week's compliment really sincere? Was your joke really funny, or was the other person's laughter a put-on? Does the other person care about you as much as he or she claimed?

Research has shown that deception does, in fact, threaten relationships (McCornack & Levine,

1990). However, not all lies are equally devastating. Feelings like dismay and betrayal are greatest when the relationship is most intense, the importance of the subject is high, and when there was previous suspicion that the other person wasn't being completely honest. Of these three factors, the importance of the information lied about proved to be the key factor in provoking a relational crisis. We may be able to cope with "misdemeanor" lying, but "felonies" are a grave threat. For example, survey respondents whose parents did not communicate about problems before announcing an impending divorce reported lower self-esteem and less satisfaction with their deceptive mothers (Thomas et al., 1995).

An occasional white lie in an otherwise honest relationship doesn't pose much threat. Major deception, though—especially when it is part of a pattern of deceit—is likely to provoke a relational crisis. In fact, the discovery of major deception can lead to the end of a relationship. More than two thirds of the subjects in McCornack and Levine's study reported that their relationship had ended since they discovered a lie. Furthermore, they attributed the breakup directly to the deception.

The lesson here is clear: Lying about major parts of your relationship can have the gravest of consequences. If preserving a relationship is important to you, then honesty—at least about important matters—really does appear to be the best policy.

## Equivocation

Lying isn't the only alternative to self-disclosure. When faced with the choice between lying and telling an unpleasant truth, communicators can—and often do—equivocate. As Chapter 5 explained, equivocal language has two or more equally plausible meanings.

Sometimes we send equivocal messages without meaning to, resulting in confusion. "I'll meet you at the apartment" could refer to more than one place. But other times we are deliberately vague. For instance, when a friend asks what you think of an awful outfit, you could say "It's really unusual—one of a kind!" Likewise, if you are too angry to accept a friend's apology but don't want to appear petty, you might say "Don't mention it."

The value of equivocation becomes clear when you consider the alternatives. Consider the dilemma of what to say when you've been given an unwanted present—an ugly painting, for example—and the giver asks what you think of it. How can you respond? On the one hand, you need to choose between telling the truth and lying. At the same time, you have a choice of whether to make your response clear or vague. Figure 10.11 (p. 308) displays these choices.

After considering the alternatives, it's clear that the first option—an equivocal, true response—is far preferable to the other choices in several respects. First, it spares the receiver from embarrassment. For example, rather than flatly saying "No" to an unappealing invitation, it may be kinder to say "I have other plans"—even if those plans are to stay home and watch TV.

A study by Sandra Metts and her colleagues (1992) shows how equivocation can save face in difficult situations. Several hundred college students were asked how they would turn down unwanted sexual overtures from a person whose feelings were important to them: either a close friend, a prospective date, or a dating partner. The majority of students chose a diplomatic reaction ("I just don't think I'm ready for this right now") as being more face-saving and comfortable than a direct statement like "I just don't feel sexually attracted to you." The diplomatic reaction seemed sufficiently clear to get the message across, but not so blunt as to embarrass or humiliate the other person. (Interestingly, men said they would be better able to handle a direct rejection than women did. The researchers suggest that one reason for the difference is that men stereotypically initiate sexual offers and thus are more likely to expect rejection.)

Besides saving face for the recipient, honest equivocation can be less stressful for the sender than either telling the truth bluntly or lying.

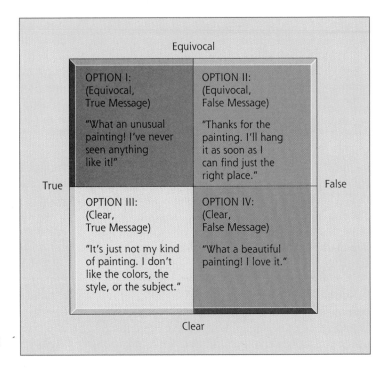

**Figure 10.11** Dimensions of Truthfulness and Equivocation

Figures 10.5 through 10.10 are from: Luft, J. *Group process: An introduction to group dynamics.* © 1963, 1970 by Joseph Luft. Used with permission of Mayfield Publishing Company.

Because equivocation is often easier to take than the cold, hard truth, it spares the teller from feeling guilty. It's less taxing on the conscience to say "I've never tasted anything like this" than to say "This meal tastes terrible," even though the latter comment is more precise. Few people *want* to lie, and equivocation provides an alternative to deceit.

Equivocal language may also save the speaker from being caught lying. If a potential employer asks about your grades during a job interview, you would be safe saying "I had a B average last semester," even though your overall grade average is closer to C. The statement isn't a complete answer, but it is honest as far as it goes. As Bavelas et al. (1990, p. 171) put it, "Equivocation is neither a false message nor a clear truth, but rather an alternative used precisely when both of these are to be avoided."

Given these advantages, it's not surprising that most people will usually choose to equivocate rather than tell a lie. In a series of experiments, subjects chose between telling a face-saving lie, the truth, and equivocating (Bavelas et al., 1990).

Only 6 percent chose the lie, and between 3 and 4 percent chose the hurtful truth. By contrast, over 90 percent chose the equivocal response. People *say* they prefer truth-telling to equivocating, but given the choice, they prefer to finesse the truth (Robinson et al., 1998).

## Hinting

Hints are more direct than equivocal statements. Whereas an equivocal message isn't necessarily aimed at changing another's behavior, a hint seeks to get the desired response from the other person. As Michael Motley (1992) suggests, some hints are designed to save the receiver from embarrassment:

| Direct Statement | Face-Saving Hint |
|---|---|
| You're too overweight to be ordering dessert. | These desserts are terribly overpriced. |
| I'm too busy to continue with this conversation. I wish you would let me go. | I know you're busy; I'd better let you go. |

DILBERT reprinted by permission of United Feature Syndicate, Inc.

Other hints are less concerned with protecting the receiver than with saving the sender from embarrassment:

| Direct Statement | Face-Saving Hint |
| --- | --- |
| Please don't smoke here; it bothers me. | I'm pretty sure that smoking isn't permitted here. |

| | |
| --- | --- |
| I'd like to invite you out for lunch, but I don't want to risk a "no" answer to my invitation. | Gee, it's almost lunch time. Have you ever eaten at that new Italian restaurant around the corner? |

The success of a hint depends on the other person's ability to pick up the unexpressed message. Your subtle remarks might go right over the head of an insensitive receiver . . . or one who chooses not to respond to them. If this happens, you still have the choice to be more direct. If the costs of a straightforward message seem too high, you can withdraw without risk.

## The Ethics of Evasion

It's easy to see why people often choose hints, equivocations, and white lies instead of complete self-disclosure. These strategies provide a way to manage difficult situations that is easier than the alternatives for both the speaker and the receiver of the message. In this sense, successful liars, equivocators, and hinters can be said to possess a certain kind of communicative competence. On the other hand, there *are* times when honesty is the right approach, even if it's painful. At times like these, evaders could be viewed as lacking either the competence or the integrity to handle a situation effectively.

Are hints, white lies, and equivocations ethical alternatives to self-disclosure? Some of the examples in these pages suggest the answer is a qualified "yes." Many social scientists and philosophers agree. For example, researchers David Buller and Judee Burgoon (1994) argue that the morality of a speaker's *motives* for lying ought to be judged, not the deceptive act itself. Another approach is to consider whether the *effects* of a lie will be worth the deception. Ethicist Sissela Bok (1978) offers some circumstances where deception may be justified: doing good, avoiding harm, and protecting a larger truth. Perhaps the right questions to ask, then, are whether an indirect message is truly in the interests of the receiver and whether this sort of evasion is the only effective way to behave. Bok suggests another way to check the justifiability of a lie: Imagine how others would respond if they knew what you were really thinking or feeling. Would they accept your reasons for not disclosing?

# Choosing the Optimal Level of Self-Disclosure

By now, it is apparent that self-disclosure is a special kind of communication that is not appropriate for every relationship or situation. In the remaining pages of this chapter we will take a look at the risks and benefits of disclosing, as well as offer some guidelines on when to reveal personal information to others.

## Risks and Benefits of Self-Disclosure

Is self-disclosure "good" or "bad"? There are two answers to this question: "Both" and "It depends." On the one hand, disclosure is both a means and an end of interpersonal relationships. Revealing important information about ourselves is a way to grow closer and build trust. The information we learn about others through disclosure is often what transforms our relationships from superficial, stereotyped role-playing arrangements into unique, deeply fulfilling ones. On the other hand, too much disclosure or disclosure that is poorly timed can lead to consequences ranging from mild annoyance and disappointment to downright rage and grief. We need to look, then, at both the benefits and risks to gain a clearer idea of when disclosing is—and isn't—an effective type of communication.

**Risks of Self-Disclosure**    The reasons for avoiding self-disclosure are summed up best by John Powell, who answers the question posed in the title of his book, *Why Am I Afraid to Tell You Who I Am?* (1968): "I am afraid to tell you who I am, because, if I tell you who I am, you may not like who I am, and that's all I have."

Revealing private information can be risky, both for the person who does the disclosing and for those who hear it. These risks fall into several categories (Derlega et al., 1993; Rosenfeld, 1979, 2000). First, self-disclosure might lead to rejection. The risk of disapproval is a powerful one. Sometimes the fear of rejection is exaggerated and illogical, but there are real dangers in revealing personal information:

**A:** I'm starting to think of you as more than a friend. To tell the truth, I think I love you.
**B:** I think we should stop seeing one another.

Even if disclosure doesn't lead to total rejection, it can create a negative impression that diminishes both the other person's respect and a basically satisfactory relational status quo. For example, one study revealed that family members withhold a great deal of personal information from one another (Guerrero & Afifi, 1995). Adolescents and young adults reported avoiding discussions of their dating and of negative life experiences with their parents, especially those of the opposite sex. Men were more reluctant than women to disclose, but neither sex revealed all personal information.

Besides affecting others' opinions of you, disclosure can lead to a decrease in the satisfaction that comes from a relationship. Consider a scenario like this, where the incompatible wants and needs of each person become clear through disclosure:

**A:** Let's get together with Wes and Joanne on Saturday night.
**B:** To tell you the truth, I'm tired of seeing Wes and Joanne. I don't have much fun with them, and I think Wes is kind of a jerk.
**A:** But they're my best friends.

Another risk of disclosure is a potential loss of influence in the relationship. Once you confess a secret weakness, your control over how the other person views you can be diminished.

## FILM CLIP

### IS IT WISE TO TELL ALL? *THE BREAKFAST CLUB*

*The Breakfast Club* is the story of five high school students who serve a Saturday detention together. The students come from different cliques in school, where each plays a stereotypical role. There is a "brain" (Michael Anthony Hall), a "prom queen" (Molly Ringwald), an "athlete" (Emilio Estevez), a "basket case" (Ally Sheedy), and a "criminal" (Judd Nelson). During their detention session, the club members expand their role repertoires. The "athlete" cries, the "basket case" comes out of her shell, the "brain" shows courage, and the "prom queen" falls for the "criminal"—all behaviors that are inconsistent with the parts they play during the week.

The students let down their guards because of the cohesiveness that develops from their mutual self-disclosures. As they discuss intimate details of their lives, they discover they're more similar than different. Each wrestles with self-acceptance; each longs for parental approval; each fights against (or succumbs to) peer pressure. Although they hate each other at the beginning of the movie, by story's end they are fast friends.

*The Breakfast Club* may end on a positive note, but is the story realistic? The film offers the best-case scenario, but consider what a less uplifting (and perhaps more realistic) one would look like. Each student will return to his or her clique after the

weekend. In those cliques, the intimate disclosures made during the detention session could easily become topics of discussion, sources of embarrassment, and weapons in the inter-clique arsenal. What seemed like a good idea on Saturday could be a nightmare on Monday. Baring your soul to virtual strangers with whom you'll have future interactions may not lead to the happy ending depicted in *The Breakfast Club*.

It would be nice if all of our intimate self-disclosures were held as trusted confidences in enduring friendships. However, that may be the case only in the movies—where we rarely get to see what happens on the Monday after.

---

**A:** I'm sorry I was so sarcastic. Sometimes I build myself up by putting you down.

**B:** Is that it? I'll never let you get away with that again!

Even if revealing hidden information leaves you feeling better, it might hurt others. It's easy to imagine yourself in a situation like this:

**A:** Well, since you asked, I have felt less attracted to you lately. I know you can't help it when your skin breaks out, but it is kind of a turnoff.

**B:** I know! I don't see how you can stand me at all!

Risks like these show that self-disclosure doesn't always lead to happily-ever-after outcomes.

In addition to these situational hazards, there are cultural dangers associated with disclosing. Like it or not, many people view revealing personal information—even in close relationships— as a kind of weakness, exhibitionism, or mental illness. Although these beliefs seem to be growing less pervasive, it is still important to consider whether the other person will welcome the information you share.

Paradoxical as it sounds, a final risk of self-disclosure is that it often leads to increased awareness. As you reveal yourself to others, you often learn more about yourself. This awareness can expose a need for you to change, and this might be difficult or painful. If ignorance is bliss, self-awareness can sometimes be quite the opposite—at least temporarily.

**Benefits of Self-Disclosure**  Although revealing personal information has its risks, the potential benefits can be at least as great. Self-disclosure—of the right type, communicated at the right time, in the right way—can be an important ingredient in interpersonal relationships.

The effect of self-disclosure on satisfying relationships works in two ways. We like people with whom we reciprocally disclose, and we disclose with people whom we like. Cozby (1972) describes a study in which subjects who had just spent a short time getting acquainted chose to disclose the greatest amount of information to partners whom they liked the most. After a period of conversation, the subjects were asked again to rate their liking for their partners. An analysis showed that the partners who had disclosed the greatest amount of information were liked the best.

Appropriate self-disclosure has been found to be positively related to marital satisfaction (Rosenfeld & Bowen, 1991; Waring & Chelune, 1983). One study revealed that distressed couples who sought counseling disclosed less information to each other and communicated more ambiguously than non-distressed couples did (Chelune et al., 1985). Couples recognize the value of disclosure: Disclosing spouses give their relationships higher evaluations and have more positive expectations than do partners who disclose less (Rosenfeld & Bowen, 1991). In one sample of fifty couples, the amount of overall disclosure in their relationships was a good predictor of whether the partners remained together over the four years in which they were studied (Sprecher, 1987).

Whether lack of self-disclosure is a cause or a symptom of troubled marriages isn't clear. However, couples who learn to change their communication styles are likely to find their relationships growing stronger. A number of studies have demonstrated that increased self-disclosure can improve troubled marriages (Vito, 1999; Waring,

1981). With the guidance of a skilled counselor or therapist, partners can learn constructive ways to open up. Many of the guidelines for constructive disclosure are contained in this chapter. Often, however, a couple with a backlog of hidden hurts and resentments needs the help of a third person to unload their emotional baggage without causing more damage.

## Guidelines for Self-Disclosure

Self-disclosure is a special kind of sharing that is not appropriate for every situation. Let's take a look at some guidelines that can help you recognize how to express yourself in a way that's rewarding for you and for the others involved.

**Is the Other Person Important to You?** There are several ways in which someone might be important. Perhaps you have an ongoing relationship deep enough so that sharing significant parts of yourself justifies keeping your present level of togetherness intact. Perhaps the person to whom you're considering disclosing is someone with whom you've previously related on a less personal level. Now you see a chance to grow closer, and disclosure may be the path toward developing that personal relationship.

**Is the Risk of Disclosing Reasonable?** Most people intuitively calculate the potential benefits of disclosing against the risks of doing so (Fisher, 1986). This approach makes sense. Even if the probable benefits are great, opening yourself up to almost certain rejection may be asking for trouble. For instance, it might be foolhardy to share your important feelings with someone whom you know is likely to betray your confidences or ridicule them. On the other hand, knowing that your partner will respect the information makes the prospect of speaking out more reasonable.

Revealing personal thoughts and feelings can be especially risky on the job (Eisenberg, 1990; Eisenberg & Witten, 1987). The politics of the workplace sometimes require communicators to keep feelings to themselves in order to accomplish both personal and organizational goals. For example, you might find the opinions of a boss or customer personally offensive but decide to bite your tongue rather than risk your job or lose goodwill for the company.

In anticipating the risks of disclosing, be sure that you are realistic. It's sometimes easy to imagine all sorts of disastrous consequences of opening up, when in fact such horrors are quite unlikely to occur.

**Is the Self-Disclosure Appropriate?** Self-disclosure isn't an all-or-nothing proposition. It's possible to reveal information in some situations and keep it to yourself in others. One important variable is the

relational stage (VanLear, 1987; Won-Doornick, 1979). Research shows that sharing personal information is appropriate during the integrating stage of a relationship, where partners grow closer by disclosing. But once the same relationship has reached a maintenance stage, the frequency of personal disclosures drops (Sillars et al., 1987). This makes sense, for by now the partners have already shared much of their private selves. Even the closest long-term relationships are a mixture of much everyday, nonintimate information and less frequent but more personal messages. Finally, realize that even intimate partners need to be sensitive to the timing of a message. If the other person is tired, preoccupied, or grumpy, it may be a good idea to postpone an important conversation.

**Is the Disclosure Relevant to the Situation at Hand?** The kind of disclosure that is often a characteristic of highly personal relationships usually isn't appropriate in less personal settings. For instance, a study of classroom communication revealed that sharing all feelings—both positive and negative—and being completely honest resulted in less cohesiveness than a "relatively" honest climate in which pleasant but superficial relationships were the norm (Rosenfeld & Gilbert, 1989).

Even in personal relationships—with close friends, family members, and so on—constant disclosure isn't a useful goal. The level of sharing in successful relationships rises and falls in cycles. You may go through a period of great disclosure and then spend another interval of relative nondisclosure (VanLear, 1987).

Even during a phase of high disclosure, sharing *everything* about yourself isn't necessarily constructive. Usually, the subject of appropriate self-disclosure involves the relationship rather than personal information (Sillars et al., 1987). Furthermore, it is usually most constructive to focus your disclosure about the relationship on the "here and now" as opposed to "there and then." "How am I feeling now?" "How are we doing now?" These are appropriate topics for sharing personal thoughts and feelings. There are certainly times when it's relevant to bring up the past, but only as it relates to what's going on in the present.

**Is the Disclosure Reciprocated?**   There's nothing quite as disconcerting as talking your heart out to someone, only to discover that the other person has yet to say anything to you that is half as revealing. You think to yourself "What am I doing?" Unequal self-disclosure creates an unbalanced relationship, one with potential problems.

The reciprocal nature of effective disclosure doesn't mean that you are obliged to match another person's revelations on a tit-for-tat basis. You might reveal personal information at one time, while the other person could open up at a later date. There are even times when reciprocal self-disclosure can be taken as stage hogging. For instance, if a close friend is talking about his opinion of your relationship, it's probably better

to hear him out and bring up your perspective later, after he's made his point.

There are few times when one-way disclosure is acceptable. Most of them involve formal, therapeutic relationships in which a client approaches a trained professional with the goal of resolving a problem. For instance, you wouldn't necessarily expect your physician to begin sharing her or his personal ailments with you during an office visit.

**Will the Effect Be Constructive?**   Self-disclosure can be a vicious tool if it's not used carefully. Every person has a psychological "beltline," and below that beltline are areas about which the person is extremely sensitive. Jabbing at an area "below the belt" is a surefire way to disable another person, usually at great cost to the relationship. It's important to consider the effects of your candor before opening up to others. Comments such as "I've always thought you were pretty unintelligent" or "Last year I made love to your best friend " may sometimes resolve old business and thus be constructive, but they also can be devastating—to the listener, to the relationship, and to your self-esteem.

**Is the Self-Disclosure Clear and Understandable?** When expressing yourself to others, it's important that you share yourself in a way that's intelligible. This means describing the sources of your message clearly. For instance, it's far better to describe another's behavior by saying "When you don't answer my phone calls or drop by to visit anymore . . ." than to complain vaguely "When you avoid me . . . ."

It's also vital to express your *thoughts* and *feelings* explicitly. "I feel worried because I'm afraid you don't care about me" is more understandable than "I don't like it . . . ."

# Summary

Intimacy comes in several forms: physical, intellectual, emotional, and shared activities. As important as intimacy is to relationships, so is distance. Intimacy is not essential to all relationships, and even in relationships where it is important, it is not important all the time. Intimacy and distance exist together in a dialectical tension—as opposing forces in a constant battle for balance. Whether in a growing relationship, a stable one, or a deteriorating one, intimacy and distance form a cyclical pattern where first one and then the other is most important.

Gender and culture exert a strong influence on both the amount of intimacy in a relationship and how that intimacy is communicated. A female intimacy style is characterized by self-disclosure, and a male intimacy style is characterized by shared activities. These differences exist within larger cultural differences. Each culture has rules that govern intimate communication, from touching in public to the disclosure of personal information. Also, each culture defines the extent to which any relationship should be formal and distant or close and intimate.

An important determinant of intimacy, although not the only determinant, is self-disclosure. Self-disclosure consists of honest, revealing messages about the self that are intentionally directed towards others. Disclosing communication contains information that is generally unavailable via other sources. Revealing personal information does not guarantee that this communication will be perceived by others as disclosing. A number of factors govern whether a communicator will be judged as being a high- or low-level discloser.

The social penetration model describes two dimensions of self-disclosure: breadth and depth. Disclosure of feelings is usually more revealing than disclosure of opinions, and disclosure of opinions is usually more revealing than disclosure of facts. Clichés are the least revealing.

The Johari Window model is a useful way to illustrate self-disclosure. A window representing a single person can illustrate the amount of information that individual reveals to others, hides, is blind to, and is unaware of. Windows representing two communicators reveal how differing levels of disclosure can affect the level of intimacy in a relationship.

Communicators disclose personal information for a variety of reasons: catharsis, self-clarification, self-validation, reciprocal obligations, impression formation, relationship maintenance and enhancement, social control, and manipulation.

The percentage of messages that are self-disclosing is relatively low. Three alternatives to revealing personal facts, feelings, and opinions are lies, equivocations, and hints. Unmalicious "white lies" serve a variety of functions: saving face for the sender or receiver, avoiding tension or conflict, guiding social interaction, managing relationships, and gaining power. When discovered by the recipient, lies have the potential to provoke a relational crisis, especially if the content of the information lied about is significant. Equivocal messages can be an attractive alternative to lying and direct honesty. They allow a communicator to be honest without being blunt and causing undesirable reaction. Hints, more direct than equivocal statements, are used primarily to avoid embarrassment. Hints are risky in that they depend on the other person's ability to pick up unexpressed messages. Lies, equivocations, and hints may be ethical alternatives to self-disclosure; however, whether they are or not depends on the speaker's motives and the effects of the deception.

Self-disclosure poses a variety of risks, both to the sender and to the recipient of the message. These potential risks are offset by the promise of many benefits. When deciding whether or not to disclose, communicators should consider a number of questions.

## Recommended Readings

**Love as a form of intimacy:**

Clyde Hendrick and Sandra Hendrick. *Romantic Love*. Newbury Park, CA: Sage, 1991.

**Self-disclosure:**

Sandra Petronio, ed. *Balancing the Secrets of Private Disclosures*. Mahwah, NJ: Lawrence Erlbaum Associates, 2000.

**Interpersonal deception:**

Michael Lewis and Carolyn Saarni, eds., *Lying and Deception in Everyday Life.* New York: Guilford, 1993.

**Equivocation as an alternative to honesty:**

Janet B. Bavelas, Alex Black, Nicole Chovil, and Jennifer Mullett. *Equivocal Communication.* Newbury Park, CA: Sage, 1990.

# Activities

1. **Invitation to Insight**
   What kinds of intimacy characterize your relationships? Answer the questions below as you think about your relationship with an important person in your life:
   a. What is the level of physical intimacy in your relationship?
   b. What intellectual intimacy do you share?
   c. How emotionally intimate are you? Is your emotional intimacy deeper in some ways than in others?
   d. What shared activities occupy an important role in this relationship?
   e. Has your intimacy level changed over time? If so, in what ways?
   After answering these questions, ask yourself how satisfied you are with the amount of intimacy in this relationship. Identify any changes you would like to occur, and describe the steps you could take to make them happen.

2. **Invitation to Insight**
   You can get a sense of how your desires for both intimacy and distance operate by following these directions:
   a. Choose an important interpersonal relationship with someone you encounter on a frequent, regular basis. You might choose a friend, family member, or romantic partner.
   b. For at least a one-week period, chart how your communication with this relational partner reflects your desire for either intimacy or distance. Use a seven-point scale in which behavior seeking high intimacy receives a 7, while behavior designed to avoid physical, intellectual, and/or emotional contact receives a 1. Use ratings from 2 through 6 to reflect intermediate stages. Record at least one rating per day, making more-detailed entries if your desire for intimacy or distance changes during that period.
   c. After charting your communication, reflect on what the results tell you about your personal desire for intimacy and distance. Consider the following questions:
      1. Was there a pattern of alternating phases of intimacy and distance during the time you observed?
      2. Was this pattern typical of your communication in this relationship over a longer period of time?
      3. Does your communication in other relationships contain a similar mixture of intimacy and distance?
      4. Most importantly, are you satisfied with the results you discovered in this exercise? If not, how would you like to change your communication behavior?

3. **Critical Thinking Probe**
   Using the definition on page 292, identify five times when you have received self-disclosing messages from others. How did these acts affect you as the recipient, how did they affect the sender, and how did they affect any other people? Combine your findings with those of your classmates. Based on the information you have collected, to what degree would you say that self-disclosure is a positive form of communication?

4. **Ethical Challenge**

   Recall three recent situations in which you used each of the following evasive approaches: lying, equivocating, and hinting. Write an anonymous written description of each situation on a separate sheet of paper. Submit the cases to a panel of "judges" (most likely fellow students), who will use the criteria of justifiable motives and desirable effects to evaluate the morality of this deception.

5. **Skill Builder**

   Use the guidelines on pages 313-314 to develop one scenario in which you *might* reveal a self-disclosing message. Create a message of this type, and use the information in this chapter to discuss the risks and benefits of sharing the message.

# CHAPTER
## 11

# Communication Climate

# After Studying the Material in This Chapter . . .

## You Should Understand:

1. The definition of communication climate.

2. The importance of being valued and confirmed.

3. The characteristics of confirming, disagreeing, and disconfirming messages.

4. The nature of positive and negative communication spirals.

5. The relationship between presenting self and defensiveness.

6. The types of messages that are likely to create positive communication climates.

7. The various ways to transform negative communication climates.

## You Should Be Able to:

1. Identify confirming, disagreeing, and disconfirming messages and patterns in your own relationships.

2. Identify the parts of your presenting self (face) that you defend, and the consequences of doing so.

3. Create messages that are likely to build supportive rather than defensive communication climates.

4. Create appropriate nondefensive responses to real or hypothetical criticisms.

## Key Terms

| | | | |
|---|---|---|---|
| Aggressiveness | Defensiveness | Face-threatening acts | Problem orientation |
| Ambiguous response | Description | Impersonal response | Provisionalism |
| Argumentativeness | Disagreeing messages | Impervious response | Spiral |
| Certainty | Disconfirming messages | Incongruous response | Spontaneity |
| Communication climate | Empathy | Interrupting response | Strategy |
| Complaining | Equality | Irrelevant response | Superiority |
| Confirming messages | Evaluation | Neutrality | Tangential response |
| Controlling communication | Face | Presenting self | |

H ow would you describe
tant relationships? Fair a
Hot? Cold? Just as physical loc
teristic weather patterns, interp
ships have unique climates, to
sure the interpersonal climate
thermometer or glancing at the
nonetheless. Every relationship
pervasive mood that colors the
participants.

*Social Tone of relationship*

*Conforming or Disconfirming*

unication climate is
:faction and perfor-
orkplace, the classroom,
for and stay in commu-
m and support them.
cal counterparts, com-
nared by everyone
ne person describing a
nositive while another
d hostile. Also, just like
on climates can change
can be overcast at one
r. Carrying the analogy
to its conclusion, we snould say that communication climate forecasting is not a perfect science.
Unlike the weather, however, people can change
their communication climates—and that's why it's
important to understand them. We'll look at several climate issues in this chapter: how communication climates develop, how and why we respond
defensively in certain climates, and what can be
done to create positive climates and transform
negative ones.

## What Is Communication Climate?

The term **communication climate** refers to the
social tone of a relationship. A climate doesn't
involve specific activities as much as the way people feel about each other as they carry out those
activities. For example, consider two interpersonal
communication classes. Both meet for the same
length of time and follow the same syllabus. It's easy
to imagine how one of these classes might be a
friendly, comfortable place to learn, whereas the
other could be cold and tense—even hostile. It's not
the course content that differs—it's the way the people in the classroom feel about and treat each other.

Just as every classroom has a unique climate,
so does every relationship. Romances, friendships,
and families—even neighborhoods, cities, and
countries—can be defined by their social tone.
Another obvious context for observing climate's
impact is the workplace, which may explain why
the topic is so widely studied (Shadur et al., 1999;
Wert-Gray et al., 1991). Think for a moment: Have
you ever held a job where backbiting, criticism,
and suspicion were the norm? Or have you been
lucky enough to work where the atmosphere was
positive, encouraging, and supportive? If you've
experienced both, you know what a difference
climate makes. Other studies (e.g., Guzley, 1992;
Odden & Sias, 1997) reinforce the fact that
employees have a higher level of commitment at
jobs in which they experience a positive communication climate. David Pincus (1986) arrived at a

## How Communication Climates Develop

Why does some communication create a positive
climate while other behavior has the opposite
effect? A short but accurate answer is that communication climate is determined by the degree to which
people see themselves as *valued*. Communicators
who perceive others as liking, appreciating, and
respecting them react positively, whereas those
who feel unimportant or abused react negatively.
Social scientists use the term **confirming** communication to describe messages that convey valuing. In
one form or another, confirming messages say "you
exist," "you matter," "you're important." By contrast,
**disconfirming** communication communicates a
lack of regard. In one form or another, disconfirming messages say "I don't care about you,"
"I don't like you," "You're not important to me."

As we have stressed throughout this book, every message has a relational dimension along with its content. This means that, whether or not we are aware of the fact, we send and receive confirming and disconfirming messages virtually whenever we communicate. Serious conversations about our relationships may not be common (Goldsmith & Baxter, 1996), but we convey our attitudes about one another even when we talk about everyday matters. In other words, it isn't *what* we communicate about that shapes a relational climate as much as *how* we speak and act toward one another.

It's hard to overstate the importance of confirming messages. For instance, a positive climate is the best predictor of marital satisfaction (Clark, 1973; Veroff et al., 1998). Satisfied couples have a 5:1 ratio of positive to negative statements, while the ratio for dissatisfied partners is 1:1 (Gottman, 1994; see also Emmers-Sommer, 1997). Positive, confirming messages are just as important in families. For example, the satisfaction that siblings feel with one another drops sharply as aggressive, disconfirming messages increase (Teven et al., 1998).

Like beauty, the decision about whether a message is confirming or disconfirming is up to the beholder (Vangelisti & Crumley, 1998). Consider, for example, times when you took a comment that might have sounded unsupportive to an outsider ("You turkey!") as a sign of affection within the context of your personal relationship. Likewise, a comment that the sender might have meant to be helpful ("I'm telling you this for your own good . . .") could easily be regarded as a disconfirming attack.

## Levels of Message Confirmation

**Types of Confirming Messages**    Even though there's no guarantee that others will regard even your best attempts at confirming messages the way you intend them, research shows that three increasingly positive types of messages have the best chance of being perceived as confirming (Cissna & Sieberg, 1990).

*Recognition*    The most fundamental act of confirmation is to recognize the other person. Recognition seems easy and obvious, yet there are many times when we do not respond to others on this basic level. Failure to write to or visit a friend is a common example. So is failure to return a phone message. Likewise, avoiding eye contact and not approaching someone you know sends a negative message. Of course, this lack of recognition may simply be an oversight. You may not notice your friend, or the pressures of work and school may prevent you from staying in touch. Nonetheless, if the other person *perceives* you as avoiding contact, the message has the effect of being disconfirming.

*Acknowledgment*    Acknowledging the ideas and feelings of others is a stronger form of confirmation than simple recognition. Listening is probably the most common form of acknowledgment. Silently and attentively paying attention to another person's words is one measure of your interest. Not surprisingly, employees give high marks to managers who solicit their opinions—even when the managers don't accept every suggestion (Allen, 1995). As you read in Chapter 7, reflecting the speaker's thoughts and feelings can be a powerful way to offer support when others have problems.

*Endorsement*   Whereas acknowledgment communicates you are interested in another person, endorsement means that you agree with her or him or otherwise find her or him important. It's easy to see why endorsement is the strongest type of confirming message, since it communicates the highest form of valuing. The most obvious form of endorsement is agreeing, but it isn't necessary to agree completely with other people in order to endorse their message. You can probably find something in the message that you endorse. "I can see why you were so angry," you might reply to a friend, even if you don't approve of his or her outburst. Of course, outright praise is a strong form of endorsement, one you can use surprisingly often once you look for opportunities to compliment others. Nonverbal endorsement can also enhance the quality of a relational climate. For example, simple acts like maintaining eye contact and nodding while someone speaks can confirm the value of a speaker's idea.

**Disagreeing Messages**   Between confirming and disconfirming lies a type of message that isn't always easy to categorize. A disagreeing message essentially says "you're wrong." How is disagreeing different from disconfirming? Most experts agree that it is psychologically healthier to have someone disagree with you than ignore you (Holte & Wichstrom, 1990; Laing, 1961). In its most constructive form, disagreement includes two confirming components: recognition and acknowledgment. At its worst, a brutal disagreeing message can so devastate another person that the benefits of recognition and acknowledgment are lost. Because there are better and worse ways to disagree with others, disagreeing messages need to be put on a positive-to-negative scale. We will do just that in this section as we discuss three types of

disagreement: argumentativeness, complaining, and aggressiveness.

*Argumentativeness*   Normally when we call a person "argumentative," we're making an unfavorable evaluation. However, the ability to create and deliver a sound argument is something we admire in lawyers, talk-show participants, letters to the editor, and political debates. Taking a positive approach to the term, communication researchers define **argumentativeness** as presenting and defending positions on issues while attacking positions taken by others (Infante & Rancer, 1982). Rather than being a negative trait, argumentativeness is associated with a number of positive attributes, such as enhanced self-concept

## FILM CLIP

### CONFIRMING AND LEARNING:
### MR. HOLLAND'S OPUS

*Mr. Holland's Opus* is another in the rich tradition of Hollywood films about teachers and their students. Movies such as *Up the Down Staircase, To Sir with Love, Educating Rita,* and *Dangerous Minds* deliver a similar message: Caring, committed instructors can and do change students' lives.

Glenn Holland (Richard Dreyfuss) is such an instructor. His first day in the profession is hardly promising; his students are as bored as he is boring. Holland slowly learns to change the climate in his classroom. He begins teaching lessons from the students' music, rock and roll. He spends countless hours working one-on-one with those who need extra help. Most important, he confirms his students' worth and dignity by investing himself in their lives.

An interesting subplot involves Mr. Holland's son, Cole. When he learns his young son is deaf, Holland is devastated because he believes they will never share a passion for music. Holland begins pouring more time and energy into his students, with little left over for Cole. He barely learns the basics of sign language, which further stifles his communication with his son. Although his students feel his constant confirmation, Holland continually disconfirms Cole by ignoring him and the events of his life.

Fortunately, Holland is awakened to the problem and redresses it in a variety of ways (including the sharing of music). By movie's end, their relationship is repaired. The story thus has many morals: A person can send both confirming and disconfirming messages; disconfirmation can be unintentional; patterns of disconfirmation can be reversed. Ultimately, *Mr. Holland's Opus* is a testimony to the transforming power of confirming communication.

(Rancer et al., 1992), communicative competence (Onyekwere et al., 1991), and positive climate in the workplace (Infante & Gorden, 1987).

The key for maintaining a positive climate while arguing a point is the *way* you present your ideas. It is crucial to attack issues, not people. In addition, a sound argument is better received when it's delivered in a supportive, affirming manner (Infante & Gorden, 1989). The supportive kinds of messages outlined on pages 330–337 show how it is possible to argue in a respectful, constructive way.

*Complaining*   When communicators aren't prepared to argue, but still want to register dissatisfaction, they often complain. As is true of all disagreeing messages, some ways of **complaining** are better than others. Jess Alberts (1988, 1990) found that satisfied couples tend to offer behavioral complaints (" You always throw your socks on the floor"), while unsatisfied couples make more complaints aimed at personal characteristics ("You're a slob"). Personal complaints are more likely to result in an escalated conflict episode (Alberts & Driscoll, 1992). The reason should be obvious—complaints about personal characteristics attack a more fundamental part of the presenting self. Talking about socks deals with a habit that can be changed; calling someone a slob is a character assault that is unlikely to be forgotten when the conflict is over.

*Aggressiveness*   The most destructive way to disagree with another person is through **aggressiveness**. Dominic Infante and his associates (1992, p. 116) define verbal aggressiveness as the tendency to "attack the self-concepts of other people in order to inflict psychological pain." Unlike argumentativeness, aggressiveness demeans the worth of others. Name calling, put-downs, sarcasm, taunting, yelling, badgering—all are methods of "winning" disagreements at others' expense.

It should come as no surprise that aggressiveness has been found to have a variety of serious consequences. Aggressive behavior is especially

## FOCUS ON RESEARCH

### THE CHILLING EFFECT: NUDGING COWORKERS OUT THE COMPANY DOOR

Have you ever wished that an unpleasant coworker would find a different job? If so, how did you treat that person? Stephen Cox found that some employees nudge unwanted coworkers toward quitting by creating a chilly communication climate.

Cox collected 126 surveys from supervisors/managers at a variety of organizations. He asked for examples of what employees said and did to their coworkers to motivate them to leave their organizations. The most common strategy was outright criticism (e.g.,

"Told him he couldn't cook a steak to save his life"). Other methods were more face-saving, such as suggesting other jobs or career alternatives ("There is a better chance for advancement elsewhere"). In extreme cases, coworkers gave ultimatums to their peers ("Get out or they will fire you").

Chilling messages can also be sent nonverbally. Respondents said that employees often avoid interaction with peers they hope will leave. Some coworkers talk about unwanted peers

behind their backs; others actually sabotage them (restrict flow of information in order to make the individual look bad).

In a perfect world, no one would use such chilling behaviors deliberately. This study shows, however, that disconfirming messages can be a powerful tool for creating organizational change. Like toxic chemicals, these sorts of strategies should be handled with care, particularly in companies that hope to maintain a warm and friendly organizational climate.

Cox, S. A. (1999). Group communication and employee turnover: How coworkers encourage peers to voluntarily exit. *Southern Communication Journal, 64,* 181–192.

hurtful when it comes from people who are close to us (Martin et al., 1996). Research shows it is associated with physical violence in marriages (Infante et al., 1989), juvenile delinquency (Straus et al., 1989), depression (Segrin & Fitzpatrick, 1992), and a negative climate in the workplace (Infante & Gorden, 1985, 1987, 1989). Chapter 12 describes how "win-win" approaches to conflict are healthier and more productive than the "win-lose" tactics of aggressiveness.

**Disconfirming Messages**   Disconfirming messages are more subtle than aggressiveness but potentially more damaging. Disconfirming communication implicitly says "you don't exist; you are not valued." As we mentioned earlier, being disconfirmed (particularly by significant others) is psychologically

unhealthy. Heineken's (1980) research suggests that people who are seriously disconfirmed may learn to treat others the same way. She found that the frequency of disconfirming responses among psychiatric patients was significantly higher than among more "normal" individuals.

Disconfirming messages are not confined to clinical situations; unfortunately, they are part of everyday life. While an occasional disconfirming message may not injure a relationship, a pattern of them usually indicates a negative communication climate. Sieberg and Larson (1971) found it was easiest to identify disconfirming communication by observing *responses* to others' messages. They noted seven types of disconfirming responses:

*Impervious Response*    An **impervious response** fails to acknowledge the other person's communicative attempt, either verbally or nonverbally. Failing to return a phone call is an impervious response, as is not responding to another's letter. Impervious responses also happen in face-to-face settings. They are especially common when adults and children communicate. Parents often become enraged when

they are ignored by their children; likewise, children feel diminished when adults pay no attention to their questions, comments, or requests.

*Interrupting Response*    As its name implies, an **interrupting response** occurs when one person begins to speak before the other is through making a point.

**Customer**: I'm looking for an outfit I can wear on a trip I'm . . .
**Salesperson**: I've got just the thing. It's part wool and part polyester, so it won't wrinkle at all.
**C**: Actually, wrinkling isn't that important. I want something that will work as a business outfit and . . .
**S**: We have a terrific blazer that you can dress up or down, depending on the accessories you choose.
**C**: That's not what I was going to say. I want something that I can wear as a business outfit, but it ought to be on the informal side. I'm going to . . .
**S**: Say no more. I know just what you want.
**C**: Never mind. I think I'll look in some other stores.

*Irrelevant Response*    It is disconfirming to respond with an **irrelevant response,** making comments totally unrelated to what the other person was just saying.

**A**: What a day! I thought it would never end. First the car overheated and I had to call a tow truck, and then the computer broke down at work.
**B**: Listen, we have to talk about a present for Ann's birthday. The party is on Saturday, and I only have tomorrow to shop for it.
**A**: I'm really beat. You won't believe what the boss did. Like I said, the computer was down, and in the middle of that mess he decided he absolutely had to have the sales figures for the last six months.
**B**: I just can't figure what would suit Ann. She's been so generous to us, and I can't think of anything she needs.
**A**: Why don't you listen to me? I beat my brains out all day and you don't give a damn.
**B**: And you don't care about me!

*Tangential Response*    Unlike the three behaviors just discussed, a **tangential response** does acknowledge the other person's communication.

*"Honey, please don't talk to Daddy when he's in a chat room."*

However, the acknowledgment is used to steer the conversation in a new direction. Tangents can come in two forms. One is the "tangential shift," which is an abrupt change in conversation. For example, a young boy runs into the house excited, showing his mother the rock he found. She says, "Wash your hands before dinner." In a "tangential drift" the speaker makes a token connection with what the other person is saying and then moves the conversation in another direction entirely. In the same scenario, the mother might say, "That's a pretty rock. But look, your hands are dirty. Go wash them before dinner."

*Impersonal Response*　In an **impersonal response**, the speaker conducts a monologue filled with impersonal, intellectualized, and generalized statements. The speaker never really interacts with the other on a personal level.

**Employee**: I've been having some personal problems lately, and I'd like to take off early a couple of afternoons to clear them up.
**Boss**: Ah, yes. We all have personal problems. It seems to be a sign of the times.

*Ambiguous Response*　An **ambiguous response** contains a message with more than one meaning. The words are highly abstract or have meanings private to the speaker alone.

**A**: I'd like to get together with you soon. How about Tuesday?
**B**: Uh, maybe so. Anyhow, see you later.

**C**: How can I be sure you mean it?
**D**: Who knows what anybody means?

*Incongruous Response*　An **incongruous response** contains two messages that seem to deny or contradict each other, one at the verbal level and the other at the nonverbal level.

**He**: Darling, I love you!
**She**: I love you too. *(giggles)*

**Teacher**: Did you enjoy the class?
**Student**: Yes. *(yawns)*

It's important to note that disconfirming messages, like virtually every other type of communication, are a matter of perception. A message that might not be intended to devalue the other person

# FOCUS ON RESEARCH

## SAYING "NO" WHEN YOU WANT TO SAY "YES"

Most people "know the drill" when someone they don't like asks them for a date: They graciously say, "I'm sorry, I already have plans." However, what happens when someone they like asks them for a date and they really *do* have plans? That was the research question posed by Amber Besson, Michael Roloff, and Gaylen Paulson to students at Northwestern University.

A pre-test determined that most heterosexual date requests at NU are initiated by males, so all of the partici-pants solicited for the study were females. The women were asked how they would respond to a date request from a man they didn't want to date, either now or in the future. Their primary responses were "apologies, statements of appreciation for the offer, and expressions of concern for the requester's feelings."

On the other hand, participants who had legitimate reasons for turning down date requests, but hoped to pursue a relationship with the requester in the future, "expressed counteroffers and expressions of interest." In other words, the women in this study were concerned about saving the face of the men they were rejecting, while sending positive mes-sages to the men about whom they were genuinely interested.

The study suggests that face-saving is a familiar social convention for refusing date requests, and that legiti-mate excuses for turning down dates need to be positively reinforced so the receivers know that the excuses are indeed genuine.

Besson, A. L., Roloff, M. E., & Paulson, G. D. (1998). Preserving face in refusal situations. *Communication Research, 25,* 183–199.

can be interpreted as disconfirming. For example, your failure to return a phone call or respond to the letter of an out-of-town friend might simply be the result of a busy schedule, but if the other person views the lack of contact as a sign that you don't value the relationship, the effect will be just as strong as if you had deliberately intended to convey a slight.

## Defensiveness

It's no surprise that disconfirming and disagreeing messages can pollute a communication climate. Perhaps the most predictable reaction to a hostile or indifferent message is **defensiveness.**

The word *defensiveness* suggests protecting yourself from attack, but what kind of attack? Seldom when you become defensive is a physical threat involved. If you're not threatened by bodily injury, what *are* you guarding against? To answer this question, we need to talk more about notions of **presenting self** and **face,** both of which were introduced in Chapter 3. Recall that the presenting self consists of the physical traits, personality charac-teristics, attitudes, aptitudes, and all the other parts of the image you want to present to the world. Actually, it is a mistake to talk about a single face: We try to project different selves to different people. For instance, you might try to impress a potential employer with your seriousness but want your friends to see you as a joker. Of course, not all parts of your presenting self are equally significant. Letting others know that you are right-handed or a Gemini is probably less important to you than convincing them you are good-looking or loyal.

When others are willing to accept and acknowledge important parts of our presenting image, there is no need to feel defensive. On the other hand, when others confront us with **face-threatening acts**—messages that seem to challenge the image we want to project—we are likely to resist what they say. Defensiveness, then, is the process of protecting our presenting self, our face.

You can understand how defensiveness operates by imagining what might happen if an important part of your presenting self were attacked. For instance, suppose an instructor criticized you for making a stupid mistake. Or consider how you would feel if a friend called you self-centered or your boss labeled you as lazy. You would probably feel threatened if these attacks were untrue. But your own experience will probably show that you sometimes respond defensively even when you know that others' criticism is justified. For instance, you have probably responded defensively at times when you *did* make a mistake, act selfishly, or cut corners in your work. In fact, we often feel most defensive when criticism is right on target (Stamp et al., 1992). The drive to defend a presenting image—even when it is false—leads some people to engage in "repetitive non-optimal behaviors" (Turk & Monahan, 1999), such as being sarcastic or verbally abusive.

So far, we have talked about defensiveness as if it is only the responsibility of the person who feels threatened. If this were the case, then the prescription would be simple: Grow a thick skin, admit your flaws, and stop trying to manage impressions. This approach isn't just unrealistic: it also ignores the role played by those who send face-threatening messages. In fact, competent communicators protect others' face needs as well as their own. For example, the people college stu-

dents judge as close friends are those who provide "positive face support" by endorsing the presenting image of others (Cupach & Messman, 1999). Findings like this make it clear that defensiveness is *interactive;* all communicators contribute to the climate of a relationship.

At this point you might be wondering how you can send a face-honoring message when you have a genuine gripe with someone. The answer to this dilemma lies in the two-dimensional nature of communication. On a content level you can express dissatisfaction with the other person, but on a relational level you can be saying—explicitly or nonverbally—that you value him or her. The second half of this chapter offers specific suggestions for creating messages that are both honest and supportive.

## Climate Patterns

Once a communication climate is formed, it can take on a life of its own. The pattern can be either positive or negative. In one study of married couples, each spouse's response in conflict situations was found to be similar to the other's statement (Burggraf & Sillars, 1987). Conciliatory statements (for example, support, accepting responsibility, agreeing) were likely to be followed by conciliatory responses. Confrontive acts (for example, criticism, hostile questions, faultfinding) were likely to trigger an aggressive response. The same pattern held for other kinds of messages: Avoidance led to avoidance, analysis evoked analysis, and so on. This was also found in a study on disagreements of married couples (Newton & Burgoon, 1990). Videotaped interactions revealed that accusations from one partner triggered accusations

| | 1 | 2 | 3 | 4 | 5 | 6 | 7 | 8 | 9 | 10 | 11 | 12 | 13 | 14 | 15 | 16 | 17 | 18 | 19 | 20 | 21 | 22 | 23 | 24 | 25 | 26 | 27 | 28 | 29 | 30 | 31 | R | H | E |
|---|---|---|---|---|---|---|---|---|---|---|---|---|---|---|---|---|---|---|---|---|---|---|---|---|---|---|---|---|---|---|---|---|---|---|
| TAT | 3 | 0 | 0 | 1 | 0 | 0 | 0 | 0 | 0 | 0 | 0 | 6 | 0 | 0 | 0 | 1 | 0 | 0 | 0 | 0 | 0 | 0 | 8 | 0 | 0 | 3 | 9 | 7 | 1 | 1 | 2 | 6 | 48 | 63 | 6 |
| TIT | 3 | 0 | 0 | 1 | 0 | 0 | 0 | 0 | 0 | 0 | 0 | 6 | 0 | 0 | 0 | 1 | 0 | 0 | 0 | 0 | 0 | 0 | 8 | 0 | 0 | 3 | 9 | 7 | 1 | 1 | 2 | 6 | 48 | 63 | 6 |

Game called on account of infinity

in response, and that communication satisfaction was highest when both partners used supportive rather than accusatory tactics.

This reciprocal pattern can be represented as a **spiral** (Wilmot, 1987). Some spirals are negative. In poorly adjusted and abusive couples, for example, one spouse's complaint is likely to produce a countercomplaint or denial by the other (Sabourin, 1995; Sutter & Martin, 1999). The cartoon on page 329 provides an amusing but sad image of how negative spirals can take on a life of their own.

Dudley Cahn (1992) summarizes studies showing that even among well-adjusted couples, negative communication is more likely to be reciprocated than positive—and that once hostility is expressed, it usually escalates. You can probably recall this sort of negative spiral from your own experience: One attack leads to another, until a skirmish escalates into a full-fledged battle:

A: (mildly irritated) Where were you? I thought we agreed to meet here a half-hour ago.
B: (defensively) I'm sorry. I got hung up at the library. I don't have as much free time as you do, you know.
A: I wasn't blaming you, so don't get so touchy. I do resent what you just said, though. I'm plenty busy. And I've got lots of better things to do than wait around for you!
B: Who's getting touchy? I just made a simple comment. You've sure been defensive lately. What's the matter with you?

Fortunately, spirals can also work in a positive direction. One confirming behavior leads to a similar response from the other person, which in turn leads to further confirmation by the first person (Le Poire & Yoshimura, 1999).

Spirals—whether positive or negative—rarely go on indefinitely. When a negative spiral gets out of hand, the partners might agree to back off from their disconfirming behavior. "Hold on," one might say, "this is getting us nowhere." At this point there may be a cooling-off period, or the partners might work together more constructively to solve their problem. If the partners pass the "point of no return," the relationship may end. As you read in Chapter 1, it's impossible to take back a message once it has been sent, and some exchanges are so lethal that the relationship can't survive them. Positive spirals also have their limit: Even the best relationships go through rocky periods in which the climate suffers. However, the accumulated goodwill and communication ability of the partners can make these times less frequent and intense. Most relationships pass through cycles of progression and regression, as illustrated in Figure 11.1.

## Creating Positive Climates

What kind of messages and behaviors create a climate that is positive, supportive, and confirming? Communication researchers have been working

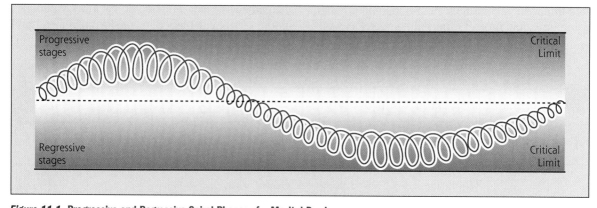

**Figure 11.1** Progressive and Regressive Spiral Phases of a Marital Dyad
From: Wilmot, W. W. (1987) *Dyadic communication* (3rd ed.) Reprinted by permission of The McGraw-Hill Companies.

**Table 11.1**

| The Gibb Categories of Defensive and Supportive Behaviors | |
|---|---|
| **Defensive Behaviors** | **Supportive Behaviors** |
| 1. Evaluation | 1. Description |
| 2. Control | 2. Problem Orientation |
| 3. Strategy | 3. Spontaneity |
| 4. Neutrality | 4. Empathy |
| 5. Superiority | 5. Equality |
| 6. Certainty | 6. Provisionalism |

for years to answer this question. One of their conclusions is that even the "best" message isn't guaranteed to create a positive climate. A comment of praise can be interpreted as sarcasm; an innocent smile can be perceived as a sneer; an offer to help can be seen as condescension. Because human communication is so complex, there aren't any foolproof words, phrases, or formulas for creating positive climates.

However, there is a helpful study that has stood the test of time: Jack Gibb's (1961) categorization of supportive and defensive behaviors. After observing groups for several years, Gibb was able to isolate six types of defense-arousing communication and six contrasting behaviors that seem to reduce the level of threat and defensiveness. The Gibb categories are listed in Table 11.1. Gibb's findings have commonsense appeal and multiple applications. As a result, they've played an important part in communication textbooks, training seminars, journals, and research studies (Moss,

1999; Proctor & Wilcox, 1993). We'll use them here to discuss how positive climates can be created by sending supportive rather than defense-provoking messages.

## Evaluation versus Description

The first type of defense-arousing message Gibb identified is **evaluation.** An evaluative message judges the other person, usually in a negative way. For instance, consider this message: "You don't care about me!" Evaluative messages like this possess several characteristics that make them so face-threatening. They judge what the other person is feeling rather than describing the speaker's thoughts, feelings, and wants. They don't explain how the speaker arrived at his or her conclusion, and they lack specifics. Furthermore, they're often phrased in the kind of defense-arousing "you" language described in Chapter 5. It's easy to understand why evaluative statements often trigger a defensive spiral.

Do the climate-threatening properties of evaluative messages mean that it's impossible to tell others how some of the things that they do bother you? No: It simply means that you must be alert to more constructive ways to do so. **Description** is a way to offer your thoughts, feelings, and wants without judging the listener. Descriptive messages make documented observations that are specific and concrete. As we mentioned earlier when discussing complaining, description focuses on behavior that can be changed rather than on personal characteristics that cannot. In addition, descriptive messages often use "I" language, which tends to provoke less defensiveness than "you" language (Proctor & Wilcox, 1993; Winer & Majors, 1981). Contrast the evaluative "You don't care about me" with this more descriptive message: "I'm sad that we don't spend as much time together as we did during the summer. When we don't talk during the week, I sometimes feel unimportant. Maybe we could set up a phone-call time on Wednesdays—that would mean a lot to me."

Note several things about this descriptive message. First, the focus is on the speaker's thoughts, feelings, and wants, with little or no judgment of the listener. Second, the message addresses specific behaviors (a desire to talk more often) rather than making sweeping character generalizations (for example, "you don't care"). The message also provides information about how the speaker arrived at this conclusion and offers a possible solution. Although it may seem ideal, even this sort of message may not get a nondefensive response. Its effectiveness will be determined by when, where, and how it is communicated (you can imagine how it would go over if said in front of a room full of relatives or in a whining tone of voice). The point is, by contrasting evaluative and descriptive messages, you can see how and why some messages are more likely to create positive climates than others.

Let's look at more examples:

| Evaluation | Description |
| --- | --- |
| You're not making any sense. | I don't understand the point you're trying to make. |
| You're inconsiderate. | I would appreciate it if you'd let me know when you're running late—I was worried. |
| That's an ugly tablecloth. | I'm not crazy about big blue stripes: I like something more subtle. |

"What do you mean, 'Your guess is as good as mine'? My guess is a hell of a lot better than your guess!"

## Control versus Problem Orientation

A second defense-provoking message involves some attempt to control another. **Controlling communication** occurs when a sender seems to be imposing a solution on the receiver with little regard for the receiver's needs or interests. The object of control can involve almost anything: where to eat dinner, what TV program to watch, whether to remain in a relationship, or how to spend a large sum of money. Whatever the situation, people who act in controlling ways create a defensive climate. Researchers Teresa Sabourin and Glen Stamp (1995) found that the communication of abusive couples was characterized by opposition to one another's viewpoints. None of us likes to feel that our ideas are worthless and that nothing we say will change other people's determination to have their way—yet this is precisely the attitude a controller communicates. Whether done with words, gestures, tone of voice, or through some other channel, whether control is accomplished through status, insistence on obscure or irrelevant rules, or physical power, the controller generates hostility wherever he or she goes. The unspoken message such behavior communicates is "I know what's best for you, and if you do as I say, we'll get along."

In **problem orientation,** however, communicators focus on finding a solution that satisfies both their own needs and those of the others involved. The goal here isn't to "win" at the expense of your partner but to work out some arrangement in which everybody feels like a winner. (Chapter 12 has a great deal to say about "win-win" problem solving as a way to find problem-oriented solutions.) Problem orientation is often typified by "we" language (see Chapter 5), which suggests the speaker is making decisions *with* rather than *for* other people.

Here are some examples of how some controlling and problem-orientation messages might sound:

| Controlling | Problem Orientation |
|---|---|
| Get off the phone—now! | I need to make an important call. If you can give me five minutes, I'll let you know when I'm off. |
| There's only one way to handle this problem . . . | Looks like we have a problem. Let's work out a solution we can both live with. |
| Either you start working harder, or you're fired! | The production in your department hasn't been as high as I'd hoped. Any ideas on what we could do? |

## Strategy versus Spontaneity

Gibb uses the word **strategy** to characterize defense-arousing messages in which speakers hide their ulterior motives. The terms *dishonesty* and *manipulation* capture the essence of strategy. Even if the intentions that motivate strategic communication are honorable, the victim of deception who discovers the attempt to deceive is likely to feel offended at being played for a sucker.

As we discussed in Chapter 7, counterfeit questions are a form of strategic communication because they try to trap others into desired responses. Indirect and double messages also can be strategic ploys that lead to defensive reactions.

In addition, many sales techniques are strategic, for they give customers limited information and then make it difficult to say no. This is not to say that all sales techniques are wrong or unethical, but most strategic ones aren't well-suited for interpersonal relationships. If you've ever gotten defensive when you thought a friend was doing a "sales job" on you, you understand the concept.

**Spontaneity** is the behavior that contrasts with strategy. Spontaneity simply means being honest with others rather than manipulating them. What it *doesn't* mean is blurting out what you're thinking as soon as an idea comes to you. As we discussed in Chapter 10, there are appropriate (and inappropriate) times for self-disclosure. You would undoubtedly threaten others' presenting selves if you were "spontaneous" about every opinion that crossed your mind. That's not what Gibb intended in using the term *spontaneity*. What he was after was setting aside hidden agendas that others both sense and resist. You can probably recall times when someone asked you a question and you suspiciously responded with "Hmmm . . . why do you want to know?" Your defensive antennae were up because you detected an underlying strategy. If the person had told you up-front why he or she was asking the question, then your defenses probably would have been lowered. That's what we mean by spontaneity.

Here are some examples:

| Strategy | Spontaneity |
|---|---|
| What are you doing Friday after work? | I have a piano I need to move Friday after work. Can you give me a hand? |
| Have you ever considered another line of work? | I'm concerned about your job performance over the last year; let's set up a time to talk about it. |
| Tom and Judy go out to dinner every week. | I'd like to go out for dinner more often. |

This is a good place to pause and talk about larger issues regarding the Gibb model. First, Gibb's emphasis on being direct is better suited for a low-context culture like the United States, which values straight talk, than for high-context cultures. Second, there are ways in which each of the communication approaches Gibb labels as "supportive" can be used to exploit others and, therefore, violate the spirit of positive climate building. For instance, consider spontaneity. Although it sounds paradoxical at first, spontaneity can be a strategy, too. Sometimes you'll see people using honesty in a calculating way, being just frank enough to win someone's trust or sympathy. This "leveling" is probably the most defense-arousing strategy of all because once we've learned someone is using frankness as a manipulation, there's almost no chance we'll ever trust that person again.

On a broader level, Ray (1993) observes that supportive communication can actually be used to restrict and control others. By creating a warm climate, we increase others' dependence on us, thereby giving us significant power over them. Before going any further, we want to say loudly and clearly that this violates the intent of climate building. If you act supportively for ulterior reasons, you've misunderstood the idea behind this chapter, and you're running a risk of causing even more defensiveness than before. None of the ideas we present in this book can go into a "bag of tricks" that can be used to control others. If you ever find yourself using them in this way, it may be time to take stock of your motives and ethical standards.

## Neutrality versus Empathy

Gibb used the term **neutrality** to describe a fourth behavior that arouses defensiveness. Probably a better word would be *indifference,* For example, 911 emergency telephone dispatchers are taught to be neutral in order to calm the caller down, but they hardly communicate indifference or a lack of caring (Shuler, 1998). Using Gibb's terminology, a neutral attitude is disconfirming because it communicates a lack of concern for the welfare of another and implies that the other person isn't very impor-

### REFLECTION

### "WHATEVER"

One word can change the whole tone of a relationship. For the past six months I have listened to my roommate talk about the problems of her job. I think she should quit, but she doesn't think she can find another job that pays as well. So, because we're friends, I've tried to listen carefully during the many times when she complains about her terrible situation—at least until last night.

For the first time I tried to tell my roommate about a problem of my own. I've got a professor whose sarcasm is starting to feel like harassment. He singles me out in a way that leaves me very uncomfortable. I would take the class next semester from another professor, but he's the only person who teaches it, and I need the course for my major.

This is a big problem for me, and I guess I spent quite a while explaining it to my roommate last night. After about a half hour of talk I wasn't any closer to a solution. I said something like, "I just don't know what to do," to which she rolled her eyes and replied "Oh, whatever."

When I heard that word, something inside me snapped. It seemed to me that she really didn't care *what* I do. This definitely has changed my feelings about her, and how I'll respond to her problems in the future. Now I can see how neutrality has such a negative effect on a communication climate.

tant to you. This perceived indifference is likely to promote defensiveness because people do not like to think of themselves as worthless, and they'll protect a self-concept that sees them as worthwhile.

The poor effects of neutrality become apparent when you consider the hostility that most people have for the large, impersonal organizations with which they have to deal: "They think of me as a number instead of a person"; "I felt as if I were being handled by computers and not human beings." These common statements reflect reactions to being handled in an indifferent way.

The behavior that contrasts with neutrality is **empathy.** Gibb found that empathy helps rid communication of the quality of indifference. When people show that they care for the feelings of another, there's little chance that the person's self-concept will be threatened. Empathy means accepting another's feelings, putting yourself in another's place. This doesn't mean you need to agree with that person. By simply letting someone know about your care and respect, you'll be acting in a supportive way. Gibb noted the importance of nonverbal messages in communicating empathy. He found that facial and bodily expressions of concern are often more important to the receiver than the words used.

We've addressed the concept of empathy in Chapter 4 and the skill of empathizing in Chapter 7; let's see what empathic messages look like when contrasted with neutral ones:

| Neutrality | Empathy |
|---|---|
| Things like this happen when you don't plan properly. | Ouch—looks like this didn't turn out the way you expected. |
| That's the way the cookie crumbles. | I know you put a lot of time and effort into this project. |
| No big deal—people get promotions here all the time. | Congratulations! I'll bet you're pretty excited about the promotion. |

## Superiority versus Equality

A fifth behavior creating a defensive climate involves **superiority.** Jake Harwood, Howard Giles, and their associates (1993) summarize a body of research which confirms that patronizing messages irritate receivers ranging from young students to senior citizens. Any message that suggests "I'm better than you" is likely to arouse feelings of defensiveness in the recipients.

Many times in our lives we communicate with people who possess less talent or knowledge than

we do, but it isn't necessary to convey an attitude of superiority in these situations. Gibb found ample evidence that many who have superior skills and talents are capable of projecting feelings of **equality** rather than superiority. Such people communicate that although they may have greater talent in certain areas, they see other human beings as having just as much worth as themselves.

Charles and Elizabeth Beck (1996) observe that equality is put to the test when a person *doesn't* have superior skills, yet is in a position of authority. Supervisors sometimes have less expertise in certain areas than their subordinates but believe it would be beneath them to admit it. Think for a moment: You've probably been in situations where you knew more about the subject than the person in charge—be it a boss, a teacher, a parent, or a salesperson—yet this person acted as if he or she knew more. Did you feel defensive? No doubt. Did that person feel defensive? No doubt as well. You both were challenging each other's presenting self, so

## FILM CLIP

### A HEALING CLIMATE: *PATCH ADAMS*

Hunter "Patch" Adams (Robin Williams) is nothing like arrogant surgeon Jack McKee (see Film Clip on *The Doctor*, p. 117). Although he's one of the top students in his class, Adams' unconventional methods get him in trouble at medical school. He clowns around with children, sings songs to dying patients, and acts silly during serious moments. This doesn't mean that Adams isn't serious about becoming a doctor. His mission is to create a medical climate where people are more important than regimen; where concern is valued over technique; where patients' emotional conditions matter as much as their vital signs; and where laughter is indeed the best medicine.

Adams works to change the school's climate by altering traditional medical communication patterns. He doesn't talk down to patients or nurses; he calls them by name and values their input. He fights against "the most terrible disease of all—indifference" by showing kindness and empathy to those around him. Early on, he identifies one of his primary professional goals: "I want to listen—really listen."

The movie *Patch Adams* is based on the true story of a doctor who is developing a "Gusundheit Hospital" in the hills of West Virginia. As the name suggests, it will be a medical center with nontraditional methods and a sense of humor. It also will have a warm and cheery communication climate.

the climate probably became hostile. A truly secure person can treat others with equality even when there are obvious differences in knowledge, talent, and status. Doing so creates a positive climate in which ideas are evaluated not on the basis of who contributed them, but rather on the merit of the ideas themselves.

What does equality sound like? Here are some examples:

| Superiority | Equality |
|---|---|
| When you get to be in my position some day, *then* you'll understand. | I'd like to hear how the issue looks to you. Then I can tell you how it looks to me. |
| You don't know what you're talking about. | I'm not sure I agree. |
| No, that's not the right way to do it! | I'd be happy to help if you'd like—just let me know. |

### Certainty versus Provisionalism

Have you ever run into people who are positive they're right, who know that theirs is the only or proper way of doing something, who insist that they have all the facts and need no additional information? If you have, you've met individuals who project the defense-arousing behavior Gibb calls **certainty.**

How do you react when you're the target of such certainty? Do you suddenly find your energy directed to proving the dogmatic individual wrong? If you do, you're reacting normally—if not very constructively.

Communicators who regard their own opinions with certainty while disregarding the ideas of others demonstrate a rather clear lack of regard for the thoughts others hold to be important. It's likely the receiver will take the certainty as a personal affront and react defensively.

In contrast to dogmatic communication is **provisionalism,** in which people may have strong opinions but are willing to acknowledge that they don't have a corner on the truth and will change their stand if another position seems more reasonable. Provisionalism often surfaces in a person's word choice. While certainty regularly uses the terms *can't, never, always, must,* and *have to,* provisionalism uses *perhaps, maybe, possibly, might,* and *may.* It's not that provisional people are spineless; they simply recognize that discussion is aided by open-minded messages. Winer and Majors (1981) found that provisional word choice does indeed enhance communication climate.

Let's look at some examples:

| Certainty | Provisionalism |
|---|---|
| That will *never* work! | My guess is that you'll run into problems with that approach. |
| You'll hate that class! Stay away from it! | I didn't like the class much at all. |
| You won't get anywhere without a college education: Mark my words. | I think it's important to get that degree. I found it was hard to land an interview until I had one. |

You've probably noticed a great deal of overlap between the various Gibb components. For instance, look at the final example under "Provisionalism." The statement is likely to create a positive climate, not only because it is provisional rather than certain, but also because it is descriptive rather than evaluative, problem-oriented rather than controlling, and equal rather than superior. You may also have noticed a tone underlying all of the supportive examples: *respect.* By valuing and confirming others—even if you disagree with them—you create a respectful climate that helps enhance a positive communication climate, both now and in future interactions. There are no guarantees of your achieving positive responses or outcomes, but by sending supportive messages, your odds for interpersonal success should improve.

# Transforming Negative Climates

The world would be a happier place if everyone communicated supportively. But how can you respond nondefensively when others use evaluation, control, superiority, and all the other attacking behaviors Gibb identified? Despite your best intentions, it's difficult to be reasonable when you're faced with a torrent of criticism. Being attacked is hard enough when the critic is clearly being unfair, but it's often even more threatening when the judgments are on target. Despite the accuracy of your critic, the tendency is either to counterattack aggressively with a barrage of verbal aggression or to withdraw nonassertively.

Since neither of these responses is likely to resolve a dispute, we need alternative ways of behaving. There are two such methods. Despite their apparent simplicity, they have proven to be among the most valuable skills communicators can learn.

## Seek More Information

The response of seeking more information makes good sense when you realize that it's foolish to respond to a critical attack until you understand what the other person has said. Even comments that on first consideration appear to be totally unjustified or foolish often prove to contain at least a grain of truth and sometimes much more.

Many readers object to the idea of asking for details when they are criticized. Their resistance

## FOCUS ON RESEARCH

### INVITATIONAL RHETORIC: AN ALTERNATIVE TO PERSUASION

According to communication professors Sonja Foss and Cindy Griffin, many people spend their lives trying to persuade others, even when they have no real stake in what those others believe or do. For example, we find ourselves in heated debates over the merits of a film, book, or athletic team when it makes no difference whether or not the other person agrees with us. While the topic may not be important, the effect of arguing can profoundly shape the climate of a relationship. Foss and Griffin attribute this argumentative approach to longstanding cultural values, including the drive toward power and domination.

But, Foss and Griffin argue, persuasion isn't the only foundation upon which communication can be based. As an alternative, they offer an approach which they term "invitational rhetoric." As its name suggests, this approach involves entering the other person's world and understanding it as he or she does. The authors explain: "The invitational rhetor does not judge or denigrate others' perspectives, but is open to and tries to appreciate and validate those perspectives, even if they differ dramatically from the rhetor's own." They point out that changing the other person may be a byproduct of invitational rhetoric, but this isn't its goal.

The authors illustrate the dramatic contrast between the traditional persuasion-oriented approach and invitational rhetoric by describing an encounter at New York's Kennedy airport between two strangers: one a feminist, pro-choice, animal rights advocate and the other a pro-life male hunter whose job involved experimenting with animals. The two began arguing so heatedly about abortion that the confrontation almost turned into a fist fight.

Later, the two combatants found themselves seated side by side on an airport shuttle bus, where the woman decided to try a more invitational approach. "I began asking him about his life and about the things that he did," she reported. As she continued to listen openly to the man, he began to do the same as she shared her own perspectives and experiences.

This exchange of invitational rhetoric brought the woman and the man together, although neither changed the other's mind. As the two crossed paths for the third time in the parking lot, waiting for their respective rides, they started walking toward each other. The woman finishes the story:

"I don't know which one of us did it first, but I guess maybe I flung open my arms and he flung open his arms and we came together in this terrific hug, both of us in tears, sobbing, crying like babies. I said, 'You know, I don't know what has happened here, but my life has been totally changed after today.' And he said, 'My life is totally changed, too, and I don't know what's happened.'"

Foss and Griffin suggest that this incident was an example of how invitational rhetoric can foster a climate of respect and understanding. As author Sally Gearhart put it: "It's a way to disagree and at the same time not to hurt each other and to respect each other and to have, actually, something very close and tender."

Foss, S. K., & Griffin, C. L. (1995). Beyond persuasion: A proposal for an invitational rhetoric. *Communication Monographs, 62,* 2–18.

grows from confusing the act of *listening open-mindedly* to a speaker's comments with *accepting* them. Once you realize that you can listen to, understand, and even acknowledge the most hostile comments without necessarily accepting them, it becomes much easier to hear another person out. If you disagree with a speaker's objections, you will be in a much better position to explain yourself once you understand the criticism. On the other hand, after carefully listening to the other's remarks, you might just see that they are valid, in which case you have learned some valuable information about yourself. In either case, you have everything to gain and nothing to lose by paying attention to the critic.

Of course, after one has spent years of instinctively resisting criticism, learning to listen to the other person will take some practice. To make matters clearer, here are several ways in which you can seek additional information from your critics.

**Ask for Specifics**   Often the vague attack of a critic is virtually useless even if you sincerely want to change. Abstract accusations such as "you're being unfair" or "you never help out" can be difficult to understand. In such cases it is a good idea to request more specific information from the sender. "What do I *do* that's unfair?" is an important question to ask before you can judge whether the accusation is correct. "When haven't I helped out?" you might ask before agreeing with or disputing the accusation.

If you already solicit specifics by using questions and are still accused of reacting defensively, the problem may be in the *way* you ask. Your tone of voice and facial expression, posture, or other nonverbal clues can give the same words radically different connotations. For example, think of how you could use the question "Exactly what are you talking about?" to communicate either a genuine desire to know or your belief that the speaker is crazy. It's important to request specific information only when you genuinely want to learn more from the speaker, for asking under any other circumstances will only make matters worse.

**Guess about Specifics**   On some occasions even your sincere and well-phrased requests for specific details won't meet with success. Sometimes your critics won't be able to define precisely the behavior they find offensive. In these instances, you'll hear such comments as "I can't tell you exactly what's wrong with your sense of humor—all I can say is that I don't like it." In other cases, your critics may know the exact behaviors they don't like, but for some reason they seem to get a perverse satisfaction out of making you struggle to figure them out. In instances like these, you can often learn more clearly what is bothering your critic by *guessing* at the specifics of a complaint. In a sense you become both detective and suspect, the goal being to figure out exactly what "crime" you have committed. Like the technique of asking for specifics, guessing must be done with goodwill if it's to produce satisfying results. You need to convey to the critic that for both of your sakes you're truly interested in finding out what is the matter. Once you have communicated this intention, the emotional climate generally becomes more comfortable because, in effect, both you and the critic are seeking the same goal.

Here are some typical questions you might hear from someone guessing about the details of another's criticism:

> "So you object to the language I used in writing the paper. Was my language too formal?"

> "OK, I understand that you think the outfit looks funny. What is it that's so bad? Is it the color? Does it have something to do with the fit? The fabric?"

> "When you say that I'm not doing my share around the house, do you mean that I haven't been helping enough with the cleaning?"

**Paraphrase the Speaker's Ideas**   Another strategy is to draw out confused or reluctant speakers by paraphrasing their thoughts and feelings and using the active listening skills described in Chapter 7. Paraphrasing is especially good in helping others solve their problems—and since people generally criticize you because your behavior creates some problem for them, the method is especially appropriate at such times.

One advantage of paraphrasing is that you don't have to guess about the specifics of your behavior that might be offensive. By clarifying or amplifying what you understand critics to be saying, you'll learn more about their objections. A brief dialogue between a disgruntled customer and a store manager who is an exceptional listener might sound like this:

**Customer:** The way you people run this store is disgusting! I just want to tell you that I'll never shop here again.

**Manager:** *(reflecting the customer's feeling)* It seems that you're quite upset. Can you tell me your problem?

**Customer:** It isn't *my* problem; it's the problem your salespeople have. They seem to think it's a great inconvenience to help a customer find anything around here.

**Manager:** So you didn't get enough help locating the items you were looking for, is that it?

**Customer:** Help? I spent twenty minutes looking around in here before I even talked to a clerk. All I can say is that it's a hell of a way to run a store.

**Manager:** So what you're saying is that the clerks seemed to be ignoring the customers?

**Customer:** No. They were all busy with other people. It just seems to me that you ought to have enough help around to handle the crowds that come in at this hour.

**Manager:** I understand now. What frustrated you the most was the fact that we didn't have enough staff to serve you promptly.

**Customer:** That's right. I have no complaint with the service I get once I'm waited on, and I've always thought you had a good selection here. It's just that I'm too busy to wait so long for help.

**Manager:** Well, I'm glad you brought this to my attention. We certainly don't want loyal customers going away mad. I'll try to see that it doesn't happen again.

This conversation illustrates two advantages of paraphrasing. First, the critic often reduces the intensity of the attack once he or she realizes that the complaint is being heard. Criticism often grows from the frustration of unmet needs—which in this case was partly a lack of attention. As soon as the manager genuinely demonstrated interest in the customer's plight, the customer began to feel better and was able to leave the store relatively calmly. Of course, this sort of active listening won't always mollify your critic, but even when it doesn't there's still another benefit that makes the technique worthwhile. In the sample conversation, for instance, the manager learned some valuable information by taking time to understand the customer. As you read earlier, even apparently outlandish criticism often contains at least a grain of truth, and thus a person who is genuinely interested in improving would be wise to hear it out.

**Ask What the Critic Wants**   Sometimes your critic's demand will be obvious:

"Turn down that music!"

"I wish you'd remember to tell me about phone messages."

"Would you clean up your dirty dishes *now!*"

In other cases, however, you'll need to do some investigating to find out what the critic wants from you:

**Alex:** I can't believe you invited all those people over without asking me first!

**Barb:** Are you saying you want me to cancel the party?

**Alex:** No, I just wish you'd ask me before you make plans.

**Cynthia:** You're so critical! It sounds like you don't like *anything* about this paper.

**Donna:** But you asked for my opinion. What do you expect me to do when you ask?

**Cynthia:** I want to know what's wrong, but I don't *just* want to hear criticisms. If you think there's anything good about my work, I wish you'd tell me that too.

This last example illustrates the importance of accompanying your questions with the right nonverbal behavior. It's easy to imagine two ways Donna could have said "What do you expect me to do when you ask?" One would show a genuine desire to clarify what Cynthia wanted, while the other would have been clearly hostile and defensive. As with all of the styles in this section, your responses to criticism have to be sincere in order to work.

### Ask about the Consequences of Your Behavior

As a rule, people complain about your actions only when some need of theirs is not being met. One way to respond to this kind of criticism is to find out exactly what troublesome consequences your behavior has for them. You'll often find that actions that seem perfectly legitimate to you cause some difficulty for your critic; once you have understood this, comments that previously sounded foolish take on a new meaning:

**Neighbor A**: You say that I ought to have my cat neutered. Why is that important to you?

**Neighbor B**: Because at night he picks fights with my cat, and I'm tired of paying the vet's bills.

**Worker A**: Why do you care whether I'm late to work?

**Worker B**: Because when the boss asks, I feel obligated to make up some story so you won't get in trouble, and I don't like to lie.

**Husband**: Why does it bother you when I lose money at poker? You know I never gamble more than I can afford.

**Wife**: It's not the cash itself. It's that when you lose, you're in a grumpy mood for two or three days, and that's no fun for me.

**Ask What Else Is Wrong**  It might seem crazy to invite more criticism, but sometimes asking about other complaints can uncover the real problem:

**Raul**: Are you mad at me?

**Tina**: No, why are you asking?

**Raul**: Because the whole time we were at the picnic you hardly spent any time talking to me. In fact, it seemed like whenever I came over to where you were, you went off somewhere else.

**Tina**: Is anything else wrong?

**Raul**: Well, I've been wondering lately if you're tired of me.

This example shows that asking if anything else bothers your critic isn't just an exercise in masochism. If you can keep your defensiveness in check, probing further can lead the conversation to issues that are the source of the critic's real dissatisfaction.

Soliciting more information from a critic sometimes isn't enough. For instance, what do you do when you fully understand the other person's objections and still feel a defensive response on the tip of your tongue? You know that if you try to protect yourself, you'll wind up in an argument; on the other hand, you simply can't accept what the other person is saying about you. The solution to such a dilemma is outrageously simple and is discussed in the following section.

## Agree with the Critic

But, you protest, how can I honestly agree with comments I don't believe are true? The following pages will answer this question by showing that there's virtually no situation in which you can't honestly accept the other person's point of view and still maintain your position. To see how this can be so, you need to realize that there are several different types of agreement, one of which you can use in almost any situation.

**Agree with the Truth**  Agreeing with the truth is easy to understand, though not always easy to practice. You agree with the truth when another person's criticism is factually correct:

"You're right; I am angry."

"I suppose I was just being defensive."

"Now that you mention it, I did get pretty sarcastic."

Agreeing with the facts seems quite sensible when you realize that certain matters are indisputable. If you agree to be somewhere at 4:00 and don't show up until 5:00, you *are* late, no matter how good your explanation for tardiness is. If you've broken a borrowed object, run out of gas, or failed to finish a job you started, there's no point in denying the fact. In the same way, if you're honest you will have to agree with many interpretations of your behavior, even when they're not flattering. You do get angry, act foolishly, fail to listen, and behave inconsiderately. Once you rid yourself of the myth of perfection, it's much easier to acknowledge these truths.

If it's so obvious that the descriptions others give of your behaviors are often accurate, why is it so difficult to accept them without being defensive? The answer to this question lies in a confusion between agreeing with the *facts* and accepting the *judgment* that so often accompanies them. Most critics don't merely describe the action that offends them; they also evaluate it, and it's the evaluation that we resist:

"It's silly to be angry."

"You have no reason for being defensive."

"You were wrong to be so sarcastic."

It's such judgments that we resent. By realizing that you can agree with—even learn from—the descriptive part of many criticisms and still not accept the accompanying evaluations, you'll often have a response that is both honest and nondefensive. A conversation between a teacher and a student illustrates this point:

**Teacher**: Look at this paper! It's only two pages long, and it contains twelve misspelled words. I'm afraid you have a real problem with your writing.
**Student**: You're right. I know I don't spell well at all.
**T**: I don't know what's happening in the lower grades. They just don't seem to be turning out people who can write a simple, declarative sentence.
**S**: You're not the first person I've heard say that.
**T**: I should think you'd be upset by the fact that after so much time in English composition classes you haven't mastered the basics of spelling.
**S**: You're right. It does bother me.

Notice that in agreeing with the teacher's comments the student did not in any way demean herself. Even though there might have been extenuating circumstances to account for her lack of skill, the student didn't find it necessary to justify her errors because she wasn't saddled with the burden of pretending to be perfect. By simply agreeing with the facts, she was able

to maintain her dignity and avoid an unproductive argument.

Of course, in order to reduce defensiveness it's important that your agreement with the facts be honest and admitted without malice. It's humiliating to accept inaccurate descriptions, and maliciously pretending to agree with these only leads to trouble. You can imagine how unproductive the above conversation would have been if the student had spoken the same words in a sarcastic tone. Agree with the facts only when you can do so sincerely. Although it won't always be possible, you'll be surprised at how often you can use this simple response.

Agreeing with criticism is fine, but by itself it isn't an adequate response to your critic. For instance, once you've admitted to another that you are defensive, habitually late, or sarcastic, you can expect the other to ask what you intend to do about this behavior. Such questions are fair. In most cases it would be a mistake simply to understand another's criticism, to agree with the accusations, and then to go on behaving as before. Such behavior makes it clear that you have no concern for the speaker. The message that comes through is "Sure, now I understand what I've done to bother you. You're right, I have been doing it and I'll probably keep on doing it. If you don't like the way I've been behaving, that's tough!" Such a response might be appropriate for dealing with people you genuinely don't care about—manipulative solicitors, abusive strangers, and so on—but it is clearly not suitable for people who matter to you.

Before reading on, then, understand that responding nondefensively to criticism is only the *first* step in resolving the conflicts that usually prompt another's attack. In order to resolve your conflicts fully, you'll need to learn the skills described in Chapter 12.

**Agree with the Odds**    Sometimes a critic will point out possible unpleasant consequences of your behavior:

"If you don't talk to more people, they'll think you're a snob."

"If you don't exercise more, you'll wind up having a heart attack one of these days."

"If you run around with that crowd, you'll probably be sorry."

Often such comments are genuinely helpful suggestions that others make for your own good. In other cases, however, they are really devices for manipulating you into behaving the way your critic wants you to. For instance, "If we go to the football game, you might catch cold" could mean "I don't want to go to the football game." "You'll probably be exhausted tomorrow if you stay up late" could be translated as "I want you to go to bed early." Chapter 12 will have more to say about such methods of indirect aggression, but for now it is sufficient to state that such warnings often generate defensiveness. A mother-son argument shows this outcome:

**Mother**: I don't see why you want to ride that motorcycle. You could wind up in an accident so easily. *(state the odds for an accident)*

**Son**: Oh, don't be silly. I'm a careful driver, and besides you know that I never take my bike on the freeway. *(denies the odds)*

**M**: Yes, but every time I pick up the paper I read about someone being hurt or killed. There's always a danger that some crazy driver will miss seeing you and run you off the road. *(states the odds of an injury)*

**S**: Oh, you worry too much. I always look out for the other driver. And besides, you have a lot better maneuverability on a motorcycle than in a car. *(denies the odds for an injury)*

**M**: I know you're careful, but all it takes is one mistake and you could be killed. *(states the odds for being killed)*

**S**: Somebody is killed shaving or taking a shower every day, but you don't want me to stop doing those things, do you? You're just exaggerating the whole thing. *(denies the odds for being killed)*

From this example you can see that it's usually counterproductive to deny another's predictions. You don't convince the critic, and your opinions stay unchanged as well. Notice the difference when you agree with the odds (though not the demands) of the critic:

**M**: I don't see why you want to drive that motorcycle. You could wind up in an accident so easily. *(states the odds for an accident)*

**S**: I suppose there is a chance of that. *(agrees with the odds)*

**M**: You're darned right. Every time I pick up the newspaper, I read about someone being hurt or killed. There's always a danger that some crazy driver will miss seeing you and run you off the road. *(states the odds for an injury)*

**S**: You're right; that could happen *(agrees with the odds)*, but I don't think the risk is great enough to keep me off the bike.

**M**: That's easy for you to say now. Someday you could be sorry you didn't listen to me. *(states the odds for regret)*

**S**: That's true. I really might regret driving the bike someday. *(agrees with the odds)*

Notice how the son simply considers his mother's predictions and realistically acknowledges the chance that they might come true. While such responses might at first seem indifferent and callous, they can help the son to avoid the pitfall of indirect manipulation. Suppose the conversation were a straightforward one in which the mother was simply pointing out to her son the dangers of motorcycle riding. He acknowledged that he understood her concern and even agreed with the possibility that her prediction could come true. If, however, her prediction was really an indirect way of saying "I don't want you to ride anymore," then the son's response would force her to clarify her demand so that he could deal with it openly. At this point they might be able to figure out a solution that lets the son satisfy his need for transportation and excitement and at the same time allows his mother to alleviate her concern.

In addition to bringing hidden agendas into the open for resolution, agreeing with the odds also helps you become aware of some possible previously unconsidered consequences of your actions. Instead of blindly denying the chance that your behavior is inappropriate, agreeing with the odds will help you look objectively at whether your course of action is in fact the best one. You might agree with your critic that you really should change your behavior.

**Agree in Principle**   Criticism often comes in the form of abstract ideals against which you're unfavorably compared:

> "I wish you wouldn't spend so much time on your work. Relaxation is important too, you know."

> "You shouldn't expect so much from your kids. Nobody's perfect."

> "What do you mean, you're not voting? The government is only going to get better when people like you take more of an interest in it."

> "You mean you're still upset by that remark? You ought to learn how to take a joke better."

In cases like these, you can accept the principle upon which the criticism is based and still

---

### REFLECTION

### COPING WITH CRITICISM AS A MARTIAL ART

I've been taking self-defense lessons for a year, and I think there are a lot of similarities between judo and agreeing with your critic. In both techniques you don't resist your attacker. Instead you use the other person's energy to your advantage. You let your opponent defeat himself.

Last week I used "verbal judo" on a very judgmental friend who called me a hypocrite because I'm a vegetarian but still wear leather shoes. I knew that nothing I could say would change his mind, so I just agreed with his perception by saying, "I can see why you think I'm not consistent." (I really *could* see how my lifestyle looks hypocritical to him, although I don't agree.) No matter what he said, I replied, "I understand why it looks that way to you."

I won't always agree with my critics this way, any more than I'll always use judo. But it sure is a useful approach to have at my disposal.

---

behave as you have been. After all, some rules *do* allow occasional exceptions, and people often *are* inconsistent. Consider how you might sincerely agree with the criticisms above without necessarily changing your behavior:

> "You're right. I am working hard now. It probably is unhealthy, but finishing the job is worth the extra strain to me."

> "I guess my expectations for the kids *are* awfully high, and I don't want to drive them crazy. I hope I'm not making a mistake."

> "You're right: If everybody stopped voting, the system would fall apart."

"Maybe I *would* be happier if I could take a joke in stride. I'm not ready to do that, though, at least not for jokes like that one."

**Agree with the Critic's Perception**   What about times when there seems to be no basis whatsoever for agreeing with your critics? You've listened carefully and asked questions to make sure you understand the objections, but the more you listen, the more positive you are that they are totally out of line: There is no truth to the criticisms, you can't agree with the odds, and you can't even accept the principle the critics are putting forward. Even here there's a way of agreeing—this time not with the critics' conclusions, but with their right to perceive things their way:

A:  I don't believe you've been all the places you were just describing. You're probably just making all this up so that we'll think you're hot stuff.

B:  Well, I can see how you might think that. I've known people who lie to get approval.

C:  I want to let you know right from the start that I was against hiring you for the job. I think the reason you got it was because you're a woman.

D:  I can understand why you'd believe that with all the antidiscrimination laws on the books. I hope that after I've been here for a while you'll change your mind.

E:  I don't think you're being totally honest about your reasons for wanting to stay home. You say that it's because you have a headache, but I think you're avoiding Mary and Walt.

F:  I can see why that would make sense to you since Mary and I got into an argument the last time we were together. All I can say is that I do have a headache.

Such responses tell critics that you're acknowledging the reasonableness of their perceptions, even though you don't agree or wish to change your behavior. This coping style is valuable, for it lets you avoid debates over who is right and who is wrong, which can turn an exchange of ideas into an argument. Notice the difference in the following scenes between Amy and Bob.

Disputing the perception:

**Amy:**  I don't see how you can stand to be around Josh. The guy is so crude that he gives me the creeps.

**Bob:**  What do you mean, crude? He's a really nice guy. I think you're just touchy.

**A:**  Touchy! If it's touchy to be offended by disgusting behavior, then I'm guilty.

**B:**  You're not guilty about anything. It's just that you're too sensitive when people kid around.

**A:**  Too sensitive, huh? I don't know what's happened to you. You used to have such good judgment about people. . . .

Agreeing with the perception:

**A:**  I don't see how you can stand to be around Josh. The guy is so crude that he gives me the creeps.

**B:**  Well, I enjoy being around him, but I guess I can see how his jokes would be offensive to some people.

**A:**  You're damn right. I don't see how you can put up with him.

**B:**  Yeah. I guess if you didn't appreciate his humor, you wouldn't want to have much to do with him.

Notice how in the second exchange Bob was able to maintain his own position without attacking Amy's in the least. Such acceptance is the key ingredient for successfully agreeing with your critics' perceptions: Using acceptance, you clarify that you are in no way disputing their views. Because you have no intention of attacking your critics' views, your critics are less likely to be defensive.

All these responses to criticism may appear to buy peace at the cost of denying your feelings. However, as you can see by now, counterattacking usually makes matters worse. The nondefensive responses you have just learned won't solve problems or settle disputes by themselves. Nevertheless, they *will* make a constructive dialogue possible, setting the stage for a productive solution. How to achieve productive solutions is the topic of Chapter 12.

## Summary

Communication climate refers to the social tone of a relationship. The most influential factor in shaping a communication climate is the degree to which the people involved see themselves as being valued and confirmed. Messages have differing levels of confirmation. We can categorize them as confirming, disagreeing, or disconfirming. Confirming messages, which communicate "you exist and are valued," involve recognition, acknowledgment, or endorsement of the other party. Disagreeing messages, which communicate "you are wrong," use argumentativeness, complaining, or aggressiveness. Disconfirming messages, which communicate "you do not exist and are not valued," include responses that are impervious, interrupting, irrelevant, tangential, impersonal, ambiguous, or incongruous. Over time, these messages form climate patterns that often take the shape of positive or negative spirals.

Defensiveness is at the core of most negative spirals. Defensiveness occurs when individuals perceive that their presenting self is being attacked by face-threatening acts. We get particularly defensive about flaws that we don't want to admit and those that touch on sensitive areas. Both the attacker and the person attacked are responsible for creating defensiveness, since competent communicators protect others' face needs as well as their own.

Jack Gibb suggested a variety of ways to create a positive and nondefensive communication climate. These include being descriptive rather than evaluative, problem oriented rather than controlling, spontaneous rather than strategic, empathic rather than neutral, equal rather than superior, and provisional rather than certain.

When faced with criticism by others, there are two alternatives to responding defensively: seeking additional information from the critic and agreeing with some aspect of the criticism. When performed sincerely, these approaches can transform an actual or potentially negative climate into a more positive one.

## Recommended Readings

**Communication climate in business:**

Charles E. Beck and Elizabeth Beck. "The Manager's Open Door and the Communication Climate." In *Making Connections: Readings in Relational Communication* edited by K. M. Galvin and P. Cooper. Los Angeles: Roxbury, 1996, pp. 286–290.

**Facework and defensiveness:**

William R. Cupach and Sandra Metts. *Facework.* Newbury Park, CA: Sage, 1994.

**Disconfirming communication:**

Anita L. Vangelisti. "Messages That Hurt." In *The Dark Side of Interpersonal Communication,* edited by William R. Cupach and Brian H. Spitzberg. Hillsdale, NJ: Lawrence Erlbaum Associates, 1994.

**Responding nondefensively to criticism:**

Theodora Wells. *Keeping Your Cool: Communicating Non-Defensively.* New York: McGraw-Hill, 1980.

## Activities

1. **Invitation to Insight**
   Identify three personal relationships that matter to you. For each relationship,
   a. Come up with a weather phrase that describes the current climate of the relationship.
   b. Come up with a weather phrase that forecasts the climate of the relationship over the next year.
   c. Consider why you chose the phrases you did. In particular, identify how feeling valued and confirmed played a part in the climates you perceived and predicted.

2. **Critical Thinking Probe**
   Mental health experts generally believe it is better to have others disagree with you than ignore you. Express your opinion on this matter, using specific examples from personal experiences to support your position. Next, discuss whether it is possible to disagree without being disconfirming.

3. **Skill Builder**
   Develop your ability to communicate supportively instead of triggering defensive reactions

in others. Restate each of the following "you" statements as "I" messages. Use details from your own personal relationships to create messages that are specific and personally relevant.

a. "You're only thinking of yourself."
b. "Don't be so touchy."
c. "Quit fooling around!"
d. "Stop beating around the bush and tell me the truth."
e. "You're a slob!"

4. **Ethical Challenge**

Gibb argues that spontaneous rather than strategic communication reduces defensiveness. However, in some situations a strategic approach may hold the promise of a better climate than a completely honest message. Consider situations such as these:

a. You don't find your partner very attractive. He or she asks "What's the matter?"
b. You intend to quit your job because you hate your boss, but you don't want to offend him or her. How do you explain the reasons for your departure?
c. You are tutoring a high school student in reading or math. The student is sincere and a hard worker, but is perhaps the most dull-witted person you have ever met. What do you say when the teenager asks "How am I doing?"

Describe at least one situation from your experience where complete honesty increased another person's defensiveness. Discuss whether candor or some degree of strategy might have been the best approach in this situation. How can you reconcile your

approach with Gibb's arguments in favor of spontaneity?

5. **Invitation to Insight**

Review the Gibb behaviors discussed on pages 331–337, and then answer the following questions:

a. Which defense-provoking behavior do you find most annoying?
b. Who in your life uses that behavior most often?
c. What part of your presenting self is threatened by that behavior?
d. How do you normally respond to that behavior?
e. What behavior do you wish that person would use instead?

6. **Skill Builder**

Practice your skill at responding nondefensively to critical attacks by following these steps:

a. Identify five criticisms you are likely to encounter from others in your day-to-day communication. If you have trouble thinking of criticisms, invite one or more people who know you well to supply some real, sincere gripes.
b. For each criticism, write one or more nondefensive responses using the categories on pages 337–345. Be sure your responses are sincere and that you can offer them without counterattacking your critic.
c. Practice your responses, either by inviting a friend or classmate to play the role of your critics or by approaching your critics directly and inviting them to share their gripes with you.

# CHAPTER
## 12

# Managing Conflict

# After Studying the Material in This Chapter . . .

## You Should Understand:

1. The four elements of conflict.

2. That conflict is natural and inevitable.

3. The characteristics of functional and dysfunctional conflicts.

4. The differences between nonassertiveness, indirect communication, passive aggression, direct aggression, and assertiveness.

5. The ways individuals interact to create relational conflict systems.

6. The characteristics of win-lose, lose-lose, and win-win problem solving.

## You Should Be Able to:

1. Recognize and accept the inevitability of conflicts in your life.

2. Identify the behaviors that characterize your dysfunctional conflicts and suggest more functional alternatives.

3. Identify the conflict styles you use most commonly and evaluate their appropriateness.

4. Use the assertive message format.

5. Describe the relational conflict system in one of your important relationships.

6. Use the win-win problem-solving approach to resolve an interpersonal conflict.

## Key Terms

| | | | |
|---|---|---|---|
| Assertion | Conflict ritual | Functional conflict | Passive aggression |
| Complementary conflict style | De-escalatory spiral | Indirect communication | Relational conflict style |
| | Direct aggression | Lose-lose problem solving | Symmetrical conflict style |
| Compromise | Dysfunctional conflict | Nonassertion | Win-lose problem solving |
| Conflict | Escalatory spiral | Parallel conflict style | Win-win problem solving |

*O*nce upon a time, there was a world without conflicts. The leaders of each nation recognized the need for cooperation and met regularly to solve any potential problems before they could grow. They never disagreed on matters needing attention or on ways to handle these matters, and so there were never any international tensions, and of course there was no war.

Within each nation things ran just as smoothly. The citizens always agreed on who their leaders should be, so elections were always unanimous. There was no social friction between various groups. Age, race, and educational differences did exist, but each group respected the others, and all got along harmoniously.

Human relationships were always perfect. Strangers were always kind and friendly to each other. Neighbors were considerate of each other's needs. Friendships were always mutual, and no disagreements ever spoiled people's enjoyment of one other. Once people fell in love—and everyone did—they stayed happy. Partners liked everything about each other and were able to fully satisfy each other's needs. Children and parents agreed on every aspect of family life and never were critical or hostile toward each other. Each day was better than the one before.

Of course, everybody lived happily ever after.

This story is obviously a fairy tale. Regardless of what we may wish for or dream about, a conflict-free world just doesn't exist. Even the best communicators, the luckiest people, are bound to wind up in situations when their needs don't match the needs of others. Money, time, power, sex, humor, aesthetic taste, and a thousand other issues arise and keep us from living in a state of perpetual agreement.

For many people the inevitability of conflict is a depressing fact. They think that the existence of ongoing conflict means that there's little chance for happy relationships with others. Effective communicators know differently. They realize that although it's impossible to *eliminate* conflict, there are ways to *manage* it effectively. The skillful management of conflict can open the door to healthier, stronger, and more satisfying relationships.

# What Is Conflict?

Stop reading and make a list of as many different conflicts as you can think of. Include conflicts you've experienced personally and those that involved other people only. The list will probably show you that conflict takes many forms. Sometimes there's angry shouting, as when parents yell at their children. In other cases, conflicts involve restrained discussion, as in labor-management negotiations or court trials. Sometimes conflicts are carried on through hostile silence, as in the unspoken feuds of angry couples. Finally, conflicts may wind up in physical fighting between friends, enemies, or even total strangers.

Whatever forms they may take, all interpersonal conflicts share certain similarities. Joyce Hocker and William Wilmot (1997) provide a thorough definition of conflict. They state that **conflict** is *an expressed struggle between at least two interdependent parties who perceive incompatible goals, scarce rewards, and interference from the other party in achieving their goals.* Let's look at the various parts of this definition to develop a better understanding of conflicts in people's lives.

## Expressed Struggle

Another way to describe an expressed struggle is to say that both individuals in a conflict know that some disagreement exists. For instance, you may be upset for months because a neighbor's loud stereo keeps you from getting to sleep at night, but no conflict exists between the two of you until the neighbor learns about your problem. Of course, the expressed struggle doesn't have to be verbal. You can show your displeasure with someone without saying a word. A dirty look, the silent treatment, and avoiding the other person are all ways of expressing yourself. One way or another, both people must know that a problem exists before their conflict surfaces.

## Perceived Incompatible Goals

All conflicts look as if one person's gain would be another's loss. For instance, consider the neighbor whose stereo keeps you awake at night. Doesn't somebody have to lose? If the neighbor turns down the noise, then he loses the enjoyment of hearing the music at full volume; but if the neighbor keeps the volume up, then you're still awake and unhappy.

The goals in this situation really aren't completely incompatible—solutions do exist that allow both people to get what they want. For instance, you could achieve peace and quiet by closing your windows or getting the neighbor to close his. You might use a pair of earplugs, or

perhaps the neighbor could get a set of earphones, which would allow the music to play at full volume without bothering anyone. If any of these solutions prove workable, then the conflict disappears.

Unfortunately, people often fail to see mutually satisfying answers to their problems. As long as they *perceive* their goals to be mutually exclusive, the conflict is real, albeit unnecessary.

## Perceived Scarce Rewards

Conflicts also exist when people believe there isn't enough of something to go around. The most obvious example of a scarce resource is money—a cause of many conflicts. If a worker asks for a raise in pay and the boss would rather keep the money or use it to expand the business, then these two people are in conflict.

Time is another scarce commodity. As authors, teachers, and family men, all of us are constantly in the middle of struggles about how to use the limited time we have at home. Should we work on this book? Spend time with our families? Enjoy the luxury of being alone? With only twenty-four hours in a day, we're bound to wind up in conflicts with our families, editors, students, and friends—all of whom want more of our time than we have available to give.

## Interdependence

However antagonistic they might feel, the people in a conflict are dependent upon each other. The welfare and satisfaction of one depends on the actions of another. If this were not true, then there would be no need for conflict, even in the face of scarce resources and incompatible goals. Interdependence exists between conflicting nations, social groups, organizations, friends, and lovers. In each case, if the two people didn't need each other to solve the problem, they would go separate ways. In fact, many conflicts remain unresolved because the people fail to understand their interdependence. One of the first steps toward resolving a conflict is to take the attitude that "we're all in this together."

## Inevitability

Conflicts are bound to happen, even in the best relationships. College students who have kept diaries of their relationships report that they take part in about seven arguments per week (Benoit & Benoit, 1987). In another survey (Samter & Cupach, 1998), 81 percent of the respondents acknowledged that they had conflicts with friends. Even the 19 percent who claimed their friendships were conflict-free used terms like "push and pull" or "little disagreements" to describe the tensions that inevitably occurred. Among families, conflict can be even more frequent. Researchers recorded dinner conversations for fifty-two families and

found an average of 3.3 "conflict episodes" per meal (Vuchinich, 1987).

Since it is impossible to *avoid* conflicts, the challenge is to handle them effectively when they do arise. Over twenty years of research shows that both happy and unhappy relationships have conflicts but that they perceive them and manage them in very different ways (Hocker & Wilmot, 1997). Unhappy couples argue in ways cataloged in this book as destructive. They are more concerned with defending themselves than with being problem oriented; they fail to listen carefully to one another, have little or no empathy for their partners, use evaluative "you" language, and ignore each other's relational messages.

Many satisfied couples think and communicate differently when they disagree. They recognize disagreements as healthy and know that conflicts need to be faced (Crohan, 1992). While they may argue vigorously, they use skills like perception checking to find out what the other person is thinking, and they let the other person know that they understand the other side of the dispute (Canary et al., 1991). These people are willing to admit their mistakes, a habit that contributes to a harmonious relationship and also helps solve the problem at hand.

Despite the fact that relationships can survive and even prosper from constructive disagreements, most people view conflict as something to be avoided whenever possible. Some common metaphors reflect this attitude (Hocker & Wilmot, 1997). It's common to talk about conflict as a kind of war: "He shot down my arguments"; "Okay, fire away"; "Don't try to defend yourself!" Another metaphor suggests that conflict is explosive: "Don't blow up!"; "I needed to let off steam"; "You've got a short fuse." Sometimes conflict seems like a kind of trial, in which one person accuses another: "Come on, admit you're guilty"; "Stop accusing me!"; "Just listen to my case." Also common is language that suggests conflict is a mess: "Let's not open this can of worms"; "That's a sticky situation"; "Don't make such a stink!" Even the metaphor of a game implies that one side has to defeat the other: "That was out of bounds"; "You're not playing fair"; "OK, you win!"

Conflicts may not always be easy, but they *can* be constructive. A more positive metaphor is to view conflict as a kind of dance in which partners work together to create something that would be impossible without their cooperation. You may have to persuade the other person to become your partner, and you may be clumsy together at first; but with enough practice and goodwill, you can work together instead of at cross-purposes.

The attitude partners bring to their conflicts can make the difference between success and failure. One study by Sandra Metts and William Cupach (1990) revealed that college students in romantic relationships who believed that conflicts are destructive were most likely to neglect or leave the relationship and less likely to seek a solution than couples who had less-negative attitudes. Of course, attitudes alone won't always bring satisfying solutions to conflicts. The kinds of skills you will learn in this chapter can help well-intentioned partners handle their disagreements constructively. But without the right attitude, all the skills in the world would be little help.

the problem at hand and often improving other areas of interaction. Other conflicts can be harmful, causing pain and weakening a relationship. Communication scholars usually describe harmful conflicts as *dysfunctional* and beneficial ones as *functional*.

What makes some conflicts functional and others dysfunctional? Usually, the difference doesn't rest in the subject of the conflict, for it's possible to have good or poor results on almost any issue. Certain individual styles of communication can be more productive than others. In other cases the success or failure of a conflict will depend on the method of resolution the communicators choose (Alberts & Driscoll, 1992). We'll talk more about types of conflict resolution later in this chapter. We want now to describe several symptoms that distinguish functional from dysfunctional conflicts.

## Integration versus Polarization

In a **dysfunctional conflict,** biases are rampant. Participants see themselves as "good" and the other person as "bad," their actions as "protective" and the other's as "aggressive," their behavior as "open and trustworthy" and the other's as "sneaky and deceitful." Researchers Robert Blake and Jane Mouton (1964) found that people engaged in this

## Functional and Dysfunctional Conflicts

Some bacteria are "good," aiding digestion and cleaning up waste, whereas others are "bad," causing infection. There are helpful forest fires, which clean out dangerous accumulations of underbrush, and harmful ones, which threaten lives and property. In the same way, some conflicts can be beneficial. They provide a way for relationships to grow by solving

kind of polarization underestimate the commonalities shared with the other person and so miss areas of agreement and goodwill.

By contrast, participants in a **functional conflict** realize that the other person's needs may be legitimate, too. A person who is allergic to cigarette smoke recognizes that smokers aren't necessarily evil people who delight in inflicting torment, while the smoker sympathizes with the other's need for cleaner air. In such issues, functional conflict is marked by mutual respect (Foss & Griffin, 1995).

## Cooperation versus Isolation

Participants in a dysfunctional conflict see each other as opponents and view the other's gain as their loss: "If you win, I lose" is the attitude. This belief keeps partners from looking for ways to agree or finding solutions that can satisfy them both. People rarely try to redefine the situation in more constructive ways, and they seldom give in, even on noncritical issues.

A more functional approach recognizes that cooperation may bring about an answer that leaves everyone happy. Even nations basically hostile to each other often recognize the functional benefits of cooperating. For example, although many member countries of the United Nations have clear-cut differences in certain areas, they work together to alleviate world hunger and to encourage peaceful solutions to world conflict. Such cooperation is also possible in interpersonal conflicts. We have a great deal to say about cooperative problem solving later in this chapter.

## Agreement versus Coercion

In destructive conflicts, the participants rely heavily on power to get what they want. "Do it my way, or else" is a threat commonly stated or implied in dysfunctional conflicts. Money, favors, friendliness, sex, and sometimes even physical coercion become tools for forcing the other person to give in. Needless to say, victories won with such power plays don't do much for a relationship.

More enlightened communicators realize that power plays are usually a bad idea, not only on ethical grounds but because they can often backfire. Rarely is a person in a relationship totally powerless; it's often possible to win a battle only to lose the war. One classic case of the dysfunctional consequences of using power to resolve conflicts occurs in families where authoritarian parents turn their children's requests into "unreasonable demands." It's easy enough to send five-year-olds out of a room for some real or imagined misbehavior, but when they grow into teenagers they acquire many ways of striking back.

## De-escalation versus Escalation

In destructive conflicts, the problems seem to grow larger instead of smaller. As you read in Chapter 9, defensiveness is reciprocal: The person you attack is likely to strike back even harder. We've all seen a small incident get out of hand and cause damage out of proportion to its importance.

One clear sign of functional conflict is that in the long run the behaviors of the participants solve more problems than they create. We say "long run" because facing up to an issue instead of avoiding it will usually make life more difficult for a while. In this respect, handling conflicts functionally is rather like going to the dentist: You may find it a little (or even a lot!) painful for a while, but you're only making matters worse if you don't face the problem.

## Focusing versus Drifting

In dysfunctional conflicts, the partners often bring in issues having little or nothing to do with the original problem. Take, for example, a couple having trouble deciding whether to spend the holidays at his or her parents' home. As they begin to grow frustrated at their inability to solve the dilemma, their interaction sounds like this:

**A:** Your mother is always trying to latch onto us!
**B:** If you want to talk about latching on, what about your folks? Ever since they loaned us that money, they've been asking about every dime we spend.

## REFLECTION

### E-MAIL DE-ESCALATES CONFLICT SPIRAL

My dad is a family law attorney who specializes in divorce cases. He says that e-mail has been a good way to get angry couples to communicate. Some husbands and wives can't be in the same room without getting into a shouting match, but e-mail slows things down and gives them a chance to think before they respond to one another. My dad asks each person in a divorcing couple to wait overnight before responding to the other's message, which cuts down on the angry and hurtful replies.

My dad says that e-mail doesn't save failing marriages, but it sure makes the breakup more civilized and less painful.

**A:** Well, if you could ever finish with school and hold down a decent job, we wouldn't have to worry about money so much. You're always talking about wanting to be an equal partner, but I'm the one paying all the bills around here.

You can imagine how the conversation would go from here. Notice how the original issue became lost as the conflict expanded. Such open-ended hostility is unlikely to solve any of the problems it brings up, not to mention its potential for creating problems that didn't even exist before.

One characteristic of communicators who handle conflict well is their ability to keep focused on one subject at a time. Unlike those dysfunctional battlers whom George Bach and Peter Wyden (1968) call "kitchen sink fighters," skillful communicators might say "I'm willing to talk about how my parents have been acting since they made us that loan, but first let's settle the business of where to spend the holidays." In other words, for functional problem solving the rule is "one problem at a time."

## Foresight versus Shortsightedness

Shortsightedness can produce dysfunctional conflicts even when partners do not lose sight of the original issue. One common type of shortsightedness occurs when disputants try to win a battle and wind up losing the war. Friends might argue about who started a fight, but if you succeed in proving that you were "right" at the cost of the friendship, then the victory is a hollow one. In another type of shortsightedness, partners are so interested in defending their own solution to a problem that they overlook a different solution that would satisfy both their goals. A final type of shortsightedness occurs when one or both partners jump into a conflict without planning the necessary steps. In a few pages, we have more to say about preventing these last two types of shortsightedness.

## Positive versus Negative Results

So far, we've looked at the differences between the *processes* of functional and dysfunctional conflicts. Now let's compare the *results* of these different styles.

Dysfunctional conflict typically has two consequences. First, no one is likely to get what was originally sought. In the short run, it may *look* as if one person might win a dispute while the other person loses, but today's victor is likely to suffer tomorrow at the hands of the original loser. Second, dysfunctional conflicts can threaten the future of a relationship. Family members, lovers, friends, neighbors, or fellow workers usually are bound together by webs of commitments and obligations that aren't easy to break. If they can't find satisfactory ways of resolving their differences, their connections will become strained and uncomfortable. Even when it is possible, dissolving a relationship in the face of a conflict is hardly a satisfying pattern.

In contrast to these dismal outcomes, functional conflicts have positive results. One benefit of skillfully handling issues is the reward of successfully facing a challenge. Finding a solution that works for you and the other person can leave partners feeling better about themselves and each other. Partners learn more about each other's needs and how they can be satisfied. Feelings are clarified. Backgrounds are shared. The relationship grows deeper and stronger. Of course, growth can occur in nonconflict situations too, but the point here is that dealing with problems can be an opportunity for getting to know each other better and appreciate each other more. Constructive conflict also provides a safe outlet for the feelings of frustration and aggression that are bound to occur. Without this kind of release, partners can build up a "gunnysack" of grudges that interfere with their everyday functioning and their goodwill toward one another.

## Individual Conflict Styles

People have their individual styles of handling conflict—characteristic approaches they take when their needs appear incompatible with what others want. As you will read, the most effective style changes from one situation to another. Despite this fact, many people have one or two "default" styles that can be effective sometimes and ineffective at others. What styles do you typically use to deal with conflict? Find out by thinking about how two hypothetical characters—Sally and Ralph—manage a problem that you might find familiar.

*Sally and Ralph have been friends for several years, ever since they moved into the same apartment building. They had always exchanged favors in a neighborly way, but lately Ralph has been depending more and more on Sally. He asks her to care for his cat and house plants almost every other weekend while he travels, borrows food and cash without returning them, and drops in to talk about his unhappy love life at least once a week. Until lately, Sally hasn't minded much, but now she's getting tired of Ralph's behavior.*

Read the five groups of responses below and rank them in the order you would be most likely

to use them. Mark your most-likely response number 1, your next-most-likely 2, and so on.

__ Steer clear of Ralph as much as possible. Pretend not to be home when he drops by. Make excuses for why you can't help him with his problems. *or* Do the favors for Ralph, hoping he'll stop imposing soon. After all, nobody's perfect, and it isn't worth making an issue.

__ Hint to Ralph that you're not happy with his behavior. When he asks you to take care of his cat, hesitate and talk about your busy schedule.

When he doesn't pay back his loans, mention that you're short of money and may need to borrow some from your friends and family. When he starts to talk about his romantic problems, mention that you need to study for an exam.

__ Do the favors for Ralph, but let him know you aren't happy. Sigh when he asks another favor. Make an occasional sarcastic remark about how much you enjoy being Ralph's housekeeper and psychotherapist. When he asks if you're upset with him, deny anything is wrong. Mention your unhappiness to some mutual friends, hoping they'll tell Ralph to back off.

__ Ralph can't take a hint, so tell him directly that you're fed up with his demands. Say you don't mind helping once in a while, but let him know he's taken advantage of your friendship. Warn him that continued impositions will threaten your friendship.

__ Tell Ralph that you're beginning to feel uneasy about his requests. Let him know that you value his friendship and want to keep feeling good about him. Explain that's why you're telling him this, and ask him to work with you to find a way to solve his problems that's less of a strain for you.

Make sure you have ranked your responses before going on. Each of the choices above represents a different style of behavior used in conflicts (Tangney et al., 1996). These five styles are explained below and summarized in Table 12.1.

**Table 12.1**

**Individual Styles of Conflict**

|  | Nonassertive | Directly Aggressive | Passive Aggressive | Indirect | Assertive |
|---|---|---|---|---|---|
| Approach to Others | I'm not OK; you're OK. | I'm OK; you're not OK. | I'm OK; you're not OK. (But I'll let you think you are.) | I'm OK; you're not OK. | I'm OK; you're OK. |
| Decision-Making | Lets others choose | Chooses for others. They know it. | Chooses for others. They don't know it. | Chooses for others. They don't know it. | Chooses for self. |
| Self-Sufficiency | Low | High or low | Looks high but usually low | High or low | Usually high |
| Behavior in Problem Situations | Flees; gives in | Outright attack | Concealed attack | Strategic, oblique | Direct confrontation |
| Response of Others | Disrespect, guilt, anger, frustration | Hurt, defensiveness, humiliation | Confusion, frustration, feelings of manipulation | Unknowing compliance or resistance | Mutual respect |
| Success Pattern | Succeeds by luck or charity of others | Beats out others | Wins by manipulation | Gains unwitting compliance of others | Attempts "win-win" solutions |

Adapted with permission from Stanlee Phelps, Nancy Austin, and Gerald Piaget, *The Assertive Woman*, 3$^{rd}$ ed. 1997. American Orthopsychiatric Association. Impact Publishers, Inc. P.O. Box 1994, San Luis Obispo, CA 93406. Further reproduction prohibited.

As you read on, see which ones best describe the way you manage your own conflicts.

## Nonassertion

The inability or unwillingness to express thoughts or feelings in a conflict is called **nonassertion.** Nonassertion sometimes comes from a lack of confidence. In other cases, people lack the awareness or skill to use a more direct means of expression. Sometimes people know how to communicate in a straightforward way but choose to behave nonassertively.

Nonassertion can take a variety of forms. One is avoidance—either physical (steering clear of a friend after having an argument) or conversational (changing the topic, joking, or denying that a problem exists). People who avoid conflicts usually believe it's easier to put up with the status quo than to face the problem head-on and try to solve it. Accommodation is another type of nonassertive response. Accommodaters deal with conflict by giving in, putting the other's needs ahead of their own.

Our example of Sally and Ralph illustrates the perils of nonassertion. Every time Sally hides from Ralph or changes the subject so he won't ask her for a favor, she becomes uncomfortable and probably leaves Ralph feeling the same way. After this avoidance goes on for a while, it's likely that whatever enjoyment Sally and Ralph had found together will be eclipsed by their new way of relating and that the friendship will degenerate into an awkward, polite charade.

Nonassertive behavior isn't always a bad idea. You might choose to keep quiet or give in if the risk of speaking up is too great—getting fired from a job you can't afford to lose, being humiliated in public, or even risking physical harm. You might also avoid a conflict if the relationship it involves isn't worth the effort. Even in close relationships, though, nonassertion has its logic. If the issue is temporary or minor, you might let it pass. It might even make sense to keep your thoughts to yourself and give in if the issue is more important to the other person than it is to you. These reasons help

explain why the communication of many happily married couples is characterized by "selectively ignoring" the other person's minor flaws (Cahn, 1992). This doesn't mean that a key to successful relationships is avoiding *all* conflicts. Instead, it suggests that it's smart to save energy for the truly important ones.

## Indirect Communication

Sometimes we choose to convey messages indirectly, hinting to others instead of expressing ourselves outright; this is **indirect communication.** Consider the case of Sally and Ralph. Rather than risk triggering a defensive reaction, Sally decides that she will try to change Ralph's bad habits with an indirect approach. If Ralph has the kind of sensitivity that characterizes most competent communicators, he may get Sally's message without forcing her to confront him.

As this example suggests, an indirect approach can save face for the other person. If your guests are staying too long at a party, it's probably kinder to yawn and hint about your big day tomorrow than to bluntly ask them to leave. Likewise, if you're not interested in going out with someone who has asked you for a date, it may be more compassionate to claim that you're busy than to say, "I'm not interested in seeing you."

Sometimes, indirect communication can be a form of self-protection. For example, you might test the waters by hinting instead of directly asking the boss for a raise or letting your partner know you could use some affection instead of asking outright. At times like these, an oblique approach may get the message across while minimizing the risk of a negative response.

The advantages of saving face for others and protecting oneself help explain why indirect communication is the most common way people make requests (Jordan & Roloff, 1990). The risk of an indirect message, of course, is that the other person will misunderstand you or fail to get the hint. There are also times when the importance of an idea is great enough that hinting lacks the necessary punch. When clarity and directness are your

## FOCUS ON RESEARCH

### STICKS AND STONES: VERBAL AGGRESSION AMONG SIBLINGS

Siblings are supposed to love one another, but even the best relationships between children in the same family include a dose of conflict. Siblings have been known to fight with fists, but more often they fight with words that sting and bruise. Matthew Martin and his colleagues wanted to know whether those "fighting words" affect long-term sibling relationships.

The researchers asked 227 college students to complete questionnaires about verbal aggression and teasing among their brothers and sisters. The respondents rated the degree to which various statements are true about their siblings and themselves, such as, "I use insults to soften my sibling when he/she is stubborn," "I talk to my sibling to make fun of him/her," and "I get a lot of pleasure out of telling my sibling off." Participants also filled out a variety of questionnaires about psychological hurt, trust, and communication satisfaction.

The researchers learned that siblings' teasing is often a form of verbal aggression, meant to hurt, not amuse. Most important, they found that "when verbal aggressiveness is present in a relationship there is less satisfaction and trust." These findings reinforce the destructive nature of aggressive and passive aggressive communication. Conflicts between siblings will always exist, but in order to keep the relationships between brothers and sisters strong and healthy, they must be handled constructively.

Martin, M. M., Anderson, C. M., Burant, P. A., & Weber, K. (1997). Verbal aggression in sibling relationships. *Communication Quarterly, 45,* 304–317.

goals, the kind of assertive approach described on the following pages is more appropriate.

## Passive Aggression

**Passive aggression** occurs when a communicator expresses dissatisfaction in a disguised manner. Passive aggression can take the form of "crazy-making" (Bach & Wyden, 1968). This term takes its name from the effect such behavior usually has on its target. There are a number of crazymaking ways to deal with conflict indirectly. One is through guilt: "Never mind. I'll do all the work myself. Go ahead and have a good time. Don't worry about me." Hinting can be another form of passive aggression: "When do you think you can get around to finishing the job?" Sometimes nonverbal behavior is a way to express aggression

indirectly: a loud sigh, a pained expression, or a disdainful laugh can get a message across. If the target of these messages asks about them, the passive aggressor can always deny the conflict exists. Even humor—especially sarcasm—can be used as passive aggression.

There are a number of risks to indirect approaches like these. First, they may not work. The other person might miss your message and continue with the undesirable behavior. On the other hand, the target of your indirect message might understand your message clearly but refuse to comply, possibly out of irritation at your underhanded style of communicating. Even when passive aggression proves successful in the short run, it can have unpleasant consequences over a longer period of time. You might get immediate compliance ("All right, I'll help you with the damn thing") but create a resentful climate that will harm the relationship in the future.

## Direct Aggression

Where a nonasserter underreacts, a directly aggressive communicator does just the opposite, lashing out to attack the source of displeasure. Dominic Infante (1987) identified nine types of **direct aggression:** character attacks, competence attacks, physical appearance attacks, maledictions (wishing the other bad fortune), teasing, ridicule, threats, swearing, and nonverbal emblems: fist-shaking, waving arms, and so on.

The results of direct aggression can have a severe impact on the target. There is a significant connection between verbal aggression and physical aggression (Infante et al., 1989). Even if the attacks never lead to blows, the psychological effects can be harmful, or even devastating. Recipients can feel embarrassed, inadequate, humiliated, hopeless, desperate, or depressed (Infante, 1987). These results can lead to decreased effectiveness in personal relationships, on the job, and in families (Beatty et al., 1996; Kinney & Segrin, 1998; O'Brien & Bahadur, 1998; Venable & Martin, 1997). Verbal aggression can affect the relationship as well as the target. One aggressive remark can lead to an equally combative reaction, starting a destructive spiral that can expand beyond the original dispute and damage the entire relationship (Infante, 1988; Turk & Monahan, 1999).

## Assertion

In **assertion,** a speaker's statement expresses thoughts and feelings clearly. Unlike an aggressive message, it does not attack the other person (Infante & Wigley, 1986). One format for an assertive message consists of five elements (Miller et al., 1975):

1. *A description of the observable behavior that prompted your message.* The key here is to describe the behavior objectively, without blaming or name-calling. Notice how each of the following statements just describes the

Get it yourself.

© 1988 by Tom Cheney. Permission courtesy of the artist.

facts: "When you didn't call me after you said you would . . ." and "Last week you asked me to buy the tickets, and now you tell me you don't want them . . . ."

2. *Your interpretation of the behavior.* Be sure to label the interpretation as subjective, not as a matter of fact. For example, "I get the idea you're mad at me" is a better statement than "Why are you mad at me?"

3. *The feelings that arise from your interpretation.* Notice the difference between saying "I get the idea you're mad at me" and the more complete description "I get the idea you're mad at me *and I feel hurt* (or *defensive, confused,* or *sorry*)." Review Chapters 5 and 8 for suggestions on how to express emotions clearly.

4. *The consequences of the information you have shared so far.* Consequences can describe what happens to *you,* the speaker ("When you tease me, I avoid you"), what happens to the *target of the message* ("When you drink too much, you start to drive dangerously"), or what happens to *others* ("When you play the radio so loud, it wakes up the baby").

5. *An intention statement.* Some intention statements are requests ("I hope you'll come again"). Others describe how you plan to act

("Unless we can work out some sort of studying arrangement, I may have to find a new place to live").

Sally could have used this format to express herself assertively to Ralph: "Ralph, I've been bothered by some things lately, and I'd like to talk them over with you. [She identifies the problem as hers and not Ralph's.] When you ask me to take care of your apartment two or three times a month and borrow food and cash without returning them [behavior], I don't think you realize the inconveniences I face [interpretation]. I didn't mind until recently—that's why I haven't said anything before—but I'm starting to feel resentful [feeling], and I'm afraid it might spoil our friendship [consequence]. I don't want that to happen [intention], so I'd like to figure out some way I can help you when you really need it but without it being quite so much of a burden on me [another intention]."

This sort of assertive message gets results, especially in our most important interpersonal relationships. While less direct forms may work in nonintimate situations, directness is more effective at getting compliance in intimate relationships (Jordan & Roloff, 1990). Furthermore, a straightforward approach is likely to result in greater relational satisfaction (Honeycutt & Wiemann, 1999; Vangelisti & Crumley, 1998). When the issue is important and the commitment between partners is high, speaking from the heart instead of beating around the bush seems to be the best approach.

Besides boosting your chances of getting what you want, an assertive approach maintains the self-respect of both people. As a result, people who manage their conflicts assertively usually feel better about themselves and each other afterward, which is not always the case with other styles.

## Which Style to Use?

Although communicating assertively might seem like the most attractive alternative to the other styles described in this chapter, it's an oversimplification to imagine that there is a single "best" way to respond to conflicts (Canary & Cupach, 1988; Canary & Spitzberg, 1987). Generally speaking, assertive tactics, such as asking for information and considering alternatives, are preferable to such aggressive tactics as shouting or blaming. But we've already seen that there are times when aggression or even nonassertion is appropriate. Occasionally, you may have to shout to get the other person's attention, and other times the smartest approach may be to swallow the other person's abuse instead of responding.

A personal conflict style isn't necessarily a personality "trait" that carries across all situations. Hocker and Wilmot (1997) suggest that roughly 50 percent of the population changes their style from one situation to another. As you learned in Chapter 1, this sort of behavioral flexibility is a characteristic of competent communicators. Several factors govern which style to use:

**The Situation**   When someone clearly has more power than you, nonassertion may be the best approach. If the boss tells you to fill that order *now!* you probably ought to do it without comment. A more assertive response ("When you use that tone of voice, I feel defensive") might be clearer, but it could also cost you your job. Likewise, an aggressive message is sometimes most appropriate. At one time or another, it will probably be necessary to raise your voice to show that you mean business.

**The Other Person**   Although assertiveness has the best chance of success with many people, some receivers respond better to other approaches. You probably know some communicators who are so sensitive or defensive that an assertive approach would be too much for them to handle. Others are so insensitive that aggressiveness is necessary, at least to get their attention.

**Your Goals**   When you want to solve a problem, assertiveness is probably the best approach. But there are other reasons for communicating in a

## MANAGING CONFLICTS IN THE HOSPITAL: PRACTICAL AND ETHICAL CHOICES

Sooner or later, almost every employee has to choose between satisfying a customer and following the boss's orders. This sort of dilemma is especially difficult when the "employee" is a nurse, the "boss" is a physician, the "customer" is a patient, and the questions involve life and death. What should a nurse do, for example, when a cancer patient who only has a short time to live asks, "How am I doing?" and the doctor has ordered the bad news to be withheld? How should a nurse respond when a patient has given "informed consent" for a surgical procedure without understanding that the results (e.g., a radical mastectomy if cancer is found) could be life-altering?

Three University of Maine researchers explored how nurses communicate when faced with this sort of dilemma. They asked thirty-three female nurses in three metropolitan hospitals to recall an incident in which a physician either withheld or distorted information given to a patient for whom she was caring. The nurses then completed a questionnaire describing their likely responses to four hypothetical situations in which their responsibilities to patients and physicians would conflict. For example, in one a doctor accidentally nicks the bladder of a patient during surgery, who is unaware of the mishap. To tell the truth means the loss of rapport between the doctor and patient, as well as a conflict between the nurse and doctor. To remain silent or lie would deny the patient his right to know about his treatment.

Dilemmas like these present both ethical and practical challenges. The nurses described them as "no-win" situations because, as one put it, "someone would end up a victim, the doctor or the patient." "You're damned if you do, damned if you don't," said another. A third comment explained: "As a patient advocate . . . it's important to tell them [patients] what their rights are, [but] it would get me into trouble with the surgeons."

An analysis of the nurses' response showed that no single conflict management style was chosen in all situations. One important factor was an individual nurse's sense of whether or not it was her obligation to question a physician's decisions. Nurses also seemed to conduct cost-benefit analysis in deciding what to do or say: If the consequences of following the doctor's orders might result in serious medical or psychological consequences, the nurses felt a greater need to speak up, either to the doctor or the patient. Practical questions also played a role in the nurses' decisions about how to respond: whether doing so would change anything, whether they could expect superiors and colleagues to back them up, and the anticipated reaction of the doctor.

The authors of the study gave an example of how the calculus of dimensions like these operates: "[If] the nurse expects little institutional support, anticipates little harm to the patient, has experienced the problem frequently in the past and has little trust in the nursing administration, there is little reason to expect success using a collaborative strategy [i.e., approaching the doctor]." In such a case, avoidance is a logical response. Given the opposite organizational situation, collaboration is a logical choice of conflict strategy.

What lessons does this study offer? It shows clearly that deciding how to manage conflict isn't a simple matter. Each communication challenge comes with its own unique set of factors that must be considered in choosing how to respond. It also suggests that competent communicators must consider a range of variables as they try to make rational, thoughtful choices about how to manage difficult situations.

Marin, M. J., Sherblom, J. C., & Shipps, T. B. (1994). Contextual influences on nurses' conflict management strategies. *Western Journal of Communication, 58,* 201–228.

conflict. Sometimes your overriding concern is to calm down an enraged or upset communicator. For example, tolerating an outburst from your crotchety and sick neighbor is probably better than standing up for yourself and triggering a stroke. Likewise, you might choose to sit quietly through the nagging of a family member rather than ruin Thanksgiving dinner. In other cases, your moral principles might compel an aggressive statement even though it might not get you what you originally sought: "I've had enough of your racist jokes. I've tried to explain why they're so offensive, but you obviously haven't listened. I'm leaving!" And your goal may be to be seen in a favorable way, in which case you may want to avoid being aggressive. In a study of university students in Turkey, friendship preferences revealed that aggression was the least preferred behavior and compromising the most preferred (Tezer, 1999).

# Conflict in Relational Systems

So far, we have been describing individual conflict styles. Even though the style you choose in a conflict is important, your approach isn't the only factor that will determine how a conflict unfolds. In reality, conflict is *relational:* Its character is usually determined by the way the people involved interact (Hocker & Wilmot, 1997; Knapp et al., 1988). For example, you might be determined to handle a conflict with your neighbors assertively, only to be driven to aggression by their uncooperative nature or even to nonassertion by their physical threats. Likewise, you might plan to hint to a professor that you are bothered by his apparent indifference but wind up discussing the matter in an open, assertive way in reaction to his constructive suggestion. Examples like these indicate that conflict isn't just a matter of individual choice. Rather, it depends on how the partners interact.

When two or more people are in a long-term relationship, they develop their own **relational conflict style**—a pattern of managing disagreements

that repeats itself over time. The mutual influence parties have on one another is so powerful that it can overcome our disposition to handle conflicts in the manner that comes most easily to one or the other (Burggraf & Sillars, 1987). As we will soon see, some relational conflict styles are constructive, while others can make life miserable and threaten relationships.

## Complementary, Symmetrical, and Parallel Styles

Partners in interpersonal relationships—and impersonal ones, too—can use one of three styles to manage their conflicts. In relationships with a **complementary conflict style,** the partners use different but mutually reinforcing behaviors. In a **symmetrical conflict style,** both people use the same tactics. Some relationships are characterized by a **parallel conflict style,** which shifts between complementary and symmetrical patterns from one issue to another. Table 12.2 illustrates how the same conflict can unfold in very different ways, depending on whether the partners' communication is symmetrical or complementary. A parallel style would alternate between these two forms, depending on the situation.

Research shows that a complementary "fight-flight" style is common in many unhappy marriages. One partner—most commonly the wife—addresses the conflict directly, while the other—usually the husband—withdraws (Krokoff, 1990; Sillars et al., 1984). It's easy to see how this pattern can lead to a cycle of increasing hostility and isolation, since each partner punctuates the conflict differently, blaming the other for making matters worse. "I withdraw because she's so critical," a husband might say. However, the wife wouldn't organize the sequence in the same way. "I criticize because he withdraws" would be her perception.

Complementary styles aren't the only ones that can lead to problems. Some distressed relationships suffer from destructively symmetrical communication. If both partners treat one another with matching hostility, one threat and insult leads

**Table 12.2**

| Complementary and Symmetrical Conflict Styles | | |
| --- | --- | --- |
| **Situation** | **Complementary Styles** | **Symmetrical Styles** |
| Wife is upset because husband is spending little time at home. | Wife complains; husband withdraws, spending even less time at home. | Wife complains. Husband responds angrily and defensively. |
| Female employee is offended when boss calls her "sweetie." | Employee objects to boss, explaining her reasons for being offended. Boss apologizes for his unintentional insult. | Employee tries to make boss understand how she feels by calling *him* "cutie." The boss gets the hint and stops using the term. |
| Parents are uncomfortable about teenager's new friends. | Parents express concerns. Teen dismisses them, saying, "There's nothing to worry about." | Teen expresses concern that parents are being too protective. Parents disagree. |

to another in an **escalatory spiral**. If the partners both withdraw from one another instead of facing their problems, a complementary **de-escalatory spiral** results, in which the satisfaction and vitality ebb from the relationship, leaving it a shell of its former self.

As Table 12.2 shows, both complementary and symmetrical behavior can produce "good" results as well as "bad" ones. If the complementary behaviors are positive, then a positive spiral results, and the conflict stands a good chance of being resolved. This is the case in the second example in Table 12.2, in which the boss is open to hearing the employee's concerns, listening willingly as the employee talks. Here, a complementary talk-listen pattern works well.

Symmetrical styles also can be beneficial, as another look at the boss-employee example shows. Many women have found that giving insensitive men a taste of their own sexist medicine is an effective way to end harassment without provoking an argument. The clearest example of a constructive symmetry occurs when both people communicate assertively, listening to one another's concerns and working together to resolve them. The potential for this sort of solution occurs in the parent-teenager conflict in Table 12.2. With

enough mutual respect and careful listening, both the parents and their teenager can understand one another's concerns and possibly find a way to give all three people what they want.

## Intimate and Aggressive Styles

Another way to look at conflict styles is to examine the interaction between intimacy and aggression. The following scheme was originally used to describe communication between couples, but it also works well for other types of relationships.

- *Nonintimate-Aggressive:* Partners fight but are unsuccessful at satisfying important content and relational goals. In some relationships, aggression is expressed directly: "Forget it. I'm not going to another stupid party with your friends. All they do is gossip and eat." In other relationships, indirect aggression is the norm: (sarcastically) "Sure, I'd *love* to go to another party with your friends." Neither of these approaches is satisfying, since there are few rewards to justify the costs of the unpleasantness.

- *Nonintimate-Nonaggressive:* The partners avoid conflicts—and one another—instead of facing issues head-on: "You won't be coming home for the holidays? Oh well, I guess that's okay. . . ."

## CONFLICT IS A WAY OF CONNECTING

My father died almost two years ago. My mom misses him—which seems logical until you take into account that their relationship was one of the most conflict-ridden I have known. They fought constantly, and about everything and anything, including money, relatives, cooking, and where to vacation.

My brothers and I never really understood what kept them together. I think now I understand: their constant bickering was their way of connecting, of saying—although in a strange way, I guess—"I love you and care about you. Why else would I take the time and energy to fight with you?" The opposite of love isn't hate, it's indifference, and my parents were anything but indifferent to each other.

I don't plan on copying their way of interacting. I won't, however, be afraid of conflict either. Done well, I guess conflict is one of the highest compliments we can pay another person—almost, but not quite as high, as saying, "I love you."

rectly, but one way or another they manage to prevent issues from interfering with their relationship.

The pattern partners choose may reveal a great deal about the kind of relationship they have chosen. Mary Ann Fitzpatrick (1977, 1988) identified three types of couples: separates, independents, and traditionals. Further research revealed that partners in each type of relationship approached conflict in a different manner (Fitzpatrick, 1988; Fitzpatrick et al., 1982). Separates took a nonintimate-nonaggressive approach (and were the least satisfied of all subjects studied). They maintained a neutral emotional climate and kept their discussion of conflict to a minimum. Successful independents were best described as intimate-aggressive. They expressed negative emotions frequently, but also sought and revealed a large amount of personal information. Satisfied traditional couples fit the intimate-nonaggressive pattern, communicating more positive and less negative information than did independents.

Information like this suggests that there's no single "best" relational conflict style. Some families or couples may fight intensely but love one another just as strongly. Others might handle issues more rationally and calmly. Even a non-intimate style can work well when there's no desire to have an interpersonal relationship. For example, you might be willing to accommodate the demands of an eccentric professor for a semester, since rolling with the punches gets you the education you are seeking without provoking a confrontation that could be upsetting and costly.

## Conflict Rituals

When people have been in a relationship for some time, their communication often develops into **conflict rituals**—unacknowledged but very real repeating patterns of interlocking behavior (Hocker & Wilmot, 1997). Consider a few common rituals:

> A young child interrupts his parents, demanding to be included in their conversation. At first the

Relationships of this sort can be quite stable, but because this pattern of communication doesn't confront and resolve problems, the vitality and satisfaction can decline over time.

- *Intimate-Aggressive:* This pattern combines aggression and intimacy in a manner that might seem upsetting to outsiders, but it can work well in some relationships. Lovers may fight like cats and dogs but then make up just as intensely. Coworkers might argue about how to get the job done but cherish their association.
- *Intimate-Nonaggressive:* This sort of relationship has a low amount of attacking or blaming. Partners may confront one another directly or indi-

parents tell the child to wait, but he whines and cries until the parents find it easier to listen to than to ignore the fussing.

A couple fights. One partner leaves. The other accepts blame for the problem and begs forgiveness. The first partner returns, and a happy reunion takes place. Soon they fight again.

One friend is unhappy with the other. He or she withdraws until the other asks what's wrong. "Nothing," the first replies. The questioning persists until the problem is finally out in the open. The friends then solve the issue and continue happily until the next problem arises, when the pattern repeats itself.

There's nothing inherently wrong with the interaction in many rituals. Consider the examples above. In the first, the child's whining may be the only way he can get the parent's attention. In the second, both partners might use the fighting as a way to blow off steam, and both might find that the joy of a reunion is worth the grief of the separation. The third ritual might work well when one friend is more assertive than the other.

Rituals can cause problems, though, when they become the *only* way relational partners handle their conflicts. As you learned in Chapter 1, competent communicators have a large repertoire of behaviors, and they are able to choose the most effective response for a given situation. Relying on one pattern to handle all conflicts is no more effective than using a screwdriver to handle every home repair, or putting the same seasoning in every dish you cook: What works in one situation isn't likely to succeed in many others. Conflict rituals may be familiar and comfortable, but they aren't the best way to solve the variety of conflicts that are part of any relationship.

## Variables in Conflict Styles

By now, you can see that every relational system is unique. The communication patterns in one family, business, or classroom are likely to be very different from any other. But along with the differences that arise in individual relationships, there are two powerful variables that affect the way people manage conflict: biological sex and culture. We will now take a brief look at each of these factors and see how they affect how conflict is managed.

### Biological Sex

Some research suggests that men and women often approach conflicts differently (e.g., Rosenfeld, 1994; Wood, 1993). Even in childhood, there is evidence that boys are (on average, of course) more likely to be aggressive, demanding, and competitive, while girls are more cooperative and accommodating. Studies of children from preschool to early adolescence have shown that boys try to get their way by ordering one another around: "Lie down." "Get off my steps." "Gimme your arm." By contrast, girls are more likely to make proposals for action that begin with the word *let's:* "Let's go find some." "Let's ask her if she has any bottles." "Let's move *these* out *first*" (Tannen, 1990). Whereas boys tell each other what role to take in pretend play ("Come on, be a doctor"), girls more commonly ask each other what role they want ("Will you be the patient for a few minutes?") or make a joint proposal ("We can both be doctors"). Furthermore, boys often make demands without offering an explanation ("Look, man, I want the wire cutters right now"). In contrast, girls often give reasons for their suggestions ("We gotta clean 'em first 'cause they got germs").

Differences like these often persist into adulthood. One survey of college students revealed that men and women viewed conflicts in contrasting ways (Collier, 1991). Regardless of their cultural background, female students described men as being concerned with power and more interested in content than in relational issues. Sentences used to describe male conflict styles included: "The most important thing to males in conflict is their egos," "Men don't worry about feelings," and "Men are more direct." In contrast, women were described as being more concerned with maintaining the relationship during a conflict. Sentences used to describe female conflict styles included: "Women are better listeners," "Women try to solve problems

## FOCUS ON RESEARCH

### FRIENDS IN CONFLICT: DOES BIOLOGICAL SEX MAKE A DIFFERENCE?

Think about recent conflicts you've had with your friends. Do you argue about the same issues with your female friends as you do with your male friends? Wendy Samter and William Cupach explored the similarities and differences between same- and opposite-sex conflicts when they asked 524 young adults to describe the nature of the disagreements with their friends.

The researchers found some differences in the topics men and women deal with in their same-sex friendships. Men argue more about shared activities than women (e.g., "Should we play tennis or go to a movie?"), while women argue more about shared space/possessions ("I wish you wouldn't borrow my clothes without asking"). By contrast, men and women who are friends with members of the opposite sex tend to struggle over different topics, including relational intimacy (e.g., "Are we just friends or something more?"), rule violations ("You didn't keep your promise to call!"), communication problems ("You don't understand me"), annoying behaviors ("I hate it when you tell those stupid jokes/talk about that soap opera"), and relationship choices ("I don't see what you like about Casey").

While there were notable differences in the conflict topics that arose between same- and opposite-sex friends, the researchers point out that they were a matter of degree, and that all friends eventually disagree about similar issues to a greater or lesser extent. Samter and Cupach concluded that "the men and women in our sample were clearly more similar than different in the sources of conflict they perceived in their same- and cross-sex friendships."

Samter, W., & Cupach, W. R. (1998). Friendly fire: Topical variations in conflict among same- and cross-sex friends. *Communication Studies, 49,* 121–138.

without controlling the other person," and "Females are more concerned with others' feelings."

Differences of this nature don't mean that men with attitudes like these are incapable of forming good relationships. Instead, their notions of what a good relationship is may be different. For some men, friendship and aggression aren't mutually exclusive. In fact, many strong male relationships are built around competition—at work or in athletics, for example. Women also can be competitive, but they are more likely to use logical reasoning and bargaining than aggression (Papa & Natalle, 1989). When men communicate with women, they become less aggressive and more cooperative than they are in all-male groups.

In contrast with the "Men are from Mars, Women are from Venus" view of conflict, another body of research suggests that the differences in how the two sexes handle conflict are rather small, and not at all representative of the stereotypical picture of aggressive men and passive women (Gayle et al., 1998). Where differences between the sexes do occur, they can sometimes be exactly the opposite of sex-role stereotypes of aggressive men and accommodating women. For example, when the actual conflict behaviors of both sexes are observed, women turn out to be more assertive than men about expressing their ideas and feelings, and men are more likely to withdraw from discussing issues (Canary et al., 1995).

"Oh, it's just more white-male stuff."

© The New Yorker Collection 1997 Edward Koren from cartoonbank.com. All Rights Reserved.

In other cases, people may *think* that there are greater differences in male and female ways of handling conflicts than actually exist (Allen, 1998). People who assume that men are aggressive and women accommodating may notice behavior that fits these stereotypes ("See how much he bosses her around. A typical man!"). On the other hand, behavior that doesn't fit these preconceived ideas (accommodating men, pushy women) goes unnoticed (Allen, 1998).

What, then, can we conclude about the influence of gender on conflict? Research has demonstrated that there are, indeed, some small but measurable differences in the two sexes. But, while men and women may have characteristically different conflict styles, the individual style of each communicator is more important than his or her sex in shaping the way he or she handles conflict.

## Culture

The ways in which people communicate during conflicts vary widely from one culture to another. As you read in Chapter 2, the kind of straight-talking, assertive approach that characterizes many North Americans is not the norm in other parts of the world (Gudykunst & Ting-Toomey, 1988). In individualistic cultures like the United States, the goals, rights, and needs of each person are considered important, and most people would agree that it is an individual's right to stand up for himself or herself. By contrast, collectivist cultures (more common in Latin America and Asia) consider the concerns of the group to be more important than those of any individual. In these cultures, the kind of assertive behavior that might seem perfectly appropriate to a North American would be rude and insensitive.

Another factor that distinguishes the assertiveness that is so valued in North American and Northern European cultures from the approaches of other cultures is the difference between high- and low-context cultural styles (Ting-Toomey, 1988). As Chapter 2 explains in detail, "low-context" cultures like the United States place a premium on being direct and literal. By contrast, "high-context" cultures like Japan value self-restraint and avoid confrontation. Communicators in these cultures derive meaning from a variety of unspoken rules, such as the context, social conventions, and hints. Preserving and honoring the "face" of the other person is a prime goal, and communicators go to great lengths to avoid any communication that might risk embarrassing a conversational partner. For this reason, what seems like "beating around the bush" to an American would be polite to an Asian. In Japan, for example, even a simple request like "close the door" would be too straightforward (Okabe, 1987). A more indirect statement, such as "it is somewhat cold today," would be more appropriate. To take a more important example, Japanese are reluctant to say "no" to a request. A more likely answer would be "let me think about it for a while," which anyone familiar with Japanese culture would recognize as a refusal.

It isn't necessary to look at Asia to encounter cultural differences in conflict. The style of some other familiar cultures differs in important ways from the Northern European and North American

## FILM CLIP

### CULTURE AND CONFLICT: *THE JOY LUCK CLUB*

*The Joy Luck Club* is not one story but many, told in film through flashbacks, narrations, and gripping portrayals. The primary stories involve four Chinese women and their daughters. The mothers all flee difficult situations in China to start new lives in the United States, where they raise their daughters with a mixture of Chinese and American styles. Many of the movie's conflicts are rooted in cultural value clashes.

The mothers were raised in the high-context, collectivist environment of China, where open conflict is discouraged and individual needs (particularly of women) are submerged for the larger good. To achieve their goals, the mothers use a variety of indirect and passive-aggressive methods. Their daughters, raised in the United States, adopt a more low-context, direct form of communication. They are also more assertive and aggressive in their conflict styles, particularly when dealing with their mothers.

The daughters have a harder time dealing with the men in their lives. For example, Rose (Rosalind Chao) begins her relationship with Ted (Andrew McCarthy) very assertively, telling him candidly what she thinks and how she feels about him (he is charmed by her directness). They marry and she becomes an accommodator, constantly submerging her needs for his. Rather than liking Rose's accommo-

dating, Ted comes to despise it. He exhorts her to be more assertive: "Once in awhile, I would like to hear what you want. I'd like to hear your voice, even if we disagree." He then suggests that they separate.

Several of the stories have happy endings. In Rose's case, she fights for her rights with Ted— and ultimately they reconcile. In fact, each woman in the movie takes a stand on an important issue in her life, and most of the outcomes are positive.

The women in *The Joy Luck Club* learn to both embrace and reject aspects of their cultural heritage as they attempt to manage their conflicts effectively.

norm. These cultures see verbal disputes as a form of intimacy and even a game. For example, Americans visiting Greece often think they are witnessing an argument when they are overhearing a friendly conversation (Tannen, 1990). A comparative study of American and Italian nursery school children showed that one of the Italian children's favorite pastimes was a kind of heated debating that Italians call *discussione* but that Americans would regard as arguing. Likewise, research has shown that in the conversations of working-class Jewish speakers of Eastern European origin, arguments are used as a means of being sociable.

Within the United States, the ethnic background of communicators also plays a role in their ideas about conflict. When a group of African-American, Mexican-American, and Euro-American college students were asked about their views regarding conflict, some important differences emerged (Collier, 1991). For example, Euro-Americans seem more willing to accept conflict as a natural part of relationships, while Mexican Americans describe the short- and long-term dangers of disagreeing. Euro-Americans' willingness to experience conflicts may be part of their individualistic, low-context communication style of speaking directly and avoiding uncertainty. It's not surprising that people from more-collective, high-context cultures that emphasize harmony among people with close relationships tend to handle conflicts in less direct ways. With differences like these, it's easy to imagine how two friends, lovers, or fellow workers from different cultural backgrounds might have trouble finding a conflict style that is comfortable for both of them.

Despite these differences, it's important to realize that culture isn't the only factor that influences the way people think about conflict or how they behave when they disagree. Some research (e.g., Beatty & McCroskey, 1997) suggests that our approach to conflict may be part of our biological makeup. Furthermore, scholarship suggests a person's self-concept is more powerful than his or her culture in determining conflict style (Oetzel, 1998). An argumentative person raised in an environment that downplays conflict is likely to be more aggressive than an unassertive one who grew up in a culture where arguments are common.

Beyond individual temperament, the environment in which we are raised can shape the way we approach conflict. Parental conflict style plays a role. Some research has revealed a significant relationship between the way a mother handles conflict and the style used by her adult children (Martin et al., 1997). Interestingly, there was no significant relationship between a father's conflict style and that of his children.

Beyond the family, the "culture" of each relationship can shape how we behave (Messman & Canary, 1998). You might handle disagreements calmly in a job where rationality and civility are the norm, but shriek like a banshee at home if that's the way you and a relational partner handle disputes.

## Methods of Conflict Resolution

Whatever the style, every conflict is a struggle to have one's goals met. Sometimes that struggle succeeds, and in other cases it fails. In the remainder of this chapter, we look at various

approaches to resolving conflicts and see which ones are most promising.

### Win-Lose

In **win-lose problem solving,** one person gets satisfaction while the other comes up short. People resort to this method of resolving disputes when they perceive a situation as being an "either-or" one: Either I get my way, or you get your way. The most clear-cut examples of win-lose situations are certain games, such as baseball or poker, in which the rules require a winner and a loser. Some interpersonal issues seem to fit into this win-lose framework: two coworkers seeking a promotion to the same job, or a couple arguing over how to spend their limited money.

Power is the distinguishing characteristic in win-lose problem solving, for it's necessary to defeat an opponent to get what you want. The most obvious kind of power is physical. Some parents threaten their children with warnings such as "Stop misbehaving or I'll send you to your room." Adults who use physical power to deal with each other usually aren't so blunt, but the threat often exists nonetheless. For instance, behind the legal system is the implied threat "Follow the rules, or we'll lock you up."

Real or implied force isn't the only kind of power used in conflicts. People who rely on authority of many types engage in win-lose methods without ever threatening physical coercion. In most jobs, supervisors have the potential to use their authority in the assignment of working hours, job promotions, desirable or undesirable tasks, and, of course, in firing an unsatisfactory employee. Teachers can use the power of grades to coerce students to act in desired ways.

Intellectual or mental power also can be a tool for conquering an opponent. Everyone is familiar with stories of how a seemingly weak hero defeats a stronger enemy through cleverness, showing that brains can triumph over brawn. In a less admirable way, crazymakers can defeat their partners by using effective, if destructive, means: inducing guilt, avoiding issues, withholding desired behaviors, false accommodating, and so on.

Even the usually admired democratic principle of majority rule is a win-lose method of resolving conflicts. However fair it may be, the system results in one group getting its way and another being unsatisfied.

The win-lose method may sometimes be necessary when there are truly scarce resources or when only one person can achieve satisfaction. For instance, if two suitors want to marry the same person, only one can succeed. To return to an earlier example, it's often true that only one applicant can be hired for a job. Still, don't be too willing to assume that your conflicts are necessarily win-lose. Many situations that seem to require a loser can be resolved to everyone's satisfaction.

There is a second kind of situation in which win-lose is the best method of conflict. Even when cooperation is possible, if the other person insists on defeating you, then the most logical response might be to defend yourself by fighting back. "It takes two to tango," the cliché goes, and it takes two to cooperate. Some people are so resistant to constructive problem solving

*"It's not enough that we succeed. Cats must also fail."*

that it may be fruitless to try that approach. In one study, employees identified by their managers as "difficult" consistently refused to cooperate in collaborative problem-solving approaches (Monroe et al., 1989). Instead, they responded with passive-aggressive strategies—refusing to accept managers' feedback, offering excuses, and using avoidance. When faced with this sort of absolute refusal to cooperate, it may be self-defeating for you to hang on to a collaborative approach.

A final and much less frequent justification for trying to defeat another person occurs when the other person is clearly behaving in a wrongful manner and when defeating that person is the only way to stop the wrongful behavior. Few people would deny the importance of restraining a person who is deliberately harming others, even if the belligerent person's freedom is sacrificed in the process. However, only in the most extreme circumstances is it productive in the long run to coerce others into behaving as we think they should.

## Lose-Lose

In **lose-lose problem solving**, neither side is satisfied with the outcome. Although the name of this approach is so discouraging that it's hard to imagine how anyone could willingly use it, lose-lose is a fairly common way to handle conflicts. In many instances the partners will both strive to be winners, but as a result of the struggle, both wind up losers. On the international scene, many wars illustrate this sad point. A nation that gains military victory at the cost of thousands of lives, large amounts of resources, and a damaged national consciousness hasn't truly won much. On an interpersonal level, the same principle holds true. Most of us have seen battles of pride in which both people strike out and both suffer.

## Compromise

Unlike lose-lose outcomes, a **compromise** gives both people at least some of what they want, although both sacrifice part of their goals. People usually settle for a compromise when it seems that partial satisfaction is the best they can hope for. Although a compromise may be better than losing everything, this approach hardly seems to deserve the positive image it has with some people. In his valuable book on conflict resolution, Albert Filley

### FILM CLIP

### COMPETING IN THE GAME OF LIFE:
### *HE GOT GAME*

Jesus Shuttlesworth (Ray Allen) is a high school basketball star who has received offers to play for universities and pro teams across the country. That's good news, right? Not for Shuttlesworth. He becomes a pawn in a greedy bidding war between coaches, agents, friends, and family members.

The most significant of his conflicts is with his father, Jake (Denzel Washington). Jake is in prison for accidentally killing his wife, and his son has never forgiven him. Jake is given a one-week parole because the governor wants him to convince Jesus to attend Big State University. If Jake succeeds, his prison sentence will be reduced—but this leads to more father-son conflict.

As Table 12.4 (see page 379) shows, win-lose competing is a good conflict strategy when sustaining or maintaining a relationship with the other person is unimportant to you. Competition is the method of choice for Jesus because he wants nothing to do with Jake. He walks away from conversations with his father, even though he holds the power to commute Jake's sentence in his hands. In a symbolic moment near the end of the story, the two men play a one-on-one basketball game to determine the fate of their relationship.

Jesus and Jake ultimately learn that win-lose solutions can end up hurting both of them, and that forgiveness can be an important part of repairing relationships damaged by years of unresolved conflict.

**Table 12.3**

| Differences between Win-Lose and Win-Win Problem Solving | |
|---|---|
| **Win-Lose** | **Win-Win** |
| Conflicting interests | Shared interests |
| Negotiations based on power | Negotiations based on trust |
| Low self-disclosure | High self-disclosure |
| Concern only for self | Concern for self and for other |

(1975, p. 23) makes an interesting observation about our attitudes toward this method. Why is it, he asks, that if someone says "I will compromise my values," we view the action unfavorably, yet we talk admiringly about people in a conflict who compromise to reach a solution? Although compromises may be the best obtainable result in some conflicts, it's important to realize that both people in a dispute can often work together to find much better solutions. In such cases, *compromise* is a negative word.

Most of us are surrounded by the results of bad compromises. Consider a common example, the conflict between one person's desire to smoke cigarettes and another's need for clean air. The win-lose outcomes on this issue are obvious: Either the smoker abstains or the nonsmoker gets polluted lungs—neither option a very satisfying one. But a compromise in which the smoker gets to enjoy only a rare cigarette or must retreat outdoors and in which the nonsmoker still must inhale some fumes or feel like an ogre is hardly better. Both sides have lost a considerable amount of both comfort and goodwill. Of course, the costs involved in other compromises are even greater. For example, if a divorced couple compromises on child care by haggling over custody and then finally grudgingly agrees to split the time with their children, it's hard to say that anybody has won.

Some compromises do leave everyone satisfied. You and the seller might settle on a price for a used car that is between what the seller was ask-ing and what you wanted to pay. While neither of you got everything you wanted, the outcome would still leave both of you satisfied. Likewise, you and your companion might agree to see a film that is the second choice for both of you in order to spend an evening together. As long as everyone is satisfied with an outcome, compromise can be an effective way to resolve conflicts.

## Win-Win

As its name suggests, the outcome of a **win-win problem-solving** style is different from the outcome of a win-lose conflict. Results that satisfy everyone are no accident: They usually result from an approach that is very different from those we've discussed so far (see Table 12.3).

In win-win problem solving, the goal is to find a solution that satisfies the needs of everyone involved. Not only do the partners avoid trying to win at each other's expense, but there's also a belief that working together can provide a solution in which all reach their goals without needing to compromise.

One way to understand how no-lose problem solving works is to look at a few examples:

■ A boss and her employees get into a conflict over scheduling. The employees often want to shift the hours they're scheduled to work so that they can accommodate personal needs, whereas the boss needs to be sure that the operation is fully staffed at all times. After some discussion they arrive at a solution that satisfies everyone:

The boss works up a monthly master schedule indicating the hours during which each employee is responsible for being on the job. Employees are free to trade hours among themselves, as long as the operation is fully staffed at all times.

- A conflict about testing arises in a college class. Due to sickness or other reasons, a certain number of students need to take exams on a makeup basis. The instructor doesn't want to give these students any advantage over their peers and also doesn't want to go through the task of making up a brand-new test for just a few people. After working on the problem together, instructor and students arrive at a no-lose solution. The instructor will hand out a list of twenty possible exam questions in advance of the test day. At examination time, five of these questions are randomly drawn for the class to answer. Students who take makeup exams will draw from the same pool of questions at the time of their test. In this way, makeup students are taking a fresh test without the instructor having to create a new exam.

- A newly married husband and wife found themselves arguing frequently over their budget. The husband enjoyed buying impractical and enjoyable items for himself and for the house, whereas the wife feared that such purchases would ruin their carefully constructed budget. Their solution was to set aside a small amount of money each month for "fun" purchases. The amount was small enough to be affordable yet gave the husband a chance to escape from their Spartan lifestyle. Additionally, the wife was satisfied with the arrangement, because the luxury money was now a budget category by itself, which got rid of the "out of control" feeling that came when her husband made unexpected purchases. The plan worked so well that the couple continued to use it even after their income rose, by increasing the amount devoted to luxuries.

Although such solutions might seem obvious when you read them here, a moment's reflection will show you that such cooperative problem solving is all too rare. People faced with these types of conflicts often resort to such dysfunctional styles of communicating as withdrawing, avoiding, or competing, and they wind up handling the issues in a manner that results in either a win-lose or lose-lose outcome. As we pointed out earlier, it's a shame to see one or both partners in a conflict come away unsatisfied when they could both get what they're seeking by communicating in a no-lose manner.

Win-win problem solving works best when it follows a seven-step approach that is based on a plan developed by Deborah Weider-Hatfield (1981):

1. **Define your needs.** Begin by deciding what you want or need. Sometimes the answer is obvious, as in our earlier example of the neighbor whose loud stereo music kept others awake. In other instances, however, the apparent problem masks a more fundamental one. Consider an example: After dating for a few months, Beverly started to call Jim after they parted for the evening—a "goodnight call." Although the calling was fine with Jim at the beginning, he began to find it irritating after several weeks.

   At first, Jim thought his aggravation focused on the nuisance of talking late at night when he was ready for sleep. More self-examination showed that his irritation centered on the relational message he thought Beverly's calls implied: that she was either snooping on Jim or was so insecure she needed constant assurances of his love. Once Jim recognized the true sources of his irritation, his needs became clear: (1) to have Beverly's trust and (2) to be free of her insecurities.

   Because your needs won't always be clear, it's often necessary to think about a problem alone, before approaching the other person involved. Talking to a third person can sometimes help you sort out your thoughts. In either case, you should explore both the apparent content of your dissatisfaction and the relational issues that may lurk behind it.

2. **Share your needs with the other person.** Once you've defined your needs, it's time to share them with your partner. Two guidelines are important here: First, be sure to choose a time and place that is suitable. Unloading on a tired or busy partner lowers the odds that your concerns will be well received. Likewise, be sure you are at your best: Don't bring an issue up when your anger may cause you to say things you'll later regret, when your discouragement blows the problem out of proportion, or when you're distracted by other business. Making a date to discuss the problem—after dinner, over a cup of coffee, or even a day in advance—often can boost the odds of a successful outcome.

   The second guideline for sharing a problem is to use the descriptive "I" language outlined in Chapter 5 and the assertive message format on pages 361-362. Rather than implying blame, messages worded in this way convey how your partner's behavior affects you. Notice how Jim's use of the assertive message format conveys a descriptive, nonjudgmental attitude as he shares his concerns with Beverly: "When you call me after every date [sense data], I begin to wonder whether you're checking up on me [interpretation of Beverly's behavior]. I've also started to think that you're feeling insecure about whether I care about you and that you need lots of reassurance [more interpretation]. I'm starting to feel closed in by the calls [feeling], and I feel myself pulling back from you [consequence]. I don't like the way we're headed, and I don't think it's necessary. I'd like to know whether you are feeling insecure and to find a way that we can feel sure about each other's feelings without needing so much reassurance [intentions]."

3. **Listen to the other person's needs.** Once your own wants and needs are clear, it's time to find out what the other person wants and needs. (Now the listening skills described in Chapter 7 and the supportive behaviors described in Chapter 11 become most important.) When Jim began to talk to Beverly about her telephoning, he learned some interesting things. In his haste to hang up the phone the first few times she called, he had given her the impression that he didn't care about her once the date was over. Feeling insecure about his love, she called as a way of getting attention and expressions of love from him.

   Once Jim realized this fact, it became clear that he needed to find a solution that would leave Beverly feeling secure and at the same time allow him to feel unpressured.

Arriving at a shared definition of the problem requires skills associated with creating a supportive and confirming climate. The ability to be nonjudgmental, descriptive, and empathic is an important, support-producing skill. Both Jim and Beverly needed to engage in paraphrasing to discover all the details of the conflict.

When they're really communicating effectively, partners can help each other clarify what they're seeking. Truly believing that their happiness depends on each other's satisfaction, they actively try to analyze what obstacles need to be overcome.

4. **Generate possible solutions.** In the next step, the partners try to think of as many ways to satisfy both of their needs as possible. They can best do so by "brainstorming"—inventing as many potential solutions as they can. The key to success in brainstorming is to seek quantity without worrying about quality. The rule is to prohibit criticism of all ideas, no matter how outlandish they may sound. An idea that seems farfetched can sometimes lead to a more workable one. Another rule of brainstorming is that ideas aren't personal property. If one person makes a suggestion, the other should feel free to suggest another solution that builds upon or modifies the original one. The original suggestion and its offshoots are all potential solutions that will be considered later. Once partners get over their possessiveness about ideas, the level of defensiveness drops and both people can work together to find the best solution without worrying about whose idea it is.

All of the supportive and confirming behaviors discussed in Chapter 11 are important during this step. However, two of them stand out as crucial: the ability to communicate provisionalism rather than certainty, and the ability to refrain from premature evaluations of any solution. The aim of this step is to generate *all* the possible solutions—whether they are immediately reasonable or not. By the partners' behaving provisionally and avoiding any evaluation until all the solutions are generated, cre-

> ## REFLECTION
>
> ### WIN-WIN SOLUTION REDUCES FRICTION
>
> After four months of living together, my two neat roommates were fed up with cleaning up after me and the other messy member of our little household, and the two of us were tired of hearing the neat freaks complain about our habits.
>
> Last week we had a meeting (again) about the dishes and glasses. But this time we didn't argue about who was right or wrong. Instead, we looked for a win-win solution. And once we started looking, we found it: Each of us gets his own dishes, glasses, and silverware—two of each item per person. We are responsible for cleaning only our own things. Now, if you look in our kitchen cabinets, you only find eight glasses, eight plates, and so on. There isn't enough stuff to make a mess, and each of us has to wash our own things if we want to eat. Everybody is happy. Some people might think our solution is silly, but it has certainly worked well for us—and that's all that matters.

ative and spontaneous behavior is encouraged. The result is a long list of solutions that most likely contains the best solution, one that might not have been expressed if the communication climate were defensive.

Jim and Beverly used brainstorming to generate solutions to their telephone problem. Their list consisted of continuing the calling but limiting the time spent on the phone, limiting the calls to a "once in a while" basis, Beverly's keeping a journal that could serve as a substitute for calling, Jim's calling Beverly on a "once in a while" basis, cutting out all calling, moving in together to eliminate the necessity for calling, getting married, and breaking up. Although some of these solutions were clearly unacceptable to both partners, they listed all the ideas they could think of, preparing themselves for the next step in no-lose problem solving.

5.  **Evaluate the possible solutions and choose the best one.** The time to evaluate the solutions is after they all have been generated, after the partners feel they have exhausted all the possibilities. In this step, the possible solutions generated during the previous step are evaluated for their ability to satisfy the mutually shared goal. How does each solution stand up against the individual and mutual goals? Which solution satisfies the most goals? Partners need to work cooperatively in examining each solution and in finally selecting the best one.

    It is important during this step to react spontaneously rather than strategically. Selecting a particular solution because the other person finds it satisfactory, while seemingly a "nice" thing to do, is as manipulative a strategy as getting the other person to accept a solution satisfactory only to you. Respond as you feel as solutions are evaluated, and encourage your partner to do the same. Any solution agreed upon as "best" has little chance of satisfying both partners' needs if it was strategically manipulated to the top of the list.

    The solution Beverly and Jim selected as satisfying her need to feel secure, his need to be undisturbed before turning in, and their mutual goal of maintaining their relationship at a highly intimate level was to limit both the frequency and length of the calls. Also, Jim agreed to share in the calling.

6.  **Implement the solution.** Now the time comes to try out the idea selected to see if it does, indeed, satisfy everyone's needs. The key questions to answer are *who* does *what* to *whom,* and *when*?

    Before Jim and Beverly tried out their solution, they went over the agreement to make sure it was clear. This step proved to be important, for a potential misunderstanding existed. When will the solution be implemented? Should Beverly wait a few weeks before calling? Should Jim begin the calling? They agreed that Jim would call after their next date.

Another problem concerned their different definitions of length. How long is too long? They decided that more than a few minutes would be too long.

The solution was implemented after they discussed the solution and came to mutual agreement about its particulars. This process may seem awkward and time-consuming, but both Beverly and Jim decided that without a clear understanding of the solution, they were opening the door to future conflicts.

Interestingly, the discussion concerning their mutual needs and how the solution satisfied them was an important part of their relationship's development. Jim learned that Beverly felt insecure about his love (sometimes); Beverly learned that Jim needed time to himself and that this need did not reflect on his love for her. Soon after implementing the solution, they found that the problem ceased to exist. Jim no longer felt the calls were invading his privacy, and Beverly, after talks with Jim, felt more secure about his love.

7.  **Follow up the solution.** To stop after selecting and implementing a particular solution assumes any solution is forever, that time does not change things, that people remain constant, and that events never alter circumstances. Of course, this assumption is not the case: As people and circumstances change, a particular solution may lose or increase its effectiveness. Regardless, a follow-up evaluation needs to take place.

    After you've tested your solution for a short time, it's a good idea to plan a meeting to talk about how things are going. You may find that you need to make some changes or even rethink the whole problem.

    Reviewing the effects of your solution does not mean that something is wrong and must be corrected. Indeed, everything may point to the conclusion that the solution is still working to satisfy your needs and the mutually shared goal, and that the mutually shared goal is still important to both of you.

It is important at this stage in the win-win problem-solving process to be honest with yourself as well as with the other person. It may be difficult for you to say "We need to talk about this again," yet it could be essential if the problem is to remain resolved. Planning a follow-up talk when the solution is first implemented is important.

Beverly and Jim decided to wait one month before discussing the effects of their solution. Their talk was short, because both felt the problem no longer existed. Also, their discussions helped their relationship grow: They learned more about each other, felt closer, and developed a way to handle their conflicts constructively.

Although a win-win approach sounds ideal, it is not always possible, or even appropriate (Budescu et al., 1999). Table 12.4 lists some factors to consider when deciding which approach to take when facing a conflict. There will certainly be times when compromising is the most sensible approach. You will even encounter instances when pushing for your own solution is reasonable. Even more surprisingly, you will probably discover that there are times when it makes sense to willingly accept the loser's role.

Some conflicts can't be resolved with win-win outcomes. Only one suitor can marry the prince or princess, and only one person can be hired for the advertised job. Much of the time, however, good intentions and creative thinking can lead to outcomes that satisfy everyone's needs.

## Summary

Despite wishes and cultural myths to the contrary, conflict is a natural and unavoidable part of any relationship. Since conflict can't be escaped, the

**Table 12.4**

**Choosing the Most Appropriate Method of Conflict**

| Consider Deferring (Lose-Win) to the Other Person | Consider Compromising | Consider Competing (Win-Lose) | Consider Cooperating (Win-Win) |
|---|---|---|---|
| When you discover you are wrong | When there is not enough time to seek a win-win outcome | When the issue is important and the other person will take advantage of your noncompetitive approach | When the issue is too important for a compromise |
| When the issue is more important to the other person than it is to you | When the issue is not important enough to negotiate at length | When sustaining or maintaining a relationship with the other person is unimportant to you | When a long-term relationship between you and the other person is important |
| To let others learn by making their own mistakes | When the other person is not willing to seek a win-win outcome | | When the other person is willing to cooperate |
| When the long-term cost of winning may not be worth the short-term gains | | | |

challenge is how to deal with it effectively so that it strengthens a relationship rather than weakens it.

All conflicts possess the same characteristics: expressed struggle, perceived incompatible goals, perceived scarce rewards, and interdependence. Functional conflicts cope with these characteristics in very different ways from dysfunctional ones. Partners strive to cooperate instead of compete; to focus on rather than avoid the issues in dispute; and to seek positive, long-term solutions that meet each other's needs.

Individuals can respond to conflicts in a variety of ways: nonassertively, indirectly, with direct or passive aggression, and assertively. Each of these approaches can be justified in certain circumstances. The way a conflict is handled isn't always the choice of a single person, since the interactants influence one another as they develop a relational conflict style. This style is influenced by the partners' genders and the influences of their cultural backgrounds.

There are four possible outcomes to a particular conflict: lose-lose, win-lose, compromise, and win-win. In most circumstances a win-win outcome is best, and it can be achieved by following the guidelines outlined in this chapter.

## Recommended Readings

**Overview of interpersonal conflict:**

Joyce L. Hocker and Willliam W. Wilmot. *Interpersonal Conflict.* 5th ed. New York: McGraw-Hill, 1997.

**Ethical conflict management:**

Roger Fisher, Elisabeth Kopelman, and Andrea K. Schneider. *Beyond Machiavelli: Tools for Coping with Conflict.* New York: Penguin, 1996.

**Conflict management in personal and work-related contexts:**

Joseph P. Folger, Marshall S. Poole, and Randall K. Stuttman. *Working through Conflict: Strategies for Relationships, Groups, and Organizations.* Reading, MA: Addison-Wesley Longman, 1996.

**Win-Win problem solving in organizations:**

Stewart D. Friedman, Perry Christensen, and Jessica DeGroot. "Work and Life: The End of the Zero-Sum Game." *Harvard Business Review,* November–December 1998: 119–129.

## Activities

1. **Invitation to Insight**
   Even the best relationships have conflicts. Using the characteristics on pages 351-354, describe at least five conflicts in one of your important relationships. Then answer the following questions:
   a. Which conflicts involve content issues? Which involve relational issues?
   b. Which conflicts were one-time affairs, and which recur?

2. **Invitation to Insight**
   From your recent experiences recall two conflict incidents, one functional and one dysfunctional. Then answer the following questions:
   a. What distinguished these two conflicts?
   b. What were the consequences of each?
   c. How might the dysfunctional conflict have turned out differently if it had been handled in a more functional manner?
   d. How could you have communicated differently to make the dysfunctional conflict more functional?

3. **Skill Builder**
   With the help of a classmate, construct an assertive message that you *could* deliver to someone in your life: a boss, professor, friend, family member, neighbor, and so on. Once you have rehearsed the message, consider the risks and benefits of delivering it. Based on your deliberations, decide whether the assertive approach is justified in this case.

4. **Invitation to Insight**

   Interview someone who knows you well. Ask your informant which personal conflict styles (nonassertive, indirect, etc.) you use most often and the effect each of these styles has on your relationship with this person. Based on your findings, discuss whether different behavior might produce more productive results.

5. **Invitation to Insight**

   This activity will be most productive if you consult with several people with whom you share an interpersonal relationship as you answer the following questions:
   a. Is your relational style of handling conflict complementary, symmetrical, or parallel? What are the consequences of this style?
   b. What combination of intimacy and aggressiveness characterizes your approach to conflict? Are you satisfied with this approach?

   c. What conflict rituals do you follow in this relationship? Are these rituals functional or dysfunctional? What might be better alternatives?

6. **Skill Builder**

   To explore how the win-win approach might work in your life, try one of the following alternatives:
   a. Use the steps on pages 376-379 to describe how you could manage a conflict by following the win-win approach. How could you try this approach in your personal life? What difference might such an approach make?
   b. Try the win-win approach with a relational partner. What parts prove most helpful? Which are most difficult? How can you improve your relationship by using some or all of the win-win approach in future conflicts?

# GLOSSARY

**Abstraction ladder**   A range of more-to-less abstract terms describing an event or object.

**Accenting**   Nonverbal behaviors that emphasize part of a verbal message.

**Achievement culture**   Term used to describe a culture that places a high value on achievement of material success and a focus on the task at hand. Also termed "masculine" cultures.

**Advising**   A listening response in which the receiver offers suggestions about how the speaker should deal with a problem.

**Affect displays**   Unintentional nonverbal behaviors that convey a sender's emotions.

**Affinity**   The degree to which persons like or appreciate one another.

**Aggressiveness**   Verbal attacks that demean others' self-concepts and inflict psychological pain.

**Ambiguous response**   A disconfirming response with more than one meaning, leaving the other person unsure of the responder's position.

**Ambushing**   A style in which the receiver listens carefully in order to gather information to use in an attack on the speaker.

**Analyzing**   A listening response in which the listener offers an interpretation of a speaker's message.

**Androgynous**   Possessing both masculine and feminine traits.

**Argumentativeness**   Presenting and defending positions on issues while attacking positions taken by others.

**Assertion**   A direct expression of a sender's needs, thoughts, or feelings, delivered in a way that does not attack a receiver's dignity.

**Assimilation to prior input**   The tendency to interpret a message in terms of similar messages remembered from the past.

**Attending**   A phase of the listening process in which the communicator focuses on a message, excluding other messages.

**Attribution**   The process of attaching meaning to another person's behavior.

**Avoiding**   A relational stage immediately prior to terminating in which the partners minimize contact with one another.

**Behavior**   Intentional and unintentional actions that can be observed and interpreted.

**Behavioral description**   An account that refers only to observable phenomena.

**Bonding**   A stage of relational development in which the partners make symbolic public gestures to show that their relationship exists.

**"But" statement**   A statement in which the second half cancels the meaning of the first, for example, "I'd like to help you, *but* I have to go or I'll miss my bus."

**Breadth**   The range of topics discussed in a relationship. Usually used to describe one dimension of self-disclosure. See *social penetration model.*

**Certainty**   Dogmatically stating or implying that one's position is correct and others' ideas are not worth considering. Likely to arouse defensiveness, according to Gibb.

**Channel**   The medium through which a message passes from sender to receiver.

**Chronemics**   The study of how humans use and structure time.

**Circumscribing** A relational stage in which partners begin to reduce the scope of their contact and commitment to one another.

**Closed questions** Questions that limit the range of possible responses, such as questions that seek a yes or no answer.

**Coculture** A group within an encompassing culture with a perceived identity.

**Cognitive complexity** The ability to construct a variety of frameworks for viewing an issue.

**Cognitive conservatism** The tendency to seek out information that conforms to an existing self-concept and to ignore information that contradicts it.

**Collective culture** A culture whose members feel loyalties and obligations to an in-group, such as one's extended family, community, and even the organization one works for.

**Communication** An ongoing, transactional process in which individuals exchange messages whose meanings are influenced by the history of the relationship and the experiences of the participants.

**Communication climate** The emotional tone of a relationship between two or more individuals.

**Communication competence** The ability to achieve one's goals in a manner that is personally acceptable and, ideally, acceptable to others.

**Complaining** A disagreeing message that directly or indirectly communicates dissatisfaction with another person.

**Complementary conflict style** When partners in a conflict use different but mutually reinforcing behaviors.

**Complementing** Nonverbal behavior that reinforces a verbal message.

**Compliance-gaining strategy** A tactic used to persuade others to think or behave in a desired way.

**Compromise** An approach to conflict resolution in which both people attain at least part of what they want through self-sacrifice.

**Confirmation** The perception of being valued.

**Confirming message** A message that expresses caring or respect for another person.

**Conflict** An expressed struggle between at least two interdependent people who perceive incompatible goals, scarce rewards, and interference from the other person in achieving their goals.

**Conflict rituals** Repeating patterns of interlocking conflict behaviors.

**Connection-autonomy dialectic** The tension between the need for integration and the need for independence in a relationship.

**Content message** A message that communicates information about the subject being discussed. See also *relational message*.

**Contradicting** Nonverbal behavior that is inconsistent with a verbal message.

**Controlling communication** According to Gibb, messages that attempt to impose some sort of outcome on another person, resulting in a defensive response.

**Conventionality-uniqueness dialectic** The tension between the need to behave in ways that conform to others' expectations, and the need to assert one's individuality by behaving in ways that violate others' expectations.

**Convergence** The process of adapting one's speech style to match that of others with whom one wants to identify. See also *divergence*.

**Counterfeit questions** Questions that are disguised attempts to send a message rather than elicit information.

**Cyclic alternation** A method to manage dialectical tensions by responding to one end of the dialectical spectrum at some times, and the other end on different occasions.

**Debilitative emotions** Emotions that prevent a person from functioning effectively.

**Deception cues**   Nonverbal behaviors that signal the untruthfulness of a verbal message.

**Decoding**   The process in which a receiver attaches meaning to a message. Synonymous with *interpreting*.

**De-escalatory spiral**   A reciprocal communication pattern in which one person's nonthreatening behavior leads to reduced hostility by the other, with the level of hostility steadily decreasing.

**Defensive listening**   A response style in which the receiver perceives a speaker's comments as an attack.

**Defensiveness**   The attempt to protect a presenting image a person believes is being attacked.

**Depth**   The extent to which information shared is highly personal. See *social penetration model*.

**Description**   Messages that describe a speaker's position without evaluating others.

**Desired self**   The person we would like to be. It may be identical to or different from the perceived and presenting selves.

**Dialectical tensions**   Relational tensions that arise when two opposing or incompatible forces exist simultaneously.

**Differentiating**   A relational stage in which the partners reestablish their individual identities after having bonded together.

**Direct aggression**   An expression of the sender's thoughts and/or feelings that attacks the position and dignity of the receiver.

**Direct request**   A compliance-gaining strategy in which the communicator directly asks another person to meet his or her needs.

**Disagreeing message**   A message that essentially communicates to another person, "You are wrong"; includes argumentativeness, complaining, and aggressiveness.

**Disclaimer**   A phrase that disqualifies the value of the following statement; for example, *"You probably won't believe this . . . ."*

**Disconfirming message**   A message that expresses a lack of caring or respect for another person.

**Disfluency**   A nonlinguistic verbalization; for example, *um, er, ah.*

**Disqualification**   A method to manage dialectical tensions by deflecting messages that would force a confrontation between the dialectical opposites.

**Divergence**   Speaking in a way that emphasizes difference from others. See also *convergence*.

**Double message**   Contradiction between a verbal message and one or more nonverbal cues.

**Dyad**   Two communicators who interact with one another.

**Dysfunctional conflict**   Harmful conflicts characterized by communication that is coercive, uncooperative, and unfocused, which often results in a win-lose outcome and the damaging of a relationship.

**Emblems**   Deliberate nonverbal behaviors with precise meanings, known to virtually all members of a cultural group.

**Emotive language**   Language that conveys the sender's attitude rather than simply offering an objective description.

**Empathizing**   A listening response that conveys identification with a speaker's perceptions and emotions.

**Empathy**   The ability to project oneself into another person's point of view in an attempt to experience the other's thoughts and feelings.

**Encoding**   The process of putting thoughts into symbols, most commonly through words.

**Environment**   Both the physical setting in which communication occurs and the personal perspectives of the people involved.

**Equality**   A type of supportive communication described by Gibb which suggests that the sender regards the receiver with respect.

**Equivocal language**   Ambiguous language that has two or more equally plausible meanings.

**Escalatory spiral**   A reciprocal communication pattern in which one person's attack leads to a counterattack by the other, with the level of hostility steadily increasing.

**Ethnic group**   A collection of people who share customs, characteristics, language, common history, or geographic origin.

**Ethnocentrism**   An attitude that one's own culture is superior to that of others.

**Euphemism**   A pleasant term substituted for a blunt one in order to soften the impact of unpleasant information.

**Evaluating response**   A listening response that appraises a sender's thoughts or behaviors and implies that the person evaluating is qualified to pass judgment on the other.

**Evaluation**   A message in which a sender judges a receiver in some way, usually resulting in a defensive response.

**Exchange theory**   The theory that people seek relationships in which the benefits they gain equal or exceed the costs they incur.

**Experimenting**   An early stage in relational development, consisting of a search for common ground. If the experimentation is successful, the relationship progresses to intensifying. If not, it may go no further.

**Expression-privacy dialectic**   The tension between the desire to be open and disclosive, and the desire to be closed and private.

**External noise**   Factors outside the receiver that interfere with the accurate reception of a message.

**Face**   The image an individual wants to project to the world. See also *presenting self*.

**Face maintenance strategies**   Strategies that lead others to act in ways that reinforce the communicator's presenting self.

**Face-threatening act**   Behavior by another that is perceived as attacking an individual's presenting image, or face.

**Facework**   Actions people take to preserve their own and others' presenting images.

**Facilitative emotions**   Emotions that contribute to effective functioning.

**Factual statement**   A statement that can be verified as true or false. See also *inferential statement, opinion statement*.

**Fallacy of approval**   The irrational belief that it is vital to win the approval of virtually every person with whom a communicator deals.

**Fallacy of catastrophic expectations**   The irrational belief that the worst possible outcome will probably occur.

**Fallacy of causation**   The irrational belief that emotions are caused by others and not by the person who has them.

**Fallacy of helplessness**   The irrational belief that satisfaction in life is determined by forces beyond one's control.

**Fallacy of overgeneralization**   Irrational beliefs in which (1) conclusions (usually negative) are based on limited evidence, or (2) communicators exaggerate their shortcomings.

**Fallacy of perfection**   The irrational belief that a worthwhile communicator should be able to handle every situation with complete confidence and skill.

**Fallacy of should**   The irrational belief that people should behave in the most desirable way.

**Feedback**   The discernible response of a receiver to a sender's message.

**Filling in gaps**   A listening habit that involves adding details never mentioned by a speaker to complete a message.

**Functional conflict**   Beneficial conflicts characterized by communication that is respectful, cooperative, and focused, which results in the resolution of a problem and the strengthening of a relationship.

**Hearing**   The first stage in the listening process, in which sound waves are received by a communicator.

**Hedges**   Words or phrases that soften the impact of a statement; for example, *"I guess I'm a little bit* disappointed. . . ."

**Hesitations**   Filler words that add no meaning to a statement; for example, *"Uh,* I'd like to talk to you about . . . *um* . . . what happened at the party last night."

**High-context culture**   A culture that relies heavily on verbal and nonverbal cues to maintain social harmony.

**"I" language**   A statement that describes the speaker's reaction to another person's behavior without making judgments about its worth. See also *"you" language.*

**Illustrators**   Nonverbal behaviors that accompany and support verbal messages.

**Impersonal communication**   Behavior that treats others as objects rather than individuals. See *interpersonal communication.*

**Impersonal response**   A disconfirming response that is superficial or trite.

**Impervious response**   A disconfirming response that ignores another person's attempt to communicate.

**Impression management**   Communication behaviors employed to ensure being perceived in a particular way by others.

**Inclusion-seclusion dialectic**   The tension between a couple's desire for involvement with the "outside world" and their desire to live their own lives, free of what can feel like interference from others.

**Incongruous response**   A disconfirming response in which two messages, one of which is usually nonverbal, contradict one another.

**Indirect appeal**   A compliance-gaining strategy based on the hope that the other person will infer or assume the communicator's unexpressed intent.

**Indirect communication**   Hinting at a message instead of expressing thoughts and feelings directly. See also *passive aggression* and *assertion.*

**Individualistic culture**   A culture in which people view their primary responsibility as being to themselves.

**Inferential statement**   A statement based on an interpretation of evidence. See also *factual statement.*

**In-group**   A group with which an individual identifies herself or himself.

**Initiating**   The first stage in relational development, in which the interactants express interest in one another.

**Insensitive listening**   Failure to recognize the thoughts or feelings that are not directly expressed by a speaker; instead, accepting the speaker's words at face value.

**Insulated listening**   A style in which the receiver ignores undesirable information.

**Integrating**   A relational stage in which the interactants begin to take on a single identity.

**Integration-separation dialectic**   The tension between the desire for connection with others and the desire for independence.

**Intensifiers**   Adjectives and adverbs that intensify the noun or verb being described, for example, a *very* bad idea, a *really* good time.

**Intensifying**   A relational stage following experimenting, in which the interactants move toward integration by increasing the amount of contact and the breadth and depth of self-disclosure.

**Interactive communication model**   A characterization of communication as a two-way event in which sender and receiver exchange messages in response to one another.

**Intercultural communication**   Communication that occurs when members of two or more cultures or other groups exchange messages in a manner that is influenced by their different cultural perceptions and symbol systems.

**Interethnic communication**   Communication that occurs when members of ethnically different groups interact.

**International communication**   Communication that occurs when citizens from different countries or other political entities meet.

**Interpersonal communication, qualitative**   Communication in which people treat each other as unique individuals as opposed to objects.

**Interpersonal communication, quantitative**   Communication between or among a small number of people, usually two.

**Interpersonal relationship**   An association in which the people meet each other's social needs to a greater or lesser degree.

**Interracial communication**   Communication that occurs when communicators from different races interact.

**Interpretation**   The process of attaching meaning to sense data. Synonymous with *decoding*.

**Interrupting response**   A disconfirming response in which one communicator interrupts another.

**Intimacy**   A state achieved by intellectual, emotional, and/or physical closeness, as well as shared activities.

**Intimate distance**   One of Hall's four distance zones, ranging from skin contact to eighteen inches.

**Irrelevant response**   A disconfirming response in which one communicator's comments bear no relationship to the previous speaker's ideas.

**"It" statement**   A statement in which "it" replaces the personal pronoun "I," making the statement less direct and more evasive.

**Johari Window**   A model that describes the relationship between self-disclosure and self-awareness.

**Kinesics**   The study of body movements.

**Leakage**   Nonverbal behaviors that reveal information a communicator does not disclose verbally.

**Lie**   A deliberate act of deception.

**Linear communication model**   A characterization of communication as a one-way event in which a message flows from sender to receiver.

**Linguistic determinism**   The notion that the worldview of a culture is shaped and reflected by the language its members speak.

**Linguistic relativism**   The notion that the language individuals use exerts a strong influence on their perceptions.

**Listening**   The process of hearing, attending, understanding, remembering, and responding to messages.

**Lose-lose problem solving**   An approach to conflict resolution in which neither party achieves its goals.

**Low-context culture**   A culture that uses language primarily to express thoughts, feelings, and ideas as clearly and logically as possible.

**Manipulators**   Movements in which one part of the body grooms, massages, rubs, holds, fidgets with, pinches, picks, or otherwise manipulates another part.

**Message**   Information sent from a sender to a receiver.

**Metacommunication**   Messages (usually relational) that refer to other messages: communication about communication.

**Microexpressions**   Brief facial expressions.

**Mixed emotions**   Emotions that are combinations of primary emotions. Some mixed emotions can be expressed in single words (that is, *awe, remorse*) whereas others require more than one term (that is, *embarrassed and angry, relieved and grateful*).

**Moderation**   A method to manage dialectical tensions by choosing to back off from expressing either end of the dialectical spectrum.

**Negotiation**   A process in which two or more people discuss specific proposals in order to find a mutually acceptable agreement.

**Neutrality**   A defense-arousing behavior described by Gibb in which the sender expresses indifference toward a receiver.

**Noise**   External, physiological, and psychological distractions that interfere with the accurate transmission and reception of a message.

**Nonassertion**   The inability to express one's thoughts or feelings when necessary. Nonassertion may be due to a lack of confidence, communication skill, or both.

**Nonverbal communication**   Messages expressed by other than linguistic means.

**Norm of reciprocity**   A social convention that obligates a communicator to return the favors extended by others.

**Nurturing culture**   A culture that regards the support of relationships as an especially important goal. Also termed "feminine" cultures.

**Openness-closedness dialectic**   The tension between the desire to be honest and open and the desire for privacy.

**Open questions**   Questions that allow for a variety of extended responses.

**Opinion statement**   A statement based on a speaker's beliefs. See also *factual statement*.

**Organization**   The stage in the perception process that involves arranging data in a meaningful way.

**Out-group**   A group that an individual sees as different from herself or himself.

**Paralanguage**   Nonlinguistic means of vocal expression: rate, pitch, tone, and so on.

**Parallel conflict style**   Partners in a conflict shift from complementary to symmetrical patterns from one conflict issue to another.

**Paraphrasing**   Restating a speaker's thoughts and feelings in the listener's own words.

**Passive aggression**   An indirect expression of aggression, delivered in a way that allows the sender to maintain a facade of kindness.

**Perceived self**   The person we believe ourselves to be in moments of candor. It may be identical with or different from the presenting and desired selves.

**Perception checking**   A three-part method for verifying the accuracy of interpretations, including a description of the sense data, two possible interpretations, and a request for confirmation of the interpretations.

**Personal distance**   One of Hall's four distance zones, ranging from eighteen inches to four feet.

**Personal space**   The distance we put between ourselves and others.

**Phonological rules**   Rules governing the way in which sounds are pronounced in a language.

**Physiological noise**   Biological factors in the receiver that interfere with accurate reception of a message.

**Polite language forms**   Overly polite terms that weaken the power of a statement, for example, *"Excuse me, please,* I'd like to talk to you for a minute, *sir."*

**Power distance**   The degree to which members of a society accept the unequal distribution of power among members.

**Powerless speech mannerisms**   Forms of speech that communicate to others a lack of power in the speaker: hedges, hesitations, intensifiers, and so on.

**Pragmatic rules**   Rules that govern interpretation of language in terms of its social context. See also *semantic rules, syntactic rules*.

**Predictability-novelty dialectic**   Within a relationship, the tension between the need for a predictable relational partner and one who is more spontaneous and less predictable.

**Prejudice**   An unfairly biased and intolerant attitude toward others who belong to an out-group.

**Presenting self**   The image a person presents to others. It may be identical with or different from the perceived and desired selves.

**Primary emotions**   Basic emotions. Some researchers have identified eight primary emotions: joy, acceptance, fear, surprise, sadness, disgust, anger, and anticipation.

**Problem orientation**   A supportive style of communication described by Gibb in which the communicators focus on working together to solve their problems instead of trying to impose their own solutions on one another.

**Provisionalism**   A supportive style of communication described by Gibb in which a sender expresses open-mindedness to others' ideas and opinions.

**Proxemics**   The study of how people and animals use space.

**Pseudolistening** An imitation of true listening in which the receiver's mind is elsewhere.

**Psychological noise** Forces within a communicator that interfere with the ability to express or understand a message accurately.

**Public distance**   One of Hall's four distance zones, extending outward from twelve feet.

**Punctuation**   The process of determining the causal order of events.

**Questioning**   A listening response in which the receiver seeks additional information from the sender.

**Race**   Physical characteristics that distinguish one group of people from another, such as skin color or facial features.

**Receiver**   One who notices and attends to a message.

**Reference groups**   Groups against which we compare ourselves, thereby influencing our self-concept and self-esteem.

**Reflected appraisal**   The theory that a person's self-concept matches the way the person believes others regard him or her.

**Reframing**   A method to manage dialectcal tensions by redefining the situation so that the apparent contradiction disappears.

**Regulating**   Nonverbal behavior that controls the flow of verbal messages in a conversation.

**Relational appeals**   Compliance-gaining strategies that rely on the target's relationship with the person making the request.

**Relational conflict style**   A pattern of managing disagreements that repeats itself over time.

**Relational message**   A message that expresses the social relationship between two or more individuals.

**Relationship**   See *interpersonal relationship*.

**Relative language**   Words that gain their meaning by comparison.

**Remembering**   A phase of the listening process in which a message is recalled.

**Repeating**   Nonverbal behaviors that duplicate the content of a verbal message.

**Respect**   The social need to be held in esteem by others.

**Responding**   A phase of the listening process in which feedback occurs, offering evidence that the message has been received.

**Revelation-concealment dialectic**   The tension between a couple's desire to be open and honest with the "outside world" and the desire to keep things to themselves.

**Segmentation**   A method to manage dialectical tensions by compartmentalizing different areas of the relationship.

**Selection**   A phase of the perception process in which a communicator attends to a stimulus from the environment. Also, a way communicators manage dialectical tensions by responding to one end of the dialectical spectrum and ignoring the other.

**Selective listening**   A listening style in which the receiver responds only to messages that interest her or him.

**Self-concept**   The relatively stable set of perceptions each individual holds of herself or himself.

**Self-disclosure**   The process of deliberately revealing information about oneself that is significant and that would not normally be known by others.

**Self-fulfilling prophecy**   The causal relationship that occurs when a person's expectations of an event and her or his subsequent behavior based on those expectations make the outcome more likely to occur than would otherwise have been true.

**Self-monitoring**   The process of attending to one's behavior and using these observations to shape the way one behaves.

**Self-serving bias**   The tendency to judge one's self in the most generous terms possible, while being more critical of others.

**Self-talk**   The nonvocal process of thinking. On some level, self-talk occurs as a person interprets another's behavior.

**Semantic rules**   Rules that govern the meaning of language, as opposed to its structure. See also *syntactic rules*.

**Sender**   The creator of a message.

**Sex role**   The social orientation that governs behavior, rather than biological gender.

**Significant other**   A person whose opinion is important enough to affect one's self-concept strongly.

**Silent listening**   Staying attentive and nonverbally responsive without offering verbal feedback.

**Sincere questions**   Genuine attempts to elicit information from others.

**Social comparison**   Evaluating oneself in terms of or by comparison to others.

**Social distance**   One of Hall's distance zones, ranging from four to twelve feet.

**Social penetration model**   A model that describes relationships in terms of their breadth and depth.

**Spiral**   A reciprocal communication pattern in which messages reinforce one another. See also *escalatory spiral, de-escalatory spiral*.

**Spontaneity**   A supportive communication behavior described by Gibb in which the sender expresses a message without any attempt to manipulate the receiver.

**Stability-change dialectic**   The tension between the desire to keep a relationship predictable and stable, and the desire for novelty and change.

**Stage hogging**   A listening style in which the receiver is more concerned with making his or her own point than in understanding the speaker.

**Stagnation**   A relational stage characterized by declining enthusiasm and standardized forms of behavior.

**Standpoint theory**   A body of scholarship that explores how one's position in a society shapes his or her view of society in general, and of specific individuals.

**Static evaluation**   Treating people or objects as if they were unchanging.

**Stereotyping**   Exaggerated beliefs associated with a categorizing system.

**Strategy**   A defense-arousing style of communication described by Gibb in which a sender tries to manipulate or deceive a receiver.

**Substituting**   Nonverbal behavior that takes the place of a verbal message.

**Superiority**   A defense-arousing style of communication described by Gibb in which the sender states or implies that the receiver is not worthy of respect.

**Supportive response**   A listening response in which the receiver reveals her or his solidarity with the speaker's situation.

**Symmetrical conflict style**   Partners in a conflict use the same tactics.

**Sympathy**   Feeling compassion for another person's emotions; less identification than empathy.

**Syntactic rules**   Rules that govern the ways symbols can be arranged, as opposed to the meanings of those symbols. See also *semantic rules*.

**Tag questions**   Questions that follow a declarative statement and relate to it; for example, "Let's get going, *okay?*"

**Tangential response**   A disconfirming response that uses the speaker's remark as a starting point for a shift to a new topic.

**Terminating**   The conclusion of a relationship, characterized by the acknowledgment of one or both partners that the relationship is over.

**Territory**   A stationary area claimed by an individual.

**Transactional communication model**   A characterization of communication as the simultaneous sending and receiving of messages in an ongoing, irreversible process.

**Uncertainty avoidance**   The tendency of a culture's members to feel threatened by ambiguous situations, and how much they try to avoid them.

**Understanding**   A stage in the listening process in which the receiver attaches meaning to a message.

**"We" language**   The use of first-person-plural pronouns to include others, either appropriately or inappropriately.

**"We" statement**   Language that implies the issue being discussed is the concern and responsibility of both the speaker and receiver of a message. See also *"I" language, "you" language*.

**White lie**   A deliberate hiding or misrepresenting of the truth, intended to help or avoid harming the receiver.

**Win-lose problem solving**   An approach to conflict resolution in which one person reaches her or his goal at the expense of the other.

**Win-win problem solving**   An approach to conflict resolution in which people work together to satisfy all their goals.

**"You" language**   A statement that expresses or implies a judgment of the other person. See also *evaluation, "I" language*.

# REFERENCES

Aboud, F. E., & Mendelson, M. J. (1998). Determinants of friendship selection and quality: Developmental perspectives. In W. M. Bukowski & A. F. Newcomb (Eds.), *The company they keep: Friendship in childhood and adolescence* (pp. 87–112). New York: Cambridge University Press.

Adamopoulos, J. (1991). The emergence of interpersonal behavior: Diachronic and cross-cultural processes in the evolution of intimacy. In S. Ting-Toomey & F. Korzenny (Eds.), *Cross-cultural interpersonal communication* (pp. 155–170). Newbury Park, CA: Sage.

Adamopoulos, J., & Bontempo, R. N. (1986). Diachronic universals in interpersonal structures. *Journal of Cross-Cultural Psychology, 17,* 169–189.

Adams, G. R., & Huston, T. L. (1975). Social perception of middle-aged persons varying in physical attractiveness. *Developmental Psychology, 11,* 657–658.

Addington, D. W. (1968). The relationship of selected vocal characteristics to personality perception. *Speech Monographs, 35,* 492–503.

Adler, R. B., & Elmhorst, J. M. (1996). *Communicating at work: Principles and practices for business and the professions* (5th ed.). New York: McGraw-Hill.

Adler, T. (1990, October). Look at duration, depth in research on emotion. *APA Monitor,* p. 10.

Adler, T. (1992, June). Enter romance, exit objectivity. *APA Monitor,* p. 18.

Adler, T. (1992, October). Personality, like plaster, is pretty stable over time. *APA Monitor,* p. 18.

Adler, T. (1993, April). Competence determined by status characteristics. *APA Monitor,* pp. 18–19.

Adler, T. (1993, February). Congressional staffers witness miracle of touch. *APA Monitor,* pp. 12–13.

Afifi, W. A., & Johnson, M. L. (1999). The use and interpretation of tie signs in a public setting: Relationship and sex differences. *Journal of Social and Personal Relationships, 16,* 9–38.

Alberts, J. K. (1988). An analysis of couples' conversational complaints. *Communication Monographs, 55,* 184–197.

Alberts, J. K. (1990). Perceived effectiveness of couples' conversational complaints. *Communication Studies, 40,* 280-291.

Alberts, J. K., & Driscoll, G. (1992). Containment versus escalation: The trajectory of couples' conversational complaints. *Western Journal of Communication, 56,* 394–412.

Alberts, J. K., Kellar-Guenther, U., & Corman, S. R. (1996). That's not funny: Understanding recipients' responses to teasing. *Western Journal of Communication, 60,* 337–357.

Albrecht, T. L., & Adelman, M. B. (1987). Communicating social support: A theoretical perspective. In T. L. Albrecht & M. B. Adelman (Eds.), *Communicating social support* (pp. 18–39). Newbury Park, CA: Sage.

Albrecht, T. L., Burleson, B. R., & Goldsmith, D. (1994). Supportive communication. In M. L. Knapp & G. R. Miller (Eds.), *Handbook of interpersonal communication* (2nd ed., pp. 419–449). Newbury Park, CA: Sage.

Allen, B. (1995). "Diversity" and organizational communication. *Journal of Applied Communication Research, 23,* 143–155.

Allen, M. (1998). Methodological considerations when examining a gendered world. In D. J. Canary & K. Dindia (Eds.), *Handbook of sex differences and similarities in communication* (pp. 427–444). Mahwah, NJ: Lawrence Erlbaum Associates.

Allen, M. W. (1995). Communication concepts related to perceived organizational support. *Western Journal of Communication, 59,* 326–346.

Almaney A., & Alwan., A. (1982). *Communicating with the Arabs.* Prospect Heights, IL: Waveland.

Altman, I. (1973). Reciprocity of interpersonal exchange. *Journal for the Theory of Social Behavior, 3,* 249–261.

Altman, I., & Taylor, D. A. *Social penetration: The development of interpersonal relationships.* New York: Holt, Rinehart and Winston.

Ambady, N., Koo, J., Lee, F., & Rosenthal, R. (1996). More than words: linguistic and nonlinguistic politeness in two cultures. *Journal of Personality and Social Psychology, 70,* 996–1011.

Andersen, P. A. (1992). Nonverbal communication in the small group. In R. S. Cathcart & L. A. Samovar (Eds.), *Small group communication: A reader* (6th ed., pp. 272–286). Dubuque, IA: Wm. C. Brown.

Andersen, P. A. (1999). *Nonverbal communication: Forms and functions*. Palo Alto, CA: Mayfield.

Andersen, P. A., Lustig, M. W., & Andersen, J. F. (1987a). *Changes in latitude, changes in attitude: The relationship between climate, latitude, and interpersonal communication predispositions*. Paper presented at the annual convention of the Speech Communication Association, Boston.

Andersen, P. A., Lustig, M. W., & Andersen, J. F. (1987b). Regional patterns of communication in the United States: A theoretical perspective. *Communication Monographs, 54,* 128–144.

Antioch College. (1996). *The Antioch College sexual offense prevention policy*. Yellow Springs, OH: Author.

Archer, R., & Berg, J. (1978, November). To encourage intimacy, don't force it. *Psychology Today, 12,* 39–40.

Argyle, M., & Henderson, M. (1985). The rules of relationships. In S. Duck & D. Perlman (Eds.), *Understanding personal relationships: An interdisciplinary approach* (pp. 63–84). Beverly Hills, CA: Sage.

Argyle, M., Alkema, F., & Gilmour, R. (1971). The communication of friendly and hostile attitudes by verbal and nonverbal signals. *European Journal of Social Psychology, 1,* 385–402.

Armstrong, G. B., Boiarsky, G. A., & Mares, M. L. (1991). Background television and reading performance. *Communication Monographs, 58,* 235–253.

Aronson, E. (1995). *The social animal* (7th ed.). New York: W. H. Freeman.

Aronson, E., Willerman, B., & Floyd, J. (1966). The effect of a pratfall on increasing interpersonal attractiveness. *Psychonomic Science, 4,* 227–228.

Aune, K. S., & Aune, R. K. (1996). Cultural differences in the self-reported experience and expression of emotions in relationships. *Journal of Cross-Cultural Psychology, 27*(1), 67–81.

Aune, R. K. (in press). A theory of attribution of responsibility for creating understanding. *Communication Monographs.*

Avtgis, T. A., West, D. V., & Anderson, T. L. (1998). Relationship stages: An inductive analysis identifying cognitive, affective, and behavioral dimensions of Knapp's relational stages model. *Communication Research Reports, 15,* 280–287.

Axelrod, R. (1984). *The evolution of cooperation*. New York: Basic Books.

Ayers, J., & Crosby, S. (1995). Two studies concerning the predictive validity of the personal report of communication apprehension in employment interviews. *Communication Research Reports, 12,* 145–151.

Ayres, J., & Hopf, T. (1993). *Coping with speech anxiety*. Norwood, NJ: Ablex.

Ayres, J., Keereetaweep, T., Chen, P., & Edwards, P. A. (1998). Communication apprehension and employment interviews. *Communication Education, 47,* 1–17.

Bach, G. R., & Wyden, P. (1968). *The intimate enemy*. New York: Avon.

Bagby, J. W. (1957). A cross-cultural study of perceptual predominance in binocular rivalry. *Journal of Abnormal and Social Psychology, 54,* 331–334.

Bales, R. (1958). Task roles and social roles in problem solving groups. In E. E. Maccoby, T. M. Newcomb, & E. L. Hartley (Eds.), *Readings in social psychology* (3rd ed., pp. 437–447). New York: Holt, Rinehart and Winston.

Balswick, J. O. (1988). *The inexpressive male: A tragedy of American society*. Lexington, MA: Lexington Books.

Banks, S. P. (1987). Achieving "unmarkedness" in organizational discourse: A praxis perspective in ethnolinguistic identity. *Journal of Language and Social Psychology, 6,* 171–190.

Barbee, P. P., Gulley, M. R., & Cunningham, M. R. (1990). Support seeking in personal relationships. *Journal of Social and Personal Relationships, 7,* 531–540.

Bargh, J. A. (1988). Automatic information processing: Implications for communication and affect. In L. Donohew & H. E. Sypher (Eds.), *Communication, social cognition, and affect* (pp. 9–32). Hillsdale, NJ: Lawrence Erlbaum Associates.

Barker, L. L. (1971). *Listening behavior*. Englewood Cliffs, NJ: Prentice-Hall.

Barker, L. L., Edwards, R., Gaines, C., Gladney, K., & Holley, F. (1981). An investigation of proportional time spent in various communication activities by college students. *Journal of Applied Communication Research, 8,* 101–109.

Barry, D. (1990). *Dave Barry turns 40*. New York: Fawcett Columbine.

Bartoshuk, L. (1980, September). Separate worlds of taste. *Psychology Today, 14,* 48–63.

Basso, K. (1970). To give up on words: Silence in Western Apache culture. *Southern Journal of Anthropology, 26,* 213-230.

Bateson, G. (1937). *Naven.* Cambridge, England: Cambridge University Press.

Bateson, G., & Jackson, D. D. (1964). Some varieties of pathogenic organization. *Disorders of Communication* [Research Publications: Association for Research in Nervous and Mental Disease], *42,* 270-283.

Battaglia, D. M., Richard, F. D., Datteri, D. L., & Lord, C. G. (1998). Breaking up is (relatively) easy to do: A script for the dissolution of close relationships. *Journal of Social and Personal Relationships, 15,* 829–845.

Baumeister, R. F., & Leary, M. R. (1995). The need to belong: Desire for interpersonal attachments as a fundamental human motivation. *Psychological Bulletin, 117,* 497–529.

Bavelas, I. (1983). Situations that lead to disqualifications. *Human Communication Research, 9,* 130-145.

Bavelas, J. B. (1990). Behaving and communicating: A reply to Motley. *Western Journal of Speech Communication, 54,* 593-602.

Bavelas, J. B., Black, A., Chovil, N., & Mullett, J. (1990). *Equivocal communication.* Newbury Park, CA: Sage.

Baxter, L. A. (1982). Strategies for ending relationships: Two studies. *Western Journal of Speech Communication, 46,* 223-241.

Baxter, L. A. (1987). Symbols of relationship identity in relationship culture. *Journal of Social and Personal Relationships, 4,* 261–280.

Baxter, L. A. (1992). Forms and functions of intimate play in personal relationships. *Human Communication Research, 18,* 336–363.

Baxter, L. A. (1994). A dialogic approach to relationship maintenance. In D. J. Canary & L. Stafford (Eds.), *Communication and relational maintenance* (pp. 233–254). San Diego: Academic Press.

Baxter, L. A., & Bullis, C. (1986). Turning points in developing romantic relationships. *Human Communication Research, 12,* 469–494.

Baxter, L. A., & Erbert, L. A. (1999). Perceptions of dialectical contradictions in turning points of development in heterosexual romantic relationships. *Journal of Social and Personal Relationships, 16,* 547–569.

Baxter, L. A., & Montgomery, B. M. (1996). *Relating: Dialogues and dialectics.* New York: Guilford Press.

Baxter, L. A., & Wilmot, W. W. (1985). Taboo topics in close relationships. *Journal of Social and Personal Relationships, 2,* 253-269.

Bazil, L. G. D. (1999). The effects of social behavior on fourth- and fifth-grade girls' perceptions of physically attractive and unattractive peers (Doctoral dissertation, California School of Professional Psychology, San Diego, 1999). *Dissertation Abstracts International, 59*(08), 4533B.

Beatty, K. J., & McCroskey, J. C. (1997). It's in our nature: Verbal aggressiveness as temperamental expression. *Communication Quarterly, 45,* 466–460.

Beatty, M. J., & McCroskey, J. C. (1998). Interpersonal communication as temperamental expression: A communibiological paradigm. In J. C. McCroskey, J. A. Daly, M. M. Martin, & M. J. Beatty, (Eds.), *Communication and personality: Trait perspectives* (pp. 41–67). Cresskill, NJ: Hampton Press.

Beatty, M. J., Burant, P. A., Dobos, J. A., & Rudd, J. E. (1996). Trait verbal aggressiveness and the appropriateness and effectiveness of fathers' interaction plans. *Communication Quarterly, 44,* 1–15.

Beatty, M. J., McCroskey, J. C., & Heisel, A. D. (1998). Communication apprehension as temporal expression: A communibiological paradigm. *Communication Monographs, 65,* 197–219.

Beck, A. T. (1976). *Cognitive therapy and the emotional disorders.* New York: International Universities Press.

Beck, C. E., & Beck. E. A. (1996). The manager's open door and the communication climate. In K. M. Galvin & P. Cooper (Eds.), *Making connections: Readings in relational communication* (pp. 286–290). Los Angeles: Roxbury.

Bell, R. A., & Buerkel-Rothfuss, N. L. (1990). (S)he loves me, s(he) loves me not: Predictors of relational information-seeking in courtship and beyond. *Communication Quarterly, 38,* 64–82.

Bell, R. A., & Healey, J. G. (1992). Idiomatic communication and interpersonal solidarity in friends' relational cultures. *Human Communication Research, 18,* 307–335.

Bell, R. A., Buerkel-Rothfuss, N. L., & Gore, K. E. (1987). Did you bring the yarmulke for the cabbage patch kid?: The idiomatic communication of young lovers. *Human Communication Research, 14,* 47–67.

Bellah, R. N., Madsen, R., Sullivan, W. M., Swidler, A., & Tipton, S. M. (1985). *Habits of the heart: Individualism and commitment in American life.* Berkeley: University of California Press.

Bem, S. L. (1974). The measurement of psychological androgyny. *Journal of Consulting and Clinical Psychology, 42,* 155–162.

Bem, S. L. (1985). Androgyny and gender schema theory: A conceptual and empirical integration. In T. B. Sonderegger (Ed.), *Nebraska symposium on motivation: Psychology and gender.* Lincoln: University of Nebraska Press.

Benoit, W. L., & Benoit, P. J. (1987). Everyday argument practices of naive social actors. In J. Wenzel (Ed.), *Argument and critical practice.* Annandale, VA: Speech Communication Association.

Berger, C. R. (1979). Beyond initial interactions: Uncertainty, understanding, and the development of interpersonal relationships. In H. Giles & R. St. Clair (Eds.), *Language and social psychology* (pp. 122–144). Oxford: Blackwell.

Berger, C. R. (1987). Communicating under uncertainty. In M. E. Roloff & G. R. Miller (Eds.), *Interpersonal processes: New directions in communication research* (pp. 39–62). Newbury Park, CA: Sage.

Berger, C. R. (1993, July). Revisiting the relationship construct. *Personal Relationship Issues, 1,* 25–27.

Berger, C. R., & Calabrese, R. (1975). Some explorations in initial interaction and beyond. *Human Communication Research, 1,* 99–112.

Berger, C. R., & diBattista, P. (1993). Communication failure and plan adaptation: If at first you don't succeed, say it louder and slower. *Communication Monographs, 60,* 220-238.

Berscheid, E., & Walster, E. H. (1978). *Interpersonal attraction* (2nd ed.). Reading, MA: Addison-Wesley.

Berscheid, E., Schneider, M., & Omoto, A. M. (1989). Issues in studying close relationships: Conceptualizing and measuring closeness. In C. Hendrick (Ed.), *Close relationships* (pp. 63–91). Newbury Park, CA: Sage.

Besson, A. L., Roloff, M. E., & Paulson, G. D. (1998). Preserving face in refusal situations. *Communication Research, 25,* 183–199.

Bharti, A. (1985). The self in Hindu thought and action. In A. J. Marsella, G. DeVos, & F. L. K. Hsu (Eds.), *Culture and self: Asian and Western perspectives.* New York: Tavistock.

Bickman, L. (1974, April). Social roles and uniforms: Clothes make the person. *Psychology Today, 7,* 48–51.

Bingham, S., & Wiemann, J. (1984). *Perceived empathy as a link between perceived communication competence and interpersonal intimacy.* Paper presented at the annual meeting of the Central States Speech Association.

Birdwhistell, R. L. (1970). *Kinesics and context.* Philadelphia: University of Pennsylvania Press.

Bischoping, K. (1993). Gender differences in conversation topic, 1922–1990. *Sex Roles, 28,* 1–18.

Blacker, L. (1999). The launching phase of the life cycle. In B. Carter & M. McGoldrick (Eds.), *The expanded family life cycle: Individual, family, and social perspectives* (3rd ed., pp. 287–306). Boston: Allyn and Bacon.

Blake, R. R., & Mouton, J. S. (1964). *The managerial grid.* Houston: Gulf Publishing.

Blank, P. D. (Ed.). (1993). *Interpersonal expectations: Theory, research, and applications.* Cambridge, England: Cambridge University Press.

Block, J., & Robins, R. W. (1993). A longitudinal study of consistency and change in self-esteem from early adolescence to early childhood. *Child Development, 64,* 909–923.

Bok, S. (1978). *Lying: Moral choice in public and private life.* New York: Pantheon.

Bolton, R. (1990). Listening is more than merely hearing. In J. Stewart (Ed.), *Bridges not walls* (5th ed., pp. 175–191). New York: McGraw-Hill.

Bond, C. F., Omar, A., Pitre, U., & Lashley, B. R. (1992). Fishy-looking liars: Deception judgment from expectancy violation. *Journal of Personality and Social Psychology, 63,* 969–977.

Booth-Butterfield, M., & Booth-Butterfield, S. (1998). Emotionality and affective orientation. In J. C. McCroskey, J. A. Daly, M. M. Martin, & M. J. Beatty (Eds.), *Communication and personality: Trait Perspectives* (pp. 171–190). Cresskill, NJ: Hampton.

Booth-Butterfield, M., & Trotta, M. R. (1994). Attribution patterns for expressions of love. *Communication Reports, 7,* 119–129.

Bordagaray-Sciolino, D. (1984). *The role of self-disclosure as a communication strategy during relationship termination.* Unpublished master's thesis, University of North Carolina at Chapel Hill.

Boster, F. J., Mitchell, M. M., Lapinski, M. K., Cooper, H., Orrego, V. O., & Reinke, R. (1999). The impact of guilt and type of compliance-gaining message on compliance. *Communication Monographs, 66,* 168–177.

Bostrom R. N. (1996). Aspects of listening behavior. In O. Hargie (Ed.), *Handbook of communication skills* (2nd ed., pp 236–259). London: Routledge.

Bostrom, R. N., &. Waldhart, E. S. (1980). Components in listening behavior: The role of short-term memory. *Human Communication Research, 6,* 221–227.

Botan, C., & Smitherman, G. (1991). Black English in the integrated workplace. *Journal of Black Studies, 22,* 165–185.

Bourhis, J., & Allen, M. (1992). Meta-analysis of the relationship between communication apprehension and cognitive performance. *Communication Education, 41,* 68–76.

Bower, B. (1990, May 19). Defensiveness reaps psychiatric benefits. *Science News, 137,* 309.

Bower, B. (1992, August 15). Truth aches: People who view themselves poorly may seek the "truth" and find despair. *Science News, 142,* 110-111.

Bower, B. (1995, March 18). Nice guys look better in women's eyes. *Science News, 147,* 165.

Bowman, B. W. (1964, January-February). What helps or harms promotability? *Harvard Business Review, 42,* 14.

Bradac, J. (1990). Language attitudes and impression formation. In H. Giles & W. P. Robinson (Eds.), *Handbook of language and social psychology* (pp. 387–412). Chichester, England UK: John Wiley.

Bradbury, T. N., & Fincham, F. D. (1990). Attributions in marriage: Review and critique. *Psychological Bulletin, 107,* 3-33.

Brashers, D. E., & Jackson, S. (1999). Changing conceptions of "message effect": A 24–year overview. *Human Communication Research, 25,* 457–477.

Brightman, V., Segal, A., Werther, P., & Steiner, J. (1975). Ethological study of facial expression in response to taste stimuli. *Journal of Dental Research, 54,* 141.

Brodsky, S. L., Hooper, N. E., Tipper, D. G., & Yates, S. B. (1999). Attorney invasion of witness space. *Law and Psychology Review, 23,* 49–68.

Broome, B. J. (1991). Building shared meaning: Implications of a relational approach to empathy for teaching intercultural communication. *Communication Education, 40,* 235–249.

Brouwer, D. (1998). The precarious visibility politics of self-stigmatization: The case of HIV/AIDS tattoos. *Text and Performance Quarterly, 18,* 114–136.

Brown, D. (1991). *Human universals.* New York: McGraw-Hill.

Brown, J. (1999, March 10). "Indian red" crayon will get new name. *Cincinnati Enquirer,* A2.

Brown, J. D., & Mankowski, T. A. (1993). Self-esteem, mood, and self-evaluation: Changes in mood and the way you see you. *Journal of Personality and Social Psychology, 64,* 421–430.

Brown, L. (1982). *Communicating facts and ideas in business.* Englewood Cliffs, NJ: Prentice-Hall.

Brownell, J. (1990). Perceptions of effective listeners: A management study. *Journal of Business Communication, 27,* 401–415.

Brownell, J. (1996). *Listening: Attitudes, principles, and skills.* Boston: Allyn & Bacon.

Bruess, C. J. S., & Pearson, J. C. (1997). Interpersonal rituals in marriage and adult friendship. *Communication Monographs, 64,* 25–46.

Budescu, D. V., Erev, I., & Zwick, R. (Eds.). (1999). Games and human behavior: Essays in honor of Amnon Rapoport. Mahwah, NJ: Lawrence Erlbaum Associates.

Buller, D. B. (1988). *Deception by strangers, friends, and intimates: Attributional biases due to relationship development.* Paper presented at the annual meeting of the Speech Communication Association, Boston.

Buller, D. B., & Aune, K. (1988). The effects of vocalics and nonverbal sensitivity on compliance: A speech accommodation theory explanation. *Human Communication Research, 14,* 301–332.

Buller, D. B., & Aune, K. (1992). The effects of speech rate similarity on compliance application of communication accommodation theory. *Western Journal of Communication, 56,* 37–53.

Buller, D. B., & Burgoon, J. K. (1994). Deception: Strategic and nonstrategic communicaton. In J. A. Daly & J. M. Wiemann (Eds.), *Interpersonal communication* (pp. 191–213). Hillsdale, NJ: Lawrence Erlbaum Associates.

Buller, D. B., & Burgoon, J. K. (1994). Deception: Strategic and nonstrategic communication. In J. A. Daly & J. M. Wiemann (Eds.), *Strategic interpersonal communication* (pp. 191–223). Hillsdale, NJ: Lawrence Erlbaum Associates.

Buller, D. B., Strzyzewski, K. D., & Hunsaker, F. (1991). Interpersonal deception: II. The inferiority of conversational participants as deception detectors. *Communication Monographs, 58,* 25–40.

Burggraf, C. S., & Sillars, A. L. (1987). A critical examination of sex differences in marital communication. *Communication Monographs, 54,* 276–294.

Burgoon, J. K., Birk, T. & Pfau, M. (1990). Nonverbal behaviors, persuasion, and credibility. *Human Communication Research, 17,* 140-169.

Burgoon, J. K., Buller, D. B., & Guerrero, L. K. (1995). Interpersonal deception: IX. Effects of social skill and nonverbal communication on deception success and detection accuracy. *Journal of Language and Social Psychology, 14,* 289–311.

Burgoon, J. K., Buller, D. B., Guerrero, L. K., Afifi, W. A., & Feldman, C. M. (1996). Interpersonal deception: XII. Information management dimensions underlying deceptive and truthful messages. *Communication Monographs, 63,* 50-69.

Burgoon, J. K., Buller, D. B., Guerrero, L. K., & Feldman, C. M. (1994). Interpersonal deception: VI. Effects of preinteractional and interactional factors on deceiver and observer perceptions of deception success. *Communication Studies, 45,* 263–280.

Burgoon, J. K., Buller, D. B., & Viprakasit, R. (1998, July). *Does participation affect deception success? A test of the inter-activity effect.* Paper presented at the conference of the International Communication Association, Jerusalem, Israel.

Burgoon, J. K., Buller, D. B., Woodall, W. G. (1996). *Nonverbal communication: The unspoken dialogue* (2nd ed.). New York: McGraw-Hill.

Burgoon, J. K., & Le Poire, B. A. (1999). Nonverbal cues and interpersonal judgments: Participant and observer perceptions of intimacy, dominance, and composure. *Communication Monographs, 66,* 105–124.

Burgoon, J. K., Parrott, R., LePoire, B. A., Kelley, D. L., Walther, J. B., & Perry, D. (1989). Maintaining and restoring privacy through different types of relationships. *Journal of Social and Personal Relationships, 6,* 131–158.

Burgoon, J. K., Walther, J., & Baesler, E. (1992). Interpretations, evaluations, and consequences of interpersonal touch. *Human Communication Research, 19,* 237–263.

Burkitt, I. (1992). *Social selves: Theories of the social formation of personality.* Newbury Park, CA: Sage.

Burleson, B. R. (1982). The development of comforting communication skills in childhood and adolescence. *Child Development, 53,* 1578–1588.

Burleson, B. R. (1984). Comforting communication. In H. Sypher & J. Applegate (Eds.), *Communication by children and adults: Social cognitive and strategic processes* (pp. 63–104). Beverly Hills, CA: Sage.

Burleson, B. R. (1994). Comforting messages: Features, functions and outcomes. In J. A. Daly & J. M. Wiemann (Eds.), *Strategic interpersonal communication* (pp. 135–161). Hillsdale, NJ: Lawrence Erlbaum Associates.

Burleson, B. R., & Caplan, S. E. (1998). Cognitive complexity. In J. C. McCroskey, J. A. Daly, M. M. Martin, & M. J. Beatty (Eds.), *Communication and personality: Trait perspectives* (pp. 233–286). Cresskill, NJ: Hampton Press.

Burleson, B. R., Delia, J., & Applegate, J. (1995). The socialization of person-centered communication: Parental contributions to the social-cognitive and communication skills of their children. In M. A. Fitzpatrick & A. Vangelisti (Eds.), *Explaining family interactions* (pp. 34–76). Thousand Oaks, CA: Sage.

Burleson, B. R., & Samter, W. (1985). Individual differences in the perception of comforting messages: An exploratory investigation. *Central States Speech Journal, 36,* 39–50.

Burleson, B. R., & Samter, W. (1994). A social skills approach to relationship maintenance. In D. J. Canary & L. Stafford (Eds), *Communication and relationship maintenance: How individual differences in communication skills affect the achievement of relationship functions* (pp. 61–90). San Diego: Academic Press.

Burleson, B. R., & Samter, W. (1996). Similarity in the communication skills of young adults: Foundations of attraction, friendship, and relationship satisfaction. *Communication Reports, 9,* 127–139.

Burns, D. D. (1999). *The feeling good handbook* (rev. ed.). New York: Plume/Penguin.

Burns, K. L., & Beie, E. G. (1973). Significance of vocal and visual channels for the decoding of emotional meaning. *Journal of Communication, 23,* 118–130.

Bushman, B. J., Baumeister, R. F., & Stack, A. D. (1999). Catharsis, aggression, and persuasive influence: Self-fulfilling or self-defeating prophecies? *Journal of Personality and Social Psychology, 76,* 367–376.

Buss, D. M. (1985, January-February). Human mate selection. *American Scientist, 73,* 47–51.

Buttny, R. (1997). Reported speech in talking race on campus. *Human Communication Research, 23,* 477–506.

Byrne, D. (1997). An overview (and underview) of research and theory within the attraction paradigm. *Journal of Social and Personal Relationships, 14,* 417–431.

Cahn, D. D. (1992). *Conflict in intimate relationships.* New York: Guilford Press.

Campbell, A., Converse, P. E., Rogers, W. L. (1976). *The quality of married life.* New York: Russell Sage Foundation.

Canary, D. J., & Cupach, W. R. (1988). Relational and episodic characteristics associated with conflict tactics. *Journal of Social and Personal Relationships, 5,* 305–325.

Canary, D. J., Cupach, W. R., & Messman, S. J. (1995). *Relationship conflict.* Newbury Park, CA: Sage.

Canary, D. J., & Emmers-Sommer, T. M. (1997). *Sex and gender differences in personal relationships.* New York: Guilford Press.

Canary, D. J., & Hause, K. (1993). Is there any reason to research sex differences in communication? *Communication Quarterly, 41,* 482–517.

Canary, D. J., & Spitzberg, B. H. (1987). Appropriateness and effectiveness perceptions of conflict strategies. *Human Communication Research, 15,* 93-118.

Canary, D. J., Weger, H., Jr., & Stafford, L. (1991). Couples' argument sequences and their associations with relational characteristics. *Western Journal of Speech Communication, 55,* 159–179.

Carbaugh, D. (1996). *Situating selves: The communication of social identities in American scenes.* Albany: State University of New York Press.

Carli, L. L. (1990). Gender, language, and influence. *Journal of Personality and Social Psychology, 59,* 941–951.

Carrell, L. J. (1997). Diversity in the communication curriculum: Impact on student empathy. *Communication Education, 46,* 234–244.

Carrell, L. J., & Willmington, S. C. (1996). A comparison of self-report and performance data in assessing speaking and listening competence. *Communication Reports, 9,* 185–191.

Carroll, J. M., & Russell, J. A. (1996). Do facial expressions signal specific emotions? Judging emotion from the face in context. *Journal of Personality and Social Psychology, 70,* 205–218.

Casmir, F. L. (1991). Culture, communication, and education. *Communication Education, 40,* 229–234.

Cawyer, C. S., & Smith-Dupré, A. (1995). Communicating social support: Identifying supportive episodes in an HIV/AIDS support group. *Communication Quarterly, 43,* 243-258.

Cegala, D. J., Savage, G. T., Brunner, C. C., & Conrad, A. B. (1982). An elaboration of the meaning of interaction involvement: Toward the development of a theoretical concept. *Communication Monographs, 49,* 229–248.

Chan, Y. K. (1999). Density, crowding, and factors intervening in their relationship: Evidence from a hyper-dense metropolis. *Social Indicators Research, 48,* 103–124.

Chandler, D. (1998). *Personal home pages and the construction of identities on the web* [On-line]. Available: http://www.aber.ac.uk/~dgc/webident.html

Chelune, G. J. (Ed.). (1979). *Self-disclosure: Origins, patterns and implications of openness in interpersonal relationships.* San Francisco: Jossey-Bass.

Chelune, G. J., Rosenfeld, L. B., & Waring, E. M. (1985). Spouse disclosure patterns in distressed and non-distressed couples. *American Journal of Family Therapy, 13,* 24–32.

Chen, G. M., & Sarosta, W. J. (1996). Intercultural communication competence: A synthesis. In B. R. Burleson & A. W. Kunkel, (Eds.), *Communication yearbook 19* (pp. 353–383). Thousand Oaks, CA: Sage.

Chen, L. (1997). Verbal adaptive strategies in U.S. American dyadic interactions with U.S. American or East-Asian partners. *Communication Monographs, 64,* 302–323.

Chovil, N. (1991). Social determinants of facial displays. *Journal of Nonverbal Behavior, 15,* 141–154.

Christopher, F. S., & Frandsen, M. M. (1990). Strategies of influence in sex and dating. *Journal of Social and Personal Relationships, 7,* 89–105.

Cialdini, R. B. (1988). *Influence: Science and practice.* Glenview, IL: Scott-Foresman.

Cissna, K. N., & Anderson, R. (1996). Communication and the ground of dialogue. In R. Anderson, K. N. Cissna, & R. C. Arnett (Eds.), *The reach of dialogue: Confirmation, voice, and community* (pp. 9–30). Cresskill, NJ: Hampton Press.

Cissna, K. N., & Sieberg, E. (1999). Patterns of interactional confirmation and disconfirmation. In J. Stewart (Ed.), *Bridges not walls* (7th ed., pp, 336–346). New York: McGraw-Hill.

Clark, R. A. (1998). A comparison of topics and objectives in a cross section of young men's and women's everyday conversations. In D. J. Canary & K. Dindia (Eds.), *Sex differences and similarities in communication: Critical essays and empirical investigations of sex and gender in interaction* (pp. 303–319). Mahwah, NJ: Lawrence Erlbaum Associates.

Clark, R. A., & Delia, J. G. (1997). Individuals' preferences for friends' approaches to providing support in distressing situations. *Communication Reports, 10,* 115–121.

Clark, R. A., Pierce, A. J., Finn, K., Hsu, K., Toosley, A., & Williams, L. (1998). The impact of alternative approaches to comforting, closeness of relationship, and gender on multiple measures of effectiveness. *Communication Studies, 49,* 224–239.

Clarke, F. P. (1973). *Interpersonal communication variables as predictors of marital satisfaction-dissatisfaction.* Unpublished doctoral dissertation, University of Denver.

Clay, R. A. (1995, November). Working mothers: Happy or haggard? *APA Monitor,* pp. 1, 37.

Clevenger, T. (1991). Can one not communicate? A conflict of models. *Communication Studies, 42,* 340-353.

Cloven, D. H., & Roloff, M. E. (1991). Sense-making activities and interpersonal conflict: Communicative cures for the mulling blues. *Western Journal of Speech Communication, 55,* 134–158.

Coates, J. (1986). *Women, men and language.* London: Longman.

Cody, M. J. (1982). A typology of disengagement strategies and examination of the role of intimacy, reactions to inequity, and relational problems in strategy selection. *Communication Monographs, 49,* 148–170.

Cody, M. J., Dunn, D., Hoppin, S., & Wendt, P. (1999). Silver surfers: Training and evaluating Internet use among older adult learners. *Communication Education, 48,* 269–286.

Cody, M. J., & McLaughlin, M. L. (1980). Perceptions of compliance gaining situations: A dimensional analysis. *Communication Monographs, 47,* 132–148.

Cody, M. J., McLaughlin, M. L., & Schneider, M. J. (1981). The impact of relational consequences and intimacy on the selection of interpersonal persuasion tactics: A reanalysis. *Communication Quarterly, 28,* 91–106.

Cody, M. J., Woelfel, M. L. , & Jordan, W. J. (1983). Dimensions of compliance-gaining situations. *Human Communication Research, 9,* 99–113.

Cohen, D., Bowdle, B. F., Nisbett, R. E., Schwarz, N. (1996). Insult, aggression, and the southern culture of honor: An "experimental ethnography." *Journal of Personality and Social Psychology, 70,* 945–960.

Cohen, S., Doyle, W. J., Skoner, D. P., Rabin, B. S, & Gwaltney, J. M. (1997). Social ties and susceptibility to the common cold. *Journal of the American Medical Association, 277,* 1940–1944.

Colbert, K. R. (1993). The effects of debate participation on argumentativeness and verbal aggression. *Communication Education, 42,* 206–214.

Coleman, L. M., & DePaulo, B. M. (1991). Uncovering the human spirit: Moving beyond disability and "missed" communications. In N. Coupland, H. Giles, & J. M. Wiemann (Eds.), *"Miscommunication" and problematic talk* (pp. 61–84). Newbury Park, CA: Sage.

Collier, M. J. (1991). Conflict competence within African, Mexican, and Anglo American friendships. In S. Ting-Toomey & F. Korzenny (Eds.), *Cross-cultural interpersonal communication* (pp.132–154). Newbury Park, CA: Sage.

Collier, M. J. (1996). Communication competence problematics in ethnic relationships. *Communication Monographs, 63,* 314–336.

Conlee, C., Olvera, J., & Vagim, N. (1993). The relationships among physician nonverbal immediacy and measures of patient satisfaction with physician care. *Communication Reports, 6,* 25–33.

Conn, M. K., & Peterson, C. (1989). Social support: Seek and ye shall find. *Journal of Social and Personal Relationships, 6,* 345–358.

Conville, R. L. (1991). *Relational transitions: The evolution of personal relationships.* New York: Praeger.

Coon, D. (1995). *Introduction to psychology* (7th ed.). St. Paul, MN: West.

Cooper, B. (1999). The relevancy of gender identity in spectators' interpretations of *Thelma and Louise*. *Critical Studies in Mass Communication, 16,* 20–41.

Cooper, J., & Jones, E. E. (1969). Opinion divergence as a strategy to avoid being miscast. *Journal of Personality and Social Psychology, 13,* 23-30.

Cooper, L. O., Seibold, D. R., & Suchner, R. (1997). Listening in organizations: An analysis of error structures in models of listening competency. *Communication Research Reports, 14,* 312–320.

Cox, S. A. (1999). Group communication and employee turnover: How coworkers encourage peers to voluntarily exit. *Southern Communication Journal, 64,* 181–192.

Cozby, P. C. (1972). Self-disclosure, reciprocity, and liking. *Sociometry, 35,* 151–160.

Cozby, P. C. (1973). Self-disclosure: A literature review. *Psychological Bulletin, 79,* 73-91.

Crane, D. R. (1987). Diagnosing relationships with spatial distance: An empirical test of a clinical principle. *Journal of Marital and Family Therapy, 13,* 307–310.

Crohan, S. E. (1992). Marital happiness and spousal consensus on beliefs about marital conflict: A longitudinal investigation. *Journal of Social and Personal Relationships, 9,* 89–102.

Cronen, V., Chen, V., & Pearce, W. B. (1988). Coordinated management of meaning: A critical theory. In Y. Y. Kim & W. B. Gudykunst (Eds.), *Theories in intercultural communication* (pp. 66–98). Newbury Park, CA: Sage.

Cronkhite, G. (1976). *Communication and awareness.* Menlo Park, CA: Cummings.

Crown, C. L., & Cummins, D. A. (1998). Objective versus perceived vocal interruptions in the dialogues of unacquainted pairs, friends, and couples. *Journal of Language and Social Psychology, 17,* 372–389.

Crowther, C. E., & Stone, G. (1986). *Intimacy: Strategies for successful relationships.* Santa Barbara, CA: Capra Press.

Crusco, A. H., & Wetzel, G. G. (1984). The Midas Touch: Effects of interpersonal touch on restaurant tipping. *Personality and Social Psychology Bulletin, 10,* 512–517.

Cupach, W. R., & Messman, S. J. (1999). Face predilections and friendship solidarity. *Communication Reports, 12,* 117–124.

Cupach, W. R., & Metts, S. (1986). Accounts of relational dissolution: A comparison of marital and non-marital relationships. *Communication Monographs, 53,* 311–334.

Davidowitz, M., & Myrick, R. (1984). Responding to the bereaved: An analysis of "helping" styles. *Death Education, 8,* 1–10.

Davidson, B., Balswich, J., & Halverson, C. (1983). Affective self-disclosure and marital adjustment: A test of equity theory. *Journal of Marriage and the Family, 45,* 93-102.

Davis, S. F., & Kieffer, J. C. (1998). Restaurant servers influence tipping behavior. *Psychological Reports, 83,* 223–226.

DeAngelis, T. (1992). Illness linked with repressive style of coping. *APA Monitor,* pp. 14–15.

DeAngelis, T. (1992, October). The "who am I" question wears a cloak of culture. *APA Monitor,* pp. 22–23.

Deaux, K. (1972). To err is humanizing: But sex makes a difference. *Representative Research in Social Psychology, 3,* 20-28.

Dennis, A. R., Kinney, S. T., & Hung, Y. T. (1999). Gender differences in the effects of media richness. *Small Group Research, 30,* 405–437.

DePaulo, B. M. (1992). Nonverbal behavior and self-presentation. *Psychological Bulletin, 3,* 203-243.

DePaulo, B. M. (1994). Spotting lies: Can humans learn to do better? *Current Directions in Psychological Science, 3,* 83-86.

DePaulo, B. M., Kashy, D. A., Kirkendol, S. E., & Wyer, M. M. (1996). Lying in everyday life. *Journal of Personality and Social Psychology, 70,* 779–795.

Derlega, V. J., Barbee, A. P., & Winstead, B. A. (1994). Friendship, gender, and social support: Laboratory studies of supportive interactions. In B. R. Burleson, T. L. Albrecht, & I. G. Sarson (Eds.), *Communication of social support: Message, interactions, relationships, and community* (pp. 136–151). Newbury Park, CA: Sage.

Derlega, V. J., & Grzelak, J. (1979). Appropriateness of self-disclosure. In G. J. Chelune (Ed.), *Self-disclosure: Origins, patterns and implications of openness in interpersonal relationships* (pp. 151–176). San Francisco: Jossey-Bass.

Derlega, V. J., Lewis, R. J., Harrison, S., Winstead, B. A., & Costanza, R. (1989). Gender differences in the initiation and attribution of tactile intimacy. *Journal of Nonverbal Behavior, 13,* 83-96.

Derlega, V. J., Metts, S., Petronio, S., & Margulis, S. T. (1993). *Self-disclosure*. Newbury Park, CA: Sage.

Derlega, V. J., Wilson, M., & Chaikin, A. L. (1976). Friendship and disclosure reciprocity. *Journal of Personality and Social Psychology, 34*, 578–582.

deTurck, M. A., & Miller, G. R. (1990). Training observers to detect deception: Effects of self-monitoring and rehearsal. *Human Communication Research, 16*, 603-620.

Dieckmann, L. E. (2000). Private secrets and public disclosures: The case of battered women. In S. Petronio (Ed.), *Balancing the secrets of private disclosures* (pp. 275–286). Mahwah, NJ: Lawrence Erlbaum Associates.

Dillard, J. P. (1990). *Seeking compliance: The production of interpersonal influence messages*. Scottsdale, AZ: Gorsuch Scarisbrick.

Dillard, J. P., Haunani, D., & Palmer, M. T. (1999). Structuring the concept of relational communication. *Communication Monographs, 66*, 49–65.

Dillard, J. P., Solomon, D. H., & Palmer, M. T. (1999). Structuring the concept of relational communication. *Communication Monographs, 66*, 49–65.

Dindia, K. (2000a). Self-disclosure research: Advances through meta-analysis. In M. A. Allen, R. W. Preiss, B. M. Gayle, & N. Burrell (Eds.), *Interpersonal communication: Advances through meta-analysis*. Mahwah, NJ: Lawrence Erlbaum Associates.

Dindia, K. (2000b). Sex differences in self-disclosure, reciprocity of self-disclosure, and self-disclosure and liking: Three meta-analyses reviewed. In S. Petronio (Ed.), *Balancing the secrets of private disclosures* (pp. 21–35). Mahwah, NJ: Lawrence Erlbaum Associates.

Dindia, K., & Allen, M. (1992). Sex differences in self-disclosure: A meta-analysis. *Psychological Bulletin, 112*, 106–124.

Dindia, K., Fitzpatrick, M. A., & Kenny, D. A. (1988). *Self-disclosure in spouse and stranger interaction: A social relations analysis*. Paper presented at the annual meeting of the International Communication Association, New Orleans, LA.

Dindia, K., Fitzpatrick, M. A., & Kenny, D. A. (1997). Self-disclosure in spouse and stranger dyads: A social relations analysis. *Human Communication Research, 23*, 388–412.

Dion, K., Berscheid, E., & Walster, E. (1972). What is beautiful is good. *Journal of Personality and Social Psychology, 24*, 285–290.

Dougherty, T., Turban, D., & Collander, J. (1994). Conforming first impressions in the employment interview. *Journal of Applied Psychology, 79*, 659–665.

Douglas, W. (1987). Affinity-testing in initial interactions. *Journal of Social and Personal Relationships, 4*, 3-16.

Douglas, W. (1990). Uncertainty, information-seeking, and liking during initial interaction. *Western Journal of Speech Communication, 54*, 66–81.

Downey, G., & Feldman, S. I. (1996). Implications of rejection sensitivity for intimate relationships. *Journal of Personality and Social Psychology, 70*, 1327–1343.

Downs, V. G. (1988). Grandparents and grandchildren: The relationship between self-disclosure and solidarity in an intergenerational relationship. *Communication Research Reports, 5*, 173-179.

Driscoll, M. S., Newman, D. L., & Seal, J. M. (1988). The effect of touch on the perception of counselors. *Counselor Education and Supervision, 27*, 344–354.

Druckmann, D., Rozelle, R. M., & Baxter, J. C. (1982). *Nonverbal communication: Survey, theory, and research*. Beverly Hills, CA: Sage.

Drullman, R., & Smoorenburg, G. F. (1997). Audio-visual perception of compressed speech by profoundly hearing-impaired subjects. *Audiology, 36*(3), 165–177.

Drummond, K., & Hopper, R. (1993). Acknowledgment tokens in series. *Communication Reports, 6*, 47–53.

Dryden, W., Neenan, M., & Yankura, J. (1999). *Counseling individuals: A rational emotive behavioural handbook* (3rd ed.). London, England: Whurr.

Duck, S. (1987). How to lose friends without influencing people. In M. E. Roloff & G. R. Miller (Eds.), *Interpersonal processes: New directions in communication research* (pp. 278–298). Beverly Hills, CA: Sage.

Duck, S. (1991a). Some evident truths about conversations in everyday relationships: All communications are not created equal. *Human Communication Research, 18*, 228–267.

Duck, S. (1991b). *Human relationships: An introduction to social psychology*. Newbury Park, CA: Sage.

Duck, S. (1992). Social emotions: Showing our feelings about other people. In *Human Relationships* (pp. 1–34). Newbury Park, CA: Sage.

Duck, S. (1994a). *Meaningful relationships: Talking, sense, and relating.* Thousand Oaks, CA: Sage.

Duck, S. (1994b). Steady as s(he) goes: Relational maintenance as a shared meaning system. In D. J. Canary & L. Stafford (Eds.), *Relational maintenance* (pp. 45–60). San Diego: Academic Press.

Duck, S. (1994c). Maintenance as a shared meaning system. In D. J. Canary & L. Stafford (Eds.), *Communication and relationship maintenance: How individual differences in communication skills affect the achievement of relationship functions* (pp. 45–60). San Diego: Academic Press.

Duck, S., & Barnes, M. K. (1992). Disagreeing about agreement: Reconciling differences about similarity. *Communication Monographs, 59,* 199–208.

Duck, S., & Miell, D. E. (1986). Charting the development of personal relationships. In R. Gilmour & S. Duck (Eds.), *The emerging field of personal relationships.* Hillsdale, NJ: Lawrence Erlbaum Associates.

Duck, S., & Pittman, G. (1994). Social and personal relationships. In M. L. Knapp & G. R. Miller (Eds.), *Handbook of interpersonal communication* (2nd ed., pp. ). Newbury Park, CA: Sage.

Duran, R. L., & Kelly, L. (1988). The influence of communicative competence on perceived task, social, and physical attraction. *Communication Quarterly, 36,* 41–49.

Eisenberg, E. M. (1984). Ambiguity as strategy in organizational communication. *Communication Monographs, 51,* 227–242.

Eisenberg, E. M. (1990). Jamming: Transcendence through organizing. *Communication Research, 17,* 139–164.

Eisenberg, E. M., & Witten, M. G. (1987). Reconsidering openness in organizational communication. *Academy of Management Review, 12,* 418–426.

Ekenrode, J. (1984). Impact of chronic and acute stressors on daily reports of mood. *Journal of Personality and Social Psychology, 46,* 907–918.

Ekman, P. (1985). *Telling lies: Clues to deceit in the marketplace, politics, and marriage.* New York: Norton.

Ekman, P., & Friesen, W. V. (1974a). Detecting deception from the body or face. *Journal of Personality and Social Psychology, 29,* 288–298.

Ekman, P., & Friesen, W. V. (1974b). Nonverbal behavior and psychopathology. In R. J. Friedman & M. N. Katz (Eds.), *The psychology of depression: Contemporary theory and research.* Washington, DC: J. Winston.

Ekman, P., & Friesen, W. V. (1975). *Unmasking the face: A guide to recognizing emotions from facial clues.* Englewood Cliffs, NJ: Prentice-Hall.

Ekman, P., Friesen, W. V., & Baer, J. (1984, May). The international language of gestures. *Psychology Today, 18,* 64–69.

Ekman, P., Levenson, R. W., & Friesen, W. V. (1983, September). Autonomic nervous system activity distinguishes among emotions. *Science, 221,* 1208–1210.

Ekman, P., Sorenson, E. R., & Friesen, W. V. (1969, April). Pan-cultural elements in facial displays of emotions. *Science, 164,* 86–88.

Elias, F. G., Johnson, M. E., & Fortman, J. B. (1989). Task-focused self-disclosure: Effects on group cohesiveness, commitment to task, and productivity. *Small Group Behavior, 20,* 87–96.

Ellis, A. (1999). Why rational-emotive therapy to rational emotive behavior therapy? *Psychotherapy, 36*(2), 154–159.

Ellis, A., & Greiger, R. (1977). *Handbook for rational-emotive therapy.* New York: Springer.

Ellis, D. G., & McCallister, L. (1980). Relational control sequences in sex-typed and androgynous groups. *Western Journal of Speech Communication, 44,* 35–49.

Endres, T. G. (1997). Father-daughter dramas: A Q-investigation of rhetorical visions. *Journal of Applied Communication Research, 25,* 317–340.

Fadiman, A. (1997). *The spirit catches you and you fall down.* New York: Farrar, Straus and Giroux.

Faul, S. (1994). *The xenophobe's guide to the Americans.* Horsham, England: Ravette.

Feeley, T. H., deTurck. M. A., & Young, M. J. (1995, May). *Baseline familiarity in lie detection.* Paper presented at the meeting of the International Communication Association, Albuquerque, NM.

Fehr, B. (1996). *Friendship processes.* Thousand Oaks, CA: Sage.

Feingold, A. (1995). Gender differences in personality: A meta-analysis. *Psychological Bulletin, 116,* 429–456.

Feldman, S. D. (1975). The presentation of shortness in everyday life. Height and heightism in American society: Toward a sociology of stature. In S. D. Feldman & G. W. Thielbar (Eds.), *Lifestyles: Diversity in American society* (2nd ed.). Boston: Little, Brown.

Felmlee, D. H. (1998). "Be careful what you wish for . . .": A quantitative and qualitative investigation of "fatal attractions." *Personal Relationships, 5,* 235–253.

Felson, R. B. (1980). Communication barriers and the reflected appraisal process. *Social Psychology Quarterly, 43,* 223-233.

Felson, R. B. (1985). Reflected appraisal and the development of self. *Social Psychology Quarterly, 48,* 71–78.

Filley, A. C. (1975). *Interpersonal conflict resolution.* Glenview, IL: Scott, Foresman.

Fincham, F. D., Beach, S. R. H., & Nelson, G. (1987). Attribution processes in distressed and nondistressed couples 3: Causal and responsibility attributions for spouse behavior. *Cognitive Therapy and Research, 11,* 71–86.

Fincham, F. D., Beach, S. R. H., & Nelson, G. (1988). Attribution processes in distressed and nondistressed couples 5: Real versus hypothetical events. *Cognitive Therapy and Research, 12,* 505–514.

Fincham, F. D., & Bradbury, T. N. (1989). The impact of attributions in marriage: An individual difference analysis. *Journal of Social and Personal Relationships, 6,* 69–85.

Finley, G. E., & Humphreys, C. A. (1974). Naive psychology and the development of persuasive appeals in girls. *Canadian Journal of Behavioral Science, 6,* 75–80.

Fischer, S. D., Delhorne, L. A., & Reed, C. M. (1999). Effects of rate of presentation on the reception of American Sign Language. *Journal of Speech, Language, and Hearing Research, 42*(3), 568–582.

Fisher, B. A. (1983). Differential effects of sexual composition and interactional content on interaction patterns in dyads. *Human Communication Research, 9,* 225–238.

Fisher, B. A., & Adams, K. (1994). *Interpersonal communication: Pragmatics of human relationships* (2nd ed.). New York: Random House.

Fisher, D. V. (1986). Decision-making and self-disclosure. *Journal of Social and Personal Relationships, 3,* 323-336.

Fisher, R., Kopelman, E., & Schneider, A. K. (1996). *Beyond Machiavelli: Tools for coping with conflict.* New York: Penguin.

Fishman, P. (1978). Interaction: The work women do. *Social Problems, 25,* 397–406.

Fitch, K. L. (1994). A cross-cultural study of directive sequences and some implications for compliance-gaining research. *Communication Monographs, 61,* 185–209.

Fitts, W. H. (1971). *The self-concept and self-actualization.* Nashville, TN: Counselor Recordings and Tests.

Fitzpatrick, J., & Sollie, D. L. (1999). Influence of individual and interpersonal factors on satisfaction and stability in romantic relationships. *Personal Relationships, 6,* 337–350.

Fitzpatrick, M. A. (1977). A typological approach to communication in relationships. In B. Rubin (Ed.), *Communication yearbook 1* (pp. 263–275). New Brunswick, NJ: Transaction Books.

Fitzpatrick, M. A. (1988). *Between husbands and wives: Communication in marriage.* Newbury Park, CA: Sage.

Fitzpatrick, M. A., Fallis, S., & Vance, L. (1982). Multifunctional coding of conflict resolution strategies in marital dyads. *Family Relations, 21,* 61–71.

Fletcher, G. J. O., Fincham, F. D., Cramer, L., & Heron, N. (1987). The role of attributions in the development of dating relationships. *Journal of Personality and Social Psychology, 53,* 481–489.

Floyd, J. J. (1985). *Listening: A practical approach.* Glenview, IL: Scott, Foresman.

Floyd, K. (1996). Communicating closeness among siblings: An application of the gendered closeness perspective. *Communication Research Reports, 13,* 27–34.

Floyd, K. (1997a). Communication affection in dyadic relationships: An assessment of behavior and expectancies. *Communication Quarterly, 45,* 68–80.

Floyd, K. (1997b). Knowing when to say "I love you": An expectancy approach to affectionate communication. *Communication Research Reports, 14,* 321–330.

Folger, J. P., Poole, M. S., & Stuttman, R. K. (1996). *Working through conflict: Strategies for relationships, groups, and organizations.* Reading, MA: Addison-Wesley Longman.

Fontaine, G. (1990). Cultural diversity in intimate intercultural relationships. In D. D. Cahn (Ed.), *Intimates in conflict: A communication perspective* (pp. 209–224). Hillsdale, NJ: Lawrence Erlbaum Associates.

Fortenberry, J. H., Maclean, J., Morris, P., & O'Connell, M. (1978). Mode of dress as a perceptual cue to deference. *Journal of Social Psychology, 104,* 131–139.

Foss, K. A., & Edson, B. A. (1989). What's in a name? Accounts of married women's name choices. *Western Journal of Speech Communication, 53,* 356–373.

Foss, S. K., & Griffin, C. L. (1995). Beyond persuasion: A proposal for an invitational rhetoric. *Communication Monographs, 62,* 2–18.

Francis, J., & Wales, R. (1994). Speech a la mode: Prosodic cues, message interpretation, and impression formation. *Journal of Language and Social Psychology, 13,* 34–44.

Friedman, S. D., Christensen, P., & DeGroot, J. (1998, November–December). Work and life: The end of the zero-sum game. *Harvard Business Review, 76*(6), 119–129.

Fromme, D. K., Jaynes, W. E., Taylor, D. K., Hanold, E. G., Daniell, J., Rountree, J. R., & Fromme, M. (1989). Nonverbal behavior and attitudes toward touch. *Journal of Nonverbal Behavior, 13,* 3-14.

Fulmer, R. (1999). Becoming an adult: Leaving home and staying connected. In B. Carter & M. McGoldrick (Eds.), *The expanded family life cycle: Individual, family, and social perspectives* (3rd ed., pp. 215–230). Boston: Allyn and Bacon.

Gadlin, H. (1977). Private lives and public order: A critical view of the history of intimate relations in the United States. In G. Levinger & H. L. Raush (Eds.), *Close relationships: Perspectives on the meaning of intimacy* (pp. 33–72). Amherst, MA: University of Massachusetts Press.

Gallois, C. (1993). The language and communication of emotion: Universal, interpersonal, or intergroup? *American Behavioral Scientist, 36,* 309–338.

Gara, M. A., Woolfolk, R. L., Cohen, B. D., Gioldston, R. B., & Allen, L. A. (1993). Perception of self and other in major depression. *Journal of Abnormal Psychology, 102,* 93-100.

Garko, M. G. (1990). Perspectives on and conceptualizations of compliance and compliance-gaining. *Communication Quarterly, 38,* 138–157.

Gass, R. (1998). *Persuasion, social influence, and compliance gaining.* Needham Heights, MA: Allyn and Bacon.

Gayle, B. M., & Preiss, R. W. (1999). Language intensity plus: A methodological approach to validate emotions in conflicts. *Communication Reports, 12,* 43–50.

Gayle, B. M., Preiss, R. W., & Allen, M. A. (1998). Embedded gender expectations: A covariate analysis of conflict situations and issues. *Communication Research Reports, 15,* 379–387.

Gayle, B. M., Preiss, R. W., & Allen, M. A. (in press). A meta-analytic interpretation of intimate and non-intimate interpersonal conflict. In M. A. Allen, R. W. Preiss, B. M. Gayle, & N. Burrell (Eds.), *Interpersonal communication: Advances through meta-analysis.* Mahwah, NJ: Lawrence Erlbaum Associates.

Gergen, K. J. (1971). *The concept of self.* New York: Holt, Rinehart and Winston.

Gergen, K. J. (1991). *The saturated self: Dilemmas of identity in contemporary life.* New York: Basic Books.

Gibb, J. R. (1961). Defensive communication. *Journal of Communication, 11,* 141–148.

Giles, H., Coupland, N., & Wiemann, J. M. (1992). "Talk is cheap . . ." but "my word is my bond": Beliefs about talk. In K. Bolton & H. Kwok (Eds.), *Sociolinguistics today: International perspectives* (pp. 218–243). London: Routledge & Kegan Paul.

Giles, H., & Franklyn-Stokes, A. (1989). Communicator characteristics. In M. K. Asante & W. B. Gudykunst (Eds.), *Handbook of international and intercultural communication* (pp. 117–144). Newbury Park, CA: Sage.

Giles, H., Henwood, K., Coupland, N., Harriman, J., & Coupland, J. (1992). Language attitudes and cognitive mediation. *Human Communication Research, 18,* 500-527.

Giles, H., & Johnson, P. (1987). Ethnolinguistic identity theory: A social psychological approach to language maintenance. *International Journal of Sociology of Language, 68,* 69–99.

Giles, H., Mulac, A., Bradac, J. J., & Smith, P. J. (1992). Speech accommodation. In W. B. Gudykunst & Y. Y. Kim (Eds.), *Readings on communicating with strangers.* New York: McGraw-Hill.

Giles, H., & Street, R. L., Jr. (1994). Communicator characteristics and behavior. In M. L. Knapp & G. R. Miller (Eds.), *Handbook of interpersonal communication* (2nd ed., pp. 103–161). Thousand Oaks, CA: Sage.

Gleason, J. B., & Greif, E. B. (1983). Men's speech to young children. In B. Thorne, C. Kramarae, & N. Henley (Eds.),

*Language, gender, and society* (pp. 140–150). Rowley, MA: Newbury House.

Goffman, E. (1959). *The presentation of self in everyday life.* Garden City, NY: Doubleday.

Goffman, E. (1971). *Relations in public.* New York: Basic Books.

Goldhaber, G. M. (1970). Listener comprehension of compressed speech as a function of the academic grade level of subjects. *Journal of Communication, 20,* 167–173.

Goldschmidt, W. (1990). *The human career.* Cambridge, MA: Basil Blackman.

Goldsmith, D. J. (1994, November). *The sequential placement of advice.* Paper presented at the meeting of the Speech Communication Association, New Orleans, LA.

Goldsmith, D. J. (2000). Soliciting advice: The role of sequential placement in mitigating face threat. *Communication Monographs, 67,* 1–19.

Goldsmith, D. J., & Baxter, L. A. (1996). Constituting relationships in talk: A taxonomy of speech events in social and personal relationships. *Human Communication Research, 23,* 87–114.

Goldsmith, D. J., & Fitch, K. (1997). The normative context of advice as social support. *Human Communication Research, 23,* 454–476.

Goldsmith, D. J., & Fulfs, P. A. (1999). "You just don't have the evidence": An analysis of claims and evidence in Deborah Tannen's *You Just Don't Understand.* In M. E. Roloff (Ed.), *Communication yearbook 22* (pp. 1–49). Thousand Oaks, CA: Sage.

Goleman, D. (1995). *Emotional intelligence: Why it can matter more than I.Q.* New York: Bantam.

Golen, S. (1990). A factor analysis of barriers to effective listening. *Journal of Business Communication, 27,* 25–36.

Goodman, G., & Esterly, G. (1990). Questions-the most popular piece of language. In J. Stewart (Ed.), *Bridges not walls* (5th ed., pp. 69–77). New York: McGraw-Hill, 1990.

Goody, E. (Ed.). (1978). *Questions and politeness.* London, UK: Cambridge.

Gordon, T. (1970). *P.E.T.: Parent effectiveness training.* New York: Wyden.

Gordon, T. (1974). *T.E.T.: Teacher effectiveness training.* New York: Wyden.

Gordon, T. (1977). *Leadership effectiveness training.* New York: Wyden.

Gorham, J. (1988). The relationship between verbal teacher immediacy behaviors and student learning. *Communication Education, 37,* 40-53.

Goss, B., & O'Hair, D. (1988). *Communicating in interpersonal relationships.* New York: Macmillan.

Gottmann, J. M. (1982). Emotional responsiveness in marital conversations. *Journal of Communication, 32,* 108–120.

Gottman, J. M., Katz, L. F., & Hooven, C. (1997). *Meta-emotion: How families communicate emotionally.* Mahwah, NJ: Lawrence Erlbaum Associates.

Graham, E. E., Papa, M. J., & Brooks, G. P. (1992). Functions of humor in conversation: Conceptualization and measurement. *Western Journal of Communication, 56,* 161–183.

Grant, C. H., III, Cissna, K. N., & Rosenfeld, L. B. (2000). Patients' perceptions of physicians' communication and outcomes of the accrual to trial process. *Health Communication, 12*(1), 23–39.

Grant, J., King, P. E., & Behnke, R. R. (1994). Compliance-gaining strategies, communication satisfaction, and willingness to comply. *Communication Reports, 7,* 99–108.

Gray, J. (1992). *Men are from Mars; women are from Venus: A practical guide for improving communication and getting what you want in your relationship.* New York: HarperCollins.

Greenwald, A. G. (1980). The totalitarian ego: Fabrication and revision of personal history. *American Psychologist, 35,* 603-618.

Greenwald, A. G., & Pratkanis, A. R. (1984). The self. In R. S. Wyer & T. K. Srull (Eds.), *Handbook of social cognition* (Vol. 3, pp. 129–178). Hillsdale, NJ: Lawrence Erlbaum Associates.

Griffin, E. M. (1994). *A first look at communication theory* (2nd ed.). New York: McGraw-Hill.

Griffin, E. M. (1997). *A first look at communication theory* (3rd ed.). New York: McGraw-Hill.

Griffin, E. M. (2000). *A first look at communication theory* (4th ed.). New York: McGraw-Hill.

Grob, L. M., Meyers, R. A., & Schuh, R. (1997). Powerful/ powerless language use in group interactions: Sex differences or similarities? *Communication Quarterly, 45,* 282–303.

Grodin, D., & Lindolf, T. R. (1995). *Constructing the self in a mediated world.* Newbury Park, CA: Sage.

Gudykunst, W. B. (1986). The influence of cultural variability on perceptions of communication behavior associated with relationship terms. *Human Communication Research,* 13, 147–166.

Gudykunst, W. B. (1993a). *Communication in Japan and the United States.* Albany: State University of New York Press.

Gudykunst, W. B. (1993b, February). *Intercultural communication as a separate area of study: Debunking the myth.* Paper presented at the meeting of the Western States Communication Association, Albuquerque, NM.

Gudykunst, W. B., & Kim, Y. Y. (1997). *Communicating with strangers: An approach to intercultural communication* (3rd ed.). New York: McGraw-Hill.

Gudykunst, W. B., & Matsumoto, Y. (1996). Cross-cultural variability of communication in personal relationships. In W. B. Gudykunst, S. Ting-Toomey, & T. Nishida (Eds.), *Communication in personal relationships across cultures* (pp. 19–56). Newbury Park, CA: Sage.

Gudykunst, W. B., & Ting-Toomey, S. (1988). *Culture and interpersonal communication.* Newbury Park, CA: Sage.

Guerrero, L. K., & Afifi, W. A. (1995). Some things are better left unsaid: Topic avoidance in family relationships. *Communication Quarterly, 43,* 276–296.

Guerrero, L. K., Andersen, P. A., Jorgensen, P. F., Spitzberg, B. H., & Eloy, S. V. (1995). Coping with the green-eyed monster: Conceptualizing and measuring communicative responses to romantic jealousy. *Western Journal of Communication, 59,* 270-304.

Guzley, R. (1992). Organizational climate and communication climate: Predictors of commitment to the organization. *Management Communication Quarterly, 5,* 379–402.

Haas, A., & Sherman, M. A. (1982a). Conversational topic as a function of role and gender. *Psychological Reports, 51,* 453-454.

Haas, A., & Sherman, M. A. (1982b). Reported topics of conversation among same-sex adults. *Communication Quarterly, 30,* 332–342.

Hackman, M., & Walker, K. (1990). Instructional communication in the televised classroom: The effects of system design and teacher immediacy. *Communication Education, 39,* 196–206.

Haefner, M. J., & Comstock, J. (1990). Compliance gaining on prime time family programs. *Southern Communication Journal, 55,* 402–420.

Hale, J. L, & Stiff, J. B. (1990). Nonverbal primacy in veracity judgments. *Communication Reports, 3,* 75–83.

Hale, J. L., Tighe, M. R., & Mongeau, P. A. (1997). Effects of event type and sex on comforting messages. *Communication Research Reports, 14,* 214–220.

Hall, E. T. (1959). *Beyond culture.* New York: Doubleday.

Hall, E. T. (1969). *The hidden dimension.* Garden City, NY: Anchor.

Hamachek, D. E. (1982). *Encounters with others: Interpersonal relationships and you.* New York: Holt, Rinehart and Winston.

Hamachek, D. E. (1992). *Encounters with the self* (3rd ed.). Fort Worth, TX: Harcourt Brace.

Hample, D. (1980). Purposes and effects of lying. *Southern Speech Communication Journal, 46,* 33-47.

Hample, D., & Dallinger, J. M. (2000). The effects of situation on the use or suppression of possible compliance gaining appeals. In M. A. Allen, R. W. Preiss, B. M. Gayle, & N. Burrell (Eds.). *Interpersonal communication: Advances through meta-analysis.* Mahwah, NJ: Lawrence Erlbaum Associates.

Harding, S. (1991). *Whose science? Whose knowledge? Thinking from womens' lives.* Ithaca, NY: Cornell University Press.

Harré, R. (1987). The social construction of selves. In K. Yardley & T. Honess (Eds.), *Self and identity: Psychological perspectives* (pp. 41–52). Chichester, England UK: John Wiley & Sons.

Haslett, B. (1983). Communicative functions and strategies in children's conversations. *Human Communication Research, 9,* 114–129.

Hatfield, E., & Sprecher, S. (1986). *Mirror, mirror: The importance of looks in everyday life.* Albany: State University of New York Press.

Hayakawa, S. I. (1964). *Language in thought and action.* New York: Harcourt Brace.

Hecht, M. L., Collier, M. J., & Ribeau, S. A. (1993). *African American communication: Perspectives, principles, and pragmatics.* Hillsdale, NJ: Lawrence Erlbaum Associates.

Hegstrom, T. G. (1979). Message impact: What percentage is nonverbal? *Western Journal of Speech Communication, 43,* 134–142.

Heineken, J. R. (1980). *Disconfirming responses in psychiatric patients.* Unpublished doctoral dissertation, University of Denver, CO.

Helmreich, R., Aronson, E., & Lefan, J. (1970). To err is humanizing-sometimes: Effects of self-esteem, competence, and a pratfall on interpersonal attraction. *Journal of Personality and Social Psychology, 16,* 259–264.

Hendrick, C., Hendrick, S. S., & Dicke, A. (1998). The love attitudes scale: Short form. *Journal of Social and Personal Relationships, 15,* 147–159.

Henneberger, M. (1999, January 29). Misunderstanding of word embarrasses Washington's new mayor. *New York Times* [On-line]. Available: http://www.nyt.com

Hewes, D. E. (Ed.). (1995). *The cognitive bases of interpersonal perception.* Hillsdale, NJ: Lawrence Erlbaum Associates.

Hocker, J. L., & Wilmot, W. W. (1997). *Interpersonal conflict* (5th ed.). New York: McGraw-Hill.

Hoffman, M. L. (1991). Empathy, social cognition, and moral action. In W. Kurtines & J. Gerwirtz (Eds.), *Moral behavior and development: Theory, research, and applications* (Vol. 1, pp. 275–301). Hillsdale, NJ: Lawrence Erlbaum Associates.

Hofstede, G. (1984). *Culture's consequences.* Newbury Park, CA: Sage.

Hoijer, H. (1994). The Sapir-Whorf hypothesis. In L. A. Samovar & R. E. Porter (Eds.), *Intercultural communication: A reader* (7th ed.). Belmont, CA: Wadsworth.

Holte, A., & Wichstrom, L. (1990). Disconfirmatory feedback in families of schizophrenics. *Scandinavian Journal of Psychology, 31,* 198–211.

Homans, G. C. (1961). *Social behavior: Its elementary form.* New York: Harcourt Brace.

Honeycutt, J. M. (1999). Typological differences in predicting marital happiness from oral history behaviors and imagined interactions. *Communication Monographs, 66,* 276–291.

Honeycutt, J. M., & Wiemann, J. M. (1999). Analysis of functions of talk and reports of imagined interactions (IIs) during engagement and marriage. *Human Communication Research, 25,* 399–419.

Horn, T. S., & Lox, C. L. (1993). The self-fulfilling prophecy. In J. M. Williams (Ed.), *Applied sport psychology: Personal growth to peak performance* (2nd ed., pp. 68–81). Mountain View, CA: Mayfield Publishing.

Hosman, L. A. (1987). The evaluational consequences of topic reciprocity and self-disclosure reciprocity. *Communication Monographs, 54,* 420-435.

Hosman, L. A. (1989). The evaluative consequences of hedges, hesitations, and intensifiers: Powerful and powerless speech styles. *Human Communication Research, 15,* 383-406.

Hoult, T. F. (1954). Experimental measurement of clothing as a factor in some social ratings of selected American men. *American Sociological Review, 19,* 326–327.

Hovarth, C. W. (1995). Biological origins of communicator style. *Communication Quarterly, 43,* 394–407.

Hubbell, A. P. (1999, November). *"I love your family-they are just like you": Lies we tell to lovers and perceptions of their honesty and appropriateness.* Paper delivered at the annual meeting of the International Communication Association, San Francisco.

Hulbert, J. E. (1989). Barriers to effective listening. *Bulletin for the Association for Business Communication, 52,* 3-5.

Ickes, W. E. (Ed.). (1997). *Empathic accuracy.* New York: Guilford Press.

Ifert, D. E., & Roloff, M. E. (1997). Overcoming expressed obstacles to compliance: The role of sensitivity to the expressions of others and ability to modify self-presentation. *Communication Quarterly, 45,* 55–67.

Ifert, D. E., & Roloff, M. E. (1998). Understanding obstacles preventing compliance: Conceptualization and classification. *Communication Research, 25,* 131–153.

Infante, D. A. (1987). Aggressiveness. In J. C. McCroskey & J. A. Daly (Eds.), *Personality and interpersonal communication* (pp. 157–192). Newbury Park, CA: Sage.

Infante, D. A. (1988). *Arguing constructively.* Prospect Heights, IL: Waveland Press.

Infante, D. A., Chandler, T. A., & Rudd, J. E. (1989). Test of an argumentative skill deficiency model of interspousal violence. *Communication Monographs, 56,* 163-177.

Infante, D. A., & Gorden, W. I. (1985). Superiors' argumentativeness and verbal aggressiveness as predictors of subordinates' satisfaction. *Human Communication Research, 12,* 117–125.

Infante, D. A., & Gorden, W. I. (1987). Superior and subordinate communication profiles: Implications for independent-mindedness and upward effectiveness. *Central States Speech Journal, 38,* 73-80.

Infante, D. A., & Gorden, W. I. (1989). Argumentativeness and affirming communicator style as predictors of satisfaction/dissatisfaction with subordinates. *Communication Quarterly, 37,* 81–90.

Infante, D. A., & Rancer, A. S. (1982). A conceptualization and measure of argumentativeness. *Journal of Personality Assessment, 46,* 72–80.

Infante, D. A., Rancer, A. S., & Jordan, F. F. (1996). Affirming and nonaffirming style, dyad sex, and the perception of argumentation and verbal aggression in an interpersonal dispute. *Human Communication Research, 22,* 315–334.

Infante, D. A., Riddle, B. L., Horvath, C. L., & Tumlin, S. A. (1992). Verbal aggressiveness: Messages and reasons. *Communication Quarterly, 40,* 116–126.

Infante, D. A., & Wigley, C. J., III. (1986). Verbal aggressiveness: An interpersonal model and measure. *Communication Monographs, 53,* 61–69.

Inman, C. (1996). Friendships among men: Closeness in the doing. In J. T. Wood (Ed.), *Gendered relationships* (pp. 95–110). Mountain View, CA: Mayfield Publishing.

Inman, M. L., & Baron, R. S. (1996). Influence of prototypes on perceptions of prejudice. *Journal of Personality and Social Psychology, 70,* 727–739.

Iverson, J. M. (1999). How to get to the cafeteria: Gesture and speech in blind and sighted children's spatial descriptions. *Developmental Psychology, 35,* 1132–1142.

Iverson, J. M., & Goldin-Meadow, S. (1997). What's communication got to do with it? Gesture in children blind from birth. *Developmental Psychology, 33,* 453–467.

Iyer, P. (1990). *The lady and the monk: Four seasons in Kyoto.* New York: Vintage.

Izard, C. E. (1971). *The face of emotion.* New York: Appleton-Century-Crofts.

Jaksa, J. A., & Pritchard, M. (1994). *Communication ethics: Methods of analysis* (2nd ed.). Belmont, CA: Wadsworth.

*Job Outlook '99,* (1999) National Association of Colleges and Employers [On-line]. Available: http://www.jobwell.org/pubs/joboutlook/want.htm

Johnson, F. (1996). Friendships among women: Closeness in dialogue. In J. T. Wood (Ed.), *Gendered relationships* (pp. 79–94). Mountain View, CA: Mayfield Publishing.

Johnson, H. M. (1998). *How do I love me?* (3rd ed.). Salem, WI: Sheffield Publishing.

Johnson, S. (1987). *Going out of our minds: The metaphysics of liberation.* Freedom, CA: Crossing.

Johnson, S., & Bechler, C. (1998). Examining the relationship between listening effectiveness and leadership emergence: Perceptions, behaviors, and recall. *Small Group Research, 29,* 452–471.

Jones, S. E. (1986). Sex differences in touch behavior. *Western Journal of Speech Communication, 50,* 227–241.

Jones, S. E. (1994). *The right touch: Understanding and using the language of physical contact.* Cresskill, NJ: Hampton Press.

Jordan, J., & Roloff, M. E. (1990). Acquiring assistance from others: The effect of indirect requests and relational intimacy on verbal compliance. *Human Communication Research, 16,* 519–555.

Judy, R., & D'Amico, C. (1997). *Work force 2020: Work and workers in the 21st century.* Indianapolis, IN: Hudson Institute.

Kalbfleisch, P. J. (1992). Deceit, distrust, and the social milieu: Applications of deception research in a troubled world. *Journal of Applied Communication Research, 20,* 308–334.

Kashy, D. A., & DePaulo, B. M. (1996). Who lies? *Journal of Personality and Social Psychology, 70,* 1037–1051.

Kassing, J. W. (1997). Development of the Intercultural Willingness to Communicate Scale. *Communication Research Reports, 14,* 399–407.

Kaufman, D., & Mahoney, J. M. (1999). The effect of waitresses' touch on alcohol consumption in dyads. *Journal of Social Psychology, 139*(3), 261–267.

Kaufmann, P. J. (1993). *Sensible listening: The key to responsive interaction* (2nd ed.). Dubuque, IA: Kendall/Hunt.

Keefe, W. F. (1971). *Listen management.* New York: McGraw-Hill.

Kellerman, K., & Cole, T. (1994). Classifying compliance-gaining messages: Taxonomic disorder and strategic confusion. *Communication Theory, 4,* 3-60.

Kellermann, K. (1989). The negativity effect in interaction: It's all in your point of view. *Human Communication Research, 16,* 147–183.

Kellermann, K. (1992). Communication: Inherently strategic and primarily automatic. *Communication Monographs, 59,* 288–300.

Kellermann, K., Reynolds, R., & Chen, J. B. (1991). Strategies of conversational retreat: When parting is not sweet sorrow. *Communication Monographs, 58,* 362–383.

Kelly, L., & Watson, A. K. (1986). *Speaking with confidence and skill.* Lanham, MD: University Press of America.

Kendon, A. (1994). Do gestures communicate? A review. *Research on Language and Social Interaction, 27,* 175–200.

Kennedy-Moore, E., & Watson, J. C. (1999). *Expressing emotion: Myths, realities, and therapeutic strategies.* New York: Guilford Press.

Kihlstrom, J. F., & Klein, S. B. (1994). The self as a knowledge structure. In R. S. Wyer & T. K. Srull (Eds.), *Handbook of social cognition, Volume 1: Basic processes* (2nd ed., pp. 153–208). Hillsdale, NJ: Lawrence Erlbaum Associates.

Kim, E. J., & Buschmann, M. T. (1999). The effect of expressive physical touch on patients with dementia. *International Journal of Nursing Studies, 36*(3), 235–243.

Kim, M. S., Hunter, J. E., Miyahara, A., Horvath, A. M., Bresnahan, M., & Yoon, H. (1996). Individual- vs. culture-level dimensions of individualism and collectivism: Effects on preferred conversational styles. *Communication Monographs, 63,* 28–49.

Kim, M. S., Shin, H. C., & Cai, D. (1998). Cultural influences on the preferred forms of requesting and re-requesting. *Communication Monographs, 65,* 47–66.

Kinney, T., & Segrin, C. (1998). Cognitive moderators of negative reactions to verbal aggression. *Communication Studies, 49,* 49–72.

Kinsley, M. (1984). It pays to be nice. *Science, 222,* 162.

Kirchler, E. (1988). Marital happiness and interaction in everyday surroundings: A time-sample diary approach for couples. *Journal of Social and Personal Relationships, 5,* 375–382.

Kirkland, S. L., Greenberg, J., & Pysczynski, T. (1987). Further evidence of the deleterious effects of overheard derogatory ethnic labels: Derogation beyond the target. *Personality and Social Psychology Bulletin, 12,* 216–227.

Kirkpatrick, D. (1992, March 23). Here comes the payoff from PCs. *Fortune,* 93-102.

Kirkwood, W. G., & Ralston, S. M. (1996). Ethics and teaching employment interviewing. *Communication Education, 45,* 167–179.

Kissling, E. A. (1996). "That's just a basic teen-age rule": Girls' linguistic strategies for managing the menstrual communication taboo. *Journal of Applied Communication Research, 24,* 292–309.

Kleinke, C. L., Peterson, T. R., & Rutledge, T. R. (1998). Effects of self-generated facial expressions on mood. *Journal of Personality and Social Psychology, 74,* 272–279.

Kleinke, C. R. (1977). Compliance to requests made by gazing and touching experimenters in field settings. *Journal of Experimental Social Psychology, 13,* 218–223.

Klopf, D. (1984). Cross-cultural apprehension research: A summary of Pacific Basin studies. In J. Daly & J. McCroskey (Eds.), *Avoiding communication: Shyness, reticence, and communication apprehension* (pp. 157–169). Beverly Hills, CA: Sage.

Kluwer, E. S., de Dreu, C. K. W., & Buunk, B. P. (1998). Conflict in intimate vs. non-intimate relationships: When gender role stereotyping overrides biased self-other judgment. *Journal of Social and Personal Relationships, 15,* 637–650.

Knapp, M. L., & Hall, J. A. (1997). *Nonverbal communication in human interaction* (4th ed.). Fort Worth, TX: Harcourt Brace.

Knapp, M. L., Putnam, L. L., & Davis, L. J. (1988). Measuring interpersonal conflict in organizations: Where do we go from here? *Management Communication Quarterly, 1,* 414–429.

Knapp, M. L., & Vangelisti, A. (2000). *Interpersonal communication and human relationships* (4th ed.). Boston: Allyn and Bacon.

Koester, J., Wiseman, R. L., & Sanders, J. A. (1993). Multiple perspectives of intercultural communication competence. In

R. L. Wiseman & J. Koester (Eds.), *Intercultural communication competence* (pp. 3–15). Newbury Park, CA: Sage.

Kolb, J. A. (1998). The relationship between self-monitoring and leadership in student project groups. *Journal of Business Communication, 35,* 264–282.

Kolligan, J., Jr. (1990). Perceived fraudulence as a dimension of perceived incompetence. In R. J. Sternberg & J. Kolligan, Jr. (Eds.), *Competence considered* (pp. 261–285). New Haven, CT: Yale University Press.

Korzybski, A. (1933). *Science and sanity.* Lancaster, PA: Science Press.

Kramer, P. D. (1997). *Should you leave?* New York: Scribner/Simon and Schuster.

Krauss, R. M., Morrel-Samuels, P., & Colasante, C. (1991). Do conversational hand gestures communicate? *Journal of Personality and Social Psychology, 61,* 743–754.

Kroeber, A. L., & Kluckholn, C. (1952). Culture: A critical review of concepts and definitions. Harvard University, Peabody Museum of American Archeology and Ethnology Papers 47.

Krokoff, L. J. (1990). Hidden agendas in marriage: Affective and longitudinal dimensions. *Communication Research, 17,* 483–499.

Kubany, E. S., Richard, D. C., Bauer, G. B., & Muraoka, M. Y. (1992). Impact of assertive and accusatory communication of distress and anger: A verbal component analysis. *Aggressive Behavior, 18,* 337–347.

Kunkel, A. W., & Burleson, B. R. (1999). Assessing explanations for sex differences in emotional support: A test of the different cultures and skill specialization accounts. *Human Communication Research, 25,* 307–340.

Kwon, Y. H., & Johnson-Hillery, J. (1999). College students' perceptions of occupational attributes based on formality of business attire. *Perceptual and Motor Skills, 87*(3, Pt 1), 987–994.

Laing, R. D. (1961). *The self and others: Further studies in sanity and madness.* London: Tavistock.

Landis, M., & Burt, H. (1924). A study of conversations. *Journal of Comparative Psychology, 4,* 81–89.

Lange, J. I., & Grove, T. G. (1981). Sociometric and autonomic responses to three levels of self-disclosure in dyads. *Western Journal of Speech Communication, 45,* 335–362.

Langer, E. J. (1978). Rethinking the role of thought in social interaction. In J. H. Harvey, W. J. Ickes, & R. F. Kidd (Eds.), *New directions in attribution research* (Vol. 2, pp. 35–58). Hillsdale, NJ: Lawrence Erlbaum Associates.

Langlois, J. H., & Roggman, L. A. (1990). Attractive faces are only average. *Psychological Science, 1,* 115–121.

Lapakko, D. (1997). Three cheers for language: A closer examination of a widely cited study of nonverbal communication. *Communication Education, 46,* 63–67.

Larkey, L. K., Hecht, M. L., & Martin, J. (1993). What's in a name? African American ethnic identity terms and self-determination. *Journal of Language and Social Psychology, 12,* 302–317.

Larose, H., & Standing, L. (1998). Does the halo effect occur in the elderly? *Social Behavior and Personality, 26,* 147–150.

Larson, J. H., Crane, D. R., & Smith, C. W. (1991). Morning and night couples: The effect of wake and sleep patterns on marital adjustment. *Journal of Marital and Family Therapy, 17,* 53-65.

Lawrence, S., & Watson, M. (1991). Getting others to help: The effectiveness of professional uniforms in charitable fund raising. *Journal of Applied Communication Research, 19,* 170-185.

Le Poire, B. A., & Yoshimura, S. M. (1999). The effects of expectancies and actual communication on nonverbal adaptation and communication outcomes: A test of interaction adaptation theory. *Communication Monographs, 66,* 1–30.

Leary, M. R., & Kowalski, R. M. (1990). Impression management: A literature review and two-component model. *Psychological Bulletin, 107,* 34–47.

Leathers, D. G. (1992). *Successful nonverbal communication: Principles and applications* (2nd ed.). New York: Macmillan.

Lebula, C., & Lucas, C. (1945). The effects of attitudes on descriptions of pictures. *Journal of Experimental Psychology, 35,* 517–524.

Lee, J. (1998). Effective maintenance communication in superior-subordinate relationships. *Western Journal of Communication, 62,* 181–208.

Lee, J. A. (1973). *The colors of love: Exploration of the ways of loving.* Don Mills, Ontario: New Press.

Leets, L. (1999, May). *When words wound: Another look at racist speech.* Paper presented at the annual conference of the International Communication Association, San Francisco.

Leets, L., & Giles, H. (1997). Words as weapons-When do they wound? *Human Communication Research, 24,* 260–301.

Lefkowitz, M., Blake, R. R., & Mouton, J. S. (1955). Status of actors in pedestrian violation of traffic signals. *Journal of Abnormal and Social Psychology, 51,* 704–706.

Lemer, R. M., & Gillert, E. (1969). Body build identification, preference and aversion in children. *Developmental Psychology, 1,* 456–463.

Levine, R. V. (1988). The pace of life across cultures. In J. E. McGrath (Ed.), *The social psychology of time* (pp. 39–60). Newbury Park, CA: Sage.

Levine, R. V., & Norenzayan, A. (1999). The pace of life in 31 countries. *Journal of Cross-Cultural Psychology, 30,* 178–205.

Levine, T. R., Park, H. S., & McCornack, S. A. (1999). Accuracy in detecting truths and lies: Documenting the "veracity effect." *Communication Monographs, 66,* 125–144.

Lewin, K. (1936). *Principles of topological psychology.* New York: McGraw-Hill.

Lewis, M. H., & Reinsch, N. L., Jr. (1988). Listening in organizational environments. *Journal of Business Communication, 25,* 49–67.

Lim, G. Y., & Roloff, M. E. (1999). Attributing sexual consent. *Journal of Applied Communication Research, 27,* 1–23.

Lippard, P. V. (1988). Ask me no questions, I'll tell you no lies: Situational exigencies for interpersonal deception. *Western Journal of Speech Communication, 52,* 91–103.

Lomranz, J. (1995). "Thus we live, forever taking leave": The launching stage in the Israeli family. *Social Behavior and Personality, 23,* 287–302.

Long, E. C. J., Angera, J. J., Carter, S. J., Nakamoto, M., & Kalso, M. (1999). Understanding the one you love: A longitudinal assessment of an empathy training program for couples in romantic relationships. *Family Relations: Interdisciplinary Journal of Applied Family Studies, 48*(3), 235–242.

Lourenco, O., & Machado, A. (1996). In defense of Piaget's theory: A reply to 10 common criticisms. *Psychological Review, 103,* 143-164.

Luce, G. G. (1971). *Body time.* New York: Pantheon Books.

Luft, J. (1969). *Of human interaction.* Palo Alto, CA: National Press Books.

Lustig, M. W., & Koester, J. (1996). *Intercultural competence: Interpersonal communication across cultures* (2nd ed.). New York: HarperCollins.

Lustig, M. W., & Koester, J. (1999). *Intercultural competence: Interpersonal communication across cultures* (3rd ed.). New York: Longman.

MacIntyre, P. D., & Thivierge, K. A. (1995). The effects of speaker personality on anticipated reactions to public speaking. *Communication Research Reports, 12,* 125–133.

Manusov, V. (1993). It depends on your perspective: Effects of stance and beliefs about intent on person perception. *Western Journal of Communication, 57,* 27–41.

Manusov, V., Winchatz, M. R., & Manning, L. M. (1997). Acting out our minds: Incorporating behavior into models of stereotype-based expectancies for cross-cultural interactions. *Communication Monographs, 64,* 119–139.

Marangoni, C., & Ickes, W. (1989). Loneliness: A theoretical review with implications for measurement. *Journal of Social and Personal Relationships, 6,* 93-128.

Marchant, V. (1999, June 28). Listen up! *Time, 153,* 74.

Marcus, M. G. (1976, October). The power of a name. *Psychology Today, 9,* 75–77, 106.

Marin, M. J., Sherblom, J. C., & Shipps, T. B. (1994). Contextual influences on nurses' conflict management strategies. *Western Journal of Communication, 58,* 201–28.

Marsh, H. W., & Holmes, I M. (1990). Multidimensional self-concepts: Construct validation of responses by children. *American Educational Research Journal, 27,* 89–117.

Martin, J. N. (1993). Intercultural communication competence: A review. In R. L. Wiseman & J. Koester (Eds.), *Intercultural communication competence* (pp. 16–29). Newbury Park, CA: Sage.

Martin, L., & Pullum, G. (1991). *The great Eskimo vocabulary hoax.* Chicago: University of Chicago Press.

Martin, M. M., Anderson, C. M., Burant, P. A., & Weber, K. (1997). Verbal aggression in sibling relationships. *Communication Quarterly, 45,* 304–317.

Martin, M. M., Anderson, C. M., & Hovarth, C. L. (1996). Feelings about verbal aggression: Justifications for sending and hurt from receiving verbally aggressive messages. *Communication Research Reports, 13,* 19–26.

Martz, J. M., Verette, J., Arriaga, X. B., Slovik, L. F., Cox, C. L., & Rusbult, C. E. (1998). Positive illusion in close relationships. *Personal Relationships, 5,* 159–181.

Maslow, A. H. (1968). *Toward a psychology of being.* New York: Van Nostrand Reinhold.

Maslow, A. H., & Mintz, N. L. (1956). Effects of aesthetic surroundings: I. Initial effects of those aesthetic surroundings upon perceiving "energy" and "well-being" in faces. *Journal of Psychology, 41,* 247–254.

Matsumoto, D. (1991). Cultural influences on facial expressions of emotion. *Southern Communication Journal, 56,* 128–137.

Matsumoto, D. (1993). Ethnic differences in affect intensity, emotion judgments, display rule attitudes, and self-reported emotional expression in an American sample. *Motivation and Emotion, 17,* 107–123.

Mayne, T. J. (1999). Negative affect and health: The importance of being earnest. *Cognition and Emotion, 13,* 601–635.

McCall, G. J. (1987). The self-concept and interpersonal communication. In M. E. Roloff & G. R. Miller (Eds.), *Interpersonal processes: New directions in communication research* (pp. 63–76). Beverly Hills, CA: Sage.

McClelland, D. C., & Atkinson, J. W. (1948). The projective expression of needs: I. The effect of different intensities of the hunger drive on perception. *Journal of Psychology, 25,* 205–222.

McConnell, J. V. (1977). *Understanding human behavior* (2nd ed.). New York: Holt, Rinehart and Winston.

McCornack, S. A. (1992). Information manipulation theory. *Communication Monographs, 59,* 1–16.

McCornack, S. A., & Levine, T. R. (1990a). When lies are uncovered: Emotional and relational outcomes of discovered deception. *Communication Monographs, 57,* 119–138.

McCornack, S. A., & Levine, T. R. (1990b). When lovers become leery: The relationship between suspicion and accuracy in detecting deception. *Communication Monographs, 57,* 219–230.

McCornack, S. A., & Parks, M. R. (1990). What women know that men don't: Sex differences in determining the truth behind deceptive messages. *Journal of Social and Personal Relationships, 7,* 107–118.

McCroskey, J. C., & Richmond, V. P. (1996). *Fundamentals of human communication: An interpersonal perspective.* Prospect Heights, IL: Waveland.

McCroskey, J. C., & Wheeless, L. (1976). *Introduction to human communication.* Boston: Allyn and Bacon.

McDaniel, E. B. (with Johnson, J.). (1975). *Scars and stripes.* Philadelphia: A. J. Holman.

McGee, D. S., & Cegala, D. J. (1998). Patient communication skills training for improved competence in the primary care medical consultation. *Journal of Applied Communication Research, 26,* 412–430.

McGuire, W. J., & Padawer-Singer, A. (1976). Trait salience in the spontaneous self-concept. *Journal of Personality and Social Psychology, 33,* 743-754.

Mehrabian, A. (1972). *Nonverbal communication.* Chicago: Aldine-Atherton.

Mehrabian, A., & Weiner, M. (1967). Decoding of inconsistent communications. *Journal of Personality and Social Psychology, 6,* 109–114.

Messman, S. J., & Canary, D. J. (1998). Patterns of conflict in personal relationships. In B. H. Spitzberg & W. R. Cupach (Eds.), *The dark side of close relationships* (pp. 121–152). Mahwah, NJ: Lawrence Erlbaum Associates.

Metts, S. (1989). An exploratory investigation of deception in close relationships. *Journal of Social and Personal Relationships, 6,* 159–179.

Metts, S., & Bowers, J. W. (1994). Emotion in interpersonal communication. In M. L. Knapp & G. R. Miller (Eds.), *Handbook of interpersonal communication* (2nd ed., pp. 508–541). Newbury Park, CA: Sage.

Metts, S., & Cupach, W. R. (1990). The influence of relationship beliefs and problem-solving relationships on satisfaction in romantic relationships. *Human Communication Research, 17,* 170-185.

Metts, S., Cupach, W. R., & Bejllovec, R. A. (1989). "I love you too much to ever start liking you": Redefining romantic relationships. *Journal of Social and Personal Relationships, 6,* 259–274.

Metts, S., Cupach, W. R., & Imahori, T. T. (1992). Perceptions of sexual compliance-resisting messages in three types of cross-sex relationships. *Western Journal of Communication, 56,* 1–17.

Milhouse, V. H. (1993). The applicability of interpersonal communication competence to the intercultural communication context. In R. L. Wiseman & J. Koester (Eds.), *Intercultural communication competence* (pp. 184–203). Newbury Park, CA: Sage.

Millar, M. G., & Millar, K. U. (1998). The effects of suspicion on the recall of cues to make veracity judgments. *Communication Reports, 11,* 57–64.

Miller, C., & Swift, K. (1973). One small step for genkind. In J. A. DeVito (Ed.), *Language: Concepts and processes* (pp. 171–182). Englewood Cliffs, NJ: Prentice-Hall. (Reprinted from the *New York Times Magazine,* April 16, 1972)

Miller, G. F. (1998). How mate choice shaped human nature: A review of sexual selection and human evolution. In C. B. Crawford & D. L. Krebs, *Handbook of evolutionary psychology: Ideas, issues, and applications* (pp. 87–129). Mahwah, NJ: Lawrence Erlbaum Associates.

Miller, G. R., & Steinberg, M. (1975). *Between people: A new analysis of interpersonal communication.* Chicago: SRA.

Miller, K. I., Stiff, J. B., & Ellis, B. H. (1988). Communication and empathy as precursors to burnout among human service workers. *Communication Monographs, 55,* 250-265.

Miller, L. C., Cooke, L. L., Tsang, J., & Morgan, F. (1992). Should I brag? Nature and impact of positive and boastful disclosures for women and men. *Human Communication Research, 18,* 364–399.

Miller, S., Nunnally, E. W., & Wackman, D. B. (1975). *Alive and aware: How to improve your relationships through better communication.* Minneapolis, MN: Interpersonal Communication Programs.

Mintz, N. L. (1956). Effects of esthetic surroundings: II. Prolonged and repeated experience in a "beautiful" and an "ugly" room. *Journal of Psychology, 41,* 259–266.

Monastersky, R. (2000, March 24). A new round of research rattles old ideas of how infants interpret the world. *Chronicle of Higher Education,* pp. A22–A23.

Monroe, C., Borzi, M. G., & DiSalvo, V. S. (1989). Conflict behaviors of difficult subordinates. *Southern Communication Journal, 34,* 311–329.

Montcrieff, R. W. (1996). *Odor preferences.* New York: Wiley.

Montgomery, B. M. (1993). Relationship maintenance versus relationship change: A dialectical dilemma. *Journal of Social and Personal Relationships, 10,* 205–223.

Montgomery, B. M., & Baxter, L. A. (Eds.). (1998). *Relating: Dilaectical approaches to studying personal relationships.* Mahwah, NJ: Lawrence Erlbaum Associates.

Montpare, J. M. (1995). The impact of variations in height on young children's impressions of men and women. *Journal of Nonverbal Behavior, 19,* 31–47.

Morris, D. (1973). *Intimate behavior.* New York: Bantam.

Morris, T. L., Gorham, J., Cohen, S. H., & Huffman, D. (1996). Fashion in the classroom: Effects of attire on student perceptions of instructors in college classes. *Communication Education, 45,* 135–148.

Moss, D. (1999). The humanistic psychology of self-disclosure, relationship, and community. In D. Moss (Ed.), *Humanistic and transpersonal psychology: A historical and biographical sourcebook* (pp. 66–84). Westport, CT: Greenwood Press.

Motley, M. T. (1990). On whether one can(not) communicate: An examination via traditional communication postulates. *Western Journal of Speech Communication, 54,* 1–20.

Motley, M. T. (1992). Mindfulness in solving communicators' dilemmas. *Communication Monographs, 59,* 306–314.

Motley, M. T. (1993). Facial affect and verbal context in conversation: Facial expression as interjection. *Human Communication Research, 20,* 3-40.

Motley, M. T., & Camden, C. T. (1988). Facial expressions of emotion: A comparison of posed expressions versus spontaneous expressions in an interpersonal communication setting. *Western Journal of Speech Communication, 52,* 1–22.

Motley, M. T., & Reeder, H. M. (1995). Unwanted escalation of sexual intimacy: Male and female perceptions of connotations and relational consequences of resistance messages. *Communication Monographs, 62,* 355–397.

Mulac, A. (1998). The gender-linked language effect: Do language differences really make a difference? In D. J. Canary & K. Dindia (Eds.), *Sex differences and similarities in communication: Critical essays and empirical investigations of sex and gender in interaction* (pp. 127–153). Mahwah, NJ: Lawrence Erlbaum Associates.

Mulac, A., Wiemann, J. M., Widenmann, S. J., & Gibson, T. W. (1988). Male/female language differences and effects in same-sex and mixed-sex dyads: The gender-linked language effect. *Communication Monographs, 55,* 315–335.

Mulford, M., Orbell, J., Shatto, C., & Stockard, J. (1998). Physical attractiveness, opportunity, and success in everyday exchange. *American Journal of Sociology, 103,* 1565–1592.

Murray, S. L., Holmes, J. G., & Griffin, D. W. (1996). The benefits of positive illusions: Idealization and the construction of satisfaction in close relationships. *Journal of Personality and Social Psychology, 70,* 79–98.

Mwakalyelye, N., & DeAngelis, T. (1995, October). The power of touch helps vulnerable babies thrive. *APA Monitor,* p. 25.

Myers, D. (1980, May). The inflated self. *Psychology Today, 14,* 16.

Myers, P. N., & Biocca, F. A. (1992). The elastic body image: The effect of television advertising and programming on body image distortions in young women. *Journal of Communication, 42,* 108–134.

Myers, S. A. (1998). Students' self-disclosure in the college classroom. *Psychological Reports, 83*(3, Pt 1), 1067–1070.

National Communication Association. (1999). *How Americans communicate* [On-line]. Available: http://www.natcom.org /research/Roper/how_americans_communicate.htm

Needleman, L. D. (1999). *Cognitive case conceptualization: A guidebook for practitioners.* Mahwah, NJ: Lawrence Erlbaum Associates.

Nellermoe, D. A., Weirich, T. R., & Reinstein, A. (1999). Using practitioners' viewpoints to improve accounting students' communications skills. *Business Communication Quarterly, 62*(2), 41–60.

Nelton, S. (1996, February). Emotions in the workplace. *Nation's Business,* pp. 25–30.

Ng, S. H., & Bradac, J. J. (1993). *Power in language: Verbal communication and social influence.* Newbury Park, CA: Sage, 1993.

Nichols, R. G. (1948). Factors in listening comprehension. *Speech Monographs, 1,* 154–163.

Nicotera, A. M. (1993). Where have we been, where are we, and where do we go? In A. M. Nicotera (Ed.), *Interpersonal communication in friend and mate relationships* (pp. 219–236). Albany: State University of New York Press.

Noller, P. (1995). Parent-adolescent relationships. In M. A. Fitzpatrick & A. L. Vangelisti (Eds.), *Explaining family interactions* (pp. 77–111). Thousand Oaks, CA: Sage.

Notarius, C. I., & Herrick, L. R. (1988). Listener response strategies to a distressed other. *Journal of Social and Personal Relationships, 5,* 97–108.

O'Barr, W. M. (1982). *Linguistic evidence: Language, power, and strategy in the courtroom.* New York: Academic Press.

O'Brien, M., & Bahadur, M. A. (1998). Marital aggression, mother's problem-solving behavior with children, and children's emotional and behavioral problems. *Journal of Social and Clinical Psychology, 17*(3), 249–272.

Odden, C. M., & Sias, P. M. (1997). Peer communication relationships and psychological climate. *Communication Quarterly, 45,* 153–166.

O'Donnell, H. S. (1973). Sexism in language. *Elementary English, 50,* 1067–1072.

Oetzel, J. G. (1998). The effects of self-construals and ethnicity on self-reported conflict styles. *Communication Reports, 11*(2), 133–144.

Officer, S. A., & Rosenfeld, L. B. (1985). Self-disclosure to male and female coaches by high school female athletes. *Journal of Sport Psychology, 7,* 360-370.

Ogden, C. K., & Richards, I. A. (1923). *The meaning of meaning.* New York: Harcourt Brace.

O'Hair, D., & Cody, M. J. (1993). Interpersonal deception: The dark side of interpersonal communication? In B. H. Spitzberg & W. R. Cupach (Eds.), *The dark side of interpersonal communication* (pp. 181–214). Hillsdale, NJ: Lawrence Erlbaum Associates.

Okabe, K. (1987). Indirect speech acts of the Japanese. In D. L. Kincaid (Ed.), *Communication theory: Eastern and Western perspectives* (pp. 127–136). San Diego: Academic Press.

Onyekwere, E. O., Rubin, R. B., & Infante, D. A. (1991). Interpersonal perception and communication satisfaction as a function of argumentativeness and ego-involvement. *Communication Quarterly, 39,* 35–47.

Orbe, M. P. (1996). Laying the foundation for co-cultural communication theory: An inductive approach to studying "nondominant" communication strategies and the factors that influence them. *Communication Studies, 47,* 157–176.

Orbe, M. P. (1998). From the standpoint(s) of traditionally muted groups: Explicating a co-cultural communication theoretical model. *Communication Theory, 8,* 1–26.

O'Sullivan, P. (1996). *An impression management model for the study of interpersonal communication.* Paper presented at the meeting of the Speech Communication Association, San Diego, CA.

O'Sullivan, P. B. (2000). What you don't know won't hurt Me: Impression management functions of communication channels in relationships. *Communication Monographs, 70.*

Palmer, J. D. (1976). *An introduction to biological rhythms.* New York: Academic Press.

Palmer, M. T., & Simmons, K.B. (1995). Communicating intentions through nonverbal behaviors: Conscious and nonconscious encoding of liking. *Human Communication Research, 22,* 128–160.

Pam, A., & Pearson, J. (1998). *Splitting up: Enmeshment and estrangement in the process of divorce.* New York: Guilford Press.

Papa, M. J., & Natalle, E. J. (1989). Gender, strategy selection, and discussion satisfaction in interpersonal conflict. *Western Journal of Speech Communication, 52,* 260-272.

Parks, M. R. (1982). Ideology in interpersonal communication: Off the couch and into the world. In M. Burgoon (Ed.), *Communication yearbook 5* (pp. 79–107). New Brunswick, NJ: Transaction.

Parks, M. R., & Floyd, K. (1996a). Making friends in cyberspace. *Journal of Communication, 46,* 80–97.

Parks, M. R., & Floyd, K. (1996b). Meanings for closeness and intimacy in friendship. *Journal of Social and Personal Relationships, 13,* 85–107.

Pasupathi, M., Stallworth, L. M., & Murdoch, K. (1998). How what we tell becomes what we know: Listener effects on speakers' long-term memory for events. *Discourse Processes, 26,* 1–25.

Patterson, M. L., & Ritts, V. (1997). Social and communicative anxiety: A review and meta-analysis. In B. R. Burleson (Ed.), *Communication yearbook 20* (pp. 263–303). Thousand Oaks, CA: Sage.

Paxton, S. J., Schutz, H. K., Wertheim, E. H., & Muir, S. L. (1999). Friendship clique and peer influences on body image concerns, dietary restraint, extreme weight-loss behaviors, and binge eating in adolescent girls. *Journal of Abnormal Psychology, 108,* 255–266.

Pearce, W. B., & Sharp, S. M. (1973). Self-disclosing communication. *Journal of Communication, 23,* 409–425.

Pearson, J. C. (1993). *Communication in the family* (2nd ed.). New York: HarperCollins.

Pearson, J. C. (2000). Positive distortion: "The most beautiful woman in the world." In K. M. Galvin & P. J. Cooper (Eds.), *Making connections: Readings in relational communication* (2nd ed., pp. 184–190). Los Angeles: Roxbury.

Pennebaker, J. W., Rime, B., & Blankenship, V. E. (1996). Stereotypes of emotional expressiveness of northerners and southerners: A cross-cultural test of Montesquieu's hypotheses. *Journal of Personality and Social Psychology, 70,* 372–380.

Person-Lynn, K. (1994, November 28). Language keeps racism alive. *Los Angeles Times,* p. B3.

Peterson, M. S. (1997). Personnel interviewers' perceptions of the importance and adequacy of applicants' communication skills. *Communication Education, 46,* 287–291.

Petronio, S. (1991). Communication boundary management: A theoretical model of managing disclosure of private information between marital couples. *Communication Theory, 1,* 311–335.

Petronio, S. (2000). The boundaries of privacy: Praxis of everyday life. In S. Petronio (Ed.), *Balancing the secrets of private disclosures* (pp. 37–49). Mahwah, NJ: Lawrence Erlbaum Associates.

Piaget, J. (1952). *The origins of intelligence in children.* New York: International Universities Press.

Pincus, D. (1986). Communication satisfaction, job satisfaction, and job performance. *Human Communication Research, 12,* 395–419.

Plax, T. G., & Rosenfeld, L. B. (1979). Receiver differences and the comprehension of spoken messages. *Journal of Experimental Education, 48,* 23-28.

Plutchik, R. (1984). Emotions: A general psychoevolutionary theory. In K. R. Scherer & P. Ekman (Eds.), *Approaches to emotion* (pp. 197–219). Hillsdale, NJ: Lawrence Erlbaum Associates.

Poole, M. S., Folger, J. P., & Hewes, D. E. (1987). Analyzing interpersonal attraction. In M. E. Roloff & G. R. Miller (Eds.), *Interpersonal processes: New directions in communication research* (pp. 220–256). Beverly Hills, CA: Sage.

Porter, L. S., Stone, A. A., & Schwartz, J. E. (1999). Anger expression and ambulatory blood pressure: A comparison of state and trait measures. *Psychosomatic Medicine, 61*(4), 454–463.

Postman, N., & Weingartner, C. (1969). *Teaching as a subversive activity.* New York: Delacorte.

Powell, J. (1969). *Why am I afraid to tell you who I am?* Niles, IL: Argus Communications.

Prager, K. J. (1995). *The psychology of intimacy.* New York: Guilford Press.

Prager, K. J., & Buhrmester, D. (1998). Intimacy and need fulfillment in couple relationships. *Journal of Social and Personal Relationships, 15,* 435–469.

Pratt, L., Wiseman, R. L., Cody, M. J., & Wendt, P. F. (1999). Interrogative strategies and information exchange in computer-mediated communication. *Communication Quarterly, 47,* 46–66.

Preto, N. G. (1999). Transformation of the family system during adolescence. In B. Carter & M. McGoldrick (Eds.), *The expanded family life cycle: Individual, family, and social perspectives* (3rd. ed., pp. 274–286). Boston: Allyn and Bacon.

Priest, P. J., & Dominick, J. R. (1994). Pulp pulpits: Self-disclosure on "Donahue." *Journal of Communication, 44,* 74–97.

Proctor, R. F. (1989). Responsibility or egocentrism?: The paradox of owned messages. *Speech Association of Minnesota Journal, 26,* 57–69.

Proctor, R. F., & Wilcox, J. R. (1993). An exploratory analysis of responses to owned messages in interpersonal communication. *ETC: A Review of General Semantics, 50,* 201–220.

Purdy, M., & Borisoff, D. (1996). *Listening in everyday life: A personal and professional approach.* Lanham, MD: University Press of America.

Ramey, E. (1972, Spring). Men's cycles. *Ms.,* pp.10–14.

Rancer, A. S., Kosberg, R. L., & Baukus, R. A. (1992). Beliefs about arguing as predictors of trait argumentativeness: Implications for training in argument and conflict management. *Communication Education, 41,* 375–387.

Rankin, P. T. (1952). The measurement of the ability to understand spoken language (Doctoral dissertation, University of Michigan, 1926). *Dissertation Abstracts, 12,* 847–848.

Raskin, R., & Shaw, R. (1988). Narcissism and the use of personal pronouns. *Journal of Personality, 56,* 393–404.

Rathus, S. A. (1993). *Psychology* (5th ed.). Fort Worth, TX: Harcourt Brace.

Rawlins, W. K. (1992). *Friendship matters: Communication, dialectics, and the life course.* New York: Aldine De Gruyter.

Ray, E. B. (1993). When the links become chains: Considering the dysfunctions of supportive communication in the workplace. *Communication Monographs, 60,* 106–111.

Redmond, M. V. (1986, November). *An inclusive conceptualization of empathy.* Paper presented at the meeting of the Speech Communication Association, Chicago.

Redmond, M. V. (1989). The functions of empathy (decentering) in human relations. *Human Relations, 42,* 593-605.

Redmond, M. V. (1995). Interpersonal communication: Definitions and conceptual approaches. In M. V. Redmond (Ed.), *Interpersonal communication: Readings in theory and research* (pp. 4–27). Fort Worth, TX: Harcourt Brace.

Regan, D. T., & Totten, J. (1975). Empathy and attribution: Turning observers into actors. *Journal of Personality and Social Psychology, 35,* 850-856.

Register, L. M., & Henley, T. B. (1992). The phenomenology of intimacy. *Journal of Social and Personal Relationships, 9,* 467–481.

Reid, T. R. (1999). *Confucius lives next door: What living in the east teaches us about living in the west.* New York: Random House.

Reissman, C. K. (1990). *Divorce talk: Women and men make sense of personal relationships.* New Brunswick, NJ: Rutgers University Press.

Richmond, V. P. (1995). Amount of communication in marital dyads as a function of dyad and individual marital satisfaction. *Communication Research Reports, 12,* 152–159.

Ricks, G. (1983). *Big business blunders.* New York: Dow Jones-Irwin.

Riggio, R. E., & Friedman, H. S. (1983). Individual differences and cues to deception. *Journal of Personality and Social Psychology, 45,* 899–915.

Ritts, V., Patterson, M. L., & Tubbs, M. E. (1992). Expectations, impressions, and judgments of physically attractive students: A review. *Review of Educational Research, 62,* 413-426.

Roach, K. D. (1997). Effects of graduate teaching assistant attire on student learning, misbehaviors, and ratings of instruction. *Communication Quarterly, 45,* 125–141.

Robinson, W. P., Shepherd, A., & Heywood, J. (1998). Truth, equivocation/concealment, and lies in job applications and doctor-patient communication. *Journal of Language and Social Psychology, 17,* 149–164.

Rockwell, P., Buller, D. B., & Burgoon, J. K. (1997). The voice of deceit: Refining and expanding vocal cues to deception. *Communication Research Reports, 14,* 451–459.

Roloff, M. E. (1981). *Interpersonal communication: The social exchange approach.* Beverly Hills, CA: Sage.

Roloff, M. E, Janiszewski, C. A., McGrath, M. A., Burns, C. S., & Manrai, L. A. (1988). Acquiring resources from intimates: When obligation substitutes for persuasion. *Human Communication Research, 14,* 364–396.

Romaine, S. (1999). *Communicating gender.* Mawah, NJ: Lawrence Erlbaum Associates.

Rosenblith, J. F. (1992). *In the beginning: Development from conception to age two.* Newbury Park, CA: Sage.

Rosenfeld, H. M. (1987). Conversational control functions of nonverbal behavior. In A. W. Siegman & S. Feldstein (Eds.), *Nonverbal behavior and communication* (2nd ed., pp. 563–601). Hillsdale, NJ: Lawrence Erlbaum Associates.

Rosenfeld, L. B. (1979). Self-disclosure avoidance: Why I am afraid to tell you who I am. *Communication Monographs, 46,* 63-74.

Rosenfeld, L. B. (1994). Sex differences in response to relationship crises: A case study of the Hill-Thomas hearing. In P. Siegel (Ed.), *Outsiders looking in: A communication perspective on the Hill/Thomas hearings* (pp. 283–301). New York: Hampton Press.

Rosenfeld, L. B. (2000). Overview of the ways privacy, secrecy, and disclosure are balanced in today's society. In S. Petronio (Ed.), *Balancing the secrets of private disclosures* (pp. 3–17). Mahwah, NJ: Lawrence Erlbaum Associates.

Rosenfeld, L. B., & Bowen, G. L. (1991). Marital disclosure and marital satisfaction: Direct-effect versus interaction-effect models. *Western Journal of Speech Communication, 55,* 69–84.

Rosenfeld, L. B., & Gilbert, J. R. (1989). The measurement of cohesion and its relationship to dimensions of self-disclosure in classroom settings. *Small Group Behavior, 20,* 291–301.

Rosenfeld, L. B., & Kendrick, W. L. (1984). Choosing to be open: Subjective reasons for self-disclosing. *Western Journal of Speech Communication, 48,* 326–343.

Rosenfeld, L. B., & Richman, J. M. (1999). Supportive communication and school outcomes, Part II: Academically at-risk low income high school students. *Communication Education, 48,* 294–307.

Rosenfeld, L. B., Richman, J. M., & Bowen, G. L. (1998). Supportive communication and school outcomes for academically "at-risk" and other low income middle school students. *Communication Education, 47,* 309–325.

Rosenthal, R., & Jacobson, L. (1968). *Pygmalion in the classroom.* New York: Holt, Rinehart and Winston.

Ross, J. B., & McLaughlin, M. M. (Eds.). (1949). *A portable medieval reader.* New York: Viking.

Rowatt, W. C., Cunningham, M. R., & Druen, P. B. (1999). Lying to get a date: The effect of facial physical attractiveness on the willingness to deceive prospective dating partners. *Journal of Social and Personal Relationships, 16,* 209–223.

Ruben, B. D. (1989). The study of cross-cultural competence: Traditions and contemporary issues *International Journal of Intercultural Relationships, 13,* 229–240.

Ruben, B. D., & Kealey, D. (1979). Behavioral assessment of communication competency and the prediction of cross-cultural adaptation. *International Journal of Intercultural Relations, 3,* 15–48.

Rubenstein, A. J., Kalakanis, L., & Langlois, J. H. (1999). Infant preferences for attractive faces: A cognitive explanation. *Developmental Psychology, 35,* 848–855.

Ruberman, R. (1992). Psychosocial influences on mortality of patients with coronary heart disease. *Journal of the American Medical Association, 267,* 559–560.

Rubin, D. L. (1986). "Nobody play by the rules he know": Ethnic interference in classroom questioning events. In Y. Y. Kim (Ed.), *Interethnic communication: Current research* (pp. 158–175). Newbury Park, CA: Sage.

Rubin, D. L., Greene, K., & Schneider, D. (1994). Adopting gender-inclusive language reforms: Diachronic and synchronic variation. *Journal of Language and Social Psychology, 13,* 91–114.

Rubin, R. B., & Graham, E. E. (1988). Communication correlates of college success: An exploratory investigation. *Communication Education, 37,* 14–27.

Rubin, R. B., Graham, E. E., & Mignerey, J. T. (1990). A longitudinal study of college students' communication competence. *Communication Education, 39,* 1–14.

Rubin, R. B., Perse, E. M., & Barbato, C. A. (1988). Conceptualization and measurement of interpersonal communication motives. *Human Communication Research, 14,* 602–628.

Rudd, J. E., & Burant, P. A. (1995). A study of women's compliance-gaining behaviors in violent and non-violent relationships. *Communication Research Reports, 12,* 134–144.

Rusbult, C. E., Bissonnette, V. L., Arriaga, X. B., & Cox, C. L. (1998). Accommodation processes during the early years of marriage. In T. N. Bradbury (Ed.), *The developmental course of marital dysfunction* (pp. 74–113). New York: Cambridge University Press.

Rymer, R. (1993). *Genie: An abused child's flight from silence.* New York: HarperCollins.

Sabourin, T. C., & Stamp, G. H. (1995). Communication and the experience of dialectical tensions in family life: An examination of abusive and nonabusive families. *Communication Monographs, 62,* 213-242.

Sachs, J. (1987). Preschool boys' and girls' language use in pretend play. In S. U. Philips, S. Steele, & C. Tanz (Eds.), *Language, gender, and sex in comparative perspective* (pp. 178–188). Cambridge, England: Cambridge University Press.

Sacks, O. (1989). *Seeing voices: A journey into the world of the deaf.* Berkeley: University of California Press.

Sadalla, E. (1987). Identity and symbolism in housing. *Environment and Behavior, 19,* 569–587.

Sagarian, E. (1976, March). The high cost of wearing a label. *Psychology Today, 10,* 25–27.

Samovar, L. A., & Porter, R. E. (1995). *Communication between cultures* (2nd ed.). Belmont, CA: Wadsworth.

Samovar, L. A., Porter, R. E., & Stefani, L. (1998). *Communication between cultures* (3rd ed.). Belmont, CA: Wadsworth.

Samter, W., Burleson, B. R., Kunkel, A. W., & Werking, K. J. (1994, May). *Gender and beliefs about communication in intimate relationships: Moderating effects of type of communication and type of relationship (or, when gender differences make a difference—and when they don't).* Paper presented at the annual meeting of the International Communication Association, Sydney, Australia.

Samter, W., & Cupach, W. R. (1998). Friendly fire: Topical variations in conflict among same- and cross-sex friends. *Communication Studies, 49,* 121–138.

Scallon, R., & Wong-Scallon, S. (1990). Athabaskan-English interethnic communication. In D. Carbaugh (Ed.), *Cultural communication and intercultural contact* (pp. 259–286). Hillsdale, NJ: Lawrence Erlbaum Associates.

Schachter, S. (1959). *The psychology of affiliation.* Stanford, CA: Stanford University Press.

Scharlott, B. W., & Christ, W. G. (1995). Overcoming relationship-initiation barriers: The impact of a computer-dating system on sex role, shyness, and appearance inhibitions. *Computers in Human Behavior, 11,* 191–204.

Schütz, A. (1999). It was your fault! Self-serving biases in autobiographical accounts of conflicts in married couples. *Journal of Social and Personal Relationships, 16,* 193–208.

Scotton, C. M. (1983). The negotiation of identities in conversation: A theory of markedness and code choice. *International Journal of Sociological Linguistics, 44,* 119–125.

Scudder, J. N., & Andrews, P. H. (1995). A comparison of two alternative models of powerful speech: The impact of power and gender upon the use of threats. *Communication Research Reports, 12,* 25–33.

Sedikides, C., Campbell, W. K., Reeder, G. D., & Elliot, A. J. (1998). The self-serving bias in relational context. *Journal of Personality and Social Psychology, 74,* 378–386.

Segrin, C., & Fitzpatrick, M. A. (1992). Depression and verbal aggressiveness in different marital couple types. *Communication Studies, 43,* 79–91.

Sennett, R. (1974). *The fall of public man: On the social psychology of capitalism.* New York: Random House.

Servaes, J. (1989). Cultural identity and modes of communication. In J. A. Anderson (Ed.), *Communication yearbook 12* (pp. 383–416). Newbury Park, CA: Sage.

Shadur, M. A., Kienzle, R., & Rodwell, J. J. (1999). The relationship between organizational climate and employee perceptions of involvement: The importance of support. *Group and Organization Management, 24,* 479–503.

Shannon, C. E., & Weaver, W. (1949). *The mathematical theory of communication.* Urbana: University of Illinois Press.

Shattuck, R. (1980). *The forbidden experiment: The story of the Wild Boy of Aveyron.* New York: Farrar, Straus & Giroux.

Shaw, C. L. M. (1997). Personal narrative: Revealing self and reflecting other. *Human Communication Research, 24,* 302–319.

Sherman, M. A., & Haas, A. (1984, June). Man to man, woman to woman. *Psychology Today, 17,* 72–73.

Sherman, M. D., & Thelen, M. H. (1996). Fear of Intimacy Scale: Validation and extension with adolescents. *Journal of Social and Personal Relationships, 13,* 507–521.

Shimanoff, S. B. (1984). Commonly named emotions in everyday conversations. *Perceptual and Motor Skills, 58,* 514.

Shimanoff, S. B. (1985). Rules governing the verbal expression of emotions between married couples. *Western Journal of Speech Communication, 49,* 149–165.

Shimanoff, S. B. (1988). Degree of emotional expressiveness as a function of face-needs, gender, and interpersonal relationship. *Communication Reports, 1,* 43-53.

Shinagawa, L. H. (1997). *Atlas of American diversity.* Newbury Park, CA: Sage/Altamira.

Sias, P. M. (1996). Constructing perceptions of differential treatment: An analysis of coworkers' discourse. *Communication Monographs, 63,* 171–187.

Sieberg, E., & Larson, C. (1971). *Dimensions of interpersonal response.* Paper presented at the meeting of the International Communication Association, Phoenix, AZ.

Siegman, A. W., & Smith, T. W. (Eds.). (1994). *Anger, hostility, and the heart.* Mahwah, NJ: Lawrence Erlbaum Associates.

Siegman, A. W., & Snow, S. C. (1997). The outward expression of anger, the inward experience of anger and CVR: The role of vocal expression. *Journal of Behavioral Medicine, 1,* 29–45.

Sillars, A. L., Folwell, A. L., Hill, K. L., Maki, B. K., Hurst, A. P., & Casano, R. A. (1992, November). *Levels of understanding in marital relationships.* Paper presented at the meeting of the Speech Communication Association, Chicago.

Sillars, A. L., Pike, G. R., Jones, T. S., & Murphy, M. A. (1984). Communication and understanding in marriage. *Human Communication Research, 10,* 317–350.

Sillars, A. L., Shebellen, W., McIntosh, A., & Pomegranate, M. (1997). Relational characteristics of language: Elaboration and differences in marital conversations. *Western Journal of Communication, 61,* 403–422.

Sillars, A. L., Weisberg, J., Burggraf, C. S., & Wilson, E. A. (1987). Content themes in marital conversations. *Human Communication Research, 13,* 495–528.

Sinclair, L. (1954). A word in your ear. In W. Goldschmidt (Ed.), *Ways of mankind* (pp. 23–32). Boston: Beacon.

Singer, J. K., Miller, L. C., & Murphy, S. (1998). *Sexual harassment and memory: How repetition of behavior and personal experience relate to judgments of sexual harassment.* Paper presented at the annual conference of the International Communication Association, Jerusalem.

Singer, M. (1998). *Perception and identity in intercultural communication.* Yarmouth, ME: Intercultural Press.

Smeltzer, L. R., & Watson, K. W. (1984). Listening: An empirical comparison of discussion length and level of incentive. *Central States Speech Journal, 35,* 166–170.

Smith, G. W. (1998). The political impact of name sounds. *Communication Monographs, 65,* 154–172.

Snodgrass, S. E. (1985). Women's intuition: The effect of subordinate role on interpersonal sensitivity. *Journal of Personality and Social Psychology, 49,* 146–155.

Snow, P. A. (1972). Verbal content and affective response in an interview as a function of experimenter gaze direction. Unpublished master's thesis, Lakehead University, Thunder Bay, Ontario, Canada.

Snyder, M. (1979). Self-monitoring processes. In L. Berkowitz (Ed.), *Advances in experimental social psychology* (Vol. 12, pp. 86–128). New York: Academic Press.

Snyder, M. (1980, March). The many me's of the self-monitor. *Psychology Today, 14,* 33-40, 92.

Solomon, D. H., & Williams, M. L. M. (1997). Perceptions of social-sexual communication at work: The effects of message, situation, and observer characteristics on judgments of sexual harassment. *Journal of Applied Communication Research, 25,* 197–216.

Sommer, R. (1969). *Personal space: The behavioral basis of design.* Englewood Cliffs, NJ: Prentice-Hall.

Speicher, H. (1999). Development and validation of intimacy capability and intimacy motivation measures. *Dissertation Abstracts International, 59*(9–B), 5172.

Spinks, N., & Wells, B. (1991). Improving listening power: The payoff. *Bulletin of the Association for Business Communication, 54,* 75–77.

Spitzberg, B. H. (1991). An examination of trait measures of interpersonal competence. *Communication Reports, 4,* 22–29.

Spitzberg, B. H. (1993). The dark side of (in)competence. In W. R. Cupach & B. H. Spitzberg (Eds.), *The dark side of interpersonal communication* (pp. 25–50). Hillsdale, NJ: Lawrence Erlbaum Associates.

Sprecher, S. (1987). The effects of self-disclosure given and received on affection for an intimate partner and stability of the relationship. *Journal of Social and Personal Relationships, 4,* 115–128.

Staffieri, J. R. (1967). A study of social stereotype of body image in children. *Journal of Personality and Social Psychology, 7,* 101–104.

Stafford, L., & Dainton, M. (1994). The dark side of "normal" family interaction. In B. H. Spitzberg & W. R. Cupach (Eds.), *The dark side of interpersonal communication* (pp. 259–280). Hillsdale, NJ: Lawrence Erlbaum Associates.

Stafford, L., & Kline, S. L. (1996). Married women's name choices and sense of self. *Communication Reports, 9,* 85–92.

Stamp, G. H. (1999). A qualitatively constructed interpersonal communication model: A grounded theory analysis. *Human Communication Research, 25,* 531–547.

Stamp, G. H., Vangelisti, A. L., & Daly, J. A. (1992). The creation of defensiveness in social interaction. *Communication Quarterly, 40,* 177–190.

Stangor, C., & Hewstone M. (Eds.). (1996). *Stereotypes and stereotyping.* New York: Guilford Press.

Stanley, J. P. (1977). Paradigmatic woman: The prostitute. In D. L. Shores & C. P. Hines (Eds.), *Papers in language variation* (pp. 303–321). Tuscaloosa: University of Alabama Press.

Stearns, C. A., & Stearns, P. (1986). *Anger: The struggle for emotional control in America's history.* Chicago: University of Chicago Press.

Steen, S., & Schwartz, P. (1995). Communication, gender, and power: Homosexual couples as a case study. In M. A. Fitzpatrick & A. L. Vangelisti (Eds.), *Explaining family interactions* (pp. 310–343). Thousand Oaks, CA: Sage.

Steil, L. K. (1997). Listening training: The key to success in today's organizations. In M. Purdy & D. Borisoff (Eds.), *Listening in everyday life: A personal and professional approach* (2nd ed., pp. 213–237). Lanham, MD: University Press of America.

Steinfatt, T. (1989). Linguistic relativity: Toward a broader view. In S. Ting-Toomey & F. Korzenny (Eds.), *Language, communica-tion, and culture: Current directions* (pp. 35–75). Newbury Park, CA: Sage.

Sternberg, R. J. (1985). *Beyond I.Q.* New York: Cambridge University Press.

Steves, R. (1996, May-September). Culture shock. *Europe Through the Back Door Newsletter, 50,* 20.

Stewart, E. C., and M. J. Bennett. (1991). *American cultural patterns: A cross-cultural perspective.* Yarmouth, ME: Intercultural Press.

Stewart, J. (1983). Interpretive listening: An alternative to empathy. *Communication Education, 32,* 379–391.

Stewart, J. (Ed.). (1994). *Bridges, not walls: A book about interpersonal communication* (6th ed.). New York: McGraw-Hill.

Stewart, J. (Ed.). (1999). *Bridges not walls: A book about interpersonal communication* (7th ed.). New York: McGraw-Hill.

Stewart, J., & Logan, C. (1993). *Together: Communicating interpersonally* (4th ed.). New York: McGraw-Hill.

Stewart, J., & Logan, C. (1998). *Together: Communicating interpersonally* (5th ed.). New York: McGraw-Hill.

Stewart, S., Stinnett, H., & Rosenfeld,L.B. (in press). Sex differences in desired characteristics of short-term and long-term relationship partners. *Journal of Personal and Social Relationships.*

Stiff, J. B., Dillard, J. P., Somera, L., Kim, H., & Sleight, C. (1988). Empathy, communication, and prosocial behavior. *Communication Monographs, 55,* 198–213.

Stiff, J. B., Kim, H. J., & Ramesh, C. N. (1989). Truth-biases and aroused suspicion in relational deception. Paper presented at the meeting of the International Communication Association, San Francisco.

Stiles, W. B., Walz, N. C., Schroeder, M. A. B., Williams, L. L., & Ickes, W. (1996). Attractiveness and disclosure in initial encounters of mixed-sex dyads. *Journal of Social and Personal Relationships, 13,* 303-312.

Strassberg, D. S., Adelstein, T. B., & Chemers, M. M. (1988). Adjustment and disclosure reciprocity. *Journal of Social and Clinical Psychology, 7,* 234–245.

Straus, M., Sweet, S., & Vissing, Y. M. (1989, November). Verbal aggression against spouses and children in a nationally representative sample of American families. Paper presented at the meeting of the Speech Communication Association, San Francisco.

Sugimoto, N. (1991, March). *"Excuse me" and "I'm sorry": Apologetic behaviors of Americans and Japanese.* Paper presented at the Conference on Communication in Japan and the United States, California State University, Fullerton, CA.

Sullins, E. S. (1991). Emotional contagion revisited: Effects of social comparison and expressive style on mood convergence. *Personality and Social Psychology Bulletin, 17,* 166–174.

Sullivan, C. F. (1996). Recipients' perceptions of support attempts across various stressful life events. *Communication Research Reports, 13,* 183–190.

Sutter, D. L., & Martin, M. M. (1999). Verbal aggression during disengagement of dating relationships. *Communication Research Reports, 15,* 318–326.

Swain, S. (1989). Covert intimacy in men's friendships: Closeness in men's friendships. In B. J. Risman & P. Schwartz (Eds.), *Gender in intimate relationships: A microstructural approach* (pp. 71–86). Belmont, CA: Wadsworth.

Swann, W. B., Jr., Wenzlaff, R. M., Krull, D. S., & Pelham, B. W. (1992). Allure of negative feedback: Self-verification strivings among depressed persons. *Journal of Abnormal Psychology, 101,* 293-306.

Swenson, J., & Casmir, F. L. (1998). The impact of culture-sameness, gender, foreign travel, and academic background on the ability to interpret facial expression of emotion in others. *Communication Quarterly, 46,* 214–230.

Sypher, B. D., & Sypher, H. E. (1983). Perceptions of communication ability: Self-monitoring in an organizational setting. *Personality and Social Psychology Bulletin, 9,* 297–304.

Tajfel, H., & Turner, J. C. (1992). The social identity theory of intergroup behavior. In W. B. Gudykunst & Y. Y. Kim (Eds.), *Readings on communicating with strangers.* New York: McGraw-Hill.

Tangney, J. P., Hill-Barlow, D., Wagner, P. E., & Marschall, D. E. (1996). Assessing individual differences in constructive versus destructive responses to anger across the lifespan. *Journal of Personality and Social Psychology, 70,* 780-796.

Tannen, D. (1986). *That's not what I meant! How conversational style makes or breaks your relations with others.* New York: William Morrow.

Tannen, D. (1990). *You just don't understand: Women and men in conversation.* New York: William Morrow, 1990.

Tannen, D. (1994a, May 16). Gender gap in cyberspace. *Newsweek,* pp. 52–53.

Tannen, D. (1994b). *Talking from 9 to 5: Women and men in the workplace: Language, sex and power.* New York: Morrow.

Taylor, A. F., Wiley, A., Kuo, F.E., & Sullivan, W. C. (1998). Growing up in the inner city: Green spaces as places to grow. *Environment and Behavior, 30,* 3–27.

Taylor, D. A., & Altman, I. (1987). Communication in interpersonal relationships: Social penetration processes. In M. E. Roloff & G. R. Miller (Eds.), *Interpersonal processes: New directions in communication research* (pp. 257–277). Newbury Park, CA: Sage.

Taylor, S., & Mette, D. (1971). When similarity breeds contempt. *Journal of Personality and Social Psychology, 20,* 75–81.

Teven, J. J., & Comadena, M. E. (1996). The effects of office aesthetic quality on students' perceptions of teacher credibility and communicator style. *Communication Research Reports, 13,* 101–108.

Teven, J. J., Martin, M. M., & Neupauer, N. C. (1998). Sibling relationships: Verbally aggressive messages and their effect on relational satisfaction. *Communication Reports, 11,* 179–186.

Tezer, E. (1999). The functionality of conflict behaviors and the popularity of those who engage in them. *Adolescence, 34*(134), 409–415.

Thibaut, J. W., & Kelley, H. H. (1959). *The social psychology of groups.* New York: Wiley.

Thomas, C. E., Booth-Butterfield, M., & Booth-Butterfield, S. (1995). Perceptions of deception, divorce disclosures, and communication satisfaction with parents. *Western Journal of Communication, 59,* 228–245.

Thourlby, W. (2978). *You are what you wear.* New York: New American Library.

Ting-Toomey, S. (1988a). A face-negotiation theory. In Y. Kim & W. Gudykunst (Eds.), *Theory in interpersonal communication.* Newbury Park, CA: Sage.

Ting-Toomey, S. (1988b). Rhetorical sensitivity style in three cultures: France, Japan, and the United States. *Central States Speech Journal, 39,* 28–36.

Ting-Toomey, S. (1991). Intimacy expressions in three cultures: France, Japan, and the United States. *International Journal of Intercultural Relations, 15,* 29–46.

Ting-Toomey, S. (1992). Identity and intergroup bonding. In W. B. Gudykunst & Y. Y. Kim (Eds.), *Readings on communicating with strangers*. New York: McGraw-Hill.

Ting-Toomey, S. (1999). *Communicating across cultures*. New York: Guilford Press.

Tipping Tips. (1996, August 27). *Wall Street Journal,* p. A1.

Tolhuizen, J. H. (1989). Communication strategies for intensifying dating relationships: Identification, use and structure. *Journal of Social and Personal Relationships, 6,* 413-434.

Touitou, Y. (1998*). Biological clocks: Mechanisms and Application.* Proceedings of the International Congress on Chronobiology, Paris, 7–11 September 1997. New York: Elsevier Science.

Tracy, K. (1984). The discourse of requests: Assessment of a compliance-gaining approach. *Human Communication Research, 10,* 513-538.

Tracy, S. J., & Tracy, K. (1998). Emotion labor at 911: A case study and theoretical critique. *Journal of Applied Communication Research, 26,* 390–411.

Trenholm, S. (1988). *Persuasion and social influence.* Englewood Cliffs, NJ: Prentice-Hall.

Trenholm, S., & Jensen, A. (1990). *The guarded self: Toward a social history of interpersonal styles.* Paper presented at the meeting of the Speech Communication Association of San Juan, Puerto Rico.

Trenholm, S., & Jensen, A. (1992). *Interpersonal communication* (2nd ed.). Belmont, CA: Wadsworth.

Trenholm, S., & Jensen, A. (2000). *Interpersonal communication* (4th ed.). Belmont, CA: Wadsworth.

Trenholm, S., & Rose, T. (1980). The compliant communicator: Teacher perceptions of appropriate classroom behavior. *Western Journal of Speech Communication, 44,* 13-26.

Triandis, H. C. (1975). Culture training, cognitive complexity and interpersonal attitudes. In R. Brislin, S. Bichner, & W. Lonner (Eds.), *Cross-cultural perspectives on learning.* New York: Wiley.

Triandis, H. C. (1990). Cross-cultural studies of individualism and collectivism. In J. Berman (Ed.), *Nebraska symposium on motivation* (pp. 41–133). Lincoln: University of Nebraska Press.

Triandis, H. C. (1992). Collectivism v. individualism: A reconceptualization of a basic concept in cross-cultural social psychology. In W. B. Gudykunst & Y. Y. Kim (Eds.), *Readings on communicating with strangers* (pp. ). New York: McGraw-Hill.

Triandis, H. C. (1994). *Culture and social behavior.* New York: McGraw-Hill.

Triandis, H. C. (1995). *Individualism and collectivism.* Boulder, CO: Westview.

Trobst, K. K., Collins, R. L., & Embree, J. M. (1994). The role of emotion in social support provision: Gender, empathy, and expressions of distress. *Journal of Social and Personal Relationships, 11,* 45–62.

Turk, D. R., & Monahan, J. L. (1999). "Here I go again": An examination of repetitive behaviors during interpersonal conflicts. *Southern Communication Journal, 64,* 232–244.

Turner, H. H., Dindia, K., & Pearson, J. C. (1995). An investigation of female/male verbal behavior in same-sex and mixed-sex conversations. *Communication Reports, 8,* 86–96.

Turner, R. E., Edgely, C., & Olmstead, G. (1975). Information control in conversation: Honesty is not always the best policy. *Kansas Journal of Sociology, 11,* 69–89.

Tusing, K. J., & Dillard, J. P. (2000). The sounds of dominance: Vocal Precursors of perceived dominance during interpersonal influence. *Human Communication Research, 26,* 148–171.

U.S. Bureau of the Census. (1998). *Statistical abstract of the United States*(118th ed.). Washington, DC: U.S. Government Printing Office.

Urberg, K. A., Degirmencioglu, S. M., & Tolson, J. M. (1998). Adolescent friendship selection and termination: The role of similarity. *Journal of Social and Personal Relationships, 15,* 703–710.

Valins, S. (1966). Cognitive effects of false heart-rate feedback. *Journal of Personality and Social Psychology, 4,* 400-408.

Vangelisti, A. L. (1994). Couples' communication problems: The counselor's perspective. *Journal of Applied Communication Research, 22,* 106–126.

Vangelisti, A. L., & Crumley, L. P. (1998). Reactions to messages that hurt: The influence of relational contexts. *Communication Monographs, 65,* 173–196.

Vangelisti, A. L., Knapp, M. L., & Daly, J. A. (1990). Conversational narcissism. *Communication Monographs, 57,* 251–274.

VanLear, C. A. (1987). The formation of social relationships: A longitudinal study of social penetration. *Human Communication Research, 13,* 299–322.

VanLear, C. A. (1991). Testing a cyclical model of communicative openness in relationship development: Two longitudinal studies. *Communication Monographs, 58,* 337–361.

Vassallo, P. (1993). The you understood. *ETC: A Review of General Semantics, 50,* 187–191.

Vaughn, D. (1987, July). The long goodbye. *Psychology Today, 21,* 37–42.

Venable, K. V., & Martin, M. M. (1997). Argumentativeness and verbal aggressiveness in dating relationships. *Journal of Social Behavior and Personality, 12,* 955–964.

Veroff, J., Douvan, E., Orbuch, T. L., & Acitelli, L. K. (1998). Happiness in stable marriages: The early years. In T. N. Bradbury (Ed.), *The developmental course of marital dysfunction* (pp. 152–179). New York: Cambridge University Press.

Vito, D. (1999). Affective self-disclosure, conflict resolution and marital quality. *Dissertation Abstracts International, 60*(3–B), 1319.

Vocate, D. R. (1994). Self-talk and inner speech: Understanding the uniquely human aspects of intrapersonal communication. In D. R. Vocate (Ed.), *Intrapersonal communication: Different voices, different minds* (pp. 3–31). Hillsdale, NJ: Lawrence Erlbaum Associates.

Voss, K., Markiewicz, D., & Doyle, A. B. (1999). Friendship, marriage and self-esteem. *Journal of Social and Personal Relationships, 16,* 103–122.

Vrij, A., & Akehurst, L. (1999). The existence of a black clothing stereotype: The impact of a victim's black clothing on impression formation. *Psychology, Crime and Law, 3*(3), 227–237.

Vuchinich, S. (1987). Starting and stopping spontaneous family conflicts. *Journal of Marriage and the Family, 49,* 591–601.

Wachs, T. D. (1992). *The nature of nurture.* Newbury Park, CA: Sage.

Waldron, V. R., & Applegate, J. L. (1998). Person-centered tactics during verbal disagreements: Effects on student perceptions of persuasiveness and social attraction. *Communication Education, 47,* 53–66.

Walster, E., Aronson, E., Abrahams, D., & Rottmann, L. (1966). Importance of physical attractiveness in dating behavior. *Journal of Personality and Social Psychology, 4,* 508–516.

Walther, J. B. (1996). Computer-mediated communication: Impersonal, interpersonal, and hyperpersonal interaction. *Communication Research, 23,* 3-43.

Walther, J. B., & Burgoon, J. K. (1992). Relational communication in computer-mediated interaction. *Human Communication Research, 19,* 50–88.

Walther, J. B., & Tidwell, L. C. (1995). Nonverbal cues in computer-mediated communication, and the effect of chronemics on relational communication. *Journal of Organizational Computing, 5,* 355–378.

Wambach, C., & Brothen, T. (1997). Teacher self-disclosure and student classroom participation revisited. *Teaching of Psychology, 24*(4), 262–263.

Waring, E. M. (1981). Facilitating marital intimacy through self-disclosure. *American Journal of Family Therapy, 9,* 33-42.

Waring, E. M., & Chelune, G. J. (1983). Marital intimacy and self-disclosure. *Journal of Clinical Psychology, 39,* 183-190.

Watzlawick, P., Beavin, J., & Jackson, D. (1967). *Pragmatics of human communication: A study of interactional patterns, pathologies, and paradoxes.* New York: W. W. Norton.

Weaver, J. B., & Kirtley, M. D. (1995). Listening styles and empathy. *Southern Communication Journal, 60,* 131–140.

Weider-Hatfield, D. (1981). A unit in conflict management skills. *Communication Education, 30,* 265–273.

Weiss, L., & Lowenthal, M. F. (1975). Life-course perspectives on friendship. In M. F. Lowenthal, M. Thurnher, & D. Chiriboga (Eds.), *Four stages of life: A comparative study of women and men facing transitions* (pp. 48–61). San Francisco: Jossey-Bass.

Weiss, R. S. (1998). A taxonomy of relationships. *Journal of Social and Personal Relationships, 15,* 671–683.

Wert-Gray, S., Center, C., Brashers, D. E., & Meyers, R. A. (1991). Research topics and methodological orientations in organizational communication: A decade in review. *Communication Studies, 42,* 141–154.

Whitman, T. L., White, R. D., O'Mara, K. M.. & Goeke-Morey, M. C. (1999). Environmental aspects of infant health and illness. In T. L. Whitman & T. V. Merluzzi (Eds.), *Life-span perspectives on health and illness* (pp. 105–124). Mahwah, NJ: Lawrence Erlbaum Associates.

Whorf, B. L. (1956). The relation of habitual thought and behavior to language. In J. B. Carroll (Ed.), *Language, thought, and reality: Selected writings of Benjamin Lee Whorf* (pp. 134–159). Cambridge, MA: MIT Press.

Wiemann, J. M., Takai, J., Ota, H. & Wiemann, M. (1997). A relational model of communication competence. In B. Kovacic (Ed.), *Emerging theories of human communication*. Albany: State University of New York Press.

Willis, F. N., & Hamm, H. K. (1980). The use of interpersonal touch in securing compliance. *Journal of Nonverbal Behavior, 5,* 49–55.

Wilmot, W. W. (1987). *Dyadic communication* (3rd ed.). New York: Random House.

Wilmot, W. W. (1995). *Relational communication* (5th ed.). New York: McGraw-Hill.

Wilson, J. M. (1982). The value of touch in psychotherapy. *Journal of Orthopsychiatry 52,* 65–72.

Winch, R. (1958). *Mate-selection: A study of complementary needs.* New York: Harper and Row.

Winer, S., & Majors, R. (1981). A research note on supportive and defensive communication: An empirical study of three verbal interpersonal communication variables. *Communication Quarterly, 29,* 166–172.

Winsor, J. L., Curtis, D. B., & Stephens, R. D. (1997). National preferences in business and communication education: An update. *Journal of the Association for Communication Administration, 3,* 170–179.

*Wisconsin State Journal,* UPI, September 7, 1978.

Wolvin, A. D. (1984). Meeting the communication needs of the adult learner. *Communication Education, 33,* 267–271.

Wolvin, A. D., & Coakley, C. (1991). A survey of the status of listening training in some Fortune 500 companies. *Communication Education, 40,* 152–164.

Wolvin, A. D., & Coakley, C. G. (1996). *Listening* (5th ed.). Boston: McGraw-Hill.

Won-Doornick, M. J. (1979). On getting to know you: The association between the stage of relationship and reciprocity of

self-disclosure. *Journal of Experimental Social Psychology, 15,* 229–241.

Wood, J. T. (1994). Gender and relationship crises: Contrasting reasons, responses, and relational orientations. In J. Ringer (Ed.), *Queer words, queer images: The (re)construction of homosexuality* (pp. 238–264). New York: New York University Press.

Wood, J. T. (1997). *Gendered lives: Communication, gender, and culture* (2nd ed.). Belmont, CA: Wadsworth.

Wood, J. T., & Dindia, K. (1998). What's the difference? A dialogue about differences and similarities between women and men. In D. J. Canary & K. Dindia (Eds.), *Sex differences and similarities in communication: Critical essays and empirical investigations of sex and gender in interaction* (pp. 19–39). Mahwah, NJ: Lawrence Erlbaum Associates.

Wood, J. T., & Inman, C. C. (1993). In a different mode: Masculine styles of communicating closeness. *Journal of Applied Communication Research, 21,* 279–295.

Woods, E. (1996). Associations of nonverbal decoding ability with indices of person-centered communicative ability. *Communication Reports, 9,* 13–22.

Woodward, M. S., Rosenfeld, L. B., & May, S. K. (1996). Sex differences in social support in sororities and fraternities. *Journal of Applied Communication Research, 24,* 260–272.

Wortman, C. B., Adosman, P., Herman, E., & Greenberg, R. (1976). Self-disclosure: An attributional perspective. *Journal of Personality and Social Psychology, 33,* 184–191.

Yingling, J. (1994). Constituting friendship in talk and metatalk. *Journal of Social and Personal Relationships, 11,* 411–426.

Yook, E. L., & Albert, R. D. (1998). Perceptions of the appropriateness of negotiation in educational settings: A cross-cultural comparison among Koreans and Americans. *Communication Education, 47,* 18–29.

Yum, J. O. (1987). The practice of Uye-re in interpersonal relationships in Korea. In D. Kincaid (Ed.), *Communication theory from Eastern and Western perspectives.* New York: Academic Press.

Zahn, C. J. (1989). The bases for differing evaluations of male and female speech: Evidence from ratings of transcribed conversation. *Communication Monographs, 56,* 59–74.

Zimbardo, P. G. (1971). *The psychological power and pathology of imprisonment.* Statement prepared for the U.S. House of

Representatives Committee on the Judiciary, Subcommittee No. 3, Robert Kastemeyer, Chairman. Unpublished manuscript. Stanford University, 1971.

Zimbardo, P. G. (1977). *Shyness: What it is, what to do about it*. Reading, MA: Addison-Wesley.

Zimmerman, B. J., Bandura, A., & Martinez-Pons, M. (1992). Self-motivation for academic attainment: The role of self-efficacy beliefs and personal goal setting. *American Educational Research Journal, 29*, 663–676.

Zimmerman, D. H., & West, C. (1975). Sex roles, interruptions, and silences in conversation. In B. Thorne & N. Henley (Eds.), *Language and sex: Difference and dominance* (pp. 105–129). Rowley, MA: Newbury House.

Zuckerman, M., & Driver, R. E. (1989). What sounds beautiful is good: The vocal attractiveness stereotype. *Journal of Nonverbal Behavior, 13*, 67–82.

Zwingle, E. (1999, August). A world together. *National Geographic Magazine, 196*, 6–33.

# NAME INDEX

# SUBJECT INDEX